"Wellum's treatment of this glorious subject is comprehensive in scope and is marked by precision, clarity, biblical fidelity, and a close acquaintance with the centuries of discussion surrounding it. It is the most helpful book on Christology I've read, and it is a pleasure to commend it to you!"

Fred Zaspel, Pastor, Reformed Baptist Church, Franconia, Pennsylvania

"Exploring our Lord's person and work from a variety of angles, Wellum engages a wide range of issues and conversation partners. Consolidating the gains of evangelical Christological reflection, this volume makes gains of its own, particularly by wrestling clearly and carefully with contemporary trends in biblical studies as well as philosophical, systematic, and historical theology."

Michael Horton, J. Gresham Machen Professor of Systematic Theology and Apologetics, Westminster Seminary California

"This is a clear, comprehensive, and compelling study. It shows Christology to be like a fabric made up of many threads all tightly woven together, a doctrine with presuppositions, connections, and consequences for the age in which we live. This doctrine is here seen in its wholeness, and that is what makes this study so theologically wholesome. It is fresh and excellent."

David F. Wells, Distinguished Senior Research Professor, Gordon-Conwell Theological Seminary

"In lucid prose, Wellum lays out the contours of a responsible Christology by tracing the arguments of the New Testament through the determinative early centuries of the Christian church, using such discussion as the jumping-off point for broader theological reflection. This is now the handbook to give to theology students and other Christians who want to understand how confessional orthodoxy regarding the doctrine of Christ developed. Highly recommended."

D. A. Carson, Research Professor of New Testament, Trinity Evangelical Divinity School; Cofounder, The Gospel Coalition

"How does the church construct its doctrine of Jesus Christ? Biblicism collects the many verses about Christ and develops a doctrine about his person and work without an overarching framework. Liberalism seeks to paint a nontraditional portrait of Jesus in order to engage with some contemporary issue or to promote a specific political agenda. Experientialism picks and chooses concepts about Jesus that conform to and confirm its idyllic vision of him. Wellum rejects these approaches and offers the church a Christology that is at once biblical, historically grounded, philosophically astute, theologically robust, covenantal, canonical, confessional, and devotional. Often as I read *God the Son Incarnate*, I had to pause to worship the God-man presented in its pages. This book is absolutely brilliant!"

Gregg R. Allison, Professor of Christian Theology, The Southern Baptist Theological Seminary

"*God the Son Incarnate* is a masterful work written by one of evangelicalism's finest theologians. In this substantial, perceptive, and faithful volume, the doctrine of Christ is ably situated in the biblical story, grounded in biblical theology, related to the historical and contemporary context, and synthesized via systematic theology. The result is that pastors, students, and church leaders alike will mature in their understanding and appreciation of Jesus's life, deity, humanity, unity, and identity."

Christopher W. Morgan, Dean and Professor of Theology, California Baptist University

"Good theology depends on good methodology, and here Wellum is second to none. After establishing a philosophical backdrop, Wellum employs exegesis, biblical theology, and historical theology to draw out systematic conclusions that apply Scripture to life. And all our doctrine, he observes, prepares us for Christology or is inferred from it. The theology and life of the church makes sense only when centered on Christ, who is God the Son incarnate, the fulfillment of divine desire and the hope of humanity. Working through these pages, the word that kept occurring to me was 'masterful.' If you only have time for one Christology, start here. I commend it without reservation."

Jonathan Leeman, Editorial Director, 9Marks; author, *Church and the Surprising Offense of God's Love*

GOD THE SON
INCARNATE

GOD THE SON INCARNATE

THE DOCTRINE OF CHRIST

STEPHEN J. WELLUM

WHEATON, ILLINOIS

Library of Congress Cataloging-in-Publication Data
Names: Wellum, Stephen J., 1964– author.
Title: God the Son incarnate : the doctrine of Christ / Stephen J. Wellum.
Description: Wheaton : Crossway, 2016. | Series: Foundations of evangelical theology series | Includes
    bibliographical references and index.
Identifiers: LCCN 2015046435 (print) | LCCN 2016003379 (ebook) | ISBN 9781581346473 (hc) | ISBN
    9781433517860 (epub) | ISBN 9781433518102 (pdf) | ISBN 9781433517853 (mobi)
Subjects: LCSH: Jesus Christ—Person and offices.
Classification: LCC BT203 .W454 2016 (print) | LCC BT203 (ebook) | DDC 232—dc23
LC record available at http://lccn.loc.gov/2015046435

To my dear wife, Karen,
Who in every way imaginable has faithfully
encouraged me to see this work completed,
And who most of all delights and glories in Christ Jesus our Lord,
As heirs together of God's sovereign grace in Christ.

To our precious children, Joel, Justin, Joshua, Janae, and Jessica,
Further evidence of God's blessing, mercy, and grace in my life.
May the Lord of Glory be your salvation, delight, and glory, and
may each of you in your own way live under Christ's Lordship
and proclaim him who is the way, the truth, and the life.

CONTENTS

PART ONE:
EPISTEMOLOGICAL WARRANT FOR CHRISTOLOGY TODAY

        I. Two Major Trends in Contemporary Christology

            A. *The Paradigm of Historical Jesus Research*

            B. *The Paradigm of Pluralism*

       II. Two Roots of Confusion in Contemporary Christology

            A. *The Impact of the Enlightenment on Christology*

                1. Enlightenment Epistemology and Worldview

                    a. The Revolution in Philosophy

                    b. The Revolution in Science

                    c. The Devolution of Religion

                2. Enlightenment Hermeneutics

                    a. The Rise of Biblical Criticism

                    b. The Rule(s) of the Historical-Critical Method

                3. The Enlightenment and Christology

                    a. The Influence of Kantianism

                    b. The Influence of Deism

                    c. The Influence of Historical Criticism

                    d. The Loss of the Revealed and Real Jesus

            B. *The Impact of Postmodernism on Christology*

                1. Postmodern Epistemology and Worldview

                2. Postmodern Hermeneutics

                3. Postmodernism and Christology

      III. One Response to Contemporary Christology

PART TWO:
BIBLICAL WARRANT FOR CHRISTOLOGY TODAY

V. The Monothelite-Dyothelite Controversy

    A. *The Importance of the "Will" Debate for Christology*

    B. *Monothelitism: Its Basic Concern and Arguments*

    C. *Dyothelitism and the Contribution of Maximus the Confessor*

PART FOUR:
A WARRANTED CHRISTOLOGY FOR TODAY

    I. Kenotic Christology (1800–1950)

        A. *Nineteenth-Century Continental Kenotic Christology*

           1. Gottfried Thomasius (1802–1875)

           2. J. H. August Ebrard (1818–1888)

           3. W. F. Gess (1819–1891)

        B. *Early Twentieth-Century British Kenoticism*

           1. Charles Gore (1853–1932)

           2. P. T. Forsyth (1848–1921)

           3. Hugh Ross Mackintosh (1870–1936)

    II. Preliminary Evaluation of Kenoticism

    I. Ontological Kenotic Christology (OKC)

    II. Functional Kenotic Christology (FKC)

        A. *Overview of FKC*

        B. *Two Representative Examples of FKC*

           1. Garrett Deweese and Klaus Issler (FKC 1)

               a. *The Chalcedonian Definition and Its Problems*

               b. *The Metaphysical and Theological Commitments of FKC 1*

           2. William Lane Craig and J. P. Moreland (FKC 2)

               a. *The Chalcedonian Definition and Its Problems*

               b. *The Metaphysical and Theological Commitments of FKC 2*

Why another series of works on evangelical systematic theology? This is an especially appropriate question in light of the fact that evangelicals are fully committed to an inspired and inerrant Bible as their final authority for faith and practice. But since neither God nor the Bible changes, why is there a need to redo evangelical systematic theology?

Systematic theology is not divine revelation. Theologizing of any sort is a human conceptual enterprise. Thinking that it is equal to biblical revelation misunderstands the nature of both Scripture and theology! Insofar as our theology contains propositions that accurately reflect Scripture or match the world and are consistent with the Bible (in cases where the propositions do not come per se from Scripture), our theology is biblically based and correct. But even if all the propositions of a systematic theology are true, that theology would still not be equivalent to biblical revelation! It is still a human conceptualization of God and his relation to the world.

Although this may disturb some who see theology as nothing more than doing careful exegesis over a series of passages, and others who see it as nothing more than biblical theology, those methods of doing theology do not somehow produce a theology that is equivalent to biblical revelation either. Exegesis is a human conceptual enterprise, and so is biblical theology. All the theological disciplines involve human intellectual participation. But human intellect is finite, and hence there is always room for revision of systematic theology as knowledge increases. Though God and his Word do not change, human understanding of his revelation can grow, and our theologies should be reworked to reflect those advances in understanding.

Another reason for evangelicals to rework their theology is the nature of systematic theology as opposed to other theological disciplines. For example, whereas the task of biblical theology is more to describe biblical teaching on whatever topics Scripture addresses, systematics should make a special point to relate its conclusions to the issues of one's day. This does not mean that the systematician ignores the topics biblical writers address. Nor does it mean that theologians should warp Scripture to address issues it never intended to address. Rather it suggests that in addition to expounding what biblical writers teach, the theologian should attempt to take those biblical teachings (along with the biblical mind-set) and apply them to issues that are especially confronting the church in the theologian's own day. For example, 150 years ago, an evangelical theologian doing work on the doctrine of man would likely have discussed issues such as the creation of man and the constituent parts of man's being. Such a theology might even have included a discussion about human institutions such as marriage, noting in general the respective roles of husbands and wives in marriage. However, it is dubious that there would have been any lengthy discussion with various viewpoints about the respective roles of men and women in marriage, in society, and in the church. But at our point in history and in light of the feminist movement and the issues it has raised even among many conservative Christians, it would be foolish to write a theology of man (or, should we say, a "theology of humanity") without a thorough discussion of the issue of the roles of men and women in society, the home, and the church.

Because systematic theology attempts to address itself not only to the timeless issues presented in Scripture but also to the current issues of one's day and culture, each theology will to some extent need to be redone in each generation. Biblical truth does not change from generation to generation, but the issues that confront the church do. A theology that was adequate for a different era and different culture may simply not speak to key issues in a given culture at a given time. Hence, in this series we are reworking evangelical systematic theology, though we do so with the understanding that in future generations there will be room for a revision of theology again.

How, then, do the contributors to this series understand the nature of systematic theology? Systematic theology as done from an evangelical Christian perspective involves study of the person, works, and relationships of God. As evangelicals committed to the full inspiration, inerrancy, and final authority of Scripture, we demand that whatever appears in a systematic theology correspond to the way things are and must not contradict any claim taught in Scripture. Holy Writ is the touchstone of our theology, but we do not limit the source material for systematics to Scripture alone. Hence, whatever information from history, science, philosophy, and the like is relevant to our understanding of God and his relation to our world is fair game for systematics. Depending on the specific interests and expertise of the contributors to this series, their respective volumes will reflect interaction with one or more of these disciplines.

What is the rationale for appealing to sources other than Scripture and disciplines other than the biblical ones? Since God created the universe, there is revelation of God not only in Scripture but in the created order as well. There are many disciplines that study our world, just as does theology. But since the world studied by the non-theological disciplines is the world created by God, any data and conclusions in the so-called secular disciplines that accurately reflect the real world are also relevant to our understanding of the God who made that world. Hence, in a general sense, since all of creation is God's work, nothing is outside the realm of theology. The so-called secular disciplines need to be thought of in a theological context, because they are reflecting on the universe God created, just as is the theologian. And, of course, there are many claims in the non-theological disciplines that are generally accepted as true (although this does not mean that every claim in non-theological disciplines is true, or that we are in a position with respect to every proposition to know whether it is true or false). Since this is so, and since all disciplines are in one way or another reflecting on our universe, a universe made by God, any true statement in any discipline should in some way be informative for our understanding of God and his relation to our world. Hence, we have felt it appropriate to incorporate data from outside the Bible in our theological formulations.

As to the specific design of this series, our intention is to address all areas of evangelical theology with a special emphasis on key issues in each area. While other series may be more like a history of doctrine, this series purposes to incorporate insights from Scripture, historical theology, philosophy, etc., in order to produce an up-to-date work in systematic theology. Though all contributors to the series are thoroughly evangelical in their theology, embracing the historical orthodox doctrines of the church, the series as a whole is not meant to be slanted in the direction of one form of evangelical theology. Nonetheless, most of the writers come from a Reformed perspective. Alternate evangelical and non-evangelical options, however, are discussed.

As to style and intended audience, this series is meant to rest on the very best of scholarship while at the same time being understandable to the beginner in theology as well as to the academic theologian. With that in mind, contributors are writing in a clear style, taking care to define whatever technical terms they use.

Finally, we believe that systematic theology is not just for the understanding. It must apply to life, and it must be lived. As Paul wrote to Timothy, God has given divine revelation for many purposes, including ones that necessitate doing theology, but the ultimate reason for giving revelation and for theologians doing theology is that the people of God may be fitted for every good work (2 Tim. 3:16–17). In light of the need for theology to connect to life, each of the contributors not only formulates doctrines but also explains how those doctrines practically apply to everyday living.

It is our sincerest hope that the work we have done in this series will first glorify and please God, and, second, instruct and edify the people of God. May God be pleased to use this series to those ends, and may he richly bless you as you read the fruits of our labors.

John S. Feinberg
General Editor

When I first agreed to undertake this project, I had no idea how difficult, challenging, and rewarding it would be. Looking back, it is not a surprise that this would be the case, given the vast scope of the subject matter. To understand our Lord Jesus Christ rightly is to understand the heart of our triune God's plan, Scripture, and the gospel itself. As an exercise in "faith seeking understanding," to think through and reflect upon our Lord's identity, the nature of the incarnation, and why he alone is the Lord and Savior, is not only challenging but glorious. It is my prayer that this work will encourage the reader to know Christ better, to be led to greater love and trust of and obedience to the Lord of Glory, and to count it a privilege to proclaim him as he truly is, the only Lord and Savior, especially in our pluralistic and postmodern age.

Many people need to be thanked, without whom this work would never have seen the light of day. We all stand on the shoulders of those who have gone before us. My understanding of the gospel, and being taught from my earliest years about the glory of Christ, is due to my faithful and godly parents, Colin and Joan Wellum. From my first breath, our Lord Jesus in all of his beauty and majesty was impressed upon my mind and heart. In addition, during my youth and teenage years, my faithful pastor, William Payne, never tired of proclaiming Christ and him crucified, and instead of capitulating to the latest fads, exhorted me to glory in Christ and him alone. This continued in my undergraduate days under the preaching ministry of John Reisinger, and later in my seminary education at Trinity Evangelical Divinity School (TEDS). There are simply too many people to thank for their influence in my life, thinking, and theology.

In addition, I want to thank the administration and trustees of The Southern Baptist Theological Seminary for granting me a number of sabbaticals to work on this project. Without their generous sabbatical policy it would have been difficult to do the research and writing of this work. I also want to thank my colleagues at Southern who have contributed to this work, especially those in the theology and tradition department—Bruce Ware, Gregg Allison, Michael Haykin, and Tom Nettles; and Peter Gentry, who teaches in the area of biblical studies. To my students over the years, first at Northwest Baptist College and Seminary and the Associated Canadian Theological Schools and Toronto Baptist Seminary, and now for these last seventeen years at Southern, I want to thank you for thinking through the glory of Christ with me in classes devoted to his person and work. May each of you never grow tired of knowing Christ who is life eternal. In addition, specific thanks go to Michael Wilkinson, one of my doctoral students at Southern, who, in a labor of love, spent countless hours editing the final work and made it a far better one, even though I take responsibility for its content. Special thanks go to John Feinberg, the editor of this series and one of my beloved theology professors at TEDS. Years ago, John invited me to be a part of the Foundations of Evangelical Theology Series, and he took a risk in doing so, for which I am truly grateful. Thank you, John, for allowing younger men like me to have an opportunity to write for the series.

Finally, I dedicate this work to my family: my wife, Karen; and our children, Joel, Justin, Joshua, Janae, and Jessica. Without their constant love, patience, and encouragement this work would not have been done. There is nothing more important in life than to know, trust, love, and obey Jesus Christ our Lord. May he be your portion, delight, and joy all the days of your life. And as Francis Schaeffer many years ago challenged a new generation, may you live your lives to the glory of our triune covenant God as radicals for truth and as those who are ambassadors of the King of kings and the Lord of lords. May Christ Jesus our Lord, God the Son incarnate, receive all praise and glory, for he is worthy!

ANF   *Ante-Nicene Fathers*, ed. Alexander Roberts, James Donaldson, Philip Schaff, and Henry Wace, 10 vols. (Peabody, MA: Hendrickson, 1994).

BECNT   Baker Exegetical Commentary on the New Testament

EBC   *The Expositor's Bible Commentary*

IJST   *International Journal of Systematic Theology*

NDBT   *New Dictionary of Biblical Theology*, ed. T. Desmond Alexander et al. (Downers Grove, IL: InterVarsity Press, 2000).

NICNT   New International Commentary on the New Testament

NIGTC   New International Greek Testament Commentary

NSBT   New Studies in Biblical Theology

NPNF[2]   *Nicene and Post-Nicene Fathers*, Series 2, ed. Alexander Roberts, James Donaldson, Philip Schaff, and Henry Wace, 14 vols. (Peabody, MA: Hendrickson, 1994).

PNTC   Pillar New Testament Commentary

WBC   Word Biblical Commentary

WTJ   *Westminster Theological Journal*

The well-known church historian Jaroslav Pelikan famously begins his book *Jesus through the Centuries* with a comment about the historical importance of Jesus Christ: "Regardless of what anyone may personally think or believe about him, Jesus of Nazareth has been the dominant figure in the history of Western culture for almost twenty centuries."[1] Pelikan's observation is not hyperbole. Even to this day, for example, a large portion of the human population continues to divide world history into BC and AD by reference to Jesus's birth in history. The importance of this particular Nazarene, however, goes far beyond natural historical observation.

Since the first few centuries AD, Jesus has been the dominant figure in religion and theological reflection. Whether out of devotion and worship or suspicion and critique, the person of Christ has held the attention of the church and the world for most of those two thousand years. And this attention is well placed. The person of Christ stands at the center of the Scriptures that reveal the purpose and plan of God for humanity and the rest of creation. According to its own claims, Scripture is God's self-revelation given progressively through the writings of human authors. As *God's* word, then, the diversity of texts come together as a unified divine communicative act[2] of the one who creates, sustains, plans, and governs all things. *This* word of *this* God declares that Jesus Christ is the focus and fulfillment of divine desire and glory and the hope of all humanity.

Jesus himself understood and taught that both Scripture and God's plan of salvation are Christocentric. Jesus chided the men on the road to Emmaus for not believing all that the prophets had spoken concerning his identity and work: "'Was it not necessary that the Christ should suffer these things and enter into his glory?' And beginning with Moses and all the Prophets, he interpreted to them in all the Scriptures the things concerning himself" (Luke 24:26–27).[3] Jesus confronted the religious leaders for not identifying him as the goal of God's revelation: "You search the Scriptures because you think that in them you have eternal life; and it is they that bear witness about me, yet you refuse to come to me that you may have life" (John 5:39–40). Jesus knew that

---

[1] Jaroslav Pelikan, *Jesus through the Centuries: His Place in the History of Culture* (New Haven, CT: Yale University Press, 1999), 1.
[2] This term is taken from Kevin J. Vanhoozer, "Exegesis and Hermeneutics," in *NDBT*, 52–64.
[3] Unless otherwise noted, all quotations of Scripture are taken from the English Standard Version (ESV).

he was the only way to life with God: "And this is eternal life, that they know you the only true God, and Jesus Christ whom you have sent" (John 17:3). And Jesus's apostles agreed that he is the focal point and fulfillment of God's plan of revelation and redemption. The book of Hebrews begins by underscoring the superiority and finality of God's self-disclosure in his Son: "Long ago, at many times and in many ways, God spoke to our fathers by the prophets, but in these last days he has spoken to us by his Son" (Heb. 1:1–2a). In Ephesians, Paul explains that, in Christ, God has made known his eternal will, "which he set forth in Christ as a plan for the fullness of time, to unite all things in him, things in heaven and things on earth" (Eph. 1:9–10).

The most important figure in the fullness of God's work, then, is the person of Jesus Christ. Paul can even describe the importance of Christ in terms of his cosmic preeminence: "For by him all things were created, in heaven and on earth, visible and invisible, whether thrones or dominions or rulers or authorities—all things were created through him and for him. And he is before all things, and in him all things hold together" (Col. 1:16–17).

The importance of the person of Christ, moreover, places Christology at the center of all theological reflection and formulation. As Herman Bavinck so aptly reminded us a century ago in his magisterial *Reformed Dogmatics*, "The doctrine of Christ is not the starting point, but it certainly is the central point of the whole system of dogmatics. All other dogmas either prepare for it or are inferred from it. In it, as the heart of dogmatics, pulses the whole of the religious-ethical life of Christianity. It is 'the mystery of godliness' (1 Tim. 3:16)."[4] The idea of a center point does not create a doctrinal hierarchy but confesses that all things theological fit together according to the pattern of Scripture. As J. I. Packer instructs, Christian theology should be viewed as "an organism, a unity of interrelated parts, a circle in which everything links up with everything else."[5] And in the center of that circle sits the discipline of Christology—the study of the person of Christ. So Packer gives us another apt metaphor: "Christology is the true hub round which the wheel of theology revolves, and to which its separate spokes must each be correctly anchored if the wheel is not to get bent."[6] We should expect, then, that when theological formulation misunderstands or distorts the identity of Christ, the entire set of related theological convictions will eventually contort or collapse completely.

Historic Christianity's most distinctive convictions are decisively shaped and determined by a proper understanding of the identity of Christ.[7] For exam-

---

[4] Herman Bavinck, *Sin and Salvation in Christ*, vol. 3 of *Reformed Dogmatics*, ed. John Bolt, trans. John Vriend (Grand Rapids, MI: Baker Academic, 2006), 274.
[5] J. I. Packer, "Uniqueness of Jesus Christ," *Churchman* 92/2 (1978): 110.
[6] J. I. Packer, "Jesus Christ the Lord," in *The J. I. Packer Collection*, comp. Alister McGrath (Downers Grove, IL: InterVarsity Press, 1999), 151.
[7] Ibid.

ple, the doctrine of the Trinity, the distinguishing feature of a Christian view of God, developed because the church rightly affirmed the incarnation of Christ from heaven, his status and title as Lord, and his relationship to the Father and the Holy Spirit. Regarding the doctrine of humanity, historic Christianity teaches that we cannot fully understand who we are apart from the identity of Christ as the Son and true image of God, his incarnation into our humanity, his life as the last Adam, and his crucifixion and resurrection for us. And the doctrine of the atonement puts Christ on the cross at the center of the triune God's work to redeem humanity. In his classic work *The Cross of Christ*, John Stott argues well that fully understanding the biblical language regarding the *death* of Christ requires correct conclusions regarding the *person* of Christ.[8] After surveying a number of options, Stott concludes that the core teaching of penal substitution is rooted in the proper identity of Christ:

> If the essence of the atonement is substitution . . . the theological inference is that it is impossible to hold the historic doctrine of the cross without holding the historic doctrine of Jesus Christ as the one and only God-man and Mediator. . . . At the root of every caricature of the cross lies a distorted Christology. The person and work of Christ belong together. If he was not who the apostles say he was, then he could not have done what they say he did. The incarnation is indispensable to the atonement.[9]

In short, we cannot afford to get Christology wrong. We simply must know and confess the person of Christ in truth.

The work of Christology, then, has crucial significance for the church and for the world. The question of Jesus's identity is not merely academic, something for theologians to ponder. Knowing who Jesus is in truth, rather, is a matter of the utmost urgency—it is literally a matter of life and death. And this great task becomes even more urgent today because the church is living and thinking amid much Christological confusion created by the misidentification of Christ. Similar to the first century (although for different reasons), our own day has seen the rise of a rampant philosophical and religious pluralism. There are many beliefs that distinguish Christianity from other worldviews, but none as important as the identity of Christ. The claim that Jesus Christ is both divine and human and the only Lord and Savior is viewed with suspicion, doubt, and even outright anger. Regardless of the response, however, the discussion always centers on the question of Jesus's identity. As Harold Netland reminds us so well, "No serious discussion of the relation of Christianity to other faiths can proceed very far without coming to grips with the towering figure of Jesus. Sooner or later, the blunt question put by Jesus to his followers—'Who do

---

[8] See John Stott, *The Cross of Christ* (Downers Grove, IL: InterVarsity Press, 1986), 149–163.
[9] Ibid., 160.

people say I am?' (Mark 8:27)—must be confronted."[10] The Jesus of the Bible is unique to Christianity, and *this* Jesus demands and deserves all of our commitment, obedience, and trust.

Given the importance of the person of Christ and Christology, this work aims to articulate a contemporary orthodox Christology that equips the church for edification in Christ and proclamation of the name of Christ. Orthodox Christology remains the most faithful to the biblical presentation of Christ and the most coherent theological formulation of his identity and significance. Such a classic Christology, however, must be articulated amid a new cultural disposition toward Christ and defended against current challenges born out of confusion regarding the identity of Christ.

The scope of such a work could stretch across multiple volumes, and it could be written for a range of readers, from laypeople to seminary students to professional academics. As part of the Foundations of Evangelical Theology series, however, the main goal here is to help equip Christians in local churches and evangelical seminaries to know the biblical presentation of Jesus Christ so that we might proclaim him with greater clarity, and delight in him with joy inexpressible and filled with glory.

Indeed, the church exists to proclaim the glory of the one who brought us out of darkness and into his marvelous light, according to which we are also conformed to that same glory and excellence. Yet as the church, our sanctification and proclamation are always situated: all that we do and say is done and said in a certain culture at a particular time in church history. What we say, moreover, is either accepted or rejected by our culture (both inside and outside the church) and either consistent or inconsistent with what the church has already said. To say anything about Jesus, then, we need to be warranted both philosophically/epistemologically and historically/ecclesiologically.[11] Ultimately, of course, we want to be biblically warranted in what we say about Jesus. The biblical presentation of Jesus Christ is the authoritative identification of our Lord, whether accepted or rejected by culture or affirmed or denied in church history. Our theology must first be correct. But it must also be cogent and must be communicated in the church's current context so that our proclamation will be both true and persuasive. We need to be extensively warranted in our conclusions regarding the one who is God and who became a man for the salvation of humanity and the glory of God.

The first three parts of this work are an effort to provide philosophical/epistemological (Part I), biblical/exegetical (Part II), and historical/ecclesiological

---

[10] Harold A. Netland, *Dissonant Voices: Religious Pluralism and the Question of Truth* (Grand Rapids, MI: Eerdmans, 1991), 235.
[11] Throughout this work, I am using warrant/warranted in the sense of providing grounds, i.e., reasons to believe what we say about who Jesus is and the identity of his person.

(Part III) warrant for the Christological conclusions at the end (Part IV). That conclusion, and the thesis of this entire volume, is that Jesus Christ is *God the Son incarnate*, one person subsisting in and acting through a fully divine nature and a fully human nature according to the attributes of each. The glorious import of this Christological identification is that, in Jesus, God himself rules sovereignly over his creation to judge the world in righteousness and that he becomes a human representative substitute for a redeemed humanity to live in covenant with God.

In Part I, we will establish the epistemological warrant for Christology. In our current context, we cannot take it for granted that everyone agrees on how we can and do come to know who Jesus is. In fact, the possibility of objective *truth* is questioned openly in today's world. It is difficult to jump into the propositional statements about the identity of Jesus Christ without first providing a well-reasoned account for how we can know anything about him. Chapter 1 will unearth the epistemological roots of current confusion regarding the identity of Jesus Christ, while chapter 2 will argue that a Christology "from above," namely a Christology rooted and grounded in Scripture, is what is necessary for a truly evangelical Christology.

In Part II, we will turn to biblical warrant for Christology by following the Bible's own presentation of who Jesus is. The Bible presents itself as one story that moves across four parts and through six covenants, unfolding the promises of God in the Old Testament and their fulfillment in the New Testament. To have biblical warrant for Christology today, what the Bible says about Jesus Christ must be read and understood according to this authoritative structure. Chapter 3 will describe the redemptive-covenantal structure of the Scriptures and place Jesus's identity within that storyline. Building on the Bible's storyline, chapter 4 will sketch the Bible's overall presentation of Christ by considering Jesus's self-understanding of who he is and how his apostles identify him according to his words and works. Chapter 5 will explore the biblical data regarding the deity of Christ, while chapter 6 will explore the full humanity of Christ by focusing on the biblical presentation of the incarnation and the rationale for God the Son adding to himself a human nature and thus becoming the man Christ Jesus.

After establishing the biblical warrant for Christology, in Part III we will develop the ecclesiological warrant. Scripture alone has magisterial authority, but the church's understanding of Scripture throughout history has ministerial authority for us today. Chapter 7 will consider the era from the first century to the Council of Nicaea and will investigate the issues and heresies that first created the need for an orthodox Christology. Chapter 8 will explore the Christological developments between Nicaea and the Council of Chalcedon, while chapter 9 will describe post-Chalcedonian developments which establish a received orthodox Christology.

In Part IV we will conclude our investigation by developing a contemporary articulation of classical Christology for evangelicals today. Chapters 10–12 take up the contemporary challenges to orthodox Christology by what has come to be known as kenotic Christology. After critiquing kenotic Christologies for failing to provide a "newer," "better," and more faithful Christology in contrast to the "older" formulation, chapters 13–14 will describe and defend a classical Christology for evangelicals today.

With that roadmap before us, we now turn to the glorious yet sobering task of thinking through the identity of our Lord Jesus Christ. Even though the task is formidable, given its importance it must be done anew for every generation. The work here can only serve as an introduction, but it is my goal to survey the crucial components of a robust evangelical Christology for today's church. My ultimate aim is not only to lay out the biblical data that grounds the church's Christology, to think through how the church has formulated Christology in the past, and to wrestle with current evangelical Christologies; I also want to proceed in such a way that we are led afresh to know Jesus Christ and to proclaim him as he truly is, the Lord of Glory who is life eternal.

I

EPISTEMOLOGICAL WARRANT
FOR CHRISTOLOGY TODAY

In general, epistemological warrant in the realm of theology amounts to a well-reasoned account of how humans can know God. Epistemological warrant for Christology should provide sound reasoning for how we can know God in the person of Jesus Christ.

In our current Christological climate, we cannot take it for granted that everyone agrees on how we can and do come to know who Jesus is. In fact, the possibility of objective *truth* is questioned openly in today's epistemological culture. It would not serve the reader, then, to jump into propositional statements about the identity of Jesus Christ without first providing a well-reasoned account for how we can know anything about him at all. Moreover, we must be able to connect *how* we can know about Jesus with *what we say* about him.

Since this is not a work on epistemology itself, the attempt at epistemological warrant here will not address the core issues and breadth of concerns related to the nature of knowledge and the means by which it can be obtained. As the Christology volume in the Foundations of Evangelical Theology series, this work begins with certain presuppositions regarding epistemology: e.g., the existence of the visible world we experience; the existence of an invisible world beyond our direct experience; the ability to know about these worlds in truth; the objectivity of truth, which is unchanged by the way we experience or know about the visible and invisible worlds. Yet building on these evangelical assumptions in epistemology, we need to give a well-reasoned account of how we can know God (invisible) in Christ (visible).

Chapter 1 will unearth the epistemological roots of current confusion regarding the identity of Jesus Christ. Epistemology shapes theological method, which then determines what we say about God. The post-Reformation changes in epistemology and method are largely responsible for the divergent views that persist in Christology today. Chapter 2 will then reach back to the insights of the Reformation to return to a Christology "from above." Revelation *from God* is the only way we can know anything *about God*. And this requires a certain attitude toward his word in Scripture and a particular method for reading it.

Contemporary Christology

Jesus of Nazareth has been and still is an enigma to many people. Even though he has been the dominant figure in the history of Western culture for almost twenty centuries, a majority of people are still confused regarding his identity. A famous poem once tried to capture something of the enigma and significance of Jesus:

> He was born in an obscure village,
>   the child of a peasant woman.
> He grew up in still another village
>   where he worked until he was thirty.
> Then for three years
>   he was an itinerant preacher.
> He never wrote a book.
> He never held an office.
> He never had a family or owned a home.
> He didn't go to college.
> He never traveled more than 200 miles
>   from the place he was born.
> He did none of the things
>   one usually associates with greatness.
> He had no credentials but himself;
>   he was only thirty-three
>   when public opinion turned against him.
> His friends ran away.
> He was turned over to his enemies
>   and went through the mockery of a trial.
> He was nailed to the cross
>   between two thieves.
> While he was dying
>   his executioners gambled for his clothing,
>   the only property he had on earth.
> When he was dead

he was laid in a borrowed grave
through the pity of a friend.
Nineteen centuries have come and gone
and today he is the central figure
of the human race,
the leader of mankind's progress.
All the armies that ever marched,
all the navies that ever sailed,
all the parliaments that ever sat,
all the kings that ever reigned,
put together,
have not affected
the life of man on earth
as much as that
One Solitary Life.[1]

Who do we say that Jesus Christ is? The question itself is not new; it has been asked ever since Jesus's earthly ministry. The writers of the four Gospels labored to impress upon us the revelation of Jesus of Nazareth, and they persist in pressing the point of his identity: *Who is* this Jesus? *Who is he* who is born the son of David, the son of Abraham (Matt. 1:1)? *Who is he* who announces the dawning of the kingdom (Matt. 4:12–17)? *Who is he* who resists every temptation of the Devil (Luke 4:1–13)? *Who is he* who commands wind and water and turns water into wine (Luke 8:22–25; John 2:6–11)? *Who is he* who pronounces the forgiveness of sins (Mark 2:1–12)? *Who is he* who raises the dead and rises from the grave (John 11:38–44; 20:1–18)?

Even Jesus himself asked his disciples, "Who do people say that the Son of Man is?" (Matt. 16:13). Similar to our own day, the responses of the people then were diverse and confused. Some identified him superstitiously with John the Baptist come back from the dead, while others thought of him as one of the great Old Testament prophets. So Jesus asked his disciples, "But who do you say that I am?" (v. 15). Speaking for them, Peter answered correctly, "You are the Christ, the Son of the living God" (v. 16). But even then, Peter did not fully grasp Jesus's identity. Immediately after his confession, Peter objected to Jesus's prediction and explanation of his own suffering and death. Peter could not yet conceive of a suffering Messiah, thinking instead of a victorious king. It was not until after the resurrection that Peter and the disciples began to understand who Jesus truly was as the Son and the Messiah. *The question of Jesus's identity could not be fully answered until all of the great events of redemptive history were fully aligned with Jesus's own life, death, and resurrection.*

---

[1] Cited in George Gallup Jr. and George O'Connell, *Who Do Americans Say That I Am?* (Philadelphia: Westminster, 1986), 14–15. The poem is an adaption from James Allan Francis, *The Real Jesus, and Other Sermons* (Philadelphia: Judson, 1926).

Even after Easter, the first-century question remains today, and unfortunately so does the confusion. Similar to the answers of old, a wide variety of responses are given today to Jesus's question about his identity: he is a sage, a prophet, a revolutionary, a cynic, and, for some, simply a failed religious leader.[2] Almost without fail, every Christmas and Easter (at least in North America) popular magazines (e.g., *Time, U.S. News & World Report, Maclean's*) and cable networks (e.g., A&E, History Channel) devote time to the question, Who is Jesus of Nazareth? Repeated Gallup polls show that people often affirm some kind of belief in Jesus, but probing deeper usually reveals that their belief is ill-informed, confused, and often contradictory to other beliefs they affirm.[3]

For Christians, this kind of confusion and uncertainty is not a benign issue. Scripture presents Jesus of Nazareth as God's own eternal Son and as a man who is appointed by God the Father to judge the living and the dead. As Stephen Clark rightly notes, Scripture is unified in its presentation of who Jesus is. As he notes, despite the diversity of the biblical material, there is a "uniform conviction that Jesus Christ is God and man."[4] In light of Scripture, the church has confessed consistently that to identify Jesus correctly we must affirm that he is the divine Son who has become incarnate, that to know him is life eternal, and that to know him not is judgment unto death. Biblically speaking, getting Christ right is a matter of life and death.

Yet even with this urgency, we must resist the temptation to move directly to the biblical foundations, historical formulations, and contemporary discussions of Christology within evangelical theology. Systematic theology does not merely *articulate* doctrines in timeless propositions; systematic theology, rather, is best understood as the *application* of Scripture to all areas of life. This articulation and application involves not only exegesis and biblical theology in light of historical theology, but also the attempt to help the church apply the biblical teaching to our current context.[5] The nature of systematic theology necessitates that we understand our present-day situation and the particular challenges it poses.

In his instructive book *Above All Earthly Pow'rs*, David Wells makes this precise point, arguing for Christology within a twofold reality: first, "the disintegration of the Enlightenment world and its replacement by the postmodern ethos"; second, the increase of religious pluralism.[6] These two intellectual

---

2 For helpful discussions of some of these current views of Jesus, see N. T. Wright, *Who Was Jesus?* (Grand Rapids, MI: Eerdmans, 1992); Gregory A. Boyd, *Cynic, Sage, or Son of God?* (Wheaton, IL: Victor, 1995); Ben Witherington III, *The Jesus Quest: The Third Search for the Jew of Nazareth*, 2nd ed. (Downers Grove, IL: InterVarsity Press, 1997).

3 For example, see Gallup and O'Connell, *Who Do Americans Say That I Am?*, 41–59.

4 Stephen Clark, "Introduction," in *The Forgotten Christ: Exploring the Majesty and Mystery of God Incarnate*, ed. Stephen Clark (Nottingham: Apollos, 2007), 9.

5 See John Frame, *The Doctrine of the Knowledge of God* (Phillipsburg, NJ: P&R, 1987), 76–88.

6 David F. Wells, *Above All Earthly Pow'rs: Christ in a Postmodern World* (Grand Rapids, MI: Eerdmans, 2005), 5. Wells develops this argument here (see ibid., 60–262). But he has also made similar points in his previous three

and cultural developments have posed a number of serious implications for doing orthodox Christology, certainly the most important being the need for a plausible defense of the uniqueness and exclusivity of Jesus Christ in a day of philosophical pluralism.[7] As Wells rightly notes, our theology must not remain merely internal to the church or to the academy; it must also address and help the church to meet the challenges we face in presenting Christ to a skeptical age that simply regards the uniqueness of Christ as highly implausible.[8]

The conditions of belief in the medieval and Reformation eras have been eclipsed today by an entirely different set of *plausibility structures.*[9] The contemporary culture does not begin with the basic propositions of Christian theology. The secularization and pluralization of the West has altered the way people think because the conditions of belief have changed. In his magisterial work on the cognitive impact of secularization, Charles Taylor traces these epistemological changes over three distinct time periods, pivoting around the Enlightenment: before the Enlightenment, people found it impossible not to believe the Christian worldview; starting with the Enlightenment, it became possible not to believe in the basic truths of Christianity; three hundred years after the Enlightenment and with the rise of postmodern pluralism, most people find it impossible to believe in the objective truths and ultimate concerns of the Christian worldview.[10] R. Albert Mohler Jr. helpfully summarizes Taylor's argument:

> In the first stage there was no rival explanation for any reality—for life, for the past, for the present, or for the future—other than Christianity. But now it is the absolute opposite. Now there are not only alternatives to the biblical worldview available, but these alternatives are declared to be superior. Indeed if nonbelief was an oddity in the first stage—so much that it was considered eccentric and even dangerous—in this third stage it is *theism* that is considered eccentric and dangerous.[11]

Obviously, what Taylor has observed in Western thought impacts how Christology will be viewed in terms of its plausibility, credibility, and logical

---

books, which reflect on the intersection of theology with contemporary culture: idem, *No Place for Truth, or Whatever Happened to Evangelical Theology?* (Grand Rapids, MI: Eerdmans, 1993); idem, *God in the Wasteland: The Reality of Truth in a World of Fading Dreams* (Grand Rapids, MI: Eerdmans, 1994); idem, *Losing Our Virtue: Why the Church Must Recover Its Moral Vision* (Grand Rapids, MI: Eerdmans, 1999).

[7] "Philosophical pluralism" can mean different things. I am using the term (along with "religious pluralism") in the same way as D. A. Carson, who uses it as an overarching term to capture the idea that "any notion that a particular ideological or religious claim is intrinsically superior to another is necessarily wrong. The only absolute creed is the creed of pluralism. No religion has the right to pronounce itself right or true, and others false, or even (in the majority view) relatively inferior" (D. A. Carson, *The Gagging of God: Christianity Confronts Pluralism* [Grand Rapids, MI: Zondervan, 1996], 19).

[8] See Wells, *Above All Earthly Pow'rs,* 6–12.

[9] See Peter L. Berger, *The Sacred Canopy: Elements of a Sociological Theory of Religion* (Garden City, NY: Doubleday, 1967); cf. Robert Wuthnow, *Rediscovering the Sacred: Perspectives on Religion in Contemporary Society* (Grand Rapids, MI: Eerdmans, 1992), 9–35.

[10] See Charles Taylor, *A Secular Age* (Cambridge, MA: Belknap, 2007).

[11] R. Albert Mohler Jr., *Atheism Remix: A Christian Confronts the New Atheists* (Wheaton, IL: Crossway, 2008), 37.

coherence. The current conditions of belief also challenge us to think through anew how best to do Christology in order to present Christ faithfully to a skeptical, pluralistic world. It would be unwise simply to work through the biblical, historical, and systematic data of Christology; doing evangelical *theology for today* requires attention to the specific *challenges of the day*. At this point, we need to remember Martin Luther's instruction to stand for the truth precisely at the point where it is being undermined and attacked:

> If I profess with the loudest voice and clearest exposition every portion of the truth of God except precisely that little point which the world and the devil are at that moment attacking, I am not confessing Christ, however boldly I may be professing Christ. Where the battle rages, there the loyalty of the soldier is proved, and to be steady on all the battle front besides, is merely flight and disgrace if he flinches at that point.[12]

Exhorted by Luther and obliged by the nature of systematic theology, we need to probe the plausibility structures that operate today, shaping the way people think. The present conditions of belief do not determine the identity of Christ that comes to us in Scripture. But where the dominant ways of thinking and knowing would make it difficult or impossible to know Christ from Scripture, we need to do some demolition work and construct the Bible's own structure of belief in an open and coherent manner. *In short, we need to lay the foundation of epistemological warrant to build an argument for an orthodox Christology for today.*

The rest of this chapter will argue that the two major trends in contemporary Christology are causing significant confusion regarding the identity of Christ because they are rooted in presuppositions that inevitably lead away from the true Jesus as he is revealed in Scripture. The epistemological changes in the Enlightenment and in postmodernity have grown throughout the areas of philosophy, science, religion, and hermeneutics to produce a skepticism toward the Bible and a rejection of its ability to identify Jesus accurately. Christology today, then, must address *how we can know* Jesus before we can say *who he is.*

Two Major Trends in Contemporary Christology

Throughout the ages, the church's confession has been uniform: Jesus is God the Son, the second person of the eternal Trinity, who at a specific point in history took to himself a human nature and was born as Jesus of Nazareth in order to accomplish our redemption. In the language of the Chalcedonian

---

[12] Cited in Francis A. Schaeffer, *No Final Conflict*, in *A Christian View of the Bible as Truth*, vol. 2 of *The Complete Works of Francis A. Schaeffer: A Christian Worldview*, 2nd ed. (Wheaton, IL: Crossway, 1985), 122. There is a legitimate dispute as to whether this was actually said by Luther. Regardless, it makes a significant point and it is the truth of the statement that I am emphasizing.

Definition, our Lord Jesus is God the Son incarnate—one person who subsists in two natures, fully God and fully man—who alone is Lord and Savior and worthy of our worship, trust, and obedience. Even though there have been various naysayers throughout church history, the Chalcedonian Confession remains the classic Christological statement accepted by virtually all segments of Christianity; the church has always confessed this basic orthodoxy as its starting point and touchstone for understanding the identity of Christ.

Today, however, the orthodox Definition is problematic for many. For a variety of reasons, many people no longer consider the orthodox understanding of Jesus's identity to be credible or plausible. Without trying to be reductionistic, we can identify two major non-orthodox trends in Christology today: first, the continued attempt to discover the historical Jesus in distinction from the biblical Jesus; second, the attempt to make Christ fit within the paradigm of religious pluralism.[13] Significantly, although proponents within these trends may differ in their motivation, methodology, and conclusions, the trends themselves lead equally to the same break from the central tradition of the church as summarized by Chalcedon. A brief description of each trend will provide for a better comprehension of the Christological confusion outside of the orthodox confession of the church.

The Paradigm of Historical Jesus Research

Many today seek to unearth the "historical Jesus" or the "real" Jesus of history.[14] Regardless of the specific viewpoint, the approaches in this trend all start with the same assumption: the "Jesus of history" is *not the same* as the "Jesus of the Bible," let alone the "Christ of Chalcedon." As Francis Watson rightly observes, modern historical Jesus research is part of "a scholarly project operating within a shared paradigm—that is, a set of assumptions, priorities, and methodological tools that inform and direct the process of research."[15] Alongside this particular project, many biblical scholars are utilizing various historical-critical tools to comprehend the literary interrelationship of the Gospels (even the entire Bible) and to discover how the ancient Christian community shaped the oral and written traditions behind the Gospels. As Watson reminds us, "Historical Jesus research is closely related to these other scholarly projects, which together constitute the modern, *wissenschaftlich* study of the Gospels."[16] Although the proponents may have different goals, they all start

---

[13] For a discussion of these two trends in Christology, see Carson, *Gagging of God*, 315–317.
[14] For the use of the term "real," see Robert B. Strimple, *The Modern Search for the Real Jesus: An Introductory Survey of the Historical Roots of Gospels Criticism* (Phillipsburg, NJ: P&R, 1995).
[15] Francis Watson, "*Veritas Christi:* How to Get from the Jesus of History to the Christ of Faith without Losing One's Way," in *Seeking the Identity of Jesus: A Pilgrimage*, ed. Beverly Roberts Gaventa and Richard B. Hays (Grand Rapids, MI: Eerdmans, 2008), 98.
[16] Ibid.

with the same working hypothesis that underlies the entire historical-critical approach to Christology: the historical Jesus is not the same as the constructed "Jesus of the Bible" or the "Christ of faith."

According to this kind of historical Jesus research, the Jesus of the Bible is simply the product of the creative imagination of the early church interpreted through the grid of a first-century cultural mind-set, which, for the most part, is not credible to us today. The biblical text in its final form cannot directly warrant our Christological reflection, as the "precritical" era of the church assumed. Instead, we must use critical tools to *get behind* the documents, peeling off layers of "dogmatic construction and legendary elaboration" that the Christian community has created. The historical-critical research is *the only valid way to discover the real Jesus* who lived in first-century Palestine.[17]

The historical Jesus research paradigm, then, produces what can be called a *critical* Christology. The historical-critical methodology it employs takes a critical, suspicious stance toward Scripture and progresses independently of the Bible's own terms. Such a critical approach stands opposite of a *confessional* Christology that commits to the full accuracy and authority of Scripture. This commitment to the reliability of the Bible's presentation of Jesus includes a rejection of any attempt to reconstruct the "real" Jesus—he has been revealed by God himself in God's own word written to man. But because the historical Jesus research paradigm operates with different theological beliefs, convictions, and worldview structures, it rejects confessional Christology as no longer credible.[18] A critical Christology assumes that Scripture actually obscures the real Jesus and that he can be identified only through historical reconstruction, not revelation.

Within the last thirty years, the historical Jesus research paradigm has been famously epitomized by two examples: *The Myth of God Incarnate* and the Jesus Seminar.[19] Significantly, both originated in the academic world but had their greatest impact in popular culture.

The Myth of God Incarnate was a 1977 symposium of essays that reflected the entire stream of historical-critical efforts in Christological construction, from the Enlightenment period through the twentieth century.[20] The seven

---

[17] Ibid., 99.
[18] For a discussion of this point, see A. T. B. McGowan, "Affirming Chalcedon," in *Forgotten Christ*, 39–40.
[19] At the popular level, this critical approach is found in Dan Brown, *The Da Vinci Code: A Novel* (New York: Doubleday, 2003). For more scholarly treatments, see Albert Schweitzer, *The Quest of the Historical Jesus: A Critical Study of Its Progress from Reimarus to Wrede*, trans. William Montgomery (New York: Macmillan, 1968); James C. Paget, "Quests for the Historical Jesus," in *The Cambridge Companion to Jesus*, ed. Markus Bockmuehl, Cambridge Companions to Religion (Cambridge, NY: Cambridge University Press, 2001), 138–155; Colin Brown, *Jesus in European Protestant Thought, 1778–1860* (Grand Rapids, MI: Baker, 1985); Alister E. McGrath, *The Making of Modern German Christology, 1750–1990*, 2nd ed. (Eugene, OR: Wipf & Stock, 2005); Witherington, *The Jesus Quest*; James Beilby and Paul Eddy, eds., *The Historical Jesus: Five Views* (Downers Grove, IL: IVP Academic, 2009).
[20] John Hick, ed., *The Myth of God Incarnate* (Philadelphia: Westminster, 1977).

authors had a twofold thesis: first, the *real, historical* Jesus, was not the Jesus of the Bible, but was a mere man approved by God for a special role; second, the orthodox conception of Jesus as God the Son incarnate is a mythological way of expressing his ultimate value for us.[21] The category of *myth* was employed to explain that the incarnation language of Scripture was part of a "story composed for the purpose of communicating a truth,"[22] not for the affirmation of historical reality.[23] Unfortunately, the authors argued, the church missed the myth and interpreted the biblical language to mean that God the Son literally became incarnate. But any credible view of Jesus today must reject the anachronous metaphysical categories of Chalcedon as the result of an outmoded way of thinking.

From 1985–1991, about two hundred mainline New Testament scholars gathered throughout the United States twice a year as the Jesus Seminar.[24] The Seminar gathered to determine which of the approximately five hundred sayings attributed to Jesus in the New Testament were actually spoken by the historical Jesus, and which ones were later "put into his mouth" by the Christian community.[25]

Ultimately, the Seminar concluded that 82 percent of the words attributed to Jesus were never actually said by him. More significantly for our purposes here, the participants drew upon the noncanonical and apocryphal *Gospel of Thomas* and their own historical reconstructions to conclude that Jesus was primarily a preacher viewed by the authorities of his day as a political subversive, which eventually led to his death.[26] Simply put, they *demythologized*

---

[21] There were a number of responses to the book. For a positive response, see Michael Goulder, ed., *Incarnation and Myth: The Debate Continued* (Grand Rapids, MI: Eerdmans, 1979); for a critical response, see Michael Green, ed., *The Truth of God Incarnate* (Grand Rapids, MI: Eerdmans, 1977).

[22] David F. Wells, *The Person of Christ: A Biblical and Historical Analysis of the Incarnation* (Westchester, IL: Crossway, 1984), 1.

[23] The notion of *myth* is not unique to these authors; it has its roots in the work of a number of people, but especially the work of David Strauss (1808–1874). In 1835, Strauss wrote *The Life of Jesus, Critically Examined*, in which he introduced the notion of *myth* into Gospel criticism (for a recent publication, see David Strauss, *The Life of Jesus, Critically Examined*, ed. Peter Hodgson, trans. George Eliot, Lives of Jesus Series [Philadelphia: Fortress, 1972]). For Strauss, the Gospels are not descriptions of events that actually happened; they are *myth*, i.e., a literary category applied to the Gospels as entire narratives. Strauss followed the lead of Georg Hegel, who argued that the religion of Christianity was one step in the development of human beings expressing universal *Ideas* of philosophy in symbolic ways. In this sense, *myths* are a suitable form of communication for human beings at an earlier stage of our development, but something we must grow beyond by *demythologizing* the truths of Christianity and demonstrating through philosophical analysis that the Gospels are simply imperfect representations of the eternal *Ideas* of reason. As applied to Christology, the God-man concept is important, not because the incarnation literally happened but because the Idea entered the world. In this way, the *myth* of the incarnation can be seen as true only if it is seen as a *symbol* of the truth concerning human beings as a whole, not as the real life of one individual man.

[24] The literature on the Jesus Seminar is legion. For a helpful overview and critique of it, see Michael J. Wilkins and J. P. Moreland, eds., *Jesus Under Fire: Modern Scholarship Reinvents the Historical Jesus* (Grand Rapids, MI: Zondervan, 1995); see also Craig A. Evans, *Fabricating Jesus: How Modern Scholars Distort the Gospels* (Downers Grove, IL: InterVarsity Press, 2006); James R. Edwards, *Is Jesus the Only Savior?* (Grand Rapids, MI: Eerdmans, 2005), 23–32; Witherington, *Jesus Quest*, 42–57.

[25] For a statement regarding this purpose of historical investigation, see Marcus J. Borg, *Jesus in Contemporary Scholarship* (Valley Forge, PA: Trinity Press, 1994), 162.

[26] For an evaluation of the *Gospel of Thomas*, see Darrell L. Bock and Daniel B. Wallace, *Dethroning Jesus: Exposing Popular Culture's Quest to Unseat the Biblical Christ* (Nashville: Thomas Nelson, 2007); Evans, *Fabricating Jesus*.

Jesus,[27] denying his deity, virginal conception, miracles, and bodily resurrection. All of these teachings are simply the result of the church's ideological construction of Jesus according to a worldview that is no longer acceptable to modern and postmodern people.[28] The cofounder of the Seminar, Robert Funk, sums up the entire stream of historical-critical Jesus research: "It is no longer credible to think of Jesus as divine. Jesus's divinity goes together with the old theistic way of thinking about God."[29]

These two examples of the historical Jesus research paradigm illustrate that a critical Christology has taken root in contemporary culture. This move away from a confessional Christology leads us away from the true identity of Christ. But the more instructive point for us here is this: *the move to a critical Christology could not have happened without a prior epistemological shift away from the biblical worldview and the basic assumptions of Christian theism.* The Myth of God Incarnate and the results of the Jesus Seminar did not change the plausibility structures for culture at large through excellent scholarship and ground-breaking research.[30] These two and the other instances of the historical-critical approach received remarkable attention, both scholarly and popular, because the fundamental restructuring of what counts as possible, plausible, reliable, and significant had already taken place.

The Paradigm of Pluralism

Although they differ situationally, the paradigms of historical Jesus research and pluralism relate symbiotically.[31] In fact, we can say that historical Jesus research is a "correlative of pluralism": the historical-critical research for the *Jesus behind* the Bible is partly a cause and partly an effect of *pluralism beyond* the Bible.[32] As a *cause*, the historical Jesus paradigm makes pluralism more

---

[27] The language of "demythologization" comes from Rudolf Bultmann, *New Testament and Mythology and Other Basic Writings*, ed. and trans. Schubert Miles Ogden (Philadelphia: Fortress, 1984); idem, *Jesus Christ and Mythology*, The Scribner Library (New York: Scribner, 1958).

[28] See, e.g., John Dominic Crossan, *Jesus: A Revolutionary Biography* (San Francisco: Harper, 1994); idem, *The Historical Jesus: The Life of a Mediterranean Jewish Peasant* (San Francisco: Harper, 1991).

[29] See Robert W. Funk, "The Coming Radical Reformation: Twenty-one Theses," *The Fourth R* 11/4 (July–August 1998), http://www.westarinstitute.org/resources/the-fourth-r/the-coming-radical-reformation/, accessed May 19, 2015.

[30] Most of the conclusions were the continuation and culmination of classic liberal theology, on which see Stanley Grenz and Roger Olson, *Twentieth-Century Theology: God and the World in a Transitional Age* (Downers Grove, IL: InterVarsity Press, 1992), 51–62. Regarding the popularity of the Jesus Seminar in particular, James Edwards makes an astute comment: "What is novel about the Jesus Seminar is not its low opinion of the historical reliability of the Gospels. Our review of critical biblical scholarship since the Enlightenment, especially in its more radical forms, reveals that similar conclusions have been reached for the past two and one-half centuries. The novelty of the Seminar consists rather in its public relations expertise and marketing savvy. The Jesus Seminar has made an end run around the sequestered scholarly guild of biblical scholars and made Jesus into a media event on television talk shows and specials at Christmas and Easter" (Edwards, *Is Jesus the Only Savior?*, 26).

[31] See Carson, *Gagging of God*, 316. Carson argues that "the sheer multiplicity of ostensibly 'historical' reconstructions has over time greatly eroded confidence in traditional Christological formulations. With confidence eroded, the stage is set to construct whatever Christology seems needed to line up with whatever the priorities of the hour happen to be. At the moment, those priorities happen to be whatever is perceived to advance pluralism" (ibid.).

[32] For "correlative of pluralism," see ibid., 37. Carson does not describe historical Jesus research as a correlative of pluralism; rather, I am employing his category and drawing my own conclusion.

plausible because the critical assumptions often lead to a denial of the biblical and historical confession of Jesus's uniqueness as the Word made flesh and the only Lord and Savior. As an *effect*, historical Jesus research naturally flows out of a paradigm that assumes philosophical pluralism and then asks "what kind of Christology would be necessary, or what kind of changes would have to be introduced into traditional Christology, in order to fit the 'given' of that pluralism."[33]

While much could be said about the paradigm of pluralism itself, we can focus here on its status as a precommitment that affects how one approaches Christology. In this regard, one of the best examples is the work of John Hick.[34] We get a sense of his prior commitment to pluralism from Hick's argument that "those who have come to see the great religions and cultures of the world, including Christianity, as different but (so far as we can tell) more or less equally valuable forms of response to the Transcendent, are inclined to read the evidence of Christian origins differently."[35] He rightly acknowledges that a traditional Christology grounds its beliefs "in the superiority of Christianity as embodied in the church and in Western civilization."[36] And, as Harold Netland observes, the superiority of Christianity is grounded in the Bible's historical claim that God the Son became incarnate: "If Jesus really was in fact the eternal creator God become man, then it becomes very difficult indeed to treat Jesus, the New Testament, and Christian faith as being on the same level as phenomena from other religious traditions. There would seem to be something inherently superior and normative, to say the least, about Jesus and the Christian faith."[37] Hick's prior commitment to pluralism (for various reasons),[38] however, commits him to a different approach to the Bible that leads him to divergent conclusions regarding the identity of Christ.

---

[33] Ibid., 316.

[34] For examples, see John Hick, "Jesus and the World Religions," in *Myth of God Incarnate*, 167–185; idem, *God Has Many Names* (Philadelphia: Westminster, 1982); idem, "An Inspirational Christology for a Religiously Plural World," in John B. Cobb et al., *Encountering Jesus: A Debate on Christology*, ed. Stephen T. Davis (Atlanta: John Knox, 1988), 5–38; idem, *The Metaphor of God Incarnate: Christology in a Pluralistic Age*, 2nd ed. (Louisville: Westminster John Knox, 2006); idem, "A Pluralist View," in John Hick et al., *Four Views on Salvation in a Pluralistic World*, ed. Dennis L. Okholm and Timothy R. Phillips, Counterpoints (Grand Rapids, MI: Zondervan, 1996), 27–59; John H. Hick and Paul F. Knitter, eds. *The Myth of Christian Uniqueness: Toward a Pluralistic Theology of Religions* (Maryknoll, NY: Orbis, 1987).

[35] Hick, *Metaphor of God Incarnate*, 175.

[36] Ibid.

[37] Harold A. Netland, *Dissonant Voices: Religious Pluralism and the Question of Truth* (Grand Rapids, MI: Eerdmans, 1991), 242.

[38] Additional reasons that Hick and other religious pluralists give for their commitment to pluralism include: (1) a traditional understanding of Christ is incoherent; (2) there is nothing unique about the Bible; (3) the sheer diversity of religions in the world, the link between ethnicity and religion, the lack of missionary success in other cultures, and the similarity of all religions in terms of their basic outlook on life are all evidence that one's adoption of religion has more to do with one's upbringing and culture than its truthfulness; (4) the universe is religiously neutral, i.e., none of the arguments for any particular religion are uniquely compelling, and even trying to argue such a case is implausible given our limited knowledge of the universe. For a helpful discussion of the challenge of pluralism for the church, see J. Andrew Kirk and Kevin J. Vanhoozer, eds., *To Stake a Claim: Mission and the Western Crisis of Knowledge* (Maryknoll, NY: Orbis, 1999).

For example, regarding the uniqueness and exclusivity of Christ, Hick urges that "in the light of our accumulated knowledge of the other great world faiths [Christian exclusivism] has become unacceptable to all except a minority of dogmatic diehards. For it conflicts with our concept of God, which we have received from Jesus, as the loving heavenly Father of all mankind; could such a Being have restricted the possibility of salvation to those who happen to have been born in certain countries in certain periods of history?"[39] The only alternative to this unthinkable conclusion is to modify the orthodox understanding of Christology to reflect the philosophical *given* of pluralism:

> The alternative to traditional orthodoxy need not be to renounce Christianity. Another more constructive possibility is to continue the development of Christian self-understanding in the direction suggested by the new global consciousness of our time. To what extent is this likely to happen? Will Christians come to see Christianity as one among several authentic ways of conceiving, experiencing and responding to the Transcendent; and will they come to see Jesus, in a way that coheres with this, as a man who was exceptionally open to the divine presence and who thus incarnated to a high degree the ideal of human life lived in response to the Real?[40]

The examples could be multiplied, but the point is this: *the paradigm of pluralism leads to a critical Christology; an a priori commitment to pluralism entails an equally a priori rejection of a confessional Christology.* This rejection of orthodoxy is the common conviction that pluralism shares with historical Jesus research. Both maintain that it is not possible to believe either what the Scriptures affirm or what the church has confessed about the identity of Jesus Christ. A basic distrust of the Bible's reliability and a dismissal of the Bible's universal authority directly effect a fundamental shift in theological convictions.

As we recognized with historical Jesus research, pluralism as a paradigm for Christology is possible only because of prior epistemological shifts. We can easily survey the landscape of current Christological discussion and describe the surface level disagreements and confusion. To produce the fruit of clarity and coherence in Christology today, however, we need to trace the roots of the current confusion to its source—we need an excavation of epistemology. Making famous the expression "ideas have consequences," Francis Schaeffer often traced the development of Western thought to demonstrate that the current mind-set did not spring up spontaneously.[41] To understand, critique,

---

[39] Hick, *God Has Many Names*, 27.

[40] Hick, *Metaphor of God Incarnate*, 176.

[41] For example, see Francis A. Schaeffer, *The God Who Is There*, in *The Francis A. Schaeffer Trilogy: The Three Essential Books in One Volume* (Wheaton, IL: Crossway, 1990); idem, *Escape from Reason*, in *Francis A. Schaeffer Trilogy*; idem, *How Should We Then Live? The Rise and Decline of Western Thought and Culture*, L'Abri 50th anniversary ed. (Wheaton, IL: Crossway, 2005).

and correct our intellectual present, then, we must first connect it with our intellectual past.

Two Roots of Confusion in Contemporary Christology

Our present-day confusion regarding the identity of Christ has a long history that is best understood by looking at pivot points that led thinking and theology away from orthodox Christology.

Historic Christianity has uniformly affirmed that Jesus is the eternal Son of God made flesh, who, as a result of the incarnation, now subsists as "one person in two natures." And until the Enlightenment era, the church invariably agreed that the "Jesus of history" is identical to the "Jesus of the Bible" or the "Christ of faith." These still dominant material understandings, along with the other tenets of orthodox Christology, follow from certain methodological convictions: Traditionally, in doing Christology, the biblical text in its final form has served as the warrant for our dogmatic constructions. Orthodoxy has been established by a "Christology from above," from the vantage point of divine revelation, where Scripture not only provides the raw data for our Christology but also provides the structure, categories, and theological framework for understanding who Jesus is. The church has argued that we can grasp Jesus's identity correctly only when he is viewed in light of the entire biblical storyline, and that any attempt to do otherwise only leads to a Jesus of our own imagination.

For many today, however, orthodoxy and its methodology are no longer viewed as credible. Those who have adopted the epistemology and hermeneutics of the Enlightenment or the postmodern period that has followed it presuppose a radically different methodology that cannot support orthodox Christology. The Enlightenment and postmodern ways of thinking and reading the Bible do not merely disagree with the way the church has understood the identity of Christ. The epistemological and hermeneutical turns characterizing the Enlightenment and postmodernism fundamentally reject orthodoxy as implausible and incoherent.

The Impact of the Enlightenment on Christology

The Enlightenment era (c. 1560–1780) saw a sea change in epistemology and methodology that spared no sector of society. But our interest in Christology limits our present investigation to the *displacement* of the medieval and Reformation worldview and the gradual *secularization* of thought and institutions in Western Europe.[42] The Enlightenment serves as the hinge that swung the

---

[42] See, e.g., W. Andrew Hoffecker, "Enlightenments and Awakenings: The Beginnings of Modern Culture Wars," in *Revolutions in Worldview: Understanding the Flow of Western Thought*, ed. W. Andrew Hoffecker (Phillipsburg,

medieval-Reformation era into the modern era, opening the door to what is now called "modernism." In noting the significance of this era, Alister Mc-Grath observes, "With the benefit of hindsight, the Enlightenment can be said to have marked a decisive and irreversible change in the political, social, and religious outlook of Western Europe and North America."[43]

Many scholars today use "Age of Reason" to describe the *nature* of the Enlightenment. In his 1784 article, "What Is Enlightenment?," Immanuel Kant sought to capture something of the *Zeitgeist* of this era:

> Enlightenment is man's emergence from his self-imposed immaturity. Immaturity is the inability to use one's understanding without the guidance of another. This immaturity is self-imposed when its cause lies not in lack of understanding but in lack of resolve and courage to use it without guidance from another. *Sapere Aude!* [dare to know] "Have courage to use your own understanding!"—that is the motto of enlightenment.[44]

The Enlightenment was the "Age of Reason," not because reason was inoperative in the Reformation and prior to it, but because reason was elevated from a ministerial instrument to a magisterial rule, especially over Scripture and tradition.[45] So Kant viewed the "enlightened" person as one who reasons autonomously, without dependence upon the authorities of the past. The mindset of "faith seeking understanding" yielded to the motto, "I believe what I can understand."[46]

A further contrast with the thought and theology of the Reformation will show us the *significance* of the Enlightenment. The Reformation is important to church history for many reasons, but here we can focus on the theological framework and epistemology of the Reformers. Even though they held many doctrinal convictions in common with the passing medieval era, as Scott Amos reminds us, "the Reformers nevertheless rejected the medieval synthesis of the human and the divine in its balance of reason and revelation."[47] This led the Reformers to emphasize *sola Scriptura*, which entailed that all beliefs, creeds, and dogmas, including church tradition, must be tested by Scripture. And this

---

NJ: P&R, 2007), 240–280; cf. John D. Woodbridge, "Some Misconceptions of the Impact of the Enlightenment on the Doctrine of Scripture," in *Hermeneutics, Authority, and Canon*, ed. D. A. Carson and John D. Woodbridge (Grand Rapids, MI: Zondervan, 1986), 241–270.

[43] McGrath, *Making of Modern German Christology*, 14.

[44] Immanuel Kant, "What Is Enlightenment?," cited in Hoffecker, "Enlightenments and Awakenings," 265.

[45] McGrath makes this same point, noting that the Middle Ages were just as much an "Age of Reason" as the Enlightenment (McGrath, *Making of Modern German Christology*, 15). However, "the crucial difference lay in the manner in which reason was used, and the limits which were understood to be imposed upon it. . . . Most medieval theologians insisted that there was a set of revealed truths, to which access could not be gained by human reason" (ibid.). On the distinction between the ministerial and the magisterial use of reason, see William Lane Craig, "Classical Apologetics," in William Lane Craig et al., *Five Views on Apologetics*, ed. Stanley N. Gundry and Steven B. Cowan (Grand Rapids, MI: Zondervan, 2000), 36–38.

[46] Stanley J. Grenz, *A Primer on Postmodernism* (Grand Rapids, MI: Eerdmans, 1996), 62.

[47] Scott Amos, "The Reformation as a Revolution in Worldview," in *Revolutions in Worldview*, 207.

commitment to Scripture meant that the Reformers constructed their Christology from a theological framework that was founded on the centrality and sovereignty of the triune God of Scripture. As a result, they had no problem affirming the Son's preexistence, virgin conception, bodily resurrection, and the uniqueness of his identity and work. Their understanding of Jesus was of one piece with their entire theological understanding of the world centered in their doctrine of God.

The Reformers, then, never separated the "Jesus of history" from the "Christ of faith." As Hans Frei observed, the Reformers believed that the Gospel narratives actually corresponded to the real world as "history-like narratives."[48] This does not deny that the biblical authors gave us an interpreted Jesus. The Reformers believed, rather, that *the interpretive framework of the biblical authors is God's own interpretive framework for the identity of Jesus*—what Scripture says about Jesus, God says about Jesus.[49] Regarding the Gospels in particular, Francis Watson sums up the Reformers' hermeneutical assumption regarding the identity of Christ: "the Jesus of whom [the Gospels] tell is maximally identified with Jesus as he really was. If the Johannine Jesus turns water into wine and speaks of himself as the light of the world, then so too did Jesus himself: the text is a window onto the historical reality."[50]

Similarly, the Reformers grounded objective truth and knowledge in the comprehensive plan of God and argued that as image-bearers we come to know truth by reasoning from divine revelation (both general and special). The Reformers, then, emphasized *a revelational epistemology in which the ministerial use of reason served theology under the authority of Scripture*. The Bible is the lens by which we rightly interpret God, the self, and the world: the word of God gives us a true (even if not exhaustive) "God's-eye point-of-view." Without this revelation, human subjectivity blinds us to the truth, and the objectivity of truth becomes questionable as the basis for theology. For the Reformers, the human creature is never autonomous, neither metaphysically nor methodologically.[51] John Calvin emphasizes this order of being and knowing in his *Institutes*, where he demonstrates that without the knowledge of God there is no knowledge of self.[52]

This relationship between knowing God and knowing self is perhaps the best point at which to begin our contrast with Enlightenment thinking. In the

---

[48] Hans W. Frei, *The Eclipse of Biblical Narrative: A Study in Eighteenth and Nineteenth Century Hermeneutics* (New Haven, CT: Yale University Press, 1974), 17–50.

[49] For a further treatment of these points, see Kevin J. Vanhoozer, *Biblical Narrative in the Philosophy of Paul Ricoeur: A Study in Hermeneutics and Theology* (Cambridge: Cambridge University Press, 1990); idem, *First Theology: God, Scripture, and Hermeneutics* (Downers Grove, IL: InterVarsity Press, 2002), 207–235.

[50] Watson, "*Veritas Christi*," 99.

[51] For this point, see Kevin J. Vanhoozer, "Human Being, Individual and Social," in *The Cambridge Companion to Christian Doctrine*, ed. Colin E. Gunton (Cambridge: Cambridge University Press, 1997), 158–159.

[52] See John Calvin, *Institutes of the Christian Religion*, 2 vols., ed. John T. McNeill, trans. Ford Lewis Battles (Philadelphia: Westminster, 1960), 1:35.

"turn to the subject" by Enlightenment philosophers such as René Descartes and Immanuel Kant, Calvin's maxim was reversed: "There is no knowledge of God except through knowledge of the self."[53] This turn gave human subjectivity a foundational status not just for theology but also for epistemology in general. And this section argues that the Enlightenment shift from a revelational epistemology to a rational epistemology created a revolution in philosophy, science, religion, and hermeneutics that made the orthodox understanding of Jesus since the early church and creeds simply incredible and incoherent.

ENLIGHTENMENT EPISTEMOLOGY AND WORLDVIEW

The epistemological changes that came during the Enlightenment did not come overnight; seeds were planted in the Renaissance, especially in the rise of humanism as an intellectual movement.[54] But in the Enlightenment, these seeds produced a radical disruption of the Reformation's theological and Christological views. The story of these changes has been told in detail elsewhere.[55] Here we need only to register how a "turn to the subject" created "a decisive shift in worldview from theocentric thinking to various degrees of anthropocentrism."[56]

As Stanley Grenz correctly reminds us, "[the Enlightenment] came as the outgrowth of various social, political, and intellectual factors that led up to and transpired during this traumatic era in human history."[57] At this time, Europe was embattled in religious wars between Protestants and Roman Catholics, and there was a desire to get beyond these debates and to arbitrate the differences through rational means. In fact, many Enlightenment thinkers came to believe that human rationality was the only way to solve problems where theology had failed. One of the reasons for this confidence stemmed from belief in "the principle of the omnicompetence and universality of human reason."[58] As a result, many began to assert that theology also derived from reason and was therefore open to critical examination. McGrath pinpoints the impact of this elevation of reason: "The ability of reason to judge revelation was affirmed. As human reason was omnicompetent it was argued that it was supremely qualified to judge Christian beliefs and practices, with a view to eliminating any irrational or superstitious elements."[59]

---

[53] Vanhoozer, "Human Being, Individual and Social," 159. In the phrase, "turn to the subject," the subject is the human subject. This is another way of speaking about the Enlightenment project, which sought to make the human subject the standard in epistemological judgment instead of God and his revelation.

[54] On humanism as an intellectual movement, see James A. Herrick, *The Making of the New Spirituality: The Eclipse of the Western Religious Tradition* (Downers Grove, IL: InterVarsity Press, 2003), 49–54; cf. also Carl Trueman, "The Renaissance," in *Revolutions in Worldview*, 178–205.

[55] See, e.g., Grenz, *Primer on Postmodernism*; cf. Hoffecker, "Enlightenments and Awakenings."

[56] Hoffecker, "Enlightenments and Awakenings," 241.

[57] Grenz, *Primer on Postmodernism*, 63.

[58] See McGrath, *Making of Modern German Christology*, 20.

[59] Ibid., 21. McGrath illustrates this point with Herman Reimarus in Germany and the *philosophes* in France. Both placed reason above revelation and introduced a critical spirit leading to the reconstruction of Christology.

We can understand the epistemological revolution—reason over revelation as the ultimate source of knowledge—by tracking changes in philosophy, science, and religion.[60]

THE REVOLUTION IN PHILOSOPHY

Often named "the father of modern philosophy," René Descartes (1596–1650) stands as the pivotal figure in philosophy who moved it from a medieval to a modern mind-set, especially through the influence of his *Discourse on the Method* (1637). Working against Pyrrhonism and its skepticism that threatened our ability to know anything with certainty, Descartes devised a method to discover indubitable truths. Instead of starting with God as the ground for his philosophy, Descartes stripped away all of his beliefs about God, the world, and the self. He was left with only one truth that he could not doubt: he existed as a thinking subject. From that starting point, then, Descartes' famous *cogito ergo sum* ("I think, therefore I am") served as the foundation for building all knowledge in every field of inquiry.

Descartes' use of the *cogito* argument, however, was not the first; in fact, it was a significant departure from Augustine's prior appropriation. "Cartesian rationalism effectively inaugurated the 'modern self' or the 'subjective turn,' a shift from knowledge as objectively rooted in biblical revelation (both general and special) to knowledge as authenticated and demonstrated by human reason."[61] Andrew Hoffecker contrasts this turn to the self with Augustine's *cogito* that centered on God:

> Augustine formulated the *cogito* in the *context* of objective Christian belief, in which knowing God took preeminence. Certainty of his own existence served the higher end of knowing God. His *cogito* formed but a small part of thought that would center on God, who alone is self-existent and self-sufficient.
>
> Descartes' use of the *cogito*, on the other hand, launched the whole project of modernity. Self-authenticating, rational self-sufficiency was the basis of Cartesian foundationalism. No matter what form epistemology took in the ensuing seventeenth- and eighteenth-century discussions, its formulators used assumptions that furthered Descartes' break from the past. Descartes' radically new method—*dubito, cogito ergo sum*—provided a subjective, rational starting point—the intellectual fulcrum of human autonomy—that set the agenda for all future philosophical discussion. Although Cartesianism was but the first of many systems that occupied European thought, it placed the debate on new ground—a human centered, secular perspective.[62]

---

[60] My presentation is indebted to Grenz, *Primer on Postmodernism*, 63–67.
[61] Hoffecker, "Enlightenments and Awakenings," 254.
[62] Ibid.

Descartes' methodological turn set the agenda for philosophy over the next few centuries, but not without serious problems. Now known as "classical foundationalism," the Enlightenment schools of epistemology—Cartesian rationalism, Continental rationalism, and British empiricism[63]—all contended that our *derived beliefs* are justified only if they are supported by an *infallible foundation*, i.e., "basic beliefs" that need no justification. Under this system, however, many beliefs—like memory beliefs, belief from logical induction, and belief in God—would not qualify as knowledge.[64] And many Enlightenment philosophers urged this kind of agnosticism, with Immanuel Kant questioning the legitimacy of the entire project of metaphysics as knowledge.

Probably no single person has had more impact on modern philosophy and theology than Immanuel Kant (1724–1804). Trying to mediate between rationalism and a strict empiricism, and working against the destructive force of Humean skepticism, Kant proposed a new approach to epistemology—his famous "Copernican revolution." Rationalism seemed arbitrary and speculative, while a consistent empiricism led to the conclusion of David Hume (1711–1776) that even such basic notions as substance, causality, and the self are questionable and can be assumed only because they cannot be established empirically. In response, Kant reversed the traditional understanding of the relationship between the subject (mind) and the object (world) in the knowing process. Instead of our minds passively conforming to objects outside of them, our minds actively schematize the sense data from the world (contra rationalism) to conform the objects of the world to our a priori categories (contra empiricism).

Working out this approach to human understanding in his *Critique of Pure Reason*, Kant limited knowledge to objects as they appear to us, which excluded the knowledge of God.[65] Human reason is limited by the fact that the a priori categories of the mind do not work beyond the sense world: mental categories without sense experience are *empty*; sense experience without categories is *blind*. The human mind is not equipped to grapple with anything beyond the range of immediate experience, and attempts to do so inevitably result in irresolvable contradictions and antinomies. Kant made a strict distinction between objects present in our experience ("phenomena") and objects lying beyond our experience ("noumena"). We can know only the phenomena; we have no *direct* knowledge of the noumena. Since the knowledge of God,

---

[63] Continental rationalism is identified with Descartes (1596–1650), Spinoza (1632–1677), and Leibniz (1646–1716); British empiricism is identified with Locke (1632–1704), Berkeley (1685–1753), and Hume (1711–1776).

[64] See, e.g., Nicholas Wolterstorff, *Reason within the Bounds of Religion*, 2nd ed. (Grand Rapids, MI: Eerdmans, 1988); Alvin Plantinga and Nicholas Wolterstorff, eds., *Faith and Rationality: Reason and Belief in God* (Notre Dame, IN: University of Notre Dame Press, 1983); John S. Feinberg, *Can You Believe It's True? Christian Apologetics in a Modern and Postmodern Era* (Wheaton, IL: Crossway, 2013), 37–76, 143–194.

[65] Immanuel Kant, *Immanuel Kant's Critique of Pure Reason*, trans., Norman K. Smith (London: Macmillan, 1929).

the self, and all other ultimate realities as they are in themselves apart from our experience of them belongs to the realm of the noumena, we must remain metaphysically and theologically agnostic.[66]

According to its major forms of philosophical thought, then, the Enlightenment constrained *knowledge in* the modern world to our *experience of* the modern world. As John Feinberg has noted, many moderns functioned in the world as if the only beliefs truly capable of being justified are the beliefs of science and not theology.[67] Theology became a *sub*-rational discipline open to critical assessment and subject to the canons of science.[68]

But this philosophical turn to science begs the question of *which* science. Is it a science grounded in a theistic view of the world, or one that is decidedly deistic and/or naturalistic? After all, science as a discipline is not presuppositionless; like theology, science is dependent upon worldview commitments. So what kind of science did the Enlightenment assume?

THE REVOLUTION IN SCIENCE

It is hard to overestimate the effects of science on the Enlightenment understanding of the world. Historic Christianity is not against science, properly understood. In fact, one can make a strong case that Christian theology provided the necessary presuppositions for an empirical science.[69] The Enlightenment, however, brought a particular combination of beliefs that set science over theology. The belief that God had created the universe in a rational, orderly, and knowable fashion was combined with the belief in reason's independent ability to understand the structure of the world. And the result was that the scientific method was applied to all disciplines of knowledge, including the human sciences—even ethics, metaphysics, and theology: "if this way of obtaining knowledge about the universe was so successful, why not apply the same method to knowledge about God?"[70]

In this regard, Isaac Newton (1642–1727) looms large in the Enlightenment and beyond. Newton was interested in both theological and scientific questions. It was his view of the physical universe, however, that transformed the thinking of the age. Newton's universe was that of a grand, orderly machine; its movements could be known because they followed certain observable

---

[66] Kant allows only a moral theology: "Now I maintain that all attempts to employ reason in theology in any merely speculative manner are altogether fruitless and by their very nature null and void, and that the principles of its employment in the study of nature do not lead to any theology whatsoever. Consequently, the only theology of reason which is possible is that which is based upon moral laws or seeks guidance from them" (ibid., 528).

[67] John S. Feinberg, *No One Like Him: The Doctrine of God*, Foundations of Evangelical Theology (Wheaton, IL: Crossway, 2001), 88.

[68] See ibid., 84–95.

[69] See, e.g., Nancy R. Pearcey and Charles B. Thaxton, *The Soul of Science: Christian Faith and Natural Philosophy*, Turning Point Christian Worldview Series (Wheaton, IL: Crossway, 1994).

[70] James W. Sire, *The Universe Next Door: A Basic Worldview Catalogue*, 4th ed. (Downers Grove, IL: InterVarsity Press, 1997), 47.

laws. Yet, while Newton was a committed theist, his successors were not. They looked at the same orderly universe but interpreted it according to a radically different worldview that separated God from his creation. Hoffecker observes that "Newton's disciples outstripped themselves as they invented metaphors to redefine the character of the universe: a vast machine or a watch designed so wisely by a watchmaker that it runs on its own without outside intervention. Nature no longer was an organism; now it had a mechanical nature and operated according to Newton's laws."[71]

This mechanistic view of the world paved the way for the rise of deism and a more naturalistic approach to science. When coupled with the revolution in philosophy, the stage was set for a growing critique of orthodox theology. Belief in "God" remained; but belief in the triune God of Scripture who creates, upholds, and acts in the world to accomplish his plan of redemption was rejected. According to the deistic view, if God acts at all in the world, it is only by upholding the natural processes, the laws of nature that he established in the first place; God does not act extraordinarily in the world. James Edwards summarizes the end result of the epistemological revolution on the mind-set of the Enlightenment:

> Committed to explaining all reality by means of the scientific method, the Enlightenment reduced all reality to naturalism, empiricism, and rationalism. Committed to naturalism as the sum of reality, the Enlightenment could not admit the possibility of a God (if there was one) who would "violate the laws of nature" by breaking into the natural order. Things that could not be explained by the scientific method—whether historical events, morality, human affection, or the existence of God—were explained *away* by it.[72]

THE DEVOLUTION OF RELIGION

Robert Funk's observation that Jesus's divinity depends upon the traditional theistic way of thinking about God is important to remember when considering that deism is already far removed from Christian theism.[73] No doubt, as Frederick Copleston notes, deism is not a *school* of thought or even an organized *religion*; rather, in the Enlightenment, deism was associated with a number of influential thinkers who (while disagreeing at points) formed a basic *system* of thought that moved the larger society from a theistic mind-set to a more secular approach.[74] At its heart, deism views religion as *natural* rather than revealed and *super*natural. Despite their diversity, therefore, all religions can be reduced to common, universal truths warranted by rational means alone.

---

[71] Hoffecker, "Enlightenments and Awakenings," 247.
[72] Edwards, *Is Jesus the Only Savior?*, 13.
[73] On this point, see Sire, *Universe Next Door*, 45–58.
[74] See Frederick Copleston, *The British Philosophers from Hobbes to Hume*, vol. 5 in *A History of Philosophy*, new rev. ed., (Garden City, NY: Doubleday, 1963), 162–163.

Most deists affirmed at least four basic points contrary to orthodox theology and Christology.[75] First, a transcendent God created the universe, but he is not now providentially active in the world: "God is thus not immanent, not fully personal, not sovereign over human affairs, not providential."[76] Second, because this transcendent God created it, the universe is rational, orderly, and law-governed, but it is best viewed as a *closed* system with no expectation that God acts in it. In fact, as Sire comments, "any tampering or apparent tampering [by God] with the machinery of the universe would suggest that God had made a mistake in the original plan, and that would be beneath the dignity of an all-competent deity."[77] Even stopping here, it is quite clear that rejecting God's activity and the miraculous raises serious doubts concerning the Bible's most significant events, including its unique and singular presentation of Jesus.

Third, humans, though personal, are part of the closed system of the universe such that, morally speaking, they are not fallen or abnormal but basically good. As McGrath notes, "Voltaire (1694–1778) and Jean-Jacques Rousseau (1712–1778) criticized the doctrine [of original sin] as encouraging pessimism in regard to human abilities, thus impeding human social and political development and promoting *laissez-faire* attitudes."[78] Fourth, the purpose of religion is to order moral behavior: "The chief role of religion, [deists] maintained, is to provide a divine sanction for morality."[79] This focus on morality enabled deists to dismiss as unreasonable and unnecessary various dogmas that traditional theology had argued were grounded in divine revelation. If deists allowed for any notion of "divine revelation," it was only that these truths were "simply a rational reaffirmation of moral truths already available to enlightened reason."[80]

Alongside the revolution in epistemology, then, religion in the Enlightenment era really underwent a *devolution*. After creating the universe, a transcendent God transferred his power to the immanent natural laws he established, thereby surrendering cosmic control to the local authority of physics, chemistry, biology, and the like. Rather than caused by or merely coordinated with the epistemological revolution, this religious devolution likely came about through an interplay of religious thought and the massive shifts in philosophy and science. Significantly for our purpose here of understanding the causes of current Christological confusion, we must learn from this brief examination of Enlightenment epistemology that theology is never insular. For good or for ill,

---

[75] Use of these points is indebted to Sire, *Universe Next Door*, 48–55.
[76] Ibid., 48.
[77] Ibid., 49.
[78] McGrath, *Making of Modern German Christology*, 24–25.
[79] Grenz, *Primer on Postmodernism*, 72.
[80] McGrath, *Making of Modern German Christology*, 20.

the prevailing intellectual conditions will influence theological construction, beginning with how we understand the nature and function of the Bible.

ENLIGHTENMENT HERMENEUTICS

Not surprisingly, the massive shift from a revelational to a strictly rational epistemology and worldview was accompanied by an equally transformative turn in the way people received and read texts. Presuppositions matter to the *way we think*, and the way we think affects *how we read* and *what we think* about what we read. Here we will look specifically at how the combination of rationalism and naturalism affected how people received and read the Bible in relation to the rise of biblical criticism and the rule (and rules) of the historical-critical method.

THE RISE OF BIBLICAL CRITICISM

For the first time since Constantine, Christian doctrine was derided openly during the Enlightenment. Not just philosophers and committed deists but also those in biblical studies scorned orthodox Christianity. In the late eighteenth century, a critical examination of the Bible, especially the four Gospels, began in earnest and culminated in yet another major shift away from the Reformation's Christianity. Prior to this time, differences between the Gospels were acknowledged, but it was assumed that such differences could be harmonized. With the epistemological revolution well under way in the Enlightenment, however, many abandoned an attitude of trust and confidence toward the Bible as God's word and viewed Scripture with suspicion. These "enlightened" hermeneuts began to criticize the reliability of the Gospels, focusing on difficulties with the miracle stories and questioning the fulfillment of prophecies, how the New Testament authors used the Old Testament, and discrepancies in the Gospel narratives. Many attribute the rise of this "biblical criticism" to the work of Richard Simon (1638–1712) and Baruch Spinoza (1632–1677),[81] but two of the most famous and significant biblical critics in the eighteenth century were Herman Reimarus (1694–1768) and Gotthold Lessing (1729–1781).[82]

As C. Stephen Evans argues, Reimarus advanced biblical criticism through two assumptions about the Bible: first, he treated the Gospels "as ordinary historical documents, with no presumption of divine inspiration or even reliability";[83] second, he approached the text with suspicion, assuming that "to learn what really happened one must look through the texts and not take them

---

[81] See Woodbridge, "Some Misconceptions of the Impact of the Enlightenment," 253–257.
[82] See McGrath, *Making of Modern German Christology*, 28–35; Strimple, *Modern Search for the Real Jesus*, 16–24; Brown, *Jesus in European Protestant Thought, 1778–1860*, 1–55.
[83] C. Stephen Evans, *The Historical Christ and the Jesus of Faith: The Incarnational Narrative as History* (Oxford: Oxford University Press, 1996), 18.

at face value."[84] With these assumptions, the "Jesus of history" versus "Christ of faith" distinction began in earnest. And with that distinction came an entire approach to Scripture that treats it "like any other book,"[85] not as what it claims to be: the God-given, reliable interpretation of the historical Jesus.

Lessing's singular contribution to the shift in Christology came when he questioned the epistemic value of history. Prior to the Enlightenment, the church argued that the identity and significance of Jesus was based upon specific historical events, like his virgin conception, miracles, death and resurrection, and his second coming. All of these events bear witness to the uniqueness of who Jesus is. In fact, the church argued that it was precisely these historical events that not only establish his *unique identity*, they also demonstrate Jesus's *universal significance* for all people. Both the uniqueness and the universality of the historical Jesus, however, came under scrutiny in the Enlightenment through interpreters like Lessing.

Lessing argued that Enlightenment epistemology inserted "an ugly, broad ditch" between the particular facts of history and the universal truths of reason.[86] In Christology, Lessing introduced the problem of how to start with the New Testament's presentation of Jesus as a historical figure who lived and ministered at a particular point in time, and then move to affirm truths about him that have universal significance for all people and all times. For Lessing and other Enlightenment interpreters, a historically mediated knowledge of God is patently unjust, and historical persons and events cannot yield universal truths: the "scandal of historical particularity"[87] is too much to overcome. The Enlightenment allowed only reason to provide the basis for establishing necessary and universal truths; the "accidental truths of history can never become the proof of the necessary truths of reason."[88]

For Lessing, this unbridgeable divide—this "ditch"—was dug by both chronology and metaphysics. In agreement with the church, Lessing acknowledged that in order to know the historical Jesus we are dependent upon written *accounts* based upon the testimony of others. In contrast with the church, however, he questioned the historical *accuracy* of these accounts. Lessing argued that human testimony cannot make a past event credible, unless we have a present experience of the exact same kind of event. So, not having firsthand experience of resurrection, we should not believe the New Testament's clear affirmation that Jesus rose from the dead, because it "rests upon the authority

---

[84] Ibid.
[85] This is an expression taken from Benjamin Jowett (1817–1893), who in an influential article in *Essays and Reviews* (1860) argued that the Bible should be treated as any other book and thus as subject to criticism.
[86] G. E. Lessing, "On the Proof of the Spirit and Power," in *Lessing's Theological Writings*, comp. and trans. Henry Chadwick, A Library of Modern Religious Thought (Stanford, CA: Stanford University Press, 1956), 53, 55.
[87] McGrath, *Making of Modern German Christology*, 32.
[88] Lessing, "On the Proof of the Spirit and Power," 53.

of others, rather than the authority of our own experience and rational reflection upon it."[89] Moreover, Lessing argued that the same testimony that *imports* the facts cannot reliably *interpret* the facts. The Gospel accounts, then, cannot prove that Jesus is unique or universally significant because historical facts are accidental and contingent, open to a variety of interpretations that must ultimately be evaluated by reason alone as conceived by the Enlightenment. We simply have no warrant to draw metaphysical conclusions from historical facts alone.

THE RULE(S) OF THE HISTORICAL-CRITICAL METHOD

Reimarus and Lessing illustrate the effect of Enlightenment thinking on how and why we read the Bible. They were standouts among many who "donned critical investigation into the origins of the Bible and the life of Jesus with intellectual legitimacy."[90] And with that recognition among the elite, the biblical criticism that began to rise during the Enlightenment reached a place of prominence in later modernity. Still today, the starting point for all biblical studies is that the Bible is untrustworthy and thus subject to critical evaluation. Evans puts it "bluntly and simply, . . . we have become unsure whether the events happened, and uncertain about whether we can know that they happened, even if they did."[91]

The rise of a general biblical criticism led to the rule and rules of a particular historical-critical method (as it has come to be called). Scholars developed and used various tools (e.g., source, form, and redaction criticism) to subject the Scriptures, especially the Gospels, to historical-critical analysis.[92] The particular use of these tools differed, and some scholars were less skeptical of the historicity of the biblical documents than others (thus, ironically, making the "assured results of scholarship" not very sure). But *they all assumed* that the Gospels do not accurately record history and that the "Jesus of history" is not the "Jesus of the Bible." Much could be said about the various critical methods employed, but our concern here is the control assumptions that led to the development and use of the various tools. No system of exegesis, including a self-consciously critical one, can proceed without presuppositions; instead, they take for granted specific philosophical and/or theological assumptions.[93]

---

[89] McGrath, *Making of Modern German Christology*, 30. Regarding miracles, for example, Lessing explains that "since the truth of these miracles has completely ceased to be demonstrable by miracles still happening at the present time, since they are no more than reports of miracles . . . , I deny that they can and should bind me in the least to a faith in the other teachings of Jesus" (Lessing, "On the Proof of the Spirit and Power," 53–55).

[90] Edwards, *Is Jesus the Only Savior?*, 14.

[91] Evans, *Historical Christ and the Jesus of Faith*, 13.

[92] On these critical tools, see, e.g., I. Howard Marshall, ed., *New Testament Interpretation: Essays on Principles and Methods* (Exeter: Paternoster, 1977).

[93] See Rudolf Bultmann, "Is Exegesis Possible without Presuppositions?," in *Existence and Faith: Shorter Writings of Rudolf Bultmann*, comp. and trans. Schubert M. Ogden (New York: Meridian, 1960), 289–296.

Taken as a whole, the historical-critical method functions on the basis of three Enlightenment principles: (1) the principle of methodological doubt; (2) the principle of analogy; and (3) the principle of correlation.[94] The principle of methodological doubt states that all historical judgments (including biblical ones) are only statements of probability and, as such, are always open to doubt, criticism, and revision. The next two principles work in tandem to determine a text's historical accuracy. The principle of analogy assumes that all historical events are in principle qualitatively similar; the principle of correlation views all historical phenomena as existing in a causal nexus, i.e., in a closed cause-effect relationship. All historical events, then, are interrelated, interdependent, and qualitatively similar.

With these three Enlightenment principles in place, only one question can legitimately lead to a proper judgment regarding a text's historical accuracy: given the causal nexus of history, is the supposed historical event analogous to our present experience? If analogous, we have warrant for historicity; if not analogous, however, we have no warrant to think that the event actually occurred. Regarding the factuality of events recorded in Scripture, specifically supernatural ones, Ernst Troeltsch argued, "Jewish and Christian history are thus made analogous to all other history."[95] So, for Christology, if presently we do not witness virgin conceptions, people walking on water, and resurrections from the dead, we must judge such things to be implausible and the biblical texts to be in error.

As many critics of the historical-critical method have observed, the nature of the historical-critical method presupposes a methodological naturalism that rejects Christian theism without examination or analysis. The three principles of the Enlightenment hermeneutic undermine three foundations of orthodox theology: (1) divine truth resides in a unique, divine revelation; (2) this divine revelation concentrates on a single redemptive incursion into the world; and (3) original sin prevents an appeal to general and necessary truths of reason as a sufficient basis for knowledge.[96] The principles underneath historical criticism, however, are not demonstrably true; they can be assumed only by first adopting a naturalistic (even if deistic) worldview that denies the possibility of unique, extraordinary, supernatural events in history. Every hermeneutical method makes assumptions; first principles are not the problem. The problem is not admitting those principles and opening them to fair scrutiny.

Even a quick critique of the first principles of the historical-critical method demonstrates their incompatibility with the self-presentation of Scripture.

---

[94] See Ernst Troeltsch, "Historical and Dogmatic Method in Theology (1898)," in *Religion in History*, trans. James Luther Adams and Walter E. Bense (Minneapolis: Fortress, 1991), 11–32.

[95] Ibid., 14.

[96] See A. O. Dyson, "Ernst Troeltsch and the Possibility of Systematic Theology," in *Ernst Troeltsch and the Future of Theology*, ed. J. P. Clayton (Cambridge: Cambridge University Press, 1976), 85–86.

Van A. Harvey identifies two ways in which they are incompatible: "(1) No critical historian can make use of supernatural intervention as a principle of historical explanation because this will shatter the continuity of the causal nexus, and (2) no event can be regarded as a final revelation of the absolute spirit, since every manifestation of truth and value is relative and historically conditioned."[97]

These insights confirm that presuppositions matter to the *way we think*, and the way we think affects *how we read* and *what we think* about what we read, including the Bible. The rise of biblical criticism represents a momentous shift in how the Bible was approached, how Christology was practiced, and ultimately how Jesus's identity was understood. Historical-critical assumptions leave the church unable to demonstrate anything qualitatively unique about Jesus. Walter Wyman states it this way: "In so far as many religions make analogous claims to being founded on the self-revelation of God, it is extremely improbable that in one case (e.g., Christianity) the claim is true, but in all other cases it is false."[98] It is no wonder that Troeltsch regarded historical criticism as a complete overturn of the pre-Enlightenment worldview: biblical criticism is "a new scientific mode of representing man and his development, and, as such, shows at all points an absolute contrast to the Biblico-theological views of later antiquity."[99] Troeltsch also characterized the rise of biblical criticism as leavening the whole of theological methodology: if the critical assumptions are admitted at one point, it changes everything and finally destroys "the dogmatic form of method that has been used in theology."[100]

THE ENLIGHTENMENT AND CHRISTOLOGY

Our brief excavation has turned up the Enlightenment roots of a revolution in epistemology, a devolution in worldview, and a suspicion toward the biblical text. We should now be able to see how these same roots are feeding today's confusion in Christology by focusing on three primary influences: Kantianism, deism, and historical criticism.

THE INFLUENCE OF KANTIANISM

Following Descartes' methodological turn to *centering* all knowledge in the reasoning power of the autonomous human subject, Immanuel Kant then *confined* all knowledge to the human subject's experience of the world according

---

[97] Van A. Harvey, *The Historian and the Believer: The Morality of Historical Knowledge and Christian Belief* (Philadelphia: Westminster, 1966), 29–30.
[98] Walter E. Wyman, *The Concept of Glaubenslehre: Ernst Troeltsch and the Theological Heritage of Schleiermacher*, American Academy of Religion Academy Series, vol. 44 (Chico, CA: Scholars Press, 1983), 7.
[99] Ernst Troeltsch, "Historiography," *Encyclopedia of Religion and Ethics*, vol. 6, ed. James Hastings (Edinburgh: T&T Clark, 1912–1915), 718.
[100] Cited in Edgar Krentz, *The Historical-Critical Method* (Philadelphia: Fortress, 1975), 55.

to a priori categories of the mind. To be sure, Kantianism has changed through criticism and reconsideration. For example, his critics have rightly charged that Kant overstepped his own philosophy by claiming to know that all of us have the same mental categories. And many post-Kantian philosophers influenced by Darwinian theory now argue that our mental categories cannot be the same because they are the product of evolution and social construction. But even as revised, Kantianism today remains true to its anti-metaphysical bias, which directly affects Christology: human autonomy is primary; knowledge of metaphysics is impossible apart from experience; and theology must be done according to an *extratextual* interpretation of Scripture. This strictly rational epistemology rejects a God's-eye viewpoint of Christ in favor of a critical approach that dichotomizes the "Jesus of history" from the "Jesus of the Bible."

In one move, Kantianism dismisses all theology throughout history, including classical Christology with its metaphysical statements. If not grounded in perception, no metaphysical or theological claim can be considered knowledge. Revelation, miracles, direct divine activity in human history, statements regarding substances and the nature of things, including the natures of Christ, are all ultimately unknowable. Since God is a *noumenal* reality, we can never *know* if God is sovereign, if he is the Creator, or whether he has disclosed himself to us. And even if God has revealed himself to us in the world, that revelation is always subjected to a natural explanation supplied by the categories and active construction of the human mind, so that any theological pursuit must proceed by methodological naturalism.

As seen in his *Religion within the Limits of Reason Alone*,[101] the application of Kant's philosophy to religion and Christology necessarily denies and reinterprets the claims that Scripture makes for itself and about Christ. Kant is left to argue that religion is important in preserving human freedom and morality, but without God in Christ defining and providing freedom and morality for us. For Kant, religion provides the ultimate goal of morality, where it speaks of a powerful moral Lawgiver whose will ought to be man's final end. In his discussion of Christianity, however, Kant (in line with other biblical critics of his day) reinterpreted the gospel in light of his "religion of reason." Jesus was the exemplar of the morally perfect human race, but not in the sense that Jesus is necessary to show us what the moral law requires—reason can do that—and certainly not as the one who meets those requirements for us. Jesus shows us, rather, that moral perfection—again, according to reason—is attainable in this life. Since we are not the authors of this idea, we may say that it has come down to us "from heaven" and has "assumed our humanity." But this kind of

---

[101] Immanuel Kant, *Religion within the Limits of Reason Alone*, trans. Theodore M. Greene and Hoyt H. Hudson (New York: Harper & Row, 1960).

incarnation has nothing to do with, and in fact specifically rejects, the claim of Scripture that the Son of God took on human flesh in history to reveal true knowledge of God otherwise unattainable by reason.

For many theologians after Kant, every major doctrine of Christianity is made to fit the a priori pattern of current experience and the rules of naturalism. After Kantian reconstruction, the truth claims of orthodox Christology regarding the identity and significance of Christ are rejected as invalid and irrelevant: the revelation of Scripture cannot be trusted and cannot tell us anything we could not discover by reason alone, apart from Scripture.

THE INFLUENCE OF DEISM

It should not surprise us that, following the Kantian turn to reason and experience, deism also radically changes how we view Jesus's identity and significance. As McGrath reminds us, "Much traditional Christian apologetic concerning the identity and significance of Jesus Christ was based upon the 'miraculous evidences' of the New Testament, culminating in the resurrection."[102] But it is exactly those unique, extraordinary, unexpected events that the closed, law-governed, machinelike universe of deism rejects. One result of such a rejection is a different understanding of salvation, in terms of both the need for it and the role Jesus plays in it. Scripture's presentation of the person and work of Christ cannot be taken on its own terms: the incarnation of the Son of God into humanity and history is impossible under deism, and the biblical link between sin and its solution in a divine-human Redeemer is incomprehensible.

In light of this thinking, at least two significant and startling entailments result for Christology. First, by engaging in a radical critique of "revealed religion" on the grounds that it is not reasonable—according to their presupposed worldview—deists discard the doctrines of the Trinity, original sin, the deity of Christ, and his substitutionary atonement for sinners. In place of orthodoxy, deists reconstruct Christology (and other doctrines) out of the observable components of the natural (albeit created) world and its inherent rationality, quite apart from Scripture and tradition and the rationality of the faith. Second, due to their conviction that rational truth must possess the qualities of necessity and universality, it is axiomatic for deists that true knowledge cannot be attained through historical religions, specifically not Christianity. Unless historical facts can be verified and generalized in the form of unchanging, universal scientific laws, they have no philosophical significance under deism. So the uniqueness of Jesus in the specific historical events of his incarnation, life, death, and resurrection cannot establish universal truths. The uniqueness and particularity of Jesus as the Son of God and the Son of Man—being the exact

---

[102] McGrath, *Making of Modern German Christology*, 23.

imprint of God's nature, and being made like humans in every respect except sin—are the very things that disqualify him under the deistic worldview from revealing anything universally true about God and man.

Methodologically, deism's approach to Christology is a perfect example of what Hans Frei labels "extratextual."[103] In such an approach, priority is given to an alien ideology, so that Christological (and all theological) claims are valid only if they fit within the *extratextual* scheme. By contrast, traditional Christology approaches the Bible *intratextually*, seeking to identify Jesus according to *the Bible's own terms*—its own categories, claims, and worldview.[104] These two methodological approaches are inherently irreconcilable because they result from two completely divergent worldviews. Deism and Christian theism both start with a God who is *ontologically* separate from his creation; but deism also maintains an *economic* separation in the sense that God does not act in his creation. Orthodox Christianity, however, confirms the witness of Scripture to God's personal governance and redemption of his creation in and through his Son, the Lord Jesus Christ.

THE INFLUENCE OF HISTORICAL CRITICISM

The Kantianism and deism of the Enlightenment each produces its own effects on Christology today, but they also combine to exert an enormous influence on the hermeneutics of Christology in particular. Kantianism privileged the power of autonomous human reason and helped develop the philosophical underpinnings of a deistic worldview, all of which creates an inherent suspicion regarding the claims of divine revelation in a historically remote and culturally unfamiliar set of writings. This root of suspicion has produced the historical-critical method that has ruled the theological landscape with its naturalistic rules for the last three centuries. And this method of biblical criticism has given us Lessing's "ugly ditch" between particular historical facts and universal truths, along with many failed attempts to cross the chasm that divides the "Jesus of history" from the "Christ of faith."

We cannot overstate the impact of Lessing's strict separation between historical testimony to particular facts and any reliable interpretation of those facts in the absence of firsthand experience. If embraced, such a separation creates a radical suspicion of Scripture that rejects its reliability and undermines the very possibility of doing orthodox Christology that attempts to draw metaphysical conclusions about Christ from the biblical documents. Many

---

[103] See Hans W. Frei, *Types of Christian Theology*, ed. George Hunsinger and William C. Placher (New Haven, CT: Yale University Press, 1992); cf. David F. Ford, ed., *The Modern Theologians: An Introduction to Christian Theology in the Twentieth Century*, 2nd ed. (Oxford: Blackwell Publishing, 1997), 1–15.

[104] I am using *intra*textual over against *extra*textual. Intratextual means that Scripture must be read *on its own terms*, not conformed to and read in light of a prior worldview. Scripture demands to be received with divine authority and read according to its own structure and categories and within its own worldview framework.

since Lessing have tried to overcome his historical-theological ditch through rigorous historical investigation.

Describing the hermeneutical impact of the historical-critical method (and not yet laying out our own method), it is sufficient in this section to note its divergence from the church's traditional way of reading the Bible and making theological conclusions regarding Jesus Christ. The church has not argued for the identity and significance of Jesus merely on the basis of historical events but has done Christology within an entire biblical-theological framework. That framework includes a specific conception of God, creation, providence, history, humans, sin, eschatology, and so on. This framework also includes an understanding that Scripture not only recounts historical persons and events but also interprets the meaning and significance of those persons and events in light of the eternal plan of God. Christian theologians have been able to make metaphysical and universal statements from history because the Scriptures are *God's own interpretation* of the persons, events, and facts of history—an interpretation that is necessarily accurate and authoritative. Orthodox Christology must demonstrate that Lessing's historical-theological ditch in modern Christology is an invention and assumption of the Enlightenment that is incompatible with the self-revelation of God in the Scriptures.

Specifically, it is the historical-critical method's *extratextual approach* to Christology that begins its radical departure from orthodoxy. Instead of doing Christology within the worldview of Scripture like the Reformers, modern critics do Christology apart from the Bible's own terms and under an Enlightenment worldview that not only is alien to the Scriptures but also is opposed to it as God's word written. Scripture at times declares and everywhere assumes that all humanity is utterly dependent upon its Creator; that our ability to reason is corrupted by sin and inherently unreliable; but that God overcomes our weakness by giving knowledge of himself and his creation through divine revelation. Rejecting Scripture's own terms at every point, the historical-critical method begins with an autonomous humanity that has the inherent power to reason reliably to the truth according to methodological naturalism, which denies even the possibility of supernatural revelation.

THE LOSS OF THE REVEALED AND REAL JESUS

To conclude our argument that the epistemological revolution of the Enlightenment continues to cause Christological confusion today, we can look briefly at the assumptions, methodology, and results of the so-called "Quests for the historical Jesus."[105] The goal of the Quests has been to recover the "Jesus of

---

[105] The specific developments within and individuals associated with the Quests are detailed in many places. See, e.g., Colin Brown, "Historical Jesus, Quest of," in *Dictionary of Jesus and the Gospels*, ed. Joel B. Green, Scot McKnight, and I. Howard Marshall (Downers Grove, IL: InterVarsity Press, 1992), 326–341; idem, *Jesus in*

history," who is different from the "Jesus of the Bible," by peeling back the bib-lical layers of legend and myth via the historical-critical method. The starting point and conclusion of the Quests represent a sharp turn away from orthodox Christology.[106]

Beginning at the end of the eighteenth century, the Old Quest (1778–1906)[107] refused to interpret the biblical text in terms of its own claims, factual content, and interpretive framework. These theologians, rather, assumed that the Bible is wholly unreliable and proceeded to reconstruct the "historical" Jesus without reliance upon and almost without reference to the biblical pre-sentation. The first half of the twentieth century brought an interim period (1906–1953)—some call it the No Quest[108]—in which some theologians de-termined that historical facts were not necessary for the Christian faith. The difficulty of establishing any historical knowledge according to an Enlighten-ment epistemology and the tools of the historical-critical method shifted the problem momentarily from the Bible's historicity to its mythology. Probably the best example, Rudolf Bultmann simply replaced (demythologized) the New Testament's mythological framework with an existential structure, asking only, "What is man?"[109] This anthropocentric framework was more congenial to modern thought and consistent with the assumed primacy and power of human reason in Enlightenment hermeneutics.

The New Quest (1953 to present) focuses on the *kerygma* about Jesus in Scripture, being dissatisfied with the doubts of the Old Quest and the disregard of historicity during the No Quest.[110] These theologians agree with the other Quests that the Gospel traditions are interpretations of the early church, but

---

European Protestant Thought; Witherington, *Jesus Quest*; Paget, "Quests for the Historical Jesus"; McGrath, *Making of Modern German Christology*; N. T. Wright, *Who Was Jesus?*; idem, *Jesus and the Victory of God*, vol. 2 in *Christian Origins and the Question of God* (Minneapolis: Fortress, 1997). For the present taxonomy of the Quests, I am following N. T. Wright's description in *Jesus and the Victory of God*, 1–124; cf. also Paget, "Quests for the Historical Jesus," 138–155.

[106] As Albert Schweitzer observes regarding the Quests, "The historical investigation of the life of Jesus did not take its rise from a purely historical interest; it turned to the Jesus of history as an ally in the struggle against the tyranny of dogma. Afterwards when it was freed from this *pathos* it sought to present the historic Jesus in a form intelligible to its own time" (Albert Schweitzer, *The Quest of the Historical Jesus: A Critical Study of Its Progress from Reimarus to Wrede*, trans. William Montgomery [New York: Macmillan, 1968], 3). N. T. Wright agrees: "Let us be clear. People often think that the early 'lives of Jesus' were attempting to bring the church back to histori-cal reality. They were not. They were attempting to show what historical reality really was, in order that, having glimpsed this unattractive sight, people might turn away from orthodox theology and discover a new freedom. One looked at the history in order then to look elsewhere, to the other side of Lessing's 'ugly ditch', to the eternal truths of reason unsullied by the contingent facts of everyday events, even extraordinary ones like those of Jesus" (Wright, *Jesus and the Victory of God*, 17–18).

[107] As the first, the Old Quest received its name from the English title of Schweitzer's book, *Quest of the Historical Jesus*. For the most part, the Old Quest starts with Reimarus, ends with Schweitzer, and includes a veritable who's who in biblical studies and classical liberal theology: e.g., David Strauss (1808–1874); F. C. Baur (1792–1860); Albrecht Ritschl (1822–1889); Adolf von Harnack (1851–1930); William Wrede (1859–1906); Wilhelm Bousset (1865–1920).

[108] W. Barnes Tatum, *In Quest of Jesus: A Guidebook* (Atlanta: John Knox Press, 1982), 71.

[109] Rudolf Bultmann, *New Testament and Mythology and Other Basic Writings*, ed. and trans. Schubert Miles Ogden (Philadelphia: Fortress, 1984), 5–6; cf. idem, *Jesus Christ and Mythology* (New York: Scribner, 1958), 11–21.

[110] For example, see Ernst Käsemann, "The Problem of the Historical Jesus," in *Essays on New Testament Themes*, trans. W. J. Montague (1964; repr., London: SCM Press, 2012), 15–47; Günther Bornkamm, *Jesus of Nazareth*, trans. Irene McLuskey, Fraser McLuskey, and James M. Robinson (Minneapolis: Fortress, 1995); James M. Rob-

they argue that this subjectivity did not prevent the Gospels from preserving authentic historical material. Yet the New Quest remains firmly committed to Enlightenment presuppositions. These theologians determine what the historical Jesus really said by applying extratextual rules: e.g., consistency and multiple attestation; the criteria of dissimilarity; various linguistic and cultural tests.

At the same time, the Third Quest (early 1980s to present)[111] applies its own, modified version of historical-critical criteria; in general, it applies the rules for authenticity more generously in an attempt to take the New Testament texts more seriously as literary documents with basic (but not full) reliability.[112] These theologians also take seriously the Jewish context of early Christianity—a context disregarded or even denigrated in the other Quests.[113] But these conciliatory efforts still come within an a priori commitment to Enlightenment epistemology and hermeneutics that cannot truly accommodate the God-givenness of Scripture and accept its accuracy and authority. James Edwards notes the problem: "to assume that a social setting—even a correctly perceived one—captures the meaning of a person in it is like supposing that a job résumé captures the essence of a person. Résumés are good at conveying *what*, but they inevitably fall short of portraying *who*. Stage sets are necessary, but on their own they cannot replace plot or actors in a play."[114]

The Quests give us a prime example of the Enlightenment's impact on Christology. As one of the major trends in Christology, the historical Jesus research paradigm separates the historical and the theological Jesus to seek the former at the expense of the latter. Seeking to excavate the historical Jesus behind the biblical text, the Quests and other critical-extratextual approaches dig deeper into Lessing's "ugly ditch" and lose the revealed Jesus made known to us through exegesis in submission to the biblical text. In his satirical critique of the Quests in *The Screwtape Letters*, C. S. Lewis uses the instruction of a veteran demon to his nephew apprentice to make the point that our Christology must take the Scriptures at face value if we are going to avoid the ultimately subjective enterprise:

> You will find that a good many Christian-political writers think that Christianity began going wrong, and departing from the doctrine of its Founder, at a very early stage. Now this idea must be used by us to encourage once again the conception of a "historical Jesus" to be found by clearing away later

---

inson, *A New Quest of the Historical Jesus and Other Essays* (Minneapolis: Augsburg Fortress, 1983); Norman Perrin, *Rediscovering the Teaching of Jesus* (New York: Harper & Row, 1976).

[111] N. T. Wright is a major figure in the Third Quest. In addition, see Ben F. Meyer, *The Aims of Jesus*, Princeton Theological Monograph Series, vol. 48 (Eugene, OR: Wipf & Stock, 2002); E. P. Sanders, *Jesus and Judaism* (Minneapolis: Fortress, 1985); J. D. G. Dunn, *Jesus Remembered*, vol. 1 in *Christianity in the Making* (Grand Rapids, MI: Eerdmans, 2003).

[112] See Brown, *Jesus in European Protestant Thought*, 338.

[113] Wright, *Who Was Jesus?*, 13.

[114] Edwards, *Is Jesus the Only Savior?*, 20.

"accretions and perversions" and then to be contrasted with the whole Christian tradition. In the last generation we promoted the construction of such a "historical Jesus" on liberal and humanitarian lines; we are now putting forward a new "historical Jesus" on Marxian, catastrophic, and revolutionary lines. The advantage of these constructions, which we intend to change every thirty years or so, are manifold. In the first place they all tend to direct men's devotion to something which does not exist, for each "historical Jesus" is unhistorical. The documents say what they say and cannot be added to; each new "historical Jesus" therefore has to be got out of them by suppression at one point and exaggeration at another, and by that sort of guessing (*brilliant* is the adjective we teach humans to apply to it) on which no one would risk ten shillings in ordinary life. . . . The "Historical Jesus" then . . . is always to be encouraged.[115]

Specific attempts within a paradigm of historical Jesus research may differ in emphases, but they all fail to find the *real Jesus* for the same reason: they reject the *revealed Jesus* because they are beholden to Enlightenment principles that are alien to the Bible and its authoritative presentation of Jesus's identity. We only know the "Jesus of history" through the biblical texts that identify him as the "Christ of faith." Focusing on just two problems with the shift from a confessional to a critical epistemology will provide a quick summary of how the Enlightenment continues to cause confusion in Christology today.

First, assuming that the historical Jesus must be a desupernaturalized Jesus and cannot be the Jesus of the Bible prevents us from ever identifying the real Jesus. The strictly rational epistemology of the Enlightenment demands a hermeneutic that simply begins with an a priori and unwarranted rejection of Scripture. And, as B. B. Warfield reminds us from a century ago, the rejection of Scripture means a rejection of the real Jesus: "It is the desupernaturalized Jesus which is the mythical Jesus, who never had any existence, the postulation of the existence of whom explains nothing and leaves the whole historical development hanging in the air."[116] The futility of the historical-critical approach is captured by Aloys Grillmeier in a few words: "The nineteenth century used all its energy to work out a purely historical picture of Jesus by means of the techniques of historical investigation. In this investigation, the dogma of the incarnation was not to be accepted as a basic presupposition: the life of Jesus was to be treated as a purely human life which developed in a human way. The attempt came to nothing."[117]

Second, committing to a historical-critical Christology prevents us from ever saying anything theological about Jesus—who he is and the meaning

---

[115] C. S. Lewis, *The Screwtape Letters* (New York: Macmillan, 1943), 116–119.

[116] B. B. Warfield, *The Person and Work of Christ*, ed. Samuel G. Craig (Phillipsburg, NJ: P&R, 1950), 22.

[117] Aloys Grillmeier, *From the Apostolic Age to Chalcedon (451)*, vol. 1 in *Christ in Christian Tradition*, trans. John Bowden, 2nd rev. ed. (Atlanta: John Knox Press, 1975), 3.

and universal significance of his life, death, resurrection, and ascension. As Francis Watson correctly observes, "Historical research is unlikely to confirm an incarnation or a risen Lord."[118] And even if some reconstructed Jesus is a figure of some significance, "he cannot be identified with the Christ of faith acknowledged by the church."[119] The heirs of the Enlightenment only exacerbate the problem of reconstructing the past by assuming that historical events are self-interpreting and transparent to historical investigation. Merely human historical research can never yield an objective and infallibly true interpretation of Jesus's identity and significance. Correctly identifying Jesus, rather, requires God himself to give us both the historical facts and the theological interpretation of those facts.

We can now say that much of the current Christological confusion regarding Jesus's identity is the rotten fruit of an Enlightenment epistemology and worldview. A strictly rational epistemology has grown through a critical hermeneutic into a paradigm of historical Jesus research that rejects the reliability of the biblical texts or reinterprets them based on extrabiblical criteria, reducing Jesus to a mere man who cannot be identified as God the Son incarnate. It remains to be seen at the close of this chapter whether the postmodern challenges to the modern epistemology can move us from a critical Christology back to a confessional Christology for today.

THE IMPACT OF POSTMODERNISM ON CHRISTOLOGY

In Western culture, most acknowledge an important shift from a modern to a postmodern society. The exact nature of the shift and its implications for theology are hotly debated, but it is certainly the case that something significant has occurred.[120] Even the terms "postmodern" and "postmodernism" are difficult to define because of their diverse use. In this regard, Kevin Vanhoozer's warning is apt:

> Those who attempt to define or to analyze the concept of postmodernity do so at their own peril. In the first place, postmoderns reject the notion that any description or definition is "neutral." Definitions may appear to bask in the glow of impartiality, but they invariably exclude something and hence are complicit, wittingly or not, in politics. A definition of postmodernity is as likely to say more about the person offering the definition than it [says] of "the postmodern." Second, postmoderns resist closed, tightly bounded "totalizing" accounts of such things as the "essence" of the postmodern. And third,

---

[118] Watson, "*Veritas Christi*," 104.
[119] Ibid., 105.
[120] For example, see six evangelical approaches to postmodernism in Myron B. Penner, ed., *Christianity and the Postmodern Turn: Six Views* (Grand Rapids, MI: Brazos Press, 2005). For the relationship between modernism and postmodernism, see Penner's three options in ibid., 18–19. I adopt the second one, which views postmodernism as different than modernism but starting from the same point, namely, human autonomy. Postmodernism, then, ought to be viewed as the logical end of modernism's assumptions, not as distinct and conceptually *beyond* modernism.

according to David Tracy "there is no such phenomenon as postmodernity." There are only postmodernities.[121]

Our purposes here, however, require not an exact definition but an educated understanding of postmodernism—an understanding actually aided by the refusal of postmodernity to be defined. James Sire notes that the term "postmodernism" was first used in reference to architecture and art. When French sociologist Jean-François Lyotard used the term to signal a shift in cultural values, however, "the term became a key word in cultural analysis."[122] Lyotard gave what is postmodern the now often-quoted descriptor "incredulity toward metanarratives."[123] The term acquired the prefix "post" because it refers to a move away from the "modern" that is associated with the prior Enlightenment ideals of rationality and progress.[124] And in this move away from modern ideals, postmodernism rejects at least three conditions of modern knowledge: "(1) the appeal to metanarratives as a foundationalist criterion of legitimacy, (2) the outgrowth of strategies of legitimation and exclusion, and (3) a desire for criteria of legitimacy in the moral as well as the epistemological domain."[125] In this light, postmodernism, especially in the area of epistemology, may be viewed as a mind-set that is suspicious of "grand narratives" and universal, objective truth; and as such, postmodernism moves away from the authority of universal science toward narratives of local knowledge.

Even though postmodernism rejects Enlightenment-modern methodology, however, it begins with the same "turn to the subject/self," only to end with the same problems. As did modernism before it, postmodernism elevates the autonomous human subject. At the same time, postmodern thought acknowledges what earlier thinkers such as Kant already taught, namely, that there are limitations to human reason, especially in making universal statements on matters such as metaphysics, ethics, and theology. Postmodernism clearly and openly critiques and rejects the hubris of the Enlightenment. But by joining modernism at the same starting point of human autonomy, postmodernism offers no better alternative. Postmodernity merely takes the Enlightenment turn to its logical conclusions:[126] starting with an independent and limited human subject leads to only a local and subjective knowledge. A postmodern

---

[121] Kevin J. Vanhoozer, "Theology and the Condition of Postmodernity: A Report on Knowledge (of God)," in *The Cambridge Companion to Postmodern Theology*, ed. Kevin J. Vanhoozer (Cambridge: Cambridge University Press, 2003), 3.

[122] Sire, *Universe Next Door*, 213.

[123] Jean-François Lyotard, *The Postmodern Condition: A Report on Knowledge*, trans. Geoff Bennington and Brian Massumi, Theory and History of Literature, vol. 10 (Minneapolis: University of Minnesota Press, 1984), 24.

[124] Vanhoozer, "Theology and the Condition of Postmodernity," 7.

[125] Ibid., 9.

[126] For a discussion of whether postmodernism is a turning away from modernism or is modernism turning in on itself, see Penner, *Christianity and the Postmodern Turn*, 16–19; Vanhoozer, "Theology and the Condition of Postmodernity," 8–9.

epistemology provides no rational way of achieving a God's-eye viewpoint of the world and history: "no longer can we aspire to the knowledge of angels, much less a God's-eye point of view."[127]

We can now trace the effects of postmodernity in contemporary culture to see its impact on Christology. This last section argues that for all of its challenges to the Enlightenment and modern mind-set, postmodernity's own assumptions and methodology still leave us on the wrong side of Lessing's ditch. With what can be called an "artificial" epistemology, we are unable to say anything certain or significant about Jesus because the Bible remains unreliable and unable to ground any theological conclusions about Jesus's identity.

POSTMODERN EPISTEMOLOGY AND WORLDVIEW

Epistemology again provides the lens through which we can see the most fundamental intellectual shifts as we move from a premodern to a modern and now to a postmodern world.[128] The premodern era was rooted in a revelational epistemology: truth is universal and objective because it is grounded in the triune God who is the source and standard of all knowledge and whose plan encompasses all things because he is the sovereign Creator and Lord of his universe. In the language of Reformed orthodoxy, God's knowledge is *archetype* (i.e., original and thus the standard) and, as his finite image-bearers, our knowledge is *ectype* (a subset of God's original knowledge and thus derivative). Our knowledge, even though limited, is a subset of his knowledge, and as we "think his thoughts after him" in nature and in Scripture, it is possible to have finite but still objective and true knowledge.

In the modern era, philosophy took a decisive "turn to the subject." Rooted in classical foundationalism, human reason sought to operate apart from divine revelation, with the goal of achieving a universal, unified explanation of all reality. Modernism believed that if human reason simply followed the correct methods, starting in human autonomy, reason could arrive at a grand theory or "metanarrative." This grand narrative would ultimately explain all reality, albeit a reality now constrained by the limits of Enlightenment thought. Myron Penner provides a helpful summary of the modern project:

> The primary objective of rational explanation in modernity is to establish a set of infallible beliefs that can provide the epistemological foundations for an absolutely certain body of knowledge. It is not that the metaphysical concern has dropped out of view, for metaphysics is very much alive in modernity (as epistemology is in premodernity); it is rather that modern metaphysics is at the mercy of theories about what knowledge is and how it is acquired. That

---

[127] Vanhoozer, "Theology and the Condition of Postmodernity," 10.
[128] For a helpful discussion of these shifts, see Feinberg, *Can You Believe It's True?*, 37–76.

is, modern theories of reality are bounded by the limits that modern theories of knowledge place on the scope and substance of human knowledge. In the end, the shift is quite dramatic. Reason (*logos*) acquires certain metaphysical rights, so to speak, in a way that premoderns did not designate. The ontological assumption of reason is intensified to the point where reason becomes its own ground. The boundaries of what may be rationally thought are determined by the nature of human rational faculties, not the extra-human rational structure of them both.[129]

This epistemological rationalism brought with it a methodological naturalism to form a whole mind-set at odds with the premodern worldview. This modern mind-set has led to a massive distrust of Scripture, including a denial of the biblical Jesus as the historical Jesus and a rejection of Chalcedonian orthodoxy and its metaphysical commitments.

Now in its own turn (to the subject-self), postmodernism rejects modern foundationalism, not by returning to premodern revelational epistemology but by pressing forward in the assumptions of rationalism. Taking seriously Kant's argument that the mind is active in structuring knowledge, and his conclusion that our minds are not objective in the knowing process, postmodernism extends this modern principle to deny the modern assumption of a common and correct set of mental categories. With subjective minds, thinking in what could be very different mental categories, we are unable to gain anything close to universal, objective truth. In place of a strict rationalism, a postmodern epistemology takes the form of coherentism or pragmatism.[130]

This is not to say that postmodernism rejects all rationality—far from it. Rather, a universal explanation is not reasonable because universal reason is not a reality. Postmodernism rejects not rationality but *Reason*. "They deny the notion of universal rationality," concludes Vanhoozer: "reason is rather a contextual and relative affair. What counts as rational is relative to the prevailing narrative in a society or institution."[131] This is why postmodernism is often associated with the attempt to undo or deconstruct anyone who thinks that they have a universal viewpoint or metanarrative.

Specifically, postmodernism attempts to break the link between language and reality, a "logocentrism" that once characterized Western thought. In the premodern era, this logocentrism was grounded in Christian theology; it was then carried over into the modern era as borrowed capital from Christianity. With the rise of Darwinism, however, and the attendant self-conscious rejection of Christian theism, the basis for logocentrism was more difficult to establish. In place of a referential view of language, postmodernism posits a constructivist

---

[129] Penner, *Christianity and the Postmodern Turn*, 22.
[130] See Feinberg, *Can You Believe It's True?*, 37–76.
[131] Vanhoozer, "Theology and the Condition of Postmodernity," 10.

view.[132] Rather than conceiving of the mind as a "mirror of nature" consistent with a correspondence theory of truth, postmodernism argues that human beings view reality through the lens of language and culture. As a result, all of our theorizing is perspectival, provisional, and incomplete. In place of comprehensive theories we now have relative confessions about how things look to us. In the end, it is all about interpretation, not about what is real, true, or good.

The movement from a modern to a postmodern outlook has also brought a corresponding change in science, beginning with the view of nature—"it is naturalism, but . . ."[133] According to the predominant scientific paradigm of modernism, the world is a closed system of causal laws. In the twentieth century, however, science switched paradigms to quantum and relativity theories that view the world as integrated, contingent, and continuously changing. John Feinberg helpfully summarizes this change in perspective:

> [I]n contrast to Newtonian physics, which saw the universe as composed of static, changeless bits of matter that interact according to set natural laws, the new science claims that things in our world are interrelated in a continuous process of change and becoming. Even in the most solid bits of matter (at the atomic and subatomic levels) things are not static but in motion. . . . Moreover, as opposed to Newtonian physics which held that physical things interact according to set physical laws, quantum physics claims that there is a certain indeterminacy at least at the atomic and sub-atomic levels of existence.[134]

At the same time that scientific paradigms have changed, however, the view of evolution remains entrenched. For most postmoderns, evolution is nonnegotiable and any opposition to it is fiercely resisted. As in the modern era, the establishment of evolution as a basic presupposition comes as a necessary part of the larger move to an a priori definition of science that rules out any consideration of the supernatural and nonmaterial. With the acceptance of quantum mechanics and relativity theory, however, some believe the door has opened for a return to an affirmation of God acting in our world.[135] But even so, most postmoderns still view the universe as a basically closed system and thus assume a methodological naturalism in their approach to all academic disciplines. The primary reason for this adherence to naturalism is a refusal to return to a full-blown Christian theism, which alone can provide the proper underpinnings for the miraculous. For its conception of God, rather, postmodernism adopts a more panentheistic alternative.[136]

---

[132] See Kevin J. Vanhoozer, *Is There a Meaning in This Text? The Bible, the Reader, and the Morality of Literary Knowledge* (Grand Rapids, MI: Zondervan, 1998), 43–147.

[133] This phrase and concept is taken from Feinberg, *No One Like Him*, 104.

[134] Ibid., 104–105.

[135] See, e.g., Evans, *Historical Christ and the Jesus of Faith*, 137–169; cf. Gregory A. Boyd, *God of the Possible: A Biblical Introduction to the Open View of God* (Grand Rapids, MI: Baker, 2000), 107–112.

[136] See John W. Cooper, *Panentheism, the Other God of the Philosophers: From Plato to the Present* (Grand Rapids, MI: Baker Academic, 2006); see also Kevin J. Vanhoozer, *Remythologizing Theology: Divine Action, Passion, and Authorship* (Cambridge: Cambridge University Press, 2010), 81–138.

Although panentheism comes in many varieties, the most rigorous theological view sees God as the universe in constant progression (as opposed to permanence), with historical events as the basic building blocks (instead of substances).[137] This kind of panentheism pictures all reality as a series of events, each of which has two poles. The mental or primordial pole is all the possibilities that actual entities can become; the physical or consequent pole is the world, God's body, which is the progressive realization of the various possibilities. In this metaphysical scheme, God is viewed as an event who is *in* everything. There is, then, no Creator-creature distinction. God and the world are not identical but neither are they inseparable; they are mutually dependent without one being subordinate to the other. The world is viewed as a moment within the divine life. In fact, because God is not only connected with but immanent to the world, he is undergoing a process of self-development and growth. God is not the supernatural, transcendent Creator of the world and Lord of history; he is (in) the natural processes of evolution by which the world and history take shape.

This view of God in the world not only fits well with current scientific conceptions of the world, but it also supports many familiar postmodern confessions of God: e.g., "a God who is immanent and relational; a God whose very being interpenetrates all things and hence underscores the connectedness of all things; a God who is not static but is constantly changing as he responds to our needs; and a God to whom we can contribute value as well as one who enhances our existence."[138] Feinberg rightly reminds us that this "process" conception of God "poses a formidable threat to traditional Christian understanding of God, and it also offers a way to synthesize various non-evangelical postmodern notions about God."[139] This process view of God predominates in non-evangelical theology today. Yet even within evangelicalism, movements such as "open theism" have embraced some tenets of postmodern panentheism.[140]

POSTMODERN HERMENEUTICS

Another contrast between modernity and postmodernity centers on the role of language and the place of hermeneutics in philosophical reflection. The modern era is identified with the "subjective turn"; the postmodern era may be identified more specifically with the "linguistic turn." Modernity assumes that reason is universal and impervious to differences of culture and language;

---

[137] See, e.g., John B. Cobb Jr. and David R. Griffin, *Process Theology: An Introductory Exposition* (Philadelphia: Westminster, 1976).

[138] Feinberg, *No One Like Him*, 142.

[139] Ibid.

[140] On open theism, see Clark H. Pinnock et al., *The Openness of God: A Biblical Challenge to the Traditional Understanding of God* (Downers Grove, IL: InterVarsity Press, 1994); John Sanders, *The God Who Risks* (Downers Grove, IL: InterVarsity Press, 1998); Boyd, *God of the Possible*. For responses, see Bruce A. Ware, *God's Lesser Glory: The Diminished God of Open Theism* (Wheaton, IL: Crossway, 2000); John M. Frame, *No Other God: A Response to Open Theism* (Phillipsburg, NJ: P&R, 2001).

postmodernity rejects this assumption as impossible. With Kant, postmoderns argue that our mental categories do not mirror the world but mold it by imposing distinctions on experience that may or may not be intrinsic to reality itself, continuing the distinction between *phenomena* and *noumena*. Postmoderns disagree with Kant, however, when it comes to the nature of our mental categories: the Kantian categories are *universal* and *necessary*; the postmodern categories are *linguistic* and *arbitrary*. It follows "that there is no commonly agreed way of interpreting reality. The distinctions that make up the 'natural order' are neither 'natural' nor 'given' but rather artificial and man-made. There is no such thing as an absolute, God's-eye point of view on reality, only a number of finite and fallible human perspectives."[141]

Postmodernism's linguistic turn and artificial (man-made) view of reality has produced an artificial approach to meaning and the biblical texts. The premodern biblical interpreters sought to discover the author's intent because they believed that thereby they would discover God's intent. As Calvin put it, "It is the first business of an interpreter to let his author say what he does say, instead 'of attributing to him what we think he ought to say."[142] Modernism rejected the Bible's inspiration and reliability and sought to discover the real Jesus behind the text, but still with the goal of interpreting the text according to the author's intent.[143] Both the premodern and modern eras, then, held to a hermeneutical realism: "the position that believes meaning to be prior to and independent of the process of interpretation."[144] The postmodern era, however, approaches the Bible with hermeneutical *non*-realism; the reader brings meaning to the text in the process of interpretation. As such, this artificial approach guarantees universal subjectivity. Vanhoozer helpfully summarizes this hermeneutical philosophy:

> Hermeneutic philosophers no longer consider knowledge as the result of a disinterested subject observing facts, but rather as an interpretive effort whereby a subject rooted in a particular history and tradition seeks to understand the strange by means of the familiar. Instead of "uninterpreted fact" serving as grist for the mill of "objective reason," both fact and reason alike are what they are because of their place in history and tradition. Hermeneutics is a cousin to historical consciousness; the realization that we do not know things directly and immediately suggests that knowledge is the result of interpretation. Reality is a text to be interpreted, mediated by language, history, culture, and tradition.[145]

---

141 Vanhoozer, *Is There a Meaning in This Text?*, 49.
142 Preface to John Calvin's *Commentary on Romans*, cited in Vanhoozer, *Is There a Meaning in This Text?*, 47.
143 Vanhoozer explains the difference between intent and truth: "In historical critical exegesis, then, the original sense is authoritative, not in the sense of being necessarily true, but insofar as it remains the norm for establishing the meaning of a passage (which may be true or false)" (Vanhoozer, *Is There a Meaning in This Text?*, 48).
144 Ibid.
145 Ibid., 20.

In the end, then, postmodernism agrees with modernism's rejection of the Bible's universal authority. Modernism denies the text's truthfulness and therefore rejects its authoritativeness. Postmodernism takes the Scriptures as authoritative, but only according to the reader's or community's interpretive experience. Rather than taking the text as the objective and universally true word of God written, the postmodern hermeneutic transforms the text into "an echo chamber in which we see ourselves and hear our own voices."[146] The modernist critic reads the Bible according to the author's intent, but then rejects the Bible's factual and theological claims. The postmodernist interpreter argues that "the text has no stable or decidable meaning, or that what meaning is there is biased and ideologically distorted. The result is that the Bible is either not recognized as making claims or, if it is, that these claims are treated as ideologically suspect."[147]

POSTMODERNISM AND CHRISTOLOGY

Postmodernism has not returned us to a revelational epistemology that will support a warranted Christology. In fact, the artificial epistemology of postmodernity moves us away from warrant as a goal or even as a possibility. The postmodern epistemology, worldview, and hermeneutic inevitably lead to a paradigm of pluralism that must accommodate all Christologies as individual stories, thereby (ironically or intentionally) rejecting orthodox Christianity.

Postmodernism has increased the confusion in Christology that first started in the Enlightenment-modern era: the problems are the same but they have been further complicated. For the most part, the Enlightenment adopted deism and a Newtonian view of physics and thereby moved to a strict naturalism, away from even the possibility of the miraculous. While the miraculous is possible in postmodernity, its possibility rests not on God's activity but on the dynamics of quantum/relativity theory. The shift from deism to Darwinism and from Newton to Einstein has moved from a *simple to a complex form of naturalism*. This new complexity has increased confusion in at least two significant aspects of Christology: the nature of humanity and the identity of Jesus.

The nature of humanity has been transformed by postmodernity's rejection of the substance-nature view of reality in favor of relationality, becoming, and emergence. In *Christology and Science*, F. LeRon Shults accepts the current views without question and challenges orthodox Christology to change from a substance-nature view to an evolutionary-biological view of the incarnation.[148] The traditional formulations of Christology that rely on the link between Jesus's personhood and the human nature of Adam before the fall must

---

[146] Ibid.
[147] Ibid., 24.
[148] F. LeRon Shults, *Christology and Science* (Grand Rapids, MI: Eerdmans, 2008).

be abandoned. Christology within the "new science" needs to be completely reformulated in ways acceptable to current thought, which, for Shults, will provide new insights and place Christ within an "emergent holist understanding of human persons."[149] Overall, Shults's reformulation entails that we must: (1) reject the notion of substance for a relational view; (2) reject a "literal reading of the story of Adam and Eve in the Garden of Eden" because it has lost its plausibility in light of discoveries about "the process of human evolution within the cosmos"; and (3) reject the virgin birth as necessary on the basis of critical scholarship and evolutionary insights.[150] Christology, rather, should aim to "uphold the intuition that Jesus Christ reveals the origin and goal of the human experience of knowing God, which is wholly dependent on the creative initiative of divine grace and cannot be achieved by human effort alone. We can accept these *theological* points of Genesis and Matthew without accepting the ancient *scientific* cosmogony and gynecology of the original authors and redactors."[151]

Christology today has been placed within an evolutionary model linked to the modern world but surpassing it in complexity and confusion. Postmodernism has not returned Christology to orthodoxy but moved it further away. The postmodern emphasis on becoming over being, existence over essence, and dynamic emergence over transcendence demonstrate that every Christology assumes a larger theology and worldview. Every Christology is constructed upon a presupposed conception of God, self, and the world.[152] To articulate and defend an orthodox Christology today, we will also need to articulate and defend an entire Christian worldview set against the overarching evolutionary paradigm of contemporary thought. The current uneasiness over the terms "substance," "nature," "person"—terms closely associated with orthodoxy— is tied to specific theological conceptions that need to be defended anew. The way forward for evangelical theology is not an appeal to current views of science but an explication and defense of a Christian-theistic view of the universe that allows for and makes sense of the personal, triune God acting uniquely and extraordinarily in his world.

Yet even more than with the transformation of human nature, postmodernity has further confused Christology by surrendering the uniqueness of Christ. During the nineteenth century, the uniqueness of Christ had already become a matter of degree only, not kind; but there was still an attempt to elevate Christianity as a religion and Jesus as a religious figure and personality.[153]

---

[149] Ibid., 37.
[150] See ibid., 21–44.
[151] Ibid., 43.
[152] For a helpful elaboration on this point, see Wells, *Person of Christ*, 148–154.
[153] Examples include the work of Friedrich Schleiermacher (Christ exhibits the highest order of God-consciousness) and the entire view of classic liberalism (Christ is the highest ideal of ethical teaching).

For example, classic liberalism rejected the historic position of the church in regard to Christ, but it still tried to maintain a unique identity for Jesus Christ in moral categories. As postmodernism has taken hold, however, Troeltsch's view now predominates so thoroughly that *Jesus is no different in kind or degree from other religious figures*. And because Jesus Christ is only one religious figure among many, Christology must be done within a pluralistic paradigm.

In fact, almost every aspect of the postmodern outlook embraces pluralism. For example, postmodernism's rejection of metanarratives also rejects a Christology from the Scriptures. The Bible cannot be received as God's word written because such a transcendent, universal perspective is a priori impossible. Without such an interpretive word grounded in God's comprehensive knowledge and plan for the world, we cannot judge between true and false, right and wrong, and so we cannot say anything definitive or unique about Christ. And the same is true with the postmodern hermeneutic applied to Christology. Modernism believed that it could reconstruct history in an objective manner, peeling off the layers of myth to rediscover the real Jesus of history. Postmodernism takes this error even further: now there is "no historical Jesus nor indeed a Christ of faith, nor any historical evidence for a clear delineation of the relationship between them. There is only Bultmann's, Schweitzer's, Käsemann's, Pannenberg's, Wright's or Crossan's constructed histories of the narratives, stories and loose causal identities that form our perception of the past."[154] Under postmodernity's epistemology and worldview and according to its hermeneutic, a pluralistic Christology is inevitable.

One Response to Contemporary Christology

The two major trends in Christology today have produced much confusion regarding the identity of Jesus Christ. The paradigms of historical Jesus research and pluralism create this confusion because they are created by epistemologies that (in different ways) reject the one reliable and authoritative source for properly identifying Jesus Christ.

From the Enlightenment era into modernity and postmodernity, the autonomous subject-self has been elevated to reign over knowledge and meaning. Modernity gives us a strictly rational epistemology and a historical-critical hermeneutic. Postmodernity gives us an artificial epistemology and hermeneutic. Both reject the revelational epistemology and hermeneutic of the premodern Reformation. The modern approach works primarily through the paradigm of historical Jesus research, resulting in a critical Christology. The postmodern approach works primarily through the paradigm of pluralism, resulting

---

[154] Colin J. D. Greene, *Christology in Cultural Perspective: Marking Out the Horizons* (Grand Rapids, MI: Eerdmans, 2003), 167.

in many personal Christologies. Both reject the confessional Christology of orthodoxy established in the early church and maintained into the premodern Reformation.

More than simply bemoan the loss of an older Christology, however, the work ahead will continue the argument for a well-warranted Christology for today. There is only one response to the two trends in contemporary Christology coming out of anti-revelational epistemologies: return to a revelational-biblical epistemology to read the Bible on its own terms and discover the identity of the real Jesus given by God himself. The Enlightenment-modern and postmodern epistemologies leave us in a legitimation crisis, asking *"whose story, whose interpretation, whose authority, whose criteria counts, and why?"*[155] To all of these questions, the next chapter argues that God himself is the answer—God himself identifies Jesus accurately and authoritatively according to his own word of interpretation in Scripture.

In this chapter, we have established only the first half of the epistemological warrant we need for Christology today. We have demonstrated that true knowledge of the true Jesus requires a revelational epistemology that looks to the Bible for God's own interpretation of who Jesus is and his significance for us and all creation. In the next chapter, we need to lay out the basic contours of this biblical epistemology so that we can be sure to follow it as we continue the work of Christology in the remaining parts and chapters.

---

[155] Vanhoozer, "Theology and the Condition of Postmodernity," 10 (emphasis his).

"Biblical" Epistemology
for Christology

David Wells rightly reminds us that Christology is now done amid the disintegration of the Enlightenment world and its replacement by the postmodern ethos and pluralism.[1] As modernism first took hold and then gave way to a postmodern mind-set, a distrust of the Scriptural view of Jesus gradually arose. This erosion of the Bible's authority in contemporary culture meant that a continued interest in Jesus would make a critical distinction: the Jesus of history is fundamentally different from the biblical Jesus. And this dichotomy has led to the futility of trying to establish the unique identity and universal significance of Christ on historical-critical grounds alone. The result is that an evangelical articulation of orthodox Christology has become both a complicated endeavor and a cardinal concern for the church in our contemporary context. Who do we—the church today—say that Jesus is?

As we have already learned, however, before we can say *who Jesus is* we must consider *how we can know* who he is. We have covered two hundred years of worldview shifts not merely for the sake of curiosity but to prepare to avoid the pitfalls of the past in our own articulation and defense of orthodox, evangelical Christology today.

This chapter will argue that to avoid the epistemological missteps of the past, we must stay the course set by a "biblical" epistemology—the only course that leads to the proper identification of Jesus Christ. Ultimately, the church needs to move from reading the Bible to thinking theologically. Taking these steps along the path laid down by a biblical epistemology requires that we read the Bible *on its own terms*: the Bible is God's word-act revelation in which God himself provides the correct interpretation of his own actions in history that

---

[1] David F. Wells, *Above All Earthly Pow'rs: Christ in a Postmodern World* (Grand Rapids, MI: Eerdmans, 2005).

climax in the historical person of Jesus Christ. So our discussion here will follow this logic: a "biblical" Christology (*who* the Lord Jesus is) depends upon a "biblical" epistemology (*how* to know who Jesus is), which is dependent upon a "biblical" doctrine of the Bible itself (*what* the Bible is).

To build our epistemological warrant for a Christology today, we will begin with how to know who Jesus is in our current culture. Then we will look more closely at what it means for Scripture to be the necessary starting point for all Christology. Finally, we will consider the particulars of the nature and function of Scripture that lead to a "biblical" Christology.

A Worldview Defense of Christianity

The current Christological confusion is not limited to the academy, but has crept out onto the streets and even into our pews. For example, *The Myth of God Incarnate*[2] and the Jesus Seminar have had such a tremendous impact not because of their scholarship but because of their popular appeal, as evidenced by the considerable amount of press they have received. On a personal note, I can still remember my brief conversation with an elderly lady in 1996 that spoke volumes regarding the pervasiveness of confusion regarding Jesus's identity. After this lady discovered that I was a pastor, we immediately began talking about the findings of the Jesus Seminar and she told me how much she had learned from the latest research. She concluded, "Isn't it wonderful how Jesus can be whoever we want him to be!" What is crucial to note is that this lady was not involved in higher education and religious studies; she was a "nonacademic" person who read nonacademic literature. But she was influenced by the academy's view of Jesus that had been picked up by popular sources. And her example is not an isolated case. The effects of two hundred–plus years of debate in academia over Jesus's identity do not remain in that laboratory; they eventually seep into the soil of the larger culture and impact people who are not aware of the nuances, history, controversy, and significance of the debate.

Evangelical theologians cannot ignore these cultural trends if we are going to present Christ faithfully to our generation. No doubt, in one sense, all of this confusion is nothing new; it goes all the way back to the early church. But in another sense, what we see today, especially in the West, is tied to a post-Christian culture, which is rooted in a massive shift away from a Christian view of the world. In fact, current Christological confusion is tied to the larger cultural and intellectual shifts (beyond epistemology)[3] that have grown in our society and even in our churches, producing a skepticism toward Scripture

---

[2] John Hick, ed. *The Myth of God Incarnate* (Philadelphia: Westminster, 1977).
[3] For a discussion of other trends that have contributed to postmodernism, see Wells, *Above All Earthly Pow'rs*, 91–262. Wells stresses that the shift to postmodern attitudes is not solely epistemological but is tied to a whole complex of social factors, including patterns of immigration, global economy, secularization, and popular culture.

and replacing revealed Christian theism with self-constructed views of God, humanity, and the world. As the plausibility structures have changed, believing in the universal significance and exclusivity of Christ has become impossible for many. An evangelical Christology cannot simply state its conclusions; it must also provide the basis for the uniqueness of Christ, which includes such perennial theological issues as the rationality, coherence, and intelligibility of our Christological formulations.

All Christological Formulations Are Worldview (Inter)Dependent

From our survey of intellectual history we also learn that Christology is never done piecemeal or in a neutral fashion—in fact, it relies on an entire nexus of theological commitments. Any attempt at Christology depends upon and presupposes an entire theological vision or worldview[4] because systematic theology does not consist of isolated parts. As noted in my Introduction, J. I. Packer has correctly observed that theology is "an organism, a unity of inter-related parts, a circle in which everything links up with everything else . . ."[5] And nowhere is this more evident than in Christology; any statement regarding Christ's identity already assumes, implicitly or explicitly, an entire theology. This insight is nothing new, but in light of the last two centuries of Christological debate, it is now more evident than ever before.

We can explore the integrated nature of Christology along two complementary paths: the presuppositions of those who depart from orthodoxy, and the interpretive framework required for an evangelical articulation and defense of orthodox Christology today.

Regarding presuppositions, our survey of Western intellectual history and its effects on Christology revealed that the primary reason for the move to non-orthodox Christologies was the a priori shifts in worldview: the Enlightenment's deism and "turn to the subject"; modernism's historical criticism, classical foundationalism, and naturalistic-evolutionary view of reality; and postmodernism's "linguistic turn" and rejection of all metanarratives. This worldview revolution ultimately turned in one direction—*away from Christian theism*. More particularly, the invalidation of the supernatural and the rejection of Scriptural authority were moves *away from the linchpins* of Christian theism. When the defining beliefs of the Enlightenment, modernity, and postmodernity are scrutinized, each can be seen as an implicit or explicit rejection

---

[4] While it is open to a number of definitions, Steven Cowan and James Spiegel capture the heart of the term "worldview": "A worldview is a conceptual scheme or intellectual framework by which a person organizes and interprets experience. More specifically, a worldview is a set of beliefs, values, and presuppositions concerning life's most fundamental issues. You might say it is a *perspective* on reality. Like tinted glasses, a worldview 'colors' the way we see things and shapes our interpretation of the world. And, it must be emphasized, *everyone* has a worldview" (Steven B. Cowan and James S. Spiegel, *The Love of Wisdom: A Christian Introduction to Philosophy* [Nashville: B&H Academic, 2009], 7, emphasis theirs).

[5] J. I. Packer, "The Uniqueness of Jesus Christ," *Churchman* 92/2 (1978): 110.

of not only the truthfulness of historic Christianity but also the worldview surrounding it and the framework supporting it. That is why we characterized the methodological approach of most modern and postmodern Christologies as *extratextual*, i.e., Christology done according to an alien ideology and within a foreign framework that rejects the revealed Jesus and constructs a pseudo-Christ.

What lesson should we learn? At the heart of our Christological confusion, and especially in our disagreement with much non-evangelical Christology, there are crucial presuppositional differences that ultimately reflect different theological visions. Until the significance of this point is sufficiently grasped, we cannot make real headway against opposing views in our articulation and defense of orthodox Christology. We must simultaneously articulate and defend an entire theology. In other words, like its rivals, orthodox Christology begins with a commitment to a specific conception of God, Scripture, human beings, sin, and so on.[6] Even Robert Funk, cofounder of the Jesus Seminar, has to admit that, "Jesus' divinity goes together with the old theistic way of thinking about God."[7] But rather than demote Jesus to a more agreeable status, we want to promote him as the Son of God revealed in the Scriptures. To that end, Christian theism must be defended not only as *basically credible* but also as *absolutely necessary*.[8]

Regarding the interpretive framework for an evangelical articulation and defense, orthodox Christology today requires an *intratextual* approach that looks for Jesus in the biblical presentation of him—according to the categories and structure of the Scriptures. Instead of removing him from the biblical storyline, as all extratextual approaches do, we must think about Jesus's identity according to and work from within the interpretive framework of Scripture.

Obviously, an intratextual approach assumes certain truths about Scripture: it is God's word written, an accurate God's-eye interpretation of who Jesus is, written though the agency of human authors. This view of Scripture acknowledges that even though the text does not say everything about Jesus's identity (cf. John 21:25), whatever it does say, it says accurately and infallibly. There is, therefore, no distinction between the "Jesus of history" and the "Christ of faith"—a distinction that assumes that the Scriptures are *not* reliable in recounting and interpreting historical events. An intratextual view

---

[6] David Wells agrees: "No Christology can be constructed which does not presuppose . . . both a clear conception of God and a clear conception of human nature" (David F. Wells, *The Person of Christ: A Biblical and Historical Analysis of the Incarnation* [Westchester, IL: Crossway, 1984], 7).

[7] Robert W. Funk, "The Coming Radical Reformation: Twenty-one Theses," *The Fourth R* 11/4 (July-August 1998), http://www.westarinstitute.org/resources/the-fourth-r/the-coming-radical-reformation/, accessed May 19, 2015.

[8] For current evangelical articulations and defenses of orthodox theism, see John S. Feinberg, *No One Like Him: The Doctrine of God*, Foundations of Evangelical Theology (Wheaton, IL: Crossway, 2001); John M. Frame, *The Doctrine of God* (Phillipsburg, NJ: P&R, 2002); Kevin J. Vanhoozer, *Remythologizing Theology: Divine Action, Passion, and Authorship* (Cambridge: Cambridge University Press, 2010).

argues that because the biblical text is God's word, it provides both accurate facts about Jesus and the authoritative framework by which we interpret those facts in order to understand Christ's identity.

It is the God-givenness of Scripture that allows us to construct an objectively grounded and warranted Christology. Scripture alone serves as our norm for grasping the identity of Christ, and the identity of Christ can be understood correctly only when viewed in light of the full biblical presentation. Attempting to remove Jesus from the storyline of Scripture, or accepting certain parts and rejecting others—something all modern and postmodern Christologies do—will only lead to a subjective, arbitrary, and ultimately false construction of Jesus's identity.

A biblical example here will help illustrate the point. Paul's famous Athenian address (Acts 17:16–32)[9] emphasizes the importance of an intratextual approach to Scripture. As one studies Paul's sermons in the book of Acts, it is important to observe *how* he proclaims the gospel and the identity of Christ, depending upon his audience. Normally, when Paul went to a city, he first went to the synagogue, where he reasoned with the Jews and God-fearers, and his proclamation of the gospel followed a basic pattern: he reasoned from the Old Testament that Jesus is the promised Messiah, who in his life, death, and resurrection, and in his sending of the Holy Spirit at Pentecost, had ushered in the long-awaited kingdom of God and new covenant era (see Acts 13:5, 14–41, 44–45; 14:1; 17:2, 10, 17). Paul could begin this way because he and his Jewish audience had a common theology. They both believed the Old Testament, and thus, when Paul spoke about "God," "Messiah," "covenants," "sin," and so on, he spoke to people who shared his worldview.

At Athens, however, Paul's audience was quite different. The Athenians, as sophisticated as they were, did not have the Old Testament; they were biblically and theologically illiterate, steeped in idolatry, pluralistic in their outlook, and ignorant of the biblical framework necessary to understand even the most rudimentary truths that Paul needed to communicate. Paul's preaching of Christ in the midst of the Areopagus, therefore, had a different starting place and structure than his preaching in the synagogues.

In Athens, Paul does not immediately begin with Jesus as the Messiah; he first builds a biblical-theological framework so that his proclamation of Jesus will make sense *on the Bible's own terms and within its own categories*. Paul first sets the Christian view as true over against the opposing non-Christian worldviews; only *then*, and only from *within* the biblical worldview does Paul proclaim Jesus as Lord and Savior. Even within the condensed address recorded

---

[9] For a helpful exposition of Acts 17, see D. A. Carson, "Athens Revisited," in *Telling the Truth: Evangelizing Postmoderns*, ed. D. A. Carson (Grand Rapids, MI: Zondervan, 2000), 384–398.

in Acts 17,[10] Paul lays down six building blocks that are foundational to the biblical worldview and essential to the correct explication and defense of Jesus's identity as the Christ.

First, Paul begins with the God of creation, explaining that this world is not the result of blind chance (contra Epicureans) or the evolution of a world-spirit (contra Stoicism), but is the creation of one sovereign, personal God who alone reigns as the Lord of heaven and earth (Acts 17:24). Second, Paul establishes that this God is independent and self-sufficient (divine aseity), meaning that he gives mankind all things and receives nothing from us to help him rule as the Lord of all history and providence (vv. 25–26).[11] Third, Paul explains that God reveals himself, creating us in his image ("offspring," not idolaters) and locating us in our exact places so that we may know him as Lord of heaven and earth (vv. 26–29). Fourth, Paul declares that mankind chooses to rebel against God as our Creator and Lord and that therefore we are justly condemned by him (vv. 30–31). Fifth, Paul then instructs the Athenians that all mankind is commanded to turn from idolatry to know God, so that on the coming day of God's final judgment they will stand before God in repentance and not in rebellion (vv. 29–31). Sixth, only after constructing this basic storyline, Paul then presents Jesus as the man whom God raised from the dead to judge the world in righteousness (v. 31).

For our present purposes, it is most important to note that before Paul presented Christ to the Athenians, he placed himself *within the framework and categories of the Christian worldview*. The only way the Athenians could know God, was for them to identify Jesus within Scripture's own interpretive framework as the sole agent of God's judgment and salvation. Jesus is the one whom God has appointed and accredited in history by his resurrection from the dead to bring about God's eternal plan. While every other man is condemned as an idolater, this one man Jesus is the standard of God's righteousness by which God himself will judge the world.

D. A. Carson nicely summarizes Paul's epistemological strategy for knowing who Jesus is:

> The good news of Jesus Christ—who he is and what he accomplished by his death, resurrection, and exaltation—is simply incoherent unless certain structures are already in place. You cannot make heads or tails of the real Jesus unless you have categories for the personal/transcendent God of the Bible; the nature of human beings made in the image of God; the sheer odium of rebellion against him; the curse that our rebellion has attracted; the spiritual, personal, familial, and social effects of our transgression; the nature of salva-

---

[10] Carson advises that speeches before the Areopagus were much longer than what is given in Acts, so what Luke has preserved is a probably condensed version in which every statement could be expanded in greater detail (ibid., 391).
[11] On the importance of divine aseity, see Frame, *Doctrine of God*, 600–616.

tion; the holiness and wrath and love of God. One cannot make sense of the Bible's plot line without such basic ingredients; one cannot make sense of the Bible's portrayal of Jesus without such blocks in place.[12]

Here is the lesson for evangelical theologians today: because the current direction of Christology is largely determined by pervasive worldview structures and presupposed ways of knowing, a truly "biblical" Christology must proceed self-consciously and explicitly from the Bible's self-presentation of Christ as the only way to identify him rightly. If we do not "interpret the biblical texts 'on their own terms,'"[13] making theological judgments according to Scripture's own structures and categories, then the Jesus constructed will not be the biblical Jesus, and there will be nothing unique about him.

"Biblical" Epistemology and the Doctrine of Scripture

Given the fact that any statement regarding the identity of Christ implicitly or explicitly assumes an entire theology, then an articulation-defense of classical Christology requires an articulation-defense of the Christian worldview. And because the Christian worldview depends entirely upon the Bible as God's revelation of that worldview, we need to discuss briefly the nature and function of the Scriptures. Our purpose is not to present a complete defense of Scripture as the word of God written, working through all the necessary affirmations and implications; other capable theologians have already done the apologetic work.[14] But we do need to sketch out the basics of an orthodox understanding of Scripture. From this outline we can then move from what Scripture is to how it functions to give us its own worldview presentation of Jesus Christ.

A high view of Scripture maintains the following: the Bible is God's

---

[12] Carson, "Athens Revisited," 386.

[13] Kevin J. Vanhoozer, "Exegesis and Hermeneutics," in *NDBT*, 52.

[14] For a helpful sample of works from the abundance of literature defending an orthodox understanding of Scripture as God's word written, see D. A. Carson and John Woodbridge, eds., *Scripture and Truth* (Grand Rapids, MI: Zondervan, 1983); idem, *Hermeneutics, Authority, and Canon* (Grand Rapids, MI: Zondervan, 1986); Timothy Ward, *Words of Life: Scripture as the Living and Active Word of God* (Downers Grove, IL: IVP Academic, 2009); Norman L. Geisler, ed., *Inerrancy* (Grand Rapids, MI: Zondervan, 1980); John M. Frame, *The Doctrine of the Word of God* (Phillipsburg, NJ: P&R, 2010). Just as I am arguing for Christology, the defense of orthodox bibliology requires a comprehensive argument that integrates other doctrines within theology (especially God, providence, and anthropology) and addresses certain philosophical, historical, archeological, and textual issues. For example, affirming that Scripture is God's inerrant word written through the free agency of human authors assumes specific conceptions of human freedom and God's sovereignty. And our view of God as triune, personal, sovereign, and omniscient also demands a specific view of Scripture: a word that is fully authoritative, infallible, and inerrant. For more discussion of these points, see Stephen J. Wellum, "The Inerrancy of Scripture," in *Beyond the Bounds: Open Theism and the Undermining of Biblical Christianity*, ed. John Piper, Justin Taylor, and Paul K. Helseth (Wheaton, IL: Crossway, 2003), 237–274; cf. Kevin J. Vanhoozer, "God's Mighty Speech-Acts: The Doctrine of Scripture Today," in *A Pathway into the Holy Scriptures*, ed. Philip E. Satterthwaite and David F. Wright (Grand Rapids, MI: Eerdmans, 1994), 143–181. Minimally, a defense of Scripture should include the Bible's claim for itself, the unity of the Bible's story, and the Bible's historical reliability. On some of these points and the interdependence of apologetics for Scripture and for Christology, see Douglas Groothuis, *Christian Apologetics: A Comprehensive Case for Biblical Faith* (Downers Grove, IL: InterVarsity Press; Nottingham: Apollos, 2011); John S. Feinberg, *Can You Believe It's True? Christian Apologetics in a Modern and Postmodern Era* (Wheaton, IL: Crossway, 2013); John M. Frame, *Apologetics: A Justification of Christian Belief*, 2nd ed. (Phillipsburg, NJ: P&R, 2015).

inerrant and infallible word; it is written through the free agency of historical human authors inspired by God; it progressively reveals God's own worldview (God's relation to and work in creation) and his authoritative interpretation of his acts within and throughout history; it culminates with the historical person and work of Jesus Christ as the fulfillment of God's promises and the completion of his eternal plan for all things.

With just these fundamental ingredients of an orthodox definition of Scripture, we gain the necessary parameters for the *how* of knowing who Jesus is. Contra the Enlightenment and its current epistemological effects, a "biblical" epistemology will confidently take the Bible on its own terms as a sure means of rightly identifying the historical person of Jesus. As Creator, God's worldview is by definition the one, true worldview. And as the one who omnisciently and omnipotently governs all things toward the end he planned from the beginning, God unfailingly communicates how things really were, are, and will be and what they really mean. When it comes to the identity and significance of the historical person of Christ, then, we should look to the Bible for the inerrant and authoritative answer from God himself.

The Necessity of Christology "From Above"

Christology "From Below" versus Christology "From Above"

Since the Enlightenment, many have advocated a "Christology from below" in contrast to a "Christology from above." While these phrases are defined in different ways, *from below* is best understood as the attempt to do Christology from the vantage point of historical-critical research, independent of a commitment to the full authority of Scripture; *from above* refers to starting with Scripture as God's own accurate and authoritative word written in texts, so that we do Christology from the point of view of those texts.[15] This distinction

---

[15] People define these expressions differently. For some, Christology *from below* is understood as an approach to Christology that concentrates on Jesus's humanity and the historical Jesus over against his deity (*from above*) (see Millard J. Erickson, *The Word Became Flesh: A Contemporary Incarnational Christology* [Grand Rapids, MI: Baker, 1991], 625–626). Ultimately, Erickson proposes that we unite both approaches in doing Christology. Veli-Matti Kärkkäinen makes a similar argument. He agrees that a Christology *from above* "begins with the confession of faith in the deity of Christ expressed in the New Testament," while a Christology *from below* begins "with an inquiry into the historical Jesus and the historical basis for belief in Christ" (Veli-Matti Kärkkäinen, *Christology: A Global Introduction* [Grand Rapids, MI: Baker Academic, 2003], 12). See also a similar point in Myk Habets, *The Anointed Son: A Trinitarian Spirit Christology* (Eugene, OR: Pickwick, 2010), 29–52, who identifies *from above* with Logos Christology, which, he argues, downplays Christ's humanity and is largely philosophically driven; and *from below*, which, he says, does Christology from how the biblical authors first encountered Jesus, namely through his humanity. Similar to Erickson, Kärkkäinen and Habets believe these two approaches are compatible. Yet in failing to outline a robust doctrine of Scripture, it is difficult to see how they are, and in fact, the main epistemological issues are blurred. No doubt, there is truth in the way these two Christological approaches are described and how they are employed, yet given our survey of intellectual history and how these expressions have been used in the actual doing of Christology, it is better and more accurate to define *from above* as Christology done from a reading of Scripture as God's own word-act revelation that gives the authoritative interpretation of Jesus in his deity *and humanity*; *from below*, in contrast, is Christology done from historical-critical reconstruction that doubts or rejects the reliability and authority of Scripture. Defining our terms this way also enables us to see better the differences between various Christological methods: e.g., a Christology *from above* sees the biblical canon as the ground and warrant of our theological formulations because Scripture provides not only the *facts* for our Christology but also

is important because it is directly linked to another one: a Christology *from below* distrusts the Bible and assumes that the historical Jesus is not one-for-one the same as the biblical Jesus; a Christology *from above* assumes the Bible is truthful in its claim that they are the same person.

Doing Christology *from below*, therefore, attempts to reconstruct the historical Jesus by critical methods to determine what we cannot know from Scripture. But before theologizing about Christ *from below*, the critic must first establish what is and is not accurate in the Bible's presentation of Jesus. This kind of critique and reconstruction leads to a "thin" reading of Scripture, i.e., viewing Scripture as a thin veil of text that hints at but ultimately hides the real historical Jesus. This approach differs from a "thick" reading, which takes Scripture in its final canonical form as the fullness of God's word that accurately and authoritatively describes and interprets the identity of the real historical Jesus.[16]

With this oppositional understanding of the two ways of doing Christology, this section argues that Jesus can be rightly identified only *from above*, never *from below*. Three concerns sufficiently demonstrate the necessity of doing Christology *from above*.

First, if Scripture is not the necessary and sufficient condition to warrant and ground our Christology, then questions of epistemology and authority will ultimately prevent us from saying anything certainly or theologically about the identity of Jesus Christ.[17] The critic looking for Christ *from below* must decide which historical facts about Jesus in Scripture are true, and more importantly, when (if ever) the biblical author's theological interpretation of Jesus is accurate. If the historical Jesus is not identical to the biblical Jesus, then critics must establish criteria *outside of Scripture* to warrant what is accurate for Christological formulation. But what exactly are those criteria, and who decides? Human rationality? Religious experience? The "assured" results of biblical scholarship? Even if a consensus is reached among critics, what warrants the choices?

In wrestling with this problem recently, Francis Watson has proposed an

---

the *God-given interpretation* of those facts; whereas a Christology *from below* grounds and warrants all theological formulation in a combination of Scripture and critical methods. In making this distinction, it becomes clear that a Christology *from below* must provide the worldview warrant for historical criticism and establish the criteria to determine what is accepted and rejected in Scripture's presentation of Jesus.

[16] For this distinction between "thin" and "thick," see Vanhoozer, "Exegesis and Hermeneutics," 57–62.

[17] In arguing for the necessity of a fully reliable Bible, I am not appealing to the fallacious argument that error in *some* places means error in *all* places. Stephen T. Davis, for example, misunderstands the epistemological argument for inerrancy in this regard (Stephen T. Davis, *The Debate about the Bible: Inerrancy versus Infallibility* [Philadelphia: Westminster, 1977], 66–82). Davis reduces the argument to the claim that if Scripture is errant at any point, then *all* statements of Scripture are in fact false. This particular argument fails as an example of the association fallacy; but it is neither my argument nor one used by other defenders of inerrancy. The argument here, rather, is this: if the Bible is *unreliable* in its factual presentation and theological interpretation of Jesus at any point, it raises the possibility that any statement about Jesus *may be false*; and if any statement about him *in Scripture* may be false, then the only way to determine what is true is by criteria *outside of Scripture*.

interesting but ultimately unsuccessful *via media* between a Christology *from above* and *from below*. Watson rightly acknowledges that, "For Christians, Jesus' true identity is established above all by the fourfold canonical Gospel. It is within this sacred textual space that we discover who Jesus is and who we are in relation to him."[18] However, Watson also endorses the Jesus of history/Christ of faith distinction.[19] He admits that this distinction operates with the working hypothesis "that the historical Jesus is other than the figure(s) we encounter in the fourfold canonical Gospel,"[20] and that the Gospels' presentation of Jesus is a combination of historical facts and "legendary motifs created by early Christian storytellers."[21] And while Watson admits that we need to identify Jesus within the "narrative framework of the Gospels,"[22] it does not appear that he believes these Gospels are *God-given*, a product of the Spirit's superintending action upon human authors that enabled them to write down *God's own* interpretation of who Jesus is. Watson believes, rather, that the Gospels are the product of *the church's* interpretation of Jesus that mixes recollections of Jesus's life and death with early Christian legends.[23] He simply assumes that the earliest Christian communities' understanding of Jesus was not revealed by God according to his own factually and theologically accurate interpretation of Jesus's identity.[24]

Ultimately, Watson's proposal leaves us with the same problem of criteria and warrant.[25] The attempt to have both *from above* and *from below* aspects to ground a Christology fails at just that point. If Scripture is somewhere/anywhere unreliable because everywhere it is a mixture of both fact and fiction,

---

[18] Francis Watson, "*Veritas Christi*: How to Get from the Jesus of History to the Christ of Faith without Losing One's Way," in *Seeking the Identity of Jesus: A Pilgrimage*, ed. Beverly Roberts Gaventa and Richard B. Hays (Grand Rapids, MI: Eerdmans, 2008), 96.

[19] Interestingly, Watson acknowledges that the historical Jesus research has been beset by serious problems, particularly issues centered on proper criteria; yet because he does not think that these problems are fatal to the entire project, he encourages us to resist the temptation to abandon the history-faith distinction (ibid., 103).

[20] Ibid., 98.

[21] Ibid., 100. Watson gives three main reasons why we should continue to endorse the dichotomy between the historical Jesus and the Christ of faith: (1) the critical paradigm possesses remarkable explanatory power in its analysis of the realities of the Gospel texts; (2) the mere fact that the Gospel story contains legends does not make it guilty of an act of willful unbelief (he appeals here to Origen, who "already knew [that] recognition of a narrative's historical implausibility may actually help the interpreter draw out its underlying theological meaning" [ibid.]); (3) we can confess that God's final, definitive saving action is in Christ, but we cannot claim that this divine saving action is such as to be empirically verifiable in principle or practice (ibid., 101).

[22] Ibid., 104.

[23] Ibid., 106–107.

[24] Ibid., 110–111. At this point, Watson is aligning himself with the post-liberal emphasis. For a critique of this view, see Kevin J. Vanhoozer, *The Drama of Doctrine: A Canonical-Linguistic Approach to Christian Theology* (Louisville: Westminster John Knox, 2005).

[25] For similar points and a varied discussion on the search for the historical Jesus, see Scot McKnight, "The Jesus We'll Never Know," *Christianity Today* 54/4 (April 2010), http://www.christianitytoday.com/ct/2010/april/15.22.html, accessed May 20, 2015; Darrell Bock, "Abandon Studying the Historical Jesus? No, We Need a Response to 'The Jesus We'll Never Know,'" n.p., http://www.christianitytoday.com/ct/2010/aprilweb-only/24-51.0.html, accessed May 20, 2015; Craig Keener, "Abandon Studying the Historical Jesus? No, Jesus Studies Matter: A Response to 'The Jesus We'll Never Know,'" *Christianity Today* 54/4 (April 2010), http://www.christianitytoday.com/ct/2010/april/17.27.html, accessed May 20, 2015; N. T. Wright, "Abandon Studying the Historical Jesus? No, We Need History: A Response to 'The Jesus We'll Never Know,'" *Christianity Today* 54/4 (April 2010), http://www.christianitytoday.com/ct/2010/april/16.27.html, accessed May 20, 2015.

then nowhere can Scripture reliably ground what we must know and confess about Christ. To state it in more philosophical language, the authority and reliability of Scripture is the *transcendental condition* for the very possibility of doing Christology in an objective, normative fashion.[26] Without a word-revelation *from above* that gives the true facts about Jesus and the authoritative interpretation of his identity, Christology loses its integrity, uniqueness, and truthfulness, and it is set adrift in our day to wander into the mire of pluralism. Evangelical theologians must not travel a path that leads away from a revelational epistemology, which alone provides an adequate basis for the supremacy and uniqueness of Christ.

A Christology *from below* undercuts the epistemological grounds for orthodoxy and leaves all Christology uncertain. Only a Christology *from above* can provide the warrant for a clear Christology for the church and bear the weight of our theological conclusions about Christ.

Second, a Christology from below fails to reach the uniqueness and universal significance of Jesus because it removes him from the Bible's own storyline and framework. Christology requires a specific soil in which to grow. Critics who distrust Scripture not only dismantle its trellis (interpretive framework), but then they remove Jesus from the life-giving soil of Scripture's storyline. All Christological formulation must take place on the Bible's own terms, according to both its structure and its storyline. We can grasp Jesus's uniqueness and universal significance only by leaving him firmly planted in the historical development of the Old Testament into the New Testament that is shaped according to the universal and eternal plan of God. If Jesus is removed from *these* facts in *this* framework, then not only will we lose his true identity, but he will simply become an enigma to us, susceptible to various imaginative and arbitrary constructions. We have already seen this inevitable quandary *from below* in the Quests for the Historical Jesus.

For example, Wolfhart Pannenberg's Christology is well known as an attempt to say something theological about Jesus on the basis of historical research.[27] Pannenberg believes that historical facts about Jesus, his bodily resurrection in particular, carry their own meaning. But to have theological significance, *the facts* of Jesus's resurrection must be interpreted within a *universal framework*: "The emergence of primitive Christianity can be understood

---

[26] The philosophical term "transcendental" refers to the task of discovering the preconditions for something to be possible. In this context, "transcendental condition" refers to the self-disclosure of the triune God in Scripture as the necessary precondition for the possibility of a normative Christology. On this point, see Kevin J. Vanhoozer, "Christ and Concept: Doing Theology and the 'Ministry' of Philosophy," in *Doing Theology in Today's World: Essays in Honor of Kenneth S. Kantzer*, ed. John D. Woodbridge and Thomas E. McComiskey (Grand Rapids, MI: Zondervan, 1991), 99–145. For a discussion on the nature of transcendental arguments, see Greg L. Bahnsen, *Van Til's Apologetic: Readings and Analysis* (Phillipsburg, NJ: P&R, 1998), 496–529.

[27] See Wolfhart Pannenberg, *Jesus: God and Man*, trans. Lewis L. Wilkins and Duane A. Priebe, 2nd ed. (Philadelphia: Westminster, 1977); idem, *Systematic Theology*, 3 vols., trans. Geoffrey W. Bromiley (Grand Rapids, MI: Eerdmans, 1992), 1:277–396.

... only if one examines it in the light of the eschatological hope for a resurrection from the dead."[28] By placing *these facts* of Jesus's resurrection within *this framework*, Pannenberg argues that Jesus's resurrection is more than a brute fact and carries something of its own interpretation.[29] Yet he finds the facts and the framework in different places: the facts come from historical research; the framework comes from Scripture.

While Pannenberg interprets "facts" regarding Jesus within a framework based on Scripture, his soil is infertile and his trellis is inadequate to support a biblical Christology. Pannenberg uses the tools of historical research to dig up facts about Jesus because he rejects Scripture as God-given and authoritative. And for the same reason, he builds only a partial framework from Scripture. Colin Gunton, therefore, has rightly criticized Pannenberg for being inconsistent in his Christology *from below*: "[he is] *either* presupposing some dogmatic beliefs ('context of meaning') and thus not arguing genuinely from below at all; *or* failing to establish what is wanted, namely, the divinity of Jesus."[30] Gunton would agree, then, with our point here that the facts and the framework of Christology are inseparable and both must be consistently justified.

Only a Christology *from above* can produce a biblical Jesus. Evangelical theologians must cultivate their Christology in the biblical storyline, supported by the biblical structures: identifying the biblical Jesus requires that both the facts and the interpretive framework of Scripture must be taken together as God-given and fully authoritative.

Third, a Christology from below cannot sustain Christian faith. As David Wells has correctly observed, "Christologies constructed from 'below' produce only a larger-than-life religious figure, the perfection of what many others already experience."[31] Doing Christology *from below* can never lead us to faith in the one who came *from above* for us and our salvation. It is simply not possible to construct a biblical and orthodox Christology out of the fabric of human experience through historical-critical reconstruction. The Jesus reconstructed *from below* will always look too much like us and will never be worthy of our worship. Wells agrees:

> Their christs might be admired, but they cannot be worshipped. They might inspire religious devotion, but they cannot sustain or explain Christian faith. They tell us very much about their authors and very little about Jesus. They are, inevitably, half-breed christs. They are half ancient and half modern.

---

[28] Pannenberg, *Jesus: God and Man*, 98.
[29] Ibid., 73.
[30] Colin E. Gunton, *Yesterday and Today: A Study of Continuities in Christology*, 2nd ed. (London: SPCK, 1997), 21.
[31] Wells, *Person of Christ*, 172.

They are constructed on the mistaken assumption that a Christ who is as baffled as we are about existence, who is as secular as we are, and who is the victim of change and circumstances as we feel ourselves to be is somehow more appealing than one who is not. These christs are impotent, and their appeal is superficial. Their appeal is not that of the biblical Christ, the One who was God with us, the means of forgiveness for our sin, and the agent of our reconciliation. Forgiveness and reconciliation are what we need centrally. We need to know there is someone there to forgive us, someone who can forgive and heal us, and that was why the Word was incarnate. Our Christology, then, must be constructed from "above."[32]

These three concerns—criteria and warrant, facts and framework, and sustaining Christian faith—help demonstrate why we must do Christology *from above*. And in doing so, we stand in the company of the historical church: the church has always begun with a Christology *from above*, grounded in the conviction that Scripture serves as the basis for all Christological reflection. And so the reflections and formulations in the rest of this work will proceed from the canonical presentation of Jesus as both historically and theologically accurate.

It must be clarified that starting *from above* does not entail the depreciation of Jesus's humanity. It is often alleged that a Christology *from below* is the only approach that does justice to Jesus's human nature.[33] The issue here and the dividing line between the various Christologies today is whether theological formulation will begin with and remain within the Scripture's storyline and structure. Taking the Bible on its own terms and speaking about Jesus according to the entire biblical presentation will necessarily do justice to both his deity *and* his humanity. In fact, Scripture demands that we wrestle with the relation between Jesus's two natures and ask the hard questions: e.g., how the persons of the Trinity relate to one another; whether we need to or even can explain the metaphysics of the incarnation; how the eternal Son lived his life as a human and achieved our salvation. Far from leading us to emphasize one over the other, a Christology *from above* will help us to affirm both Jesus's deity and his humanity as we learn to articulate just how the "Christ of faith" is the "Jesus of history."

Evangelical theologians, then, must look to Scripture and its own plausibility structures to serve as the foundation for all of our theologizing about Christ. Lesslie Newbigin is helpful here with his contention that the *reasonableness* of

---

[32] Ibid., 172–173. Basically making the same point in his discussion of various Christologies *from below*, Gunton concludes, "one thing is becoming clear: in Christology, matters of method and content are closely related: the way a Christology is approached cannot be separated from the kind of Christology that emerges, and a Christology from below is hard put to avoid being a Christology of a divinized man" (Gunton, *Yesterday and Today*, 17–18).

[33] For the charge that a Christology *from above* does not/cannot do justice to Jesus's humanity, see Maurice Wiles, "Christianity without Incarnation?," in *The Myth of God Incarnate*, 4; Raymond Brown, *Catholic Biblical Quarterly* 42/3 (1980): 414. For a response to this charge, see Robert L. Reymond, *Jesus, Divine Messiah: The New Testament Witness* (Phillipsburg, NJ: P&R, 1990), 16–21.

Christianity, specifically Christology, must be understood in *Christian* terms, i.e., within the biblical-theological framework of Scripture:

> The story the church is commissioned to tell, if it is true, is bound to call into question any plausibility structure which is founded on other assumptions. The affirmation that the One by whom and through whom and for whom all creation exists is to be identified with a man who was crucified and rose bodily from the dead cannot possibly be accommodated within any plausibility structure except one of which it is the cornerstone. In any other place in the structure it can only be a stone of stumbling.[34]

In other words, philosophically speaking, there is not something more basic or foundational than the revelation of God in Jesus Christ from which we can do Christology. In fact, as soon as we say there is something else we are back to the quandary of the Quests, tangled in the roots of the Enlightenment that have grown throughout modernism into our own postmodern era.

Scripture as God's Word-Act Revelation

One immediate entailment of doing Christology *from above* is that we must take *sola Scriptura* seriously. Scripture is not the church's book; the church did not create and does not control Scripture. According to its own self-testimony, rather, Scripture is God's word written, his own self-revelation to his church as its Creator and Lord.

No doubt, starting from a *revelational foundation* involves a commitment to both general and special revelation, but priority is always given to Scripture.[35] The revelation of God in his creation is true, but Scripture alone comes to us as God's own interpretation of his redemptive acts in creation that gives us a true and objective basis for knowing him. Moreover, while Scripture does not provide an *exhaustive* revelation of God, it does give us the *authoritative* interpretation of what it does reveal. General revelation gives us truth, but without telling us the meaning of the truth; special revelation gives us both and without error.

As special revelation, Scripture should be viewed as first-order, the authoritative "spectacles" by which we view the world. Scripture provides both our foundation and our metanarrative for theology, including our Christology. Scripture is best understood, then, as a word-act revelation that requires a "thick" reading. We must read Scripture as an entire canon and take seriously not only what it says about God's mighty acts but also how it interprets them, especially in regard to Christ.[36] This means that Scripture not only describes

---

[34] Lesslie Newbigin, *Proper Confidence: Faith, Doubt, and Certainty in Christian Discipleship* (Grand Rapids, MI: Eerdmans, 1995), 93.

[35] See John Frame, *The Doctrine of the Knowledge of God* (Phillipsburg, NJ: P&R, 1987), 62–75.

[36] On this point, see Peter J. Gentry and Stephen J. Wellum, *Kingdom through Covenant: A Biblical-Theological Understanding of the Covenants* (Wheaton, IL: Crossway, 2012), 87–89. To say that Scripture is a word-act revela-

the facts of history with accuracy; it also explains those facts in such a way that we can rightly know Christ and formulate correct doctrine regarding his identity. In doing Christology, *sola Scriptura* demands that we move carefully from Scripture's own interpretive framework and categories (first-order) to theological formulation (second-order).[37]

This is not to say that tradition and historical theology are not important, but they are important *as a rule of faith*. D. A. Carson rightly reminds us that, "Historical theology, though it cannot in itself justify a belief system, not only sharpens the categories and informs the debate but serves as a major checkpoint to help us prevent uncontrolled speculation, purely private theological articulation, and overly imaginative exegesis."[38] So we must confess that Scripture alone has *magisterial authority* and always reigns over tradition; but we should also say that tradition functions in a *ministerial capacity* to aid our interpretation and application of Scripture. Stating the relationship between Scripture and tradition this way does not deny that reading the Bible involves what is famously called a "hermeneutical spiral." No one approaches Scripture as a *tabula rasa*; we all interpret Scripture with viewpoints, assumptions, and even biases inherited from our various traditions, cultures, and backgrounds. But Scripture is able to confirm or correct our views as needed precisely because Scripture itself is not the interpretation of the church but the written word of God himself that interprets his own acts in history and their significance for his church and the world.

In doing Christology, then, we start *from above* with God's word written and continue reading Scripture as God's word-act revelation that provides both the facts and the interpretation of those facts for an accurate and authoritative identification of Jesus Christ. How can we know who Jesus is? The church submits to the magisterial authority of Scripture and leans on the ministerial aid of tradition and historical theology.

A "BIBLICAL" CHRISTOLOGY

Just as a commitment to Christology *from above* entails a reading of Scripture as God's word-act revelation, this submission to God's own interpretation requires that we recognize the particular ways in which Scripture demands to

---

tion is to affirm that Scripture is God's own interpretation of his redemptive acts through the agency of human authors. While God's redemptive acts are revelatory in themselves, they are not self-interpreting. For example, in the Old Testament, the greatest redemptive act of God was his deliverance of Israel from their slavery in Egypt. But the meaning of this *act* had to be given by God's *word* (cf. Ex. 6:6–7; Deut. 4:32–35). The New Testament presents the death and resurrection of Jesus Christ as the final redemptive act of God. But again, for this *act* of God to be "good news," God himself had to supply a *word* about its significance and implications for all persons throughout all history (cf. Matt. 27:45–28:10; Acts 2:22–24; 3:11–16; 10:34–43; 13:26–35; Rom. 6:1–11; 1 Cor. 15:1–8). God's *acts* in redemptive history are never separated from God's *word* of interpretation.

[37] These concepts are taken from Richard Lints, *The Fabric of Theology: A Prolegomenon to Evangelical Theology* (Grand Rapids, MI: Eerdmans, 1993), 259–336.

[38] D. A. Carson, "Recent Views of Scripture," in *Hermeneutics, Authority, and Canon*, 18.

be read. At the heart of evangelical theology is the attempt to be biblical and to "take every thought captive to obey Christ" (2 Cor. 10:5). But what does it mean to be "biblical"? In Christology, how do we know that our theological formulations are true to Scripture and thus biblically warranted?[39] This question may seem strange to ask, especially for evangelicals, since many view the task of doing theology in a fairly straightforward fashion. In recent years, however, many have acknowledged that doing theology is not at all obvious. For example, is our Christology "biblical" if we merely find various texts to back up our assertions? Is doing "biblical" Christology simply a matter of collecting texts and arranging them properly, according to a certain logic or a central theme (or various themes)?[40] Or is it more than this?

We are not tackling head-on the whole subject of theological method and hermeneutics, so the discussion here will be brief. The brevity of discussion, however, does not reflect the importance of methodology for Christology. We must be clear-minded and convictional about a "biblical" methodology before we endeavor toward a "biblical" Christology in the following chapters. This section, then, will simply describe the theological-Christological method underlying the work ahead. We need to see that articulating a God-given Christology according to a God-given methodology (on the Bible's own terms) is both possible and necessary.

We begin with a basic definition of systematic theology from John Frame. Systematic theology is "the application of God's Word by persons to all areas of life."[41] No doubt many points could be developed from this definition, but for our purposes we will develop it by emphasizing two concepts in order to describe the nature and task of systematic theology as a discipline.

Systematic theology is a twofold task. First, we must properly *interpret Scripture* as God's self-revelation; second, we must *apply Scripture* by means of theological construction and defense. Stated another way, the twofold task of systematic theology is moving from "canon to concept."[42] In Christology, then, we must first engage the Bible's full-orbed teaching regarding Jesus's identity as the Christ and then make theological conclusions by thinking through, reflecting upon, and putting together the diverse data. When done this way, theology becomes an exercise of "faith seeking understanding" that enables us not only *to know the real Jesus, but also to proclaim and defend him as God the Son incarnate, the Lord of Glory.*

---

[39] I have addressed this issue in Gentry and Wellum, *Kingdom through Covenant*, 81–108.

[40] This is often the criticism against Charles Hodge. Hodge's methodology is briefly discussed in Charles Hodge, *Systematic Theology*, 3 vols. (Grand Rapids, MI: Eerdmans, 1981), 1:9–17. For a similar methodology used by a contemporary theologian, see Wayne Grudem, *Systematic Theology: An Introduction to Biblical Doctrine* (Grand Rapids, MI: Zondervan, 1994), 21–43.

[41] Frame, *Doctrine of the Knowledge of God*, 76.

[42] This expression is from Kevin J. Vanhoozer, "From Canon to Concept: 'Same' and 'Other' in the Relation between Biblical and Systematic Theology," *Scottish Bulletin of Evangelical Theology* 12/2 (1994): 96–124.

As we look a bit more closely at how to interpret Scripture to identify Jesus, let us keep our eyes on the need for warrant in our theology. As we have seen, a "biblical" epistemology (how we know Jesus) requires a Christology *from above*—God's own revelatory interpretation of Jesus's identity. Because this God-given interpretation is written, identifying Jesus requires reading *from above*—reading that obeys the rules of Scripture. *It is this relation between how we know Jesus and how we read Scripture that establishes epistemological warrant for Christology.*

Interpreting Scripture: Biblical Theology and Christology

As the first part of the twofold task of systematic theology, interpreting Scripture requires that we understand the proper role of biblical theology as a discipline. In terms of Christology and for our purposes here, we can define biblical theology as the hermeneutical discipline of reading the Bible as God's word on the Bible's own terms, which requires theological and typological interpretation.[43]

BIBLICAL THEOLOGY AND THEOLOGICAL INTERPRETATION

A theological interpretation of Scripture focuses on what God has revealed to be true and significant by allowing the textual features of Scripture to determine the meaning of every reading. Because the Bible is God's word written through human authors, a biblical hermeneutic will see an overall *unity and coherence to textual diversity* that declares God's unfailing plan and purposes in this fallen world. In this sense, Scripture should be read as "a unified communicative act, that is, as the complex, multileveled speech act of a single divine author."[44] And because Scripture is God's word written through human authors, *his revelation has progressively unfolded* to us step-by-step over time along with redemptive history. This progressive revelation of God's plan and purposes *takes shape through redemptive covenants* between God and his people across separate but related epochs in redemptive history, culminating in the person and new covenant work of Christ (cf. Heb. 1:1–2; Col. 1:15–20).[45]

Our task in reading Scripture, then, is carefully and faithfully attending to the biblical plot and pattern of God's revelatory redemption in Christ. Because the God of salvation is the sovereign Lord of history, both redemption

---

[43] "Biblical theology" means different things to different people. On the discipline of biblical theology, see Edward W. Klink III and Darian R. Lockett, *Understanding Biblical Theology: A Comparison of Theory and Practice* (Grand Rapids, MI: Zondervan, 2012); Gentry and Wellum, *Kingdom through Covenant*, 21–38; Charles H. H. Scobie, *The Ways of Our God: An Approach to Biblical Theology* (Grand Rapids, MI: Eerdmans, 2003).

[44] Vanhoozer, "Exegesis and Hermeneutics," 61; cf. idem, *First Theology: God, Scripture, and Hermeneutics* (Downers Grove, IL: InterVarsity Press, 2002), 159–203; Michael S. Horton, *Covenant and Eschatology: The Divine Drama* (Louisville: Westminster John Knox, 2002), 123–276.

[45] On this point, see Lints, *Fabric of Theology*, 259–336; cf. D. A. Carson, *The Gagging of God: Christianity Confronts Pluralism* (Grand Rapids, MI: Zondervan, 1996), 141–335.

and revelation move providentially toward a goal that Scripture says is summed up and fulfilled in Jesus Christ (Eph. 1:9–10). Given this nature of Scripture, Michael Horton correctly proposes that a proper method of interpretation is "redemptive-historical-eschatological," which requires that we must interpret Scripture according to its own intrasystematic categories.[46] Scripture uses many literary forms—e.g., narrative, law, apocalyptic, psalm, wisdom, gospel, letter—to unfold a plot centered in Christ. As D. A. Carson reminds us, "the fact remains that the Bible as a whole document tells a story, and, properly used, that story can serve as a metanarrative that shapes our grasp of the entire Christian faith."[47] *The systematic theologian must first interpret Scripture as a biblical theologian so that the structure of Scripture itself structures all theological formulations.*

As a helpful guide at this point, Richard Lints proposes that the methodology of "biblical" systematic theology must interpret Scripture along its redemptive-historical plotline according to three horizons: textual, epochal, and canonical.[48] In reading any text, then, we not only exegete it in terms of its syntax, literary context, historical setting, and genre (textual horizon), we also locate it in redemptive-history (epochal horizon), and then finally we read the text in light of the whole canon (canonical horizon). It is only when we read Scripture in terms of the canonical horizon that we are interpreting it in a fully "biblical" manner—according to its God-givenness in both nature and function. In fact, to read the Bible canonically as a unified whole is not just one approach among other possibilities; reading Scripture according to all three horizons is the interpretive strategy that best corresponds to the nature of the text itself, given its divine inspiration.[49]

Furthermore, as Lints correctly notes, "Essential to the canonical horizon

---

[46] See Horton, *Covenant and Eschatology*, 1–19, 147–276. For Horton, the terms "eschatological" and "redemptive-historical" capture the heart of Scripture's own intrasystematic categories. The *eschatological* is more than a mere locus of theology; rather, it is a lens by which we read Scripture and do our theology. Scripture itself comes to us as a redemptive revelation that is rooted in history. God's eternal plan unfolds and is worked out in time in such a way that the very form and shape of Scripture is eschatological. Scripture, then, is more than a storehouse of facts or propositions; Scripture also unfolds a storyline with a plot and a divine interpretation of the drama of redemption. This dramatic story is eschatological at heart and Christological in focus, and our doing of theology must reflect what Scripture *is*. For Horton, Scripture's own self-presentation is *redemptive-historical* in that it comes to us as "the organic unfolding of the divine plan in its execution through word (announcement), act (accomplishment), and word (interpretation)" (ibid., 5). Redemption progresses and unfolds, and revelation follows its pace and contours as God interprets his actions and the human responses in actual historical contexts. For Horton, the nature of Scripture has at least three important implications for theological method. First, epistemologically speaking, a redemptive revelation entails that even though God's knowledge is exhaustive and is progressively revealed to us over time, our knowledge, while true, is always finite, incomplete, and dependent upon God's first-order revelation. Second, our reading of Scripture and our doing of theology must attend to the historical unfolding of redemptive history that is *organically* related to and ultimately centered on Christ. The very form and shape of Scripture reminds us that God did not disclose himself in one exhaustive act but in an organic, progressive manner that explains the Bible's diversity. Theology must be careful not to proof-text, i.e., use texts without considering their redemptive-historical location. Third, theology must avoid speculation. It must attend to what God has actually said and done.
[47] Carson, *Gagging of God*, 194.
[48] See Lints, *Fabric of Theology*, 259–311.
[49] For a development of the horizons interpretive strategy, see Vanhoozer, *First Theology*, 194–203.

of biblical interpretation is the continuity between the promises of God and his fulfillment of those promises."[50] God has glued together the diverse epochs of redemptive history by a "promise-fulfillment" motif, which becomes a crucial part of reading Scripture correctly. The God who created the world is the same God who made covenant promises to his people, and the same God who faithfully keeps his promises across the ages, ultimately bringing them to fulfillment in Jesus Christ (see 2 Cor. 1:20). So we must look for the biblical authors to unpack both the continuity of God's plan (tied to his promises) and its discontinuity (fulfillment in Christ).

Lints helps us see the significance of this promise-fulfillment dynamic: "The biblical authors frame their writings with the assertion that God has been faithful to his promises in times past, and so he shall be faithful in the future. The promise-fulfillment model is a thread that secures the unity of the diverse collection of these writings. It provides meaning in the midst of present circumstances and hope for future deliverance."[51] As we trace out the storyline of Scripture, moving from promise to fulfillment, we are better able to see how all of Scripture hangs together and reaches its consummation in Christ—and we begin to appreciate even more that the diverse stories of Scripture are not randomly juxtaposed but are knit together as parts of a larger tapestry that ultimately displays God's glory in Christ.

BIBLICAL THEOLOGY AND TYPOLOGY

Interpreting types follows the intentional, intertextual development of persons, events, and institutions to their final, full meaning and significance in the person and work of Christ. Scripture unfolds God's redemptive-historical plan through the promise-fulfillment motif in many ways, but typology provides a centering trajectory for God's progressive revelation. No doubt, typology is a disputed topic in biblical and theological studies, and it means different things to different people. As Paul Hoskins reminds us, "Studies in biblical typology have been complicated by the use of the terms 'typology' and 'type' where no definitions of these terms are given."[52] But before defining *typology*, we must first distinguish it from *allegory*.

---

[50] Lints, *Fabric of Theology*, 303.

[51] Ibid.

[52] Paul M. Hoskins, *Jesus as the Fulfillment of the Temple in the Gospel of John* (Eugene, OR: Wipf & Stock, 2007), 18. Hoskins describes two different conceptions of typology within contemporary biblical studies: a traditional view that sees the correspondence between type and antitype as God-given, intentional, and predictive versus a critical view that is more skeptical about the predictive and prospective significance of the types (ibid., 18–36). I follow the traditional understanding of typology. For its defense, see Richard Davidson, *Typology in Scripture: A Study of Hermeneutical ΤΥΠΟΣ Structures*, Andrews University Seminary Doctoral Dissertation Series, vol. 2 (Berrien Springs, MI: Andrews University Press, 1981); see also John H. Stek, "Biblical Typology Yesterday and Today," *Calvin Theological Journal* 5/2 (1970): 133–162; Leonhard Goppelt, *Typos: The Typological Interpretation of the Old Testament in the New*, trans. Donald H. Madvig (Grand Rapids, MI: Eerdmans, 1982); Douglas J. Moo, "The Problem of *Sensus Plenior*," in *Hermeneutics, Authority, and Canon*, 175–212; Lints, *Fabric of Theology*, 304–310; G. K. Beale, "Did Jesus and His Followers Preach the Right Doctrine from the Wrong Texts?

The major difference between typology and allegory is that typology is grounded in authorial intent. Typology looks to the *text* for an *intertextual*[53] development of *historical* persons, events, and institutions intended by God to correspond to each other; allegory does not assume this. Also, since allegories are not grounded in authorial intent that is (inter)textually warranted, allegorical interpretation depends on some kind of *extratextual* grid to warrant its explanation. As Kevin Vanhoozer notes, allegorical interpretation depends on the strategy of declaring, "*This* (word) means *that* (concept),"[54] with *that* being determined by something *outside* the text. To the contrary, typology is determined by what is *in* the text. An investigation of the six explicit New Testament texts that deal with typology (Rom. 5:14; 1 Cor. 10:6, 11; Heb. 8:5; 9:24; 1 Pet. 3:21) produces a consistent picture of typology that clearly distinguishes it from allegory.

After investigating the biblical dynamic of typology, Richard Davidson defines it as a New Testament hermeneutical endeavor that studies the Old Testament salvific-historical realities, or "types" (persons, events, institutions), that God has specifically designed to correspond to and predictively prefigure their intensified antitypical fulfillments (inaugurated and consummated) in New Testament salvation history.[55] Three features in particular will help keep us "biblical" in the interpretive work ahead.

First, typology is symbolism rooted in *historical* and *textual* realities. Both the type and the antitype exist in real time and space and both have clear and concrete references in biblical texts. So typology makes intertextual connections between earlier and later historical realities.[56] Second, typology is *prophetic* and *predictive*.[57] While the type has significance for its own time, its greater significance is directed toward the future; it testifies to something greater than itself that is still to come. But the future antitype *will surely come*, because God omnisciently predicted it and omnipotently fulfills it in Christ

An Examination of the Presuppositions of Jesus' and the Apostles' Exegetical Method," in *The Right Doctrine from the Wrong Texts? Essays on the Use of the Old Testament in the New*, ed. G. K. Beale (Grand Rapids, MI: Baker, 1994), 387–404; Graeme Goldsworthy, *Gospel-Centered Hermeneutics: Foundations and Principles of Evangelical Biblical Interpretation* (Downers Grove, IL: IVP Academic, 2006), 234–257.

[53] I am using "intertextual" in distinction from "intratextual." "Intratextual" refers to interpreting Scripture in terms of its own interpretive framework—the structure and storyline *within* Scripture—while "intertextual" refers to textual developments *across* that structure and storyline.

[54] Kevin J. Vanhoozer, *Is There a Meaning in This Text? The Bible, the Reader, and the Morality of Literary Knowledge* (Grand Rapids, MI: Zondervan, 1998), 119.

[55] My treatment of typology is indebted to a number of people, specifically Richard Davidson. Davidson investigates all uses of *typos* in the New Testament and then draws conclusions regarding the "biblical" nature of typology (see Davidson, *Typology in Scripture*). The present definition is compiled from his summary discussion in ibid., 397–408.

[56] Regarding the function of typology, Lints explains that, "The typological relation is a central means by which particular epochal and textual horizons are linked to later horizons in redemptive revelation. It links the present to the future, and it retroactively links the present with the past. It is founded on the organic connection of God's promises with his fulfillment of those promises (Lints, *Fabric of Theology*, 304).

[57] Typology is not a kind of *verbal* prediction, but a prediction built from a *model/pattern* that God himself has established and that gradually appears as later texts reinforce the model/pattern. A type appears and becomes more clear through intertextual developments across redemptive history, ultimately culminating in Christ.

according to his eternal plan. Third, typology functions by *repetition* and *escalation*. A type (e.g., Adam) will appear at least one more time in later persons (e.g., other Adam-like figures such as Noah, Abraham, Israel, and David), events, or institutions before finding its ultimate fulfillment in Christ (the last Adam). And each repetition has an *a fortiori* quality, moving from lesser to greater (e.g., from Adam as son to Christ as Son).

BIBLICAL THEOLOGY AND CHRISTOLOGY

We can now see how interpreting the Bible on its own terms applies directly to Christology: a Christology *from above* will identify Jesus by interpreting Scripture theologically (an intrasystematic and ultimately canonical reading) and typologically. For a theological understanding of Christ, we must locate him within the worldview and storyline of the Bible. A "biblical" Christology requires biblical theology to attend closely to the Bible's content by following its own contours in its own categories. And this intrasystematic reading of Scripture will also involve an ultimately canonical interpretation of Jesus. To draw correct conclusions regarding Christ's identity according to the Bible's own structure, texts must be interpreted along the textual, epochal, and canonical horizons. All three are important, but the first two horizons build up into the last horizon such that the canonical level presents the truest, fullest, divine intention regarding the identity of Christ.

We can look briefly at Psalm 2 for a helpful illustration of theological interpretation for proper Christological formulation. Through numerous allusions and four direct quotes, the New Testament uses Psalm 2 to demonstrate diverse truths about Jesus: his resurrection (Acts 13:33); his superiority to angels (Heb. 1:5); his appointment as our great High Priest (Heb. 5:5). But from the early church to today, one of the more difficult questions asks how to understand "today" in Psalm 2:7: "I will tell of the decree: The LORD said to me, 'You are my Son; today I have begotten you.'" In the Patristic era, it was common to interpret Psalm 2 as a direct prophecy about Christ, in which case the "today" of verse 7 is an "eternal today" that supported the church's discussion of the "eternal generation of the Son" and its rejection of adoptionism.[58] It is difficult, however, to interpret Psalm 2:7 in its textual and epochal horizon as anything less than a reference to the historical-covenantal enthronement of the Davidic king and the promises of the Davidic covenant. But when the New Testament applies Psalm 2 to Jesus, does this *functional* understanding of "today" necessitate a denial of Jesus's *eternal, ontological* sonship? Absolutely not.

---

[58] See Robert L. Reymond, *Jesus, Divine Messiah: The New and Old Testament Witness* (Fearn, Ross-shire, Scotland: Mentor, 2003), 77–81. For Psalm 2:7 and adoptionism (Jesus's sonship is not eternal but is entered into upon his resurrection), see J. D. G. Dunn, *Christology in the Making: A New Testament Inquiry into the Origins of the Doctrine of the Incarnation*, 2nd ed. (Grand Rapids, MI: Eerdmans, 1996), 12–64.

Psalm 2 must be read within its immediate context (textual horizon) and its redemptive-historical context (epochal horizon), and both of these readings must then be taken into a consideration of the New Testament's diverse application of Psalm 2 (canonical horizon). Reading canonically this way allows us to look through Psalm 2 to see a functional development of Jesus's sonship that neither contradicts nor diminishes his ontological sonship. The *functional* stream of Christology stresses that Jesus in his humanity is appointed as Son by virtue of what he does in his earthly ministry: Jesus's victorious work on our behalf not only secures our redemption but also earns the exaltation and enthronement of a man as Son and Lord (Rom. 1:3–4). The *ontological* stream of Christology stresses that Jesus is the divine Son of God from eternity by virtue of who he has always been.

By reading Psalm 2 within its textual horizon and the epochal context of the Davidic covenant, we can say that the "Lord" enthroned David as his king, thereby establishing him as God's son (Ps. 2:7). But then we must also read Psalm 2 within its canonical context by following the typological trajectory from the Davidic covenant into the new covenant in Christ. Then we can say that God has finally fulfilled his covenantal promise by enthroning the man Jesus to function as Son and king over his people through his victorious resurrection from the dead (Acts 13:33).[59] And because the nature of typology is not to say everything but to highlight certain aspects of a greater reality, we can also still say that this same Jesus is the eternal Son, who he has always been ontologically (John 1:1–2; Col. 1:15–17; Heb. 1:1–3).

Interpreting Psalm 2 in light of its three horizons helps us see the whole canonical presentation of Jesus as the God-man who is God's Son-King promised to rule forever in righteousness over God's people. Ultimately, a theological interpretation does justice to both the functional and the ontological sonship of Christ, which allows us to affirm these theological realities: the Son's eternal deity; the need for his historical incarnation; and the uniqueness and significance of Christ as the Lord of Glory, the Word made flesh, Messiah, and King.

And, as we have just seen, a theological reading of Scripture will often involve a typological interpretation of Jesus. The dynamic of intertextual typology develops the identity of Christ through the intrasystematic categories of Scripture across the textual, epochal, and canonical horizons as redemptive history passes through each interrelated covenant unto the new covenant and finally the new creation. Just think of how Jesus is described in the New Testament: the son of Abraham (Matt. 1:1); the son of David (Matt. 1:1; cf. 2:6; 9:27, etc.); the last Adam (Rom. 5:12–21; 1 Cor. 15:21–28; cf. Heb. 2:5–18); the

---

[59] On this point, see Peter T. O'Brien, *The Letter to the Hebrews*, PNTC (Grand Rapids, MI: Eerdmans, 2010), 66–68, 194–197; see also Vern S. Poythress, "What Does God Say through Human Authors?," in *Inerrancy and Hermeneutic: A Tradition, A Challenge, A Debate*, ed. Harvie M. Conn (Grand Rapids, MI: Baker, 1988), 81–99.

servant of the Lord (Matt. 12:17–21). All of these diverse titles and descriptions are built on typological structures that are developed through the biblical covenants in the Old Testament. For example, as we discussed regarding Psalm 2, the title "Son" carries with it typological overtones tied to Israel and the Davidic kings as "sons," with the title finding its fulfillment in Christ—one who is son in his human ancestry and, in a far greater way, God the Son from all eternity.[60]

The theological and typological interpretation of biblical theology is *necessary* for a "biblical" identification of Jesus. Only by tracing out what the Bible says and how it says it do we discover what God intended all along: all of Scripture leads us to behold the glory of God in the person and work of Christ. But biblical theology alone is *not sufficient*. In addition to interpretation, the church is called to the application of Scripture. Even with the results of reading the Bible on its own terms, we must still make theological conclusions that make the best sense of the Bible's own presentation of Christ.

Applying Scripture: From Canon to Christology

Systematic theology, and thus doing Christology, takes the results of biblical theology and goes one step further to apply the entire canon of Scripture to all areas of life.[61] More than simply repeating Scripture through biblical interpretation and exposition, theology moves from the canon (biblical theology) to concept (systematic theology) as a full exercise in "faith seeking understanding." Through biblical theology, then, the interpretive framework of Scripture becomes our "spectacles" for systematic theology by which we seek to live and act biblically in the world as we "think God's thoughts after him."[62] To be in the world but not of the world, the church needs more than biblical data from biblical theology. *Living in the world and resisting the world requires the church to move beyond theological description to theological formulation that meets the needs of discipleship in the faith and defense of the faith.*

As part of the task of application, then, systematic theology involves both constructive and apologetic work. First, in moving from canon to concept, the *constructive work* of theology takes the results of biblical theology and "puts together" all the data in a coherent fashion. So, for example, we learn through biblical theology that Scripture presents Jesus as utterly unique, one who is both divine and human. But this biblical presentation raises some legitimate

---

[60] On this point, see D. A. Carson, *Jesus the Son of God: A Christological Title Often Overlooked, Sometimes Misunderstood, and Currently Disputed* (Wheaton, IL: Crossway, 2012).

[61] For a discussion of the concept of *application*, see Frame, *Doctrine of the Knowledge of God*, 81–88. Horton and Vanhoozer each speak of application as *performance* (see Horton, *Covenant and Eschatology*, 265–276; Vanhoozer, *Drama of Doctrine*, 363–457).

[62] Theology as "thinking God's thoughts after him" is a nice summary of the theological task. See Herman Bavinck, *Prolegomena*, vol. 1 of *Reformed Dogmatics*, ed. John Bolt, trans. John Vriend (Grand Rapids, MI: Baker, 2003).

systematic questions. For example: How do we make sense of this presentation of Jesus in Trinitarian terms, i.e., the precise relations of the Father, Son, and Spirit? What about the relation between the Son's deity and his humanity (cf. John 1:1, 14)? And how do we reconcile that Jesus is God the Son and yet he informs his disciples that he does not know certain things (e.g., Mark 13:32)?[63] Many more questions like these arise naturally from biblical theology and require the church to think constructively about the biblical data. Answering these questions requires the church to make certain conclusions from the diverse data of biblical theology in order to articulate in one place the full identity of Christ.

Second, systematic theology also distinguishes itself from biblical theology by the addition of *apologetic work*. As the church has constructed its systematic theology through reflection upon and proclamation of the biblical Christ, the church also has had to defend the entire presentation as theologically coherent. From the earliest years until today, critics have challenged the church at this very point. Whether in response to Celsus in the second century or John Hick today, it is not enough for systematic theology merely to say, "Here is the biblical Christ." Theology must also honor the biblical Christ and defend the biblical presentation of him as our hope (1 Pet. 3:15). As with any doctrine, but especially in Christology, it is incumbent upon the theologian to show why the canonical presentation of Christ is coherent and consistent. To be sure, no theologian will be able to explain how all of the data fit together; an exhaustive theology is not possible or expected, given our finitude and sin and because God has not given us an exhaustive revelation.[64] But we are required to show why it is that what we are called to say is not self-contradictory.

At this point, with the whole constructive-apologetic endeavor of systematic theology before us, one final issue needs to be addressed: the use of extrabiblical language. Given these moves from canon to concept and from concept to apologetics, the use of extrabiblical language in our theological formulations has been an important concern from the beginning. As the early church wrestled with the biblical data and sought to explain coherently the doctrine of God, Trinitarian relations, and the nature of Christ and his identity, the church employed concepts and terminology of the day that were outside of Scripture. Two issues arose then and remain today: *whether* we can and should use extrabiblical terminology in our biblical-theological formulations, and if so, *which* terms advance the constructive and apologetic tasks.

---

[63] These are not the only issues that Christology must address in a constructive fashion. Other examples include: the *nature* of God and human beings, especially when affirming that Christ has both a divine nature and a human nature; the definition and constitution of a *person*; the nature of the *incarnation* and what it means for the eternal Son to live an incarnate life (including the reality of self-consciousness, the will, and the mind); the *cosmic functions* of the Son, who upholds the universe while he lives an incarnate life.

[64] This is another way of speaking of the archetype versus ectype distinction in epistemology. On this point, see Paul Helm, *John Calvin's Ideas* (Oxford: Oxford University Press, 2004), 11–34.

First, is it legitimate to explain the content of biblical theology using extrabiblical terminology that inevitably brings philosophical baggage? If all extrabiblical frameworks for interpretation are illegitimate—as previously argued—then can extrabiblical terminology in formulation be legitimate? Even in the first century, the church's use of extrabiblical terminology led, ironically, to heretics charging the church with departing from Scripture. And this criticism has continued into our day, probably represented best by Adolf Harnack, the nineteenth-century theologian who charged the church with the "acute Hellenization" of Christianity in the early centuries.

As David Wells identifies it, "The problem which is raised is whether language that is nonbiblical and, in these cases, philosophical can be used to define and explore the meaning of the Christian faith without in some way perverting it."[65] Because of the very nature of systematic theology, the church has responded that the use of extrabiblical concepts and terminology is inevitable as we move from canon to concept; and such use is legitimate *as long as* those concepts and terms faithfully represent and do not distort the biblical teaching.[66] The use of extrabiblical words and concepts—e.g., "Trinity," "person," "nature," "*communicatio idiomatum*," "hypostatic union"—are both helpful and legitimate if they explain or clarify Scripture to make sense of it in the world while remaining submissive to the authoritative interpretation in the word. Systematic theology does not simply repeat Scripture; it attempts to *apply* Scripture in terms of both theological construction and apologetic interaction.[67]

Second, if it is possible and even necessary to use extrabiblical terms, which ones can be used without distorting biblical teaching? This issue gets further complicated when we remember that words are not neutral; they have a history and thus a lot of philosophical and theological baggage. And this linguistic freight quickly became a concern for the early church amid its Trinitarian and Christological debates. Looking at an example of the church choosing

---

[65] Wells, *Person of Christ*, 91.
[66] I use the term "extrabiblical" in order not to confuse it with "nonbiblical" or "unbiblical."
[67] Two more points need to be stated. First, Scripture does not give us a technical Christology that is designed to answer every question. Scripture does, however, give us a worldview by which we think about God and the world, and correspondingly about Christ. This framework, though it is not in the technical vocabulary of philosophers or theologians, nonetheless implies positions on philosophical issues. In this sense Scripture speaks on all matters—not as a textbook on all matters—but as providing an overall perspective that can be rendered conceptually, suggesting some formulations and ruling out others—all of which applies to doing Christology. Second, we must reject the Greek versus Hebrew language dichotomy that prevails in so much of this discussion. This distinction goes back to the Biblical Theology Movement made popular in North America in the 1940s and 1950s. This movement was preoccupied with biblical *words* and *language*. The proponents believed that word studies and etymologies gave access to the distinctive *mentality* and *theology* of the biblical authors. On the basis of word studies, it was then argued that the biblical notions of divine action, time, and so on were dynamic and concrete, in contrast to the static and abstract concepts of the Greeks. This movement then concluded that Christology is more *functional* than *ontological*. James Barr, however, has thoroughly dismantled this argument and put this false dichotomy to rest (see James Barr, *The Semantics of Biblical Language* [Eugene, OR: Wipf & Stock, 2004]). All of this is to say that the early church did not distort the biblical data by using extrabiblical terminology.

certain extrabiblical terms will give us a principle for our own Christological formulation.

As we will discuss more in Part III, one of the great accomplishments of the early ecumenical councils was to solidify the use of certain terms and to "Christianize" them. For example, *ousia* in classical philosophy denoted a single existence or individual entity; it was not used for "nature." In early Christian use, however, *ousia* was eventually used to denote the *nature* of a thing (Latin: *essentia*). Conversely, *hypostasis* in classical philosophy was used to describe something's real essence, that which undergirds and holds together its outer, empirical qualities, similar to the meaning of *ousia*. In early Christian use, however, *hypostasis* was uncoupled from *ousia* to refer more to an individual, concrete existence that was identified with the Latin *persona*, meaning *person*.

The use of these particular extrabiblical terms and concepts has led to the essential Trinitarian affirmation that God is *three persons* in *one nature*, and to the crucial Christological confession that our Lord Jesus is *one person* in *two natures*. And yet, the historical use of these good and necessary terms and concepts has not settled the issues. As will be covered in Part IV, the apologetic task of theology continues today concerning *person* and *nature* in reference to God and Christ.

Here, then, is our principle for using extrabiblical language in the service of systematic theology: choose carefully and faithfully, and expect disagreement. Church history teaches us that just as the church has always endured disagreement over words inside the Bible, it will certainly suffer disagreement over words outside of the Bible. But church history also teaches us that words outside of the Bible can be faithful to those inside the Bible and that finding those words is possible, good, and necessary. We must constantly ask which terms and concepts will help the church and the world understand the biblical presentation of Jesus as the Christ. And in this, our goal is not inventiveness but faithfulness.[68]

As it turns out, a "biblical" Christology depends both on the Bible's own terms (i.e., framework and function) for the interpretation of biblical theology, and on extrabiblical terms (i.e., words and concepts not used in the Bible) for the formulation of systematic theology. Both are required to move from reading the Bible to thinking and speaking theologically along the path of a "biblical" epistemology that leads us to the proper identification of Christ.

---

[68] On this point, see David S. Yeago, "The New Testament and the Nicene Dogma: A Contribution to the Recovery of Theological Exegesis," in *The Theological Interpretation of Scripture: Classic and Contemporary Readings*, ed. Stephen Fowl (Oxford: Blackwell, 1997), 87–102.

In chapter 1, we saw that the two major trends in Christology today have produced much confusion regarding the identity of Jesus. The paradigms of historical Jesus research and pluralism create this confusion because they are created by two epistemologies that (in different ways) reject the one reliable and authoritative source for true knowledge of Jesus Christ. In fact, the current epistemological climate makes knowledge of God in Christ impossible for some humans and irrelevant or insignificant for many more.

The Enlightenment raised the status of human reason to omnicompetence, positioning humanity to reign over every aspect of life. And this enthronement of reason led to radical changes in philosophy, science, religion, and hermeneutics. Ultimately, as the Enlightenment moved into modernity, the reign of human reason led to the dethronement of the God of Christian theism and the rejection of his inerrant instruction in his written word. In short, the Enlightenment-modern epistemology limits knowledge to what can be directly experienced by the autonomous human subject as he experiences and interprets the physical world according to the control of presuppositions of methodological naturalism. This strictly rational epistemology, of course, rejects as a priori unreasonable the existence of God—at least a God who acts in the world in a way that would be considered supernatural—and the possibility that ancient texts reporting ancient events concerning historically unique individuals can provide true accounts that have any significance beyond their time and location.

Postmodernism critiques the Enlightenment-modern confidence in reason, but only to move from other presuppositions to reject the God of the Bible and the Bible's authority as God's own objective interpretation of reality. Postmodernism presupposes the impossibility of a God who is absolute in his being—independent of creation—and of a God's-eye point of view on reality. According to the postmodern worldview, the categories we use to talk about reality are man-made and artificial; there is no "real" connection between language and reality.

So, modernity presupposes a strictly rational epistemology and a historical-critical hermeneutic, while postmodernity presupposes an artificial epistemology and a reader-centric hermeneutic. What both have in common is that they reject the revelational epistemology and hermeneutic of the Reformation. The modern approach works primarily through the paradigm of historical Jesus research, resulting in a critical Christology that remains suspicious of the biblical texts and constantly looks behind them for the "real" Jesus. The postmodern approach works primarily through the paradigm of pluralism, resulting in many personal Christologies based on the meaning brought into the biblical texts by each individual reader. Both reject the confessional Christology of orthodoxy established in the early church and maintained into the Reformation.

There can be only one response to the two trends in contemporary Christology coming out of anti-revelational epistemologies: return to a revelational-biblical epistemology to read the Bible on its own terms and discover the identity of the real Jesus given by God himself.

In chapter 2, we began with this lesson for evangelical theologians today: a truly "biblical" Christology must proceed self-consciously and explicitly from the Bible's self-presentation of Christ as the only way to rightly identify him. A "biblical" Christology is one that constructs the identity of Jesus from the Bible and on the Bible's own terms. Rightly identifying Jesus, then, requires doing Christology "from above," starting with Scripture as God's own accurate and authoritative word written in texts that interpret one another. Scripture not only describes the facts of history with accuracy; it also explains the meaning and significance of those facts in such a way that we can know Jesus in truth and formulate correct doctrine regarding his identity.

Systematic theology, then, has a twofold task: *interpreting Scripture* as God's self-revelation through biblical theology and *applying Scripture* through theological construction and defense. Interpreting the Bible requires a theological reading. Theological interpretation focuses on what God has revealed to be true and significant by allowing the textual features to determine the meaning of every reading. A theological reading attends to the biblical plotline that develops along three horizons: syntax, literary context, and genre (textual horizon); location in redemptive-history (epochal horizon); integration with the rest of the canon as a whole (canonical horizon).

While necessary, biblical theology alone is not sufficient. Systematic theology takes the biblical data from biblical theology and formulates them for application to every area of life. Living in the world and resisting the world requires the church to move beyond theological description to theological formulation that meets the needs of discipleship in the faith and defense of the faith. The task of applying Scripture, then, requires *constructive* and *apologetic* work. All three horizons of interpretation are important, but the textual and epochal horizons build up into the canonical horizon in such a way that the canonical level presents the truest, fullest, divine intention regarding the identity of Christ. Systematic theology moves from canon to concept by putting together the descriptions of biblical theology into a coherent whole. And amid this constructive work, challenges to the faith require various defenses that further sharpen theological formulation to best understand and proclaim the biblical Christ.

11

BIBLICAL WARRANT FOR
CHRISTOLOGY TODAY

All Christians want to be biblical in handling the Scriptures. But what counts as "biblical" does not enjoy the kind of consensus we might expect and even assume. In theory and in practice, those who seek to "rightly divide the word of truth" approach the text with different motivations for their work, employ different means in their interpretation, and reach different conclusions at the end.

At the center of these differences in methodology and interpretation often lies a difference in understanding and responding to the Bible's self-presentation. In keeping with a Christology "from above" (Part I), the next few chapters will argue that *the Bible demands to be read on its own terms*. The Bible presents itself as one story that moves across four parts and through six covenants, unfolding the promises of God in the Old Testament to their fulfillment in the New Testament. To have biblical warrant for Christology today, what the Bible says about Jesus Christ must be read and understood according to this authoritative structure.

As we will see, when the Bible is read on its own terms, it presents Jesus as God the Son incarnate—the thesis of this volume. Chapter 3 will describe the redemptive-covenantal structure of the Scriptures. The biblical storyline develops across four major parts or epochs: creation, fall, redemption, and inauguration-consummation. These parts form the epochal horizon that gives every particular reading a specific redemptive-historical context. And as the biblical storyline unfolds, the plotline progresses through six covenants: God covenants with Adam/creation, Noah/creation, Abraham, Israel, and King David before the new covenant then comes in Christ. Chapter 4 sketches the Bible's overall presentation of Christ according to this structure and its typological dynamic by considering Jesus's self-understanding of who he is and how his apostles identify him according to his words and works. Working within the biblical framework themselves, Jesus and his apostles reach the same conclusion: he is both God and man. Chapter 5 then explores the God-equal deity of Christ by looking at his divine status, works, and titles. And chapter 6 discusses the full humanity of Christ by focusing on the biblical presentation of the incarnation and the rationale for God the Son coming in our flesh.

THREE

THE AUTHORITATIVE STRUCTURE

OF THE BIBLICAL STORYLINE

Francis Schaeffer once wrote,

> I have come to the point where, when I hear the word "Jesus"—which means so much to me because of the Person of the historic Jesus and His work—I listen carefully because I have with sorrow become more afraid of the word "Jesus" than almost any other word in the modern world. The word is used as a contentless banner. . . . [T]here is no rational scriptural content by which to test it. . . .
>   Increasingly over the past few years the word "Jesus," separated from the content of the Scriptures, has been the enemy of the Jesus of history, the Jesus who died and rose and is coming again and who is the eternal Son of God.[1]

More than four decades ago, Schaeffer put his finger on a serious problem that remains today: "Jesus" has almost become a meaningless word due to its separation from the content and framework of Scripture. When this occurs, the unfortunate result is that Jesus becomes anything we want him to be except the Jesus of the Bible.[2] In our survey of the epistemological and hermeneutical developments since the Enlightenment, we have already seen that all *extratextual* approaches to Christology fail to bring us to the real Jesus. Imposing a foreign worldview on the text necessarily obscures and obviates the clear and authoritative revelation of Jesus's identity by God himself. To proceed *intratextually* toward the Bible's Jesus—who the real Jesus of history *is*—we now need to trace out the structure and storyline of the Scriptures.

David Wells helps us transition from the broad strokes of a biblical

---

[1] Francis A. Schaeffer, *Escape from Reason* (London: InterVarsity Fellowship, 1968), 78–79.
[2] For a popular treatment of how "Jesus" has been removed from the categories, content, and structure of the Bible, and thus distorted within American society, see Stephen J. Nichols, *Jesus Made in America: A Cultural History from the Puritans to the Passion of the Christ* (Downers Grove, IL: IVP Academic, 2008).

epistemology to a finer sketch of the Bible's own terms: After noting a number of epistemological assumptions which are crucial for our understanding of Jesus's identity, Wells astutely observes that, "Almost as important as these [epistemological presuppositions], however, are the choices that we make with respect to the interpretive framework, the categories of understanding, which we employ in our analysis of the biblical material."[3] In other words, in order to grasp the Jesus of the Bible correctly, we must place him within the larger biblical-theological framework of Scripture, which, for Wells, is the eschatological framework of the kingdom of God. As Wells correctly maintains, the eschatological framework of Scripture rooted in the Bible's entire storyline is the "interpretive framework within which [Jesus's] birth, death, and resurrection assume their proper meaning."[4] And the storyline of Scripture does move from the promise to the realization of God's kingdom—from the garden of Eden, through Old Testament Israel, into the New Testament church, unto the new creation. While this much is true and helpful, however, a closer look at the Bible's internal structure will yield more clarity when it comes time to place Jesus within this authoritative storyline.[5] D. A. Carson reminds us that even with all of its diversity, "the Bible as a whole document tells a story, and, properly used, that story can serve as a metanarrative that shapes our grasp of the entire Christian faith."[6] And this surely includes an entire Christology.

The goal of this chapter is to lay out the four major parts and six progressive covenants of the biblical metanarrative so that we can later see how the Bible itself presents Jesus to us. These parts and covenants work together to form the Bible's own theological framework that puts all of the intervening biblical data into place to display a clear and correct picture of Jesus. Apart from placing Jesus within this framework, we will fail to understand *who* he is, let alone what he has done. Furthermore, to understand how each part and covenant functions in the biblical identification of Christ, in the following discussion we will resist an explicit connection to the person of Christ as long as possible; even by the end of this chapter, many questions will await answers

---

[3] David F. Wells, *The Person of Christ: A Biblical and Historical Analysis of the Incarnation* (Westchester, IL: Crossway, 1984), 21.

[4] Ibid., 32. Colin Gunton also argues that to understand who Jesus is we must place him within the context of the Old Testament: "Israel, we might say, provides the logic of Christology, so that the Old Testament lays down the framework within which both Jesus himself, so it would appear, and his first interpreters understood his significance" (Colin Gunton, *The Christian Faith: An Introduction to Christian Doctrine* [Oxford: Blackwell, 2002], 80). See also N. T. Wright, "Jesus," in *New Dictionary of Theology*, ed. Sinclair Ferguson, David F. Wright, and J. I. Packer (Downers Grove, IL: InterVarsity Press, 1988), 348–351; idem, *Jesus and the Victory of God*, vol. 2 in *Christian Origins and the Question of God* (Minneapolis: Fortress, 1997), 147–653.

[5] For other helpful examples of placing Jesus within the interpretive framework of Scripture, see Graeme Goldsworthy, *According to Plan: The Unfolding Revelation of God in the Bible* (Downers Grove, IL: InterVarsity Press, 1991); Stephen G. Dempster, *Dominion and Dynasty: A Biblical Theology of the Hebrew Bible*, NSBT 15 (Downers Grove, IL: InterVarsity Press, 2003); Paul R. House, *Old Testament Theology* (Downers Grove, IL: InterVarsity Press, 1998); Thomas R. Schreiner, *New Testament Theology: Magnifying God in Christ* (Grand Rapids, MI: Baker Academic, 2008).

[6] D. A. Carson, *The Gagging of God: Christianity Confronts Pluralism* (Grand Rapids, MI: Zondervan, 1996), 194.

to come in the following chapters that consider *specifically what* the Bible says about Jesus. To have proper *biblical* warrant for our Christology, we first need to know *precisely how* the Bible speaks about Jesus. We must proceed deliberately and carefully to take the Bible on its own terms—the only authoritative terms for the proper identification of Christ.

FOUR PARTS TO THE STORY

This section will sketch the four major parts that support the metanarrative of Scripture, its overarching scheme that holds all of the smaller parts and stories together in their proper place to make sense of God's revelation. More specifically, plotting the course of redemptive-history from creation to fall to redemption to inauguration-consummation provides the theological points that tell us about God, creation, and humanity so that in the end we find our way to Jesus who is God the Son incarnate, the eternal Word made flesh for us and for our salvation, our glorious Lord who renews both creation and humanity.

Creation

It is difficult to overestimate the importance of the doctrine of creation. Many Christians are naturally interested in the doctrine of salvation, but without creation there is no understanding of the Christian faith as the Bible describes it. In terms of Christology, as the first major part of the biblical storyline, creation establishes a unique theistic, eschatological, typological framework for the identification of Christ. And quite properly, the entire framework is first grounded in the identification of God himself.

Scripture presents God as the uncreated, independent, self-existent, self-sufficient, all-powerful Lord who created the universe and governs it by his word (Genesis 1–2; Ps. 50:12–14; 93:2; Acts 17:24–25). And this reality gives rise to the governing category at the heart of all Christian theology: the Creator-creature distinction. God alone is God; all else is creation that depends upon God for its existence. But the transcendent lordship of God (1 Kings 8:27; Ps. 7:17; 9:2; 21:7; 97:9; Isa. 6:1; Rev. 4:3) does not entail the remote and impersonal deity of deism.

Scripture stresses that God is both transcendent *and* immanent with his creation. As Creator, God is also the Covenant Lord[7] who is fully present in this world and intimately involved with his creatures: he freely, sovereignly, and purposefully sustains and governs all things to their eternally planned end

---

[7] For an extended discussion of how creation identifies God as the Covenant Lord, see John M. Frame, *The Doctrine of God* (Phillipsburg, NJ: P&R, 2002), 1–115. For the expression "the covenant Lord" as a summary way of talking and thinking about the triune God of Scripture, see idem, *The Doctrine of the Knowledge of God* (Phillipsburg, NJ: P&R, 1987), 11–61. For another excellent treatment of the doctrine of God, see John S. Feinberg, *No One Like Him: The Doctrine of God*, Foundations of Evangelical Theology (Wheaton, IL: Crossway, 2001).

(Ps. 139:1–10; Acts 17:28; Eph. 1:11; 4:6). And yet this immanent lordship does not entail the abstract and evolving deity of panentheism. Even though God is deeply involved with his world, he is not part of it or developing with it.

As Creator and Covenant Lord, rather, God rules over his creation perfectly and personally.[8] He rules with perfect power, knowledge, and righteousness (Ps. 9:8; 33:5; 139:1–4, 16; Isa. 46:9–11; Acts 4:27–28; Rom. 12:33–36) as the only being with divine aseity.[9] And in this rule, God loves, hates, commands, comforts, punishes, rewards, destroys, and strengthens, all according to the personal, covenant relationships that he establishes with his creation. God is never presented as some mere abstract concept or impersonal force. Indeed, as we progress through redemptive-history, God discloses himself not merely as uni-personal but as tri-personal, a being-in-relation, a unity of three persons: Father, Son, and Spirit. In short, as the Creator–Covenant triune Lord, God acts in, with, and through his creatures to accomplish all he desires to do in the way he desires to do it.

Scripture also presents this one Creator–Covenant Lord as the Holy One over all his creation (Gen. 2:1–3; Ex. 3:2–5; Lev. 11:44; Isa. 6:1–3; 57:15; cf. Rom. 1:18–23). The common understanding for the meaning of holiness is "set apart," but holiness conveys much more than God's distinctness and transcendence.[10] God's holiness is particularly associated with his aseity, sovereignty, and glorious majesty.[11] As the one who is Lord over all, he is exalted, self-sufficient, and self-determined both metaphysically and morally, and thus *categorically different in nature and existence* from everything he has made. He cannot be compared with the "gods" of the nations or be judged by human standards. God alone is holy in himself; God alone is God. Furthermore, intimately tied to God's holiness in the metaphysical sense is God's personal-moral purity and perfection. He is "too pure to behold evil" and unable to tolerate wrong (Hab. 1:12–13; cf. Isa. 1:4–20; 35:8). God must act with holy justice when his people rebel against him; yet he is the God who loves his people with a holy love (Hos. 11:9), for he is the God of "covenant faithfulness" (*hesed*). Often,

---

[8] For a discussion of God's existence and actions as a personal being, see Feinberg, *No One Like Him*, 225–231; Frame, *Doctrine of God*, 602; see also Herman Bavinck, *God and Creation*, vol. 2 of *Reformed Dogmatics*, ed. John Bolt, trans. John Vriend (Grand Rapids, MI: Baker, 2004), 15–19; cf. Carson, *Gagging of God*, 222–238.

[9] Aseity is more than a metaphysical attribute that stresses God's self-existence; it also refers to epistemological and ethical categories. As Frame notes, "God is not only self-existent, but also self-attesting and self-justifying. He not only exists without receiving existence from something else, but also gains his knowledge only from himself (his nature and his plan) and serves as his own criterion of truth. And his righteousness is self-justifying, based on the righteousness of his own nature and on his status as the ultimate criterion of rightness" (*Doctrine of God*, 602).

[10] See Willem VanGemeren, *New International Dictionary of Old Testament Theology and Exegesis*, 3 vols. (Grand Rapids, MI: Zondervan, 1997), 3:879; see also Feinberg, *No One Like Him*, 339–345. For a discussion of the belief by past theologians that holiness is the most fundamental characteristic of God, see Richard A. Muller, *The Divine Essence and Attributes*, vol. 3 of *Post-Reformation Reformed Dogmatics* (Grand Rapids, MI: Baker Academic, 2003), 497–503. Even though we must demonstrate care in elevating one perfection of God, there is a sense in which holiness defines the very nature of God. In fact, whenever we combine God's holiness with love, justice, or goodness, we always say that it is a holy love, holy justice, or holy goodness.

[11] See Muller, *Divine Essence and Attributes*, 497–503.

divine holiness and love are set against each other, but Scripture never presents them as being at odds. We not only see this taught in the Old Testament, but the New Testament, while maintaining God's complete holiness (see Rev. 4:8), also affirms in 1 John 4:8 that "God is love." But it is important to note, an incredible *tension* results in how God will simultaneously demonstrate his holy justice and covenant love, which is truly resolved only in the person and work of Christ—God the Son incarnate who becomes our propitiatory sacrifice and reconciles divine justice and grace in his cross (Rom. 3:21–26).[12]

As the first major part of the biblical storyline, then, creation presents *the fundamental identity of God himself*. And it is God's identity as the holy Creator–Covenant Lord that gives a particular theistic shape to Scripture's interpretive framework[13]—an identity and shape within which ultimately Jesus is placed. In fact, because there is no other being like God, his transcendent, immanent, perfect, personal, covenantal, and holy lordship over all creation determines the meaning and significance of all that happens in history. In our survey of intellectual history, we discovered that a major cause of current Christological confusion is the adoption of viewpoints that presuppose different understandings of God and the God-world relationship. According to a biblical epistemology, however, there are no abstract events or brute facts to be interpreted according to either the strict rationalism of the Enlightenment or the absolute relativity of postmodern-pluralistic thinking. All that happens in creation comes by the design of the holy Creator–Covenant Lord who reveals and interprets his own works along the storyline of Scripture.

Creation also establishes that this particular theistic framework that supports the Bible's metanarrative is *eschatological*. Things are not now what they were or what they will be. Creation begins an entire drama that drives the course of history to the end designed for it by its Creator–Covenant Lord. God spoke his creation into existence as "very good" (Gen. 1:1–3, 31; cf. John 1:1–3)[14] and started building his kingdom from the beginning. Graeme Goldsworthy helps us locate the kingdom of God even in the garden:

---

[12] On this point, see D. A. Carson, *The Difficult Doctrine of the Love of God* (Wheaton, IL: Crossway, 2000).

[13] All other "theistic" frameworks (deism, panentheism, etc.) are incompatible with the unique biblical-theological framework of Scripture established by its specific metaphysical-moral identification of God. And so only the Bible's particular theistic framework can provide the correct identification of Christ. For a development of this point, see Millard J. Erickson, *The Word Became Flesh: A Contemporary Incarnational Christology* (Grand Rapids, MI: Baker, 1991), 507–530. Moreover, to remove Jesus from the Bible's overall presentation of God is to fail to understand how New Testament Christology is presented within its Jewish context. And even before the New Testament, Richard Bauckham rightly argues that Second Temple Judaism held to a strict monotheism similar to the above discussion of God as the Creator–Covenant Lord, and that as such, it was "impossible to attribute real divinity to any figure other than the one God" (Richard Bauckham, *Jesus and the God of Israel: God Crucified and Other Studies on the New Testament's Christology of Divine Identity* [Grand Rapids, MI: Eerdmans, 2008], 2).

[14] Some argue that *goodness* is merely the complete correspondence between divine intention and the universe. This view, however, does not necessitate a perfect world and thus allows for death in the nonhuman world before the fall (see William J. Dumbrell, *The Search for Order: Biblical Eschatology in Focus* [Grand Rapids, MI: Baker, 1994], 20–22; Hugh Ross, *Creation and Time: A Biblical and Scientific Perspective on the Creation-Date Controversy* [Colorado Springs: NavPress, 1994], 62ff). The better option links *goodness* with *moral realities* to argue

The *kingdom of God* is a name that is not used in the Bible until much later, but the idea of it immediately comes to mind as we think of creation. . . .

How may we describe the kingdom of God as it has been revealed up to this point in Scripture? God's rule involves the relationships that he has set up between himself and everything in creation. In other words, God makes the rules for all existence. Both accounts of creation show mankind as the center of God's attention and the recipient of a unique relationship with him. Thus the focus of the kingdom of God is on the relationship between God and his people. Man is subject to God, while the rest of creation is subject to man and exists for his benefit. The kingdom means God ruling over his people in the material universe.[15]

In short, God made a good creation as the proper physical habitation in which his kingdom people could live under his covenant rule.[16] And because this state of affairs is central to the desire of the Lord of history, the goodness of creation and the presence of his kingdom are central to the storyline that unfolds his plan. The fact that rebellion within God's kingdom corrupted all creation means that the events of history are moving under the governance of the Creator–Covenant Lord in an eschatological direction toward a "new creation" and the consummation of an eternal kingdom (see Isa. 65:17–25; Rom. 8:19–22; Rev. 21:1–4).

This is not to say that the coming creation replaces an original creation that God somehow failed to keep on course. Renewal of both creation and humanity, rather, was part of God's eternal plan (1 Cor. 2:7; Eph. 1:5–11; 2 Tim. 1:9; Titus 1:2); the "new creation" represents the original eschatological goal of the old creation. The week of creation itself culminated in the rest of God on the seventh day (Gen. 2:1–3). And this one day of completion and rest became a pattern that grounds observance of the Sabbath day under the old covenant (see Ex. 20:8–11) but ultimately points to a final "Sabbath rest for the people of God" (Heb. 3:7–4:13) under the new covenant that will never end (see Rev. 21:22–25), associated with the great salvation rest inaugurated by Jesus himself.

---

that death, pain, and suffering did not exist prior to the fall and that they are a result of Adam's sin (cf. Gen. 2:17; 3:19; Rom. 5:12; 6:23) (see, e.g., Andrew S. Kulikovsky, *Creation, Fall, Restoration: A Biblical Theology of Creation* [Fearn, Ross-shire: Mentor, 2009], 204–220). Also, a *good* world entails that both physical and spiritual realities were created good and, sadly, in light of the fall, both are corrupted by sin and in need of redemption. As Scripture later speaks of the Redeemer and his incarnation, it does so by stressing the need for Christ to become flesh in order to redeem. In this light, it is important to remember that the first Christological heresy in the church denied not Christ's deity but his humanity. Docetism, which rejected the original goodness of created physical reality, also denied the reality of a real incarnation. The church, conversely, starting with a proper view of creation, realized that without a real incarnation, the Redeemer could not fully redeem us.

[15] Goldsworthy, *According to Plan*, 94–95. God's rule is key in the Old Testament: "The idea of the rule of God over creation, over all creatures, over the kingdoms of the world, and in a unique and special way, over his chosen and redeemed people, is the very heart of the message of the Hebrew scriptures" (idem, "Kingdom of God," in *NDBT*, 618).

[16] For a detailed treatment of God's plan to have a people for himself in a place for themselves, as it develops through the Old Testament, see Dempster, *Dominion and Dynasty*.

Finally, creation establishes that this particular theistic-eschatological framework of Scripture is also *typological*. As we have seen, according to a biblical epistemology, numerous people, events, and institutions follow a typological trajectory through the Scriptures unto a final fulfillment—various types move to their appointed antitypes. But creation gives us one of the first types that has a distinctive effect on the interpretive framework of Scripture in general and on Christology in particular.

Humanity created in God's image (*imago Dei*) functions as an important *metatype* that stretches across the metanarrative of Scripture and takes up other types along the way. This *imago* metatype, moreover, comes imbedded within the Bible's eschatological presentation of the goodness of creation and the presence of God's kingdom: "Then God said, 'Let us make man in our image, after our likeness. And let them have dominion over . . . all the earth'" (Gen. 1:26).[17] The climax of what God as Creator called "very good" was that he gave subordinate rule to a humanity made in the *imago Dei*, designed to be vice-regents of God as Covenant Lord.[18] Along with the goodness of creation and the presence of God's kingdom, then, the image of God in man becomes central to the desire and plan of the Lord of history and thus central to the biblical storyline. Also, given humanity's role in God's plan, and especially the unique role of the first man, Adam, it is not surprising that Scripture draws a tight relation between Adam-Christ, as both are identified as *imago* (Gen. 1:26; Col. 1:15), and Christ, as the divine Son, becomes flesh in order to reverse Adam's failed representational headship. In fact, apart from the Bible's teaching regarding humans as image-bearers, it is difficult to make coherent and plausible the very idea of an incarnation.[19] Additionally, it is also important to see how as a metatype, the *imago Dei* moves to its own typological fulfillment in and through two other types.

---

[17] "Image" and "likeness" are synonyms (see Anthony Hoekema, *Created in God's Image* [Grand Rapids, MI: Eerdmans, 1986], 11–101) both here and in related texts (e.g., Gen. 5:1; 9:6; 1 Cor. 11:7; Col. 1:15; 3:10), although a slight nuance can be detected. On this point, see Peter J. Gentry and Stephen J. Wellum, *Kingdom through Covenant: A Biblical-Theological Understanding of the Covenants* (Wheaton, IL: Crossway, 2012), 181–202.

[18] The terms "image" (*selem*) and "likeness" (*demut*) are rare in the Old Testament as applied to humans (see Gen. 1:26–27; 9:6; cf. a similar phrase in Gen. 5:3; cf. 1 Cor. 11:7; James 3:9). In the ancient Near East, however, the image was a physical *representation* of the "god," specifically the king who possessed the spirit of the "god." And this provides a key point of departure from the biblical use. Scripture teaches that man (collectively) is made in God's image. Not just the king but *all* humans are vice-regents made to rule as God's representatives. Dominion is not *the* definition of the *imago* but a consequence of it (cf. Psalm 8). Scripture later teaches that in redemption, humans are renewed in the "image/likeness" of God (Col. 3:10; Rom. 8:29; cf. Eph. 4:24; 2 Cor. 3:18), which is then linked to Christ, the Son, who is the true "image" of God, thus the archetype of our being created in God's image (Col. 1:15; cf. Heb. 1:3).

[19] Wells, *Person of Christ*, 7, argues that Christology requires a clear conception not only of God but also of humans. Why? Because the nature of the incarnation requires that we think about the nature of God *and* humans since our Lord is, in the words of the Chalcedonian Definition, one person who is truly God and *truly man* in two natures forever. It is important to think of Islam at this point. Islam's rejection of the very possibility of an incarnation is tied to their view of God *and* man. In regard to God, Islam denies the Trinity and has a different view of the entire God-world relation. In terms of humans, Islam denies that we are image-bearers. Given these differences, it is not surprising that they reject the incarnation as impossible and inconceivable.

First, the *imago Dei* takes up *son/sonship*. Stephen Dempster explains the image-son connection in Genesis 5:

> By juxtaposing the divine creation of Adam in the image of God and the subsequent human creation of Seth in the image of Adam, the transmission of the image of God through this genealogical line is implied, as well as the link between sonship and the image of God. As Seth is a son of Adam, so Adam is a son of God. Language is being stretched here, as a literal son of God is certainly not in view, but nevertheless the writer uses an analogy to make a point.[20]

Moving from the Old Testament into the New Testament, Luke refers explicitly to Adam as the "son of God" (Luke 3:38). This image-son connection is possible because, like image-bearing, sonship carries a strong representational significance in Scripture. After Adam, both Israel (Ex. 4:22; cf. Hos. 11:1) and the Davidic kings (2 Sam. 7:14ff; Psalm 2) bear this image-sonship precisely because each was made to represent the Covenant Lord and carry out his rule in the world in a special way, thus carrying on the Adamic role and function.

Second, this typological trajectory of the image-son also picks up the Adam–last Adam connection. The New Testament (especially Paul's letters) divides all humanity under the representative headship of two men: Adam and the "last Adam" (1 Cor. 15:45; cf. Rom. 5:14). In this sense, *Adam* is a special case of image-sonship. The first Adam had the dignity of representing what it means to be human—to be the vice-regent of God. But he also functioned as the first man to represent all humanity before God. In short, to be *Adam* is to be a human covenantal head of humanity under the Creator–Covenant Lord.

Taken together, then, the image-son-Adam type established in creation increases along a typological trajectory unto fulfillment in the antitype: the true image-Son and last Adam. The first, earthly image-son-Adam's rebellion under the first covenant brought sin, judgment, and death to all humanity and corruption to all creation. So the true image-Son and last Adam must bring righteousness and eternal life to a new humanity under a new covenant in a new creation.

In sum, creation establishes a particular theistic-eschatological-typological framework that brings every reading of Scripture into a singular plan of God that carries certain expectations for humanity and all creation. The Creator–Covenant Lord is bringing the goodness of his creation and the presence of his kingdom to its completion in a true and final image-Son-Adam. This coming *imago Dei* will precisely represent God; this coming Son will perfectly obey him; this coming Adam will provide faithful covenant headship—all for the

---

[20] Dempster, *Dominion and Dynasty*, 58–59.

sake of God's glory in a new humanity that will reign over a new creation according to the provisions of a new covenant.

Fall

As the second major part of the biblical metanarrative, the fall forges a tension into the interpretive framework established by creation. After Genesis 3, the world and the people in it are no longer "very good." No one can honestly examine human history, or even one human life, and fail to conclude that we have missed the mark in some way. But not everyone explains the human problem in the same way. Without overly simplifying the matter—allowing for much nuance—we can divide the understanding of human failure into two explanations: intrinsic and moral. Non-Christian worldviews consider the human problem to be intrinsic to the human condition. Our failure is linked to our finitude as an essential and necessary product of our natural makeup. But the church has traditionally rejected the intrinsic argument in light of the biblical storyline and the *historicity* of Adam and the fall.

Almost immediately after creation,[21] Genesis 3 presents a space-time epochal shift caused by the immoral act of man who was created "very good."[22] After receiving every provision and the blessing of God to obey and enjoy him in vice-regent reign, Adam willfully rebelled against the Creator–Covenant Lord. After rejoicing in God's provision of a "helper fit for him" (Gen. 2:20–23), Adam became dissatisfied with vice-regency under God and fell to Satan's temptation to rule without God by "be[coming] like God, knowing good and evil" (3:4–7). The fall shows us that the entrance of human sin into God's creation was *internal* or *moral*, but not *intrinsic* or part of our original creation. The temptation to sin came externally, from Satan. The desire and will to act in disobedience to God, however, came from within Adam himself. Yet this same Adam was not made with such a moral defect; otherwise the metaphysically and morally perfect God could not have looked on everything he had made, including Adam and his mandate to spread God's image over the earth, and called it "very good" (1:26–31).[23]

---

[21] This sense of timing is certainly true from a narrative perspective. Regardless of the possible lapse of time after the first Sabbath and Adam's rebellion, the text emphasizes a drastic shift from goodness to corruption.

[22] Scripture never reduces the human problem to an issue of biology or social conditions, contra Karl Giberson, *Saving the Original Sinner* (Boston: Beacon, 2015); Peter Enns, *Evolution of Adam* (Grand Rapids, MI: Brazos, 2012). Without denying complex connections with our physical bodies and social interactions, our root problem is willful and responsible sin before God—a *moral* problem in need of a *moral* solution. The unrighteous must be made righteous by one who was never unrighteous.

[23] For a defense of the historicity of Adam and the fall, see Henri Blocher, *Original Sin: Illuminating the Riddle*, NSBT 5 (Downers Grove, IL: InterVarsity Press, 2000); C. John Collins, *Did Adam and Eve Really Exist? Who They Were and Why You Should Care* (Wheaton, IL: Crossway, 2011); Hans Madueme, ed., *Adam, the Fall, and Original Sin: Theological, Biblical, and Scientific Perspectives* (Grand Rapids, MI: Baker Academic, 2014); cf. Matthew Barrett and A. B. Caneday, eds., *Four Views on the Historical Adam* (Grand Rapids, MI: Zondervan, 2013). Only a *historical* Adam and fall into sin and its corruption can be overcome. Denial of the historical Adam and his original sin makes sin and evil part of what it means to be human, with two unbiblical consequences: (1) responsibility for

Once sin entered the garden, moreover, it expanded over all creation through Adam's covenant headship. God appointed Adam to stand on our behalf as a human race such that, "just as sin came into the world through one man, and death through sin, . . . so death spread to all men because all sinned . . ." (Rom. 5:12). Regardless of the specific view regarding the spread of sin and its effects, the "original sin"[24] of Adam as the representative of humanity has corrupted the entire human race throughout all of human history. Beginning with murder in Adam's immediate family (Gen. 4:6–8), sin multiplied and expanded until "every intention of the thoughts of [man] was only evil continually. . . . for all flesh had corrupted their way on the earth" (6:5, 12). And this human problem of sin with its corruption of all thoughts and desires has continued from the time of Noah into our own day. Accordingly, the apostle Paul summarizes that "all [members of humanity] have sinned and fall short of the glory of God" (Rom. 3:23).

In short, God's original vice-regent and covenant head of humanity failed, with tragic and universal consequences. The first image-son-Adam, who was created and blessed to represent the righteous rule of God over all of his "very good" creation, rebelled and plunged all humanity into moral corruption that sets them against the Creator–Covenant Lord. And because all humanity was given dominion over the earth, the whole creation has been subjected to futility, bound to the impotence of its immoral rulers (Rom. 8:18–23).[25]

It is this basic *tension* between God's original creation and the subsequent fall of humanity that adds another dimension to the theistic-eschatological-typological framework of Scripture. We must soberly recognize that God cannot abide with a sinful humanity, and a sinful humanity cannot bring forth the plan of God to have a people for himself in a place of perfect provision. As the Creator–Covenant Lord, God is intrinsically holy, righteous, and just, such that his own perfect nature requires that he perfectly judge and punish his rebellious vice-regents. From the beginning, the wages of sin has been exile and death under the wrath of God (Rom. 6:23; see Adam and Eve's exile from the garden and the refrain of death in Adam's genealogy; the death of every Davidic king and the exile of Israel from the Promised Land).[26] But it

---

sin and evil traces back to our Creator, who must have made us "flawed" from the outset; (2) all ground is lost for the hope that our fallen condition can be reversed. This is one of the problems with treatments of Genesis 3 that do not view the fall as historical. For example, Paul Ricoeur does not want to equate finitude and sin, yet he denies the historicity of the fall (Paul Ricoeur, *The Symbolism of Evil*, trans. Emerson Buchanan [Boston: Beacon, 1986]). For a critique of this position, see Blocher, *Gagging of God*, 212–221.

[24] For a helpful discussion of original sin, see Blocher, *Original Sin*; Hoekema, *Created in God's Image*, 133–167.

[25] Some describe the effects of sin in terms of a fivefold alienation or separation involving God, self, others, creation, and inheritance of paradise. For a development of this point, see Kulikovsky, *Creation, Fall, Restoration*, 201–204.

[26] Closely related to God's holiness is his wrath—his holy reaction to evil. Scripture speaks of divine wrath using high-intensity language, and a substantial part of the Bible's storyline turns on God's wrath. God is forbearing, gracious, and longsuffering, but he is also a God of holiness, wrath, and judgment (see Carson, *Gagging of God*, 232–234; idem, *Difficult Doctrine of the Love of God*, 65–84). The wrath of God, unlike his love or holiness, is not an intrinsic perfection; rather, it is an expression of his holiness in reaction against sin. Where there is no sin, there

is precisely this necessity of God to judge and punish human sin that twists a tension into the biblical metanarrative, what John Stott calls the "problem of forgiveness":

> The problem of forgiveness is constituted by the inevitable collision between divine perfection and human rebellion, between God as he is and us as we are. The obstacle to forgiveness is neither our sin alone, nor our guilt alone, but also the divine reaction in love and wrath towards guilty sinners. For, although indeed "God is love," yet we have to remember that his love is "holy love," love which yearns over sinners while at the same time refusing to condone their sin. How, then, could God express his holy love?—his love in forgiving sinners without compromising his holiness, and his holiness in judging sinners without frustrating his love? Confronted by human evil, how could God be true to himself as holy love? In Isaiah's words, how could he be simultaneously "a righteous God and a Saviour" (45:21)?[27]

Whereas *sin* is an *internal* moral problem for humanity, *forgiveness* is an *intrinsic* moral problem for God.[28] Of course, in the end, there is no real problem for God, but at this point in the storyline, it remains unclear how two necessities will both become reality: the punishment of sinful humanity and the forgiveness of sinful humanity to fulfill God's creation plan. How can God save us and satisfy himself simultaneously? Or, how can God who is righteous forgive sinners he created for righteousness and be both "just and the justifier" (Rom. 3:25–26)?[29]

With the first two major parts of the biblical storyline in place, then, we can sketch the first lines of the interpretive framework with a question: how can the metaphysically-morally perfect Creator–Covenant Lord manifest his glory in the righteous rule of humanity over creation by forgiving humanity for sinful rebellion and restoring man from internal corruption to live with God as his glorious vice-regents?

---

is no wrath, but there will always be love and holiness. Where God in his holiness confronts his image-bearers in their rebellion, there must be wrath, otherwise God is not the personal and self-sufficient God he claims to be (see Carson, *Gagging of God*, 232–234; Muller, *Divine Essence and Attributes*, 476–503).

[27] John Stott, *The Cross of Christ* (Downers Grove, IL: InterVarsity Press, 1986), 88–89; cf. Donald Macleod, *Christ Crucified: Understanding the Atonement* (Downers Grove, IL: IVP Academic, 2014), 79–100; Geerhardus Vos, *Christology*, vol. 3 of *Reformed Dogmatics*, trans. and ed. Richard B. Gaffin Jr. (Bellingham, WA: Lexham, 2014), 20–84.

[28] Clarity on this point is crucial: God is never dependent upon or required to act or not act in accordance with anything external to his own nature. And the inability to act contrary to his perfect nature marks no deficiency in God. The inability to act against his metaphysical and moral perfection is part of that very same perfection.

[29] For a discussion of the tension between God's wrath and mercy, see Stott, *Cross of Christ*, 232–234; Garry Williams, "The Cross and the Punishment of Sin," in *Where Wrath and Mercy Meet: Proclaiming the Atonement Today*, ed. David Peterson (Carlisle, UK: Paternoster, 2001), 68–99. It is crucial to note that this biblical tension does not arise for the modern or postmodern mind-set. Worldviews mixed with naturalistic and individualistic axioms do not view sin/evil in relation to God but reduce them to the things of this world. Unbiblical worldviews cannot make true sense of the essence and extremity of the human problem and the glory and graciousness of its solution brought by God himself. See David Wells, *Losing Our Virtue: Why the Church Must Recover Its Moral Vision* (Grand Rapids, MI: Eerdmans, 1999) for a helpful discussion of the biblical relation between God, humans, and sin.

Redemption

As the third major part of the biblical metanarrative, redemption resolves the tension forged into the interpretive framework by the fall of humanity. With God's plan for the world moving forward from creation, the disastrous events of the fall force us to ask how the Creator–Covenant Lord can forgive sinful humanity when his perfection requires punishment. How can God be both subject and object in salvation, i.e., how can he take the initiative yet satisfy his own righteous requirements? Redemption answers that *God himself* will take the initiative and accomplish our salvation. The fall drama makes an epochal shift away from the goodness of creation and the presence of God's kingdom through the righteous reign of his human vice-regents; redemption shows us that this shift in the storyline is not a departure from God's plan but the unfolding of it in accordance with the mystery of his will to unite all things in heaven and earth "to the praise of his glorious grace" (Eph. 1:6).

Even amid his curses after Adam's rebellion, God demonstrated his commitment to the goodness of his creation and the rule over it by humanity: "I will put enmity between you [Satan] and the woman, and between your offspring and her offspring; he shall bruise your head, and you shall bruise his heel" (Gen. 3:15).[30] In this *protevangelium* (i.e., the first gospel proclamation),[31] God promised that "someone out of the human race itself ('the woman's offspring'), although fatally 'wounded' himself in the conflict, would destroy the serpent (Satan)."[32] The dominion of the original vice-regent was lost and all humanity and creation were corrupted through the rebellious covenant headship of the first Adam. But as Graeme Goldsworthy rightly observes, this rebellion took place according to God's plan, and there is no hint that God created in the beginning "on a trial basis, or with a view to scrapping it after a period of time."[33]

And so another Adam, the promised "offspring" or "seed" of the woman,[34] must restore both humanity and creation through an obedient covenant headship. Stephen Dempster rightly observes that in this seed-Adam, "human—and therefore divine—dominion will be established over the world. The realization

---

[30] See Goldsworthy, *According to Plan*, 112, who connects creation and salvation as an unfolding drama by observing that "the background to God's work of rescuing sinners is his commitment to his creation" (ibid.).

[31] For a helpful connection between the good news of Eve's offspring and the gospel of salvation in Christ, see T. D. Alexander, *The Servant King: The Bible's Portrait of the Messiah* (Leicester: Inter-Varsity Press, 1998), 16–19; Geerhardus Vos, *Biblical Theology: Old and New Testaments* (Grand Rapids, MI: Eerdmans, 1948).

[32] Robert L. Reymond, *Jesus, Divine Messiah: The New Testament Witness* (Phillipsburg, NJ: P&R, 1990), 69; see also House, *Old Testament Theology*, 65; John H. Sailhamer, *The Pentateuch as Narrative: A Biblical-Theological Commentary* (Grand Rapids, MI: Zondervan, 1992), 106–109.

[33] Goldsworthy, *According to Plan*, 112.

[34] "Seed" (*zera'*) is a key word in Genesis, occurring 59 times compared to 170 times in the rest of the Old Testament. Although the noun does not have distinctive singular and plural forms, one can make a strong case that it is singular in Genesis 3, especially since the rest of Genesis focuses on a single line of seed descended from Eve that carries on through Noah and Abram and on to Christ (cf. Gal. 3:16) (see T. D. Alexander, "Seed," in *NDBT*, 769–773; Reymond, *Jesus, Divine Messiah*, 69–71).

of the kingdom of God is linked to the future of the human race."[35] The freedom of creation from "its bondage to corruption" depends upon "the freedom of the glory of the children of God" (Rom. 8:21). And as Genesis 3 unfolds, there is evidence that Adam lays claim on the promise when he names his wife "Eve," because "she was the mother of all living" (v. 20). In this context, Adam appears to be reclaiming dominion in faith "through *naming* his wife *the mother*, which cannot help but allude to the more specific role she will have as the one who will provide a seed who will strike the serpent."[36] In addition, God provides clothes to cover the shame and nakedness of Adam and Eve (v. 21), which signifies that God will not let his creation project be lost.

But here again we face the fall: how can sinful, rebellious humanity that lives in opposition to God under his wrath bring forth obedient sons of God to manifest his glory in their reign under God's blessings? While much more can be said and will be developed through the next chapters in this part, here we simply need to highlight two dimensions that shape the biblical metanarrative into a redemptive framework for interpretation in general and the identification of Jesus in particular.

First, the redemption and reign of humanity on the Bible's terms will come by the work of *God himself*. The prophets proclaim this word of the Creator–Covenant Lord himself: "I, I am the LORD, and besides me there is no savior" (Isa. 43:11); "I myself will be the shepherd of my sheep" (Ezek. 34:15). The psalmists declare it plainly: "Salvation belongs to the LORD; your blessing be on your people" (Ps. 3:8). And John's vision reveals that the redeemed in heaven exult in the salvific work of God himself with great joy: "Hallelujah! Salvation and glory and power belong to our God, for his judgments are true and just" (Rev. 19:1–2). The Scriptures allow no creature—not even the mightiest angel!—to rescue sinful humanity from the wrath of God and restore God's rule over his creation. God himself must deliver a people from his own wrath while satisfying the requirements of his intrinsic holiness, righteousness, and justice.

Second, the redemption and reign of humanity on the Bible's terms will come *by a man*. And this man will come as the promised offspring of Eve and as the last Adam, who will establish the eternal and righteous reign of God on the earth. The prophets proclaim the coming of this man by the word of the Creator–Covenant Lord: "But he [the servant of the LORD] was pierced for our transgressions; he was crushed for our iniquities; upon him was the

---

[35] Dempster, *Dominion and Dynasty*, 69. Dempster observes further that "the triumph of the woman's seed would suggest a return to the Edenic state, before the serpent had wrought its damage, and a wresting of the dominion of the world from the serpent" (ibid., 68). In other words, it is through the seed of the woman that the Adamic role in creation will be restored, that the curses will be removed, and that the serpent will be destroyed.

[36] Ibid., 68–69; cf. Gerhard von Rad, *Genesis: A Commentary*, trans. John H. Marks, Old Testament Library (Philadelphia: Fortress, 1976), 96.

chastisement that brought us peace, and with his wounds we are healed" (Isa. 53:5); "And I will set up over them one shepherd, my servant David, and he shall feed them. . . . And I, the LORD, will be their God, and my servant David shall be prince among them" (Ezek. 34:23–24). The psalmists declare it plainly: "'As for me [the LORD], I have set my King on Zion, my holy hill.' I will tell of the decree: The LORD said to me [the anointed king], 'You are my Son; . . . Ask of me, and I will make the nations your heritage, and the ends of the earth your possession'" (Ps. 2:6–8). And John's vision reveals that the redeemed in heaven exult in it with great joy: "Salvation belongs to our God . . . *and to the Lamb,*" who is "one like a son of man" (Rev. 7:10; 1:13). The Bible allows no other scenario: a man will redeem humanity to restore God's creation rule. Because of who he is, this one man's death for many will secure God's forgiveness of their sins and bring them into God's kingdom to reign under him and over the earth (Eph. 1:7; Rev. 5:9–10).

In sum, redemption shapes the Bible's theistic-eschatological-typological framework to bring into every reading the expectation that both God himself *and* a man of his choosing will act to redeem humanity and restore all creation.

Inauguration-Consummation

As the fourth major part of the biblical metanarrative, inauguration-consummation adds a distinctive feature to the eschatological aspect of the interpretive framework by bridging from "this present age" into "the age to come." The storyline of Scripture divides all history into these two ages. "This present age" began when God created all things and continued through humanity's corruption of all things, such that this age is characterized by sin, death, and opposition to God. "The age to come," though it sounds entirely future-oriented, has already broken into the present (inauguration) with the coming, redemption, and reign of God's new man. Yet this final, eternal age will come into its final fulfillment at the *telos* of all history (consummation).

This two-sided reality of redemptive history leads to an *already–not yet* dynamic in the structure of the Bible's self-presentation. To be clear, the *already* is not "this present age" in itself but the presence of "the age to come" *in* "this present age." Theologians use the concept of *inaugurated eschatology* to describe the significance of the fact that the final fulfillment of God's plan for humanity and all creation has begun: the way things will be forever has crashed into the way things are now temporarily.[37] Two brief examples will help make this point.

---

[37] For an in-depth treatment of inaugurated eschatology, see Gentry and Wellum, *Kingdom through Covenant,* 591–602; Schreiner, *New Testament Theology,* 41–116; see also Herman Ridderbos, *Paul: An Outline of His Theology,* trans. John Richard deWitt (Grand Rapids, MI: Eerdmans, 1975), 44–90.

First, the eternal kingdom of the Creator–Covenant Lord has come already, and its king sits on his throne even now. At this point, it is no longer possible to talk about the general structure of Scripture without reference to the specific person of Christ. The New Testament so clearly and explicitly presents Jesus as the fulfillment of the entire course of the biblical storyline that he demands to be named even before we can fully identify him by working through the metanarrative.[38] As a witness to the historical and narrative power of Jesus's presence, the apostle Matthew tells us that John the Baptist responded to the coming of Jesus of Nazareth by declaring, "the kingdom of heaven is at hand" (Matt. 3:2).[39] The kingdom came with the coming of the king himself. As Isaiah had prophesied he would do (Isa. 40:3), John the Baptist recognized Jesus as the righteous king promised throughout the Old Testament who would bring justice to God's people and to all the earth (Matt. 3:11–12; Isa. 40:9–17; John 1:14–18). Jesus himself understood that, in him, God's kingdom had truly come to earth (Matt. 4:12–17; Mark 1:15). And Jesus's disciples watched him literally ascend into heaven (Luke 24:51; Acts 1:9), where, Paul tells us, Jesus sits on God's throne with dominion over all creation (Eph. 1:20–22). And yet, Jesus taught his disciples to pray for God's kingdom to come (Matt. 6:10) and to look and prepare for his own second coming, this time in majestic glory, judgment, and power (Matt. 24:29–31; 25:31–46; Mark 9:1).

D. A. Carson captures this inaugurated eschatology of the kingdom in terms of its unfolding from the Old Testament into the New Testament:

"Kingdom" no longer primarily conjures up a theocratic state in which God rules by his human vassal in the Davidic dynasty. It conjures up the immediate transforming reign of God, dawning now in the ministry, death, resurrection, ascension, and session of Jesus, the promised Messiah, and consummated at his return. Eschatology is thereby transformed. The locus of the people of God is no longer national and tribal; it is international, transracial, transcultural. If the Old Testament prophets constantly look forward to the day when God will act decisively, the New Testament writers announce that God has acted decisively, and that this is "good news," gospel, of universal, eternal significance and stellar importance.[40]

---

[38] I am using "fulfillment" not in the sense of direct (e.g., Mic. 5:2; Matt. 2:1–12) but in the sense of indirect prophecy, to indicate that the typological patterns in the Old Testament point to the person and work of Jesus in the New Testament—he is the accomplishment of all that has been anticipated. For a helpful discussion of these points, see D. A. Carson, *Matthew*, in *EBC*, vol. 8 (Grand Rapids, MI: Zondervan, 1984), 27–29; Schreiner, *New Testament Theology*, 70–79. Anthony Hoekema provides a helpful list of examples where the New Testament presents the entire Christ event—from incarnation to ascension—as the fulfillment of Old Testament expectations (Anthony Hoekema, *The Bible and the Future* [Grand Rapids, MI: Eerdmans, 1979], 15). For example: (1) Jesus's birth (Isa. 7:14; Mic. 5:2; Matt. 1:20–23; 2:5–6); (2) his flight into Egypt (Hos. 11:1; Matt. 2:14–15); (3) his triumphal entry into Jerusalem (Zech. 9:9; Matt. 21:4–5); (4) his innocent and intentional crucifixion (Isaiah 53; Zech. 12:10; John 19:34); (5) his resurrection and ascension (Ps. 16:10; 68:18; Acts 1:9; 2:24–32) (ibid.).

[39] Jonathan Pennington argues that "kingdom of heaven" signifies that God's kingdom is from above, and as such, it represents God's sovereign rule over all the kingdoms of this world (Jonathan T. Pennington, *Heaven and Earth in the Gospel of Matthew*, Supplements to Novum Testamentum, vol. 126 [Leiden and Boston: Brill, 2007], 67–76).

[40] Carson, *Gagging of God*, 254.

Second, the Spirit has come as a gift of God's kingdom given by the king from his throne. In accordance with Joel's prophecy, Peter recognized that the Spirit of God came with the kingdom of God to the people of God (Acts 2:14ff.). Specifically, the crucified Jesus was raised and exalted to the promised Davidic throne—the eternal throne over creation—where he received the promise of the Holy Spirit and from where he "poured out [the Spirit of God]" (Acts 2:32–35; cf. Luke 24:46–51; John 14:15–17). Yet the present gift of the Spirit is a deposit and guarantee of a future inheritance for God's kingdom people (Eph. 1:13–14). As Anthony Hoekema summarizes, "we may say that in the possession of the Spirit we who are in Christ have a foretaste of the blessings of the age to come, and a pledge and guarantee of the resurrection of the body. Yet we have only the firstfruits. We look forward to the final consummation of the kingdom of God, when we shall enjoy these blessings to the full."[41]

Another way to understand inauguration-consummation is to look at "the age to come," moving from the Old Testament to the New Testament perspective. The Old Testament anticipates only one coming of the Lord and Messiah—a coming in power and might. And his coming would usher in "the last days" and "the age to come" to realize the eschatological hope and expectation of the prophets. As David Wells describes it, "These two ages were related to one another in a chronological sequence. This αἰών ended with the coming to earth of the Messiah, and with his arrival there began the heavenly αἰών."[42] The appearing of the Lord *and* Messiah would bring the fullness of God's saving rule and reign: his kingdom would extend through a new covenant with all God's people, throughout a new creation, and without the presence of God's enemies. Never contradicting this Old Testament anticipation, the New Testament modifies it to reveal not one but two comings of the Lord and Messiah. In his *first* coming, Jesus appears as Lord and Christ, and brings all that the Old Testament associates with "the age to come" into "this present age" *in principle*. The *consummation* of "the age to come" awaits the *second* coming of Jesus. "This present age" continues even with the decisive enthronement of Christ until he comes again—this last time in manifest power and glory.

And in the midst of these two comings, Scripture stresses that Christ is both currently and eschatologically reigning over his creation-kingdom. The realities of life in "the age to come" have already come from the future into "this present age," but not in full. Because it is in "the present evil age" (Gal. 1:4) that Christ sits on the throne of heaven, "far above all rule and authority and power and dominion . . . not only in this age but also in the one to come" (Eph. 1:21), there is both continuity and discontinuity between his present and

---

[41] Hoekema, *Bible and the Future*, 67.
[42] Wells, *Person of Christ*, 29.

future kingdoms. The future kingdom of Christ is here *in kind* (continuity), and the present kingdom of Christ will increase *unto completion* (discontinuity) at his return. William Manson describes this reality of the future kingdom in the present in terms of the *"Eschaton"*—the final, designed end of the world:

> When we turn to the New Testament, we pass from the climate of prediction to that of fulfillment. The things which God had foreshadowed by the lips of His holy prophets He has now, in part at least, brought to accomplishment. The *Eschaton*, described from afar . . . has in Jesus registered its advent. . . . The supreme sign of the *Eschaton* is the Resurrection of Jesus and the descent of the Holy Spirit on the Church. The Resurrection of Jesus is not simply a sign which God has granted in favour of His Son, but is the inauguration, the entrance into history, of *the times of the End.*
>
> Christians, therefore, have entered through the Christ into the New Age. Church, Spirit, life in Christ are eschatological magnitudes. Those who gather in Jerusalem in the numinous first days of the Church know that it is so; they are already conscious of tasting the powers of the World to Come. What has been predicted in Holy Scripture as to happen to Israel or to man in the *Eschaton* has happened to and in Jesus. The foundation-stone of the New Creation has come into position.[43]

At the end of the biblical metanarrative, inauguration-consummation overlaps the two ages of the Scripture's eschatology. Creation establishes an overall eschatological framework for interpreting the content of Scripture across its structured storyline. After moving through the tension of fall and the resolution of redemption, however, the storyline reaches forward to bring part of the new creation into the present. Looking for the identity of Jesus on the Bible's own terms, then, requires that we ask: *Who* can accomplish such a task? What kind of person is he? What does it mean for who he is that Jesus has brought God's kingdom in kind into "this present age" and that he is taking all creation to the completion of God's kingdom in "the age to come"?

The Biblical Framework for Authoritative Identification

These four major parts of the biblical storyline support the entire metanarrative and form the basic framework for interpreting the biblical revelation. More specifically for our purposes, creation, fall, redemption, and inauguration-consummation shape the way the Scriptures present and identify Jesus. Reading the Bible on *these terms* is the only authoritative framework for identifying who Jesus is. Even regarding the basic structure of the Bible, we either submit to God's own interpretation of Jesus Christ in its entirety or we reject God's revelation and forfeit a full knowledge of his Son. Put simply, faithfully reading

---

[43] William Manson, *Eschatology in the New Testament*, ed. T. F. Torrance and J. K. S. Reid, Scottish Journal of Theology Occasional Papers, vol. 2 (Edinburgh: Oliver & Boyd, 1953), 6.

along the four-part self-presentation of Scripture determines whether we find or lose the Jesus of history who is the Jesus of the Bible.

As part of the task of building biblical warrant for Christology, then, it will help to consider briefly how each part contributes to the identity of Christ.

First, we have seen that *creation* establishes a particular theistic-eschatological-typological framework for identifying the person of Christ. As David Wells noted, "No Christology can be constructed which does not presuppose . . . a clear conception of God."[44] Beginning with creation's theism has implications for both the general plausibility and the specific features of Christology. If the transcendent, metaphysically-morally perfect and personal God is eliminated a priori as unreasonable, then so too is the historical ground for Christology as a whole and the uniqueness of Christ in particular. As Robert Funk rightly noted but for the wrong reasons, "Jesus' divinity goes together with the old theistic way of thinking about God."[45] In an age where most Christological work is done from within a *postmodern and pluralistic* framework which is highly indebted to panentheistic and evolutionary constructs—where change and development are viewed as fundamental—it is not surprising that most current Christological discussion does not reflect the teaching of Scripture, let alone the history of the church.[46]

That is why, before we can accurately conceive of Jesus's identity, we must firmly fix in our minds the understanding of the biblical God who is Creator, Lord, sovereign, and personal. Without this, not only will our Christology be unfaithful to the Bible's presentation, but also, orthodox Christology will seem quite implausible from the outset as it becomes difficult to sustain anything unique about Christ.[47] In other words, if from the outset the unique God of Scripture is eliminated as unreasonable, then so is the classical understanding of the incarnation and the basis for establishing and grounding Christ's uniqueness.[48] In truth, differences in Christology are also differences in theology proper. Frances Young is an apt example:

---

[44] Wells, *Person of Christ*, 7.

[45] Robert W. Funk, "The Coming Radical Reformation: Twenty-one Theses," *The Fourth R* 11/4 (July–August 1998), http://www.westarinstitute.org/resources/the-fourth-r/the-coming-radical-reformation/, accessed June 17, 2015.

[46] Wells, *Person of Christ*, 7–8, develops this point further, noting that since the twentieth century, philosophy has increasingly stressed "becoming over being, existence rather than essence, dynamic emergence within the world rather than abstract aloofness from the world. It is a shift to broadly existential motifs. . . . Consequently, the idea of evolution—that unfolding of reality which itself exhibits something of the divine—is far more likely today to provide the immediate matrix of Christological thought than the older ideas of God and man which now seem unreal and abstract." All of this greatly affects how Christ is interpreted and how Christology is formulated, and—it must be stressed—this entire approach to Christology is alien to the biblical-theological categories of Scripture.

[47] Stuart C. Hackett, *The Reconstruction of the Christian Revelation Claim: A Philosophical and Critical Apologetic* (Grand Rapids, MI: Baker, 1984), 219. Hackett describes the impact on Christology of denying the biblical view of God: "since from this perspective there is no transcendent God in the theistic sense, the supposition that Jesus could be God incarnate becomes unintelligible and is therefore dismissed on principles as pure mythology" (ibid.).

[48] For a development of some of these ideas, see Carson, *Gagging of God*, 200–203.

Christians of the early church lived in a world in which supernatural causation was accepted without question, and divine or spiritual visitants were not unexpected. Such assumptions, however, have become foreign to our situation. . . . supernatural causation or intervention in the affairs of this world has become, for the majority of people, simply incredible. . . . There is no room for God as a causal factor. . . . like the Fathers, we find that the problem of Christology is intimately related with the more general problem of God's relationship with the world.[49]

At the heart of Young's rejection of classical Christology is her rejection of the biblical God.

Moreover, Jesus's identity is tied not to a generic God but to the one Creator–Covenant Lord introduced at creation and followed through the history of Israel and on to the first and second comings of Christ. Donald Macleod helpfully summarizes this God-Christ identification:

It is only in the light of this doctrine of God that we can understand the doctrine of the incarnation. When the New Testament calls Christ *theos* it means this *theos*: the God of Genesis One; the God of Abraham, Isaac and Jacob; the God of Horeb and the Burning Bush; the God of the soaring prophecies of Isaiah. When it calls him *kurios* it means that he is Jahweh, that he possesses all the attributes of the God of Israel and that his earthly story is but the continuation of that divine story which began in the Beginning and ran through the call of Abraham, the Exodus and the miracle of Mount Carmel to the mission of the last of the Prophets, John the Baptist. And the most remarkable thing about the Continuation is that the New Testament does not seem to think it remarkable at all and shows not a trace of consternation or embarrassment over being called to bear witness to this seismic modification of the Old Testament doctrine of God.[50]

Second, Scripture ties its eschatology of a "very good" creation and the kingdom of God on earth to the Son of God who came from heaven to the earth. In Ephesians, Paul explains that "before the foundation of the world" (1:4), God planned to "unite all things in [Christ], things in heaven and things on earth" (vv. 9–10). And this great reconciliation throughout creation (see Col. 1:20) takes place through the particular redemption and universal rule of Christ (Eph. 1:5–10, 20–23). So even before he created all things "very good" under the vice-regency of man, God purposed to display his glory in his creation and kingdom by giving both creation and redemption to his Son, who would come into the world to take the world to its eschatological end. In Colossians, Paul sums up the creation-kingdom-Christ connection by declaring

---

[49] Frances Young, "A Cloud of Witnesses," in *The Myth of God Incarnate*, ed. John Hick (Philadelphia: Westminster, 1977), 31–32.
[50] Donald Macleod, "The Doctrine of the Trinity: Some Preliminaries," 2, at http://www.reformation21.org/Past_Issues/April_2006/Trinity_Some_Preliminaries_/167/.

that "all things were created through him and for him . . . and in him all things hold together" (1:16–17). As Carson reminds us, "Ultimately [the] plotline [of Scripture] anticipates the restoration of goodness, even the transformation to a greater glory, of the universe gone wrong (Rom. 8:21), and arrives finally at the dawning of a new heaven and a new earth (Revelation 21–22; cf. Isa. 65:17), the home of righteousness (2 Pet. 3:13)."[51] The interpretive framework of Scripture connects this ultimate goodness and righteousness with the utterly unique and incomparable Jesus of the Bible.

Third, the image-son-Adam typology shows us that this righteous rule of God must come through a righteous, obedient man. This typological trajectory that begins in creation ends in Christ. We will look at the specific development of this typology when we transition to the six covenants that progress through the four major parts of Scripture. Here we simply need to understand that the first part of the biblical metanarrative gives us a determinative typology for understanding the identity of Christ: he is the true image-Son and last Adam. In short, the reign of Christ will be righteous because he is the exact image of God, the obedient Son of God, and the faithful Adam of a new humanity. Christ is "the image of the invisible God . . . in [whom] all the fullness of God was pleased to dwell" (Col. 1:15, 19), being "the exact imprint of his nature" (Heb. 1:3). Moreover, Jesus is the true image of God both as the "Son of the Most High" and as the Son who sits on "the throne of his father David" (Luke 1:32). Jesus is the Son loved by the Father, who "has given all things into his hand" (John 3:35; cf. 17:2), including judgment and eternal life (5:21–24), which authority the Son exercises in perfect obedience to the Father (5:19; 8:28). And this image-Son came from heaven to earth as the last Adam and covenant head who redeems a sinful people to share in his own sonship to God (Eph. 1:3–7), conforming them into his own image (Rom. 6:4; 8:29; Eph. 4:24; Col. 3:10), and bringing them into his own obedience (John 15:1–11; 1 Cor. 1:30).

Fourth, and building on the previous point, the *imago Dei* in humanity also grounds the logical plausibility of the very idea of an incarnation. Probably the most difficult question in Christology is how the two natures of Christ's deity and humanity are united in the person of the Son, given the Creator-creature distinction. How can we make sense of the orthodox confession of the church that God the Son, the second person of the Godhead took to himself a human nature without a human person, and yet not think that there is something lacking in regard to that human nature? A lot of ink has been expended on that very question, and later we will return to it in detail. However, at this stage, my point is simply this: as difficult as these concepts are, given the biblical teaching

---

[51] Carson, *Gagging of God*, 202.

on the *imago Dei*, there is an internal logic and coherence that is able to make sense of how an incarnation is possible.

As David Wells rightly insists, that which undergirds and makes sense of the incarnation and especially our understanding of the hypostatic union, i.e., how the two natures of Christ are united in the person of the divine Son, is the *imago Dei*. Even though the *imago Dei* has been understood in a variety of ways, at its heart, Wells notes, "is the idea that what constitutes humanity, what sets it apart from mere animal life, are capacities and perhaps resultant roles in creation the originals of which are to be found in God. Human nature as created is the echo of which the Creator is sound. He is the original, and we are derivative."[52] Given this fact, then, to speak of an incarnation, as incredible as it is, is not implausible since what it means to be truly human is revealed in and by the divine Son who is described as the *true* image of God. As Wells comments, "That being the case, a perfect humanity, one unspoiled by sin, would not only coalesce naturally with the divine but would, in fact, find its perfection in the divine from which it was derived. . . . The divine Word, then, was not united to a human nature that was antithetical to its own life, but rather the divine Word already possessed everything that was necessary to be human."[53]

In this way, the Scriptural teaching of humans created as the *imago Dei* is foundational to a biblical Christology. As we walk through the storyline of Scripture, we, who are created after the divine pattern, ultimately are created after the image of the Son, who in his deity is the exact "image of the invisible God" (Col. 1:15), and who in his humanity takes on our image, becomes the last Adam, the true man, and the head of a new humanity. In this way, the divine Son as "image" is the archetype, the full display and exact correspondence of God (see John 14:9; Heb. 1:3); while as the incarnate one, our Lord Jesus Christ, he is the Son incarnate so that, as Wells so aptly states, "In Christ, we see all that Adam was intended to be, but never was, all that we are not but which we will become through resurrection."[54] In this sense our creation as *imago Dei* is more fully revealed by the person and work of the incarnate Son. This is why our salvation is partly described as being conformed to the image of God's own dear Son (Rom. 8:29; 2 Cor. 3:18; 4:4; Eph. 4:21–24; Col. 3:10).

Fifth, taking the next two parts together, the biblical metanarrative moves toward the identification of Christ through the tension of *fall* and the resolution of *redemption*. We have seen that the sinful rebellion of the first, earthly image-son-Adam moved both humanity and creation away from the righteousness and goodness that God planned in the beginning. But we have also seen that this movement was not a departure or modification of God's plan but the

---

[52] Wells, *Person of Christ*, 177–178.
[53] Ibid., 178.
[54] Ibid.

predestined means for unfolding it. God chose to allow the fall of his human vice-regents and the corruption of his creation so that he might demonstrate his manifold wisdom in the manifestation of his glory: God glorifies himself through both judgment and grace, condemnation and justification, eternal destruction and eternal life. And as we just recognized from the typology rooted in creation, this is the very authority given to Jesus as the true image-Son and last Adam.

But even more revealing is that the particular tension in the "problem of forgiveness" will be resolved by *God himself through the Son himself.* God's perfection and his plan for the righteous reign of humanity over a "very good" creation require both the punishment and the forgiveness of sinful humanity. And God himself accomplishes both in Christ. It was Christ himself whom God "put forward as a propitiation by his blood" (Rom. 3:25) and who "died for the ungodly" (Rom. 5:6)—"the righteous for the unrighteous" (1 Pet. 3:18)—having "appeared once for all at the end of the ages to put away sin by the sacrifice of himself" (Heb. 9:26). And it is in Christ himself that an unrighteous humanity has now been "justified by his blood, . . . [and] saved by him from the wrath of God" (Rom. 5:9), having been reconciled to God and having "become the righteousness of God" (2 Cor. 5:19, 21) to "walk in newness of life" (Rom. 6:4). And yet, the Scriptures maintain that if such a righteous humanity is to rise out of a corrupted race to rule over his creation, God himself must do it.

Finally, the biblical metanarrative brings this redemptive resolution in Christ via the two-stage *inauguration-consummation.* We can see the overlap of "the present age" and "the age to come" by looking quickly at the re-creation and rule of humanity and the renewal of creation under that reign. Hebrews tells us *both* that those in Christ "have been sanctified through the offering of the body of Jesus Christ once for all" *and* that "by a single offering he has perfected for all time those who are being sanctified" (Heb. 10:10, 14). Paul explains in Romans that those in Christ *both* "have received the Spirit of adoption as sons" *and* "wait eagerly for adoption as sons, the redemption of [their] bodies" (Rom. 8:15, 23). And in Ephesians, Paul tells us that those in Christ *both* are "seated . . . with him in the heavenly places" above all other power and authority *and* are vulnerable to failure "by human cunning, by craftiness in deceitful schemes" because of those who still follow "the prince of the power of the air, the spirit that is now at work in the sons of disobedience" (Eph. 1:20–21; 2:2, 6; 4:14).

Moreover, the creation under the reign of Christ and his new humanity is "in the pains of childbirth until now" before the transition is complete (Rom. 8:22; see Rev. 21:1): the new creation is both here and coming. While much more can be said, here it is important to understand the importance of both eschatological elements: both the reality of inauguration and the certainty of consummation point to the identity of Christ. Simply put, because of *who* he is, Christ brought the kingdom of God in kind by his first coming and guarantees its completion at his second coming.

The most basic structure of Scripture, then, brings us to identify the person of Jesus, the Son, with God himself. Creation, fall, redemption, and inauguration-consummation work together not just to align but to equate the promised work of God and the accomplished work of Christ. The Son incarnate ushers in the kingdom of God, redeems and shepherds the people of God, and gives them the Spirit of God. And at the center stands the cross of Christ, where Scripture presents not three parties—God, Jesus, and humanity—but only two, God and sinners. John Stott helps us make sense of this drama by emphasizing that the cross does not hold "God as he is in himself (the Father), but God nevertheless, God made-man-in-Christ (the Son)."[55]

Six Covenants through the Story

The four major parts of the biblical storyline establish the authoritative framework apart from which Christ cannot be known. But these parts do not say everything. Christology does not reduce to judgments based only on the juxtaposition of texts according to each biblical epoch. A biblical Christology will do no less, but it must do more, to read the Bible on its own terms. The Bible's terms include six covenants that progressively develop in more detail all that the basic four-part framework begins to demonstrate. Each covenant belongs to a particular part/epoch of the biblical storyline and drives the plotline within each part and from one epoch to the next. In this sense, *covenant* is more than a unifying theme of Scripture or even the central narrative element necessary to understanding what the Bible reveals about Jesus. Covenant is the backbone to the entire storyline of Scripture, the relational reality that moves redemptive history forward according to God's design and final plan for humanity and all creation.

The concept of *kingdom through covenant* captures the fundamental dynamic at work as God's redemptive plan unfolds across the canon of Scripture.[56] God's kingdom comes through covenants, both by means of them and in their succession. In assembling the basic biblical framework, we saw that the kingdom of God began in the garden under the first Adam and was corrupted through sin until the last Adam inaugurated the kingdom of "the age to come."

---

[55] Stott, *Cross of Christ*, 158. As already noted, it is very important to observe that the doctrine of the Trinity is foundational in making sense of the Bible's presentation of the person of Christ as the divine persons are unfolded across the four-part structure of the Bible and the six-part progression of the biblical covenants.
[56] For a complete discussion of this point, see Gentry and Wellum, *Kingdom through Covenant*.

We now need to add that after God's initial promise in Genesis 3:15 that a man would come to restore humanity and its rule over creation, God's plan for this redemptive reign works out through election and covenant. God first chose Noah and his family to escape the flood of God's wrath and repopulate the earth. Out of all the nations, God then chose Abraham and his seed, to multiply them and make them into a great nation. When Israel, as God's son, had multiplied under Egyptian slavery, God brought them out to be his people within the land he gave them. And within the nation of Israel, God chose David to be king over his people and chose all of the Davidic kings to be his sons. Finally, God chose people from "among all the nations" in Christ (Rom. 1:5–6) to be his "holy nation, a people for his own possession" (1 Pet. 2:9).

Each election, moreover, came with a specific covenant. In short, the Bible presents each covenant as a formal relationship between two parties, God and his human partner (individual or corporate), that establishes obligations and expectations.[57] We cannot fully explore the biblical covenants here. But in this section we will cover the basic terms of each covenant and consider how it functions in the Bible's storyline. More specifically, the following discussion will pursue two goals: understanding each covenant in its immediate context, and relating each covenant to its predecessor(s). Most evangelicals agree that our triune God has one plan of salvation, centered in Christ and the new covenant, a covenantal salvation that has been foreshadowed in various ways by the preceding covenants. But the precise relationship between the covenants remains a disputed issue within evangelical theology, most notably among covenant theology and dispensationalism.[58] While this work does not attempt a resolution of those disputes, the Bible's own terms require that we make a decision and work consistently toward the identity of Christ.

The description and synthesis below understands that the Scriptures present a *plurality* of covenants (cf. Gal. 4:24; Eph. 2:12; Heb. 8:7–13) that *progressively* reveal God's one plan of salvation and which reach their fulfillment, *telos*, and terminus in Christ and the new covenant. God reverses the disastrous effects of sin and ushers in his saving reign *through*—instrumentally and diachronically—the biblical covenants. So as we trace how each covenant develops, we need to see both its continuity and its discontinuity with the previous covenant(s) to grasp the covenantal progression of the plotline aimed at the person of Christ.

Tracing the six biblical covenants through the four parts of Scripture will complete the interpretive framework we need to understand the Bible's own presentation of Jesus. Filling in the biblical metanarrative and worldview re-

---

[57] For more on the nature of covenants in Scripture, see ibid., 129–145.
[58] For a description of these theological systems and their differences, see ibid., 21–126, 591–716.

garding the redemptive-restorative reign of God himself through Christ himself will help establish the biblical warrant we need to conclude that, as the true image-son and last Adam, Jesus Christ is God the Son incarnate.

Adam and the Covenant of Creation[59]

In the garden, God established a formal relationship with Adam as his covenant partner–mediator on behalf of the entire human race, a relationship that created obligations and expectations for the two parties. God promised to give Adam and his posterity the blessing of eternal life with God in a place of perfect provision if Adam perfectly obeyed the law of God. Covenant theology speaks of the relationship in Genesis 1–2 as the "covenant of works." Many theologians, however, have questioned the *existence of a covenant* here based on the absence of the word "covenant" (*berit*),[60] and others have refuted this *kind of covenant* due to problems with the idea of Adam *working* to gain favor with God. Yet Scripture gives us at least three reasons to contend for there having been a covenant with Adam, one that is best described as the "covenant of creation."

First, the absence of the word "covenant" in Genesis 1–2 does not prevent the reality of a covenant. The immediate context and other parts of Scripture indicate that God in fact established a covenant with Adam (cf. Hos. 6:7: "But like Adam they transgressed the covenant").[61] Second, the immediate context contains covenantal elements: the Lord/vassal relationship and the obedience-disobedience motif (Gen. 2:16–17); God identifies himself by his covenantal name, Yahweh (e.g., vv. 4, 5, 7, 8); God creates Adam as God's image-bearer, which Scripture describes as a covenantal relationship.[62] Third, the canonical context reveals that the storyline of Scripture divides humanity under the headship of two individuals, Adam and Christ (Rom. 5:12–21), and the covenant headship of Christ as the last Adam in the new covenant makes little sense without the covenant headship of the first Adam.

As God's image-bearer, Adam was blessed by God and was given the mandate to rule over God's creation, to put all things under his feet (cf. Psalm 8) and to establish the pattern of God's kingdom in this world. We can call this the covenant of creation for at least three reasons: God established it within the first days of creation; he extended its terms to all that Adam and the rest of humanity were to do "over all the earth" (Gen. 1:26); and he excluded nothing on the earth from the corruption of Adam's disobedience (Rom. 5:12–14;

---

[59] For a more detailed discussion, see ibid., 177–221.

[60] *Berit* is not used until Genesis 6:18, and thus some have concluded that we should not speak of a covenant prior to Noah (see, e.g., Paul R. Williamson, *Sealed with an Oath: Covenant in God's Unfolding Purpose*, NSBT 23 [Downers Grove, IL: InterVarsity Press, 2007], 44–58).

[61] For an extended defense of this point, see Gentry and Wellum, *Kingdom through Covenant*, 147–221.

[62] For a development of these points, see ibid.

8:18–22). The Adamic covenant, then, was a covenant of creation in which God as the Creator–Covenant Lord obligated himself to Adam and all of humanity through blessing, provision, and the promise of eternal life; and he obligated humanity to multiply the divine image over all creation as his righteous vice-regents.

Yet before Adam had fathered any children, he rebelled against God, breaking the covenant of creation. And the terms of the covenant called for death and exile, the exclusion of Adam and his descendants from eternal life with God in paradise. Moreover, Adam's sin corrupted his image-bearing and sonship such that, when Adam fathered children "in his own likeness, after his image" (Gen. 5:3), his posterity spread a fallen *imago Dei* over the whole earth that was incapable of the required righteousness. All humanity would suffer exile and death as covenant breakers, and all creation would groan under their corruption, without the hope of restoration except for the *protevangelium* of Genesis 3:15—God's promise that an obedient and victorious offspring of Eve would come.

The Noahic Covenant[63]

God's gracious promise of restoration in the face of Adam's rebellion and the fall of humanity leads directly to God's covenant with Noah. In fact, Scripture presents the Noahic covenant as God's reaffirmation of his commitment to his creation and a continuation of the Adamic covenant. After describing the cycle of death among Adam's descendants that proves that the covenant of creation was broken, Scripture moves to a scene that seems to threaten God's plan for a righteous humanity over a "very good" creation. The wickedness of sin had filled all humanity and the violence of man had filled all the earth such that God determined to "'blot out man whom I have created from the face of the land, man and animals and creeping things and birds of the heavens, . . .'" (Gen. 6:7). But even so, God spared Noah and his family from the flood that "destroy[ed] all flesh in which is the breath of life under heaven" (v. 17).

God established a formal relationship with Noah as his covenant partner–mediator on behalf of the entire human race to continue the prior covenant of creation, a relationship that created obligations and expectations for the two parties. As he did with the first Adam, God blessed Noah as *another Adam*, made provision for him, and commanded him to fill the earth with humans who would have dominion over the earth (Gen. 9:1–7). And in demonstration of his self-obligation to his own creation, the Creator–Covenant Lord promised to endure the internal sinfulness of man for a time (cf. 8:21) and to never again destroy all life by an earth-consuming flood (9:8–17). This covenantal

---

[63] For a more detailed discussion, see ibid., 147–176.

commitment by God, however, did not negate the requirement for covenantal obedience by humanity. As a continuation of the Adamic covenant, the terms of the Noahic covenant required full obedience to God in all his ways.

But also like the first Adam, Noah failed to walk with God in righteousness (Gen. 9:18–28). And so sin and death would continue to ruin humanity's rule as God's vice-regents. In fact, by the time we reach Genesis 11, we have Genesis 3 all over again. The tower at Babel was a rebellious attempt by humanity to set up their own kingdom—to make a name for themselves in one place in direct opposition to God and his command that they represent him in every place over the whole earth (11:1–9).

So the Noahic covenant tells us that the promised offspring of Eve will come, but he will come through Noah's descendants. Noah himself is not the promised *Adam*. In accord with the tension in the biblical storyline as it moves from creation to fall—from goodness to corruption—the progression of God's plan from the Adamic covenant to the Noahic covenant raises the question of who can possibly stand as God's faithful covenant partner–mediator on behalf of all humanity. Scripture maintains this tension but signals its certain resolution through another call with another covenant.

The Abrahamic Covenant[64]

Scripture juxtaposes and contrasts the rebellion at Babel under the Noahic covenant (Genesis 11) with the call of Abram and God's promise to make him into a great nation to bless all the nations (Genesis 12). More specifically, God establishes a formal relationship with Abram-Abraham to make his offspring a *gôy*, i.e., a world community, a political entity, a *kingdom* under God for the sake of all humanity. Similar to the Noahic covenant, the Abrahamic covenant does not present a new plan of God for his creation but presents his original plan anew.

In Genesis 12, the storyline of Scripture recapitulates the important elements in God's original creation of human beings in Adam and his repopulation of the earth in Noah. God blesses Abraham and promises to multiply his offspring and make provision for them in the land of Canaan with the goal of a peaceful relationship between God and humanity through the restoration of the nations (Gen. 12:1–3, 6–7; cf. 15:4–5; 17:1–8; 18:18–19; 22:16–18). So as with Noah, Abraham functions as *another Adam* through whom the promised offspring of Eve will come to reverse the sin and death of the first Adam. Making this point, N. T. Wright correctly summarizes the importance of the Abrahamic covenant: "Abraham emerges within the structure of Genesis as the answer to the plight of all humankind. The line of disaster and of the 'curse,' from Adam,

---

[64] For a more detailed discussion, see ibid., 223–299.

through Cain, through the Flood to Babel, begins to be reversed when God calls Abraham and says, 'in you shall all the families of the earth be blessed.'"[65]

Yet in addition to this continuity with the Noahic covenant, Scripture develops the Abrahamic covenant with important elements of discontinuity. God *spared* Noah (and his family) to covenant with him for *repopulation* after the *destruction* of wicked humanity. In contrast, God *separates* Abraham to covenant with him for *restoration* during the *preservation* of the wicked nations. This discontinuity signals that the Abrahamic covenant functions parallel to the Adamic covenant with creation that was reaffirmed in the Noahic covenant. The Noahic covenant preserves the line for the man of promise to come and continues for the sake of every living creature "while the earth remains" (Gen. 8:21–22). Alongside this covenant of preservation, the Abrahamic covenant narrows the line of descent and the particular blessings of God to one family and nation.

The Abrahamic covenant and lineage will surely bring forth the one who will fulfill all of God's promises for humanity and creation. As with every covenant, however, Scripture describes the Abrahamic covenant as having both unconditional/unilateral and conditional/bilateral elements. The inauguration ceremony in Genesis 15 clearly communicates, by the dread symbol of a divine dismemberment (Gen. 15:7–21; cf. Jer. 34:18–20), that God unilaterally obligates himself to accomplish his promise to make Abraham and his offspring into a great nation and to give them a place to live with God in peace and prosperity. God will keep his promises regardless of what Abraham does. In keeping his covenant promises, however, God still demands complete obedience from his covenant partner (Gen. 17:1; 18:19; 22:16–18).[66] And just like Adam and Noah before him, Abraham fails to meet this demand.

The Abrahamic covenant, then, creates an antinomical tension in the coming of God's kingdom through his covenants with man. God will act unilaterally to keep his unconditional promise to bless all nations through the offspring of Abraham (Gen. 12:3), the promised offspring of Eve. *And yet*, God will always demand perfect obedience from a faithful covenant partner that sinful humanity cannot produce. Scripture keeps both of these ostensibly opposing elements at work as it narrows the offspring of Abraham to the nation of Israel.

The Covenant with Israel or "Old Covenant"[67]

According to his covenant with Abraham, God declared that he would make Abraham and his descendants into a great nation by bringing them out of four

---

[65] N. T. Wright, *The New Testament and the People of God* (Minneapolis: Fortress, 1992), 262.

[66] See Williamson, *Sealed with an Oath*, 84–91.

[67] For a more detailed discussion, see Gentry and Wellum, *Kingdom through Covenant*, 301–388.

hundred years of slavery in a foreign nation (Gen. 15:13–14). In Genesis 35, God affirms the pattern of promises he made to Abraham and his offspring to show that God is narrowing his covenant blessings and purposes to the line of Jacob, whom he had renamed Israel (32:28). The Lord himself declares and promises, "I am God Almighty: be fruitful and multiply. A nation and a company of nations shall come from you, and kings shall come from your own body. The land that I gave to Abraham and Isaac I will give to you, and I will give the land to your offspring after you" (35:11–12). So it was out of covenant loyalty to Abraham (Ex. 19:4; Deut. 7:8) that God delivered Israel out of Egyptian slavery through Moses (Ex. 3:6; cf. 2:24–25; Deut. 4:36–38). God would keep his covenant promise to bless the nations through Abraham by covenanting with the people of Israel.

God establishes a formal relationship with Israel to make them his first-born son and his kingdom people governed by his written law among the pagan nations that oppose him (Ex. 19:5–6; 20:1–17). As a nation, then, Israel functions as *another Adam* through whom the promised offspring of Eve and Abraham will come to restore God's kingdom that was corrupted by the sinful rebellion of the first Adam. And the terms of the old covenant indicate that God's kingdom must come through an obedient covenant partner. God will bless his people with life if they obey him, and he will curse them with death and destruction if they disobey him.

Yet, while the law-covenant held out the promise of life (Lev. 18:5), Israel broke the law and came under its curse of death and exile. The law was "holy and righteous and good" (Rom. 7:12), but Israel was internally corrupt with sinful desires and thus incapable of keeping the law. The law graciously provided a system of sacrifices to atone for the people's sins under Israel's covenant with God, but "it is impossible for the blood of bulls and goats to take away sins" (Heb. 10:4). Human sin requires human death. So God did not design his law-covenant with Israel to provide a permanent solution to the "problem of forgiveness" or to restore the nation from its corruption into a righteous kingdom that would spread over the earth (Gal. 3:10–11, 21–22).

The old covenant, rather, functions in Scripture to heighten the antinomical tension in the coming of God's kingdom through his covenants with man. God continues in his unilateral determination to keep his unconditional promise to bring forth the offspring of Abraham, now through an Israelite. *And yet*, by breaking the bilateral terms of the covenant, Israel proves that it cannot produce such a man to be the obedient son and faithful covenant partner that God demands. The Old Testament prophets tell us that the temporary covenant with Israel would become the "old covenant" that points to the coming of a permanent "new covenant" (see Jer. 31:31–34; 2 Cor. 3:5–11). Looking back on the law-covenant, the New Testament apostles reveal that it functions to intensify sin and prepare God's people for his righteousness to come apart from the law, in a man "from heaven" (Rom. 3:21; 5:20–21; 7:13; 1 Cor. 15:47–49; Gal. 4:4).

But before God's kingdom comes through this new and better covenant in this man who will descend from heaven (cf. John 3:13), the Scriptures tell us that he will be a son of David, the king of Israel.

The Davidic Covenant[68]

Within the covenant with Israel, God covenants with King David and his sons by making two main promises: to relate to the Davidic kings as a father to a son (2 Sam. 7:14; 1 Chron. 17:13; cf. Psalm 2; 89:26–27) and to establish David's house forever (2 Sam. 7:12–16; 1 Chron. 17:11–14). The sonship that was applied to the nation of Israel (Ex. 4:22–23; cf. Hos. 11:1) is now applied to David and his sons. As an individual, the Davidic king takes on the representative role of Israel as a nation. The king of Israel becomes the administrator and mediator of God's covenant with Israel, thus representing God's rule to the people and representing the people as a whole to God (2 Sam. 7:22–24). And this representative role of the Davidic king takes on significant implications for the coming of God's kingdom when God himself promises, "your house and your kingdom shall be made sure forever before me. Your throne shall be established forever" (v. 16).

The eternal reign of the Davidic king, moreover, takes on a universal dimension. The Davidic covenant further narrows and defines the lineage of the promised offspring of Eve and Abraham: he will be not just any Israelite, but a king of Israel and a son of David. But the Davidic king also inherits the role of Adam as son of God and covenant head of all humanity. Walter Kaiser rightly argues that, in 2 Samuel 7:19b, David refers to the promises God makes to him as "the charter by which humanity will be directed."[69] David himself understands what this covenant means for the entire human race: the Davidic king's eternal rule on the throne of Israel will effect God's rule over the entire world as God has intended it for humanity since he created Adam in the garden. God's plan to restore humanity's vice-regent role in creation by making Israel into a great nation will be accomplished in the person of a Davidic king who will reign forever over all nations (see Psalms 2; 8; 45; 72).

The Davidic covenant, however, also carries forward the antinomical ten-

---

[68] For a more detailed discussion, see ibid., 389–431.
[69] See Walter C. Kaiser Jr., "The Blessing of David, The Charter for Humanity," in *The Law and the Prophets: Old Testament Studies Prepared in Honor of Oswald Thompson Allis*, ed. John H. Skilton (Nutley, NJ: P&R, 1974), 311–314; cf. William J. Dumbrell, *Covenant and Creation: A Theology of Old Testament Covenants* (Carlisle, UK: Paternoster, 1984), 151–152.

sion in the coming of God's kingdom through his covenants with man.[70] God continues in his unilateral determination to keep his unconditional promise to bring forth the offspring of Abraham, now more specifically a Davidic king, who will reign under God over the whole world. *And yet*, as with God's previous covenant partners—Adam, Noah, Abraham, and Israel as a nation—every Davidic son–king fails to rule in the perfect obedience and covenant loyalty that God demands. And so the curse of the old covenant with Israel would carry the king and the people into exile for their idolatry. *But still*, Isaiah prophesies under the old covenant with Israel that the Davidic king, who is identified as the "servant of the LORD,"[71] will restore Zion from exile (Isa. 2:1–5), delight in the "fear of the LORD" (11:1–10), represent the Lord in justice and righteousness (11:3–5), and become a banner to the nations (see 11:10), teaching and ruling them (42:1, 3–4; 49:1, 6). God will make a new and "everlasting covenant" based on "the sure mercies [or faithfulness] performed by David" (55:3).[72]

The Davidic covenant, then, functions to heighten both the hopes of God's covenants with man and the questions regarding what kind of man can fulfill those hopes. God will provide a righteous king for Israel and all the nations. But if Israel cannot produce the promised Davidic son–king and "servant of the LORD," then where will he come from? God will bring forth the long-awaited offspring of Eve-Abraham-David to restore humanity's vice-regency over all creation. But if all of the offspring down the entire chosen line of descent have failed, then who can walk with God in perfect obedience and covenant loyalty? God will raise up a man to represent the entire human race in righteousness. But if all *other Adams* after the first Adam have been disqualified because of their inherited corruption, then who will the "last Adam" be?

The storyline of Scripture finally answers these questions with the coming of Christ and the new covenant.

The New Covenant[73]

Tracing the progression of the biblical covenants now allows us to set the new covenant in Christ at the end of a covenantal-typological trajectory. And this

---

[70] Most biblical theologians rightly emphasize the royal grant style of the Davidic covenant; the issue is whether it is *solely* this kind of covenant (see, e.g., Craig A. Blaising and Darrell L. Bock, *Progressive Dispensationalism* [Wheaton, IL: BridgePoint, 1993], 159–165; Michael S. Horton, *God of Promise: Introducing Covenant Theology* [Grand Rapids, MI: Baker, 2006], 43–50). For a demonstration that the Davidic covenant includes elements of both a royal grant and a suzerain-vassal covenant, see Gentry and Wellum, *Kingdom through Covenant*, 389–431.
[71] For a persuasive argument that the "servant of the LORD" in Isaiah is the Davidic king, see, e.g., Daniel I. Block, "My Servant David: Ancient Israel's Vision of the Messiah," in *Israel's Messiah in the Bible and the Dead Sea Scrolls*, ed. Richard S. Hess and M. Daniel Carroll (Grand Rapids, MI: Baker Academic, 2003), 17–56; J. Alec Motyer, *The Prophecy of Isaiah: An Introduction and Commentary* (Downers Grove, IL: InterVarsity Press, 1993).
[72] Peter Gentry's translation. *Hasdê dāwîd* in Isaiah 55:3 is often translated the "sure mercies for David" or "faithfulness promised to David." It is better to see that David is the agent or subject, not the object, and thus the phase should be translated "sure mercies [or faithfulness] performed by David." See Gentry and Wellum, *Kingdom through Covenant*, 389–427.
[73] For a more detailed discussion, see Gentry and Wellum, *Kingdom through Covenant*, 433–564.

terminal position is key to understanding not just the new covenant but all of the covenants before it. One biblical covenant leads to the next, and *each plays its part* in progressing the plan of God for humanity and creation. But God's kingdom comes through the covenants as an *integrated scheme* that finds its fulfillment, terminus, and *telos* in the new covenant (see Jer. 31:29–34; cf. Luke 22:20; 2 Corinthians 3; Hebrews 8; 10). The Old Testament prophets anticipated a new and everlasting covenant that would bring with it the new creation, the Spirit of God, and the saving rule and reign of God among the nations.[74] And the postexilic prophets expected that the new covenant would have a purpose similar to the covenant with Israel: the new covenant would bring the Abrahamic blessing back into the present experience of Israel and the nations.[75] Yet along with this continuity, the new covenant would also bring significant discontinuity. Three main features will demonstrate what is new in the new covenant. And considering this newness will help us understand the uniqueness of God's new covenant partner–mediator.

First, the new covenant changes the *structure* of God's covenant people. Under the old covenant, God dealt with his people in a mediated or "tribal" fashion.[76] Despite a remnant theme, the Old Testament pictures God working with his people as a tribal grouping whose knowledge of God and whose relations with God were uniquely dependent on specially endowed leaders. Under the old covenant there was a strong emphasis on the Spirit of God being poured out, not on each believer but distinctively on prophets, priests, kings, and a few designated special leaders. Given this hierarchical structure of the covenant community, when these leaders obeyed God, the entire nation benefited; when they disobeyed, the entire nation suffered. But as D. A. Carson observes, the prophet Jeremiah signals a structural shift in the covenant community:

> In short, Jeremiah understood that the new covenant would bring some dramatic changes. The tribal nature of the people of God would end, and the new covenant would bring with it a new emphasis on the distribution of the knowledge of God down to the level of each member of the covenant community. Knowledge of God would no longer be mediated through specially endowed leaders, for *all* of God's covenant people would know him, from the least to the greatest. Jeremiah is not concerned to say there would be no teachers under the new covenant, but to remove from leaders that distinctive mediatorial role that made the knowledge of God among the people at large a secondary knowledge, a mediated knowledge.[77]

---

[74] On this point, see ibid.

[75] See ibid., 433–564, 644–652.

[76] See D. A. Carson, *Showing the Spirit: A Theological Exposition of 1 Corinthians 12–14* (Grand Rapids, MI: Baker, 1987), 150–158; cf. idem, "Evangelicals, Ecumenism, and the Church," in *Evangelical Affirmations*, ed. Kenneth S. Kantzer and Carl F. H. Henry (Grand Rapids, MI: Zondervan, 1990), 347–385.

[77] Carson, *Showing the Spirit*, 152. It is clear from the context that the knowledge spoken of here is a salvific knowledge (see Dumbrell, *Covenant and Creation*, 177–178; House, *Old Testament Theology*, 317–321). This is *not* to

The new covenant raises every member of the new covenant to the same relationship with God, through the universal distribution of the Spirit (see Joel 2:28–32; Acts 2). Being the first to be filled with the Spirit of God (see Isa. 11:1–3; 49:1–2; 61:1ff.), the new covenant mediator would then pour out his Spirit on all flesh, namely, all those within the covenant community (see Ezek. 11:19–20; 36:25–27; Joel 2:28–32; cf. Num. 11:27–29).[78] And because all those under the new covenant enjoy the promised gift of the eschatological Holy Spirit (see Eph. 1:13–14), Paul explains that, "Anyone who does not have the Spirit of Christ does not belong to him" (Rom. 8:9).

Second, the new covenant changes the *nature* of God's covenant people. The prophet Jeremiah distinguishes between the old covenant and the new covenant based on the heart condition of the covenant members (Jer. 31:31–34). Whereas only a remnant under the old law-covenant truly knew the Lord, God changes the heart of every new covenant member: "I will write [my law] on their hearts. And I will be their God, and they shall be my people. And no longer shall each one teach his neighbor . . . , for they shall all know me, from the least of them to the greatest, declares the LORD" (Jer. 31:33–34). Describing the law as written on the heart mirrors "circumcision of the heart" (cf. Deut. 30:6; cf. Deut. 10:16; Jer. 4:4; 9:25–26), which minimally but not exclusively refers to regeneration (Rom. 2:29). This does not mean that no one in the Old Testament ever experienced regeneration. But under the new covenant, God's people will no longer be a mixed community—"not all who are descended from Israel belong to Israel" (Rom. 9:6)[79]—but the entire community will be regenerate and obedient from the heart.[80] The Spirit of God who is distributed universally under the new covenant enables every member to follow God's word, helping them to be covenant keepers and not covenant breakers.[81]

Third, the new covenant changes the *sacrifice* made for God's covenant people. The old covenant provided for the forgiveness of sins through a system of animal sacrifices. But "it is impossible for the blood of bulls and goats to take away sins" (Heb. 10:4). The old covenant sacrifices were designed to remind God's covenant people of their sinfulness through repetition. The sacrifice under the new covenant, however, was offered once for all time because

---

say that the new covenant is not a mediated covenant; it is mediated, in and through Christ. The point is that the new covenant he mediates is structurally different than the previous covenant communities.

[78] On this point, see Max Turner, "Holy Spirit," in *NDBT*, 551–558; David F. Wells, *God the Evangelist: How the Holy Spirit Works to Bring Men and Women to Faith* (Grand Rapids, MI: Eerdmans, 1987), 1–4; Geerhardus Vos, "The Eschatological Aspect of the Pauline Conception of the Spirit," in *Redemptive History and Biblical Interpretation: The Shorter Writings of Geerhardus Vos*, ed. Richard B. Gaffin Jr. (Phillipsburg, NJ: P&R, 1980), 91–125; Hoekema, *Bible and the Future*, 55–67.

[79] Under the old covenant, both the elect and non-elect within Israel received the covenant sign of circumcision and both were viewed as full covenant members in the national sense. It was only the believers, however, the remnant, who were the spiritual seed of Abraham, the true Israel, the "Israel of God" in a salvific sense (cf. Rom. 2:28–29; Gal. 6:15–16).

[80] For a more detailed discussion, see Gentry and Wellum, *Kingdom through Covenant*, 483–530, 644–652.

[81] On this point, see Thomas R. Schreiner, *Romans*, BECNT (Grand Rapids, MI: Baker, 1998), 395–468.

it was sufficient to remove the sins of every member of the covenant community (vv. 12–17). As prophesied under the old covenant, the sacrifice of the new covenant mediator himself brings the promise of God himself, that "I will remember their sins and their lawless deeds no more" (Heb. 10:17; cf. Jer. 31:33–34). In the Old Testament, "remembering" is not simple recall (cf. Gen. 8:1; 1 Sam. 1:19). That God "will remember their sins no more" means that no action against sin will need to be taken under the new covenant. In short, based on the single sacrifice of the new covenant, all of its members experience the full and complete forgiveness of all sins.[82]

By changing the structure and nature of God's covenant people and the sacrifice made on their behalf, the new covenant helps us understand what it means for Jesus to be its mediator. The newness of the new covenant helps explain the uniqueness of Christ.

The person of Christ is unique as the man who fulfills all of the promises and types working through the biblical covenants. For example, the New Testament presents Jesus as the long-awaited typological fulfillment of the offspring of Eve (Gen. 3:15), who crushes Satan by a single sacrificial death, setting a new humanity free from the corruption and death of sin. Jesus is the true offspring of Abraham who received the promise of God to be a blessing to all the nations, which he accomplishes by redeeming his new covenant people from the curse of the old covenant and by giving them the Spirit (Gal. 3:10–18).[83] And Jesus is the promised Son of David who is seated on the throne of heaven above all other powers and dominion, ruling over all nations and all things for the sake of his new covenant people (Eph. 1:20–23; 2:4–7).

The person of Christ is unique as a man who is identified with God himself. For example, as just observed, Christ has ascended to the throne of heaven and reigns as the king of God's own kingdom, yet the Scriptures are clear that God does not share his throne. God does delegate vice-regent authority to humanity on earth, but he alone sits on the throne of heaven (cf. Revelation 4). Even though he is the Son of David, this king of promise will also be David's Lord and will share in the divine rule (Ps. 110:1; cf. Matt. 22:41–46), even bearing the very titles and names of God himself: "Wonderful Counselor, Mighty God, Everlasting Father, Prince of Peace" (Isa. 9:6). And still, Paul boldly and clearly proclaims that the person of Christ has taken his place on the throne of God, "far above all rule and authority and power and dominion, and above every name that is named, not only in this age but also in the one to come" (Eph. 1:21).

But perhaps what identifies Christ with God most clearly is the full and

---

[82] See Dumbrell, *Covenant and Creation*, 181–185.

[83] For a more detailed discussion, see Thomas R. Schreiner, *Paul, Apostle of God's Glory in Christ: A Pauline Theology* (Downers Grove, IL: InterVarsity Press, 2001), 73–85.

complete forgiveness of sins. In the beginning, humanity is at covenantal rest with God, who pronounces that all things are "very good." Immediately following the original sin of Adam, however, humanity falls into covenantal unrest, alienated from God and condemned. And while the successive biblical covenants promise a restoration of covenantal harmony with increasing specificity, each also increases the covenantal tension by demonstrating that there is no man on earth who is qualified to forgive sins and establish a covenant of peace with God. On certain occasions even before the cross, however, Jesus exercised the authority given to him by the Father to pronounce, "your sins are forgiven," for those who had faith in who he is (Matt. 9:2, 5; Luke 7:48). And Paul tells us both that "there is one mediator between God and men, the man Christ Jesus . . ." (1 Tim. 2:5) and that in Christ, God himself was reconciling the world to himself, not counting their sins against them (see 2 Cor. 5:19).

By identifying the person of Christ with God himself, then, the new covenant resolves the tension in the biblical storyline that serves both redemption and revelation. As the biblical covenants progress, the plan of God for humanity and all creation becomes more clear and yet more constrained to a set of antinomical propositions: God will keep his unconditional promise to redeem humanity through the offspring of Eve-Abraham-David, yet humanity cannot produce this true image-son-Adam; God himself will save his people, yet a man will redeem them and sit on God's throne. The terms and function of the new covenant reveal that the man Christ Jesus comes as the exact representation of God, the perfectly obedient Son, and the faithful last Adam *precisely because he comes "from heaven,"* not as part of the original now sinful humanity that is "from the earth" (1 Cor. 15:47). And this same Jesus brings the redeemed kingdom of God himself *precisely because he is God the Son.*

Covenantal Progression for Authoritative Identification

Working through the six biblical covenants, God moves his one plan for humanity and all creation from his initial promises in the Adamic covenant to their fulfillment in Christ and the new covenant. In creation, the first major part-epoch of the drama to unfold, God obligates himself to creation in general and to humanity in particular and never turns back. The Creator–Covenant Lord who set humanity over a "very good" creation responds in holy wrath to the rebellion of his vice-regents by destroying them and all life corrupted by them—but not completely. God's curse under the terms of the covenant with creation moves the plotline of Scripture from creation to fall. But God covenants with Noah to preserve the line for the man of promise to come who will restore all things. And with the Noahic covenant, God has already moved the drama of Scripture into redemption by his promise to preserve the earth until his plan is accomplished. God chooses to covenant with Abraham, Israel, and then the Davidic kings not to *find* the true image-Son and last Adam but to bring him forth.

By covenanting with humanity in more specific relationships, the Creator–Covenant Lord does not labor to redesign his original plan that has failed. Through the development of one covenant into the next, rather, God constructs the relational realities necessary to rightly identify the one who will complete God's design for his glory in his creation. The entire covenantal scheme must be considered as it develops through creation, fall, and redemption and into inauguration-consummation if we are to understand fully who Jesus is as the final mediator for men and covenant partner with God. Only by placing the new covenant in Christ at the end of the Bible's covenantal-typological trajectory can we see most fully Jesus's identity, which is his identification with God himself.

Only this particular covenantal progression along these particular part-epochs of the biblical storyline will reveal the true identity of Christ. The Lord of history has worked covenantally, successively, and progressively throughout each epoch in history to both redeem a people for himself and reveal himself to them as their God. But the divine framework is not coextensive with the divine revelation. In fact, the structure of the storyline raises as many questions as it answers. For example: What exactly does it mean that the man Jesus is identified with God himself? If God's final covenant partner–mediator is God the Son, then how can he also be the man Jesus? How does the man Jesus come both "from heaven" and from the chosen line of sinful humanity? And how is one who is identified in any way with sinful humanity able to redeem them and make them into a new humanity? To answer these questions and more, and to continue building the biblical warrant necessary for a contemporary Christology, we must now read *what* the Bible says according to *how* the Bible says it—on its own epochal-covenantal terms.

FOUR

THE IDENTITY OF JESUS FROM

THE STORYLINE OF SCRIPTURE

As the Creator–Covenant Lord, God has moved throughout history to both redeem a people for himself and reveal himself to his people. As the Lord of Scripture—both its subject and its object—God has provided and preserved the written revelation of his redemption in a particular form that shapes every reading. To understand what God has revealed in his word, we must read every text according to the Bible's own epochal-covenantal terms.

As we have seen in the last chapter, the four biblical part-epochs fit together and the six biblical covenants progress through them to provide an authoritative structure to the storyline of Scripture. Moving from creation to inauguration-consummation and from the covenant of creation to the new covenant in Christ, the biblical metanarrative provides the context for understanding the smaller stories along the way. So it is along *this* way that we must read Scripture—following the texts along the typological plotline laid down by the progression of one covenant into the next through the epochal shifts that unfold to reveal the sin and rebellion of humanity and the redemption and reconciliation of God. And the path along this interpretive storyline leads us in line with and to the consummation of God's plan for humanity and all creation.

When readings are faithful to the Bible's own terms, each text and each episode within the metanarrative plays its role to meet the expectations established by the storyline itself. The promised true image-Son and last Adam will come to represent God exactly, obey him perfectly, and live in covenant with him faithfully as the mediator of a new and eternal covenant for the sake of a new humanity. God himself will act sovereignly and unilaterally to save and recreate this new humanity from his throne in heaven. And the promised

Messiah himself ("Christ" in the New Testament) will redeem this people from their sins to sit on the throne of God in heaven. Christ will inaugurate God's own kingdom on the earth in "this present age" to then consummate his kingdom throughout a new earth in the "age to come."

To understand the identity of Christ Jesus when he arrives in *this* storyline of Scripture, then, we must read the New Testament texts according to their terminal position: the last epoch that sees the inauguration of God's kingdom and the new covenant between God and man with terms for their reconciliation. In pursuit of biblical warrant for the present Christological work, the previous chapter constructed the interpretive framework necessary for the exegetical and theological task undertaken in this and the next chapters of Part II. Here we need to press for greater biblical warrant by considering key texts in the New Testament that shed light on the contours of Jesus's identity. Read within the Bible's own interpretive framework, these texts will identify Jesus as both the divine Son of God and the human Messiah-Christ promised to come from God.

Both Jesus and his apostles understood the uniqueness of the Christ to come, and bore witness to him. As we come upon their Christological conclusions in the New Testament at the end of the biblical metanarrative, it is crucial for biblical warrant that we note *how* they came to identify the Christ. The Christology of the first century followed the same structured storyline of Scripture that we must follow for a Christology for today. Jesus and his apostles followed the epochal shifts and covenantal progression of redemptive history up to their own place in the plotline.

Jesus understood that he came as the promised Christ and the eternal Son of the Father. He did not see himself and his role in redemptive history apart from all that the triune God had been doing in the world from its original creation. Jesus knew, rather, that he came as the one sent by his Father to accomplish the entire divine plan for the vice-regent rule of a righteous humanity over a "very good" creation. And Jesus understood that in him all of the promises maintained throughout all of the covenantal hostility between God and man would be fulfilled so that the Creator–Covenant Lord himself could dwell with man in covenantal peace. Jesus knew that he would bring the promised kingdom of God and that as the Son of God he would redeem a people for that kingdom. In sum, the New Testament gives us Jesus's own witness that he came as both God and man. More specifically, Jesus understood that he came as the Christ who is God the Son who has become incarnate according to the Scriptures, thus fulfilling God's eternal plan.

And the men that Jesus authorized to continue bearing witness that he is *this* Christ also continued to think and speak in terms of the metanarrative coming through the Old Testament Scriptures.[1] In fact, Jesus's self-identification and self-witness grounded the apostolic identification and witness to Jesus as both God and man. The New Testament writings form a pattern that puts the man Jesus Christ at the center of divine redemption and revelation as God the Son who came to reconcile humanity and all creation to himself (cf. Eph. 1:7–10; Col. 1:15–20). Because the New Testament presents the identity of Jesus in accord with the structure and storyline of the Old Testament, many theologians refer to the whole of Scripture as *Christocentric*. The entire plan of God for humanity and all of creation centers in the person of Christ. But because God's plan unfolds progressively through the development of epochs and covenants, we must also recognize that Scripture is *Christotelic*: The entire plan of God moves to its conclusion in Christ. The focus of the apostolic witness in the New Testament and the key to their understanding of Jesus's identity is who the Christ would be according to the redemptive drama unfolding out of the Old Testament. In sum, the apostolic Christology is concerned with where Jesus came from, why he came, and what he has accomplished in his coming according to the Scriptures. And in short, all of these parts to the epochal-covenantal equation add up to identify Jesus as God the Son incarnate.

As we consider the self-understanding of Jesus and the apostolic understanding of his identity, the thesis of this chapter—and of this entire work of Christology—is that *Jesus is God the Son incarnate*. The particulars and implications of this identity will be developed later, especially in Part IV. But to have the necessary biblical warrant for those final conclusions, we need to listen to the witness of Jesus himself and of his apostles. First we will consider the implicit and explicit witness of Jesus to his own identity by considering how he understood certain events in his life, his relationship to the Father, and his place in the plan and purpose of God. Then we will take up four key New Testament texts that demonstrate who the apostles think Jesus is according to how his teaching and works aligned with the specific promises and expectations for the coming of God's kingdom and the redemption of God's people.[2]

---

[1] For a helpful discussion regarding the nature and importance of apostolic authority for the nature and importance of the Bible's authority, see Herman N. Ridderbos, *Redemptive History and the New Testament Scriptures*, trans. H. De Jongste, rev. Richard B. Gaffin Jr., Biblical and Theological Studies (Phillipsburg, NJ: P&R, 1988).

[2] For a similar development of biblical Christology, see Richard Bauckham, *Jesus and the God of Israel: God Crucified and Other Studies on the New Testament's Christology of Divine Identity* (Grand Rapids, MI: Eerdmans, 2008). Bauckham rejects the evolutionary and developmental approaches to Christology in contemporary scholarship. An *evolutionary* approach represents the Enlightenment and classic liberal theology, which argued that the earliest Christology evolved by adding on new ideas and claims that were not found in the historical Jesus but were later placed on his lips by the church. A *developmental* approach argues that the earliest Christology was simply the outworking of what was always there in principle. Instead, Bauckham argues for a divine identity Christology, namely that the New Testament authors related Jesus to the strict monotheism of the Old Testament by including him within the divine *identity* rather than as a second, separate "divine" figure. Given the strict monotheism of Israel, to identify Jesus with the name, character, and works of Yahweh is indeed staggering and it helps explain how

The Self-Understanding of Jesus

Did Jesus understand himself to be God the Son incarnate? What is the biblical evidence that Jesus self-identified as the promised Messiah-Christ, the man who would come to do the works of God himself? Before we answer these questions, it is necessary to make an important distinction. We must distinguish between Jesus's self-consciousness and his self-identity.[3] *Self-consciousness* is a psychological term that refers to a person's inner awareness, which includes multiple aspects, such as moral and religious desires, fears, joys, and anxieties. Most acknowledge that access to a person's self-consciousness is nearly impossible, especially in the case of historical individuals who no longer can be interviewed. If we are trying to determine Jesus's self-consciousness, we will be disappointed or deceived because it is simply not available to us.[4]

Instead, we should think in terms of Jesus's self-identity/understanding. We do have access to what a person thinks about himself because, barring disability or deceit, people tend to act according to their self-identity. So we can interpret a person's words and deeds in order to understand that person's self-understanding of who they are. But even with self-identity we must be careful to interpret what the person says and does within the proper context. Generally, it is doubtful that we ever know the entire context of an event in a person's life. Apart from a clear and explicit statement, then, we usually lack certainty in our interpretation of another person's self-identity. But regarding the self-identity of Jesus, we have all the context we need. Jesus's self-understanding of his person and purpose comes to us within the storyline of Scripture that forms the entire interpretive framework in which Jesus understands his own identity. It is both ironic and gracious that the most complex person in history should be made known to us so clearly through the revealed and written word of God.

---

monotheistic Jews could identify Jesus with Yahweh and view him as God-equal with Yahweh. Bauckham's view also stands against much of contemporary scholarship. He rightly argues that the entire New Testament views Jesus in the highest of terms. In addition, Bauckham's view avoids the misleading dichotomy between a "functional" and "ontological" Christology. As these terms have been used, a "functional" Christology interprets various texts as affirming that Jesus exercises the *functions* of divine lordship, but they do not affirm that he is *ontologically* deity (e.g., Oscar Cullmann, *The Christology of the New Testament*, trans. Shirley C. Guthrie and Charles A. M. Hall [London: SCM, 1959], 3–4). This dichotomy has been a crucial way that many biblical scholars set New Testament Christology over against Chalcedonian Christology. As the story goes, in Chalcedon there was an unbiblical preoccupation with the *nature* or ontology of Jesus, not his function. The Patristic era was too indebted to Greek philosophy thus modifying New Testament Christology. But, as Bauckham shows, this construction is false. To speak of God's identity and Christ's *divine identity*, is to say something about who he is *and* what he does. God's sovereign rule is a function of who he is as the true God, and Jesus's participation in God's rule is not just a matter of what Jesus does but of who Jesus is in relation to God. This entails, then, that there is much more continuity between New Testament Christology and Patristic Christological formulation.

[3] For this distinction, see David Wells, *The Person of Christ: A Biblical and Historical Analysis of the Incarnation*, Foundations for Faith (Westchester, IL: Crossway, 1984), 36–37; cf. J. D. G. Dunn, *Christology in the Making: A New Testament Inquiry into the Origins of the Doctrine of the Incarnation*, 2nd ed. (Grand Rapids, MI: Eerdmans, 1996), 22–33.

[4] Contra Dunn in *Christology in the Making*, 22–33. In seeking to answer the question, "Did Jesus speak or think of himself as God's Son?," Dunn constantly frames the discussion in terms of "Jesus' consciousness of divinity" or "Jesus' messianic consciousness" (ibid., 23), and seemingly equates self-consciousness and self-understanding (ibid., 25). These two cognitive phenomena, however, are significantly different, and it is a mistake to conflate them, especially in the task of interpretation.

Jesus's Implicit Witness to Himself

In one sense, Jesus's entire life bore witness to who he understood himself to be. But to bring his self-identity into focus, it will be helpful to consider the five most significant aspects of his time in "this present age": his baptism, his life and ministry, his death and resurrection, the worship he received, and the kingdom he inaugurated. As we will see, Jesus understood himself to be God the Son incarnate so clearly that even his actions implied this particular divine-human identity.[5]

THE BAPTISM OF JESUS

Jesus came to the Jordan and John the Baptist with the understanding that "it is fitting for us to fulfill all righteousness" (Matt. 3:15). And upon his baptism, "immediately he went up from the water, and behold, the heavens were opened to him, and he saw the Spirit of God descending like a dove and coming to rest on him; and behold, a voice from heaven said, 'This is my beloved Son, with whom I am well pleased'" (vv. 16–17). Jesus knew that to have the Spirit from the Father for the sake of righteousness signaled that he was the promised Messiah and that the messianic age had dawned—an age identified, as we saw in previous chapters, with God's sovereign, saving rule (Isa. 61:1–2; Luke 4:16–21; cf. Ezekiel 34; Jonah 2:9).[6] As such, to be the Spirit-anointed Messiah according to the storyline of Scripture is to be identified with God himself, who must act to fulfill the Old Testament expectation of redemption and restoration (Isa. 9:6–7).

Significantly, the Gospel accounts make the man Jesus the recipient of the divine action at his baptism and focus our attention on Jesus's understanding of the event: "he saw the heavens being torn open and the Spirit descending on him" (Mark 1:10). Jesus joined other people in John's "baptism of repentance" (Acts 13:24) to sympathize and align himself with their plight in his ministry of reconciliation between God and man. At the same time, however, God spoke to *this* man to declare, "You are my beloved Son; with you I am well pleased" (Mark 1:11). As a combination of Psalm 2:7 and Isaiah 42:1,[7] these words confirm that Jesus heard the Father tell him directly that he is the Son-King who will bring justice and righteousness to all the nations through the sovereign

---

[5] For the important distinction between the implicit and explicit disclosure of Jesus's self-identification, see Wells, *Person of Christ*, 37; Dunn, *Christology in the Making*, 22–25.

[6] See R. T. France, *The Gospel of Matthew*, NICNT (Grand Rapids, MI: Eerdmans, 2007), 121–122; D. A. Carson, *Matthew*, in *EBC*, vol. 8 (Grand Rapids, MI: Zondervan, 1984), 106–110; Thomas R. Schreiner, *New Testament Theology: Magnifying God in Christ* (Grand Rapids, MI: Baker, 2008), 172–173; Max Turner, *The Holy Spirit and Spiritual Gifts: In the New Testament Church and Today* (Peabody, MA: Hendrickson, 1997), 19–30; Sinclair B. Ferguson, *The Holy Spirit*, Contours of Christian Theology (Downers Grove, IL: InterVarsity Press, 1996), 45–52; Graham A. Cole, *He Who Gives Life: The Doctrine of the Holy Spirit*, Foundations of Evangelical Theology (Wheaton, IL: Crossway, 2007), 149–177.

[7] See France, *Matthew*, 123–124; Carson, *Matthew*, 106–110; Schreiner, *New Testament Theology*, 172–173.

and saving reign of the Creator–Covenant Lord himself.[8] This event certainly signals a functional identity with God. But given Jesus's virginal conception (Matt. 1:18–25; Luke 1:26–38), the typological significance of his status as the "beloved" (*agapētos*) Son, and his ability to inaugurate the kingdom rule of God, the baptism of Jesus also implicitly bears witness to his ontological identification with God (see also Matt. 11:25–27).[9]

In the event of his baptism and the affirmation of the Father, then, the New Testament presents Jesus with the self-understanding that he comes as the promised Davidic Son–King to fulfill God's covenantal promises that culminate in the coming of God himself to save a people for himself. As David Wells comments, "It was visibly signaled and audibly declared. And the Synoptic authors plainly wanted their readers to understand this."[10] Even at his baptism and the beginning of his earthly ministry, Jesus self-identified as God the Son incarnate, the one man anointed and able to do what only God can do.[11]

THE LIFE AND MINISTRY OF JESUS

Not only at his baptism but also throughout his life and ministry, Jesus understood himself to be the eternal Son in unique relation to the Father, and the only man to share the authority and power of God himself. While we cannot here consider every work of Christ between his baptism and ascension, Matthew gives us a clue that much of Jesus's ministry was encapsulated in his teaching and miracles. On two occasions, Jesus "went throughout all Galilee, teaching in their synagogues and proclaiming the gospel of the kingdom and healing every disease and every affliction among the people" (Matt. 4:23; cf. 9:35). As Murray Harris observes, Matthew carefully places the two verses in the narrative as an *inclusio* to bookend and characterize Jesus's ministry up to his death.[12] And we must also recognize that the New Testament presents the works of Jesus as qualitatively (not just quantitatively) greater than everything that preceded him.

In short, Jesus's teaching (Matthew 5–7) and healing/miracles (Matthew

---

[8] See France, *Matthew*, 119–121; Carson, *Matthew*, 107–108.

[9] See Carson, *Matthew*, 109–110.

[10] Wells, *Person of Christ*, 39.

[11] This divine-human identity affirmed at Jesus's baptism is reaffirmed at his transfiguration (Matt. 17:1–8; Mark 9:2–8; Luke 9:28–36). Although many have questioned it, there is no reason to deny the authenticity of this account, where Jesus is "transfigured" before his disciples (see Carson, *Matthew*, 383–384; Robert Reymond, *Jesus, Divine Messiah: The New Testament Witness* [Phillipsburg, NJ: P&R, 1990], 316–325). The transfiguration fits literarily and logically in the biblical narrative. The only reason to reject its historicity is to assert that Jesus had no understanding of his deity or preexistence. But such an assertion is an assumption about the issue in debate. Within the plotline of Scripture, there is no reason to doubt the historical reality of Jesus's transfiguration. And given this event, it seems clear that Jesus understands himself to be the Messiah-Christ, the suffering servant, God's Son both functionally and ontologically, one who is superior to all the Old Testament forerunners represented by Moses and Elijah. Jesus understands himself to be uniquely different and in another category altogether. For a helpful discussion of the transfiguration, see Wells, *Person of Christ*, 39–40; Reymond, *Jesus, Divine Messiah*, 316–325.

[12] See Murray J. Harris, *Three Crucial Questions about Jesus* (Grand Rapids, MI: Baker, 1994), 82–83.

8–9) are set within the context of the kingdom of heaven to imply that Jesus is God the Son incarnate. Jesus's teaching ministry highlights the authority he shares with God himself. It is through his teaching (in part) that Jesus brings the kingdom of God into this world in "this present age." Jesus is not presented as a mere man—even a sinless man—who is specially endowed by the Spirit with incredible wisdom and power. The Old Testament brings forth numerous Spirit-empowered men who performed mighty works of God (e.g., Moses, Elijah). And in the New Testament, the apostles are commanded "to heal every disease and every affliction" (Matt. 10:1) and to teach and preach (28:20). The crucial difference, however, is that none of these forerunners or followers of Jesus inaugurated God's long-awaited and promised kingdom in their own words and works. But Jesus did, placing him in a different category than any previous prophet, priest, or king. And everything that the apostles would say and do later was based solely on the authorization and power they received from Jesus (Acts 3:6; 4:10; 9:34; Matt. 28:18–20). Jesus gave his own teaching on his own authority—"I say to you"—and he viewed his miracles as evidence that in him God's supernatural reign had arrived.

A good example of how Jesus understood the dominical import of his teaching comes in how he related it to the Old Testament law. One of the most important texts in this regard is Matthew 5:17–20. Debate has surrounded how best to interpret Jesus's words, "I have not come to abolish [the Law or the Prophets] but to fulfill them" (Matt. 5:17).[13] But the best interpretation stresses the *antithesis* between *abolish* and *fulfill*, showing that Jesus claimed to be the prophetic end toward whom all of the teaching under the old covenant with Israel pointed for its ultimate significance.[14] This interpretation understands *fulfill* to have the exact same meaning as its use in Matthew 1–2 (and elsewhere in Matthew), which relies on the prophetic function of the Old Testament. The Old Testament anticipates the Messiah and leads us to him in the person of Jesus Christ, particularly through typological persons, events, and institutions. Jesus was not abolishing the canonical authority of the Old Testament but correctly orienting it to terminate in his own authority. D. A. Carson explains that "the OT's real and abiding authority must be understood through the person and teaching of him to whom it points and who so richly fulfills it."[15]

Implied though it may be, the Christological claim here is simply staggering. Jesus understood himself to be the eschatological goal of the entire Old Testament and the sole authoritative interpreter of its teaching. In other words, Jesus self-identified as a man who shared authority with God, the author of the Law under his covenant with Israel.

---

[13] For a discussion of the various options, see Carson, *Matthew*, 140–147; France, *Matthew*, 177–191.
[14] For a defense of this view, see Carson, *Matthew*, 143–145; cf. France, *Matthew*, 182–184.
[15] Carson, *Matthew*, 144.

Along with his teaching, Jesus's miracles bear witness to his unique relation to God the Father. In fact, the healing and nature miracles performed by Jesus display both the authority and the power of God himself. His healing miracles evidence the arrival of the messianic age (Luke 7:22–23; cf. Isa. 29:18–19; 35:5–6; 61:1) and manifest the supernatural rule of God coming in and through Jesus. Jesus exercised authority over nature when he rebuked the stormy sea and it obeyed with a great calm (Matt. 8:26). He walked on the sea, and the waters were obliged to support him (14:25, 28–30). While these acts of authority and power simply amaze in isolation, they take on crucial Christological significance as the storyline of Scripture comes out of the epochs and covenants of the Old Testament. The development of the drama of redemption reveals that the Lord alone triumphs over the stormy sea (see Ps. 65:7; 107:23–31) and treads upon its waters (Job 9:8, LXX; cf. Ps. 77:19; Isa. 51:9–10).[16] And in similar manner, the New Testament presents many other healings and miracles and even the exorcism of demons (Matt. 4:23; 9:35; 10:7–8; Luke 9:11; 10:9, 17; 11:20) as an indication of Jesus's self-identification with God in authority and power.

So, based on the miracles he performed, we can say that the man Jesus implicitly but quite convincingly identified himself as God by doing what God alone can do.

Finally, in addition to his teaching and miracles, Jesus exercised the authority and power of God himself through judgment and resurrection. Jesus understood himself to be the man appointed by his Father to exercise divine judgment (Matt. 7:22–23; 16:27; 25:31–33, 41; cf. John 5:22–23). But Scripture is clear that judgment is the work of God alone (Deut. 1:17; Jer. 25:31; Rom. 2:3, 5–6; 14:10; 1 Pet. 1:17). And yet, Jesus knew that he came as the appointed judge of all humanity and that his verdict assigns every person to either eternal punishment or eternal life (Matt. 25:46; cf. John 5:29; 2 Cor. 5:10).[17] And in relation to this judgment, Jesus understood that he had the authority and power of resurrection. The prophetic anticipation of God's kingdom and the new covenant age contains the hope of resurrection life (Ezek. 37:1–23; cf. Dan. 12:2; Isa. 25:6–9), a hope based on the singular ability of God to raise the dead to new life (1 Sam. 2:6; Ezekiel 37). But even so, Jesus knew that he had received this authority and power unique to God directly from the Father: "For as the Father raises the dead and gives them life, so also the Son gives life to whom

---

[16] As Simon Gathercole explains, "The reference to walking on the sea is a 'theophany' motif which is taken over from Yahweh to Jesus. . . . the combination of the two passages showing Jesus' mastery of the sea (Matt 14:22–33; Mark 6:45–52) points very strongly to a close identification of him with Yahweh in the OT" (Simon J. Gathercole, *The Preexistent Son: Recovering the Christologies of Matthew, Mark, and Luke* [Grand Rapids, MI: Eerdmans, 2006], 64).

[17] By speaking of the judgment seat of God (Rom. 14:10) and the judgment seat of Christ (2 Cor. 5:10) together, Paul depicts not two judgments but one, which again highlights the close identity between the Father and the Son.

he will. . . . Truly, truly, I say to you, an hour is coming, and is now here, when the dead will hear the voice of the Son of God, and those who hear will live" (John 5:21, 25).[18] Throughout his entire life and ministry, then, from his earliest teaching and miracles to his final acts of eternal judgment and resurrection to eternal life, the man Jesus self-identified as God himself—he knew he was God the Son incarnate.

JESUS'S DEATH AND RESURRECTION

Jesus also self-identified as God the Son incarnate in his death and resurrection. As he approached his death, Jesus did not view it as martyrdom but as central to his divinely planned messianic mission. At Caesarea Philippi, after he blessed Peter for identifying him as the Christ, Jesus then explained to his disciples that he *must* (*dei*) suffer and die and in three days rise again (Matt. 16:21–23). Jesus knew that he would die. As John Stott comments, "the Synoptic evangelists bear a common witness to the fact that Jesus both clearly foresaw and repeatedly foretold his coming death."[19] But Jesus did not react with fatalistic resignation. Rather, he embraced his death as a voluntary, obedient act according to the will of his Father that was planned before the foundation of the world (Mark 10:45; cf. John 10:17–18).

Jesus understood, moreover, that by his death, "everything that is written about the Son of Man by the prophets will be accomplished" (Luke 18:31). Thinking along the epochal and covenantal development of the Old Testament, Jesus knew that as the Son of God his death would bring divine judgment upon the world, depose Satan as "the ruler of this world," and install himself as king over all creation for the sake of all people (John 12:31–33). And as the Son of Man, Jesus understood that he could accomplish these divine works that would reconcile God and man because he had authority on earth to forgive sins (Mark 2:5–12; Luke 5:20–26).

Wells sums up the identifying power of Jesus's death and resurrection with a rhetorical question: "His actions, in this regard, had an implied Christological significance, for who can forgive sin but God alone? (Mark 2:7/Luke 5:21)."[20]

THE PRAISE AND WORSHIP OF JESUS

As we have seen, God alone is worthy of worship, because of his metaphysical-moral perfections, and as the one Creator–Covenant Lord he demands this worship from his creatures. Indeed, no other being can cross the Creator-

---

[18] Jesus also says, "I am the resurrection and the life" (John 11:25). In the context of John's Gospel, D. A. Carson explains that Jesus is claiming not merely that he has the power to resurrect and give life, but that "there is neither resurrection nor eternal life outside of him" (D. A. Carson, *The Gospel according to John*, PNTC [Grand Rapids, MI: Eerdmans, 1991], 412), which must be understood as a claim to deity.

[19] John Stott, *The Cross of Christ* (Downers Grove, IL: InterVarsity Press, 1986), 28.

[20] Wells, *Person of Christ*, 41.

creature divide, and God is unwilling to share his glory and worship with any created thing (Isa. 42:8). In fact, to worship the creature rather than the Creator is blasphemy (see Acts 14:14–15; Rom. 1:18–23; Rev. 19:10) and high treason against the Covenant Lord (Deut. 4:16–20; 1 Kings 11:1–11; cf. John 19:15).

As a man, however, Jesus received the praise of man and never rebuked his worshipers (Matt. 14:33; 21:15–16; 28:9, 17; John 20:28). A person might bow down (*proskyneō*, sometimes translated "worship") before Jesus out of deep respect. But Peter rebuked someone who bowed down to *him* in a similar context (Acts 10:25–26), and the angels know that it is categorically improper to bow to anyone other than God himself (Rev. 19:10; 22:8–9). And yet, Jesus never rejected this kind of worship when it was given to him on earth.[21] In fact, knowing that the Father had committed divine authority to him to judge as God himself, Jesus also understood the purpose of this power: "that all may honor the Son, just as they honor the Father. Whoever does not honor the Son does not honor the Father who sent him" (John 5:23).

So Jesus not only received the honor, praise, and worship that should be given only to God himself; Jesus demanded it, because he self-identified as God the Son incarnate.

JESUS AND THE INAUGURATION OF GOD'S KINGDOM

In the Gospels, especially the Synoptics, the life and ministry and the death and resurrection of Jesus all focus on the kingdom of God.[22] As we have just seen, all that Jesus taught, all of the miracles he performed, and all of the authority and power he exercised related to and helped to bring the kingdom of the "age to come" into "this present age." And as we saw in chapter 3, the coming of the kingdom of heaven has been the plan of God throughout all the epochs of redemptive history and in the promise of God as it developed through all of the Old Testament covenants. By the time this plotline reaches into the New Testament, we expect that this kingdom will come as *God's* kingdom, which he himself initiates *through* the Davidic king. It is God who must act in power and grace to save his people, yet he will do so through a human king—and thus the close identification of Yahweh and the king. It is quite revealing, then, for Jesus to appear, knowing these kingdom expecta-

---

[21] The rest of the New Testament and the practice of the apostolic church was to worship Jesus as God. For the best treatment of the worship of Jesus in the early church, see Larry W. Hurtado, *Lord Jesus Christ: Devotion to Jesus in Earliest Christianity* (Grand Rapid, MI: Eerdmans, 2003); idem, *How on Earth Did Jesus Become a God?* (Grand Rapids, MI: Eerdmans, 2005).

[22] Kingdom is mentioned thirteen times in Mark (nine of them in common with Matthew and Luke); twenty-seven times in Matthew (not in common with Mark); twelve times in Luke (not in common with Mark), and twice in John. John's Gospel speaks of these same realties in the language of "eternal life," which belongs to the "age to come" (see I. Howard Marshall, *New Testament Theology: Many Witnesses, One Gospel* [Downers Grove, IL: InterVarsity Press, 2004], 498; cf. Carson, *John*, 187–190). And as Andreas Köstenberger instructs, "That the expressions 'kingdom of God' and 'eternal life' are essentially equivalent is suggested by their parallel use in Matthew 19:16, 24 pars" (Andreas J. Köstenberger, *John*, BECNT [Grand Rapids, MI: Baker Academic, 2004], 123).

tions, and to claim to meet them all. In fact, the works Jesus claimed to do were so clearly linked to the inauguration of God's kingdom that if Jesus did not think he was doing the work of God himself it would have been deceptive for him to remain silent. As Wells observes,

> This "age" . . . was supernatural, could only be established by God himself, would bring blessings and benefits which only God could give, would achieve the overthrow of sin, death, and the devil (which only God could accomplish), and was identified so closely with God himself that no human effort could bring it about and no human resistance turn it back. If Jesus saw himself as the one in whom this kind of Kingdom was being inaugurated, then such a perception is a Christological claim which would be fraudulent and deceptive if Jesus was ignorant of his Godness.[23]

Much of Jesus's implicit witness to his self-identity, then, depends upon this incredible but unavoidable deduction: if the works that Jesus claimed he did could be accomplished only by God himself, then by claiming to do those works, the man Jesus implied that he is God himself. This divine-human implication by deduction should not be disregarded for its indirection. It might seem counterintuitive, but the indirect nature of Jesus's claim to be God the Son incarnate reveals the depth and truth of his self-identity. The reality of his deity and humanity pressed into every aspect of Jesus's life on this earth to such an extent that every word was spoken and every work was performed with the understanding that he was fulfilling the promise that the Creator–Covenant Lord himself would redeem humanity and reign over his creation in perfect righteousness.

Although Jesus never said, "I am God the Son incarnate," his implicit witness to this self-identity is no less clear and convincing. The clarity and weight of Jesus's self-identity comes not from his words and works alone, but from their place in the interpretive framework of Scripture. Jesus knew the structure and expectations of the Old Testament, and he knew that he was the one to accomplish the works and receive the worship that is unique to God himself. So even though he never used these exact words, Jesus certainly self-identified as God the Son incarnate—so much so that every significant aspect of his life and death bore witness to it.

Jesus's Explicit Witness to Himself

In addition to the implicit witness of Jesus, the New Testament also gives us explicit statements by Jesus regarding his unique relationship with the Father

---

[23] Wells, *Person of Christ*, 38. For a similar view, see Reymond, *Jesus, Divine Messiah*, 239–241; George E. Ladd, "Kingdom of Christ, God, Heaven," in *Evangelical Dictionary of Theology*, ed. Walter A. Elwell (Grand Rapids, MI: Baker, 1984), 609.

and connection with his works. More specifically, the Gospels demonstrate that Jesus quite intentionally and knowingly self-identified as God the Son incarnate.

JESUS'S SELF-IDENTITY IN HIS USE OF ABBA

In each of the Synoptics, Jesus addresses God by the Aramaic term *Abba*, which reveals how he perceived his relationship to the Father (see Matt. 6:9; 11:25–26; 26:39, 42; Mark 14:36; Luke 10:21; 11:2; 22:42; 23:34, 46). As Joachim Jeremias has shown in his study of the contemporary Jewish literature, "there is *no analogy at all* in the whole of Jewish prayer for God being addressed as Abba."[24] The reason for this reticence was due to the fear that one might fail to give proper deference to God's holiness and majesty. Yet Jesus, as Wells notes, "with utmost regularity, addresses God by this term of intimacy and familiarity."[25]

Also important to note is how Jesus distinguishes his use of *Abba* from that of his disciples when he teaches them to pray, "Our Father" (Matt. 6:9; John 20:17). Later in Scripture, Paul says that Christians, as adopted sons of God, are free to call God *Abba* (see Rom. 8:15; Gal. 4:6), but it is only through Jesus that this is possible. In other words, it is only because we are united by faith to the Son that we have access to the Father by the Spirit (John 1:12; cf. 14:6; 17:26; Rom. 8:15). Our use of the term is made possible only because of the Son in relation to his Father, which is another way of underscoring Jesus's unique sonship.

Jesus, then, by the use of this term understands himself to be the unique Son in relation to the Father. The precise nature of this sonship is not explained by the term *Abba* alone; ultimately, the nature of Jesus's sonship is revealed in the entire plotline of Scripture. But when read within the structure and story-line of Scripture, it is clear that Jesus's sonship is not merely functional but also ontological. This point is demonstrated in Jesus's use and understanding of the title "Son" and in his application of the title to himself.

JESUS'S SELF-IDENTITY AS THE "SON OF GOD"

Far more than a generically descriptive phrase, *Son of God* functions in Scripture as a title that discloses the identity of the one who bears it.[26] The title appears throughout the Synoptic Gospels (Matt. 3:17; 11:25–27; 28:19; Mark 1:1, 11; 9:7; Luke 1:32; 3:38; 9:35) and occupies a central role in John's Gospel

---

[24] Joachim Jeremias, *The Prayers of Jesus* (Philadelphia: Fortress, 1989), 57.

[25] Wells, *Person of Christ*, 43."

[26] For a detailed treatment of the title "Son," see D. A. Carson, *Jesus the Son of God: A Christological Title Often Overlooked, Sometimes Misunderstood, and Currently Disputed* (Wheaton, IL: Crossway, 2012); Graeme Goldsworthy, *The Son of God and the New Creation* (Wheaton, IL: Crossway, 2015); for a discussion of *Son* in John's Gospel, see Andreas J. Köstenberger and Scott R. Swain, *Father, Son, and Spirit: The Trinity and John's Gospel*, NSBT 24 (Downers Grove, IL: InterVarsity Press, 2008), 75–92; cf. Carson, *John*, 246–259.

(John 3:16, 17, 35–36; 5:19–23; 6:40; 8:36; 14:13; 17:1). *Son of God* is applied to Jesus at his baptism (Mark 1:11), temptation (Luke 4:9), and transfiguration (Mark 9:7; Matt. 17:5; Luke 9:35). And the title is used to address Jesus by the centurion (Mark 15:39), the high priest (Mark 14:61), and the demons (Mark 3:11; 5:7). In fact, the title *Son of God* is so central to the identity of Jesus Christ that John wrote his Gospel "so that you may believe that Jesus is the Christ, the Son of God" (John 20:31).

To grasp the significance of what Jesus meant by calling himself the Son of God, it will be helpful to think in both functional and ontological terms. First, the New Testament does not hesitate to emphasize a strong functional aspect to Jesus's sonship, rooted in the typological figures of the Old Testament—Adam, Israel, and the Davidic king. Building on this pattern, Jesus is the true Son who is the Last Adam, true Israel, and David's greater Son. In addition, by virtue of *what he does*, Jesus is appointed to be Son and Lord. By becoming incarnate (John 1:1, 14) and obediently identifying with us and representing us as our covenant head and substitute, Jesus brings about our eternal redemption, and as a result of his work, he takes up the title *Son of God* at a particular time in history (see Rom. 1:3–4; Phil. 2:6–11).[27] But Jesus's incarnational sonship culminating in his representative and substitutionary death for us is only half of the story. By virtue of *who he is*, Jesus has been the Son of God from eternity. In fact, Jesus's eternal sonship provides the basis for his incarnational and redemptive sonship.

Jesus regularly addressed God directly as "Father" (e.g., Matt. 11:25; Luke 23:46; John 11:41; 12:28) and referred to him as "my Father" (e.g., Matt. 16:17; 26:29; Luke 22:29; John 15:8). Even by themselves, these expressions go beyond a relationship of obedience to one of begottenness. As a child, before he had accomplished the works given to him by the Father, Jesus spoke of his heavenly sonship to his earthly parents: "Did you not know that I must be in my Father's house?" (Luke 2:49). And just before his death, Jesus prayed to God on the basis of his own life as the eternal Son of God: "And now, Father, glorify me in your own presence with the glory that I had with you before the world existed" (John 17:5).

Jesus certainly knew that he was appointed to be the Son of God in his incarnate life. By considering how Jesus addressed and referred to God as his Father, we can say Jesus also knew that he had always been the Son of God from eternity. And by reading Jesus's own words within the plotline of Scripture that he knew he was bringing to completion, we can see deeper into Jesus's self-identification as God the Son incarnate. Two examples will suffice.

In John 5:16–30, after healing a crippled man, Jesus responds to those who

---

[27] See Douglas Moo, *The Epistle to the Romans*, NICNT (Grand Rapids, MI: Eerdmans, 1996), 44–53; Peter T. O'Brien, *The Epistle to the Philippians: A Commentary on the Greek Text*, NIGTC (Grand Rapids, MI: Eerdmans, 1991), 205–253.

criticize him for working on the Sabbath: "My Father is working until now, and I am working" (v. 17). In Jesus's time, the rabbis agreed that God worked on the Sabbath without becoming a Sabbath-breaker. After all, if he did not, who would uphold the universe? In other words, God's working on the Sabbath is an exception to the Sabbath law.[28] So Jesus not only calls God his own Father in intimate terms; he also makes himself equal with God by claiming the same authority as God to work on the Sabbath. And in the following verses, Jesus will explain that the validity of his Sabbath work is based on the divine nature of all his works, the divine worship warranted by these works, and the divine aseity of the one who performs these works.

The literary structure of John 5:19–23 is framed around four *gar* ("for" or "because") statements. The first *gar* statement introduces the last clause of verse 19: "So Jesus said to them, 'Truly, truly, I say to you, the Son can do nothing of his own accord, but only what he sees the Father doing. For [*gar*] whatever the Father does, that the Son does likewise.'" Jesus here makes three points about his sonship grounded in his dependence upon the Father: the Son is *not* the Father; the Son does *only* what the Father does; the Son does *all* that the Father does. The Father and the Son are distinct from each other yet perform the same works. The Son does no less and no more than the Father— they are perfectly united in their work. As Carson observes, "Jesus is not equal with God as *another* God or as a *competing* God."[29] Rather, the Father always "initiates, sends, commands, commissions, grants; the Son responds, obeys, performs his Father's will, receives authority."[30] It is *this* eternal and intimate Father-Son relationship that accounts for Jesus's authority and ability to do as the Son all that the Father does as the Father. And it is *this* Son, the promised image-Son whose identity has been progressively unfolded through the biblical storyline, who finally comes in the person of Jesus Christ.

The second *gar* statement explains the fundamental dynamic of this unique Father-Son relationship: "For [*gar*] the Father loves the Son and shows him all that he himself is doing" (John 5:20). Jesus speaks here of an intimate life with the Father that far surpasses any Creator-creature covenantal relationship. The relational dynamic that moves the Father to bring the Son into all that the Father is doing is divine love. This love is eternal and infinite; the Son has shared the Father's will, desires, and power without any limits of time or capacity. And yet this love is also temporal and incarnational in that some of the works given

---

[28] After laying out the argument of the rabbis, Carson explains that even though God works on the Sabbath, he cannot be charged with violating it, because "(1) the entire universe is his domain (Is. 6:3), and therefore he never carries anything outside of it; (2) otherwise put, God fills the whole world (Je. 23:24); and in any case (3) God lifts nothing to a height greater than his own stature" (Carson, *John*, 247).

[29] Carson, *John*, 250; cf. Köstenberger and Swain, *Father, Son, and Spirit*, 87–90.

[30] Carson, *John*, 251.

by the Father to the Son are to be accomplished as a man on the earth in the fullness of time.

The first two *gar* statements of John 5:19–20, then, establish that Jesus understood the divine nature of his own works that are possible for God alone. The next two *gar* statements will show that Jesus knew that his works would bring him the worship that is proper for God alone.

In verses 21–23, Jesus explains in particular that the Father has given the Son the divine works of resurrection from the dead and judgment upon all humanity. Resurrection and judgment are the sole prerogatives of God (see Gen. 18:25; 2 Kings 5:7; Ezek. 37:13; cf. Rev. 20:11–15). For example, even the powerful prophet Elijah did not himself raise the Zarephath widow's son, but he prayed to the Lord as a "man of God" (1 Kings 17:19–24). In the third *gar* statement of John 5, however, Jesus claims the authority and power of resurrection as the *Son of God*: "For as the Father raises the dead and gives them life, so also the Son gives life to whom he will" (v. 21). Moreover, closely linked to the divine power of resurrection is the prerogative of divine judgment. In the New Testament, resurrection prepares all humanity to stand before God for judgment and proves that those raised with Christ (see Rom. 6:4; Eph. 2:6; Col. 3:1) will not be condemned (see Rom. 8:1). And the fourth *gar* statement shows us that Jesus understood that *both* resurrection and judgment were given to him *for* God-only worship: "For [*gar*] not even the Father judges anyone, but He has given all judgment to the Son, so that all will honor the Son even as they honor the Father. He who does not honor the Son does not honor the Father who sent Him" (John 5:22–23, NASB).

It is important to pause here to grasp fully the Christological significance of Jesus's claim for himself. This open claim by Jesus to receive the honor due the Father is based not on ambassadorial authority under God but on ontological equality with God. As Carson concludes,

> This goes far beyond making Jesus a mere ambassador who acts in the name of the monarch who sent him, an envoy plenipotentiary whose derived authority is the equivalent of his master's. That analogue breaks down precisely here, for the honour given to an envoy is never that given to the head of a state. The Jews were right in detecting that Jesus was "making himself equal with God" (vv. 17-18). But this does not diminish God. Indeed, the glorification of the Son is precisely what glorifies the Father, just as in Philippians 2:9-11, where at the name of *Jesus* every knee bows and every tongue confesses that Jesus Christ is Lord, and all this is to the glory of God the Father. Because of the unique relation between the Father and the Son, the God who declares "I am the LORD; that is my name! I will not give my glory to another" (Is. 42:8; *cf.* Is. 48:11) is not compromised or diminished when divine honours crown the head of the Son.[31]

---

[31] Ibid., 254–255.

Based on the connections between the four *gar* statements in John 5:19–23, then, we can summarize Jesus's self-identity as follows: he is the Son loved eternally and infinitely by the Father, such that the Father has sent his Son to do the works of God himself temporally and incarnationally, specifically exercising the authority and power of resurrection and judgment, all so that the Son will receive worship as God himself. In other words, Jesus understood that he was God the Son incarnate come to do the works of God as a man.

Moreover, in a later *gar* statement, Jesus explains further why he is able to give resurrection life: "For as the Father has life in himself, so he has granted the Son also to have life in himself" (John 5:26). In the context of John's Gospel and the metanarrative coming out of the Old Testament, this claim to divine aseity must refer to the Son's eternal ontology, not to a function of his incarnation. As we discussed in chapter 3, aseity is one of the fundamental attributes that highlights the Creator-creature distinction. God alone exists by his own nature and power; all creatures, including all humanity, exist as a prerogative of God. Without at this time entering into the debate regarding the eternal generation of the Son (but see Part IV), we must at least agree with Carson that Jesus understood that his power of resurrection flowed from divine aseity: "it is this eternal impartation of life-in-himself to the Son that grounds his authority and power to call the dead to life by his powerful word."[32] Simply put, the man Jesus understood that, as the Son of God, he shared in the divine nature.

Jesus also speaks of his divine-human sonship in Matthew 11:25–27, this time in terms of mutual knowledge and shared sovereignty with the Father. After addressing God as "Father, Lord of heaven and earth" (v. 25), Jesus thanks God for concealing the significance of his miracles from some as an act of judgment upon their sin and revealing it to others as an act of grace. But then Jesus turns the spotlight on himself as the exclusive agent of God's self-revelation: "All things have been handed over to me by my Father, and no one knows the Son except the Father, and no one knows the Father except the Son and anyone to whom the Son chooses to reveal him" (v. 27). In an explicit claim to deity, Jesus affirms two realities that are unique to the Father-Son relationship.[33] First, Jesus's claim to mutual knowledge with the Father, as Robert Reymond argues, "lifts Jesus above the sphere of the ordinary mortal and places him in a position, not of equality merely, but of absolute reciprocity and interpenetration of knowledge with the Father."[34] This intimate and comprehensive knowledge of the Father cannot come to Jesus as a man in consequence of his incarnational sonship and messianic mission. The finite cannot

---

[32] Ibid., 257; cf. Kevin Giles, *The Eternal Generation of the Son: Maintaining Orthodoxy in Trinitarian Theology* (Downers Grove, IL: IVP Academic, 2012).
[33] For further discussion on this point, see Reymond, *Jesus, Divine Messiah*, 206–210.
[34] Ibid., 207.

comprehend the infinite. Rather, as George Eldon Ladd has argued, "sonship precedes messiahship and is in fact the ground for the messianic mission."[35] Second, Jesus claims to share sovereignty with the Father whereby both must take the initiative to reveal each other in order for anyone to come to a saving knowledge of God.

Simply put, Jesus's self-identity as the Son must be understood in divine terms. In B. B. Warfield's words,

> Not merely is the Son the exclusive revealer of God, but the mutual knowledge of the Father and Son is put on what seems very much a par. The Son can be known only by the Father in all that He is, as if His being were infinite and as such inscrutable to the finite intelligence; and His knowledge alone—again as if He were infinite in His attributes—is competent to compass the depths of the Father's infinite being. He who holds this relation to the Father cannot conceivably be a creature.[36]

And yet, Jesus's divine self-identity does not contradict or diminish his self-identity as the Son of God in human terms.

So we can now bring together the ontological and functional aspects of Jesus's self-identity: Jesus understood that he is the eternal Son of God and that he became the incarnational Son of God. Jesus knew that he has always been the Son by eternal dependence upon the Father. And Jesus also knew that he came to fulfill the covenantal promise of the Father to bring forth his true image-Son and the last Adam of the human race. In short, Jesus intentionally and explicitly identified himself to be God the Son incarnate.

JESUS'S SELF-IDENTITY AS THE "SON OF MAN"

Jesus also testified to his identity as God the Son incarnate by his most common self-designation, the *Son of Man*. The title is used in all the Gospels and in every case by Jesus himself.[37] In order to grasp what Jesus meant by calling himself the Son of Man, it is crucial to understand it within the storyline of Scripture and its Old Testament background.[38]

---

[35] George Eldon Ladd, *A Theology of the New Testament* (Grand Rapids, MI: Eerdmans, 1974), 167.

[36] B. B. Warfield, *The Lord of Glory* (repr., Grand Rapids, MI: Baker, 1974), 83. There is even more in this text that could be developed in terms of Jesus's divine self-identity. For example, in verses 28–30, Jesus invites the burdened to come to him, which in itself is an incredible Christological statement. Jesus's invitation is an echo of Jeremiah 31:25, where the Old Testament prophet anticipates the arrival of the new covenant age—an age which only Yahweh can usher in. On this point, see Carson, *Matthew*, 277–279.

[37] The title appears thirty times in Matthew, fourteen in Mark, twenty-five in Luke, and thirteen in John. Outside the Gospels, the term is used with reference to Jesus only in Acts 7:56, Hebrews 2:6, and Revelation 1:13 and 14:14. The title is not used at all after Jesus's death, except in Acts 7:56. David Wells draws an insightful conclusion from the title's absence in the apostolic letters: "[it] suggests that this was *his* term and not a formulation placed on his lips by the early church as Rudolf Bultmann and Norman Perrin propose. If this title was the creation of the church, we would also expect to encounter it in the epistles" (Wells, *Person of Christ*, 78).

[38] See Schreiner, *New Testament Theology*, 213–231; cf. Gathercole, *Preexistent Son*, 253–271; C. F. D. Moule, *The Origin of Christology* (Cambridge: Cambridge University Press, 1977), 11–22.

In the Old Testament, "son of man" is used as a synonym for humans within the context of our role in creation (see Ps. 8:4; cf. Num. 23:19; Job 25:6; Isa. 51:12; 56:2; Jer. 49:18, 33(NASB); 50:40; 51:43).[39] But as the biblical meta-narrative unfolds through God's covenants with man, "son of man" refers more specifically to one who is unique among humanity. In Daniel 7, the title takes on the significance of a superhuman figure who functions alongside the "Ancient of Days," who is God seated for judgment. In Daniel's vision, four kingdoms of man appear as four beasts that terrorize the peoples of the earth. The kingdom of God, however, ultimately triumphs and destroys all rival kingdoms. And yet, in an unexpected turn after the destruction of every kingdom of man, God gives his own kingdom and all dominion over the nations to "one [who is] like a son of man" (Dan. 7:13–14). But *this* son of man is different than all others: he comes on the "clouds of heaven" (v. 13); his reign lasts forever (v. 14); and his reign gives dominion over the whole earth to his kingdom people (vv. 18, 22, 27). So we have in this son of man who comes from heaven the promised Son-king who will bring covenantal reconciliation between God and man, restoring man's righteous vice-regent rule over God's creation. Thomas Schreiner gives us the overall significance of Daniel's vision: "Indeed, the son of man in Daniel does not grasp rule through military conquest by which he brutally rules over other human beings. He is given the kingdom of God himself, and thereby he fulfills the role for which human beings were created (Psalm 8)."[40]

So when Jesus steps into *this* storyline as the self-designated Son of Man, he makes a clear statement regarding his identity. Jesus refers to himself as the Son of Man in (1) his ministry (Mark 2:10, 28; Luke 7:34; 9:58; 19:10); (2) his suffering and resurrection (Mark 10:45; Luke 17:24–25; 22:48; 24:7; John 3:14; 6:53; 8:28; 12:23; 13:31); and (3) his future coming (Matt. 10:23; 19:28; 24:30; 25:31; Mark 8:38; 13:26; 14:62; Luke 12:8–10, 40; 17:22–30; 18:8).[41] And putting these Son of Man sayings together, we can conclude that "Jesus employed a term which has specific content in the Old Testament, but in applying it to himself and his work it came to have a meaning both larger and more complex than it does in the Old Testament."[42] To become the

---

[39] In Psalm 80:17, there is a dispute as to the referent of "son of man." This psalm recounts God's saving acts on behalf of Israel and its present devastation under foreign nations. Israel is compared to a vine that the Lord planted but has now cut down. The Lord is petitioned to show regard for "the son whom you made strong for yourself" (v. 15). And later a similar request is made: "[L]et your hand be on the man of your right hand, the son of man whom you have made strong for yourself!" (v. 17). In this context, "man" and "son of man" could refer to Israel in connection with the earlier reference to Israel as God's "son" (Ex. 4:22) and "vine" (Isa. 5:1–7). Yet in the context of the entire Psalter, it may also refer to the anointed king who represents Israel as a whole. If the latter, which is quite probable, then "son of man" should be understood in terms of the function of *son* within an entire typological pattern—Adam to Israel to David. *Son of man*, then, carries messianic overtones and speaks of a unique representative human. For further discussion, see Schreiner, *New Testament Theology*, 213–216; cf. Stephen G. Dempster, *Dominion and Dynasty: A Biblical Theology of the Hebrew Bible*, NSBT 15 (Downers Grove, IL: InterVarsity Press, 2003), 194–202, 215–217.

[40] Schreiner, *New Testament Theology*, 216.

[41] See Wells, *Person of Christ*, 80; Schreiner, *New Testament Theology*, 219–221.

[42] Wells, *Person of Christ*, 80.

promised Son of Man, the Son of God came from heaven through incarnation, conquered Satan, sin, and death through crucifixion and resurrection, gives victory to his people through vicarious suffering and justification, and will return to bring eternal judgment upon all his enemies and to reign forever with his people in righteousness.

As the Son of Man, Jesus again self-identifies as both God and man. Jesus uses the title in his humiliation as a man to save the lost (Matt. 8:20; Mark 10:45) and in his divine authority to forgive sins and his divine power to resurrect the dead (Mark 2:10; Matt. 17:9). Jesus refers to himself as the Son of Man in his resurrected-incarnational ascension to the throne of heaven (Matt. 19:28) and in his future return as the king of heaven, "coming on the clouds of heaven with power and great glory" (24:30).

JESUS'S SELF-IDENTITY IN THE PURPOSE AND WORK OF GOD

Even more explicit evidence of Jesus's self-identity as God the Son incarnate comes in how he understands the purpose of his coming. On numerous occasions in the New Testament, Jesus offers "I have come to" statements (or an equivalent phrase) in which he reveals the various reasons for his advent and work on the earth. Simon Gathercole has provided what is probably the best treatment of these purpose statements in *The Preexistent Son*. While Gathercole reaches many conclusions and implications, we can only consider his main arguments here by looking at a few examples.[43]

The New Testament gives us eight statements by Jesus that declare why he has come. In two of these purpose statements, Jesus reveals that he came to serve others and offer his life as a ransom (Matt. 20:28); and to seek and save the lost (Luke 19:10). As we have just seen, Jesus's self-identification as the Son of Man within the storyline of Scripture shows that he understood himself to be both God and the man to whom God would give his own kingdom for the sake of his own people. In these two Son of Man purpose statements, Jesus specifies that he came to do the God-only work of pastoral care for his people. According to the unfolding metanarrative of the Creator–Covenant Lord's commitment to humanity, God himself promised to seek his sheep and shepherd his flock (Ezekiel 34). According to Jesus's self-understanding, he came as the Son of Man to fulfill this promise. As the divine-human Lord of the earth, Jesus says that he came to gather God's own people to himself.

In the six remaining purpose statements, Jesus declares that he came to preach the good news of the kingdom in Israel (Mark 1:38); to fulfill rather than to abolish the Old Testament (Matt. 5:17); to call sinners to himself (Matt. 9:13); to bring a sword and division rather than peace to the earth

---

[43] See Gathercole, *Preexistent Son*, 83–189.

(Matt. 10:34); to divide family members against one another (Matt. 10:35); and to cast a fire onto the earth (Luke 12:49). In each case (especially Luke 12:49), Jesus understands his own identity in divine terms. Jesus came and preached with divine authority that was confirmed by attendant miracles; he came as the embodied righteousness of the kingdom of heaven; and he came to purify the earth by separating a people for himself in that righteousness.

Even more than these explicit statements, however, perhaps the most significant indication of Jesus's self-identity concerning the purpose and work of God comes in his forgiveness of sins.[44] In Mark 2, Jesus tells a paralytic, "Son, your sins are forgiven" (v. 5). The religious leaders who charge Jesus with blasphemy are correct that God alone can forgive sins (v. 7), so Jesus does not challenge their theological reasoning. But he does challenge their theological conclusion that Jesus is not God: "Why do you question these things in your hearts? Which is easier, to say to the paralytic, 'Your sins are forgiven,' or to say, 'Rise, take up your bed and walk'?" (vv. 8–9).

In explaining the point of Jesus's rhetorical question, R. T. France argues that "if the 'harder' of the two options can be demonstrated, the 'easier' may be assumed also to be possible."[45] Forgiving sins is harder because only God has the requisite authority and power. But Jesus's question "is not about which is easier to *do*, but which is easier to *say*, and a *claim* to forgive sins is undoubtedly easier to make, since it cannot be falsified by external events, whereas a claim to make a paralyzed man walk will be immediately proved true or false by a success or failure which everyone can see."[46] It logically follows, then, that "Jesus' demonstrable authority to cure the disabled man is evidence that he also has authority to forgive sins."[47]

France's explication is certainly true, but there seems to be more here. Jesus has stepped into the plotline of Scripture at a point where he can fulfill the plan of God by inaugurating the kingdom of God. Everything that Jesus says and does must be interpreted within this overarching purpose and work. Healing the paralytic, then, is proof that Jesus has authority to forgive sins *as the man in whom the saving rule and reign of God himself has finally come into the world* (see Matt. 8:17; cf. Jer. 31:34; Isa. 35:5–6; 53:4; 61:1). As Carson notes, "This is the authority of Emmanuel, 'God with us' (Matt. 1:23), sent to 'save his people from their sins' (Matt. 1:21)."[48] Even the location of Jesus's

---

[44] In light of the fall, humanity's greatest problem is sin against a holy and righteous God. Ultimately, God is the only one with the authority to forgive sin, because first and foremost all sin is against God. In fact, at the heart of the "newness" of the new covenant is the promise of the full forgiveness of sin (see Jer. 31:34). Under the old covenant, sin was forgiven, but only in a temporary, anticipatory, typological fashion. It is only with the arrival of the new covenant that God is said to remember our sin no more.

[45] France, *Matthew*, 346.

[46] Ibid.

[47] Ibid.

[48] Carson, *Matthew*, 222.

claim reinforces his self-identification as God the Son incarnate. Jesus proves that he has the divine authority to forgive sins *outside the temple*.

The plotline, the scene, and the dialogue combine to reveal that the promised forgiveness of sin and covenantal reconciliation between God and man is fulfilled in the person of Jesus. The temple, priesthood, and sacrificial system played their typological function to set the stage for God himself to come as the man Jesus to redeem a people for himself.

JESUS'S USE OF "I AM"

In addition to the purpose statements in the Synoptics, John's Gospel gives us the eminent "I am" (*egō eimi*) statements by which Jesus identifies himself with the Creator–Covenant Lord of the Old Testament. When Jesus refers to himself as "I am" without a predicate (John 6:20; 8:24, 28, 58; 18:6), he connects his personal identity with the covenantal identity of Yahweh. In Exodus 3, God identifies himself to Moses as the "I am" (Ex. 3:6, 14), which becomes the unique and personal name for God in his covenant with Israel and with David. And in Isaiah 40–48, the prophet uses God's covenantal name to make the point that, as the one true and living God, Yahweh is unique and incomparable by nature (Isa. 41:4; 43:10, 25; 45:8, 18, 19, 22; 46:4, 9; 48:12, 17). The "I am" is in a category by himself as the eternally self-existent being who alone is sovereign, omniscient, and omnipotent in contrast to the idols and false gods. The Old Testament reserves "I am" for Yahweh; by definition, this name cannot apply to any mere man.

So when Jesus steps into the storyline coming out of the Old Testament and refers to himself as "I am," he is making an explicit statement regarding his identity. In John 8, for example, Jesus concludes a particular controversy with the Jews about his origin and identity by declaring, "Truly, truly, I say to you, before Abraham was, I am" (v. 58). At this point in the developing covenantal plotline, the Jews are clinging to their descent from Abraham, who received the covenant promise of blessing from God. Jesus explicitly refers to himself as "I am" to reveal himself to be the God of Abraham.

As another example, in John 13, Jesus begins predicting the events leading up to his death, so that "when it does take place you may believe that *egō eimi*" (v. 19). Schreiner makes the case that Jesus uses *egō eimi* here as the unique name of God—so "I am," not "I am he," as in most translations—and notes the Christological significance: "The use of 'I am' demonstrates that such predictions are not merely the prophecies of an ordinary prophet. Jesus demonstrates his deity by proclaiming what will happen before it occurs."[49] In short, the man Jesus claims to be standing before the Jews as their Creator–Covenant Lord.

---

[49] See Schreiner, *New Testament Theology*, 253.

Jesus also identifies with Yahweh of the Old Testament by referring to himself as the typological fulfillment of certain Old Testament persons, events, and institutions. These particular "I am" statements, therefore, have predicates: the bread of life (John 6:35); the light of the world (8:12); the door (10:7, 9); the good shepherd (10:11, 14); the resurrection and the life (11:25); the way, the truth, and the life (14:6); and the true vine (15:1, 5). In John 6, for example, Jesus declares, "I am the bread of life" (vv. 35, 48) to reveal that he is greater than the manna that sustained Israel in the wilderness because he gives eternal life to the people of God as a work of God himself (vv. 51, 58). And in John 10, Jesus declares, "I am the good shepherd" (v. 11), in contrast to a thief or mere hired hand. By using this predicate within the plotline of Scripture, Jesus is claiming to fulfill the role of Israel's kings to shepherd the people where all of those kings failed (Ezek. 34:1–10). But Jesus also identifies with Yahweh, who promised, "I, I myself will search for my sheep and will seek them out. . . . And I will bring them out from the peoples . . . and will bring them into their own land" (vv. 11–13).

In all of Jesus's "I am" sayings, then, he continues to bear witness intentionally and explicitly to his self-identification as God the Son incarnate.

JESUS AS THE OBJECT OF FAITH

Finally, Jesus explicitly makes himself the object of the saving faith and trust that is reserved for God alone. The Old Testament affirms repeatedly that "salvation belongs to the LORD" (Jonah 2:9); "He only is my rock and my salvation" (Ps. 62:2, 6); "On God rests my salvation and my glory" (v. 7). The New Testament certainly does not contradict this convention; but the covenant security offered to God's people does expand to include the salvation, blessings, and peace available in Jesus Christ (see John 14:1; Acts 10:43; 16:31; Rom. 10:12–13). In fact, the New Testament signals the significance of this expansion by focusing saving faith on Jesus while referring to God as the proper object of faith on only twelve occasions.[50]

This shift to Jesus, however, does not mean that Jesus becomes a rival object of faith. Rather than replace God as the one worthy of our trust for our salvation, Jesus reveals himself to be God in the flesh, divine yet distinct from the Father. For example, in John 14 Jesus tells his disciples, "Let not your hearts be troubled. Believe in God; believe also in me" (v. 1). As Jesus has moved ever closer to the cross, he has become deeply troubled in heart (12:27) and spirit (13:21). His disciples are greatly troubled, but for entirely different reasons. They are not facing the horrors of crucifixion like Jesus and cannot understand

---

[50] John 12:44; 14:1; Acts 16:34; Rom. 4:3, 5, 17, 24; Gal. 3:6; 1 Thess. 1:8; Titus 3:8; Heb. 6:1; 1 Pet. 1:21; see Harris, *Three Crucial Questions about Jesus*, 77.

what Jesus will experience. It is enough, however, that Jesus's disciples know that he is leaving, for them to fear losing him. The disciples have set their hopes fully on Jesus as the Christ, even if they do not yet fully grasp his identity. And rather than redirect them to God, Jesus encourages them that their belief in *him* is belief in God.

Within the developing storyline and covenants of the Old Testament, which Jesus knows well, he can so confidently center his disciples' faith in him only because he knows he is God the Son incarnate. The New Testament presents Jesus as a model of faith in his relationship as a man with God. But before we can model our faith after Jesus, the New Testament and Jesus himself command us to trust Jesus as the object of our faith in his coming as the God of our salvation. As the apostles testify in light of the advent of Christ, "there is no other name under heaven given among men by which we must be saved" (Acts 4:12; cf. Acts 10:43; 16:31; Rom. 10:9–11; 1 Cor. 1:2; 1 John 3:23; 5:13).[51]

The Apostolic Understanding of Jesus

As we now consider the Christology of the apostles, it is important to realize that their understanding was based on Jesus's understanding of his own identity. The New Testament does not present the apostolic identification of Jesus as different or even apart from Jesus's witness to himself. In fact, what we have seen in Jesus's implicit and explicit words and works as God the Son incarnate forms the theological foundation and evangelical motivation for the apostles' witness to him—to his uniqueness among men and his significance for all mankind.

The Pattern of the New Testament's Christology

It is also important to recognize that as the apostles fill out the Christology of the New Testament, they develop Jesus's identity according to both his deity and his humanity. Many theologians have tried to identify Jesus according to

---

[51] Our conclusion that Jesus understands himself to be God the Son incarnate differs from N. T. Wright. Wright has done a superb work turning back unwarranted skepticism among biblical scholars regarding the historicity and accuracy of the New Testament's presentation of Jesus, but he denies that Jesus knew that he was God the Son (see N. T. Wright, *The Challenge of Jesus* [Downers Grove, IL: InterVarsity Press, 1999], 96–125; cf. idem, *The New Testament and the People of God* [Minneapolis: Fortress, 1992]; idem, *Jesus and the Victory of God* [Minneapolis: Fortress, 1996]). Wright, similar to Richard Bauckham, asserts that Jewish monotheism was strict and that within Second Temple Judaism there was the twin belief that Yahweh would return to Zion and that Yahweh would be enthroned along with his Messiah. Wright also contends that Jesus viewed himself as carrying out the vocation of Yahweh, yet awareness of vocation is not the same thing as Jesus knowing he is God the Son. As Wright states, we should "forget the pseudo-orthodox attempts to make Jesus of Nazareth conscious of being the second person of the Trinity" (*Jesus and the Victory of God*, 653; cf. *Challenge of Jesus*, 120–125). Even though there is much to commend in Wright's work, his conclusion does not do justice to Jesus's self-identity and the entire biblical storyline. It is certainly the case that Jesus sees himself as the antitype of the Temple and Torah and that in his coming he was inaugurating God's kingdom. But given the biblical-theological framework that identifies Jesus and interprets his person and work, we must also say that Scripture presents all of Jesus's works to be the actions of Yahweh himself, something which Jesus himself knows. Jesus does not view himself merely as a messianic "son," but also as the eternal Son who has come and taken on our humanity in order to fulfill his Father's will and to redeem God's people. For a contrary view to Wright, see John Murray, *Systematic Theology*, vol. 2 of *Collected Writings of John Murray* (Carlisle, PA: Banner of Truth Trust, 1977), 138, who contends that Jesus's self-identity is as the *divine* Son.

a dominant but ultimately unhelpful dichotomy between his ontology and his function. And this dichotomy is often used to drive a wedge between the divine and human natures of Jesus that often results in the depreciation or complete loss of his divinity. In short, many current attempts at Christology argue that Jesus exercised the functions of deity without having the ontology of deity.[52] The New Testament, however, holds together the ontology and function of Jesus to bear witness to his deity and humanity as complementary and necessary to understanding his identity.

The New Testament's refusal to pit Jesus's ontology over against his function is grounded in the Bible's storyline. Because the storyline moves from the Old Testament to the New Testament, Christ's identity is first understood in terms of Old Testament messianic expectation which unites the eschatological hope of the Lord's coming to save his people with the coming of the Davidic king. In the New Testament, we discover who this Messiah is: the eternal Word made flesh (John 1:1–3, 14), the one who has come to save his people from their sins as the "son of David" (Matt. 1:1, 21). The Old Testament, then, anticipates and promises the Messiah, while the New Testament announces his arrival and identifies him as the Lord who is the great King. Thus, the overall pattern of biblical Christology does not pit Christ's ontology and function against each other; instead, it unites them in the person and work of Christ.

The thesis of this section is that the apostles present Jesus according to this very same storyline, hence the reason why they present Christ as both God and man by linking *what Jesus does* (function) to *who he is* (ontology).[53] The apostles do not see the divine works performed by the man Jesus as a problem; instead they view them as the key to understanding his true and full identity. For the apostles, Jesus's actions do not speak louder than his words, but Jesus's works do combine with his words in the context of certain kingdom promises and expectations to say something astounding about Jesus: he is the divine Son, the Creator–Covenant Lord, come now as a man to redeem humanity and restore the divine rule over all creation, for eternal life with his people in complete covenant reconciliation.

The Apostolic Witness to Jesus Christ

The men whom Jesus authorized and enabled to bear faithful witness to him (cf. Luke 24:45–49; Acts 1:8) have done so in the New Testament Gospels and

---

[52] Or as Oscar Cullmann states, "When it is asked in the New Testament 'Who is Christ?' the question never means exclusively, or even primarily, 'What is his nature?' but first of all, 'What is his function?'" (Cullmann, *Christology of the New Testament*, 3–4). Behind this dichotomy of the ontological and functional lies another debate. Individuals such as Cullmann contend that ontological considerations are indebted to Greek philosophy and are foreign to a Jewish or Hebrew way of looking at the world. For an excellent critique of this view, see James Barr, *The Semantics of Biblical Language* (Eugene, OR: Wipf & Stock, 2004).

[53] As already noted, Bauckham, *Jesus and the God of Israel*, 31, argues that rather than ontology and function, thinking in terms of *identity* better captures the New Testament presentation of Jesus.

Epistles. A survey of Christological thought working through each Gospel and every epistle would exceed the limitations of the present project. But a consideration of four key passages will provide the main apostolic argument for the identity of Christ, an argument which unpacks Christ's unique identity in two complementary ways: Jesus is *God the Son* and thus Lord by virtue of who he has always been, *and* Jesus *now becomes Lord and Christ* by virtue of his incarnation and cross work. In his humanity, the Son fulfills the roles of previous sons (e.g., Adam, Israel, David) by inaugurating God's kingdom and the promised new covenant age, *and* he is able to do so precisely because he is the *divine* Son.

ROMANS 1:3–4

[1] Paul, a servant of Christ Jesus, called to be an apostle, set apart for the gospel of God, [2] which he promised beforehand through his prophets in the holy Scriptures, [3] concerning his Son, who was descended from David according to the flesh [4] and was declared to be the Son of God in power according to the Spirit of holiness by his resurrection from the dead, Jesus Christ our Lord . . .

It is certain that the first verses of Romans have something significant to say about the identity of Christ. But what exactly is Paul saying? Is he saying that Christ is the Son of God from eternity, or that he only became the Son at a certain point in history? Appealing to verse 4 and its participle *horisthentos*—from the verb *horizō*, "to appoint"—some scholars argue that Jesus first became the Son at his resurrection. For example, James Dunn argues this view by linking Romans 1:3–4 with Acts 13:32–33 and its use of Psalm 2. Appealing to Psalm 2:7—"I will tell of the decree: The LORD said to me, 'You are my Son; today I have begotten you'"—Dunn argues that early Christians interpreted "today" as a temporal trigger such that Jesus's divine sonship should be viewed "principally as a role and status he had entered upon, been appointed to, at his resurrection."[54] On this view, Jesus's relation to God as his Son was something he gained, and therefore something he previously did not have.

Conversely, Robert Reymond resists the specter of adoptionism by translating *horisthentos* as "marked out" or "designated," and by interpreting "the Spirit of holiness" in verse 4 as a reference to Christ's divine nature.[55] Reymond then argues that it was not at the resurrection that Jesus took on a new role and entered into a new state (exaltation from humiliation); the resurrection simply

---

[54] Dunn, *Christology in the Making*, 36. Dunn argues further that *"the language of the earliest post-Easter confession of Jesus' sonship and the earliest use of Ps. 2:7 certainly seem to have placed the decisive moment of 'becoming' quite clearly in the resurrection of Jesus"* (ibid., 46, emphasis his); see also John A. T. Robinson, *The Human Face of God* (London: SCM, 1973), 161.

[55] See R. L. Reymond, *Jesus, Divine Messiah: The New and Old Testament Witness* (Fearn: Mentor, 2003), 378–379.

marked out Jesus as the Son "in accordance with what he is on his divine side (that is, 'according to the spirit of holiness')."[56]

But the *adoption* of Jesus as the Son and the *display* of his sonship via his divinity are not the only two options for understanding Paul's Christology here. The adoption option stresses his *deity* at the expense of his humanity; the display option stresses his *divinity* at the expense of his humanity. A third option, however, holds together Jesus's divine and human sonship according to the apostles' pattern of Christology in the New Testament. Three observations about Romans 1:3–4 will help us see that Paul understands Jesus to be the Son of God both because of who he has always been—even before his incarnation—and because of what he has done as a man.

First, as we have seen, the title *Son* works at two levels: it designates Jesus as the eternal Son *and* as the human son who is the antitype of previous "sons"—Adam, Israel, and David. Applying the typological function of *Son*, Schreiner concludes, "The one who existed eternally as the Son was appointed the Son of God in power as the Son of David. . . . In other words, the Son reigned with the Father from all eternity, but as a result of his incarnation and atoning work he was appointed to be the Son of God as one who was now both God and man."[57]

Second, it is best to render the participle *horisthentos* (Rom. 1:4) as "appointed" or "designated" and not "declared" or "marked out."[58] The emphasis of the verse, then, is on a unique appointment based on a unique work. This appointment, however, does *not* entail a merely functional Christology. Douglas Moo helpfully highlights the plain grammar of the text: "the Son is the subject of the entire statement in vv. 3–4: It is the *Son* who is 'appointed' Son."[59] Recognizing the significance of this grammatical feature, Moo then argues that "[t]he tautologous nature of this statement reveals that being appointed Son has to do *not* with a change of essence—as if a person or human messiah becomes Son of God for the first time—but with a change in status or function."[60] And following the plain sense of Paul's thought here clears the way to see that he is presenting Christ at the termination of a typological trajectory that runs through the enthronement of the Davidic king. The divine Son comes

---

[56] Reymond, *Jesus, Divine Messiah*, 382. Reymond also argues the following two points, which are difficult to sustain exegetically. First, "flesh" (*sarx*) in verse 3 is a reference to Christ's human nature that is contrasted in verse 4 with "according to the spirit of holiness" (ibid., 376–381). Second, Reymond rejects that verses 3–4 teach "successive stages" in the life of Christ or insert a contrast between what Jesus was before and what he was after his resurrection (ibid., 381–384). Thus, the relation between the two participial phrases of verses 3–4 is one of climax not contrast, so that, at the resurrection, Jesus was not appointed as Son but displayed or demonstrated his sonship in accordance with his divine nature (ibid., 381–384).

[57] Thomas R. Schreiner, *Romans*, BECNT (Grand Rapids, MI: Baker, 1998), 38–39.

[58] In its seven other New Testament occurrences, the verb means "to determine" or "to appoint," and there is no compelling reason to think Paul is using the word here in a different way (see Moo, *Romans*, 47–48; Schreiner, *Romans*, 42).

[59] Moo, *Romans*, 48.

[60] Ibid.

as the *incarnate* Lord Jesus Christ to accomplish certain works that lead to his *incarnate* enthronement-appointment as the true Davidic Son–King. So Moo is correct in his conclusion that "[t]he transition from v. 3 to v. 4 . . . is not a transition from a human messiah to a divine Son of God (adoptionism) but from the Son as Messiah to the Son as both Messiah *and* powerful, reigning Lord."[61]

Third, this typological understanding of the text is confirmed by the antithetical parallel between "according to the Spirit of holiness" (*kata pneuma hagiōsunēs*; v. 4) and "according to the flesh" (*kata sarka*; v. 3). Some scholars suggest that *flesh* and *spirit* mark a contrast between Jesus's *human* and *divine* natures.[62] Others argue that "spirit of holiness" is a reference to Christ's obedient, consecrated spirit that he manifested throughout his earthly life.[63] A better suggestion, however, accounts for the framework established by the biblical storyline that governs Paul's identification of Christ: *flesh* and *spirit* mark a contrast between the *old* and *new* eras of redemptive history. The old era is characterized by the covenant mediation of Adam and dominated by sin, death, and the *flesh*; the new era is characterized by the covenant mediation of Christ, the last Adam, and brings forth the blessings of salvation, life, and the *Spirit*.[64]

In his earthly life—his life in the realm of the flesh—the eternal Son of God is the promised Messiah-Christ. And by his powerful work epitomized in his victorious resurrection, the Son has brought with him in his reign the Spirit of God. Paul's contrast between *flesh* and *spirit*, then, focuses not on the two natures of Christ, human and divine, but on the two states of Christ, his *humiliation* and *exaltation*.

---

[61] Ibid., 49. This understanding is further grounded in an allusion to Psalm 2:7: "You are my Son; today I have begotten you." In the New Testament, Psalm 2 is quoted a number of times and in quite diverse ways (see Acts 4:25–26; 13:33; Heb. 1:5; 5:5; Rev. 2:27; 12:5; 19:15). Consistent with his interpretation of Romans 1:3–4, Reymond argues (along with many in the early church) that Psalm 2:7 does not apply to the Davidic king but refers directly to Christ (Reymond, *Jesus, Divine Messiah*, 77–81). It is an address of the Father to the Son in eternity past, which for many in the early church was used as one of the textual proofs for the doctrine of the eternal generation of the Son. In its immediate context, however, it is difficult *not* to read Psalm 2 as a reference to the Davidic king. A better interpretation is to read Psalm 2 typologically. As each Davidic king was enthroned, this Psalm continued to point forward to the day when the Messiah would usher in God's kingdom and all that it entails through his triumphant cross work and resurrection that would exalt him to sit at God's right hand with a name above every name. In this way, as Schreiner notes, the new dimension that results by virtue of Jesus's work "was not his sonship but his heavenly installation as God's Son by virtue of his Davidic sonship" (Schreiner, *Romans*, 39).

[62] For this interpretation, see the discussion in Moo, *Romans*, 49.

[63] See, e.g., Reymond, *Jesus, Divine Messiah*, 378–381.

[64] See Moo, *Romans*, 49–50; Schreiner, *Romans*, 43–45; Herman Ridderbos, *Paul: An Outline of His Theology*, trans. John Richard deWitt (Grand Rapids, MI: Eerdmans, 1975), 64–68. The use of "flesh" (*sarx*) in Paul is diverse, but predominantly it is tied to the old age associated with Adam, sin, and death. The more neutral uses of *sarx* (e.g., Rom. 3:20; 4:1; 9:3, 5; 11:14; 1 Cor. 1:26, 29) carry a nuance of weakness. The reason for this, as Schreiner explains, is "that the flesh participates in the old age of sin and death" (Schreiner, *Romans*, 43). Thus, as Paul states elsewhere, Jesus was born "in the likeness of sinful flesh" (Rom. 8:3)—that he was born not fallen, but weak, taking on a human nature associated with this old age in order to inaugurate the new age that is characterized by the life and power of the Holy Spirit. Thus, in the incarnation and state of humiliation, Christ becomes one with us, though without sin. But by his obedience, even obedience to death on a cross and then resurrection from the dead, he who has the Spirit is exalted, and as such, his resurrection marks the beginning of the new age and era. His resurrection signals that the new age has begun and that God's promises from the Old Testament have now become a reality, at least in an inaugurated form.

We can now summarize Paul's witness to the identity of Christ in Romans 1:3–4 by pulling together these three observations from the text: the eternal Son of God became the incarnate Son of God to then become the Davidic Son of God through his life, death, and resurrection. The Redeemer we need—one who can undo the work of Adam, accomplish our forgiveness, and usher in God's kingdom and the new creation—must be God the Son incarnate.

PHILIPPIANS 2:5–11

> [5] Have this mind among yourselves, which is yours in Christ Jesus, [6] who, though he was in the form of God, did not count equality with God a thing to be grasped, [7] but emptied himself, by taking the form of a servant, being born in the likeness of men. [8] And being found in human form, he humbled himself by becoming obedient to the point of death, even death on a cross. [9] Therefore God has highly exalted him and bestowed on him the name that is above every name, [10] so that at the name of Jesus every knee should bow, in heaven and on earth and under the earth, [11] and every tongue confess that Jesus Christ is Lord, to the glory of God the Father.[65]

Paul also teaches the divine-human identity of Christ by means of another contrast: the forms of *God* and *servant* in Philippians 2. Some scholars argue that the text depends on an Adam-Christ contrast that would restrict the difference between them—and the point of the passage—to the divergent attitudes and actions of two men made in the image of God.[66] But as the following five observations will demonstrate, Paul traces a trajectory not from the first to the last Adam, but from the eternal exaltation of the preexistent and divine Son of God to the historical exaltation of Jesus Christ via the humiliation of the Son's incarnation, death, and resurrection.

First, the two-part literary structure of the passage guides the nature and direction of the action. In verses 6–7, two verbs describe Jesus's self-humbling in connection with his taking our human nature (i.e., the state of humiliation); in verses 9–11, two verbs describe the Father's exaltation of Jesus due to his victorious work as a man (i.e., the state of exaltation).[67] The action of the text, then, moves from the Son's preincarnational existence in equality with God to his lowly incarnational existence as a condemned and executed criminal. But

---

[65] Scholars disagree whether this text is Pauline or a pre-Pauline hymn. Either way, however, most acknowledge that we must accept this text as Paul's own view—he either authored it or accepted it as true—and interpret it accordingly (see O'Brien, *Philippians*, 188–202).

[66] For an example of this Adam-Christ argument in biblical studies, see Dunn, *Christology in the Making*, 114–121. In theological studies, this text serves as an important but misused proof-text for kenotic Christologies, which argue that, in the incarnation, the Son "emptied" himself of some of his divine attributes. For a critique of the various kenotic approaches, see Part IV; see also N. T. Wright, *The Climax of the Covenant: Christ and the Law in Pauline Theology* (Minneapolis: Fortress, 1992), 56–98; O'Brien, *Philippians*, 196–198; Gordon D. Fee, *Pauline Christology: An Exegetical-Theological Study* (Peabody, MA: Hendrickson, 2007), 375–393; Schreiner, *New Testament Theology*, 323–327.

[67] See O'Brien, *Philippians*, 205–232; Schreiner, *New Testament Theology*, 324.

the action continues as God exalts Jesus in his incarnational existence to his preincarnational honor and glory that he shared with God.

Second, in verse 6 Paul points to the preexistence and deity of Christ by the phrase "who, though he was in the form of God" (*hos en morphē theou huparchōn*).[68] Many scholars have attempted to define the precise meaning of "form of God," but Peter T. O'Brien's recent treatment of the term stands out as the most helpful.[69] After surveying the term, O'Brien concludes that *morphē* refers to that "form which truly and fully expresses the being which underlies it."[70] In general, then, Paul uses *morphē* to explain that Jesus truly and fully expresses the essence of God (v. 6) and the essence of a servant (v. 7).

O'Brien's conclusion builds off the work of R. P. Martin, who focused on the use of *morphē* in the LXX.[71] Martin discovered in the LXX that: (1) *morphē* denotes the appearance or form of something by which we describe it; (2) *morphē* and *eikōn* ("image") are used interchangeably; and (3) *eikōn* and *doxa* ("glory") are also equivalent terms. Taken together, this means that *morphē* belongs to a group of words "which describes God not as he is in himself but as he is to an observer."[72] *Morphē*, then, does not describe God's nature per se, but it presents a form that truly and fully expresses the underlying divine nature.[73]

So in Philippians 2:6–7, we can now see that Paul uses the conceptual and communicative power of *morphē* to affirm the full deity (*morphē theou*)[74] and humanity (*morphēn doulou*)[75] of Christ. The preincarnational person of Christ has always existed as the full expression of what it means to be God. And this same divine person became incarnate, so that Jesus now also exists as the full expression of what it means to be a man-servant. As will be explained below, the movement between these two forms is not subtraction or transformation but addition for salvation and glorification. Macleod captures the heart of this contrast in the *morphēs* of Christ:

> The subject of the *kenōsis*, therefore (the one who "emptied himself"), is one who had glory with the Father before the world began (Jn. 17:5). . . . He possessed all the majesty of deity, performed all its functions and enjoyed all

---

[68] O'Brien rightly observes that the relative pronoun *hos* ("who") links and identifies the historical Jesus with God the Son who existed prior to the incarnation (O'Brien, *Philippians*, 206).

[69] See ibid., 205–211.

[70] Ibid., 210.

[71] See Ralph P. Martin, *Carmen Christi: Philippians ii. 5–11 in Recent Interpretation and in the Setting of Early Christian Worship* (Cambridge: Cambridge University Press, 1967), 99–120.

[72] Donald Macleod, *The Person of Christ*, Contours of Christian Theology (Downers Grove, IL: InterVarsity Press, 1998), 212.

[73] For his helpful survey of the meaning of *morphē*, see O'Brien, *Philippians*, 207–221.

[74] Ibid., 211. The use of *morphē theou* in verse 6 functions similarly to John 17:5 and Hebrews 1:3 in establishing the deity of Christ. In John, Jesus says that he shared in the glory of the Father before the world began; in Hebrews, the emphasis is on the Son sharing the radiance of God's glory and the exact representation of his being.

[75] The meaning of *morphēn doulou* in verse 7 is clarified by the prepositional phrase *en homoiōmati anthrōpōn genomenos*, "being born in the likeness of men." In this context, to be in the form of a servant is to be fully human.

its prerogatives. He was adored by his Father and worshipped by the angels. He was invulnerable to pain, frustration and embarrassment. He existed in unclouded serenity. His supremacy was total, his satisfaction complete, his blessedness perfect. Such a condition was not something he had secured by effort. It was the way things were, and had always been; and there was no reason why they should change. But change they did, and they changed because of the second element involved in the *kenōsis*: Christ did not insist on his rights . . . he did not regard being equal with God as a *harpagmos*.[76]

Third, it is best to translate the difficult phrase *ouch harpagmon hēgēsato to einai isa theō* in verse 6 as, "He did not think equality with God something to be used for his own advantage."[77] The issue is not whether Jesus gains or retains *equality* with God. The text is clear that the Son exists in the "form of God" and thus shares "equality with God" (v. 6).[78] Instead, the issue is one of Jesus's *attitude* in regard to his divine status.[79] As Schreiner rightly points out, "Paul *assumes* that Jesus is equal with God. The verse does not teach that Jesus quit trying to attain equality with God. Rather, Paul emphasizes that Jesus did not take advantage of or exploit the equality with God that he already possessed."[80] In other words, the grasping or advantage-taking does not move toward equality with God as its goal but begins with God-equality and moves toward others.[81] The text, then, emphasizes the selfless attitude of the preincarnational Christ: he regarded his equality with God not as excusing him from but as uniquely qualifying him for the task of redemptive suffering and death as a man.[82]

Fourth, we should understand "but [he] emptied himself" in verse 7 as a metaphorical expression that refers not to the subtraction or reduction of divine attributes but to the addition of a human nature.[83] Contrary to the more extreme kenotic Christologies, the text does not support the position that the

---

[76] Macleod, *Person of Christ*, 213–214.

[77] Bauckham, *Jesus and the God of Israel*, 41. This translation is dependent upon the work of R. W. Hoover, who translates *harpagmos* as an idiom to mean "something to use for his own advantage" (R. W. Hoover, "The Harpagmos Enigma: A Philological Solution," *Harvard Theological Review* 64/1 [1971]: 95–119). For other discussions of *harpagmos* in Philippians 2:6, see O'Brien, *Philippians*, 211–216; Wright, *Climax of the Covenant*, 77–82; Schreiner, *New Testament Theology*, 325.

[78] For the argument that to exist in the "form of God" is parallel to being "equal with God," see Schreiner, *New Testament Theology*, 325; O'Brien, *Philippians*, 216; Wright, *Climax of the Covenant*, 72, 75, 80–83.

[79] See Bauckham, *Jesus and the God of Israel*, 41.

[80] Schreiner, *New Testament Theology*, 325.

[81] O'Brien reinforces this understanding by following C. F. D. Moule's suggestion that the participial clause in verse 6 should not be viewed as concessive (i.e., who, *though* he was in the form of God), but as causal (i.e., "precisely *because* he was in the form of God he did not regard this equality with God as something to be used for his own advantage") (O'Brien, *Philippians*, 216).

[82] On this point, Macleod makes an astute observation: "The conclusion to which this leads us is that the impulse to serve lies at the very heart of deity. God is not self-centred and self-absorbed. As love, he is pure altruism, looking not on (or at) his own things, but at the things of others. From this point of view the idea of *kenōsis* is revolutionary for our understanding of God. It is his very form to forego his rights" (Macleod, *Person of Christ*, 215).

[83] It should not be missed that this text also implies that Jesus made an intentional and informed decision on his part not to take advantage of his position and status, which is possible only for one who actually has personal preexistence before taking on our humanity. For a discussion of this point, see Schreiner, *New Testament Theology*, 325; cf. Gathercole, *Preexistent Son*, 25.

preincarnational person of Christ emptied himself of his divine attributes or of his *morphē theou*. Paul uses the verb *ekenōsen* as an idiomatic expression: to empty in the sense of giving up one's rights (cf. ESV and NIV). And Paul clearly explains the nature of this *kenōsis* by two participial phrases that describe the manner in which Christ "emptied" himself: by "taking the form of a servant" (*morphēn doulou labōn*); and by "being made in human likeness" (*en homoiōmati anthrōpōn genomenos*).[84] The grammar and context of verses 6–8 equate the *emptying* of Christ with *taking on the lowly status* of a human servant (v. 7) who *humbles himself in death* for the sins of others (v. 8).

Paul's point, then, is not that Christ *exchanged* the "form of God" *for* the "form of a servant" but that he now *manifests* the "form of God" *in* the "form of a servant." The text says nothing about Christ emptying his divine attributes. Rather, he empties himself by adding to himself a complete human nature and a willingness to undergo the agony of death for our sake and for our salvation.[85]

To get a better sense of what the *kenōsis* of Christ reveals about his identity, we can follow Macleod's observation that verses 7–9 stress three movements in the Son's humiliation. In the first movement, the preincarnational Christ took the form of a servant (*morphēn doulou*; v. 7): "He became a slave, without rights: a non-person, who could not turn to those crucifying him and say, 'Do you not know who I am?'"[86] In other words, the eternal Son, who had all the rights of deity, became a nobody and willingly submitted to his Father's will for us. In the second movement, Christ took on our human likeness (*homoiōma*) to be found in human form (*kai schēmati heurtheis hōs anthrōpos*; v. 8), which entails that he became all that we are as humans except without sin (cf. Rom. 8:3). In the third and final movement, Christ obediently submitted himself to death on a cross (Phil. 2:8) in the likeness of sinful humanity. The limit of the *kenōsis* of Christ, then, was not incarnation but crucifixion.

Taken together, these three movements of the divinely exalted Son into the humiliation of Christ become three layers of veiling that temporarily hide his God-equal glory. In this sense, then, we can say that the full *kenōsis* of Christ involved the near complete *krypsis* ("hiddenness") of his divine glory, but not the loss of his divine nature and attributes.[87] So according to the apostolic

---

[84] The two aorist participles *labōn* and *genomenos* are both modal and coincident with the verb *ekenōsen*, grammatically equating the emptying of Christ with "humbling himself" and taking on our human nature (see O'Brien, *Philippians*, 218–223).

[85] The kenotic views will be discussed and critiqued at length in Part IV. Here we need only to say that proper exegesis disallows the kenotic interpretation of Philippians 2:5–11, and orthodox theology prohibits severing the divine attributes from the divine nature. Additionally, verses 9–11 speak of Christ's exaltation with no hint that he thereby regained divine attributes lost in the incarnation. Making this point, Schreiner argues that "Paul utilizes paradoxical language by describing Christ's emptying in terms of adding" (Schreiner, *New Testament Theology*, 325).

[86] Macleod, *Person of Christ*, 216.

[87] See Oliver D. Crisp, *Divinity and Humanity* (Cambridge: Cambridge University Press, 2007), 118–153; Macleod provides a graphic account of the *kenosis-krypsis* of Christ: "In becoming incarnate God not only accommodates himself to human weakness: he buries his glory under veil after veil so that it is impossible for flesh and blood to

understanding, the nature and goal of Jesus's emptying himself was to place God the Son incarnate on a cross, willingly and obediently enduring not only the burden of human weakness and sin but also the full weight of the Father's divine wrath with all of its physical, spiritual, and relational agony.

Fifth, in verses 9–11 God exalts Christ back to his God-equal glory on the basis of and in response to the Son's incarnational obedience. As we have seen, the Son lost none of his deity in his incarnation. But his deity alone does not warrant his *incarnational* exaltation. Rather, it was the Son's obedience *as a man*, indeed as the Son *incarnate*, climaxing on the cross, that merited his bearing "the name that is above every name." Macleod provides a well-composed portrait of Jesus's incarnate obedience:

> Never once does he in his own interest or in his own defence break beyond the parameters of humanity. He had no place to lay his head; but he never built himself a house. He was thirsty; but he provided for himself no drink. He was assaulted by the powers of hell; but he did not call on his legions of angels. Even when he saw the full cost of *kenōsis*, he asked for no rewriting of the script. He bore the sin in his own body, endured the sorrow in his human soul and redeemed the church with his human blood. The power which carried the world, stilled the tempest and raised the dead was never used to make his own conditions of service easier. Neither was the prestige he enjoyed in heaven exploited to relax the rules of engagement. Deploying no resources beyond those of his Spirit-filled humanness, he faced the foe as flesh and triumphed as man.[88]

Based on *this* obedience, the Father exalted God the Son incarnate to his pre-incarnational glory so that every knee in heaven and on earth will bow to a man. As Dan McCartney rightly insists, in Christ we have "the restatement of the originally intended divine order for earth, with man properly situated as God's vicegerent."[89]

All creation will worship and submit to the man Jesus Christ. By resurrection from crucifixion and enthronement in heaven, the Father has stripped away every veil of the incarnation so that all will see that the man Jesus Christ is God himself. The name that is above every name is not Jesus. The peerless name of heaven and earth is Yahweh, the name of the Creator–Covenant Lord. Isaiah prophesied that Yahweh himself would save his people and that all creation would submit to him (Isa. 45:22–23). And Paul applies this prophecy to the incarnational obedience and exaltation of Christ (Phil. 2:9–11).[90] In other

---

recognize him. As he hangs on the cross, bleeding, battered, powerless and forsaken, the last thing he looks like is God. Indeed, he scarcely looks human" (Macleod, *Person of Christ*, 218).

[88] Macleod, *Person of Christ*, 220.

[89] Dan G. McCartney, "Ecce Homo: The Coming of the Kingdom as the Restoration of Human Viceregency," *WTJ* 56 (1994): 2.

[90] The apostles repeatedly emphasize this uniqueness of Jesus by applying to him numerous Old Testament texts about Yahweh (see Ex. 3:14 with John 8:58; Isa. 44:6 with Rev. 1:17; Ps. 102:26–27 [LXX] with Heb. 1:11–12; Isa.

words, Jesus Christ reigns now over all creation from the throne of heaven as God the Son incarnate.[91]

COLOSSIANS 1:15–20

[15] He is the image of the invisible God, the firstborn of all creation. [16] For by him all things were created, in heaven and on earth, visible and invisible, whether thrones or dominions or rulers or authorities—all things were created through him and for him. [17] And he is before all things, and in him all things hold together. [18] And he is the head of the body, the church. He is the beginning, the firstborn from the dead, that in everything he might be preeminent. [19] For in him all the fullness of God was pleased to dwell, [20] and through him to reconcile to himself all things, whether on earth or in heaven, making peace by the blood of his cross.[92]

As "one of the christological high points of the New Testament,"[93] Colossians 1:15–20 gives us great insight into the identity of Christ by presenting him in unique categories. The text is rich with Christological nuance and import, all of which can be studied at length. But for our purposes here, we can focus on what Paul means by referring to Jesus in these terms: "the image of the invisible God"; "the firstborn of all creation"; the agent and center of all creation; "the firstborn from the dead"; the one with "the fullness of God"; the agent and center of cosmic reconciliation. The simplest approach is to follow the basic structure of the passage. The first main stanza (vv. 15–16) focuses on the representative and creative functions of Christ; a transitional stanza (vv. 17–18a) links his roles in creation and redemption; the second main stanza (vv. 18b–20) takes us into the reconciling work of Christ.

Paul begins his Christology in verses 15–16 by identifying Christ as "the image of the invisible God" (*eikōn tou theou tou aoratou*) (v. 15). *Image* carries the sense of "something that looks like, or represents, something else."[94] As in 2 Corinthians 4:4, the stress is on the Son as the perfect revelation of God. "No one has ever seen God," writes John, but "the only God, who is at the Father's side, he has made him known" (John 1:18). Here, Paul makes the same point by declaring that the Son has perfectly reflected the Father from eternity and

---

45:23 with Phil. 2:10–11). The apostles also identify Jesus with God by applying the title *theos* to Jesus (see John 1:1, 18; 20:28; Rom. 9:5, Titus 2:13; Heb. 1:8–9; 2 Pet. 1:1).

[91] It is important here to agree with Schreiner regarding the equality and distinction of Father and Son: "Clearly, Paul teaches that Jesus shares in the same divine nature as Yahweh himself, but Paul does this without denying monotheism or the distinctions between the Father and the Son" (Schreiner, *New Testament Theology*, 326–327; cf. Bauckham, *Jesus and the God of Israel*, 41–45; O'Brien, *Philippians*, 241–243; Wells, *Person of Christ*, 64–66).

[92] Scholars disagree as to whether this text is original to Paul or was an early hymn circulating when Paul was writing his epistle. Either way, we should interpret the text as part of Paul's Christological thought: he either wrote it as true about Christ or incorporated it because it is true about Christ.

[93] Douglas Moo, *The Letters to the Colossians and to Philemon*, PNTC (Grand Rapids, MI: Eerdmans, 2008), 107. N. T. Wright states that this text is "reckoned among the most important Christological passages in the New Testament" (N. T. Wright, *The Epistles of Paul to the Colossians and Philemon: An Introduction and Commentary*, Tyndale New Testament Commentaries [Leicester; Grand Rapids, MI: Eerdmans, 1986], 64).

[94] Moo, *Colossians and Philemon*, 117.

now perfectly reveals the invisible God in the incarnate Christ. Only a divine Son can be *this* image.

The use of "image" (*eikōn*) also links back to the creation of humanity "in the image of God." We have seen in chapter 3 that God created man with the express purpose that in the vice-regent rule of humanity the *imago Dei* would be faithfully spread over the whole earth. While the first humans were created in the image of God, however, they were not the original *imago Dei*. The eternal Son is the archetype image; humanity is the ectype image.[95] So we can agree with N. T. Wright that from all eternity, Jesus "held the same relation to the Father that humanity, from its creation, had been intended to bear."[96] And this function as the eternal image of God grounds the role of Christ as the incarnational image of God. By being made in the image of God as a man, God the Son has come as the last Adam, to restore the vice-regent reign of humanity and spread the *imago Dei* throughout a new humanity. As Wright argues, the Son is "the climax of the history of creation, and at the same time the starting-point of the new creation."[97]

Still within the first main stanza, verses 15–16 connect the imaging function of Christ to his role in creation by Paul's reference to Christ as "the firstborn of all creation" (*prōtotokos pasēs ktiseōs*) (v. 15) in terms of *rank* and *authority*.[98] Paul's use of *firstborn* comes out of the Old Testament. Israel's identity as God's "firstborn" son (Ex. 4:22) entailed the nation's status as representative and ruler for God in the world. And the Davidic king also received the title: "I will make him the firstborn, the highest of the kings of the earth" (Ps. 89:27). *Firstborn*, then, has the connotation of *supreme over*, which is precisely its meaning in Colossians 1:15.[99] Confirming this interpretation in verse 16, Paul explains why he can call Christ the firstborn of creation: "for [*hoti*] by him all things were created, . . . whether thrones or dominions or rulers or authorities."

As the firstborn, Christ existed before creation, functioned as the agent of creation, and therefore stands supreme over creation. All things were made "in him" (*en autō*) (Col. 1:16), meaning all of God's creative work was "in terms of" or "in reference to" Christ.[100] All things were made "through him" (*di' autou*)

---

[95] See ibid., 118–119; see also Schreiner, *New Testament Theology*, 327.

[96] Wright, *Colossians and Philemon*, 70.

[97] Ibid. For further discussion of how Christ as the image of God fulfills the purposes of God in humanity, see Lane G. Tipton, "Christology in Colossians 1:15–20 and Hebrews 1:1–4: An Exercise in Biblico-Systematic Theology," in *Resurrection and Redemption: Theology in Service of the Church: Essays in Honor of Richard B. Gaffin, Jr.*, ed. Lane G. Tipton and Jeffrey C. Waddington (Phillipsburg, NJ: P&R, 2008), 193–194.

[98] "Firstborn" (*prōtotokos*) can convey the idea of priority in both time and rank. Ultimately, context determines its use (see Moo, *Colossians and Philemon*, 119–124). For a discussion of how the church through the Nicene Creed rightly rejected the Arian heresy that "firstborn of all creation" means Christ is the first creature, see Part III.

[99] See Moo, *Colossians and Philemon*, 119–120; Schreiner, *New Testament Theology*, 327; cf. Peter T. O'Brien, *Colossians, Philemon*, WBC (Waco, TX: Word, 1982), 44–45.

[100] Some scholars argue that the preposition *en* should be taken in the instrumental sense: "by him all things were created." Moo and O'Brien make the case that *en* should be taken in the sense of sphere: "in him all things were created" (Moo, *Colossians and Philemon*, 120–121; O'Brien, *Colossians, Philemon*, 45–46).

(v. 16), meaning Christ acted with God and as God in the work of creation that is possible for God alone. And all things were made "for him" (*eis auton*) (v. 16), meaning Christ is the reason for all of God's creative work—the identity of Christ is tied to the *telos* of the entire universe.[101] Schreiner summarizes the Christological implication: "Jesus is the goal as well as the agent of all creation. The glory that belongs to the only God also belongs to Jesus as creator and Lord."[102]

In verses 17–18a, Paul makes a transition by linking the role of Christ in creation with his work of redemption. Paul first reaffirms that Christ is the agent and Lord of creation: "And he is before all things" (*kai autos estin pro pantōn*) (v. 17). Then Paul confirms that even now, Christ is the Lord of cosmic preservation and providence: "and in him all things hold together" (*kai ta panta en auto synestēken*) (v. 17).[103] And this staging of Christ's identity allows Paul to make the point that it is the Lord of creation and providence who is "the head of the body, the church" (v. 18a). Paul intentionally connects the cosmic work and glory of the preincarnate Christ with his incarnate work and glory in creation and redemption.

Then in the second main stanza (vv. 18b–20), Paul explains that this Christ who is the "firstborn of all creation" is also the "firstborn from the dead" (*prōtotokos ek tōn nekrōn*) (v. 18b). Firstborn, of course, has the same sense of rank and authority as with the lordship of Christ over all creation. Paul now stretches the sovereignty and supremacy of Christ from creation to the new creation in the death and resurrection of God the Son incarnate. As Schreiner explains, "Jesus rules over death because he was the first to conquer death."[104] Because Christ inaugurates a new creation, a new order, a new humanity, "[h]e is the beginning" (*hos estin hē archē*) (v. 18b).[105] And Christ accomplishes this work "that in everything he might be preeminent" (*hina genētai en pasin autos prōteuōn*) (v. 18b). The incarnation and crucifixion of Christ, then, has served to extend the image and glory of God himself into humanity and the rest of creation. The lordship over all creation that belongs to Christ by right of his deity becomes his by right of his incarnate-redemptive work that inaugurates the new creation.[106]

---

[101] In verse 16, the verb *ktizō* ("create") is first used in the aorist passive tense (*ektisthē*) and then in the perfect tense (*ektistai*) (Harris, *Three Crucial Questions about Jesus*, 80–81). Far more than a stylistic maneuver, Paul's shift in verb tense emphasizes that creation not only came to exist by the Son but also continues to exist by him (cf. Moo, *Colossians and Philemon*, 124).

[102] Schreiner, *New Testament Theology*, 327.

[103] The verb *sunestēken* is in the perfect tense. As Moo notes, "the use of the perfect tense suggests a stative idea: the universe owes its continuing coherence to Christ" (Moo, *Colossians and Philemon*, 125). The cosmic functions of the *incarnate* Son are at the center of debate regarding a classical Christology versus various kenotic versions. As we will discuss in detail in Part 4, most versions of kenoticism cannot account for the incarnate Son continuing to exercise his divine attributes, especially during the state of humiliation.

[104] Schreiner, *New Testament Theology*, 328.

[105] For further discussion of Christ as the "beginning" (*archē*), see Schreiner, *New Testament Theology*, 328; Moo, *Colossians and Philemon*, 128–129; O'Brien, *Colossians, Philemon*, 50–51.

[106] See Wright, *Colossians and Philemon*, 73–75.

Finally, in verses 19–20, Paul explains that all of the creative and redemptive work and glory of Christ is possible because he is God the Son incarnate: "For in him all the fullness of God was pleased to dwell" (*hoti en auto eudokēsen pan to plērōma katoikēsai*) (v. 19).[107] In other words, the man Jesus Christ is the place where God in all of his fullness was pleased to take up his residence and display his glory. Moo observes that "[i]n typical New Testament emphasis, Christ replaces the temple as the 'place' where God now dwells."[108] And O'Brien rightly adds that "[a]ll the attributes and activities of God—his spirit, word, wisdom and glory—are perfectly displayed in Christ."[109] Paul makes clear that the deity of Christ is a present reality by using the present tense: the fullness of God "dwells" or "lives" (*katoikeō*) in Christ. But the adverb "bodily" (*sōmatikōs*) is separated from the verb, a grammatical feature that, as Harris argues, entails two distinct affirmations: "that the entire fullness of the Godhead dwells in Christ eternally and that this fullness now permanently resides in Christ in bodily form."[110]

The same eternal divine fullness of the Son continues to fill his incarnational existence as Jesus Christ, so that there is no sphere of life in heaven and earth over which he is not sovereign and supreme.[111] This comprehensive and cosmic reign of God would mean the destruction of all creation but for God's plan and promise to redeem and restore all things. So Paul concludes his Christology in Colossians 1:15–20 by explaining that God chose to work "through [Christ] to reconcile to himself all things, whether on earth or in heaven, making peace by the blood of his cross" (v. 20).

According to the apostolic understanding, then, in the man Jesus Christ has come the revelation and reign of God to accomplish the recreative and redemptive work of God for the reflection of God throughout all creation. There is no sphere of existence over which he is not sovereign and supreme. No wonder that all people are summoned to submit to him in trust, love, worship, and obedience.

Hebrews 1:1–4

[1] Long ago, at many times and in many ways, God spoke to our fathers by the prophets, [2] but in these last days he has spoken to us by his Son, whom he appointed the heir of all things, through whom also he created the

---

[107] Paul's use of this phrase comes out of the Old Testament, where "fullness" is a reference to God (see O'Brien, *Colossians, Philemon*, 52; Moo, *Colossians and Philemon*, 130–133). And the Old Testament is filled with the refrain that God chooses and is pleased to display his glory in the universe (see Ps. 72:19; Jer. 23:24; cf. Isa. 6:3; Ezek. 43:5; 44:4) and uniquely in the temple (see Ps. 68:16; 132:13–14; Isa. 8:18). Moo rightly argues that "was pleased" is very close to the idea of "choose" or "elect" (cf. Luke 12:32; 1 Cor. 1:21; Gal. 1:15) (Moo, *Colossians and Philemon*, 131–132).

[108] Moo, *Colossians and Philemon*, 133.

[109] O'Brien, *Colossians, Philemon*, 53.

[110] Harris, *Three Crucial Questions about Jesus*, 66; cf. O'Brien, *Colossians, Philemon*, 110–114.

[111] Wright, *Colossians and Philemon*, 79.

world. [3] He is the radiance of the glory of God and the exact imprint of his nature, and he upholds the universe by the word of his power. After making purification for sins, he sat down at the right hand of the Majesty on high, [4] having become as much superior to angels as the name he has inherited is more excellent than theirs.

It is not an overstatement to say that the entire book of Hebrews is centered in Christology. From the opening verses to the close of the book, the main subject matter of the letter is the majesty, supremacy, and glory of the Son, our Lord Jesus Christ.

Probably first written to Jewish Christians living in Rome (see Heb. 13:24) before the fall of Jerusalem, Hebrews seeks to encourage and warn these believers who seemingly had begun well but are now in danger of compromising their commitment to Christ. They have been Christians for some time (5:12) and have even experienced persecution for their faith (10:32–34), but some of these Christians are now drifting away (2:1–4). So the author writes to warn them and to encourage them.[112]

To encourage these weary and wavering Christians, the author of Hebrews gives them the glorious and unwavering truth that Jesus Christ has come as the fulfillment of all the promises and expectations of the Old Testament because he has come as God the Son incarnate. By expounding text after text from the Old Testament, the author presents Jesus as the Son, Lord, and High Priest who is greater than angels (Heb. 1:5–2:18), Moses (3:1–6), Joshua (3:7–4:12), and the priests and old covenant sacrifices (2:17–19; 4:14–10:39). As Richard Bauckham notes, the author applies these titles to Christ because he assumes that the Son shares both the unique identity of God and the fullness of humanity: "In each category Hebrews portrays Jesus as both truly God and truly human, like his Father in every respect and like humans in every respect."[113]

So the Christology of Hebrews continues the apostolic pattern of New Testament Christology: Jesus is Son and Lord because of who he has always been (Heb. 1:2–3) *and* because of his work in taking on our humanity and fulfilling the role of Adam (2:5–18), David (1:4–14), and the high priest (4:14–10:39) to secure our redemption and inaugurate the promised age to come. David Wells correctly notes that, while the author does not lay out a theory of the incarnation, he affirms that the supremacy and finality of the Son in redemption requires his full deity and full humanity:

---

[112] For a discussion of some of this background, see William L. Lane, *Hebrews 1–8*, WBC (Dallas: Word, 1991), xlvii–clvii; George H. Guthrie, *Hebrews*, NIV Application Commentary (Grand Rapids, MI: Zondervan, 1998), 17–38.

[113] Bauckham, *Jesus and the God of Israel*, 236.

The author offers no theory as to how the divine became enfleshed. The process of incarnation is referred to (2:9; 10:5), but not explored. Yet it remains clear that for the author this process did not involve diminution of or modification in that Godness which had been the Son's. In the midst of describing Jesus' very human cries and tears, the author insists that it was the same divine Son who was experiencing this pain.[114]

To bring true comfort and encouragement to the struggling people of God, the author knows that he must emphasize the dual identity of Christ. To have an all-sufficient Lord and Savior, the Christ must be both divine and human. For the sacrifice of Christ to be efficacious, he must be God the Son incarnate. As Wells observes, the divine-human identity of Jesus "was not an incidental matter (4:15; 7:26); it was the sine qua non for the Son's sacrificial mission. His pure humanity was as much necessitated by his pretemporal appointment as was his full divinity, for each was indispensable to his saving work."[115]

The Christological truths developed in Hebrews deserve a full-length treatment. But we must focus here on the highlights that help us understand the uniqueness and significance of the person of Christ. We can see the author's main presentation by considering three contrasts that reveal the superiority of Christ and five identity statements that describe who Jesus is in himself and in terms of creation and redemption.

The author first contrasts the timing of God's revelation to stress the *chronological* superiority of his revelation in Christ. God spoke "long ago" (Heb. 1:1), but in his Son he has spoken finally and definitively "in these last days" (v. 2). The point is that there will be no more "days" in "this present age" and thus no further revelation is coming to supplement what God has now fully revealed in his Son.[116] Moreover, focusing on the eras of God's revelation to his people divides redemptive history into two successive ages (in agreement with the rest of the New Testament) and presents the Son as the one who inaugurates the "last days,"[117] i.e., the overlap of "this present age" and the "age to come" created by the in-breaking of God's sovereign rule and reign. And as we have already seen according to the epochal-covenantal structure of Scripture, bringing the kingdom of "the age to come" into "this present age" and "these last days" is a work of God himself that identifies the Son with the Creator–Covenant Lord.[118]

The second contrast stresses the *qualitative* superiority of God's revelation in Christ: "God spoke to our fathers by the prophets, but in these last

---

[114] Wells, *Person of Christ*, 55.
[115] Ibid., 54–55.
[116] We should understand "these last days" in the context of "this present age," not in contradiction to the fact that there is a coming age of consummation.
[117] See Lane, *Hebrews 1–8*, 10–12; Wells, *Person of Christ*, 52–53.
[118] See Wells, *Person of Christ*, 21–66; Bauckham, *Jesus and the God of Israel*, 233–241.

days he has spoken to us by his Son" (Heb. 1:1–2). This is not to say that the Old Testament prophetic revelation is inferior in the sense of less authoritative than later revelation. But the previous revelation was deliberately incomplete and anticipatory, i.e., God spoke "at many times and in many ways" (v. 1). As William Lane comments, "The fragmentary and varied character of God's self-disclosure under the old covenant awakened within the fathers an expectation that he would continue to speak to his people. . . . The ministry of the prophets marked the preparatory phase of that history."[119] What God says by his Son does not contradict or supplant but fulfills and completes God's progressive revelation.

The third contrast stresses the *personal* superiority of God's revelation in Christ: God spoke previously "by the prophets" (Heb. 1:1), but now he has spoken "by his Son" (v. 2).[120] Once again, the purpose is not to downplay the authority of the Old Testament prophets but to show the superiority of the Son—he is no less than a prophet, but he is infinitely more. God's previous revelation was incomplete because it was intended to point beyond itself to its fulfillment in the Christ. The Son is greater than the Old Testament prophets because he is the one about whom they prophesied. Even more, the Son is greater than the Old Testament prophets because he is the one in whom all of God's revelatory and redemptive purposes culminate (cf. Eph. 1:9–10). In fact, the author uses the rest of Hebrews to unpack how the Son accomplishes the divine plan that was progressively revealed through the covenantal-typological development of God's promises through the Old Testament prophets, priests, and kings.

With these three contrasts in place to present the superiority of the Son, the author of Hebrews then provides five identity statements that describe who Jesus is in himself and in terms of creation and redemption.

First, the Son is the one "whom [God] appointed the heir of all things" (Heb. 1:2b). In this first of two relative clauses, we should understand *appointment* in a way similar to what we saw in Romans 1:3–4 and in light of Old Testament texts like Psalm 2. Specifically, Psalm 2:7 should guide our interpretation because the author quotes it in verse 5 to argue that Christ is greater than the angels.[121] As seen earlier in the discussion of Jesus's self-identification, we should interpret Psalm 2 as a reference to the Davidic king who is a type and pattern of the king to come.[122] In fact, we must read Psalm 2 typologically to keep in step with the apostolic understanding of how to read Scripture and how to identify the Christ. The apostles repeatedly apply Psalm 2 to Jesus in terms

---

[119] Lane, *Hebrews 1–8*, 11.

[120] For a discussion of the significance of God's speaking literally "in Son" (*en huiō*), see Lane, *Hebrews 1–8*, 11; Guthrie, *Hebrews*, 46–47.

[121] See Lane, *Hebrews 1–8*, 12; Guthrie, *Hebrews*, 47; Schreiner, *New Testament Theology*, 380–381.

[122] For a defense of this view, see Reymond, *Jesus, Divine Messiah*, 77–81.

of his appointment as the antitype of David (see Heb. 1:2, 5, 8–9, 13; 5:5; cf. Acts 13:33; Rom. 1:3–4).[123] So in Hebrews 1:2b, we should understand that the Son was "appointed the heir of all things" not as *merely another* but as a *far greater* Davidic king (1:5; 5:5), the one who by virtue of his incarnation, death, and resurrection has inherited the rule of God over all things.

Second, the Son is the one "through whom also [God] created the world" (v. 2b). Noting the grammatical force of the *kai*, "*and* through whom," William Lane argues that it links this second relative clause with the first to explain that the one who has inherited all things is the same one who was involved in the creation of all things.[124] Moreover, this economy of creation sheds light on the Father-Son relationship: the Father makes the world *through the Son*. In fact, God makes the world in a triune work of the Father through the Son by the Spirit (cf. Gen. 1:2). The point here is that the Son is the agent of creation who came into creation to rule over creation as the promised Davidic king and Christ.

Third, the Son is "the radiance of the glory of God and the exact imprint of his nature" (Heb. 1:3a). This language so strongly affirms the full deity of the Son that in church history the Arians refused to recognize the authenticity of Hebrews on the basis of this text alone.[125] The author uses synonymous parallelism to form one idea at the heart of Christ's identity: he is the radiance (*apaugasma*)[126] of God's glory and (*kai*) the exact imprint (*charaktēr*) of his nature (*hupostaseōs*).[127] In other words, these two parts of this one identity statement present the incarnate Son as the one who makes visible the very glory of God himself, which is obviously something only God can do (cf. John 1:14–18). As Macleod helpfully clarifies, "[The Son] is the glory made visible: not a different glory from the Father's but the same glory in another form. The Father is the glory hidden: the Son is the glory revealed. The Son is the Father repeated, but in a different way."[128] All of who God is and all that enables him to be known in truth is found in Christ (see John 14:9).[129]

Fourth, the Son is the one who "upholds the universe by the word of his power" (Heb. 1:3). Similar to Colossians 1:15–17, the Son is presented as the Lord of providence. And to stress that this providential power is not static but

---

[123] See Schreiner, *New Testament Theology*, 380–381.

[124] Lane, *Hebrews 1–8*, 12.

[125] See Wells, *Person of Christ*, 53. The Arians denied the eternal preexistence and deity of the Son.

[126] The term is best translated "radiance" or "effulgence" and not "reflection" (see Lane, *Hebrews 1–8*, 12–13).

[127] It should be noted that as Christological reflection developed through the fourth and fifth centuries, *hypostasis* came to bear the meaning of *person* and not *nature*. But the New Testament use of the term (2 Cor. 9:4; 11:17; Heb. 3:14; 11:1) does not refer to *person*. For a discussion and defense of the early church's development and use of *hypostasis* to defend the truth of Scripture against heresy, see Part IV.

[128] Macleod, *Person of Christ*, 80.

[129] The overall thought here is very similar to the prologue of John's Gospel (see Philip E. Hughes, *A Commentary on the Epistle to the Hebrews* [Grand Rapids, MI: Eerdmans, 1987], 41–42; Carson, *John*, 111–139). And the representative function of the Son here is parallel to other New Testament texts "that speak of Jesus as the 'form,' 'likeness,' or 'image' of God (e.g., John 1:2; Phil. 2:6; Col. 1:15)" (Guthrie, *Hebrews*, 48).

dynamic, the author uses the verb *pherōn* ("upholds"), which conveys the idea of carrying something from one place to another.[130] Even in his incarnation as the Christ, then, the Son through whom all things were created now sustains all things and is bringing them to their appointed end.

And fifth, the Son is the one who, "[a]fter making purification for sins, [has] sat down at the right hand of the Majesty on high, having become as much superior to angels as the name he has inherited is more excellent than theirs" (Heb. 1:3b–4). The author of Hebrews moves from creation to the Son's work of redemption to present him as the human High Priest and King of our salvation who bears the name of Yahweh. The Son's incarnation is not explained but is assumed as the means of his reign as the only Redeemer of humanity. The author uses the aorist participle—"having made" (*poiēsamenos*) purification for our sins—to emphasize that the single sacrificial work of Christ is effective in "these last days" and into the eternal age to come.[131] The point is simple but staggering: the incarnation of God the Son, his all-sufficient sacrifice on our behalf, and his heavenly reign over all the earth will endure forever. And as we have seen in Philippians 2 above, this incarnate accomplishment merits *the man* Christ Jesus the name above every name—the name of Yahweh, the Creator–Covenant Lord himself. A human is now superior to angels because the eternal Son has become the eternal man, which means that Yahweh has come in the flesh to do what only he can do: cosmic redemption, reconciliation, and rule.[132]

THE BIBLE'S SELF-PRESENTATION OF JESUS

Through Jesus's own words and works—both implicit and explicit—he knowingly and intentionally identified himself as the divine Son of God and the eternal *imago Dei*. In the same way, he also identified himself as the incarnational *imago Dei* and the man who would fulfill all of God's covenant promises as his true Son-King and the last Adam. Following these words and works and the self-identification of Christ, his apostles came to the same conclusion. They looked along the redemptive drama unfolding out of the Old Testament and recognized Jesus as the one who would meet the growing expectation that God

---

[130] See Hughes, *Hebrews*, 45–46.

[131] See Lane, *Hebrews 1–8*, 15.

[132] For further discussion of the incarnate Son's identity with Yahweh, see Bauckham, *Jesus and the God of Israel*, 21–23, 233–253. As discussed in the consideration of Romans 1:3–4 above, we must reject the argument of Dunn and others that inheriting the name of Yahweh means Jesus was adopted as the Son of God. Dunn believes the author of Hebrews uses adoptionist language, awkwardly merging the incompatible Hebraic and Platonic worldviews (Dunn, *Christology in the Making*, 52–56). But the text shows that the thought-world of the author is thoroughly Hebraic and not Platonic. He presents Christ as God the Son incarnate within the structured storyline coming out of the Old Testament. And as we have just seen, the author clearly affirms the preincarnational deity of the Son in the very first verses. As Macleod nicely summarizes, the Jesus of Hebrews "was the Son of God. This was what distinguished him from the prophets and set him above the angels. He performed the functions of God (creation and providence); he enjoyed the prerogatives of God ('Let all God's angels worship him'); he inherited the titles of God; and he was exclusively related to God as the shining of his glory and the very image of his being. He was, and is, *God* (1:8)" (Macleod, *Person of Christ*, 85).

himself would save his people and set his servant-shepherd-king over them. The apostles placed what Jesus did and who Jesus said he was within the epochal-covenantal storyline of Scripture and identified him as the Son of God come as a man to do what only God can do and all that God requires of man.

For our purpose in this chapter of establishing biblical warrant for the coming Christological conclusions, we need to make a simple but pivotal deduction from what Jesus and his apostles have said and how they came to say it. The self-identification of the Lord Jesus Christ and the apostolic understanding of Jesus's identity come to us in the Gospels and Epistles of the New Testament. And as we have seen, this New Testament material continues and concludes the storyline from the Old Testament documents. With the Old Testament and the New Testament linked through the dominical and apostolic teaching, then, what we have considered in this chapter is the Bible's self-presentation of Jesus's identity. This might seem elementary, but it is nonetheless crucial. We must have the Bible's self-presentation of Jesus to know the real Jesus. As we discussed throughout Part I and in chapter 3, the only authoritative interpretation of Jesus is the one given by God himself. And God has revealed the identity of Jesus only in Scripture and through its structured storyline.

What we have in this chapter, then, is the authoritative interpretation and biblical identity of Jesus: he is God the Son incarnate. The implications and significance of this conclusion, however, need to be worked out in the next two chapters. Specifically, we need to examine what it means that Jesus is fully God and fully man. First we will look at the deity of Christ; then we will take up the humanity of Christ.

THE DEITY OF CHRIST:
GOD THE SON FROM ETERNITY

In the last chapter, we came to the biblical identity of Christ: he is God the Son incarnate. The Lord Jesus Christ and his apostles understand his coming in terms of the Old Testament storyline and its covenantal-typological expectations. And as Jesus fulfills all of those expectations, it becomes clear that he is the promised Messiah, the Christ who would teach with the authority of God, do the works of God, and inaugurate the kingdom of God, all as the man that God would bring forth from humanity to be his true image-son-king and the last Adam. By his words and works, then, Jesus identifies himself to be God the Son come in the flesh. Beginning with Jesus's self-identification, the apostles reach the same conclusion by interpreting all that Jesus said and did in terms of the plotline developing out of the Old Testament. So the New Testament completes the entire metanarrative in such a way that the whole Bible on its own terms presents Jesus as God the Son incarnate.

As we saw in the last chapter, Philippians 2:5–11 is a central Christological text that gives us a clear picture of the full deity and full humanity of Christ Jesus. Christ is and has always been *en morphē theou* ("in the form of God"; v. 6), displaying all that makes God recognizable as God. And by his incarnation, this same Christ took on *morphēn doulou* ("form of a servant"; v. 7), having been made in the likeness of humans in every way (except sin). It was as the God-man, then, that the Son obediently humbled himself by dying on a cross in the place of sinful humanity that had rejected the rule of the Creator–Covenant Lord (v. 8). This obedient end to his humiliation, however, merited the exaltation of Christ by the Father. So it was also as the God-man that Christ rose from the dead, ascended to the throne of heaven, and received the peerless name of the Creator–Covenant Lord—Yahweh. Simply put, the

Son as the Son in relation to his Father and the Spirit has always been Lord; but now, as a result of his incarnation, he has become the Lord in the flesh, namely the Son *incarnate*.

Based on this identification of Christ, we can say that his deity enjoys an *ontological priority* that deserves special attention. This priority does not deny or diminish the fullness, reality, and significance of Christ's humanity. As we will explore in the next chapter, the humanity of Christ is equally necessary for all that he has accomplished for our salvation and for the consummation of God's kingdom on earth. But in this chapter, we need to consider the truth and significance of the fact that Christ was the divine Son *before* he was the *incarnate* Son. Even while the New Testament fully affirms the full humanity of Christ, the uniqueness of his identity depends upon his deity. It was *God the Son* who became incarnate (John 1:14), not vice versa. Scripture does not teach that the man Jesus grew into deity or that he was adopted into the divine life. And Scripture does not present Jesus as another Spirit-empowered man like Moses, Joshua, and Elijah, only quantitatively greater than these.

The deity of Christ also needs special attention due to an *epistemological priority*. In the first century, Christ died for the sake of a rebellious humanity that rejected the rule of the Creator–Covenant Lord. In our own century, however, the same rebellious humanity rejects not only the rule but even the existence of the Creator–Covenant Lord. The contemporary culture has developed epistemologically under a steady diet of secular and naturalistic perspectives produced by the Enlightenment-modern and postmodern worldviews. The result has been that most people reject the category of deity or dismiss the supernatural as unimportant or unknowable. Even in Christology, most offerings today deny or deemphasize the deity of Christ.

A biblical Christology, then, will stand in direct contrast to most contemporary Christologies that view Christ primarily in human terms, reducing and denuding his uniqueness and making him more congenial to our postmodern and religiously pluralistic age. David Wells gives us a good sense of this current Christological humanism:

> [Contemporary Christology] often takes on the form of orthodoxy, insisting that Christ must, first and foremost, be said to be fully human. The word *human* is then transformed into a synonym for twentieth-century, secular modernity. It is then assumed that to be human, such a Christ must be as fallible as we are, as confused, as filled with doubts, as unsure about the future, as agnostic about the purposes and plans of God, as diffident about the possibilities of knowing God, and as baffled about ethical norms and the possibility of absolutes. To present a Christ who is the exegesis of God's character and plans, who acts and speaks as God, who knows from whence

he came and why, and who did on the cross what only God could do is, it is argued, to present a Christ who is not human![1]

These non-evangelical Christologies not only do not present the real Jesus, they cannot do so because they either ignore the Scriptures or read them according to an unbiblical worldview. As we saw in chapter 3, an evolutionary framework for interpreting the world and its events dominates the epistemological landscape. So it is no surprise that laypeople and scholars alike deny or diminish the deity of Christ and elevate his humanity even as they transform it to fit the categories of current thought.[2]

A biblical Christology, moreover, will be an evangelical Christology that knows the necessity of identifying Jesus "from above," according to the authoritative interpretation revealed to us by God himself in the Scriptures. Wells, again, helps us pinpoint the significance of looking for the real Jesus in the right way:

> It is not possible to construct such a figure from "below," to create him out of the fabric of human experience. There are no analogies in human experience for this role. Christologies constructed from "below" produce only a larger-than-life religious figure, the perfection of what many others already experience. . . . Their christs might be admired, but they cannot be worshipped. They might inspire religious devotion, but they cannot sustain or explain Christian faith. They tell us much about their authors and very little about Jesus. . . . They are constructed on the mistaken assumption that a christ who is as baffled as we are about existence, who is as secular as we are, and who is the victim of change and circumstances as we feel ourselves to be is somehow more appealing than one who is not. These christs are impotent, and their appeal is superficial. Their appeal is not that of the biblical Christ, the One who was God with us, the means of forgiveness for our sin, and the agent of our reconciliation. Forgiveness and reconciliation are what we need centrally. We need to know there is someone there to forgive us, someone who can forgive and heal us, and that was why the Word was incarnate. Our Christology, then, must be constructed from "above."[3]

There is no substitute for reading the Bible on its own terms to identify the real Christ. The worldview and theology that develops from the structure

---

[1] David F. Wells, *The Person of Christ: A Biblical and Historical Analysis of the Incarnation* (Westchester, IL: Crossway, 1984), 173–174.
[2] Even some recent evangelical Christologies overemphasize Jesus's humanity to the detriment of his deity. For example, Gerald F. Hawthorne, *The Presence and the Power: The Significance of the Holy Spirit in the Life and Ministry of Jesus* (Eugene, OR: Wipf & Stock, 2003), affirms Christ's full deity, but he insists that in becoming human, the Son "willed to renounce the exercise of his divine powers, attributes, prerogatives, so that he might live fully within those limitations which inhere in being truly human" (ibid., 208). The result is that "the divine attributes of omniscience, omnipotence, and omnipresence are potential and latent during the Son's earthly life" (ibid., 211). Thus, Jesus performed miracles not by his own divine power but by the Spirit. The New Testament, however, presents Jesus's divine works not merely as a sign of his Spirit-filled humanity but as a testimony to his divine sonship. For a detailed discussion and critique of some of these evangelical Christologies, see Part IV.
[3] Wells, *Person of Christ*, 172–173.

and storyline of the Scriptures cannot be ignored or altered without losing the ability to see Jesus for who he really is.

Attending to the ontological and present epistemological priorities, then, this chapter will explore the deity of Christ according to the Scripture's presentation of it. As John Frame notes, the Old Testament uses "Yahweh is Lord" to summarize its presentation of God as "the one who controls all things, speaks with absolute authority, and enters creation to draw creatures into covenant relation with him."[4] So it is with possibly the greatest Christological import that the New Testament repeatedly presents Jesus as Lord and identifies him with Yahweh (e.g., Rom. 10:9; 1 Cor. 12:3; Phil. 2:11). We will look at the evidence for this presentation and identification of Christ under three basic categories: his divine status, his divine works, and his divine titles.[5]

The Divine Status of Christ

We have seen that, as the eternal Son, Christ has the very same status and prerogatives as God himself. We can now further explore his divine status by examining his divine attributes, rule, and worthiness of worship.

Divine Attributes

The New Testament teaches that Christ possesses all of the divine attributes. In Colossians 2:9, Paul explains why the believers in Colossae should break loose from the teaching of this world and submit themselves to Christ alone: "For in him the whole fullness of deity dwells bodily." Paul's contrast and reasoning would make no sense if Christ existed—even in part—according to or at the pleasure of human philosophy or traditions or the elemental spirits of the world (Col. 2:8). Rather, by ontology and function, Christ is "the head of all rule and authority" (v. 10). In other words, all of the divine attributes that make God who he is and enable him to work as only he does are found in Christ—God the Son incarnate. Paul does not say that in Christ is found a plenitude of deity, as if he had a sufficient amount of divine attributes for the task at hand. Leaving out no excess of attributes, Paul declares that the *plērōma*, the entire fullness and sum total of deity inhabits the Son, who has added to himself a human nature.[6]

---

[4] John M. Frame, *The Doctrine of God* (Phillipsburg, NJ: P&R, 2002), 650.

[5] For a more detailed discussion of the material, see, e.g., Richard Bauckham, *Jesus and the God of Israel: God Crucified and Other Studies on the New Testament's Christology of Divine Identity* (Grand Rapids, MI: Eerdmans, 2008); Robert M. Bowman Jr. and J. Ed Komoszewski, *Putting Jesus in His Place: The Case for the Deity of Christ* (Grand Rapids, MI: Kregel, 2007); Gordon D. Fee, *Pauline Christology: An Exegetical-Theological Study* (Peabody, MA: Hendrickson, 2007); Richard N. Longenecker, ed. *Contours of Christology in the New Testament* (Grand Rapids, MI: Eerdmans, 2005); Thomas R. Schreiner, *New Testament Theology: Magnifying God in Christ* (Grand Rapids, MI: Baker Academic, 2008), 305–338, 380–430.

[6] Cf. Peter T. O'Brien, *Colossians, Philemon*, WBC (Waco, TX: Word, 1982), 110–113; Douglas J. Moo, *The Letters to the Colossians and to Philemon*, PNTC (Grand Rapids, MI: Eerdmans, 2008), 193–195.

We can see this fullness of deity in Christ with taxonomical assistance from the traditional communicable and incommunicable attributes of God.[7] The New Testament presents Jesus as having the moral attributes of God, which he has shared in some measure by making man in his image: e.g., Jesus is the definition and measure of God as *love* (Rom. 8:35–39; Gal. 2:20; Eph. 3:17–19; 5:2, 25; cf. 1 John 3:16; 4:10–12); Jesus is the *righteous* one (Acts 3:14; 7:52; 22:14; James 5:6); Jesus is the *holy* one (Acts 3:14; 4:27, 30; 2 Cor. 5:21; Heb. 4:15; 7:26; 1 Pet. 2:22);[8] and the wrath of Jesus is the same as the *wrath* of God (Rev. 6:16). Even as the Old Testament presents the Lord as "the God of *truth*" (e.g., Ps. 31:5, NASB; Isa. 65:16) in terms of his authority (source and standard of truth) and character (upright, trustworthy, consistent), the New Testament claims that the Son came "full of grace and truth" (John 1:14)—an allusion to the Lord himself (cf. Exodus 34). In fact, Jesus *is* the truth (John 14:6)—he is the embodiment of all that "the God of truth" has revealed to man.[9] Jesus came as the wisdom of God (1 Cor. 1:24, 30; Col. 2:3) with the authority of God (Eph. 1:22; Col. 2:10) such that all of his teaching was (and is!) trustworthy (Matt. 22:16; Luke 20:21; John 8:40, 45). In his being, words, and works, Jesus is the eternal *imago Dei*.

The New Testament authors also ascribe to Christ the incommunicable attributes of God. For example, the Son shares in the Father's eternity.[10] He existed with the Father before creation (John 1:1, he was "with God"; cf. 12:41; 1 Cor. 10:4; Heb. 1:2); he shared glory with the Father before the world existed (John 17:5); the Father sent him, and he came into the world (Rom. 8:3; 2 Cor. 8:9; Gal. 4:4; cf. John 1:9; 3:17; 1 John 4:9), to appear on earth at the end of the ages (Heb. 9:26; cf. 1 Pet. 1:20). And the Son come in the flesh possesses omnipotence (Matt. 8:26–27; 1 Cor. 1:18, 23–25; Eph. 1:19–20; Phil. 3:21; Col. 2:10), omnipresence (cf. 1 Kings 8:27; Ps. 139:7–10; Matt. 18:20; 28:20; Eph. 4:10), immutability (cf. Num. 23:19; Mal. 3:6; 2 Cor. 1:20; Heb. 1:10–12; 13:8; James 1:17), and omniscience (cf. Ps. 139:1–3; Isa. 46:8–13; 48:3–6; Mark 2:8; John 1:48; 2:25; 6:64; 21:17; Acts 1:24; 1 Cor. 4:5; Col. 2:3, 9; Rev. 2:23).

Reconciling the *plērōma* deity of Christ with his true and complete humanity requires more than simply juxtaposing divine and human attributes.

---

[7] On the classifying of divine attributes see John S. Feinberg, *No One Like Him: The Doctrine of God*, Foundations of Evangelical Theology (Wheaton, IL: Crossway, 2001), 233–276; Frame, *Doctrine of God*, 387–401.

[8] Scripture does present Jesus's sinlessness as a quality of his perfect humanity. However, Jesus is not merely the perfect man. He has a quality of perfection that identifies him with God. As God the Son, Christ's moral perfection transcends every human category (cf. Frame, *Doctrine of God*, 675).

[9] See D. A. Carson, *The Gospel according to John*, PNTC (Grand Rapids, MI: Eerdmans, 1991), 129–130, 491. Carson helpfully explains that "Jesus is the truth, because he embodies the supreme revelation of God—he himself 'narrates' God (1:18), says and does exclusively what the Father gives him to say and do (5:19ff; 8:29), indeed he is properly called 'God' (1:1, 18; 20:28). He is God's gracious self-disclosure, his 'Word,' made flesh (1:14). Jesus is the life (1:4), the one who has 'life in himself' (5:26), 'the resurrection and the life' (11:25), 'the true God and eternal life' (1 Jn. 5:20)" (ibid., 491).

[10] On this point, see Simon J. Gathercole, *The Preexistent Son: Recovering the Christologies of Matthew, Mark, and Luke* (Grand Rapids, MI: Eerdmans, 2006).

For example, in addition to his omniscience, the New Testament presents a Jesus who grew in knowledge and suffered ignorance at times (see Luke 2:52; Mark 13:32). Making sense of how the same person can have seemingly mutually exclusive attributes—omniscience and ignorance—at the same time makes for some of the most difficult Christological reflection and reasoning. We will take up this particular complexity (and others) in Parts III and IV by considering the nature of the incarnation, the eternal relations of the divine persons, and how those relations are manifest in the external work of God. At this point, however, we simply need to acknowledge that the Scriptures present the incarnation of God the Son with all of the divine attributes and without losing any of their perfection.[11]

Divine Rule

Along with the divine attributes, the New Testament also affirms that Christ shares equally with God in his divine rule and reign over all of creation.[12] The Old Testament repeatedly celebrates the universal lordship of Yahweh. As a summary, Israel was taught to sing, "For you, O Lord, are most high over all the earth; you are exalted far above all gods" (Ps. 97:9). Attributing this same universal supremacy to Jesus, then, the New Testament makes an astonishing claim regarding his deity. Christ exercises unrivaled dominion over "all things" (Rom. 14:9; 1 Cor. 15:27–28; Eph. 1:22; Phil. 2:10; 3:21; Heb. 1:2; 2:8; 1 Pet. 3:22; Rev. 1:5),[13] including all human and angelic authorities (Eph. 1:21; Phil. 2:10; Heb. 1:4–6, 13). As a result of his triumphant work in redemption and reconciliation, Jesus now sits on God's throne (2 Cor. 5:10; Heb. 1:3; 8:1; 12:2; cf. Rev. 22:1), at "the right hand of the Majesty on high" (Heb. 1:3; Rom. 8:34; Col. 3:1; Heb. 8:1; 10:12), sharing the universal lordship of Yahweh over every created rule, authority, power, and dominion (Rom. 9:5; Eph. 1:20–21; 4:10; Phil. 2:9–11; Heb. 1:3; 7:26).

In short, the New Testament conclusion to the biblical storyline puts Jesus "in the place that in the Old Testament and ancient Judaism belonged to God alone. . . . Jesus is utterly unique in this shared position. No one else shares God's throne and rules over all creation."[14] The categories and expectations

---

[11] Frame captures the details of Jesus's omniscience: "Like God, Jesus knows all things (Matt. 11:25–27; John 2:24–25; 16:30; 21:17; Col. 2:3). There is no record of his ever having made an error or mistake. He has a supernatural knowledge of events and facts (John 4:16–19, 29). He knows the thoughts, even the hearts, of human beings (Matt. 9:4; 12:25; Mark 2:8; Luke 6:8; 9:47; John 1:47; 2:24–25; 21:17; Rev. 2:23). He knows the future. He knows that he must die at the hands of sinners (Matt. 16:21; Mark 8:31; Luke 9:22). He knows in advance who will betray him (Matt. 26:24), Peter's denial (John 13:38), the kind of death Peter will die (John 21:18–19), and the future of the kingdom (Matt. 8:11). He knows the Father as the Father knows him, and he is sovereign in revealing the Father to human beings (Matt. 11:25–27; Luke 10:22; John 10:15)" (Frame, *Doctrine of God*, 676).
[12] On this point, see the discussion of John 5 in chapter 4.
[13] For further discussion of Jesus's universal rule, see Bauckham, *Jesus and the God of Israel*, 18–25.
[14] Bowman and Komoszewski, *Putting Jesus in His Place*, 256. The authors also cite Martin Hengel, *Studies in Early Christology* (Edinburgh: T&T Clark, 1995), 225.

that develop across the epochs and covenants of Scripture lead us to con-clude that "he with whom God shares his throne must be equal with God."[15]

Divine Worship

If Christ does have all of the divine attributes, and exercises the divine rule of God himself, then it makes sense that he should receive the worship, devotion, confidence, and trust that God alone demands and deserves. But to appreciate that a mere man could not receive such divine worship, we need to recognize that for hundreds of years, the people of Israel recited the *Shema'* (Deut. 6:4) twice daily. This foundational confession affirmed that Yahweh is the one true and living God and that he alone is the proper object of worship. The worship of a creature, any creature, even the highest and most powerful angel, brought an individual and ultimately the nation under the covenant curse of exile and death (Ex. 20:1–7). And the early church continued this same understanding, specifically rejecting the idea that a human being should be worshiped (cf. Acts 14:14–15; Rev. 19:10).

When Jesus walks onto this theo-dramatic stage, the New Testament shines a spotlight on his deity by making him the *proper* recipient of divine worship. Jesus received the praise and worship of his disciples in response to his works on earth and he never rebuked one of them (Matt. 14:33; 21:15–16; 28:9, 17; John 20:28; cf. 5:22–23). And after Jesus ascended back to heaven as the exalted Lord, his praise and worship intensified throughout the church (Eph. 5:19; Phil. 2:9–11; Heb. 1:6; cf. Rev. 5:11–12). John Stott connects the Old Testament worship of God and the New Testament worship of Christ: "Nobody can call himself a Christian who does not worship Jesus. To worship him, if he is not God, is idolatry; to withhold worship from him, if he is, is apostasy."[16]

Moreover, to round out our understanding of Jesus's deity in his worthi-ness of divine worship, we need to consider how the New Testament presents Jesus as the proper object of prayer and faith. All the formal prayers recorded in the New Testament are addressed to God the Father. But this only amplifies the deity of Christ on those occasions when individuals and groups of believers prayed to Jesus (Acts 1:24–25; 7:59–60; 9:10, 13; 22:17–19; 1 Cor. 1:2; 16:22; 2 Cor. 12:8; Rev. 22:20). In short, by praying to Jesus for salvation, forgiveness of sin, deliverance from evil, healing for sickness, providential guidance and pro-tection, and security after death, these people identified Jesus with God himself.

Similarly, turning to Jesus as one worthy of our trust for our salvation

---

[15] Ibid.
[16] John R. W. Stott, *The Authentic Jesus* (London: Marshall, Morgan & Scott, 1985), 34. For a detailed treat-ment of the worship theme applied to Jesus in earliest Christianity, see Larry W. Hurtado, *Lord Jesus Christ: Devotion to Jesus in Earliest Christianity* (Grand Rapids, MI: Eerdmans, 2003); Bauckham, *Jesus and the God of Israel*, 127–181.

recognizes his deity. The Old Testament repeatedly affirms that "Salvation belongs to the LORD" (Jonah 2:9); "He only is . . . my salvation" (Ps. 62:2, 6); "On God rests my salvation and my glory" (Ps. 62:7). The New Testament, however, introduces the Lord Jesus Christ as a proper object of saving faith (see John 3:15–16; 14:1; Acts 3:16; 4:12; 10:43; 16:31; Rom. 10:12–13; 1 Cor. 1:2).[17] In fact, the New Testament only occasionally holds up God the Father as an object of faith.[18] Rather than creating a contest between God and Christ, however, the New Testament explains that faith in Christ *is* faith in God.[19]

Jesus can be an object of our faith because he is *one* of the divine subjects of the *one* source of divine blessings in God himself. For example, notice how Paul begins his letters: "Grace to you and peace from (*apo*) God our Father and the Lord Jesus Christ" (Rom. 1:7; 1 Cor. 1:3; 2 Cor. 1:2; Gal. 1:3; Eph. 1:2; Phil. 1:2; 1 Thess. 1:1; 2 Thess. 1:2; Philem. 3; 1 Tim. 1:2; 2 Tim. 1:2; Titus 1:4). Paul uses the preposition *from* only once and places it before the Father and Son to affirm that both the Father and the Son form a single source of divine grace and peace. Given his deep commitment to the *Shema'* as a Jew, Paul could not place Jesus on par with the Father as the fount of spiritual blessing without confessing the full deity of Christ.[20] As Murray Harris notes, "This is not because Jesus has displaced God the Father as the one we must trust, but because it is in Christ that God meets us in salvation. There are not two competing personal objects of saving faith. Only because Jesus is fully divine, intrinsically sharing God's nature and attributes, does he become a legitimate object of trust."[21]

THE DIVINE WORKS OF CHRIST

As we have now seen by considering his divine status, the Scriptures present the Lord Jesus Christ as equal and one with the Father in nature, or *ontology*. Alongside this evidence of deity, we can now focus on the divine works of Christ, his divine *function*. It will be helpful to divide the biblical data to consider the divine works of Christ under two headings.

---

[17] Jesus is also presented as the object of numerous doxologies. A doxology is a formal ascription of praise, honor, glory, or blessings given to a divine person, but never to a merely human figure. New Testament doxologies are regularly addressed to God, sometimes through Jesus Christ (Luke 2:14; Rom. 11:36; 16:27; 2 Cor. 11:31; Gal. 1:5; Eph. 3:21; Phil. 4:20; 1 Tim. 1:17; 1 Pet. 4:11; 5:11; Jude 24–25; Rev. 5:13; 7:12). But on at least four occasions, a doxology is addressed directly to Christ (2 Tim. 4:18; 2 Pet. 3:18; Rev. 1:5–6; 5:13), recognizing his God-equal divine status.

[18] Murray J. Harris lists only twelve texts that present the Father as an object of faith (John 12:44; 14:1; Acts 16:34; Rom. 4:3, 5, 17, 24; Gal. 3:6; 1 Thess. 1:8; Titus 3:8; Heb. 6:1; 1 Pet. 1:21) (*Three Crucial Questions about Jesus* [Grand Rapids, MI: Baker, 1994], 77, 118).

[19] See this discussion in terms of Jesus's self-identification as God the Son in chapter 4.

[20] Similarly, Paul affirms the deity of Christ in 1 Thessalonians 3:11 and 2 Thessalonians 2:16–17. In the first text, Paul uses God and Jesus as two different subjects but with a singular verb ("direct"). In the second text, Paul again uses God and Jesus as two different subjects, this time with multiple singular verbs ("loved," "gave," "encourage," "strengthen"). Paul thus distinguishes the divine persons of the Father and the Son but he also equates them in their divine nature such that he could trace a single action to a single, unified source (cf. Harris, *Three Crucial Questions*, 75–79).

[21] Harris, *Three Crucial Questions*, 77.

First, Christ is the agent of creation and the providential Lord of heaven and earth. As we discussed in chapter 4, Colossians 1:15–20 and Hebrews 1:1–3 tell us that Jesus is both the eternal Son through whom God created and sustains all things and the incarnate Son who continues to hold all things together on earth and now rules and orders all things from heaven. These works, quite obviously, belong to God alone (see Genesis 1; Ps. 102:25; 104:24, 27, 30). The New Testament continues to affirm the God-only work of creation and providence (see Rom. 1:18–23; 4:17; 11:36; Heb. 2:10; 11:3). But the New Testament adds that these are the works of God *as a trinity of divine persons.* More specifically, the Father always works *through* the Son by the power of the Holy Spirit (John 1:3; Col. 1:16; Heb. 1:1–3; cf. Gen. 1:2). So the Son reigns not as a separate God of creation and providence but as a distinct person of the one Creator–Covenant Lord.

We can get an even better sense of Jesus's deity in his divine works by considering how Paul develops the *Shema'* of Deuteronomy 6:4 in 1 Corinthians 8:6: "Yet for us there is one God, the Father, from whom are all things and for whom we exist, and one Lord, Jesus Christ, through whom are all things and through whom we exist." N. T. Wright correctly observes that Paul intentionally links the identity of Christ with the God of the Old Testament: "Paul has placed Jesus *within* an explicit statement, drawn from the Old Testament's quarry of emphatically monotheistic texts, of the doctrine that Israel's God is the one and only God, the creator of the world."[22]

In a dramatic development, Paul takes the foundational confession of Israel that there is only one God and stretches it over the works of Jesus Christ. Paul continues to confess only one God, but as Gordon Fee points out, "[Paul] insists that the identity of the one God also includes the one Lord."[23] With the arrival and revelation of God the Son incarnate, it is impossible to think of the one God without thinking of the one Lord Jesus Christ. As Richard Bauckham observes, "in Paul's quite unprecedented reformation of the Shema', the unique identity of the one God *consists of* the one God, the Father, *and* the one Lord, his Messiah . . . [Paul] maintains monotheism not by adding Jesus to but by including Jesus in his Jewish understanding of the divine uniqueness."[24]

Second, Christ is the inaugurator of the kingdom of God and the age to come. Jesus did not come to perform signs and wonders as just another but greater Moses; he did not come to heal as just another but greater Elisha or to prophesy as just another but greater Isaiah; he did not come to rule over Israel as just another but greater Davidic king. Jesus came to do all of these works,

---

[22] N. T. Wright, *The Climax of the Covenant: Christ and the Law in Pauline Theology* (Minneapolis: Fortress, 1992), 128.

[23] Fee, *Pauline Christology,* 91.

[24] Bauckham, *Jesus and the God of Israel,* 28, 30.

but not as a mere man empowered by the Spirit of God. Jesus came as the Son of God to bring the new creation, new covenant, and eschatological kingdom of the Creator–Covenant Lord. Jesus came to redeem, judge, and rule as God himself. As Schreiner concludes, "Jesus' miracles are not just the promise of the kingdom; they are themselves the actualization, at least in part, of the kingdom."[25]

The only one who can bring *God's* kingdom into reality is *God himself.* Scripture presents the kingdom of God primarily in terms of the rule of God, the obedience of his people, and the judgment of his enemies. By definition, these three components of God's kingdom require the presence and power of the divine king. So when Jesus ascends to the throne of heaven, demands and enables the obedience of the church, and triumphs over all of his enemies, including Satan, sin, and death, we must understand that *these* divine works of Christ bear witness to his deity.[26]

To see more clearly the full deity of Christ in his kingdom work, we can consider a few specific examples related to the coming of the Spirit of God, the judgment of God, and eternal life with God.

Jesus dispenses the promised eschatological Spirit. The Old Testament promises that the new covenant age will be marked by God's giving of his Spirit (Joel 2:28–29; Ezek. 36:25–27; cf. John 3:1–10). The New Testament then explains that this promise is fulfilled in the work of Christ: the Gospels tell us that Jesus was anointed as the one to give God's Spirit to God's people (Matt. 3:11, 13–17; John 14–16); Luke writes that fulfillment of the prophecy began at Pentecost (Acts 2); and the entire New Testament argues that the giving and coming of the Spirit depends upon the person and work of Christ (e.g., Acts 2:32–33; Romans 7–8; 1 Corinthians 2; 3:16–17; 2 Corinthians 3; Gal. 3:14; 4:6; 4:21–6:10; Eph. 1:13–20; 2:18–22; 3:14–19; 4:1–16). Based on Jesus's fulfillment of this Old Testament promise, Peter announces the Christological significance: "'Being therefore exalted at the right hand of God, and having received from the Father the promise of the Holy Spirit, [Jesus] has poured out this [the coming of the Spirit] that you yourselves are seeing and hearing. . . . Let all the house of Israel therefore know for certain that God has made him both Lord and Christ" (Acts 2:33, 36). Being the one who pours out the Spirit of God proves that Jesus is not only the Christ but also the Lord, i.e., Yahweh, the LORD.[27]

Jesus raises the dead and executes final judgment. The Old Testament makes it abundantly clear that God alone has the authority and power to resurrect and to assign each man to eternal life or death (Deut. 1:17; 1 Sam. 2:6; Jer. 25:31; Rom. 14:10), divine works associated with the dawning of the eternal

---

[25] Schreiner, *New Testament Theology*, 64.
[26] Wells, *Person of Christ*, 171–175.
[27] See the section below on "Lord" as a divine title that identifies Christ as Yahweh.

age to come (Ezek. 36:25–27; Ezekiel 37; Dan. 12:2). Yet the New Testament tells us on three occasions that Jesus brought a person from death to physical life (Mark 5:21–24, 35–43; Luke 7:11–17; John 11:1–44). And going still further, the New Testament reveals that Jesus himself *is* the resurrection and the life (John 11:25–26), who will raise those who believe in him to eternal life and raise those who reject him to eternal judgment on the last day (John 5:21–23, 28–29; cf. 6:39–44, 54; Acts 10:42; 17:31; Rom. 14:10 with 2 Cor. 5:10). Jesus, then, has sole authority over the eternal destiny of all the living and the dead, to "repay each person according to what he has done" (Matt. 16:27; 2 Thess. 1:8–9).

More specifically, Jesus forgives sins as God and Savior. The Old Testament teaches that only God can forgive sins because only God is the Creator–Covenant Lord who deserves and demands obedience from all of his creatures. Every sin is, first and foremost, an act of rejection and rebellion against the lordship of Yahweh. And because forgiveness of sins belongs to God alone, salvation belongs to God alone (Jonah 2:9). But after the New Testament agrees that forgiveness of sins is a divine work (Mark 2:7), it then presents Jesus as the Son of God with authority on earth to forgive sins (Mark 2:10; Acts 5:31; Col. 3:13). Making the obvious Christological implication most explicit, Paul and Peter each refer to the Son as our "God and Savior Jesus Christ" (Titus 2:13; 2 Pet. 1:1). Even when Paul refers to God alone as "our Savior" in his letter to Titus, he immediately adds that Jesus is "our Savior" (Titus 1:3–4; 3:4–6). Moreover, it is crucial to understand that the New Testament presents Jesus forgiving sins not as another God or as God the Father but as God the Son who shares in the work of the Father. For example, God the Father "predestined us for adoption as sons through Jesus Christ"; in the Son, "we have redemption through his blood, the forgiveness of our trespasses . . ." (Eph. 1:5, 7).

THE DIVINE TITLES OF CHRIST[28]

Given the divine attributes and works of Jesus, it is not surprising that the New Testament attributes numerous titles to Christ that also indicate his deity. In fact, *Christ* is a title, not a personal name. Calling Jesus "the Christ" or referring to him as "Christ Jesus" does reveal him as the man promised to appear as God's Messiah for the salvation of God's people. Understood according to the storyline coming out of the Old Testament, however, using the title *Christ* indicates that this man would also be divine. And other titles function similarly to present these two parts to Jesus's identity: e.g., Son, Son of Man, even Son of God.

---

[28] For a helpful discussion of the names and titles of Christ, see Geerhardus Vos, *Christology*, vol. 3 of *Reformed Dogmatics*, trans. and ed. Richard B. Gaffin Jr. (Bellingham, WA: Lexham, 2014), 5–19.

To look through the titles of Christ to see his deity most clearly, then, we need to consider how the New Testament refers to him as "Lord" (*kurios*) and "God" (*theos*).

The Son as "Lord"

It is true that the New Testament authors and those they write about use "Lord" (*kurios*) in different ways, including in reference to Jesus. For example, "Lord" is sometimes used as a polite form of address directed at Jesus (e.g., Matt. 8:8, 21; 15:27; 17:15; 18:21), which, of course, does not imply his deity. The predominant use of "Lord" in reference to Christ, however, does not fit this social convention. To understand what it usually means to say that Jesus is "Lord," we need to begin by observing with Wells that the Septuagint uses *kurios* in more than six thousand instances as a linguistic substitute for Yahweh.[29] Interesting in its own right, this linguistic phenomenon becomes a hermeneutical key when we remember that the New Testament authors relied heavily on the Septuagint in their reading of the Old Testament and their interpretation of Jesus's identity, and thus, when *kurios* is applied to Jesus, it is an unambiguous affirmation of deity, with only a few exceptions.[30]

In short, as we have already seen in our discussion of Philippians 2:9–11, the New Testament authors often use "Lord" to identify Jesus as Yahweh according to the storyline, promises, and expectations of the Old Testament.[31] For example, what the Old Testament says regarding Yahweh, the New Testament says regarding Jesus in terms of his character (cf. Ex. 3:14 and John 8:58; cf. Isa. 44:6 and Rev. 1:17; cf. Ps. 102:26–27 [LXX] and Heb. 1:11–12; cf. Isa. 28:16 and Rom. 9:33; 10:11; 1 Pet. 2:6), his holiness (cf. Isa. 8:12–13 and 1 Pet. 3:14–15), the worship of Jesus (cf. Isa. 45:23 and Phil. 2:10–11; cf. Deut. 32:43 [LXX]; Ps. 97:7 [LXX] and Heb. 1:6), prayer to Jesus (cf. 1 Cor. 16:22), and the works of Jesus (creation, cf. Ps. 102:25 [LXX] and Heb. 1:10; salvation, cf. Joel 2:32 and Rom. 10:12–13; Acts 2:21; and cf. Isa. 40:3 and Matt. 3:3; judgment, cf. Isa. 8:14 and 1 Pet. 2:8; see also Rom. 9:33; and ultimate triumph, cf. Ps. 68:18 and Eph. 4:8).[32] On the basis of this evidence, Wells rightly concludes that "[t]o speak of Christ as Lord, then, is to identify him ontologically with Yahweh, to ascribe to him the worship which rightly belongs only to God, to acknowledge him as sovereign in his church and in his creation, and to see him as the vindicator of God's character in the world."[33]

---

[29] See Wells, *Person of Christ*, 74–77.
[30] This point is stressed throughout Fee, *Pauline Christology*.
[31] For a full treatment of Paul's application of *kurios* to Christ, see Fee, *Pauline Christology*; David B. Capes, *Old Testament Yahweh Texts in Paul's Christology*, Wissenschaftliche Untersuchungen zum Neuen Testament 2/47 (Tübingen: Mohr-Siebeck, 1992).
[32] For a summary of the biblical data from Fee and Capes, see Bauckham, *Jesus and the God of Israel*, 182–232.
[33] Wells, *Person of Christ*, 77.

The Son as "Theos"

As another indication of Jesus's deity, the New Testament applies the title *theos* ("God") to him at least seven times (John 1:1, 18; 20:28; Rom. 9:5; Titus 2:13; 2 Pet. 1:1; Heb. 1:8). Almost half of these divine appellations occur within John's Gospel, which sets the pattern for the rest of the occurrences. So we can trace the Christological significance of *theos* applied to Jesus by first taking up John's use and then quickly considering the use of *theos* by Paul, Peter, and the writer of Hebrews.[34]

JOHN 1:1–18

[1] In the beginning was the Word, and the Word was with God, and the Word was God. [2] He was in the beginning with God. [3] All things were made through him, and without him was not any thing made that was made. [4] In him was life, and the life was the light of men. . . . [14] And the Word became flesh and dwelt among us, and we have seen his glory, glory as of the only Son from the Father, full of grace and truth. . . . [18] No one has ever seen God; the only God, who is at the Father's side, he has made him known.

It would be difficult to overstate the importance of the first few verses of John's Gospel for the rest of the book and for the rest of the New Testament. D. A. Carson argues that the prologue (John 1:1–18) "summarizes how the 'Word' which was with God in the very beginning came into the sphere of time, history, tangibility—in other words, how the Son of God was sent into the world to become the Jesus of history, so that the glory and grace of God might be uniquely and perfectly disclosed. The rest of the book is nothing other than an expansion of this theme."[35] In fact, the entire motivation for John to write his Gospel was "so that you may believe that Jesus is the Christ, the Son of God, and that by believing you may have life in his name" (20:31). And in many ways, the entire New Testament flows out of Jesus's command that disciples of all nations would be brought under the one divine name "of the Father and of the Son and of the Holy Spirit" (Matt. 28:19) revealed in the person and work of Christ.

For our purposes here, we can concentrate on how John understands the identity and revelatory role of Jesus Christ as "the Word (*logos*) [who in the beginning] was God (*theos*)" (John 1:1). Using *logos* to describe the person of Christ is unique in the New Testament to the apostle John. The isolated use of the term, however, does not mean that we must look outside of Scripture to determine its meaning. Given the widespread use of *logos* ideas in Hellenism, many biblical scholars have argued in the past century that John's use of

---

[34] For a complete treatment of all of these texts see Murray J. Harris, *Jesus as God: The New Testament Use of Theos in Reference to Jesus* (Grand Rapids, MI: Baker, 1992).

[35] Carson, *John*, 111.

logos is completely indebted to Greek philosophy. But it has been repeatedly and convincingly demonstrated that John does not think in terms of a Greek worldview but according to the Bible's own terms—according to the categories, structures, and framework of the Old Testament.[36]

The Old Testament, in fact, affords a rich theology of the "word"/"word of God" in three areas. First, God's word is active and powerful in creation; he literally spoke the world into existence (Gen. 1:3ff; Ps. 33:6, 9; 147:15–18; 148:5–6). Second, God's word reveals and redeems. God speaks to communicate his existence, character, and purposes and to guide his people in his ways (Gen. 3:8–19; 12:1; 15:1; 22:11; Ps. 119:9, 25, 28, 65, 107, 160, 169, 170; Isa. 9:8; Jer. 1:4; Ezek. 33:7; Amos 3:1, 8). And God saves, delivers, and judges through his Word (Isa. 55:11; cf. Ps. 29:3ff; 107:20). Third, God's word is so closely identified with God himself that Scripture presents his word as eternal (Ps. 119:89). Frame argues that "God's word . . . is his self-expression."[37] Especially in creation, revelation, and salvation, God gives himself by giving us his word.[38] But God performs all of his mighty acts and is present to his creation by his word. Frame sums up the matter in a sentence: "Where God is, his word is, and vice versa."[39]

So it makes perfect biblical sense that if Christ is the one who became incarnate to make God known to man through the reconciliation of God and man, then John should identify him as the Word of God. Jesus Christ is "God's ultimate self-disclosure."[40] But John goes further in his identification of this Word: "In the beginning was the Word, and the Word was with God . . ." (John 1:1). In other words, the *logos* who became a man is no mere personification of God but a person who has existed from all eternity with God. Wells connects the eternality of this Word that has always been with God and his incarnational revelation of God: "In the Word, then, we are met by the personal and eternal God who has joined himself to our flesh. In Jesus, the permanent and final unveiling of God has taken place, and the center of this truth is coincidental with the life

---

[36] On this point, see ibid., 114–118. As an example of the dissimilarity between the Hellenistic concepts of *logos* and John's use of *logos*, consider Stoicism and its denial of the Creator-creature distinction. According to a generally pantheistic outlook, the Stoics taught that the *logos* was the rational principle by which everything exists and which composes the essence of the human soul. *Logos* as reason, then, permeates all things, and the goal of human life is to live in harmony with reason according to nature. This framework leaves no room for a personal God, especially one who providentially rules over and reveals himself to his creation. Or consider Philo, the Jewish philosopher who sought to unite a Middle Platonic conception of God with a Jewish worldview. Philo viewed the *logos* as a kind of intermediary between the transcendent God and the world. According to this deistic framework, God remains separate from the world, connected only indirectly via the *logos*. The *logos* here is not a person or even fully divine but more akin to the relationship between a human speaker and his words: the words of a speaker express the speaker's mind and intention without having a separate personal existence.

[37] Frame, *Doctrine of God*, 471.

[38] See Carson, *John*, 116; F. F. Bruce, *The Gospel of John* (Grand Rapids, MI: Eerdmans, 1983), 29.

[39] Frame, *Doctrine of God*, 472. Frame also notes many biblical correlations between God's word and his Spirit (Gen. 1:2–3; Deut. 30:11–14; Ps. 33:6; Isa. 34:16; 59:21; John 6:63; 16:13; Acts 2:1–4; 1 Thess. 1:5; 2 Tim. 3:16; 2 Pet. 1:21).

[40] Carson, *John*, 116.

of this man. Jesus is the means through which and in conjunction with whom God has made known his character, his will, and his ways (cf. John 14:6)."[41]

The eternality and personality of the Word, however, are not the climax of John's identification of Christ. John uses a triadic structure in verse 1 to create a sense of escalation as the identity of the Word becomes more clear. Each of the three clauses has the same subject, Word (*logos*), and an identical verb "was" (*ēn*).[42] And one clause progresses to the next until they reach the full deity of the *logos*: "the Word was God" (*theos ēn ho logos*). "Having distinguished the Word from God, John shows what they both have in common: they are God."[43] In one amazing verse, John declares that the Word has an eternal existence in personal intercommunion with God and shares the intrinsic nature of God.[44]

We can now summarize what John means by referring to Christ as the *logos* and ultimately giving him the title *theos*: Christ is eternal ("In the beginning was the Word"; v. 1a); Christ is a distinct person from God the Father ("the Word was with God," v. 1b; cf. "the only Son from the Father," v. 14); Christ shares the full deity of God ("the Word was God"; v. 1c). And with the eternality, personality, and deity of the Word-Son-Christ in view, we can now understand just who it is that John says became incarnate: *theos* himself.

God's own self-expression became flesh: "And the Word became (*egeneto*) flesh (*sarx*) and dwelt among us" (John 1:14a). Carson captures John's clarity at this point: "If the Evangelist had said only that the eternal Word assumed manhood or adopted the form of a body, the reader steeped in the popular dualism of the Hellenistic world might have missed the point. But John is unambiguous, almost shocking in the expressions he uses: *the Word became flesh*."[45] We will take up the full humanity of Christ in the next chapter. Here we need to recognize the purpose that John gives us for the full enfleshment of full deity: "we

---

[41] Wells, *Person of Christ*, 69–70.

[42] In John 1:1, three times the imperfect *ēn*, "was," is employed, signifying the Word's continuous, or open-ended state of existence. In this way, as Macleod notes, "It corresponds to the *I am* of John 8:58 ('before Abraham was born, I am') and to the *ho ōn* ('the Being One', Rev. 1:8) of the Apocalypse" (Donald Macleod, *The Person of Christ*, Contours of Christian Theology [Downers Grove, IL: InterVarsity Press, 1998], 46). For a further discussion of John's use of *ēn*, see Carson, *John*, 114.

[43] Andreas J. Köstenberger and Scott R. Swain, *Father, Son, and Spirit: The Trinity and John's Gospel*, NSBT 24 (Downers Grove, IL: InterVarsity Press, 2008), 49.

[44] From the patristic era (Arius) to the present (Jehovah's Witnesses), some have argued that John 1:1c should be translated, "the Word was *a* god," because the definite article is missing before *theos*. This argument, of course, would extend to deny the eternality and the full deity and equality of the Son with the Father. This translation must be rejected for several reasons: (1) No monotheistic Jew would affirm the real existence of "a god," because the *Shema'* confesses only one true and living God. (2) In Greek syntax, as Daniel Wallace notes, an anarthrous preverbal predicate nominative is rarely indefinite, sometimes definite, and normally qualitative (Daniel Wallace, *Greek Grammar beyond the Basics* [Grand Rapids, MI: Zondervan, 1997], 256–270). (3) Placing a definite article before *theos* would equate God and the Word without distinction, destroying the distinction John intentionally makes in verse 1b ("the Word was *with* God"). Moreover, using the definite article would make room for the error of modalism, where God and the Word are only different manifestations of the same one person. (4) John uses the anarthrous *theos* on many other occasions (e.g., John 1:6, 12–13, 18) without the slightest hint that he is referring to "a god." For a more detailed treatment of John 1:1, see Köstenberger and Swain, *Father, Son, and Spirit*, 28–50; Carson, *John*, 117; Harris, *Jesus as God*, 51–71.

[45] Carson, *John*, 117. It is possible that John is responding to an incipient gnosticism, or better, docetism (Gk. *dokeō*, to appear; Christ only *appeared* to be human). Note John's emphasis in 1 John 1:1–4; 4:1–3 on the genuineness of the incarnation and that a denial of Christ's true humanity is to deny the gospel.

have seen his glory, glory as of the only Son from the Father, full of grace and truth" (v. 14b). The *subject* of the incarnation was *not* the divine nature itself, and it was neither God the Father nor God the Holy Spirit; it was specifically the Word, or divine Son who united himself to a human nature for the purpose of revealing the divine glory that he shares with the Father.[46] Any change in the deity of the Son, then, would preclude him from displaying the fullness of the Father's glory. The Son makes God known precisely because he remains fully divine in his incarnation. To accomplish the mission of incarnation, the Son must continue to possess all the attributes of God, exercise his divine preroga-tives, and perform his divine works, including his cosmic functions.

Finally, John concludes his prologue with an *inclusio* by once again apply-ing the title *theos* to the Son: "No one has ever seen God; the only God, who is at the Father's side, he has made him known" (John 1:18). Although some in the Old Testament saw visions of God (e.g., Exodus 33–34; Isa. 6:5), no one ever actually saw God himself before the incarnation of Christ. John now tells us that the unique Son (*monogenēs*) from the Father is the unique God (*monogenēs theos*) at the Father's side who makes God known to humans in grace and truth.[47] John places *theos* in apposition to *monogenēs* to call Jesus Christ the "one-of-a-kind Son, God [in his own right]."[48]

JOHN 20:28

Thomas answered him, "My Lord and my God!"

At the end of his Gospel, John records a third application of the title *theos* to Jesus, forming a book-length *inclusio* with the very first verse. This intentional literary device frames the entire Gospel with the confession that Jesus is *God* the Son.[49]

Having just seen the risen Christ, Thomas cries out in worship: "My Lord and my God [*theos*]!" (John 20:28). It is important to note that John has re-

---

[46] See Macleod, *Person of Christ*, 185–186.

[47] John 1:18 has an important textual variant. Some manuscripts read *monogenēs huios* ("the only Son") while others read *monogenēs theos* ("the only Son, who is God"). Most scholars agree that the latter is original because (in part) it is the more difficult reading (see Köstenberger and Swain, *Father, Son, and Spirit*, 78).

[48] Ibid. A comment needs to be made regarding the meaning of *monogenēs*. Historically, *monogenēs* has been translated, "only begotten" (KJV) and has been used to explain the Son's "eternal generation" from the Father. Today, many doubt whether *monogenēs* by itself refers to uniqueness of origin (see Carson, *John*, 111–139). Usage in the New Testament does demonstrate semantic overlap among *monogenēs*, *prōtotokos* ("firstborn"; cf. Col. 1:15; Ps. 89:27) and *agapētos* ("beloved"; cf. Mark 1:11; 9:7; 12:6; Luke 3:22; 9:35; 20:13). However, the etymology of *monogenēs* connects it to *ginomai* ("become"), not *gennaō* ("beget"). So it is best to understand *monogenēs* as "the only member of a kin or kind" (Carson, *John*, 128), and thus when applied to Jesus, it means that he is utterly unique, a "one-of-a-kind Son" (Köstenberger and Swain, *Father, Son, and Spirit*, 76; cf. Macleod, *Person of Christ*, 72–73). Macleod draws the following conclusions: "First, *monogenēs* says nothing about origins because the Son is unoriginated. Secondly, it emphasizes the uniqueness of Jesus' sonship. Thirdly, this uniqueness consists of four things: he is an object of special love, he is the Father's equal, he is the Father's likeness and he is an eternal, not an adopted, Son" (72–73). And *monogenēs* has the same effect when applied to the Son of God: he stands at the Father's side as God himself, without equal and parallel.

[49] See Schreiner, *New Testament Theology*, 259; Carson, *John*, 657–659.

corded a conversation: "[Jesus] said to Thomas" (v. 27); then "Thomas answered [Jesus]" (v. 28); and in response, "Jesus said to [Thomas]" (v. 29). The simple but crucial point here is that Thomas is speaking directly to Jesus when he says, "My Lord and my God!" Thomas is not praising God for Christ's resurrection; he is claiming Christ as his God because of the resurrection. He recognized that Jesus, now alive from the dead, was supreme over all physical and spiritual life ("Lord") and shared the divine nature ("God"). And Jesus does not rebuke Thomas for his worship and confession of Jesus's deity. In fact, since the Jews regarded worship of anything other than God himself as blasphemous, Jesus's silence amounts to agreement. Even more, Jesus then acknowledges and accepts Thomas's confession of faith (v. 29a) and commends the same faith to others (v. 29b). And John endorses Thomas's confession of Jesus's deity by making it his last and highest Christological affirmation immediately before explaining that he wrote his Gospel so that others would believe in the fully divine Son of God (vv. 30–31).

ROMANS 9:5

> To them belong the patriarchs, and from their race, according to the flesh, is the Christ, who is God over all, blessed forever. Amen.

In addition to John, the apostle Paul also applies the title *theos* to Christ. Expressing deep sorrow for the majority of his fellow Jews because they have failed to embrace their Messiah in saving faith, Paul lists the incredible privileges of the Jewish people: "[T]o them belong the adoption, the glory, the covenants, the giving of the law, the worship, and the promises" (v. 4). The highest privilege however, centers in Christ: "To them belong the patriarchs, and from their race, according to the flesh, is the Christ, who is God over all [*ho ōn epi pantōn theos*], blessed forever. Amen" (v. 5).[50] Using a term that in the New Testament usually refers to God the Father, Paul applies *theos* directly to Christ, specifically affirming by the title that he is "over all" and "blessed forever." As Harris explains, Paul identifies Christ as *theos* because "Christ is a universal sovereign and the object of eternal adoration."[51]

TITUS 2:13 AND 2 PETER 1:1

> . . . waiting for our blessed hope, the appearing of the glory of our great God and Savior Jesus Christ . . . (Titus 2:13)

---

[50] The text can be punctuated in various ways. Some editors of the Greek text put a semicolon or period after 5a, making the last part of the verse a doxology addressed to God the Father: "God who is over all be blessed for ever. Amen" (RSV). However, most scholars acknowledge this is not correct. The word order in Greek reads far more naturally as a description of or doxology to the Messiah, Jesus Christ (see NRSV). In fact, the editors of the most recent Greek New Testament texts (e.g., Nestle-Aland 28th edition and UBS 4th edition) punctuate the text to reflect the Christological doxology: "the Messiah, who is God over all, blessed forever." For a thorough treatment of these options, see Harris, *Jesus as God*, 143–172; cf. Schreiner, *New Testament Theology*, 335–337.

[51] Harris, *Jesus as God*, 165.

> To those who have obtained a faith of equal standing with ours by the righteousness of our God and Savior Jesus Christ . . . (2 Pet. 1:1)

These two texts are written by different authors—Paul and Peter—but make a similar claim: Jesus Christ is "our God and Savior" (*tou theou hēmōn kai sōtēros*). Harris notes that in the first century, the formula "God and Savior" was a common religious expression used by both Palestinian and Diaspora Jews in reference to Yahweh, the one true God.[52] Moreover, the anarthrous *sōtēros* should be understood in connection with *tou theou* to form one title, "God and Savior," applied to one person, Jesus Christ.

HEBREWS 1:8–9

> [8] But of the Son he says, "Your throne, O God, is forever and ever, the scepter of uprightness is the scepter of your kingdom. [9] You have loved righteousness and hated wickedness; therefore God, your God, has anointed you with the oil of gladness beyond your companions."

In the overall context for this text (Heb. 1:4–14), the author makes the argument that Jesus is greater than angels. In short, angels were created to serve God (v. 7); the Son is God (vv. 8–9); therefore, as the Son, Jesus is greater than the angels who serve him. To ground his argument, the author quotes Psalm 45:6–7, which in its original context celebrates the wedding of the Davidic king. In Hebrews, however, this psalm functions as a typological prophecy that is fulfilled by Christ. As the true Davidic king, Jesus fulfills the promise of the Davidic covenant to be a king who rules forever.[53] Moreover, this eternal king is the eternal Son who bears the title *theos*. Christ comes with a twofold sonship: he is the human antitype of David, and he is God himself.[54]

CHRISTOLOGICAL CONCLUSIONS ON THE SON AS THEOS

Given that the title *theos* makes such a strong affirmation of the deity of Christ, some have questioned why it is not used more extensively in the New Testament. Why, for example, do we not find statements such as "Jesus is God" throughout the New Testament writings? Three points will not only provide an answer but they will take us to the heart of New Testament Christology. First, the New Testament does in fact use *theos* in reference to Jesus throughout the New Testament and in key places. Not only do four different authors apply the title to Jesus (John, Paul, Peter, and the author of Hebrews), but they do so

---

[52] Ibid., 178–182, 232–234. The phrase "God and Savior" was a common formula in the Greco-Roman world, and it regularly referred to one deity, but obviously with different meaning than in a biblical context. There is no reason to think that Paul departs from this standard usage.

[53] For a full treatment of the difficult issues related to reconciling the Old Testament context of Psalm 45 and its use in Hebrews, see Harris, *Jesus as God*, 205–227; William L. Lane, *Hebrews 1–8*, WBC (Dallas: Word, 1991), 29–33.

[54] See Harris, *Jesus as God*, 205–227.

consistently and purposefully.[55] For example, as noted in the discussion of John 1:1–18 and 20:28, *theos* forms a book-length *inclusio* to frame the entire Gospel in terms of the full deity of Christ. Moreover, application of the title was not restricted to Christians who lived in one geographical region. The apostolic testimony that Christ is *theos* comes in letters written in Asia Minor (John, Titus), Greece (Romans), and possibly Judea (Hebrews) and Rome (2 Peter); and these letters addressed Christians living in Asia Minor (John, 2 Peter), Rome (Romans, Hebrews), and Crete (Titus). And the confession that Christ is *theos* comes out of both the Jewish Christian (John, Hebrews, Peter) and Gentile Christian (Rome, Titus) theological settings.

Second, *theos* is *not* used repeatedly because the identity of Jesus taught by the New Testament is that of God the Son in relation to his Father and the Spirit, thus preserving Trinitarian relations. The God of the Bible is a triune God, and repeated use of the title *theos* could lead to confusion. Normally in the New Testament, *theos* refers to God the Father, and in Trinitarian formulas "God" always denotes the Father, never the Son or the Spirit (e.g., 2 Cor. 13:14). The New Testament repeatedly distinguishes the Father, Son, and Spirit, while also affirming the full equality of each of the divine persons. That is why, in the salutations of many New Testament letters, "God" is distinguished from "the Lord Jesus." As a result of this distinction, *theos* virtually becomes a proper name for God the Father. Thus, if *theos* was used in reference to the Son as his proper name as well, linguistic ambiguity would emerge. For example, how could one make sense of 2 Corinthians 5:19 if it read, "God was in *God*, reconciling the world to himself"? In order to preserve the personal distinctions within God, *theos* predominantly denotes the Father and not the Son. Nowhere is this distinction more evident than where the Father is called "the God of our Lord Jesus Christ" (Eph. 1:17), or "his God and Father" (Rev. 1:6), and where Jesus speaks of "my God." The New Testament, then, is very careful in how *theos* is applied to Jesus in order to underscore Trinitarian relations.

Third, in addition to preserving Trinitarian relations, the New Testament also wants to preserve the fact that Jesus is God the Son incarnate. If "God" had become a personal name for Christ, interchangeable with "Jesus," it is not hard to imagine that the humanity of Christ could have been diminished. But instead, the New Testament presents *theos* as the proper name for God the Father so that its use as a divine title for Jesus bears clear witness to the fullness of his deity without overshadowing his full humanity.

The New Testament, then, carefully teaches that Jesus is not God in the

---

[55] Depending on the dating of the New Testament books, the use of *theos* for Christ begins immediately after his resurrection in AD 30 (John 20:28), continued during the 50s (Rom. 9:5) and 60s (Titus 2:13; Heb. 1:8; 2 Pet. 1:1) and into the 90s (John 1:1, 18).

sense of being the same person as the Father (or Spirit), but he is God in that he shares the same divine nature.

Jesus as God the Son

As we have seen, the New Testament makes a cumulative-case argument for the deity of Christ. First, the New Testament gives divine status to the man Jesus by affirming his divine attributes, divine rule, and divine worship. Already in this first category we can see the logic and coherence of the New Testament's argument. Starting with the most basic idea, Jesus has in full all of the characteristics and capacities that make God who he is. Being the very image and essence of God, then, Jesus acts *as God*: he rules with universal authority, power, and dominion. And because he is God by nature and in his rule, Jesus receives the worship of his disciples and stands as the proper object of their faith for salvation. Second, the New Testament emphasizes that Jesus not only has divine status but he also performs specific divine works that only God can do. In sum, Christ is the agent of creation and the providential Lord of heaven and earth who inaugurates the kingdom of God and brings the age to come into the present, most dramatically in the forgiveness of sins. And third, consistent with his divine ontology and function, the New Testament crowns Christ with certain divine titles. He is both Lord and God, titles that refer and belong to Yahweh alone.

Murray Harris summarizes the biblical evidence this way:

> Jesus is not only God in revelation, the revealer of God (an official title)—he is God in essence. Not only are the deeds and words of Jesus the deeds and words of God—the nature of Jesus is the nature of God. By nature, as well as by action, Jesus is God. Other New Testament titles of Jesus, such as "Son of God" or "Lord" or "Alpha and Omega," imply the divinity of Jesus, but the title *God* explicitly affirms his deity.[56]

But Harris also rightly notes that we must be careful in our conclusion that "Jesus is God." The nearest comparable statements in the New Testament are "the Word was God" (John 1:1) and "the only Son, who is God" (John 1:18). The theological proposition "Jesus is God" is a necessary and true inference from the New Testament evidence. But if we make this inference and state this proposition without qualification, we risk telling less than the whole truth about Jesus: he is now the Son *incarnate*. And in his permanent incarnate existence, God the Son retains both his deity and his humanity. Jesus is neither only God nor merely human. To preserve Trinitarian relations and the reality of the incarnation, it is better to say that Jesus is *God the Son incarnate*. It is to the subject of Jesus's full and complete humanity that we now turn.

---

[56] Harris, *Three Crucial Questions*, 101.

THE HUMANITY OF CHRIST: GOD THE SON *INCARNATE*

In the last chapter, we saw that Scripture establishes the full deity of Christ as a necessary part of his identity. In this chapter, we will see that Scripture insists that the full humanity of Christ is just as necessary for us to know who he is. While most people today more quickly deny or diminish Jesus's divinity and accept his humanity, this has not always been the case. In fact, the early church first struggled against heresies that rejected the real and complete humanity of Christ.[1] Moreover, while accepting Christ as a man comes more easily to a culture that largely scoffs at the supernatural, this does not entail that the nature of Jesus's humanity is accepted or understood on the Bible's own terms.

So once again we need to look at how the authoritative storyline of Scripture presents God the Son incarnate. God created man in his image to spread the rule and glory of God over all creation. The first man and vice-regent of God, however, rebelled against the Creator–Covenant Lord and brought all of humanity and the rest of creation into ruin under the divine curse. Yet God remained committed to his original plan and promised to reverse the effects of sin and death, redeem a new humanity, and restore all of creation. As the divine plan developed through the biblical covenants, each covenant mediator entered the stage of redemptive history with the hope of bringing forth the promised true image-son-king who would restore God's rule over creation through a righteous humanity. But every mediator failed as a covenant partner with God and as a representative of humanity.

By the time Jesus comes on the scene, the identification of the man of God's promise has become more specific even as the anticipation of his appearance

---

[1] See Part III for a full discussion of docetism and the problems associated with its position that the divine Son only appeared to take on humanity.

has become more desperate. As God progressively revealed himself through his covenants with Adam, Noah, Abraham, Israel, and then David, it became clear that God himself would have to act in order to redeem humanity and restore creation through the coming of his own kingdom. But the covenantal developments also revealed that a man—a son, the king—must redeem humanity through suffering, to then reign over a restored creation as God's righteous vice-regent and faithful covenant partner. A man must come to represent God on the earth; a man must live in covenant obedience to God; a man must bear the covenant curse on behalf of a disobedient humanity; and a man must rule with the character of God over the earth.

The New Testament presents Jesus as *this* man: he is the true image of God (Col. 1:15; Heb. 1:3), the promised offspring of Abraham (Gal. 3:16), the obedient Son of God (Heb. 5:7–10), the great High Priest (Heb. 5:1–10; 7:1–28), the great Davidic king (Matt. 1:1), and the last Adam (1 Cor. 15:45; cf. Rom. 5:15). The typological trajectories that come through the Old Testament terminate in one who can stand in the place of sinful humanity yet without sin, sympathize with the weakness and temptations of humanity, and provide a model life for a redeemed humanity. Jesus could fulfill these roles only as one who was fully human. In the previous chapter, we discussed the biblical emphasis on the Son's eternal ontology and function. But because God requires a man to fulfill his plans and purposes for his creation, the New Testament also insists on the Son's incarnational ontology and function. The eternal Son of God *became a man* to accomplish the will and plan of God *as a man*.

In the rest of this chapter, we will examine the full humanity of Christ by considering the biblical presentation of the incarnation, the biblical rationale and reasons for the incarnation, and the necessity of Jesus's sinlessness during his incarnation.

The Biblical Presentation of the Incarnation[2]

The Scriptures present us with the real enfleshment of the eternal Son who now has a full and complete human nature. The New Testament does not equivocate on this truth or leave the humanity of Christ as a matter of implication. The Gospels lay the foundation for the incarnation: "the Word became flesh" (John 1:14). John even ascribes the spirit of antichrist to anyone who does *not* confess that Jesus has come "in the flesh" (1 John 4:2).[3] Paul teaches that Jesus accomplished his reconciling work "in his body of flesh" (Col. 1:22; cf. Eph.

---

[2] This section is indebted to the work of David Wells and Herman Bavinck (see David F. Wells, *The Person of Christ: A Biblical and Historical Analysis of the Incarnation* [Wheaton, IL: Crossway, 1984], 41–65; Herman Bavinck, *Sin and Salvation in Christ*, vol. 3 of *Reformed Dogmatics*, ed. John Bolt, trans. John Vriend [Grand Rapids, MI: Baker, 2006], 295–298).

[3] First John 4:2 uses the perfect participle, *elēluthota*, which assumes that Christ's enfleshment is now permanent.

2:14, "in his flesh"), and that in sending his Son "in the likeness of sinful flesh," God "condemned sin in the flesh" (Rom. 8:3). Peter speaks of Christ dying for us "in the flesh" (1 Pet. 3:18; cf. 4:1). And according to Hebrews, Christ was "made lower than the angels" and shared in our humanity in order to bring "many sons to glory" (Heb. 2:9–10). The entire weight of the New Testament, then, bears witness to the *genuineness* of Jesus's humanity.

Moreover, the New Testament tells us much about the *fullness* of Jesus's humanity. With so much biblical data to consider, it will be helpful to look at the human nature of Christ according to his outer life (physical, functional) and his inner life (mental, emotional, spiritual).[4]

The outer life of Jesus demonstrates that he had a body and grew and developed like all other human beings. For example, Jesus spoke of his body, head, hands, feet, blood, and bones, both before and after his resurrection (see Matt. 26:12, 26–28; Mark 14:8, 24; Luke 7:44–46; 22:20; 24:39; John 6:53–56; cf. John 19:34, 37). Jesus was born like all human babies, even though his conception was unique (Luke 2:7); he grew from childhood to adulthood, both physically and mentally (Luke 2:40); and he suffered in his body and died (Matt. 27:32–61; Mark 15:21–47; Luke 23:26–56; John 19:28–42). The so-called apocryphal gospels offer fanciful details to fill in the "gaps" in Jesus's childhood. These writings, however, come well after the New Testament era and go far beyond the New Testament narrative. Even though we have little data regarding Jesus's childhood, what the New Testament authors were authorized to say presents Jesus undergoing the normal stages of human development. He was born as an infant (Luke 2:16), grew into childhood (Matt. 2:11, 14, 16, 19–23; Luke 2:39), entered his teenage years (Luke 2:42–43), and then developed into a grown adult of about thirty years (Luke 3:23). Philip Eveson observes how the Gospels view Jesus's human development as similar to that of his cousin, John:

> As John the Baptist "grew and became strong in spirit" (Luke 1:80), so the child Jesus "grew and became strong, filled with wisdom. And the favour of God was upon him" (Luke 2:40). Then, as he grew from boyhood to manhood, he "increased in wisdom and in stature and in favour with God and man" (Luke 2:52).
>
> Not only so, but Luke's presentation is very reminiscent of the descriptions of the growth of Old Testament figures such as Isaac and Ishmael (Gen. 21:8, 20), Samson (Judg. 13:24), and particularly Samuel, who also grew "both in stature and in favour with the LORD and also with man" (1 Sam. 2:26).[5]

---

[4] Although scholars disagree on the matter, this discussion assumes that a human nature consists of a body-soul duality, or what Anthony Hoekema calls a psychosomatic unity. For a defense of this view, see John Cooper, *Body, Soul, and Life Everlasting: Biblical Anthropology and the Monism-Dualism Debate*, 2nd ed. (Grand Rapids, MI: Eerdmans, 2000); Anthony A. Hoekema, *Created in God's Image* (Grand Rapids, MI: Eerdmans; Exeter: Paternoster, 1986); William Hasker, *The Emergent Self* (Ithaca, NY: Cornell University Press, 1999).

[5] Philip H. Eveson, "The Inner or Psychological Life of Christ," in *The Forgotten Christ: Exploring the Majesty and Mystery of God Incarnate*, ed. Stephen Clark (Nottingham: Apollos, 2007), 66–67.

The apostle Paul emphasizes the human birth, descent, and role of Christ. Galatians 4:4 speaks of Jesus being "born [*genomenon*] out of [*ek*] a woman"[6] rather than through (*dia*) her. Paul uses the preposition *ek* to stress that in his birth, Jesus did not merely use Mary's humanity as an instrument for entering the world but shared in her human nature so that he would live as all Jewish men, "born under the law" (v. 4b).[7] Similarly, Romans 1:3 tells us that the Son "was descended [*genomenou*] from [*ek*] the seed [*spermatos*] of David, according to the flesh."[8] Paul again uses the preposition *ek* to deliberately affirm Jesus's human nature: he is a man who belongs to and shares in the same lineage as David's descendants. And Paul both assumes and explains the importance of Jesus's humanity when he compares the "one man" Adam and the "one man Jesus Christ" (Rom. 5:14–16; cf. 1 Cor. 15:21), and in his confession that there is only one mediator between God and man, "the man Christ Jesus" (1 Tim. 2:5; cf. Acts 17:31). So we can conclude with Wells that "[t]hese affirmations appear to rule out any possibility that Paul's view of Jesus was that he was in any way less than fully human."[9]

The author of Hebrews then presents the human life of Jesus. The author presents the Son in the most exalted of terms, but he also insists on Christ's full humanity. Jesus was from the tribe of Judah (Heb. 7:14); was tempted like us (yet without sin) (4:15); he learned obedience as we do (5:8); and he took on our "flesh and blood" (2:14) in order to become our perfect High Priest and accomplish our eternal salvation (2:17–18; 5:1–10; 7:1–28). Moreover, the author stresses that the Son was "made like his brothers in every respect" (2:17) and that he "learned obedience through what he suffered" (5:8). It was precisely this human development that qualified Jesus to become the human priest and covenant mediator required to reconcile man to God (8:6; 9:15, 24; 12:24).

Without the eternal Son's fully human birth, growth, and development, we would not have an all-sufficient Savior whose sacrificial death achieved for us the full forgiveness of our sins and whose sympathetic service helps us to walk in the power of that forgiveness. The outer life of Christ presented to us according to the Bible's own terms demonstrates that he came into this world with a fully human nature to accomplish as a man all that God required of and planned for humanity.

The inner life of Jesus demonstrates that he had a mind, will, and soul,

---

[6] Author's translation.

[7] Wells, *Person of Christ*, 58, contends that "born of a woman" is idiomatic for what was fully human (cf. Job 14:1, 2; 15:14, 15; 25:4, 5; Matt. 11:11). Whether this statement implies that Paul has knowledge of the virgin conception is debated, but it is possible (see J. Gresham Machen, *The Virgin Birth of Christ* [Grand Rapids, MI: Baker, 1930], 259–265). Jesus's humanity, then, would have an anatomy, physiology, biochemistry, and genetic code similar to ours. The means by which this took place was the virgin conception that resulted in the Son being particularized as a man, and, through the genetic contribution of Mary, that gave Jesus a specific genetic history, even though some of that genotype was provided miraculously by the agency of the Spirit.

[8] Author's translation.

[9] Wells, *Person of Christ*, 58.

and experienced life like all other human beings. Along with Jesus's outer life, Oscar Cullmann argues for "an inner human development" that qualified Jesus to fulfill the roles and perform the works given to him in his incarnation.[10] The New Testament portrays Jesus exhibiting a full range of human emotions, needs, and characteristics.[11] He was moved to pity, compassion, love, and affection (Matt. 9:36; Mark 1:41; 8:2; Luke 7:36–50; John 11:5; 13:34; 15:9–13); he was distressed (Mark 7:34; 8:12; Luke 22:15, 44); he became angry (Mark 3:5; John 11:33, 38); he experienced joy (Luke 10:21; John 15:11); he got annoyed (Mark 10:14); he was surprised (Matt. 8:10; Mark 6:6) and disappointed (Mark 8:17; 9:19); he remained subject to his parents (Luke 2:51); he suffered hunger and thirst (Matt. 4:1–2; Mark 11:12; John 19:28), fatigue and weariness (Matt. 8:23–24; John 4:5–6), and temptation (Luke 4:2, 13; 22:28), and he offered up prayers with loud cries and tears (Matt. 26:36–46; cf. Heb. 5:7).

Jesus was able to have these human experiences because his human nature included a human soul (see Matt. 27:50; Luke 23:46; John 12:27; 13:21) and a human psychology, including a human mind and will.[12] For example, the New Testament tells us that as Jesus grew into an adult, he learned to think better than he did as a child: he "increased in wisdom and in stature" (Luke 2:52). The Gospels do present Jesus with extraordinary knowledge. People are amazed at his understanding, even at twelve years old (Luke 2:47). Having never met her or heard about her, Jesus knew that the Samaritan woman had had five husbands (John 4:18). And before he reached Bethany and the tomb of Lazarus, Jesus knew that Lazarus was dead (John 11:14).[13] But Jesus also admitted that he did not know when he would return because the timing was known only by the Father. To see that an increase in his human wisdom and knowledge works together with supernatural knowledge to present Jesus with a human mind, "we must distinguish between supernatural knowledge and infinite knowledge."[14] In the Old Testament, prophets sometimes had supernatural knowledge (e.g., 2 Kings 6:12). These men were not omniscient, however, but received divine revelation by the action of the Spirit. Similarly, the extraordinary knowledge of Christ is best understood as revelation from his Father through the Spirit.

---

[10] Oscar Cullmann, *The Christology of the New Testament*, trans., Shirley C. Guthrie and Charles A. M. Hall (Philadelphia: Westminster, 1963), 97.

[11] On the emotional life of Christ, see B. B. Warfield, "The Emotional Life of Our Lord," in *The Person and Work of Christ*, ed. Samuel G. Craig (Philadelphia: P&R, 1980), 93–145; see also the helpful discussion in Donald Macleod, *The Person of Christ* (Downers Grove, IL: InterVarsity Press, 1998), 170–178.

[12] For a helpful discussion of the psychological life of our Lord, see Eveson, "Inner or Psychological Life of Christ," 48–92. This discussion assumes that the biblical terms for soul, spirit, and heart are interchangeable, that these terms refer to the immaterial part of our being, and that a human nature consists of a distinct capacity for thought (mind) and volition (will). In historical and contemporary theology, the issue of the will has been debated in terms of dyothelitism's "doctrine of two wills" and monothelitism's "doctrine of one will." For a treatment of this debate and the importance of Jesus's human will for Christology, see Parts III and IV.

[13] Other examples of Jesus's supernatural knowledge include knowing the character of Nathaniel before he meets him (John 1:47); knowing there is a coin sufficient to pay the temple tax inside the fish's mouth (Matt. 17:27); and knowing that there is a shoal of fish beside his disciples' boat when they had caught nothing (John 21:5–6).

[14] Macleod, *Person of Christ*, 166.

In fact, Jesus himself says, "the Son can do nothing of his own accord, but only what he sees the Father doing" (John 5:19); "I can do nothing on my own. As I hear, I judge, and my judgment is just, because I seek not my own will but the will of him who sent me" (5:30); "My teaching is not mine, but his who sent me" (7:16); "For I have not spoken on my own authority, but the Father who sent me has himself given me a commandment—what to say and what to speak. . . . What I say, therefore, I say as the Father has told me" (12:49, 50).[15] Jesus indicates here that his teaching and his own understanding of it comes not from the divine nature he shares with the Father but from the Father to Jesus's human mind and capacity to know, learn, and understand. This does not mean that as God the Son, Jesus was not omniscient.[16] We will reconcile Jesus's divine and human knowledge in Part IV. Here we simply need to recognize that God the Son incarnate lived (and still lives) a fully human life, and that in obedience to his Father and for our salvation, Jesus chose to live within the limitations of his humanity unless his Father allowed otherwise.[17] D. A. Carson helpfully explains this general principle of limitation:

> [Jesus] therefore would not use his powers to turn stones into bread for himself: that would have been to vitiate his identification with human beings and therefore to abandon his mission, for human beings do not have instant access to such solutions. His mission prohibited him from arrogating to himself the prerogatives rightly his. But if that mission required him to multiply loaves for the sake of the five thousand, he did so. Even his knowledge was self-confessedly limited (Matt. 24:36).[18]

---

[15] See D. A. Carson, *The Gospel according to John*, PNTC (Grand Rapids, MI: Eerdmans, 1991), 246–259; Andreas J. Köstenberger and Scott R. Swain, *Father, Son, and Spirit: The Trinity and John's Gospel*, NSBT 24 (Downers Grove, IL: InterVarsity Press, 2008), 111–133.

[16] For a discussion of the deity of Christ in general and the divine attribute of omniscience in particular, see chapter 5 and Part IV.

[17] In Part IV, this point will be developed in terms of Trinitarian relations and Christ's mission as the last Adam. In theological studies, scholars continue to debate whether the Son's dependence upon the Father is limited in duration (i.e., the state of humiliation) or whether it is the outworking of an eternal *taxis* (ordering) or relations between the divine persons. For an example of an argument for limited dependence, see Millard J. Erickson, *Who's Tampering with the Trinity? An Assessment of the Subordination Debate* (Grand Rapids, MI: Kregel, 2009); for an argument for eternal-relational dependence, see Robert Letham, *The Holy Trinity: In Scripture, History, Theology, and Worship* (Phillipsburg, NJ: P&R, 2004); Kyle Claunch, "God Is the Head of Christ: Does 1 Corinthians 11:3 Ground Gender Complementarity in the Immanent Trinity?," in *One God in Three Persons: Unity of Essence, Distinction of Persons, Implications for Life*, ed. Bruce A. Ware and John Starke (Wheaton, IL: Crossway, 2015), 65–93. The discussion in Part IV will develop this debate further. Here it is sufficient to say that according to the axiom that the economic relations between the divine persons reflect prior immanent relations, the eternal-relational dependence of the Son makes the best biblical-theological sense (see my "Irenic and Unpersuasive: A Review of Millard Erickson, *Who's Tampering with the Trinity?*," *Journal of Biblical Manhood and Womanhood* 15:2 [2010]: 37–47). Regarding Jesus's human knowledge, J. I. Packer explains, "His knowing, like the rest of his activity, was bounded by his Father's will. And therefore the reason why he was ignorant (for instance) the date of his return was not that he had given up the power to know all things at the Incarnation, but that the Father had not willed that he should have this particular piece of knowledge while on earth, prior to his passion. . . . Jesus's limitation of knowledge is to be explained, not in terms of the mode of the Incarnation, but with reference to the will of the Father for the Son while on earth" (J. I. Packer, *Knowing God*, 20th Anniversary ed. [Downers Grove, IL: InterVarsity Press, 1993], 62).

[18] D. A. Carson, *The Farewell Discourse and Final Prayer of Jesus: An Exposition of John 14–17* (Grand Rapids, MI: Baker, 1980), 36.

Although the New Testament does not give us a lot of information, it provides enough to agree with Macleod that Jesus "had a human mind, subject to the same laws of perception, memory, logic and development as our own."[19] Jesus learned by studying the Scriptures and the world as we do, unless his Father allowed otherwise. But given his sinlessness and the fact that he is the eternal Son, Jesus's intellect would have been perfectly attuned to the Father. Given Jesus's unique intimacy in relation to his Father, Macleod suggests that as a man, Jesus may have "lived in a thought-world of pure revelation so that to an extent that we cannot fathom God disclosed himself not only to his thinking but *in* his thinking. In this respect, revelation, in the case of Christ, was concurrent with his own thought-processes."[20] Yet we must still affirm that *as a man*, whether in the state of humiliation or exaltation, Jesus was not omniscient, thus preserving the genuineness and fullness of his humanity according to the theological insight that, the "finite is not capable of [containing] the infinite" (*finitum non capax infiniti*).[21]

Finally, in addition to the human mind of Christ, we also need to recognize that the incarnation provided God the Son with a human will. Through centuries of debate, the consistent witness of the church is that Christ has two wills: a divine will according to his divine nature and a human will according to his human nature.[22] Denying that Christ has a distinct human will and the ability to choose as a man according to it endangers the full humanity of Christ. Indeed, Scripture's entire storyline requires an obedient Son who actively obeys *as a man*, and as such, a biblical Christology requires that the Son wills *as God* and also wills *as a man*.[23] As Michael Horton explains, "Jesus is therefore not merely the Son of God as to his divinity, but is the true and faithful Son of Adam who always obeys his Father's will in the power of the Holy Spirit. This meritorious human life lived in full dependence on the Spirit (recapitulation) is not extrinsic but intrinsic to redemption; it is not merely a necessary prerequisite of a sacrificial offering, but part and parcel of that offering."[24]

Jesus's ordeal in the garden of Gethsemane brings his outer and inner life together to illustrate his full humanity as God the Son incarnate. Jesus has come to the brink of the cross, where he will bear the sins of the world and

---

[19] Macleod, *Person of Christ*, 164.
[20] Ibid., 167.
[21] Bavinck, *Sin and Salvation in Christ*, 258. For a further discussion of the complexities involved in the knowledge capacity and function of God the Son incarnate, see Part IV.
[22] Monothelitism (*one* will located in the *person* of Christ) was rejected by the early church at the Third Council of Constantinople (the Sixth Ecumenical Council, in 681) in favor of dyothelitism (*two* wills, one located in each of Christ's *natures*, hence Christ had a divine and a human will). For a further discussion of the debate regarding the will(s) of Christ, see Parts III and IV; see also Thomas A. Watts, "Two Wills in Christ? Contemporary Objections Considered in the Light of a Critical Examination of Maximus the Confessor's *Disputation with Pyrrhus*," *WTJ* 71 (2009): 455–487.
[23] On this point, see Michael S. Horton, *Lord and Servant: A Covenant Christology* (Louisville: Westminster John Knox, 2005), 159–177.
[24] Ibid., 172.

suffer crucifixion and death under the wrath of God. He has come to the lowest point of his *kenōsis* in his identification with humanity and obedience to the Father. Here he prays, "My Father, if it be possible, let this cup pass from me; nevertheless, not as I will, but as you will" (Matt. 26:39; see Mark 14:36; Luke 22:42). But this distinction between Jesus's will and the will of the Father is not a private matter. Jesus has already told his disciples, "I have come down from heaven, not to do my own will but the will of him who sent me" (John 6:38). In taking on our humanity, the Son is now able to make human choices according to human desires, longings, aspirations, and aversions. As Macleod observes,

> Such language presupposes not only a metaphysical distinction between the will of Jesus and the will of the Father, but also the logical possibility that Jesus' natural preferences (based on personal self-interest) might not always coincide with the wishes of the Father. Indeed, it is this fact which creates the whole possibility of *kenōsis* or self-emptying. The Servant consults not his own interests but the interests of others (Phil. 2:4). This climaxes in Gethsemane, where the dilemma becomes almost unbearably acute.[25]

We can probe deeper into Jesus's humanity by considering separately the two petitions in his Gethsemane prayer. In his first petition, Jesus prays, "My Father, if it be possible, let this cup pass from me; nevertheless, not as I will" (Matt. 26:39). Far from opposing God's will for him, Jesus is expressing the natural fear of death and aversion to pain and suffering that is quite proper for a human facing crucifixion. In this sense, Jesus does not want this "cup"; everything in him shrinks from it. The words used to describe Jesus's mental state are graphic: "troubled" (*adēmonein*), "greatly distressed" (*ekthambeisthai*), and "sorrowful (*perilupos*), even to death" (Mark 14:33–34). This is the inner life of a man facing a cruel and horrible death, and this for the sins of his enemies.[26] As Macleod notes, not only the specific words but the entire narrative describes the agony of the moment: "The whole account resonates the acutest torment and anguish."[27] Jesus is physically exhausted. As he tells his disciples, "the flesh is weak" (Matt. 26:41). But as his disciples sleep, Jesus takes his body to the point of breaking down: "his sweat became like great drops of blood falling down to the ground" (Luke 22:44). In fact, amid Jesus's struggle, "there appeared to him an angel from heaven, strengthening him" (Luke 22:43). This is the outer life of a man facing execution by crucifixion, with the choice either to save himself or to win the eternal salvation of many.

In his second petition, Jesus prays, "but as you [Father] will" (Matt. 26:39).

---

[25] Macleod, *Person of Christ*, 179.
[26] See ibid., 173; cf. Warfield, *Person and Work of Christ*, 129–137.
[27] Macleod, *Person of Christ*, 173.

Even with certain terror and agony hanging on his decision, Jesus aligns his human will to the divine will and submits *in his humanity* to the Father. Just as he embraced his messianic mission at his baptism and during his temptation in the wilderness, Jesus once again chooses as a man to willingly obey his Father. As the author of Hebrews explains, "Although he was a son, he learned obedience through what he suffered. And being made perfect, he became the source of eternal salvation to all who obey him" (Heb. 5:8–9). To learn obedience as a man, Jesus had to make human choices. And to make human choices, Jesus must have had a human will distinct from the divine will. In fact, if Jesus did not have a human will, then the agonizing drama of Gethsemane is a complete farce and we are left without a human representative substitute to suffer for our human sins and make us part of a new humanity. But the humanity of Christ on display in Gethsemane is not fictional. God himself has revealed through the New Testament authors that the divine Son who became incarnate chose to bear the cross out of love for the Father and for his people. We can have confidence that Christ hung on the cross in the fullness of humanity by considering how he made that decision. Jesus willed to do as a man what he initially and rightly did not want to do as a man, such that a man lived and died in perfect obedience to God for our salvation and the completion of God's glorious plan for humanity and the rest of creation.[28]

In Christ, then, we meet God the Son incarnate, fully God and *fully man*. As Paul describes him, the eternal Son is now "the *man* Christ Jesus" (1 Tim. 2:5). The Bible presents the incarnation as true and as the voluntary action of the Son to become like us in our humanity in every respect, having a human body, soul, and psychology.

To understand better how the full humanity of Christ shapes his identity, we now need to move from the biblical presentation of the incarnation as true to the biblical rationale for the incarnation as necessary.

CUR DEUS HOMO? WHY THE GOD-MAN?

In the eleventh century, Anselm of Canterbury famously asked, "Why did God become man?"[29] It is an important question to ask since it takes us into the rationale for the incarnation, and thus into the heart of the gospel. Anselm's answer was that God the Son became man to fulfill God's plan to save sinners by making satisfaction for their sin. No less can be said. But Scripture gives a number of reasons for why the incarnation was a necessity in the divine plan. The complexity of the incarnation itself and the attending issues deserve a full-

---

[28] On this point, see Watts, "Two Wills in Christ?," 455–487.
[29] See Anselm's classic work, *Why God Became Man*, in Brian Davies and Gillian R. Evans, eds., *Anselm of Canterbury: The Major Works* (Oxford: Oxford University Press, 2008).

length treatment. But for our purposes here, we can trace the biblical rationale as it is summed up in Hebrews 2:5–18, probably the most detailed discussion in a single text of Scripture.

The Biblical Rationale for the Incarnation

As discussed in chapter 5, the entire book of Hebrews focuses on the majesty, supremacy, and glory of the Son, our Lord Jesus Christ. By expounding multiple Old Testament texts, and by a series of contrasts with various Old Testament figures, the author encourages a group of predominantly Jewish Christians with the truth that Jesus has come as the Lord in the flesh to fulfill all of the promises and expectations of the Old Testament.

Beginning in the opening verses, the author uses a series of comparisons and contrasts to unpack his thesis that Jesus is superior to all of the Old Testament figures before him, including Moses, Joshua, and the high priests. But he begins by demonstrating that Jesus is superior to angels. First, Jesus is greater than angels who serve God because he is the Son of God (Heb. 1:5–14). In contrast to angels, the Son is identified with the LORD due to his greater name (vv. 4–5), the worship he receives (v. 6), his unchanging existence as the universe's Creator and Lord (vv. 10–12), and the rule and reign he shares with his Father (vv. 7–9, 13). Angels, on the other hand, are simply creatures and ministering servants (vv. 7, 14); they are not in the same transcendent category as the Son. Second, Jesus is superior to angels because he has come to do the work that no angel could ever do. By taking on our humanity, the Son becomes the representative man of Psalm 8—the last Adam—who undoes the first Adam's failure and ushers in the new creation by bringing all things into subjection under his rule and reign.[30]

For our purposes here, we need to focus on the centrality of the incarnation to the fulfillment of God's redemptive plan, which is the author's final argument for the superiority of the Son. The author of Hebrews gives us a four-part rationale for the purpose and necessity of the incarnation in 2:5–18:

[5] For it was not to angels that God subjected the world to come, of which we are speaking. [6] It has been testified somewhere,

"What is man, that you are mindful of him,
  or the son of man, that you care for him?
[7] You made him for a little while lower than the angels;
  you have crowned him with glory and honor,
    [8] putting everything in subjection under his feet."

---

[30] For a helpful article on this point, see A. B. Caneday, "The Eschatological World Already Subjected to the Son: The *Oikoumenē* of Hebrews 1.6 and the Son's Enthronement," in *A Cloud of Witnesses: The Theology of Hebrews in Its Ancient Contexts*, ed. Richard Bauckham et al. (Edinburgh: T&T Clark, 2008), 28–39.

THE HUMANITY OF CHRIST: GOD THE SON *INCARNATE* □ 219

Now in putting everything in subjection to him, he left nothing outside his control. At present, we do not yet see everything in subjection to him. [9] But we see him who for a little while was made lower than the angels, namely Jesus, crowned with glory and honor because of the suffering of death, so that by the grace of God he might taste death for everyone.

[10] For it was fitting that he, for whom and by whom all things exist, in bringing many sons to glory, should make the founder of their salvation perfect through suffering. [11] For he who sanctifies and those who are sanctified all have one source. That is why he is not ashamed to call them brothers, [12] saying,

"I will tell of your name to my brothers;
in the midst of the congregation I will sing your praise."

[13] And again,

"I will put my trust in him."

And again,

"Behold, I and the children God has given me."

[14] Since therefore the children share in flesh and blood, he himself likewise partook of the same things, that through death he might destroy the one who has the power of death, that is, the devil, [15] and deliver all those who through fear of death were subject to lifelong slavery. [16] For surely it is not angels that he helps, but he helps the offspring of Abraham. [17] Therefore he had to be made like his brothers in every respect, so that he might become a merciful and faithful high priest in the service of God, to make propitiation for the sins of the people. [18] For because he himself has suffered when tempted, he is able to help those who are being tempted.

First, the Son became a man to fulfill God's original intention for humanity (see Heb. 2:5–9). The author demonstrates this point by an appeal to Psalm 8. In its Old Testament context, Psalm 8 celebrates both the majesty of God as the Creator and the exalted position humans have in creation. The psalm leads us back to God's original design of creation and to remember that God created us in his image and bestowed on us glory and honor by giving us the right to exercise dominion over the world as his vice-regents (Genesis 1–2).[31] By transitioning from the quotation of Psalm 8:4–6 to Jesus, the author of Hebrews argues that the proper vice-regency of humanity is restored in the Son

---

[31] It is proper to speak in the plural here because *anthrōpos* ("man") in Hebrews 2:6 is a collective noun referring to all of humanity: "What is man, that you are mindful of him, or the son of man, that you care for him?" Some interpret "son of man" as a direct reference to Christ, but given its Old Testament context and synonymous parallelism, "son of man" is best viewed as a reference to Adam and the human race. However, in the storyline of Scripture, the typological trajectory that begins with the first Adam terminates in Christ, who fulfills the role of humanity as the last Adam (see Peter T. O'Brien, *The Letter to the Hebrews*, PNTC [Grand Rapids, MI: Eerdmans, 2010], 95–96).

who became incarnate: "Now in putting everything in subjection to him, he left nothing outside his control" (Heb. 2:8b). This restoration of humanity to the glory and honor of dominion over the earth under God, however, has not come all at once: "At present, we do not yet see everything in subjection to him" (v. 8b). When we look at the world, we know that God's original design for the human race has been frustrated; we do not rule as God intended us to rule.

But just as the use of Psalm 8 here in Hebrews leads us to look back to the original intention for humanity that was corrupted by sin, the same psalm also encourages us to look forward to God's completion of his plan and his enthronement of a righteous humanity over the earth. Given its position in the Old Testament, especially in light of God's *protevangelium* promise (Gen. 3:15) and the unfolding development of his promises through the biblical covenants, Psalm 8 speaks prophetically. David looks forward to a day when God will restore humans to his original intention for us, a restoration that will take place through another man—one who comes from the human race to act on our behalf to reverse the curse of the first Adam. Instead of failure and corruption through disobedience, this last Adam will bring victory and righteousness through obedience to God.

This is precisely how Hebrews 2:9 applies Psalm 8 to Christ: "But we see him who for a little while was made lower than the angels, namely Jesus, crowned with glory and honor because of the suffering of death, so that by the grace of God he might taste death for everyone." Jesus is presented as the antitype of Adam. He is the representative human being whose obedient humiliation in his incarnation and death merited his exaltation that he will share with his people. As Thomas Schreiner concludes, "In that sense, [Jesus] is the true human being, the only one who has genuinely lived the kind of life that humans were intended to live under God."[32] The rule promised to humanity has been taken up by the man Christ Jesus. This man is restoring a people to bear the image of God in truth, making them truly human again.

Second, the Son became a man to bring many sons to glory (see Heb. 2:10–13). In the context of Hebrews 2, the word "glory" is not a reference to heaven; rather, it is a term from Psalm 8 referring to God's intention to restore us to what he originally created us to be. The imagery identifies Jesus with Yahweh who led Israel out of Egypt in the first exodus to make them into a people for his own possession and purposes. Jesus has now brought about the new exodus through his death and resurrection. As the "founder [*archēgon*] of their salvation" (Heb. 2:10)—a word which conveys the idea of "pioneer" (leader/forerunner and founder/victor)—Jesus is now leading a people out of

---

[32] Thomas R. Schreiner, *New Testament Theology: Magnifying God in Christ* (Grand Rapids, MI: Baker Academic, 2008), 382.

slavery to sin and death (vv. 14–15) and into the covenant life and representative reign under God that he has planned from the beginning.[33] Jesus is the first man of the new creation. He is the trailblazer and the champion who has won the victory for new humanity by opening up new territory through his redemptive work.

This new exodus and the glory of a new humanity, then, depend upon the Son's suffering, which requires his incarnation. To bring many sons to glory, "it was fitting that he [God] . . . should make the founder of their salvation perfect through suffering" (Heb. 2:10). As Peter O'Brien rightly observes, the idea that the suffering of the Son "was fitting" corresponds to the fact that to help the offspring of Abraham, the Son "had to be" made like them "in every respect" (v. 17).[34] Unless the Son took upon himself our humanity and suffered for us, there would be no suffering to help humanity, no fulfillment of God's promises for humanity, and no return to the planned glory of humanity. Jesus's suffering and death, then, was not a failed end to the incarnation but the precise purpose of the incarnation, all of which fulfills the Creator–Covenant Lord's plan to perfect a new humanity to rule over his good creation.

Moreover, Jesus himself was made "perfect through suffering," or better, "through sufferings" (*dia pathēmatōn*; Heb. 2:10). The precise meaning of "perfection" (*teleiōsai*) in Hebrews remains a matter of much debate.[35] In the present context, however, it is best to understand *perfection* vocationally. As O'Brien argues, "Christ's being perfected is a vocational process by which he is made complete or fully equipped for his office."[36] In addition, "through sufferings" is not synonymous with "the suffering of death" (v. 9), but it "designates the sufferings *through* which Christ had to pass."[37] And this entails the entire experience of suffering associated with and leading up to Christ's death.[38] In other words, in order for Christ to accomplish his work and to fulfill his office of Redeemer for us, he had to become one with us, and his entire incarnate experience qualified him to become our "merciful and faithful high priest" (v. 17).

Finally, this incarnate identification and suffering was necessary for "bringing many sons to glory" (Heb. 2:10). God's fitting action of perfecting the Son by the incarnation and his suffering serves as the basis for his forming a community of sons and daughters who are beginning to be restored to the very purpose of their creation. Both the Son as sanctifier and the sons who are sanctified are all of one origin (*ex henos pantes*, v. 11). And "that is why he is not ashamed

---

[33] See O'Brien, *Hebrews*, 103–108.
[34] See ibid., 102–103.
[35] For the various options, see ibid., 107–108. For a detailed discussion of "perfection" in Hebrews, see David G. Peterson, *Hebrews and Perfection: An Examination of the Concept of Perfection in the "Epistle to the Hebrews,"* Society for New Testament Studies, vol. 47 (Cambridge: Cambridge University Press, 1982).
[36] O'Brien, *Hebrews*, 107.
[37] Ibid.
[38] See ibid.; cf. Peterson, *Hebrews and Perfection*, 69.

to call them brothers" (v. 11b). In other words, through the incarnation the Son came to share in the source and suffering of our human nature. And this incarnate identification and suffering was the only way to bring a ruined humanity into the glory of a new humanity. As F. F. Bruce explains, "since those who are sanctified to God through His death are sons and daughters of God, the Son of God is not ashamed to acknowledge them as His brothers—not only as those whose nature He took upon Himself, but those whose trials He endured, for whose sins He made atonement, that they might follow Him to glory on the path of salvation which He Himself cut."[39]

Third, the Son became a man to destroy the power of death and the Devil (see Heb. 2:14–16). The author of Hebrews directly connects the incarnation with the destruction of all that holds the new humanity back from its divinely planned and promised glory: "Since therefore the children share in flesh and blood, he himself likewise partook of the same things, that through death he might destroy the one who has the power of death, that is, the devil, and deliver all those who through fear of death were subject to lifelong slavery" (vv. 14–15). In short, the destruction of our slave-master and our deliverance from the cage of fear requires that, like us, the Son would come to "share in flesh and blood." According to Scripture, death is not normal to God's original creation; rather, it is the result of sin (Gen. 2:17). Death is God's penalty for our disobedience (cf. Rom. 6:23). In judgment against his rebellious vice-regents, God gave mankind over to the power of Satan (cf. 2 Cor. 4:4; Eph. 2:1–3; Col. 1:13). Created to rule over God's creation as his image-bearers, we now cower in fear before God as those who are spiritually dead, which ultimately shows itself in our physical death. Our only hope is found in a deliverer, a "pioneer" (Heb. 2:10) who goes before us and defeats our enemies. We need a Savior who can deal with sin, death, and Satan by first sharing our common humanity and then, in that humanity, suffering and dying so that by his death the power of death is destroyed. As O'Brien explains, "Only through his incarnation and death could the Son effect God's ultimate purpose for these members of his family—a purpose that is described in terms of their being glorified (v. 10), sanctified (v. 11), liberated (v. 15), and purified from sins (v. 17)."[40]

The incarnation was the necessary means by which the eternal Son became our all-sufficient Redeemer and Lord. Jesus is able to redeem humanity precisely because he came to share in our common human nature. It is not angels he helps, or better, "takes hold of" (*epilambanomai*), since he does not identify with or take on the nature of an angel. Rather, the Son identifies with the offspring of Abraham, his people, and leads them to glory in a new exodus of

---

[39] F. F. Bruce, *The Epistle to the Hebrews: The English Text with Introduction, Exposition, and Notes*, NICNT (Grand Rapids, MI: Eerdmans, 1964), 45.
[40] O'Brien, *Hebrews*, 113.

victory and triumph.[41] By his incarnation and cross work, the Son becomes our victor who wins the battle, and apart from this there is no salvation. Our plight is so desperate due to sin that it requires nothing less than the enfleshment of God's own unique Son. His humanity cannot be an appearance; it must be genuine and full to bring forth the glory of a new humanity.

Fourth, the Son became a man to become a merciful and faithful high priest (see Heb. 2:17–18). The mention of Jesus as our High Priest introduces the office and work of Christ that the author of Hebrews will explore in great detail throughout the rest of the book (4:14–5:10; 7:1–10:25). More importantly for our current interest, the High Priesthood of Christ places a capstone on the argument for the purpose and necessity of the incarnation. The author begins by stressing both the mandatory and the comprehensive nature of the incarnation: "Therefore (*hothen*, "for this reason") he had (*ōpheilen*) to be made like (*homoiōthēnai*) his brothers in every respect (*kanta panta*)" (Heb. 2:17a). In other words, to come according to the plan of God, the Son could not take on a partial or pseudo human nature. The Son was under obligation (*ōpheilen*) by the Father to take on a human nature (*homoiōthēnai*) that exactly corresponds to every aspect of our human nature (*kanta panta*), but of course without sin.[42]

More specifically, two purpose clauses tell us that God the Son had to become a man, (1) "so that he might become a merciful and faithful high priest in the service of God"; and (2) "to make propitiation for (*hilaskesthai*) the sins (*tas hamartias*) of the people" (Heb. 2:17b).[43] Or, to state it in the language of the early church, the Son had to become flesh because "he could not redeem what he did not assume"; representation requires identification.[44] If the Son did not become one with us in every way, he could not redeem us in every way. Along with Hebrews, then, we must emphasize that it was this incarnation—the genuine enfleshment of the Son in a fully human nature—that was necessary for our salvation and the fulfillment of all that God planned before the foundations of the world.[45]

---

[41] On the exodus theme, see ibid., 116–118.

[42] See ibid., 118–122.

[43] There is considerable debate over how the verb *hilaskesthai* with the object "sins" should be understood. Does it mean: (1) "to make expiation for" (RSV); (2) "to make atonement for" (NIV); (3) "to make propitiation for" (ESV)? It is best not to pit these options against one another. It first and foremost refers to expiation, but expiation in Scripture is only through propitiation. On this point, see Donald Macleod, *Christ Crucified: Understanding the Atonement* (Downers Grove, IL: IVP Academic, 2014), 101–150. Cf. Leon Morris, *The Apostolic Preaching of the Cross* (Grand Rapids, MI: Eerdmans, 1965), 125–160, 202–205.

[44] John of Damascus represents this view: "For the whole Christ assumed the whole me that he might grant salvation to the whole me, for what is unassumable is incurable" (cited in Bavinck, *Sin and Salvation in Christ*, 297).

[45] As the argument for the superiority of Christ continues in Hebrews, the author develops the connection between a full incarnation and complete reconciliation in terms of the typological fulfillment of the high priesthood (Heb. 5:1–10; 7:1–10:25). Hebrews 5:1 summarizes the priestly office: the high priest is (1) chosen from among the people and identifies with them (within Israel this right and privilege was reserved for Aaron and his direct descendants); (2) appointed to act as a mediator and representative of the people before God; and (3) the one who represents the people before God on behalf of their sin. The full incarnation of the Son was necessary for him to come as the fulfillment of *this* kind of priest.

With this four-part rationale from Hebrews 2:5–18, we can now summarize the purpose and necessity of the Son's incarnation. The Son was obligated by the Father to take on a genuine and full human nature because a complete incarnation was the only way that the Son could: (1) rule as God's obedient vice-regent over creation; (2) bring many disobedient sons into the glory of his own obedient vice-regency through sufferings that fit him for the vocation; (3) suffer the death penalty on behalf of the disobedient, releasing them from fear of death under divine judgment; (4) and represent sinners before God as reconciled to him through the forgiveness of their sins.

The Incarnation of the Son and the Redemption of Man

With the purpose and necessity of the incarnation summarized for us by Hebrews 2, we can now correlate the different parts with the rest of the New Testament under six headings.

Human Rule over Creation

Paul develops the restoration of human rule under God over his creation by tracing the typological trajectory from Adam to Christ (Rom. 5:12–21; 1 Corinthians 15). As the first vice-regent and covenant head of the human race, Adam rebelled against the Creator–Covenant Lord and brought sin into the world with all of its disastrous effects. Reversing these effects requires a new covenant and a faithful covenant mediator. Paul presents Jesus as this last Adam (1 Cor. 15:45; cf. Rom. 5:14), the promised Messiah-Christ by way of the eternal Son's incarnation and assumption of a fully human nature (Phil. 2:7). As the incarnate Son, Christ has redeemed a people for God and raised them up to rule with him in righteousness over all creation (Eph. 1:7–10, 20–23; 2:6).

Representative Obedience

A righteous vice-regency requires a righteous humanity. From the creation of man and the first covenant, the holy Creator–Covenant Lord has demanded obedience from his human covenant partners. But a sinful humanity is unable to produce even one righteous man. Finally in Christ, however, the obedient son has come, through the incarnation of the eternal Son. And the point of his incarnation was representation. God the Son incarnate obeyed the Father perfectly in life and in death *on our behalf as our representative*. The Son became a man to serve as the last Adam and our great High Priest, thus accomplishing our redemption and justification (Phil. 2:6–8; Rom. 5:18–19).

SUBSTITUTIONARY SACRIFICE

The Son's representative and priestly incarnation was also substitutionary. As our great High Priest, Jesus identifies with us, represents us, and ultimately fulfills the typological promise of every priest and every sacrifice in the Old Testament by offering himself as the perfect and sufficient sacrifice for the forgiveness of our sins: "But as it is, he has appeared once for all at the end of the ages to put away sin by the sacrifice of himself" (Heb. 9:26b). God the Son incarnate entered into the presence of God as a man on our behalf, "not by means of the blood of goats and calves [which cannot take away sins] but by means of his own blood, thus securing an eternal redemption" (v. 12). It is this obedient (10:9), substitutionary sacrifice, in fact, that merited the exaltation of the incarnate Son to rule over creation and ensure the sanctification of his people: "But when Christ had offered for all time a single sacrifice for sins, he sat down at the right hand of God, waiting from that time until his enemies should be made a footstool for his feet. For by a single offering he has perfected for all time those who are being sanctified" (vv. 12–14).

SYMPATHETIC SERVICE

Through his incarnation, the eternal Son knows our temptations and struggles not only in terms of his omniscience but now *by experience* (Heb. 2:17–18; 4:14–15). Jesus is our "merciful and faithful high priest" (2:17), which is more a description of Yahweh (see Ex. 34:6) than of Old Testament priests. God is merciful. God the Son, who is the exact representation of God, also became a merciful (*eleēmōn*) priest *as a man* through his experience of suffering and temptation.

Macleod rightly insists,

> Nevertheless, there is real change. . . . He experiences life in a human body and in a human soul. He experiences human pain and human temptations. He suffers poverty and loneliness and humiliation. He tastes death. . . . Before and apart from the incarnation, God knew such things by observation. But observation, even when it is that of omniscience, falls short of personal experience. That is what the incarnation made possible for God: real, personal experience of being human.[46]

Jesus's incarnational experience and suffering perfectly qualified him to save us completely (Heb. 7:25). Even though he "has passed through the heavens" (4:14) and is now seated at the Father's right hand as the victorious Lord, he is not removed from our human experience of living in this fallen world: "for we do not have a high priest who is unable to sympathize with our weaknesses,

---

[46] Macleod, *Person of Christ*, 186.

but one who in every respect has been tempted as we are, yet without sin" (v. 15). This empathy extends beyond mere compassion to Jesus's ability to save us and care for us. Macleod captures the beauty and wonder of the Son's incarnational sympathy for us:

> [Jesus] lived not in sublime detachment or in ascetic isolation, but "with us", as "the fellow-man of all men", crowded, busy, harassed, stressed and molested. No large estate gave him space, no financial capital guaranteed his daily bread, no personal staff protected him from interruptions and no power or influence protected him from injustice. He saved us from alongside us.[47]

The Son now serves us as a sympathetic priest through his personal experience of the same weaknesses and temptations that are ours. And as the faithful (*pistos*) priest, the incarnate Son perfectly reflects the faithfulness of the Lord (see Ps. 145:13b) even in the face of temptation and suffering. Christ has been faithful to the end, even suffering the wrath of God in our place; he experienced our God-forsakenness so we might become the reconciled and the righteousness of God (2 Cor. 5:21).

Provision and Pattern for Redeemed Lives

The imitation of Christ is an important biblical theme that is directly linked to the incarnation of the Son. In John's Gospel, Jesus describes his washing of the disciples' feet as an example (*hupodeigma*) for them to follow (John 13:15, 34). In Philippians 2:5–11, Paul exhorts the church to have the same attitude as Christ, and in Romans 8:29 he describes our growth in sanctification as conformity to Christ. Peter also uses the example of Christ's conduct in his sufferings as paradigmatic (*hupogrammon*) for us (1 Pet. 2:21–23). And Hebrews presents Christ as our example in how to run the race set before us: "looking to Jesus, the founder [*archēgos*] and perfecter of our faith" (Heb. 12:2). As David Peterson points out, "[Jesus] is the perfect example—perfect in realization and in effect—of the faith we are to imitate, trusting in him. He is the supreme pioneer and the perfect embodiment of faith. He has realized faith to the full from start to finish."[48]

We do need to exercise care at this point. Scripture teaches that Jesus is our example in many ways, yet he is not our example in every way. In his suffering, for example, the achievement of his work as God the Son incarnate is unique and incomparable, totally different from our suffering in terms of its accomplishment and effect. Even the example of Christ's faithfulness is singular since it is by *his* faithfulness alone that we are redeemed: he alone

---

[47] Ibid., 180.
[48] David Peterson, "The Incarnation and Christian Living," in *The Word Became Flesh: Evangelicals and the Incarnation*, ed. David Peterson (Carlisle, UK: Paternoster, 2003), 91.

makes faith possible, grounded in his unique identity and work. As Peterson insists regarding Hebrews 2, "As the pioneer of *their* salvation (2:10), he accomplished a deliverance for his people which they could not accomplish for themselves. . . . Jesus is the one who has given faith its perfect basis by his high-priestly work. . . . His faith is thus qualitatively and not just quantitatively greater than theirs."[49] Moreover, we must recognize that even Jesus's temptations are unique to him. Ordinary humans are not tempted to turn stones to bread or to throw themselves down from a great height to have angels catch us. These kinds of temptations were aimed directly and uniquely at Jesus *as the incarnate Son of God*. Even so, the Son does serve as our example in his humanity: how he depends on the Father and obeys him; how he relies on the power of the Spirit; how he glorifies God in all he does.

In addition, it is also crucial to affirm that the incarnation was not a temporary act: Jesus the Christ is now and forevermore the incarnate Son. At his exaltation, Jesus did not give up his human nature. He appeared to his disciples as a man after the resurrection, even with his visible wounds (John 20:25–27). He had "flesh and bones" and ate food (Luke 24:39, 41–42). At the ascension, Jesus ascended into heaven in his resurrection body and he will return in the same way (Acts 1:11). Jesus was seen by Stephen standing at God's right hand (Acts 7:56), by Paul on the Damascus road (Acts 9:5), and by John in his vision (Rev. 1:13–17). In fact, Jesus promises to feast with us again in the new creation (Rev. 19:9). All of these facts together assume the permanency of the incarnation. Wayne Grudem summarizes the data this way: "All of these texts indicate that Jesus did not *temporarily* become man, . . . he lives forever not just as the eternal Son of God, the second person of the Trinity, but also as Jesus, the man who was born of Mary, and as Christ, the Messiah and Savior of his people. Jesus will remain fully God and fully man, yet one person, forever."[50]

PROVISION AND PATTERN FOR REDEEMED BODIES

The incarnation is certainly confirmation of the incredible value of humanity, but it is still more. Christ's glorified human nature also sets the pattern for our glorified humanity. This point is uniquely developed in 1 Corinthians 15. In response to the Corinthians' confusion regarding their future bodily resurrection, Paul explains the intimate relationship between Christ's resurrection and ours.[51] As Paul lays out his overall argument, he works with three crucial assumptions.

First, Paul (along with the entire New Testament) views Christ's coming

---

[49] Ibid., 92–93.
[50] Wayne Grudem, *Systematic Theology* (Grand Rapids, MI: Zondervan, 1994), 543.
[51] For a more detailed treatment of 1 Corinthians 15, see my article, "Christ's Resurrection and Ours: A Study in 1 Corinthians 15," *Southern Baptist Journal of Theology* 6/3 (2002): 76–93.

and work in redemptive-historical and eschatological categories.[52] As God's Son, the Last Adam (1 Cor. 15:21–22), Christ has inaugurated a new creation, supremely evidenced in his death, resurrection, and giving of the Spirit. As such, he has ushered in the "age to come," that which the Old Testament prophets longed for and anticipated, an age characterized by the defeat of God's enemies—sin, death, and Satan. Even though this age has "not yet" been consummated in its fullness, nevertheless it is "already" here in reality and power; the resurrection and the gift of the Spirit are guarantees. That is why Paul conceives of the resurrection of Christ (and the gift of the Spirit) in the category of "firstfruits" (vv. 20, 23; cf. Rom. 8:23). Just as the firstfruits of the harvest are a foretaste of the full harvest (Lev. 23:9–14), so Christ's resurrection anticipates and ensures the believer's resurrection. It is God's "down payment" (*arrabōn*), a pledge that the final eschatological end is surely coming.[53] Even though the believer's resurrection does not come until the *parousia*, Christ's resurrection is the guarantee that those "in Christ" shall be raised, patterned after his glorious resurrection.

Second, Paul assumes an indissoluble union between Christ's resurrection and the believer's bodily resurrection. This union makes sense in light of the Adam-Christ typological contrast in 1 Corinthians 15:21–22. Just as Adam was the covenant head of the old creation and by his disobedience brought death to us all, so Christ is the new covenant head who brings life and salvation for all those who believe in him. The use of this typology underscores both the *indissoluble union* between these two heads and their people and the *inevitability of resurrection* for the believer who, "in Christ," shares in Christ's own resurrection from the dead. As Fee correctly notes, "Thus Christ is the firstfruits; he is God's pledge that all who are his will be raised from the dead. The inevitable process of death begun in Adam will be reversed by the equally inevitable process of 'bringing to life' begun in Christ. Therefore, it is not possible for the Corinthians to say there is no resurrection of the dead. Such a resurrection is necessitated by Christ's."[54]

Third, in 1 Corinthians 15:24–28, Paul views the resurrection of Christ in light of God's sovereign purposes. In this interim period between the first and second coming of the Lord Jesus, not all of God's enemies have been subjected to him and destroyed; specifically, the enemy of death remains for now. The day when God is "all in all" has not yet arrived. That is why Paul elsewhere can speak of believers and the whole creation groaning as we await the consummation that will bring the resurrection of our bodies (see Rom. 8:18–27).

---

[52] See Gordon D. Fee, *The First Epistle to the Corinthians*, NICNT (Grand Rapids, MI: Eerdmans, 1987), 746.
[53] On "firstfruits," see Anthony C. Thiselton, *The First Epistle to the Corinthians*: A Commentary on the Greek Text, NIGTC (Grand Rapids, MI: Eerdmans, 2000), 1223–1224; Fee, *First Epistle to the Corinthians*, 749.
[54] Fee, *First Epistle to the Corinthians*, 751.

But precisely because God[55] raised Jesus triumphantly from the dead, Paul is confident that God has set in motion an "inevitable chain of events"[56] that will be completed only when all of God's enemies are destroyed, including death itself. That is why Christ's resurrection *demands* our resurrection: if we are not raised bodily from the grave, then death is never truly defeated and God is never "all in all." Our greatest hope as those "in Christ" is that our death and corruption stand between the Creator–Covenant Lord and his glory in creation and covenant, and he will not give his glory to another (cf. Isa. 48:11)!

After establishing the *necessity* of the believer's future resurrection, Paul turns to the *nature* of the resurrection body, in 1 Corinthians 15:35–49: we will have a body that is both *physical* and *transformed*, patterned after the resurrection body of Christ. In verse 45, Paul quotes from Genesis 2:7 to make the point that Adam was given a certain kind of body at creation; it was a natural (*psychē*) body; a body of the earth; a body which, as a result of sin, is subject to death and decay. Since Adam is the covenant head of the old creation, we bear his likeness in our fallen state. But Christ is different. He is a life-giving spirit (*pneuma zōopoioun*). His life is the life of heaven itself, for he is God the Son incarnate. And as the new covenant head of his people, his resurrection body becomes the pattern of our resurrection body, a "spiritual" (*pneumatikon*) body, supernatural and glorified. Because of Christ's resurrection and glorification, we will have bodies that are appropriate for the "sons of God, being sons of the resurrection" (Luke 20:36), who will "reign forever and ever" with the risen God-man (cf. Rev. 22:3–5), under the Lord God and in the light of his glory (Rev. 21:23–24; 22:5), over a new and perfected creation (21:1–3).

While the New Testament does not give us great detail regarding what to expect of our resurrection bodies, 1 Corinthians 15:53 does tell us there will be some continuity and some discontinuity. We shall be raised imperishable (*phtharton*) and immortal (*athanasian*). Like Christ's resurrection body, our resurrection bodies will be fitted for the new creation. They will not be susceptible to disease; they will not be susceptible to death; they will be physical bodies that are raised in "glory" and "power" (v. 43) and will be "dominated and directed by the Holy Spirit" (*pneumatikos*; v. 44). The fact that we are raised assumes some kind of continuity between our present body and our resurrection body. In fact, as Anthony Hoekema insists, "the very language of v. 53 implies and demands continuity: 'For this perishable nature must *put on* the imperishable, and this mortal nature must *put on* immortality.'"[57] Yet there

---

[55] In the text, the emphasis is on God's action in raising Christ Jesus from the dead and putting all things under his feet. Regarding 1 Corinthians 15:27, it is debated whether "he" refers to God or to Christ. Given what Paul has outlined in chapter 15, it is best to take it as referring to God the Father, as the ESV does. On this point, see ibid., 757–759.

[56] Ibid., 747.

[57] Anthony Hoekema, *The Bible and the Future* (Grand Rapids, MI: Eerdmans, 1979), 251–252.

is discontinuity as well, as seen in the risen Lord himself. As we compare and contrast his preresurrection and postresurrection body, there are some obvious differences. Presently, however, we know little about the exact nature of our future resurrection body. We must be content with knowing only that it will be perfectly fitted to live in the new creation, a reality so glorious that it surpasses our imagination.

THE SINLESSNESS OF CHRIST

As we have seen, the Scriptures maintain that the genuineness and fullness of Christ's humanity are necessary for our salvation and for the fulfillment of God's entire plan for humanity and the rest of creation. The genuineness and fullness of his humanity, however, would not matter if Christ's humanity was not also sinless. As we complete our work of biblical warrant in the identification of God the Son incarnate, we need to consider how and why the Bible presents Christ as sinless.

The Biblical Presentation of Jesus's Sinlessness

The New Testament teaches that Jesus shares fully in our human nature, but not in our sin nature. The Son had to become all that it means to be human, but the corruption of sin is not essential to humanity. God created Adam to be fully human—indeed, the Hebrew word *'ādām* is first the generic term for mankind that then becomes the proper name for the first man. Before Adam's rebellion, sin was not part of his human nature. God originally created all things, including humanity, to be "very good" (Gen. 1:31). And God created the first man in his own image to represent God's own righteous rule over this very good creation (vv. 26–28). Moreover, we know that sin was not part of God's original creation of humanity because the divine punishment for sin did not come until after Adam's rebellion (2:16–17; 3:11b–19). Sin and death came into the world and spread to all mankind not as part of God's original design for man but as a result of the original man's rebellion against his Creator and rejection of the divine design for humanity (cf. Rom. 5:12, 15, 17).

While sin was not part of God's original creation of humanity, however, Scripture tells us that, as a result of Adam's disobedience, sin corrupted every part of every human born in the image of Adam. God himself bore witness to the totality of man's sinfulness by destroying all humanity in the flood, save for one man and his family. The waters of judgment and the salvation of Noah, however, were not God's solution for cleansing humanity of its sinfulness. Before the flood, "every intention of the thoughts of [man's] heart was only evil continually" (Gen. 6:5). And well after the world was repopulated through Noah, the apostle Paul agrees with the psalmist of Israel that "None is righteous, no, not one; . . . All have turned aside; together they have become worthless; no one does good, not even one" (Rom. 3:10–12).

When Jesus enters into this plotline with a claim to sinlessness, then, he makes a clear and shocking statement regarding his own human nature. Jesus recognized sin in others but never in himself. He showed no consciousness of sin, never prayed for his own forgiveness, and commanded others to repent of their sins without ever repenting himself. Jesus even challenged his enemies to find fault with him: "Which one of you convicts me of sin?" (John 8:46). Moreover, Jesus claimed to have kept all of his Father's commands (John 15:10) and to have fulfilled all righteousness (Matt. 3:15). Jesus saw himself as neither a sinner by nature nor a sinner by transgression.

The rest of the New Testament also bears witness to the sinlessness of Christ. For example, the author of Hebrews views Jesus as "one who in every respect has been tempted as we are, yet without sin" (Heb. 4:15). Jesus is able to help sinners in the suffering of temptation precisely because he himself suffered temptation sinlessly (cf. 2:16–18). Moreover, Jesus became a far greater high priest than those under the old covenant and offered himself as a perfect sacrifice on our behalf because he was "holy, innocent, unstained, separated from sinners, and exalted above the heavens" (7:26)—he had no need to offer sacrifices for his own sins (v. 27), but "offered himself without blemish to God" (9:14).

As one who spent three intimate years with Jesus, Peter presents Jesus as the "lamb without blemish or spot" (1 Pet. 1:19), by which he picks up on Old Testament imagery to affirm that Jesus did not sin during his lifetime and that he was also free from any inherited sin or moral defilement. It is Jesus's moral perfection that grounds Peter's confession that, "[Jesus] committed no sin, neither was deceit found in his mouth" (2:22); and that Jesus died as "the righteous for the unrighteous, that he might bring us to God" (3:18).

In his first epistle, John assures his readers that "if anyone does sin, we have an advocate with the Father, Jesus Christ the righteous" (1 John 2:1). To explain why those who follow Christ will not make a practice of sinning, John explains that "[Jesus] appeared in order to take away sins, and in him there is no sin" (3:5). And in a letter to the Corinthian church, Paul connects the sinlessness of Jesus in life and the effectiveness of his sacrificial death: "For our sake he made him to be sin who knew no sin, so that in him we might become the righteousness of God" (2 Cor. 5:21). Even when Paul speaks of Jesus coming to live as a man, he is careful not to say that he *took on* sinful flesh; rather, Paul says that God sent his own Son "in the *likeness* of sinful flesh and *for* sin" (Rom. 8:3). And just before Jesus took his sinless humanity to the cross for the sake of our sins, Pilate who sentenced him to death and the criminal who died beside him had to confess that Jesus was faultless (John 18:38; cf. Luke 23:4, 14–15, 22, 41, 47).

Texts could be multiplied, but it is already clear from Scripture that Jesus himself and the apostles he authorized to tell the truth about him all declare that Jesus neither sinned nor had a sin nature. Reflecting on the sinlessness of Christ, Macleod observes, "Nowhere in the structures of his being was there any sin. Satan had no foot-hold in him. There was no lust. There was no affinity with sin. There was no proclivity to sin. There was no possibility of temptation from within. In no respect was he fallen and in no respect was his nature corrupt."[58]

Sinless but Fallen?

In the last two hundred years, some scholars have attempted to maintain the *sinlessness* of Christ but argue that in his incarnation he assumed a *fallen* human nature. In general, those who make this argument rely on the affirmation that Christ became *fully* human like us and then assume that to be human like us requires a *fallen* human nature.[59] In New Testament studies, C. E. B. Cranfield endorsed this view by insisting that the phrase "in the likeness of sinful flesh" (Rom. 8:3) equates to the assumption of sinful flesh.[60] In theological studies, Thomas Torrance has argued (quite ironically) that redemption of our fallen nature requires Christ's assumption of our fallen nature:

> There can be no doubt that the New Testament speaks of the flesh of Jesus as the concrete form of our human nature marked by Adam's fall . . . if Jesus Christ did not assume our fallen flesh, our fallen humanity, then our fallen humanity is untouched by his work—for *"the unassumed is the unredeemed"*, as Gregory Nazianzen put it. . . . Thus Christ took from Mary a corruptible and mortal body in order that he might take our sin, judge and condemn it in the flesh, and so assume our human nature as we have it in the fallen world that he might heal, sanctify and redeem it.[61]

---

[58] Macleod, *Person of Christ*, 222.

[59] Edward Irving first advocated this view in the nineteenth century (see Edward Irving, *The Doctrine of the Incarnation Opened in Six Sermons,* vol. 1 of *Sermons, Lectures, and Occasional Discourses* [London, Seeley & Burnside, 1828]; idem, *The Orthodox and Catholic Doctrine of Our Lord's Human Nature Set Forth in Four Parts* [London, Baldwin & Cradock, 1830]; idem, *The Opinions Circulating Concerning Our Lord's Human Nature, Tried by the Westminster Confession of Faith* [London, John Lindsay, 1830]). More recently, Karl Barth has given prominence to the argument that a full humanity entails a fallen humanity: "There must be no weakening or obscuring of the saving truth that the nature which God assumed in Christ is identical with our nature as we see it in the light of the fall. If it were otherwise, how could Christ be really like us? What concern could we have with Him? We stand before God characterized by the fall. God's Son not only assumed our nature but He entered the concrete form of our nature, under which we stand before God as men damned and lost" (Karl Barth, *Church Dogmatics,* 1.2, trans. G. T. Thomson [Edinburgh: T&T Clark, 1956], 153).

[60] C. E. B. Cranfield, *A Critical and Exegetical Commentary on the Epistle to the Romans,* 2 vols., 6th ed., International Critical Commentary (Edinburgh: T&T Clark, 1975), 379.

[61] Thomas F. Torrance, *Incarnation: The Person and Life of Christ,* ed. Robert T. Walker (Downers Grove, IL: IVP Academic, 2008), 61–62. See also the recent work, John C. Clark and Marcus Peter Johnson, *The Incarnation of God: The Mystery of the Gospel as the Foundation of Evangelical Theology* (Wheaton, IL: Crossway, 2015), 103–125, who argue for this view within evangelical theology.

While the motivation is positive, the argument that Christ became a fallen human to redeem fallen humanity misreads the Scriptures and misunderstands the biblical rationale for the incarnation.[62] The advocates of Christ's fallenness certainly do not intend to disparage our Lord; in fact, they are trying to honor his work in their reasoning that if Christ did not assume a fallen human nature then he is not fully like us, he was not tempted like us, and thus he cannot help or redeem us. They argue that the Son became incarnate in a fallen human nature and relied upon the Spirit to resist temptation and the commission of sin. The Son won our salvation by his Spirit-empowered obedience in a fallen human nature. The problem, however, is that this argument falters at the precise points it seeks to affirm. We can see the errors of a fallen incarnation in six steps.

First, a fallen incarnation lacks biblical support. As we have already seen in the biblical presentation, the sinlessness of Christ extends to both his actions and his nature. Pauline expressions such as "born in the likeness of men" (Phil. 2:7), "being found in human form" (Phil. 2:8), and "in the likeness of sinful flesh" (Rom. 8:3) refer to our common human nature, not our corrupt human nature. In Scripture, the object of the incarnation is always humanity, not sin. Christ came to represent a new humanity. We already have a representative of fallen humanity: the first Adam, in whose transgression we all sinned and came under the penalty of death (see Rom. 5:12). The Pauline contrast between the first Adam and Christ as the last Adam makes sense only if Christ does not partake of the corrupted Adamic nature. Jesus in not "in Adam" as we are, and thus he is not fallen. The New Testament acknowledges that Christ fully entered into the human condition, thus exposing himself to this fallen world, yet it avoids any suggestion that "Christ so participated in this realm that he became imprisoned 'in the flesh' and became, thus, so subject to sin that he could be personally guilty of it."[63]

Second, a fallen incarnation implies that corruption is essential to humanity. To argue that unless Christ was fallen he cannot be fully like us seems to require the assumption that to be human is to be fallen. We do live in fallen natures within a fallen world, but both are aberrations of God's original creation. As Oliver Crisp reminds us, "'being fallen' or 'fallenness' is not an essential property of all human beings *per se*. That is, it is not a property that an entity

---

[62] For a helpful analysis of this view's strengths and weaknesses, see Kelly M. Kapic, "The Son's Assumption of a Human Nature: A Call for Clarity," *IJST* 3/2 (2001): 154–166.

[63] Douglas J. Moo, *The Epistle to the Romans*, NICNT (Grand Rapids, MI: Eerdmans, 1996), 480; cf. Peter T. O'Brien, *The Epistle to the Philippians: A Commentary on the Greek Text*, NIGTC (Grand Rapids, MI: Eerdmans, 1991), 224–226; Gordon D. Fee, *Pauline Christology: An Exegetical-Theological Study* (Peabody, MA: Hendrickson, 2007), 246–247; 387–388. Regarding Romans 8:3, Fee makes an astute observation: "Had Paul intended a more complete identification with us in our sinfulness itself, he could easily have said simply 'in sinful flesh.' But in fact all the words of this phrase are necessary here (i.e., 'likeness,' 'flesh,' 'of sin') because of the preceding argument. Christ must effectively deal with sin, thus come in 'our flesh' (which in our case is full of sin), but only in the 'likeness' of such because, though 'in the flesh,' he was not in sin (as 2 Cor. 5:21 makes clear)" (247).

has to exemplify in order to be counted part of a particular kind (of thing), in this case the kind 'humanity'."[64] To make fallenness *essential* to humanity is, in reality, to misread the biblical presentation and to compromise the integrity of God's creation and of God himself as the Creator. Making fallenness essential to humanity entails that the humanity created by God *must necessarily sin*. And such an entailment would mean that God did not (could not?!) create a humanity that truly was "very good" (Gen. 1:31). Moreover, the essentiality of corruption to humanity and the inevitability of sin would destroy any hope of an eternal freedom from sin and death, in Christ. Thankfully, Scripture assures us that Christ was sinless in both his actions and his nature. Rather than bringing the fullness of his humanity into question, the functional and ontological sinlessness of Christ's humanity guarantee the pattern of our new and true humanity. As the last Adam and new covenant head of the new creation (cf. 2 Cor. 5:17), Christ restores and transforms us to what we were originally created to be.

Third, a fallen incarnation is not required for the temptations of Christ to be real. Macleod rightly notes that "unfallen" and "not liable to temptation" are not interchangeable terms.[65] We must affirm that the Son was tempted and that his temptations were genuine, yet this does not require that Christ had to be fallen or that all of his temptations were identical to ours. Jesus experienced temptation, yet "without sin" (Heb. 4:15). Unlike us, he was not tempted by anything within himself. He was not enticed by sinful desires (cf. James 1:14) because there was no sin in him, not even a predisposition to sin. Jesus was tempted, rather, in terms of normal *sinless* human weaknesses. He could be tempted through hunger, through fear of pain, and as Macleod observes, through "holy affections, feelings and longings which, in the course of his work, he had to thwart."[66] Foremost among these longings was his perfect fellowship with his Father. In Gethsemane, Jesus was overwhelmed by the thought of losing his Father's communion as he bore our sins on the cross. "He was not being called upon to mortify a lust. He was being called upon to frustrate the holiest aspiration of which man is capable. What he wanted and what his Father directed were in conflict. Hence the 'loud cries and tears' (Heb. 5:7)."[67] In many ways, then, Jesus's sinless nature ensured that his temptations far surpassed anything we will encounter in our sinful natures.[68]

---

[64] Oliver D. Crisp, *Divinity and Humanity* (Cambridge: Cambridge University Press, 2007), 95.
[65] Macleod, *Person of Christ*, 226.
[66] Ibid.
[67] Ibid.
[68] For a helpful description of this point, see ibid., 226–228. Macleod writes, "We must be careful not to misconstrue the effect of Jesus's sinless integrity at this point. Far from meaning a shorter, painless struggle with temptation it involved him in protracted resistance. Precisely because he did not yield easily and was not, like us, an easy prey, the devil had to deploy all his wiles and use all his resources. The very fact that he was invincible meant that he endured the full force of temptation's ferocity, until hell slunk away, defeated and exhausted. Against us, a little temptation suffices. Against him, Satan found himself forced to push himself to his limits" (ibid., 227–228).

Fourth, a fallen incarnation is not required by Torrance's appeal to the Patristic maxim, "the unassumed is the unredeemed." Gregory, in fact, deployed this principle against the heresy of Apollinarianism, which denied that Christ assumed a human mind and thus denied he had a full and complete human nature. At stake was whether Christ had a full human nature, not whether that nature was fallen.[69]

Fifth, a fallen incarnation risks separating the human *nature* of Christ from his *person*, inviting the charge of Nestorianism.[70] Typically, those who argue that Christ assumed a fallen *nature* still affirm that the *person* of Christ was not subject to the same corruption. The difficulty with such a distinction, however, is that we cannot separate the eternal person of the Son from the human nature that he assumed.[71] Simply put, the corruption of the Son's human nature cannot be quarantined but would implicate his divine person. The only way to avoid such a disastrous implication is to move in a Nestorian direction, with equally disastrous implications. A Nestorian separation of person and nature would either make Christ's humanity an agent in its own right, acting independently of the Son, or would reject the hypostatic union of the person of the Son with the human nature he assumed. The only options involve either two persons or two acting subjects in Christ in contradiction of the Scriptures and in violation of the church's historical confession.[72]

Sixth, a fallen incarnation requires that Christ is sinful or has the property of original sin. For Jesus to have a fallen nature and yet never sin seems to require that we separate *fallen* from *sinful*; but such a move is difficult to warrant both biblically and theologically. According to the biblical presentation, a corrupt nature is the result of sin against God that places us in a metaphysical and judicial state of sinfulness under God's curse and judgment. Christ came as the last Adam and our Savior, however, precisely because he did not sin in Adam and does not exist in a human nature under the curse and judgment of God (cf. Rom. 5:12–21).

Jesus's Sinlessness and His Virgin Conception

Finally, we come to the question of *how* the Son assumed a sinless nature through incarnation. Once again, Scripture does not lay the answer open to us as in a textbook. But the storyline of Scripture does connect the continuity and

---

[69] See Gregory of Nazianzen, *To Cledonius the Priest Against Apollinarius* (NPNF[2] 7:440).

[70] The "nature-person" distinction is at the heart of Trinitarian and Christological formulation. For a development of the distinction, see Parts III and IV of this work.

[71] For example, Edward Irving argued that the *person* of Christ was holy while the human *nature* was not: "Whenever I attribute sinful properties and dispositions and inclinations to our Lord's human nature, I am speaking of it considered as apart from Him, in itself. . . . We can assert the sinfulness of the whole, the complete, the perfect human nature, which He took, without in the least implicating Him with sin" (Edward Irving, *The Collected Writings of Edward Irving*, 5 vols., ed. Gavin Carlyle [London, Strahan 1865], 5:563, 565).

[72] See Crisp, *Divinity and Humanity*, 113–117; Macleod, *Person of Christ*, 228.

discontinuity of Jesus's humanity and ours to his virgin conception.[73] Being "born of the Virgin Mary," as the Apostles' Creed confesses, does not provide the sole explanation for Jesus's full and sinless humanity.[74] But the Gospel accounts do present the virgin conception as the incarnational ingress point of God the Son into the world such that he would be called "holy" (Matt. 1:18–25; Luke 1:26–38; 2:1–21). As James Orr observes, "It is objected that birth from a Virgin does not itself secure sinlessness. But turn the matter round, and ask: Does not perfect sinlessness, on the other hand, imply a miracle in the birth?"[75] Or, in the words of A. B. Bruce, "A sinless man is as much a miracle in the moral world as a Virgin birth is a miracle in the physical world."[76]

There is, then, a significant link between the full and sinless incarnation of Christ and his virgin conception. How he came in the flesh tells us something instructive for the identification of God the Son incarnate. A quick look at the birth narratives will position us to consider the Christological import of the Son's incarnation through virgin conception.

MATTHEW'S ACCOUNT

Matthew begins his Gospel with a genealogy (1:1–17) that describes Jesus as "the son of David, the son of Abraham" (v. 1). Most commentators note that this genealogy is purposefully structured in terms of David the king, the exile of Israel, and the fulfillment of God's promises in the birth of this child.[77] In other words, the unique birth of Jesus is not some strange occurrence in history; it is part of the plan and promises of God now coming to fulfillment. Specifically, Matthew links Jesus to the promises of God that have developed through the biblical covenants of the Old Testament to create the expectation

---

[73] Most correctly observe that the term "virgin birth" is something of a misnomer. There is no textual evidence to indicate that the birth itself was supernatural or unique. At issue is not the birth of Christ but the *conception* of his human nature. The birth event was ordinary in every way. The conception, however, was supernatural: Mary became pregnant by the direct power of the Holy Spirit and without intercourse with a man.

[74] It is best *not* to make the virgin conception the *sole* explanation for Christ's sinlessness, even though many have tried to do so. As the argument goes, all human beings have imputed legal guilt and an inherited corrupt moral nature from Adam. Adam's sin is transmitted to every human being through procreation where both the male and female are present. In the case of Christ, however, the male is absent, and this becomes the explanation for Christ's sinless humanity. However, there are some problems with this view, especially if it functions as the *sole* explanation for Christ's sinlessness. First, this view requires that the transmission of sin is *only* through the male, but this is hard to support from Scripture. Second, unless one affirms an Augustinian realist view of sin's transmission, it is not sufficient to say that sin is transmitted *merely* in terms of physical relations; it also involves legal relations such as the imputation of Adam's guilt to his progeny (Rom. 5:12–21). Third, one still has to explain why Christ did not inherit sin from his mother Mary. Mary was neither sinless (contrary to Roman Catholic theology, which, by declaration of Pope Pius IX on December 8, 1854, has dogmatized the "immaculate conception" of Mary), nor did she act merely as a surrogate. Instead, as Sinclair B. Ferguson, *The Holy Spirit* (Downers Grove, IL: InterVarsity Press, 1997), 41, notes, "The human nature which was assumed by the Son of God was not created *ex nihilo*, but was inherited through Mary."

[75] James Orr, *The Virgin Birth of Christ* (London: Hodder & Stoughton, 1907), 189. Ferguson, *Holy Spirit*, 41.

[76] A. B. Bruce, *Apologetics: Or, Christianity Defensively Stated*, 8th ed. (New York; Scribner, 1905).

[77] For example, the use of three fourteens is artificially constructed for a theological point. It highlights the significance of David and the exile, since the number fourteen probably represents the numerical value of "David" by *gematria*. On this point, see D. A. Carson, *Matthew*, in *EBC*, vol. 8 (Grand Rapids, MI: Zondervan, 1984), 60–69; R. T. France, *The Gospel of Matthew*, NICNT (Grand Rapids, MI: Eerdmans, 2007), 26–33.

that the Creator–Covenant Lord himself will come in and through the Davidic king to redeem humanity and restore his creation.[78]

In this redemptive-covenantal context, Matthew emphasizes the work of God through the Holy Spirit in the conception of Christ (see 1:18–25). Joseph and Mary were engaged, and "before they came together" (*prin ē sunelthein autous*) (v. 18) Mary was found to be pregnant. This text stresses that Mary became pregnant *without sexual intercourse*. And verses 24–25 make the same point: "[Joseph] took his wife, but knew her not [*ouk eginōsken autēn*] until [*heōs*] she had given birth to a son." When Joseph discovers that Mary is pregnant, his reaction is quite normal: he resolved to divorce her, since he assumed that she had been unfaithful to him. But an angel of the Lord appeared to him and explained *the conception of Jesus* in divine and Davidic terms: "that which is conceived in [Mary] is from the Holy Spirit" (v. 20); and "you shall call his name Jesus, for (*gar*) he will save his people from their sins" (v. 21).

In other words, God himself worked supernaturally to conceive in Mary the human nature of the eternal Son, such that as a man he would take up the Davidic-messianic vocation of saving the people of God. Anyone steeped in the Old Testament would immediately recognize two important points: (1) the stress on the agency of the Holy Spirit tied to the expectation of the coming Messiah and messianic age (see Isaiah 11; 42; 61; Joel 2:28–32); (2) the fact that this child will save his people from their sins according to the new covenant promise of Jeremiah 31:34. The angels' announcement and the virginal conception are interpreted within the promise-plan of God according to which God's long-awaited King and kingdom are now at hand.[79] And, citing Isaiah 7:14,[80] Matthew confirms that we should interpret the conception and birth of Christ in terms of God himself coming in the flesh to be with his people through their deliverance: "All this took place to fulfill what the Lord had spoken by the prophet: 'Behold, the virgin shall conceive and bear a son, and they shall call his name Immanuel' (which means, God with us)" (Matt. 1:22–23).[81]

---

[78] For a further discussion of this point and the covenantal-typological function of Scripture, see chapters 4–5.

[79] France, *Matthew*, 50–51.

[80] Two major issues are debated regarding Matthew's use of Isaiah 7:14: first, questions over the use of "virgin" (*parthenos*) for the Hebrew *'almâ*; second, how Matthew sees this prophetic text fulfilled in Jesus. In regard to the former, Carson correctly observes that "the Hebrew word *'almâ* is not precisely equivalent to the English word 'virgin' (NIV), in which all the focus is on the lack of sexual experience; nor is it precisely equivalent to 'young woman,' in which the focus is on age without reference to sexual experience" (Carson, *Matthew*, 77). Yet, as Macleod notes, "the point is rather academic since young, unmarried women would be expected to be virgins. If they were not, their prospects of marriage would be seriously compromised (Dt. 22:13ff)" (Macleod, *Person of Christ*, 26). In addition, the LXX translates *'almâ* as "virgin" (*parthenos*), and Matthew certainly understands it as such. Ultimately, Matthew should be understood to interpret Isaiah 7:14 as a *direct* prophecy regarding Christ. For a defense of this view, see J. Alec Motyer, *Isaiah*, Tyndale Old Testament Commentaries (Downers Grove, IL: InterVarsity Press, 1999), 77–90.

[81] Even though complex issues have surrounded Matthew's use of this text, the history of interpretation affirms that Matthew is presenting the virgin conception as the fulfillment of God's prophetic word—a word rooted in the Old Testament storyline, centered on the coming of the King who is also the Lord.

LUKE'S ACCOUNT

Luke's presentation of the virgin conception is similar to Matthew's in many respects. But Luke comes closer to telling us how it happened. The angel Gabriel explains to Mary that "[t]he Holy Spirit will come upon you, and the power of the Most High will overshadow [*episkiasei*] you; therefore [*dio*] the child to be born will be called holy—the Son of God" (Luke 1:35). This description is not mythological or even primarily metaphysical; rather, the angel of the Lord is explaining the conception of Christ in redemptive-historical and eschatological terms.[82]

First, the divine explanation places the virgin conception in the context of creation and new creation realities. Genesis 1:2 presents the Spirit of God hovering in divine power over the waters as God begins the creation of the world. Matthew now presents the Spirit of God covering a virgin with the power of the Most High as God conceives a human nature into the world. God himself worked as the efficient cause in the conception of Christ as the head of the new creation. As a further parallel to the Spirit's work in the first creation, God produces what he calls "good" or "holy." The virgin conception of Jesus, then, is not a progressive, natural development; it did not originate in the will of man. Rather, the conception of Christ is a divine intrusion—the last great culminating eruption of the power of God into the plight of humanity as the first man of the new creation now arrives in fulfillment of all Old Testament expectations.

Second, the "overshadowing" work of the Spirit connects the conception of Christ to God's unique covenantal presence. In the LXX, the verb *episkiazō* translates the Hebrew *sākak*, which is used for the hovering of the cloud of God's glory-presence under the old covenant (Ex. 40:35; cf. LXX; see Ps. 91:4; cf. LXX). Later known as the *shekinah*, this glory of God guarded and guided Israel through the wilderness and reappeared in the cloud representing the presence of God in the tabernacle (Ex. 40:34–38) and in the temple (Isa. 6:1–4). Significantly, in response to Israel's idolatry, the *shekinah*-glory departs from the temple (Ezek. 10:1–22) and does not reemerge until the coming of Christ (John 1:14–18), the Lord of Glory and the fulfillment of the temple (John 2:19–22).[83]

Through the virgin conception of Christ, then, God's glory-presence breaks into the world to indwell a human nature such that, in a man, God is with us as Immanuel.[84]

---

[82] See Graham Cole, *He Who Gives Life: The Doctrine of the Holy Spirit* (Wheaton, IL: Crossway, 2007), 156.

[83] On Jesus as the antitypical fulfillment of the temple, see Paul M. Hoskins, *Jesus as the Fulfillment of the Temple in the Gospel of John* (Eugene, OR: Wipf & Stock, 2007).

[84] On these points, see Ferguson, *Holy Spirit*, 38–45.

A Sinless Incarnation

With the biblical presentation of the birth narratives, we can now summarize the virgin conception of Christ and consider how it helps us understand the sinlessness of his humanity. In short, Jesus was *not* conceived "in Adam" but by the divine power of the Holy Spirit, so that the glory-presence of God the Son assumed a human nature. Jesus descended from the line of Adam, but not in exactly the same way we do. Every human born after Adam was born "in Adam" and stands guilty and corrupted because of Adam's sin (Rom. 5:12–21). But not the last Adam. As Macleod writes, "Adam begot a son in his own image (Gen. 5:3). But Adam did not beget Christ. The Lord's existence has nothing to do with Adamic desire or Adamic initiative. . . . Christ is new. He is from outside."[85] The creative and consecrating power of the Holy Spirit created and sanctified the human nature that the Son assumed in his incarnation. And what God creates is very good—holy, pure, and uncorrupted. As Sinclair Ferguson concludes, "Only by the work of the Spirit could the divine person of the Logos assume genuine human nature, come 'in the likeness of sinful man' (Rom. 8:3), and yet remain 'holy, harmless, undefiled' (Heb. 7:26, AV), 'the holy one' (Lk. 1:35)."[86] The same Spirit and sovereign power that created the first Adam has now created the last and greater Adam, who is holy, righteous, and good in his humanity.[87]

Moreover, the human nature created by the Spirit of God was made for the glory-presence of God himself. Not only does God not create in corruption, but he cannot dwell with or in what is corrupted, defiled, or sinful (cf. 1 John 1:5). God provided an entire priesthood and sacrificial system to make this very point under his covenant with Israel. And as the typological trajectory moves from the priesthood, sacrifices, and temple in the Old Testament to the person of Christ in the New Testament, the storyline of Scripture tells us to expect an increase in the demonstration of God's holiness in the midst of his people. When God the Son becomes incarnate as our Immanuel, then, we should expect that his dwelling place will be holy, pure, and undefiled. And indeed, "in [Christ] all the fullness of God was pleased to dwell" (Col. 1:19); "the Word became flesh and dwelt among us, and we have seen his glory, glory as of the only Son from the Father" (John 1:14). Simply put, God could not assume a fallen human nature.

---

[85] Macleod, *Person of Christ*, 41.

[86] Ferguson, *Holy Spirit*, 42.

[87] Scripture is careful in how it relates the virgin conception to Jesus's sinlessness. As noted in note 73, above, Scripture does not make the virgin conception the *sole* explanation for Christ's sinlessness. Instead, Scripture emphasizes two truths simultaneously: first, because he had no human father, Jesus was not "in Adam" like we are in Adam; and second, the sovereign action of the Spirit was at work, creating and sanctifying Christ's human nature (Luke 1:35). Since Jesus is God the Son who assumed our human nature by the Spirit, and it is the Spirit who sanctified this union from the moment of conception, Jesus the Messiah is capable of bearing our sin and guilt not only because he himself is sinless but also because he is *God the Son* who can satisfy his own righteous requirements on our behalf.

The all-glorious Creator–Covenant Lord assumed a full and sinless human nature, such that the eternal Son became a man in order to restore humanity to its vice-regent glory and to inaugurate the new creation, over which the new humanity will rule in righteousness in the age to come. In this way and by these glorious means, our Lord Jesus Christ becomes our great prophet, priest, and king, the head of the new creation, the Lord of glory, who is worthy of all our worship, adoration, and praise.[88] In fact, it is only as God the Son incarnate that Jesus can achieve his great work for us. To deny either Christ's deity or his humanity is to deny the Jesus of the Bible and to rob us of our Redeemer.

Excursus: Is It Tenable to Believe in the Virgin Conception Today?

This question must be asked in light of centuries of skepticism regarding the historicity of the virgin conception. Ever since the Enlightenment, critics have treated the virgin conception as a myth or a legend.[89] That Jesus was truly conceived by a virgin has been the dominant confession of the church in the early creeds and throughout church history. But those in the broadly liberal tradition have rejected it for a variety of reasons. The reasons for rejecting the virgin conception are diverse, often contradictory, and have more to do with the intrusion of unbiblical theological assumptions. In this excursus we will briefly describe three main reasons why critics deny the supernatural conception of God the Son incarnate.

The Historicity of the Biblical Accounts

There are a number of related issues under this heading. First, some question the historicity of the birth narratives due to the challenge of reconciling the genealogical accounts in Matthew and Luke, specifically the records from David on (cf. Matt. 1:6–16; Luke 3:23–31).[90] The differences between the two accounts are well known, but it is important to begin with what they have in common: Jesus is God's Son, who has entered this world and become human, and even though he is physically Mary's son, he is also Joseph's legal son and thus heir to the Davidic throne (see Matt. 2:15; Luke 1:35). The differences, then, are seen in the details of the genealogies: Matthew begins with Abraham and moves forward to Jesus; Luke begins with Jesus and moves backward to Adam. Matthew traces the line through Jeconiah, Shealtiel, and Zerubbabel;

---

[88] Since ancient times, and especially in the work of John Calvin, a famous way for thinking through the work of Christ is by employing the concept of Christ's threefold office: prophet, priest, and king. Each of these roles presuppose the need for the full humanity of Christ. For a helpful discussion of Christ's work developed in this way, see Robert Letham, *The Work of Christ* (Downers Grove, IL: InterVarsity Press, 1993); Geerhardus Vos, *Christology*, vol. 3 of *Reformed Dogmatics*, trans. and ed. Richard B. Gaffin Jr. (Bellingham, WA: Lexham, 2014), 85–182.

[89] It was not only the Enlightenment era, but some in the early church also denied the virgin conception of Christ, e.g., the Ebionites, Cerinthus, and Celsus.

[90] See Carson, *Matthew*, 62–81; France, *Matthew*, 26–40; Machen, *Virgin Birth of Christ*, 188–237.

Luke traces it through Neri, Shealtiel, and Zerubbabel. More significantly, Matthew traces Jesus's ancestry through the kingly line of Solomon; Luke traces the line through David's son Nathan (Luke 3:31; cf. 2 Sam. 5:14). Given these differences, many contend that these accounts are incompatible.

How should we respond? Initially, it is implausible to think that these accounts are irreconcilable given that both Matthew and Luke were recognized by the church as authoritative Scripture. Why would the church have received both of these Gospels if there were obvious contradictions between them? In terms of various reconciliation attempts, some have argued that Luke traces Mary's line but substitutes Joseph's name (Luke 3:23) to avoid mentioning a woman and to show that Jesus is a descendant of David (cf. Luke 1:32), while Matthew traces the legal line from Joseph to David. However, this theory is *prima facie* problematic: on the face of it, Luke seems to give Joseph's genealogy, not Mary's line.[91]

A better explanation is that Luke traces Joseph's actual physical descent (moving from David to Nathan), while Matthew provides the line of kingly succession (moving from David to Solomon), and both lines converge at Joseph.[92] If this is so, then Luke provides Joseph's actual descent back to David through his physical father Heli, to his father Matthat, and then further back to Nathan and David; and Matthew provides the kingly succession by starting with David and working to Joseph. In this view, there are a number of suggestions to help explain the two different men, Jacob (in Matthew) and Heli (in Luke), named as Joseph's father. In most proposed solutions, they are regarded as different people based on the assumption of a second marriage (sometimes a levirate marriage; cf. Deut. 25:5–10; Matt. 22:24). In this case, Joseph would be the legal son of Jacob but the physical son of Heli, hence the reason for two lines of ancestry. This account is not without questions, but as J. Gresham Machen argued many years ago, its plausibility is enough to show "that the differences between the two genealogies are not irreconcilable."[93]

---

91 See Carson, *Matthew*, 61–65; France, *Matthew*, 26–33.
92 See Carson, *Matthew*, 64; Machen, *Virgin Birth of Christ*, 188–209.
93 Machen, *Virgin Birth of Christ*, 209. For a discussion of the problems, see Raymond E. Brown, *The Birth of the Messiah: A Commentary on the Infancy Narratives in Matthew and Luke* (Garden City, NY: Doubleday, 1977), 503–504. The main problem with this view is that it requires Jacob, Joseph's father in Matthew 1:16, to be the full brother of Heli, Joseph's father mentioned in Luke 3:23. This is possible if Jacob, the royal heir, died without offspring and Heli married Jacob's widow according to the laws of levirate marriage (Deut. 25:5–10). But if Jacob and Heli are full brothers, then Matthan (in Matthew) and Matthat (in Luke) must be the same man, even though Matthan's father is Eleazar (in Matthew) and Matthat's father is Levi (in Luke). Can we make sense of this? Machen lays out some alternatives that reconcile the accounts: (1) Assuming that Matthan and Matthat refer to the same person, then either (a) we have Heli marrying his brother Jacob's widow, as noted above, or (b) Heli's physical son, Joseph, Jacob's nephew, becomes the legal heir of Jacob due to Jacob's dying without children. Given these possible scenarios, however, an explanation is still required for Matthan's father being Eleazar and Matthat's father being Levi (Machen, *Virgin Birth of Christ*, 188–209). As a solution regarding this alternative, Machen proposes, "It seems best to explain the divergence regarding their father, not by Levirate marriage, but by the fact that the kingly line became extinct with Eleazar, who is said by Matthew to have 'begotten' Matthan (Matthat), so that a scion of a widely divergent collateral line became his heir. Matthat (Matthan) would thus be the legal heir of Eleazar, but the actual son of Levi, who appears in the genealogy of Luke" (ibid., 208). (2) Assuming that Matthan and Matthat

Second, the historicity of the narratives is also doubted on the basis of literary questions. For example, some have identified the genre of the birth narratives as "midrash," thus concluding that the texts were never intended to tell "real" history; instead, they were written as imaginative stories reflecting on Old Testament texts in light of Jesus.[94] The problem with this suggestion is that the birth narratives do not fit the genre of midrash: there is no running commentary of an Old Testament text and, at face value, they make historical claims.[95] Related to the midrash objection is the claim that the birth narratives are more kerygmatic than historically accurate, suggesting that the intent of the authors is to proclaim the truth of who Jesus is rather than recount factual information.[96] But, as D. A. Carson notes, this suggestion necessitates an indefensible "rigid dichotomy between proclamation and teaching."[97] Even more to the point, the birth narratives are not saying something vague but something specific about Jesus, namely that he is the promised Messiah from David's line, which is a claim that is rooted in historical realities.

Third, in a more radicalizing version of the argument, some argue that the birth narratives are simply imaginative constructions borrowed from ancient myths and legends.[98] In the Hellenistic world, there were stories of Zeus fathering Hercules, Perseus, and Alexander, and of Apollo fathering Ion, Asclepius, and Pythagoras. It is for this reason that Robert Stein contends that "probably the most frequent argument raised against the virgin conception is that too many other parallels exist in ancient literature to allow [one] to take the Christian account seriously."[99] Yet the problem is that a careful reading of the Gospels demonstrates that they are not Greek in origin but Jewish, and the parallels between these other ancient accounts and the New Testament are nonexistent.[100] The biblical account is set in the context of an entirely different worldview that gives no hint of any sexual activity between God and Mary; nothing in Scripture is even remotely close.[101]

---

are *not* the same person, Machen proposes an ancient solution, namely, "Jacob and Heli were half-brothers—that is, that they had the same mother but not the same father" (ibid.). The point is that with either solution, there are possible ways to relieve the charge of contradiction.

[94] See, e.g., M. D. Goulder, *Midrash and Lection in Matthew* (London: SPCK, 1974); W. D. Davies, *The Setting of the Sermon on the Mount* (Cambridge: Cambridge University Press, 1964); J. S. Spong, *Born of a Woman: A Bishop Rethinks the Birth of Jesus* (New York: HarperOne, 1994).

[95] On this point, see N. T. Wright, *Who Was Jesus?* (Grand Rapids, MI: Eerdmans, 1992); P. S. Alexander, "Midrash and the Gospels," in *Synoptic Studies: The Ampleforth Conferences of 1982 and 1983*, ed. C. M. Tuckett, Journal for the Study of the New Testament 7 (Sheffield: JSOT, 1984); idem, "Midrash," in *The SCM Dictionary of Biblical Interpretation*, 2nd ed., ed. R. J. Coggins and J. L. Houlden (London: SCM, 2003).

[96] See, e.g., Davies, *Setting of the Sermon on the Mount*, 67.

[97] Carson, *Matthew*, 72.

[98] See, e.g., John Hick, ed. *The Myth of God Incarnate* (Philadelphia: Westminster, 1977).

[99] R. H. Stein, *Jesus the Messiah: A Survey of the Life of Christ* (Downers Grove, IL: InterVarsity Press, 1996), 65.

[100] See, e.g., Ronald H. Nash, *The Gospel and the Greeks: Did the New Testament Borrow from Pagan Thought?* 2nd ed. (Phillipsburg, NJ: P&R, 2003).

[101] Millard Erickson argues that these ancient world myths "are nothing more than the stories about fornication between divine and human beings, which is something radically different from the biblical accounts of the virgin birth" (Millard Erickson, *Christian Theology* [Grand Rapids, MI: Baker, 1986], 752).

Fourth, some question the historical reliability of the birth narratives because of the overall silence about the virgin conception in the rest of the New Testament. If the virgin conception actually occurred, why is it not mentioned repeatedly in the New Testament? However, even though Matthew and Luke are the only places that explicitly reference the virgin conception, it is possible to read Galatians 4:4 as consistent with it: "God sent forth his Son, born [*genomenos*] of a woman, born under the law."[102] In addition, one must also consider these facts: (1) no author in the New Testament contradicts or denies the virgin conception; (2) the only two places in the entire New Testament that describe the birth and infancy of Jesus are unanimous in their attestation of it; (3) if the story was legendary, then John, writing his Gospel later, could have corrected it; (4) as Luke was Paul's traveling companion, it is highly unlikely that there would be a fundamental divergence between them at this point.[103]

From the evidence, then, we can conclude that there is no good reason to question the historical accuracy of the biblical birth narratives. In fact, there is every reason to accept them as accurately telling us the means by which God the Son became incarnate.

The Uniqueness of the Biblical Accounts

Others deny the virgin conception based on their rejection of historic Christian theology, specifically that God can act unilaterally and effectively in the world.[104] Because the plausibility or even possibility of a virgin conception is directly tied to our worldview, our response to this objection also requires an entire Christian worldview defense.[105] For our purposes, we will focus on the fact that *Scripture itself* presents the virgin conception as a mighty act of God rooted in his covenantal promises to bring about our redemption through the promised Messiah. The supernatural conception of God the Son in the womb of a virgin is extraordinary, but it is *not* implausible—indeed, "nothing will be impossible with God" (Luke 1:37).

After all, the God who creates *ex nihilo*, who upholds and sustains the universe by his word, and who directs all things toward their appointed end, is certainly able to bring about a virgin conception, and in many ways, it is

---

[102] Paul does not use the usual word for "born" (*gennētos*); rather, he uses *genomenos* ("become"). This strange variation may not explicitly assert a virginal conception, but it is consistent with such a phenomenon (cf. Rom. 1:3; Phil. 2:7). Macleod, *Person of Christ*, 29, observes that "if Paul had wanted to avoid contradicting the doctrine of the virgin birth, he could have chosen his language more felicitously than he does in Galatians 4:4." Or as James Orr, *The Virgin Birth of Christ* (New York: Charles Scribner, 1907), 117, observes, "There is hardly an allusion to Christ's entrance into our humanity in the Epistles which is not marked by some significant peculiarity of expression."

[103] For a full discussion of this issue, see Macleod, *Person of Christ*, 29–32.

[104] See Eduard Schweizer, *The Good News according to Matthew*, trans. David E. Green (Atlanta: John Knox, 1975); Goulder, *Midrash and Lection in Matthew*, 33; Hick, *Myth of God Incarnate*.

[105] See, e.g., R. Douglas Geivett and Gary R. Habermas, eds., *In Defense of Miracles: A Comprehensive Case for God's Action in History* (Downers Grove, IL: InterVarsity Press, 1997).

what you would expect should God the Son become incarnate. Yet, it must be acknowledged that trying to understand this mighty act apart from the Bible's worldview does render it quite implausible. Years ago, B. B. Warfield nicely reminded us of this fact:

> These can appear strange (namely the virginal conception, the miraculous life of Christ, and his resurrection) only when the intervening life is looked upon as that of a merely human being, endowed, no doubt, not only with unusual qualities, but also with the unusual favor of God, yet after all nothing more than human and therefore presumably entering the world like other human beings. . . . From the standpoint of the evangelical writers, and of the entirety of primitive Christianity, which looked upon Jesus not as a merely human being but as God himself come into the world . . . [t]he entrance of the Lord of Glory into the world could not but be supernatural; . . . There is no reason for doubting the trustworthiness of the narratives at these points, beyond the anti-supernaturalistic instinct which strives consciously or unconsciously to naturalize the whole evangelical narrative.[106]

Theological Objections to the Biblical Accounts

Finally, some reject the virgin conception for various theological reasons. For example, even though Wolfhart Pannenberg affirms the bodily resurrection of Christ, he denies the historicity of the virgin conception because he thinks it is inconsistent with Jesus's preexistence. Pannenberg believes that the birth narratives arose as legends from within the Hellenistic Jewish community and that they stand "in an irreconcilable contradiction to the Christology of the incarnation of the preexistent Son of God found in Paul and John."[107] In a similar way, J. D. G. Dunn argues that the birth narratives portray the virgin conception as "Jesus' *origin*, as the *begetting* (becoming) of Jesus to be God's Son,"[108] and that the birth narratives do not present "the transition of a pre-existent being to become the soul of a human baby or the metamorphosis of a divine being into a human foetus."[109] In short, the argument is that within the New Testament there are inconsistent Christologies. This argument, however, will not stand. The entire pattern of New Testament Christology presents Christ's identity as God the Son incarnate, fully God and fully man. One cannot pit the Son's preexistence over against his becoming incarnate *and the means by which he did so.*[110]

Ironically, Emil Brunner rejects the virgin conception because it is incon-

---

[106] Warfield, *Person and Work of Christ*, 32.

[107] Wolfhart Pannenberg, *Jesus: God and Man*, 2nd ed., trans. Lewis L. Wilkins and Duane A. Priebe (Philadelphia: Westminster, 1977), 143.

[108] J. D. G. Dunn, *Christology in the Making: A New Testament Inquiry into the Origins of the Doctrine of the Incarnation*, 2nd ed. (Grand Rapids, MI: Eerdmans, 1989), 50.

[109] Ibid., 51; cf. Pannenberg, *Jesus: God and Man*, 143.

[110] On this point, see Macleod, *Person of Christ*, 33–34. Erickson also says there is "no reason why the preexistence [of God's Son] and the virgin birth should be in conflict if one believes that there was a genuine incarnation at the beginning of Jesus's earthly life" (Erickson, *Christian Theology*, 753).

sistent not with the Son's preexistence but with Christ's full humanity. For Brunner, procreation by a human father is part of what it means to be human, and therefore a virgin conception would compromise the full humanity of Christ.[111] Even though procreation by a human father is the norm for a vast percentage of humans, it is not essential or necessary to our humanity.[112] Given the development in scientific technology in the areas of artificial insemination and *in vitro* fertilization, it is now possible to think of procreation apart from sexual relations without even considering the mighty action of God. One may be fully human and share all that humanity shares without having come into the world through the normal means God has established. But to prove that human fatherhood is not essential to full humanity by the normal means of procreation, we simply need to recognize that the first *Adam* did not come into the world through a human father in this way—and neither did the last Adam.

Arthur Peacocke has recently argued that a virgin conception creates a docetic Christ: "In light of our biological knowledge it is then impossible to see how Jesus could be said to share our human nature, if he came into existence by a virgin conception of the kind traditionally proposed."[113] Peacocke's argument is that if Jesus was virginally conceived, then he would not have sufficient genetic material to be counted truly human and thus he would only *appear* to be human. But this argument is a *non sequitur*. All one has to argue is that Mary's contribution of an ovum had within it the necessary genetic material that true human beings need.[114]

These objections are not an exhaustive list, but they are some of the more dominant ones. In the end, the biblical record stands. Matthew and Luke clearly teach the virgin conception of Christ, and nothing in the New Testament disputes this fact; biblical-theological reasoning supports it; the historical creeds and confessions of the church have affirmed it. There is simply no good reason to reject the supernatural conception of God the Son incarnate in a virgin womb. In fact, as we have argued above, the virgin conception is an important aspect of the structure and storyline of Scripture that identifies the uniqueness and significance of the person and work of Christ.[115] We cannot deny one without affecting the other.

---

[111] Emil Brunner, *The Mediator: A Study of the Central Doctrine of the Christian Faith*, trans. Olive Wyon (London: Lutterworth, 1934), 325, insists: "The Son of God assumed the whole of humanity; thus he took on himself all that lies within the sphere of space and time. Procreation through the two sexes forms part of human life."

[112] It is important to distinguish between being "fully human" and "merely human." See Thomas V. Morris, *The Logic of God Incarnate* (Ithaca, NY: Cornell University Press, 1986), 56–70.

[113] Arthur Peacocke, "DNA of our DNA," in *The Birth of Jesus: Biblical and Theological Reflections*, ed. George J. Brooke (Edinburgh: T&T Clark, 2000), 65.

[114] For a development of this argument, see Oliver D. Crisp, *God Incarnate: Explorations in Christology* (New York: T&T Clark, 2009), 79–87; Michael D. Bush, "Christology and the 'Y' Chromosome," in *Unapologetic Apologetics: Meeting the Challenges of Theological Studies*, ed. William A. Dembski and Jay Wesley Richards (Downers Grove, IL: InterVarsity Press, 2001), 144–155.

[115] Bavinck, *Sin and Salvation in Christ*, 290, nicely summarizes the significance of Jesus's virgin conception: "The supernatural conception, therefore, is not a matter of indifference and without value. It is more intimately tied to the deity of Christ, to his eternal preexistence, his absolute sinlessness, and is therefore of great importance for the faith of the church."

In chapter 3, we saw that the four major parts of the biblical storyline support the entire metanarrative and form the basic framework for interpreting the biblical revelation. More specifically for our purposes of establishing biblical warrant for Christology, we saw that the epochs of creation, fall, redemption, and inauguration-consummation shape the way the Scriptures present and identify Jesus. And across these part-epochs, God works through six biblical covenants to move his one plan for humanity and all creation from his initial promises in the creation covenant to their fulfillment in Christ and the new covenant. This particular covenantal progression along these particular part-epochs of the biblical storyline more fully reveals the true identity of Christ.

In creation, God obligates himself to creation in general and humanity in particular and never turns back. The Creator–Covenant Lord who set humanity over a "very good" creation responds in holy wrath to the rebellion of his vice-regents by destroying them and all life corrupted by them—but not completely. God's curse under the terms of the covenant with creation moves the plotline of Scripture from creation to fall. But God covenants with Noah to preserve the line for the man of promise to come who will restore all things. And with the Noahic covenant, God moves the drama of Scripture into redemption by his promise to preserve the earth until his plan is accomplished. God chooses to covenant with Abraham, Israel, and then the Davidic kings not to *find* the true image-Son and last Adam but to *bring him forth*.

By covenanting with humanity in more specific relationships, the Creator–Covenant Lord does not labor to redesign his original plan that has failed. Through the development of one covenant into the next, rather, God constructs the relational realities necessary to rightly identify the one who will complete God's design for his glory in his creation.

In chapter 4, we considered how the Bible uses its epochal-covenantal structure and storyline to develop the identity of Christ as God the Son incarnate. Through Jesus's own words and works—both implicit and explicit—he knowingly and intentionally identified himself as the divine Son of God and the *eternal imago Dei*. In the same way, he also identified himself as the *incarnational imago Dei* and the man who would fulfill all of God's covenant promises as his true Son-King and the last Adam. Following these words and works and the self-identification of Christ, his apostles came to the same conclusion. They looked along the redemptive drama unfolding out of the Old Testament and recognized Jesus as the one who would meet the growing expectation that God himself would save his people and set his servant-shepherd-king over them. The apostles placed what Jesus did and who Jesus said he was within the storyline of Scripture and identified him as the Son of God come as a man to do what only God can do and all that God requires of man.

For the purpose of establishing biblical warrant for the coming Christological conclusions, we need to make a simple but pivotal deduction. The self-identification of the Lord Jesus Christ and the apostolic understanding of Jesus's identity come to us in the Gospels and Epistles of the New Testament, which continue and conclude the storyline from the Old Testament documents. With the Old Testament and the New Testament linked through the dominical and apostolic teaching, then, the witness of Jesus and his apostles give us the Bible's self-presentation of Jesus's identity. This might seem simple, but it is no less crucial. The God-given, inerrant, authoritative, biblical identity of Jesus is that he is God the Son incarnate—he is both God and man.

In chapter 5, we laid out the New Testament's cumulative-case argument for the deity of Christ. First, the New Testament gives divine status to Jesus by affirming his divine attributes, divine rule, and divine worship. Jesus has, in full, all of the characteristics and capacities that make God who he is. Being the very image and nature of God, then, Jesus acts *as God*: he rules with universal authority, power, and dominion. And because he is God by nature and in his rule, Jesus receives the worship of his disciples and stands as the proper object of their faith for salvation. Second, the New Testament emphasizes that Jesus not only has divine status but he also performs specific divine works that only God can do. Christ is the agent of creation and the providential Lord of heaven and earth who inaugurates the kingdom of God and brings the age to come into the present. And third, consistent with his divine ontology and function, the New Testament crowns Christ with certain divine titles. He is both Lord and God, titles that refer and belong to Yahweh alone. Yet while Christ is God, he is not God the Father—he is God the Son. To preserve Trinitarian relations and the reality of the incarnation, then, it is better to say that Jesus is *God the Son incarnate*.

Accordingly, in chapter 6 we took up the full humanity of Christ. The outer life of Jesus demonstrates that he had a body and grew and developed like all other human beings. And the inner life of Jesus demonstrates that he had a mind, will, and soul and experienced life like all other human beings. The New Testament does not leave the full humanity of Christ to speculation and uncertainty, because his incarnation in the likeness of humanity was necessary to fulfill the storyline of God's redemption coming out of the Old Testament. The Son was obligated by the Father to take on a genuine and full human nature because a complete incarnation was the only way that the Son could: (1) rule as God's obedient vice-regent over creation; (2) bring many disobedient sons into the glory of his own obedient vice-regency through sufferings that fit him for the vocation; (3) suffer the death penalty on behalf of the disobedient, releasing them from the fear of death under divine judgment; (4) represent sinners before God as reconciled to him through the forgiveness of their sins.

This work of redemption and restoration, moreover, was possible because Jesus's humanity was not only full but also sinless. Through the virgin conception, the Holy Spirit created and sanctified the human nature that the Son assumed in his incarnation. Jesus descended from the line of Adam, but not in exactly the same way we do. Every mere human born after Adam was born "in Adam" and stands guilty and corrupted because of Adam's sin. But not the last Adam. As full and sinless man, Jesus was perfectly qualified to fulfill the promise of God to redeem a new humanity.

III

ECCLESIOLOGICAL WARRANT
FOR CHRISTOLOGY TODAY

INTRODUCTION TO PART III

The church exists to proclaim the glory of God in Christ, who brings the church out of darkness and into his marvelous light (1 Pet. 2:9). In every generation, Christians confess and profess Jesus Christ our Lord. Yet because the authoritative interpretation of Jesus's identity is given to us in Scripture (Part II), Christians today should not say anything substantially different from what the church has said faithfully throughout history.

Scripture alone has magisterial authority; but the church's understanding of Scripture throughout history has ministerial authority for us today. To have ecclesiological warrant for Christology, a contemporary articulation of the doctrine must be governed by Scripture and guided by church history. In particular, the universal and enduring attestation to the biblical sense and to the conceptual superiority of the early church councils should accord them deference and allow them to correct any substantial differences in our contemporary doctrinal conclusions.

The chapters in this part will use the Council of Chalcedon as a focus and fulcrum. The significance of this ecumenical council was its formulation of an orthodox Christology that accounted for the witness of Scripture to the deity and humanity of Jesus Christ and refuted the false witness of various heresies that diminished one nature or the other.

Chapter 7 considers the issues and heresies that first created the need for an orthodox Christology. The early Christological formulations by a number of theologians leading up to and including the affirmations made by the Council of Nicaea resolved only some of the issues. Chapter 8 then discusses the crucial Christological developments from Nicaea to the Council of Chalcedon. The Definition of Chalcedon regarding the person and natures of Christ marked the emergence of an orthodox Christology. And chapter 9 gives attention to the post-Chalcedonian developments that clarified the necessary implications of the Definition, thereby establishing an orthodox Christology. As we will see, this survey of historical Christology will help in correcting current confusion and protecting a contemporary articulation of orthodox Christology (Part IV).

SEVEN

ANTE-NICENE CHRISTOLOGY:
THE NEED FOR ORTHODOXY

From Genesis to Revelation, Scripture presents a unique and incomparable Jesus. In the Old Testament we anticipate his coming in a variety of ways. In the Gospels, Jesus is human in his birth although his conception is utterly unique. He grows physically, mentally, and spiritually, and in every way he is like us, except without sin. Yet this same Jesus is uniquely *identified* with God—the Son in relation to his Father (and the Spirit)—and as such, he is God-equal with the Father as the universe's Creator and Lord, and now, due to his incarnation and work, our glorious Redeemer. As Part II has demonstrated, the biblical warrant is strong and well grounded for the church's confession that Jesus is nothing less than God the Son incarnate.

This confession regarding Jesus's identity, however, is not the end of Christological reflection. In fact, given *all* of the biblical data and taking that data seriously, in one sense Christological reflection only now begins. As a result of the biblical teaching, it is legitimate to ask, as an exercise in "faith seeking understanding," how do we make sense of it? Given the Creator-creature distinction, how is it possible for the Creator to become the creature? Is such a thing logically coherent? If Jesus is fully God and thus omniscient, why then does he confess his lack of knowledge on certain matters? Who is the subject of the incarnation? Is it God the Son, or a composite of a divine and human person? Scripture affirms that Jesus was tempted as we are, but does this entail that he could have sinned as we do, or not?

Such theological questions are not always answered by chapter and verse, even though Scripture is the epistemological warrant for answering such questions. Scripture clearly states who Jesus is; it unpacks for us his work in all of its glory and splendor; it describes the personal relations between the Father,

Son, and Spirit; it concludes that Jesus alone is Lord and Savior, but not every question we ask in regard to how all the biblical data coherently fit is answered by a specific text. This is where the church, rooted in Scripture, begins to further theologize about Christ by "thinking God's thoughts after him." As biblical exegesis leads to biblical theology, so the application of the canon to these questions necessarily spawns systematic theology. The church, in light of questions from believers, denials from unbelievers, and even false conclusions drawn from Scripture from within the church—what we label heresies—gladly confesses Christ.

This is precisely how Christological formulation developed in church history. From her inception, as the church confessed Jesus as God the Son incarnate, she also sought to understand in greater ways her glorious Redeemer and the entire message of God's saving grace. As the church carried out the Great Commission by proclaiming Christ to the nations, training believers, and defending the gospel to unbelievers, Christological reflection took place. In fact, in the first five hundred years of the church, theological thinking primarily occurred in two crucial, interrelated areas.

First, theological reflection focused on theology proper, specifically Trinitarian formulation. Given Jesus's self-identity as God the Son in relation to the Father and the Spirit, how do we make sense of who God is? How do we conceptualize the fact that there is one true and living God while simultaneously affirming the distinctness of Father, Son, and Holy Spirit, and the full equality of the Son and Spirit with the Father? What exactly is the relation between the Father, Son, and Spirit in eternity past and in time? Should we confess that the Son and the Spirit are God-equal (*homoousios*) with the Father, or are they of a lesser nature? In the fourth century, after the church's rejection of gnosticism, she found herself in a life-and-death battle with a very subtle and sophisticated heresy known as Arianism. Similar to gnosticism, if embraced, Arianism would have destroyed biblical Christianity at its very core. When the church rejected it at the Council of Nicaea (325), not only was Trinitarian theology reaffirmed but so was the corresponding truth of Christ's deity. It was out of this battle that we have the formulation of the orthodox doctrine of the Trinity as represented by the Nicene Creed.[1]

Second, and interrelated with Trinitarian reflection, was Christological formulation. Even though the church rejected Arianism and affirmed the full deity of Christ, Christological questions remained. How are Christ's deity and humanity related to each other? How do we preserve the unity of the incarnate Son in regard to one personal subject, while simultaneously making sense of

---

[1] The Nicene Creed represents the confessions of the first two councils of the church: Nicaea (325) and Constantinople (381). For more on these councils as they relate to the doctrine of the Trinity, see Robert Letham, *The Holy Trinity: In Scripture, History, Theology, and Worship* (Phillipsburg, NJ: P&R, 2004).

his full deity and humanity? Who is the acting subject of the incarnation? Is it the eternal Son who took to himself a complete human nature, or is it the uniting of two personal subjects (the Son and a man) to form a single subject? These kinds of Christological questions led to further reflection, articulation, and defense of the biblical Jesus epitomized by the Council of Chalcedon (451) over against various challenges and false understandings of Christ.

In fact, Trinitarian and Christological formulation matured and developed over against what Harold O. J. Brown labeled the "positive" side of heresy.[2] Ironically, as dangerous as heresy is, it also serves a purpose. Not only does heresy presuppose that orthodoxy exists; it also forces the church to respond to it by articulating in a more precise and coherent manner the "faith that was once for all delivered to the saints" (Jude 3), which is precisely what happened in the Patristic era.

In the development of theology, this is not to say that the church's doctrinal formulations are beyond dispute; only Scripture serves that role. Yet, historical theology, what we are calling the *ecclesiological warrant*, serves a critical role in our theologizing which we ignore to our peril. No theologian today approaches Christology *de novo*; rather, we stand on the shoulders of giants and learn from the past's mistakes *and* from its constructive doctrinal formulations. In this way church councils and confessions serve as secondary standards to Scripture; doctrine is worked out in the laboratory of history, where ideas are tested for their faithfulness to Scripture. Previous doctrinal formulations, especially ones which receive catholic consent, help function as guardrails for us today. This is uniquely true of the early ecumenical councils, which established the basic parameters within which Trinitarian and Christological theologizing operates. The Nicene and Chalcedonian Creeds, which established Trinitarian and Christological orthodoxy, help us today in doing theology and legitimately serve as "rules of faith."

In saying this, two points are assumed. First, there is a definable orthodox Christology of the church regarding Christ's identity as represented by the Chalcedonian Definition, and to depart from it, or to revise it, is very unwise unless we have strong biblical warrant to do so. No doubt, Chalcedon is not the final word on Christology, yet it provides the church with the basic guardrails within which we theologize about the incarnation. In fact, the main reason for the next three chapters of Part III is to unpack the *ecclesiological warrant* for Christology and to discover how the church arrived at her conclusions in order not to "reinvent the wheel" and repeat history's mistakes. Oliver Crisp states it this way: "Theology should not be novel—or, at least, it should not

---

[2] See Harold O. J. Brown, *Heresies: The Image of Christ in the Mirror of Heresy and Orthodoxy from the Apostles to the Present* (Garden City, NY: Doubleday, 1984), 1–5.

be novel for the sake of novelty. To my mind, systematic theology should be faithful to Scripture and take seriously the chorus of voices that constitute the Christian tradition."[3] Once again, this does *not* mean that we do not critically evaluate the tradition, yet it does demand that we do so first, consistent with Scripture, and second, standing on the shoulders of the tradition unless there is reason not to.

Second, it is assumed that Christological development, as represented by the Chalcedonian Definition, is in *continuity* with Scripture and is *not* a distortion of it. Early heretics often charged the church with departing from Scripture, since she employed extrabiblical terminology in her creeds. In the nineteenth century this charge was famously made by Adolf von Harnack, who claimed that patristic theology was infected by "acute Hellenization." Harnack was not simply saying that the church employed extrabiblical terms in their creeds; rather he charged the church with adopting a Hellenistic mind-set, one that was alien to Scripture, and thus distorting the biblical data.

Throughout the ages, the church has given two responses to this charge. First, the church affirmed that extrabiblical terminology can (and must) be used in doctrinal development as long as the terms and ideas faithfully reflect the biblical teaching. Thus, the use of extrabiblical words such as Trinity, person, nature, *anhypostasia*, *communicatio idiomatum*, and so on, are legitimate if they help explain and make sense of the biblical data without distorting them. Second, the church strongly rejected the claim that she was distorting the Bible; in fact, she argued that by the use of these terms she was faithfully communicating the Bible's teaching.

Richard Bauckham, in reflecting on the charge that the early church departed from biblical categories in her Christological formulation and thus distorted who Jesus truly is, notes the two broad ways it is often argued, both of which are flawed in their interpretation of the data: "The first sees the New Testament as containing, in embryonic form, the source of the development which culminated in the Nicene theology of the fourth century."[4] What this amounts to is the affirmation that in the New Testament there is a kind of trajectory of thought that affirms that Jesus is fully God and fully human, but "it is left to the theologians of the fourth century to bring such fully divine Christology to full expression and to find adequate ways of stating it within the context of a Trinitarian doctrine of God."[5] The second way of interpreting the data is more radical: it "supposes that a Christology which attributed true divinity to Jesus

---

[3] Oliver D. Crisp, *Divinity and Humanity: The Incarnation Reconsidered* (Cambridge: Cambridge University Press, 2007), xiii. For a very helpful discussion on this point, see David F. Wells, *The Person of Christ: A Biblical and Historical Analysis of the Incarnation* (Westchester, IL: Crossway, 1984), 86–91.

[4] Richard Bauckham, *Jesus and the God of Israel: God Crucified and Other Studies on the New Testament's Christology of Divine Identity* (Grand Rapids, MI: Eerdmans, 2008), 57–58.

[5] Ibid., 58.

could not have originated within a context of Jewish monotheism."[6] The implication of this view is that a high Christology is possible only as Christianity transitions from a Jewish theological background to a Hellenistic religious and philosophical background which is much more amenable to a divine Christology. On this interpretation, Nicaea and Chalcedon represent "the triumph of Greek philosophy in Christian doctrine."[7]

The problem, however, with both of these interpretations is that they fail to do justice to the New Testament *and* to Patristic Christology. The first view fails to recognize, as Part II demonstrated, that from the outset the New Testament presents the highest Christology imaginable, not merely seeds of it. The second interpretation, as Bauckham notes, is "virtually the opposite of the truth."[8] The high Christology of the New Testament is rooted in a Jewish theological context *and* it was not Jewish but Greek philosophical categories that made it difficult to attribute full humanity and/or deity to Jesus. In other words, unless Platonism was reformed and substituted by biblical-theological categories, the tendency in gnosticism and Arianism was to make Jesus no more than semi-divine—neither truly God nor truly human—something that the church rejected. The confession, then, of *homoousios* identifies God as Father, Son, and Holy Spirit, and identifies God from the narrative of the history of Jesus to ensure that this divine identity is truly the identity of the one and only God. It is for this reason that the Chalcedonian Definition gives us a Jesus in continuity with the New Testament, albeit by employing different terminology, but not in continuity with Greek philosophy.[9]

With those important points noted, let us begin to sketch the basic contours of Christological development in historical theology and thus establish the ecclesiological warrant for Christology. Obviously the amount of material is vast. Entire volumes have traced the development of Christological reflection, so our discussion will discuss only the key points.[10] In this chapter, we will

---

[6] Ibid.

[7] Ibid.

[8] Ibid.

[9] On this point, see Aloys Grillmeier, *From the Apostolic Age to Chalcedon (451)*, vol. 1 in *Christ in Christian Tradition*, trans. John Bowden, 2nd rev. ed. (Atlanta: John Knox, 1975), 7–9. Grillmeier insists that the charge that Patristic Christology is more concerned with ontology than with function is incorrect because the "question of Jesus's nature was precisely the question of his soteriological function and meaning" (ibid., 7). He concludes with this important point: "Nicaea and Chalcedon did not see their formulations as a distortion of the *kerygma*, but as its defence and its confirmation. The content of the *kerygma*, however, was always the person of Christ and his uniqueness. The theological struggles of the patristic period are nothing else than an expansion of this central question; this gives them their continuity" (ibid., 9). For additional clarity on this point, see David S. Yeago, "The New Testament and the Nicene Dogma: A Contribution to the Recovery of Theological Exegesis," in *The Theological Interpretation of Scripture: Classic and Contemporary Readings*, ed. Stephen E. Fowl, Blackwell Readings in Modern Theology (Malden, MA: Blackwell, 1997), 87–102. Yeago argues that the Nicene *homoousion* is neither imposed on the New Testament texts nor distantly deduced from the texts, "but rather describes a pattern of judgements present *in* the texts, in the texture of scriptural discourse concerning Jesus and the God of Israel" (ibid., 88).

[10] The most detailed treatment of the development of Christology in church history is Aloys Grillmeier's work. See especially his *From the Apostolic Age to Chalcedon (451)*; idem, *From the Council of Chalcedon (451) to Gregory the Great (590–604)*, vol. 2, part 1 in *Christ in Christian Tradition*, trans. Pauline Allen and John Cawte (Atlanta: John Knox, 1987); idem, *The Church of Constantinople in the Sixth Century*, vol. 2, part 2 in *Christ in Christian Tradition*,

describe Christological development from the second century to the Council of Nicaea. In chapter 8, we will highlight the central points from Nicaea to the Chalcedonian Definition, while chapter 9 will focus on post-Chalcedonian developments. Part III, then, will provide the basic components of an orthodox, catholic Christology, at least until the rise of the Enlightenment.

Throughout our journey, we will employ the image of a traveled road. Every road leads to a specific destination, and every road establishes set parameters within which to travel. Going too far on either side of the road puts a traveler in the ditch and thus in grave danger. By analogy, the road to Chalcedon and beyond leads to the establishment of the church's catholic confession: Jesus is God the Son, who has always subsisted, along with the Father and Spirit, in the divine nature, but now, for our salvation, has taken to himself another nature, and as a result of that action, he now subsists in two natures. As the church formalized this conclusion, she did so by rejecting various heresies that have one thing in common despite their differences: each heresy failed to do justice to *all* of the biblical data. In one way or another, the humanity, the deity, or the single subject of Christ was compromised or denied, which then undercut the biblical Jesus. In rejecting these views, the church remained faithful to the biblical presentation of Christ *and* gained greater theological clarity in her confession and proclamation of God the Son incarnate.

In traversing the Christological development from the second century to the fourth century, we will proceed in three steps. First, we will discuss some key terminological issues that are crucial to all Christological reflection, ancient and contemporary. Second, we will highlight the emergence of orthodoxy over against various heresies during this era. Third, we will describe the unique contribution of the Council of Nicaea in its rejection of the Arian heresy.

Key Terminological Issues in Christological Formulation

One of the positive results of heresy was that it forced the church to define terms carefully and to produce a common vocabulary by which greater theological precision occurred. In fact, one of the crowning achievements of the ecumenical councils was precisely this point, even though it was difficult. There are two aspects of this development.

The "Nature-Person" Distinction

In order to make sense of the biblical data and to respond to various heresies in regard to the Trinity and Christology, the church had to make a crucial

---

trans. Pauline Allen and John Cawte (Louisville: Westminster John Knox, 1995); see also Jaroslav Pelikan, *The Emergence of the Catholic Tradition (100–600)*, vol. 1 in *The Christian Tradition: A History of the Development of Doctrine* (Chicago: University of Chicago Press, 1971); J. N. D. Kelly, *Early Christian Doctrines*, 5th rev. ed. (London: A & C Black, 1977); Gerald Bray, *God Has Spoken: A History of Christian Theology* (Wheaton, IL: Crossway, 2014).

"nature-person" distinction. Scripture teaches that God is one, yet it also teaches that God is three and that there is a difference between the way he is one and the way he is three. To deny or even minimize this difference is fundamentally to misunderstand the biblical teaching and to open the door to false views of God.

The vocabulary that expressed God's oneness was "being" and more commonly his "nature," while his threeness was expressed in the language of "person." Technically, as Gerald Bray points out, *being* refers to "what a thing *is*" and *nature* refers to "what a thing *is like*,"[11] but throughout the centuries these subtleties have mostly disappeared in Christian theology, and the words "being" and "nature" are now used synonymously. Thus when speaking of God, we say that he is the supreme Being, the Creator of the universe and thus distinct from his creation and in a category all by himself, who has a nature which is then described in terms of his attributes.[12]

Historically, especially in the medieval era, theologians have spoken of God's attributes as those things that are *essential* to him in contrast to accidental, i.e., God has his attributes necessarily; he cannot set aside or lose his attributes and still be God. Thus, God's nature is immaterial, eternal, omnipotent, omniscient, omnipresent, etc., and necessarily so. Today, some speak of the divine attributes within the conceptual thought of "essentialism."[13] "Essentialism" distinguishes between essential and contingent attributes. Essential attributes are attributes God has by necessity, i.e., what he has in every possible world (e.g., infinity, eternality, aseity, simplicity, immutability, immensity, holiness, triunity, etc.). Contingent attributes or perfections are attributes God has, but not in every possible world (e.g., creator, redeemer, sustainer, since God chooses to become these things in conjunction with his free decision to create, sustain, and redeem). Whatever way we employ to think of God's attributes, to speak of the nature of God (or of the nature of anything), is to describe "that by which a thing is what it is."[14]

"Person," on the other hand, cannot be reduced to "nature." Scripture teaches that the "persons" of the Trinity—Father, Son, and Holy Spirit—cannot be confused with or submerged in the single "nature" of God; otherwise they lose their distinctness. But what exactly is a *person*? This is not an easy

---

[11] Gerald Bray, *Creeds, Councils, and Christ: The Continuity between Scripture and Orthodoxy in the First Five Centuries* (Downers Grove, IL: InterVarsity Press, 1984), 147. Cf. idem, *God Has Spoken*, 293–322.

[12] On these points, see Bray, *Creeds, Councils, and Christ*, 146–151; cf. John S. Feinberg, *No One Like Him: The Doctrine of God*, Foundations of Evangelical Theology (Wheaton, IL: Crossway, 2001), 37–80, 204–231.

[13] For a discussion of Medieval and Reformation ways of thinking about the divine attributes, see Richard A. Muller, *The Divine Essence and Attributes*, vol. 3 of *Post-Reformation Reformed Dogmatics* (Grand Rapids, MI: Baker Academic, 2003). For a discussion of "essentialism," see Jay Wesley Richards, *The Untamed God: A Philosophical Exploration of Divine Perfection, Simplicity, and Immutability* (Downers Grove, IL: InterVarsity Press, 2003); cf. K. Scott Oliphint, *Reasons for Faith: Philosophy in the Service of Theology* (Phillipsburg, NJ: P&R, 2006), 191–255.

[14] Herman Bavinck, *Sin and Salvation in Christ*, vol. 3 of *Reformed Dogmatics*, ed. John Bolt, trans. John Vriend (Grand Rapids, MI: Baker, 2006), 306.

question to answer, and even today this question is still debated. At this juncture, however, it is important to stress two points.

First, Scriptural fidelity requires us to distinguish "person" from "nature." Second, in the Patristic era, "person" could be understood in two very distinct ways, but it is the second way that is crucial to understanding orthodox Christology as defined by Chalcedon. The first way viewed "person" merely as a united personal appearance (Gk.: *prosōpon*). As Donald Fairbairn explains, "In this understanding, one could say that Christ was a single person, but this would mean little more than the obvious fact that the Jesus whom people could see, hear, and touch appeared as one man. In actuality, this understanding asserts, he was really two different subjects, the Logos and the man Jesus, appearing together as one *prosōpon*."[15] The second way—crucial to Christology—viewed "person" as "an active subject who *does things* and *to whom things happen*."[16] This understanding of "person" acknowledges that Christ appeared as a single character, but it goes further. It asks the important question, *who* was the active subject (i.e., person) of the incarnation? Scripture is clear: the *person* of the incarnation is the divine Son who assumed a human nature without a human subject—"the *Word* became flesh" (John 1:14)—hence the affirmation that Jesus is *one* person in *two* natures.

As we will discuss throughout Part III, this understanding of "person" was later given specific definition by the church.[17] For example, John Calvin defines a divine person as a "subsistence in God's essence, which, while related to the others, is distinguishable by an incommunicable quality"[18]—an incommunicable quality or property that was spoken of in terms of that which uniquely pertains to the Father, Son, and Spirit.[19] Or, as Herman Bavinck explains, a "person" is "what exists in and for itself, the owner, possessor, and master of a nature, a completion of existence, sustaining and determining the existence of a nature, the subject that lives, thinks, wills, and acts through nature with all its abundant content, by which nature becomes self-existent and is not an accident of another entity."[20]

As the "person-nature" distinction was employed in theology proper and

---

[15] Donald Fairbairn, "The One Person Who Is Jesus Christ: The Patristic Perspective," in *Jesus in Trinitarian Perspective: An Intermediate Christology*, ed. Fred Sanders and Klaus D. Issler (Nashville: B&H, 2007), 83.

[16] Ibid. Cf. Bray, *God Has Spoken*, 316–322.

[17] Boethius's definition is often seen as a standard definition: "A person is an individual substance of a rational nature" (cited in Gilles Emery, "The Dignity of Being a Substance: Person, Subsistence, and Nature," *Nova et Vetera*, 9/4 (2011): 994 (English edition). For the original source, see Boethius, *Liber de Persona et Duabus Naturis*, chapter 3, "A Treatise against Eutyches and Nestorius," 85, in his *Theological Tractates*.

[18] John Calvin, *Institutes of the Christian Religion*, ed. John T. McNeill, trans. Ford Lewis Battles (Philadelphia: Westminster, 1960), 1.13.6.

[19] Historically, the way the persons of the Godhead were distinguished was in terms of the internal, eternal relationships or properties of the persons: ingenerateness (Father), begottenness or eternal generation (Son), and eternal procession (Spirit). On this point, see Robert Letham, *Holy Trinity*, 108–268; Brown, *Heresies*, 104–157.

[20] Bavinck, *Sin and Salvation in Christ*, 306. For a similar definition, see Geerhardus Vos, *Christology*, vol. 3 of *Reformed Dogmatics*, trans. and ed. Richard B. Gaffin Jr. (Bellingham, WA: Lexham, 2014), 39–84.

in Christology, the church affirmed that in God there are three persons—acting subjects—who subsist in one, single nature, and that in Christ there is one person who subsists in two natures. Bavinck summarizes these truths in this way: In terms of the Trinity, "the unity of the three persons in the divine being is in the full sense natural, consubstantial, coessential"; and in terms of Christ, "the unity of the two natures in Christ is personal,"[21] so that in the incarnation, the second person of the Godhead assumed a human nature and gave to that nature its person as its active subject, who "lived, thought, willed, acted, suffered, died, and so on in and through it with all of its constituents, capacities, and energies."[22] Or, as Thomas Aquinas stated it, "The assumed [human] nature does not have its own proper personality, not because some perfection of human nature is wanting, but because something surpassing human nature is added, i.e., union to a divine person."[23]

Even though the "nature-person" distinction was assumed by the church from the start, it took time to reach conceptual clarity.[24] In fact, debate over competing views of the Trinity and Christology center on different understandings of this distinction—an issue which the church has had to think through carefully even to our present day.

Terminological Developments in Communicating the "Nature-Person" Distinction

The second positive contribution of heresy was to help the church wrestle with how best to communicate the "nature-person" distinction by adopting a common vocabulary. For example, in the Nicene Creed, contra Arian theology, the church affirmed that Christ was *homoousios* with the Father (i.e., of the same substance). Or, in the Chalcedonian Creed, contra Nestorianism and Apollinarianism, the church argued that Christ had one person (*prosōpon* or *hypostasis*) who existed in two natures (*physis*). None of these words appears directly in Scripture except in Hebrews 1:3 (*hupostaseōs*), and even there it is not used in the way it is used in the Creed.

The church's challenge in using such terminology was twofold. First, she had to translate terms from Greek to Latin, which was not easy. As one translates from one language to another, ambiguities and misunderstanding often result. Second, the terms employed were not neutral; they came with a history of usage and thus brought philosophical baggage with them, and if one was

---

[21] Bavinck, *Sin and Salvation in Christ*, 306.
[22] Ibid., 307.
[23] Thomas Aquinas, *Summa Theologica*, 3.4.2.2.
[24] Jean Galot argues this point: "Greek philosophy had not provided theology with concepts suitable for expressing the distinction. In the history of human thought, this distinction was developed by theology in its efforts to give valid expression to the message of Revelation" (Jean Galot, *Who Is Christ? A Theology of Incarnation* [Chicago: Franciscan Herald, 1981], 288); see also Gerald Bray, *God Is Love: A Biblical and Systematic Theology* (Wheaton, IL: Crossway, 2012), 118–133.

not careful, that baggage could lead to great confusion and misunderstanding.[25] For example, to describe God's oneness, eventually the Greek word *ousia* was employed by the church to denote "being" and the "nature" of a thing, so that in Trinitarian thought, God had one nature (*ousia*).[26] In reference to the three persons, the Greek word *hypostasis* was utilized. In this way, the terms *ousia* and *hypostasis* were viewed as words referring to distinct aspects of God, the former to God's oneness (being, nature) and the latter to God's threeness (persons). However, in classical philosophy *ousia* and *hypostasis* were synonyms. Given this use of the words in classical philosophy, even at Nicaea, where it was confessed that the Son was "of the substance (*ousia*) of the Father," if not careful, this could be understood by some to say that the Son and the Father were the same individual entity, hence the charge of modalism.[27] In addition, the term *prosōpon* was also used by the early church. Originally it was used "either of a face of or the face's expression, which revealed what was within the person. It was also used in a legal context for the person who held the right to a property."[28] When applied Christologically, when used in the first sense, it was applied to the Son, who visibly represented what was hidden in the Godhead; when used in the second sense, it was used of Christ as having an individual, concrete existence—a meaning that was later assumed by *hypostasis*.

Eventually, by the Synod of Alexandria (362), the church resolved the terminological confusion and standardized the use of the terms as applied to the Trinity and Christology. When speaking of God's oneness (being, nature) the Greek word *ousia*, and sometimes *physis*, was used. In reference to God's threeness (person), the Greek word *hypostasis* was employed, and *prosōpon* was now viewed as a synonym of *hypostasis*. When the church translated the Greek words into Latin, *ousia* equaled *essentia*, *hypostasis* and *prosōpon* equaled *persona*, and *hypostasis/persona* was understood as an active or personal subject who subsists in a nature who lives, thinks, wills, and acts in and through the nature.[29] "Person" was not used in the contemporary psychological sense of "person" associated with one's personality, or as a term that referred to the entire individual, or as a synonym for the soul. As this terminology was employed in theology, it led to the consistent Trinitarian affirmation that God, as the one true and living God, exists as three "persons" (active subjects) subsisting in one "nature," and in Christology, the Lord Jesus is one "person"—the eternal Son—subsisting in two "natures."[30]

---

[25] For a fine discussion of these issues, see Brown, *Heresies*, 127–131; Bray, *God Has Spoken*, 293–322.
[26] In Greek, *ousia* denoted "being" and *physis* denoted "nature."
[27] See Letham, *Holy Trinity*, 115–118.
[28] Wells, *Person of Christ*, 94.
[29] See Bray, *God Has Spoken*, 316–322; cf. Geerhardus Vos, *Theology Proper*, vol. 1 of *Reformed Dogmatics*, trans. and ed. Richard B. Gaffin Jr. (Bellingham, WA: Lexham, 2014), 45–49.
[30] Bray, *Creeds, Councils, and Christ*, 151.

With these terminological distinctions in place, let us now outline the high points of Christological development from the second century to Nicaea, as the church was led to greater understanding of Jesus's identity, especially in the mirror of heresy.

Ante-Nicene Christological Formulation (c. 100–325)

Aloys Grillmeier observes that "no epoch of christology displays such numerous and so different currents of thought as the second century."[31] At first glance this may seem disconcerting, but it should not surprise us, for two reasons: First, we must remember that even though the New Testament was written by this time, it was not circulating as an entire canon. Second, as the church spread and became universal throughout the Roman Empire, she not only faced opposition in terms of persecution but also challenges "from within." Already in the New Testament, even when the apostles existed, we have those from "within" the church who preached the gospel for their own profit and distorted it. But now, as people from biblically illiterate and alien worldview backgrounds are converted, they inevitably import a lot of baggage, which increases the danger of syncretism. Many who thought they were proclaiming Christ were in reality obscuring the very gospel they sought to proclaim. As "faith seeks understanding" in the face of legitimate questions, from within and without, true and false understanding results—the latter known as "heresies."[32]

Jeremy Jackson suggests that what unites *all* heresies is the denial of Christ and his work.[33] As we embark on describing various false views of who Jesus is, we need to keep this in mind. At the heart of the gospel is Jesus, and at the heart of all heresy is a misunderstanding and/or denial of him. Why is this so? Probably because the idea of salvation by God's sovereign grace, achieved by the incarnate Son, who lived a life we could not live and died as our penal substitute—something we could not do—is offensive to rebellious man. It removes from us any ability to contribute to our salvation, and it drives us to raise the empty hands of faith and to receive what God has graciously and powerfully done for us in Christ. If we want to distinguish true Christianity from false in any era, we must ask, "Who do you say that Jesus is and does?" Our response to this question reveals what we think Christianity is, and it ultimately discloses what we believe in other doctrinal areas as well.

---

[31] Grillmeier, *From the Apostolic Age to Chalcedon (451)*, 37.

[32] Our English word "heresy" is a transliteration of both the Greek and the Latin word. As Brown explains, "In Christian usage, the term 'heresy' refers to a false doctrine, i.e. one that is simply not true and that is, in addition, so important that those who believe it, whom the church calls heretics, must be considered to have abandoned the faith" (Brown, *Heresies*, 1). Like true belief, of which heresy is a distortion, heresies are always lived and thought. Heresies, then, are never merely intellectual, and the only antidote to them is right belief according to Scripture, repentance, and faith. For a helpful discussion of heresy, see Stephen J. Nichols, *For Us and for Our Salvation: The Doctrine of Christ in the Early Church* (Wheaton, IL: Crossway, 2007), 20.

[33] See Jeremy C. Jackson, *No Other Foundation* (Westchester, IL: Crossway, 1980), 31–42.

False Steps: Early Departures from the Jesus of the Bible

In this period of time, there were two ways in which people departed from the biblical Jesus: they denied and/or minimized either his deity or his humanity. Interestingly, and unlike our own day, the first significant heresy, associated with gnosticism, denied Christ's full humanity, but other groups also denied his deity. Following are three examples.

Heresies Associated with Judaism

The first number of Christological heresies is associated with Judaism.[34] In the New Testament era, the Jewish community for the most part rejected the deity of Jesus and denied that he was the Messiah promised from the Old Testament. From the second until the early fifth century, there existed a Jewish-Christian group known as the Ebionites—a group associated with the continuation of the Judaistic opponents of Paul. This group denied Jesus's virgin conception along with his deity. In their view, Jesus was an ordinary man who possessed unusual but not supernatural gifts. Jesus distinguished himself from others by a strict observance of the law, and the Ebionites taught that, due to his observance of the law, "Christ" descended on Jesus by the Spirit of God at his baptism, which meant that God's presence and power were with him in unique ways, primarily in terms of influence. Near the end of his life, "Christ" conceived in messianic terms withdrew from Jesus, thus his cry of abandonment on the cross.

Another Jewish-Christian group, known as the Elkesaites, held a similar view. They too rejected the virgin conception and Jesus's deity and spoke of Christ as a higher spirit or angel. Instead of viewing Jesus as God the Son incarnate, they regarded him as an incarnation of the ideal Adam, and also called him the highest archangel; but God the Son he was not. These early views were a far cry from the Jesus presented in the New Testament.

Heresies Associated with Monarchianism

A second variety of Christological (Trinitarian) heresies was associated with monarchianism.[35] This position rightly sought to preserve monotheism and thus the divine unity, or *monarchia* (*monos*, one; *archos*, ruler, source), but to the exclusion of the full and coequal deity of the Son (and Spirit). This exclusion of the deity of the Son (and Spirit) was done in one of two ways, both of which departed from the biblical teaching.

---

[34] For a detailed discussion of these views, see Grillmeier, *From the Apostolic Age to Chalcedon (451)*, 37–77; Nichols, *For Us and for Our Salvation*, 17–26; cf. Louis Berkhof, *The History of Christian Doctrines* (Grand Rapids, MI: Baker, 1937), 43–45; Galot, *Who Is Christ?*, 213–249.

[35] On monarchianism, see Brown, *Heresies*, 95–103; Berkhof, *History of Christian Doctrines*, 77–80; Kelly, *Early Christian Doctrines*, 115–123.

The first way was the position of adoptionism[36] or dynamic monarchianism. In order to preserve the divine unity, this view argued that Jesus was not God the Son. Instead, the Logos—a kind of power or reason identified and consubstantial with the Father but *not* a distinct person—came upon the man Jesus at his baptism. Prior to Jesus's baptism, he was wholly human, but as a reward for his exceptional moral virtue, Jesus was "adopted" as God's Son and empowered by God and thus able to perform his many miracles. In this sense, Jesus was "deified" by virtue of a received power, not because of any supposed equality of nature with the Father. Because it was believed that God could not suffer, this position maintains that the Logos flew back to God before Jesus died on the cross, thus the explanation for Jesus's cry of abandonment. Paul of Samosata, bishop of Antioch (c. 200–275) was a famous proponent of this view. His views were rejected by the church in the third century. In the next century, Paul's views influenced later figures such as Lucian of Antioch and his pupil, Arius, who denied the deity of the Son. Over a millennium later, this view was taught by Socinianism and Unitarianism, and today many within the liberal tradition of the church are adoptionistic in their Christology.[37]

The second way monarchianism developed and excluded the deity of the Son by excluding his personal distinctness from the Father was modalism, also known as Sabellianism (named after Sabellius). It was a very influential view in the early church. It had the twin conviction that God is one and that Jesus is God, yet modalists were uncomfortable with Tertullian's suggestion that the Father and Son shared the same substance, arguing that this entailed "bitheism." So they conceived of the Father, Son, and Spirit as "modes" in which God manifested himself. It was suggested that God manifested himself differently in each of the three phases of world history—as Father in the Old Testament (Creator), as Son in the Gospel period (as Redeemer), and as Spirit since the time of Pentecost (role of Sanctifier). In this way they denied the personal distinctions between the Father, Son, and Spirit within the Godhead. No doubt, modalism affirmed the full deity of Christ, yet it denied his distinct person within the Godhead. One disastrous implication of modalism is that the events of redemptive history become a charade. Not being a distinct person, the Son cannot really represent us to the Father nor accomplish a substitutionary atonement on our behalf. Modalism is necessarily docetic, teaching that Christ was human in appearance only, unless one affirms—which some modalists did—that the Father suffered on the cross (Patripassianism), since the Son is not actually distinct from the Father.

---

[36] Technically, the word is *adoptianism*, but we will use the more common spelling. See Bray, *God Has Spoken*, 227.
[37] For examples of adoptionistic Christologies, see the works of Friedrich Schleiermacher, Albrecht Ritschl, and John A. T. Robinson, as well as John Hick, editor of *The Myth of God Incarnate* (Philadelphia: Westminster, 1977).

Both of these views veered off the road into the ditch. The unity of God was preserved but the deity of the Son was denied, and as a result Jesus was viewed either as an empowered man or as a mere manifestation of God, but certainly not God the Son incarnate.

Heresies Associated with Gnosticism

Without question, the most serious distortion of biblical thought during this time was the heretical worldview of gnosticism and its Christological counterpart, docetism.[38] Gnosticism was part of a large and complex religious and philosophical movement that swept through the Hellenistic world at the beginning of the second century. It was based on the Platonic dualism of matter and spirit; Gnostics argued that the material world was inherently evil while the spirit world was potentially good. In addition, gnosticism offered people a detailed, secret knowledge (Gk. *gnosis*) of reality, claiming to know and to be able to explain things of which ordinary people, including Christians, were ignorant. It divided humans into various classes, and only those in the highest and most spiritual class could attain this secret knowledge. At every point, gnosticism was a worldview alien to Christianity, and if accepted or mixed with biblical faith, the truth of the gospel would have been destroyed.

For example, Gnostics viewed God as one, yet remote and unknowable—wholly other and thus removed from this fallen, material universe, which he did not create. Since in Gnostic thought there is a distance between God and the world, the "gap" is filled by a strange host of intermediaries. In fact, it was one of these intermediaries, a lesser power or god, the "Demiurge," who created this material, fallen universe, including human beings. When it comes to humans, we are comprised of the same spiritual substance that God is, but we have become trapped in physical bodies, which are like tombs that we must escape. Our "fall" into sin is not a historic fall; rather, it is identical to our "fall" into matter and thus becoming trapped in our physical bodies. In this way, creation and fall coincide, due to the work of the Demiurge. Therefore sin is viewed as the alienation of our soul from the true God, while we exist in our physical bodies. As long as our souls are trapped in physical bodies and materiality, we will be subject to "sin." Salvation is an escape from the bondage of material existence and a journey back to the home from which our souls have fallen. This possibility is initiated by the great Spirit—God—who wishes to draw back into itself all the stray bits and pieces. God sends forth an emanation of himself—a spiritual redeemer—who descends through layers and

---

[38] For a detailed discussion of gnosticism and docetism, see Grillmeier, *From the Apostolic Age to Chalcedon (451)*, 79–85; Brown, *Heresies*, 38–69; Robert M. Grant, ed. *Gnosticism: A Source Book of Heretical Writings from the Early Christian Period* (New York: Harper & Row, 1961); Pelikan, *Emergence of the Catholic Tradition (100–600)*, 81–97.

layers of reality from pure spirit to dense matter and attempts to teach some of the divine sparks of Spirit their true identity and home. Once awakened by knowledge, we are able to begin the journey back.

In this view, then, who is Jesus? Despite their diversity, Gnostics taught that Jesus was the human vehicle for this heavenly messenger, "Christ," who was sent by God to rescue the soul from the body. All forms of gnosticism denied that "Christ"—this heavenly, spiritual redeemer—became incarnate, given their antithesis between spirit and matter. So they argued that "Christ" either temporarily associated himself with the man Jesus (adoptionism) or he simply took the appearance of a physical body (docetism; Gk. *dokeō*, "to appear"). For most Gnostics, the heavenly redeemer entered Jesus at his baptism and left him before he died on the cross.[39]

Gnosticism radically departed from the biblical teaching of Jesus and ended up in the ditch. It denied the entire biblical conception of God as the Creator and Lord who shares his rule with no one, and the reality of God the Son as coequal with the Father. Additionally, gnostics denied the reality of the incarnation including the full and complete humanity of the incarnate Son. As such, gnosticism left us with an entirely different conception of sin and salvation. It is not surprising that the early church fathers such as Ignatius, Irenaeus, and Tertullian tirelessly argued against it. They correctly realized that gnosticism was a heresy that had to be rejected *in toto*.

Early Orthodox Christological Formulation

Many early church fathers could be discussed, and we have already mentioned Ignatius, Irenaeus, and Tertullian, who strongly rejected gnosticism and docetism. Regardless of who we discuss, what united the orthodox development of Christology was the keeping together of the biblical teaching regarding the full deity and full humanity of Christ in one active subject. Here are some of the key people during this time, noting what they have in common and their unique contributions.

IGNATIUS OF ANTIOCH (D. C. 115)

Ignatius was a contemporary of the apostle John. He was martyred c. 115. While awaiting his death, he wrote seven epistles that have been preserved. As noted, Ignatius wrote strongly against docetism, thus stressing the reality of the incarnation and the full humanity of Christ. Ignatius famously writes,

---

[39] The more famous docetists include Valentinus (c. 136–165), Basilides (died c. 140), and Marcion (died 160). Early church fathers such as Ignatius (died c. 115), Irenaeus (130–202), and Tertullian (c. 200s) responded strongly to this false teaching. Even though gnosticism was not full-blown until the second century, there is an incipient form of it in view in John 1:14; 1 John 1:1–3; 4:1–3, where John is clear that anyone who denies the humanity of Christ denies the gospel.

> Turn a deaf ear therefore when any one speaks to you apart from Jesus Christ, who . . . was really born, who both ate and drank; who really was persecuted under Pontius Pilate; who really was crucified and died . . . who, moreover, really was raised from the dead when his Father raised him up. . . . But if, as some atheists (that is, unbelievers) say, he suffered in appearance only, . . . why am I in chains. And why do I want to fight with wild beasts? If that is the case, I die for no reason.[40]

Ignatius also affirms the full deity of the Son. In *Eph*. 7:2, Ignatius sets two series of statements about the one Christ side by side. On the left are statements about Christ in the flesh as man; on the right are those that are made of him as the preexistent Son.[41] There can be no doubt that Ignatius, immediately after the apostolic age, believed in the full deity and humanity of Jesus Christ. Grillmeier also observes that Ignatius affirms the unity in Christ: "This theological understanding of the unity in Christ finds its clearest expression in Ignatius in his use of the so-called 'exchange of predicates', where the divine is predicated of the man Christ and the human of the Logos, while the distinction between the two kinds of being is clearly maintained. This way of speaking is possible only because the unity of the subject is recognized."[42]

Justin Martyr and Logos Christology (c. 100–165)

As Christians proclaimed Christ to their culture, they experienced intellectual opposition. A number of Christian writers, known as the "apologists," sought to explain and defend the faith to its cultured despisers.[43] One of the most famous of these early apologists was Justin Martyr (c. 100–165), and in regard to Christology he is especially important for the development of what is called "Logos Christology."[44]

As an apologist, Justin believed that the "Logos" was an important link between Christian and Hellenistic thought. As a student of the philosophers, Justin claimed that the philosophers were basically correct on many points,

---

[40] Ignatius, *Epistle of Ignatius to the Trallians* 9 (ANF 1:66–72).

[41] See Grillmeier's discussion in *From the Apostolic Age to Chalcedon (451)*, 86–89.

[42] Ibid., 89.

[43] "Cultured despisers" is taken from Friedrich Schleiermacher, *On Religion: Speeches to Its Cultured Despisers*, Cambridge Texts in the History of Philosophy, trans. and ed. Richard Crouter (Cambridge: Cambridge University Press, 1996).

[44] At the beginning of the second century, the apologists not only attempted to explain Christianity in response to many misunderstandings, but they also tried to demonstrate that it was intellectually credible. Some of the early opponents of Christianity include Fronto, Tacitus, Lucian, Porphyry, and Celsus. Probably the best known is Celsus and his work, *The True Doctrine: A Discourse against the Christians* (c. 175–180). The entire book is preserved by Origen, who responded to it in the third century in his *Contra Celsus* (see Origen, *Origen against Celsus* (ANF 4:395–670). For a modern attempt to restore the main order of Celsus's argument, see *The True Doctrine: A Discourse against the Christians*, trans. R. Joseph Hoffmann (Oxford: Oxford University Press, 1987). Some early Christian apologists include Justin Martyr, Tatian, Athenagoras of Athens, Theophilus of Antioch, Aristides, and Melito of Sardis, as well as later theologians such as Origen, Tertullian, and Irenaeus. In addition to Justin, other apologists developed Logos Christology as well, including Tatian, Athenagoras, and Theophilus of Antioch.

although their overall view was incomplete since it lacked Christ. Thus, in spite of the differences between pagan philosophical thought and Christianity, Justin maintained that the philosophers had glimpses of the truth and that this was more than a mere coincidence. How, then, did he explain the partial agreements between the philosophers and Christian theology? Justin's answer centered in the "Logos." According to Greek thought, a human mind can understand reality because it shares in the Logos or universal reason that undergirds all reality. But for the Christian, especially in light of John's Gospel, we affirm that in Jesus of Nazareth the "Logos" was made flesh (John 1:1–3, 14). In the incarnation, then, the underlying reason of the universe, the Logos, has come to this earth and lived among us. Justin appeals to this truth, thus linking together Christian and Hellenistic thought in Christ.

With his use of Logos Christology, Justin strongly affirms the deity of the Logos and the reality of the incarnation. He teaches that the Logos is God's preexistent Spirit—a second God—who now has become incarnate in Jesus Christ. In this way, two truths are stressed—the Logos's eternal oneness with the Father and also his appearance in human history as the Logos emitted or expressed. In addition, Justin wants to speak of the relation between the Logos and the Father as eternal, and even though the Father generates the Logos, this in no way diminishes the Father or the Logos because, like fire kindled from fire, that from which many can be kindled is by no means made less, but remains the same. In this explanation, Justin is seeking to make sense of how God is one, yet the Father and Son are both deity and share the divine nature.[45]

To further explain the Logos's relation to God, Justin speaks of the Logos as the "cosmic Logos," who is God's offshoot and agent in creation. The Logos, then, was in the world before Jesus; he spoke through the Jewish prophets and Greek philosophers. In this way, the Logos, literally, *logos spermatikos*, is the one who is in every human being and is the source of all truth whenever it is understood and uttered (cf. John 1:3ff.). But now, in time, this Logos has taken on flesh and come to dwell among us as Jesus the Messiah.

By the use of Logos Christology Justin seeks to achieve a number of things. First, he seeks to explain why Christians may embrace "all truth as God's truth." Second, he explains why Christians can believe in and worship Jesus Christ as God (a "second God") without rejecting monotheism. Christ as the universal Logos preexisted Jesus as God's Son, as fire taken from fire—somewhat less than God himself but of God's own nature and substance. Third, he explains why people must become Christians: the same Christ as universal Logos is the source of all truth, beauty, and goodness, but only Christians know the Logos

---

[45] See Sara Parvis and Paul Foster, eds., *Justin Martyr and His Worlds* (Minneapolis: Fortress, 2007).

fully by faith in Christ. In the end, Justin argues, all thought apart from Christ is incomplete.[46]

One of the problems that Justin bequeaths later generations, however, is subordinationism, i.e., viewing the Logos as ontologically subordinate to the Father by making the procession of the Logos from the Father dependent on creation. This will open the door for some to say that there is no eternal preexistence of the Logos in a distinct personal existence—a door, sadly, that later Arian theology walks through.

IRENAEUS OF LYONS (c. 130–202)[47]

Irenaeus was born in Asia Minor. He spent his Christian training as a disciple of Polycarp and was then sent as a presbyter to Gaul, where he was appointed bishop of Lyons in 177. Probably his best-known apologetic work is his defense of Christianity against gnosticism—*Against Heresies*. In his response to gnosticism, he presents an entirely different theology. For example, in contrast to gnosticism, Irenaeus affirms the *one* God, who exists as Father, Son, and Holy Spirit, who is the Creator of heaven and earth, *ex nihilo* by his Word and by the Spirit, his "two hands." For Irenaeus, God has direct contact with his creation and he has not brought it to pass through a range of intermediaries. Some argue that Irenaeus's "two hands" view treats the Son and Spirit as subordinate to the Father, which is possible since he writes in the ante-Nicene era. Yet, he clearly places this subordination *within* God's being and does not treat the Son and the Spirit as external to the Father but as one with him. For Irenaeus, the Son and the Spirit are fully God, yet for him this affirmation does not detract from the divine unity. The Father, Son, and Spirit are viewed as working in union and harmony in creation, providence, and redemption, for they are *in* each other prior to creation.

In terms of his view of human beings and God's plan of salvation, Irenaeus follows the storyline of Scripture—creation, fall, and redemption—and argues that humans were created good but they became corrupt by a voluntary act of the will, tied to Adam and a historic fall. Furthermore, precisely because the entire human race is "in Adam," all humans enter the human race as fallen. Our predicament, in the end, is not metaphysical but moral, and thus the need for God to bring about our salvation by his own provision of himself.[48]

---

[46] For a more detailed description of Justin, see Grillmeier, *From the Apostolic Age to Chalcedon (451)*, 98–104; Letham, *Holy Trinity*, 90–97; Galot, *Who Is Christ?*, 220–223.

[47] See Sara Parvis and Paul Foster, eds., *Irenaeus: Life, Scripture, Legacy* (Minneapolis: Fortress, 2012); Eric F. Osborn, *Irenaeus of Lyons* (Cambridge: Cambridge University Press, 2005).

[48] As we will discuss in chapter 8 regarding Nestorius, a nuance is necessary to understand Christological reflection in the fifth century. Even though creation, fall, redemption is the dominant way Irenaeus reads Scripture, Donald Fairbairn argues that there is tension in Irenaeus, Origen, and later Christian thinkers between what he calls a three-act versus a two-act scheme of redemptive-history (Donald Fairbairn, *Grace and Christology in the Early Church*, Oxford Early Christian Studies [Oxford; New York: Oxford University Press, 2003]). Fairbairn explains,

In regard to Christology, Irenaeus was the first to formulate the meaning of the person and work of Christ in a systematic way. He did so by following the structure and framework of Scripture. He clearly affirmed that Jesus is fully man and fully God. He did not discuss at length the relations of the Son and Spirit with the Father, or their preexistence; however, he viewed both as deity and he rejected the Logos as merely an emanation or merely an attribute or expression of God. Instead he argued that the Logos has always existed as the One who reveals the Father and thereby is personally distinct from him, and *not* as a mode of the Father—which helps clarify some of the problems that Logos Christology bequeathed the church. For Irenaeus, the Son is true God by nature. Furthermore, Irenaeus strongly emphasized the unity of Christ's person.[49] Against the Gnostics, who distinguished between Christ, the being of heavenly origin, and Jesus, the earthly being, Irenaeus declared that "Jesus Christ is one and the same" (*heis kai ho autos*),[50] an expression later incorporated in the Chalcedonian Definition.

It is precisely because of who Jesus is that he can do the work that Scripture attributes to him. In unpacking the doctrine of salvation, Irenaeus rejected the spirit-flesh dualism of gnosticism and instead spoke of "recapitulation," in the sense that salvation is a renewal and restoration of creation, not its abrogation. Since all humanity is "in Adam," Christ must "recapitulate" Adam, and to do so, Jesus must be fully God *and* fully man—hence the rationale for the incarnation.[51]

"The three-act scheme sees humanity as created (the first act) in the state of immortality and fellowship with God and views the fall (the second act) as a radical departure from the good condition in which God had originally placed Adam and Eve. Salvation (the third act) is understood primarily as a restoration of people to the original condition of perfect fellowship" (ibid., 17–18). This is the majority view of the church. However, in contrast, the minority view is two-act, which "sees humanity's original created state (the first act) more as one of opportunity than as one of perfection. God created people with the capacity for immortality and fellowship with himself and gave them the vocation of obtaining these things. This view places less emphasis on the fall than a three-act scheme does, and it sees redemption (the second act) as the work of the incarnate Christ in leading humanity to a higher level, assisting people in fulfilling their vocation, rather than as a restoration to a previous condition. This scheme sees the key acts as *creation* and *elevation*" (ibid., 18). Irenaeus mostly opts for the three-act view, yet in *Against Heresies* he seems to portray a two-act view of salvation (Irenaeus, *Against Heresies* 4.38.3 [ANF 1:521–522]; see Fairbairn, *Grace and Christology*, 19). Why is this important? For those who opt for a three-act scheme, as orthodoxy does, much more emphasis is placed on God's action in accomplishing our salvation than on our own action, and on the need for a divine Son to step into history in order to redeem us. However, for those who opt for a two-act scheme, as is later stressed by Theodore of Mopsuestia and Nestorius, Fairbairn explains, "salvation is largely the human task, with God's assisting grace, of ascending from an imperfect human age to a perfect human age. In this understanding, there is no particular need for God to enter human life personally in order to save humanity. We need a human example and trailblazer, not a divine Savior. As a result, Theodore and Nestorius write of Christ as the man who has received aid and cooperation from the Logos, so that he can himself ascend to the second age and blaze the trail that we will follow in ascending to that age ourselves.... [In terms of the personal subject of the incarnation, this kind of Christology] sees that person as the man Jesus, who is indwelt by God the Son in order to receive the aid he needs to blaze the trail we follow" (idem, "One Person Who Is Jesus Christ," 96).

[49] Galot, *Who Is Christ?*, 220–223.

[50] Irenaeus, *Against Heresies* 3.16.2; 3.17.4 (ANF 1:440–441, 445).

[51] Grillmeier observes that Irenaeus frequently speaks as though Christ consisted only of Logos and *sarx* ("flesh"), yet "he certainly does not deny the soul of Christ. His is a theology of antithesis, which lets the glory of the divine Logos become visible simply by joining it to its most extreme opposite, the sinful corruptible flesh" (Grillmeier, *From the Apostolic Age to Chalcedon (451)*, 103–104). Later reflection would unpack more the relation between the Son and his human nature.

In addition, Irenaeus gave us two crucial phrases: *Filius dei filius hominis factus*—"The Son of God [has] become a son of man," and *Jesus Christus vere home, vere deus*—"Jesus Christ, true man and true God." For Irenaeus, the redemptive work of Christ depends fully on the identity between his humanity and our humanity. This is a high point of Christological clarity that will be attained again, but not surpassed, almost three centuries later at Chalcedon.

Tertullian (c. 160–230)

Tertullian was born and lived in Carthage, North Africa. He was born into a pagan Roman family and educated in rhetoric and law. Sometime before 197, he became a Christian. He is the first notable representative of the Latin-speaking church, dubbed by many as the "father" of Latin or Western theology, and he also wrote as an apologist against Marcion and other heretical groups (e.g., *Prescription of Heretics*; *Against Marcion*; *Against Praxeas*).

Tertullian, along with Irenaeus, opposed gnosticism using many of the same arguments. Tertullian also wrote against modalism. In answering modalism, Tertullian anticipates the later formulations of Nicaea and Chalcedon, and, as Jean Galot notes, he "anticipated the answers later provided in the Eastern church to three great Christological errors: Apollinarianism, Nestorianism, and Monophysitism."[52] In fact, he coins the very terms that will be used in those later Councils. He is the first to use the word *trinitas* (Trinity) to refer to God, and he argues that God is one "substance" (*una substantia*) in three "persons" (*tres personae*). The names "Father," "Son," and "Spirit" are not modes but represent real, eternal distinctions, yet this threeness does not deny God's oneness. Tertullian is also helpful in explaining what he means by his terms. By "substance" he means that fundamental ontological being-ness that makes something what it is, while "person" (*persona*) refers to the identity of action that provides distinctness.[53]

Also, as with others in this time period, there is a subordinationist strand in Tertullian's thinking.[54] He argues for a divine ordering among the persons; the Father is "greater" than the Son, who is second, while the Spirit is third from the Father and the Son,[55] but this ordering seems to be explained in more ontological than functional terms. For example, as Robert Letham explains, Tertullian suggests that before all things were made God was alone—"yet not alone, for he had with him his own reason (*ratio*), which he possessed in himself, that is, his own thought, which the Greeks call *logos*."[56] Technically,

---

[52] See Galot, *Who Is Christ?*, 223.
[53] See Grillmeier, *From the Apostolic Age to Chalcedon (451)*, 121–131.
[54] See ibid., 118–121.
[55] Tertullian, *Against Praxeas* 7–8 (ANF 3:601–603); cf. Grillmeier, *From the Apostolic Age to Chalcedon (451)*, 120.
[56] Letham, *Holy Trinity*, 99.

however, Tertullian argues, "God did not have his Word (*sermo*) at this time, only reason. God sent out his Word at creation."[57] But does this mean that the Word came into existence only at creation, and had no preexistence? Tertullian distinguishes between the immanent Word and the emitted Word: "the Word was always inherent in reason, and reason was within God, but is explicitly a person only from creation."[58] It is hard to avoid the conclusion that Tertullian is advocating an ontological subordination, yet, in other places he insists on the real personal distinctions of the Father, Son, and Spirit, and that they all share fully in the one being of God.[59] This tension is not fully resolved; maybe it is too much to ask, since further reflection has to take place.

When turning to Christology, Tertullian affirms that the subject of the incarnation is the Logos, who has taken on flesh.[60] In thinking through the relation between the deity and humanity of Christ, Tertullian does not discuss the issue in depth, but he does use the same basic concepts of substance (nature) and person: Jesus Christ was of a divine substance and human substance, yet only one person.[61] In this way he affirms two natures in Christ yet united in one subject, who is the divine Son. Against what would later become Nestorianism, Tertullian clearly argues that the person of Christ was not the result of the conjunction of two substances thus forming a "composite" person, "but a single divine person who possesses a twofold state or a twofold substance."[62] But as noted above, Tertullian is unclear in regard to the subordinationist issue, and he seems to hold that the Son is a derivation of the Father's substance, yet he does place these relations *within* the Godhead and does not want to imply inequality of being, but explanation of relations and origin.[63] Tertullian's unique contribution to Christology is his concept of "person," which in future years is developed with more sophistication. Tertullian clearly preserves the unity of the Son in the person and the subsistence of that person in two natures so that Jesus is now fully God and fully man; yet he is not always crystal clear on these concepts.[64]

Furthermore, against gnosticism/docetism, Tertullian affirmed that Christ had a human soul, a truth Irenaeus did not discuss but which became crucial in later Christological reflection.[65] For Tertullian, a human nature was comprised of a body *and* a soul, and thus for Christ, since he was fully man—and

---

[57] Ibid.
[58] Ibid.
[59] Tertullian, *Against Praxeas* 8 (ANF 3:602–603).
[60] Ibid., 27 (ANF 3:623–624), in Grillmeier, *From the Apostolic Age to Chalcedon (451)*, 121n50).
[61] For a discussion on this point, see Grillmeier, *From the Apostolic Age to Chalcedon (451)*, 121–131.
[62] Galot, *Who Is Christ?*, 226.
[63] Tertullian, *Against Praxeas* 9 (ANF 3:603–604); Kelly, *Early Christian Doctrines*, 114; Letham, *Holy Trinity*, 99–101.
[64] See Grillmeier, *From the Apostolic Age to Chalcedon (451)*, 129.
[65] Tertullian argued, "But in Christ we find the soul and the flesh expressed in simple unfigurative terms; that is to say, the soul is called soul, and the flesh, flesh" (Tertullian, *On the Flesh of Christ* 13 [ANF 3:533]).

in order to save us—he had to assume a body-soul composite. As Galot notes, this soteriological argument "was invoked more than a century later against Apollinarianism,"[66] which denied Christ's human soul, and it also allowed Tertullian to account for Jesus's emotions and passions, which he experienced in his human soul. Also, Tertullian's strong affirmation of Christ's two natures—natures which retained their own properties and were not confused or mingled—was also important in the church's stand against monophysitism, which contended for one blended nature as a result of the incarnation.

Origen (c. 185–254)

Origen was the son of Christian parents from Alexandria and served as a representative of Eastern theology within the church. His father suffered martyrdom during the persecution of Septimius Severus. Origen, who was still a young child, wished to offer himself for martyrdom, but his mother forced him to remain home by hiding his clothes. Origen was a brilliant thinker. At age eighteen, he was already a teacher at the school of Clement, who trained catechumens, i.e., candidates for baptism. After doing this for a number of years, Origen then devoted himself entirely to running a school of Christian philosophy. There he lectured to both Christians and non-Christians, and became quite famous. Origen moved his teaching and writing headquarters to Caesarea in 233. During the persecution under Decius, he was tortured to such a point that he died shortly after having been released from prison. Origen's literary output was vast: he wrote eight hundred treatises, compiled the *Hexapla*,[67] wrote numerous commentaries, debated the Roman philosopher Celsus (*Contra Celsum*), and wrote a systematic theology (*De principiis*).

Origen was favorable to Hellenistic philosophy and particularly Neoplatonism, and he was a controversial figure for a variety of reasons. However, in terms of Trinitarian and Christological thought, many later orthodox theologians were highly indebted to him, particularly Athanasius and the Cappadocians—Basil and the two Gregorys. His most noteworthy and controversial Trinitarian contribution was his doctrine of the eternal generation of the Son by the Father. It was not anything new, but for Origen it was utilized to explain the relations between the Father and the Son. He distinguishes what he means from human generation, and argues that it does not happen by any outward act but according to God's nature and eternally, having no beginning other than in God.[68] There is no point, then, at which the Son is nonexistent or the Father is without the Son; the Son in no way can be viewed as a creature, contra

---

[66] Galot, *Who Is Christ?*, 223.
[67] The Hexapla was the Old Testament text in six columns: Hebrew, Greek transliteration, plus four Greek translations.
[68] Origen, *De Principiis* 1.2.4 (*ANF* 4:247).

later Arian theology. As Robert Letham explains, "It follows that the genera-tion of the Son is continuous; the Father communicates his divinity to the Son at every instant."[69] But there is a problem in Origen's explanation: He thinks that the generation of the Son occurs by the free act of the Father's will; but if it is entirely free, is it possible to think that the Son might not have been? If so, does this mean that the Son is of lesser status and substance than the Father? Origen tries to avoid this conclusion by stressing the *eternal* character of the generation, and that we must not understand this act in human terms. For Origen the Father and Son have a unity of nature[70] and share one and the same power,[71] for there is no unlikeness between them.[72] Also, as Letham points out, Origen has an early version of *perichoresis* where he stresses, "the mutual indwelling of the three persons in the one divine being."[73] Yet, Origen does say that the Son derives his deity from the Father, and he would deny what Calvin later taught, that the Son is *autotheos* (God of himself), since for Origen, the Son (and Spirit) share in the Father's deity by derivation.[74] Unfortunately in later years, Origen's stress on the subordination of the Son (and Spirit) opened the door to a denial of the deity of the Son by the Arians, even though this was not Origen's intent.[75]

In terms of Christology, Origen argued that the unity in Christ was achieved through the mediacy of the soul of Christ between his flesh and the Logos. This idea was tied to Origen's unbiblical belief in the preexistence of the soul, and thus, in the case of Christ, there was one particular soul, due to its purity and dedication, which was able to enter into a union with the Logos. God then created for it a pure, noncorrupt human body, which was able to encompass the Logos-soul pair and allow him to suffer and die as a man. After the resur-rection, Jesus's humanity was glorified and divinized in such a way that the stress was not on the Logos becoming man but on the man becoming Logos.[76] At this point, Origen's theologizing was not helpful, since he was in danger, as Grillmeier points out, of making Christ "only a 'quantitatively' different exceptional case of the universal relationship of the 'perfect' to the Logos, however mystically deep Origen may wish to make the relationship between Logos and soul in the God-man."[77] Furthermore, Origen opened the door to later Nestorian Christology by viewing the soul as a center of activity, which

---

[69] Letham, *Holy Trinity*, 103; Origen, *Homily on Jeremiah* 9.4, in Origen, *Homilies on Jeremiah and Homily on 1 Kings 28*, trans. John Clark Smith, The Fathers of the Church, vol. 97 (Washington, DC: Catholic University of America Press, 1998).
[70] See Origen, *De Principiis* 1.2.6 (*ANF* 4:247–248).
[71] See ibid., 1.2.10 (*ANF* 4:250–251).
[72] See ibid., 1.2.12 (*ANF* 4:251).
[73] Letham, *Holy Trinity*, 104.
[74] See Origen, *De Principiis* 1.2.13 (*ANF* 4:251); idem, *Origen Against Celsus* 5.39 (*ANF* 4:561).
[75] For a helpful discussion of this point, see Letham, *Holy Trinity*, 106–107.
[76] See Brown, *Heresies*, 93–94.
[77] Grillmeier, *From the Apostolic Age to Chalcedon (451)*, 147.

seemed to imply that in Christ there was some kind of "double personality."[78] At this stage in Christological reflection, Origen did not make a clear "nature-person" distinction and thus did not locate the unity of Christ in the "person" of the Son—something later Christology did. As a result, Origen opened the door for later heresies which the church would have to think through and reject, and probably the most significant heresy on the horizon was that of Arianism, a heresy to which we now turn.

The Council of Nicaea and the Arian Challenge

After gnosticism, the second great heresy of the early church was Arianism, a view promoted by Arius (c. 256–336), a presbyter in Alexandria, and then promulgated by others who argued a similar position.[79] Arianism was condemned at the Councils of Nicaea (325) and Constantinople (381), even though its influence continues to this day as represented by the Jehovah's Witnesses. Similar to gnosticism, if accepted by the church, Arianism would have destroyed the gospel and the Christian faith root and branch. Yet, in spite of its serious nature, Arianism did help the church define Christ's identity with more precision and sophistication.[80]

Since no theological view or movement begins in a vacuum, it is important to set the larger context in which Arianism arose. Coming from third-century discussion, and given the church's wrestling with making coherent God's unity and diversity, especially vis-à-vis the Father-Son relation, the monarchian and Logos Christology paradigms carried a lot of weight. Those who sought to preserve God's unity within the monarchian paradigm, if not careful, veered toward modalism. Others, influenced by Logos Christology, if not careful, veered toward ontological subordinationism by "according a lower status to the Son and the Spirit, maintaining the unity of God with the Father imparting deity to the Son and Spirit,"[81] as taught by Origen. No doubt, these thinkers spoke of the relations between the Father, Son, and Spirit *within* the Godhead, but as Letham notes, it resulted in "an unstable and explosive situation."[82] By the late third century, modalism was resolved, but the subordinationist issue was unresolved, and people like Arius took this unstable position where no previous theologian had gone: Arius reduced the Son to a creature, albeit the

---

[78] For a discussion of this point, see ibid., 147; Brown, *Heresies*, 94.

[79] Even though the heresy of Arianism is drawn from Arius's name, we have very little of his writing, and he probably played a minor role in the theological debates that eventually bore his name. However, his views represented an influential train of thought that we now call "Arianism." See Letham, *Holy Trinity*, 109–111; cf. Lewis Ayres, *Nicaea and Its Legacy: An Approach to Fourth-Century Trinitarian Theology* (Oxford: Oxford University Press, 2006); Michel R. Barnes and Daniel H. Williams, eds., *Arianism after Arius: Essays on the Development of the Fourth Century Trinitarian Conflicts* (Edinburgh: T&T Clark, 2000); R. P. C. Hanson, *The Search for the Christian Doctrine of God: The Arian Controversy, 318–381* (Edinburgh: T&T Clark, 1988).

[80] See Brown, *Heresies*, 104–106.

[81] Letham, *Holy Trinity*, 109.

[82] Ibid.

most exalted creature; he considered the Son the first-begotten of the Father, but he rejected his eternal preexistence and his coequal status with the Father. Such a view, the church insisted, was a denial of the Jesus of the Bible and of Scripture's teaching regarding God and salvation. Here, in a nutshell, are the basic contours of Arius's thought.

Arius's Theology and Christology

Arius was concerned to preserve the transcendence of God and his absolute unity, which for him eliminated any possibility of God sharing his being with another person—otherwise the unity of God would be compromised.[83] How, then, should we conceive of the Father-Son relation?

Arius affirmed that it is only the Father who is eternal, thus the Son (and the Spirit) had an origin; "there was a time when the Son was not." Similar to the rest of creation, the Son was "begotten" from God (which for Arius is a synonym of "created"), even though he viewed the Son as the highest of all created beings.[84] Given God's absolute transcendence, in order to create, God first had to create a spiritual being that could act as a mediator—an intermediary figure—a kind of Platonic demiurge. In Scripture this figure was called "wisdom," "image," or "word," but not because the Son is God-equal with the Father or shares the divine nature: for Arius, the Son is simply a creature, and it is only God (the Father) who is true deity, Word, and Wisdom. The reason the Son, as a creature, is called God's "word" and "wisdom" is that he shares, by grace and participation, the wisdom of God. The same explanation is given for why Scripture attributes to the Son the title *theos*; it does so only by analogy.[85]

Given this understanding, Arius taught that the Son is not worthy of divine worship. For him, Christ is the perfect creature and our Savior because he constantly grows in his commitment to the good and thus serves as our example of how we can attain perfection and partake of divinity as he did. The Son, then, is viewed as only *quantitatively* greater than us. Additionally, Arius denies that the Son fully reveals the Father, since he is only the mediator of creation. As Grillmeier astutely observes, for Arius, the Father-Son relation is simply another aspect of the God-world relationship, and in his presentation of Christ, unlike what we find in Scripture, "we hear nothing of soteriology or a theology of revelation. The Son is typically understood as a cosmological intermediary."[86] But one thing he is not: a divine Savior who acts on our behalf by taking on our human nature and doing all that is necessary to redeem us

---

[83] See, Grillmeier, *From the Apostolic Age to Chalcedon (451)*, 219–228; Brown, *Heresies*, 104–116; Bray, *God Has Spoken*, 232–246; cf. Gregg R. Allison, *Historical Theology: An Introduction to Christian Doctrine* (Grand Rapids, MI: Zondervan, 2011), 368–371.
[84] See Brown, *Heresies*, 112–116; cf. Galot, *Who Is Christ?*, 226–228.
[85] See Grillmeier, *From the Apostolic Age to Chalcedon (451)*, 227–232.
[86] Ibid., 231.

from the ravages of sin and death. Thus, for Arius, the incarnation is not the self-emptying of God the Son for us and our salvation (Phil. 2:6–11), but the means of glorification of the created son. In truth, Arianism is a bridge view between polytheism and monotheism in its presentation of Christ as a semi-divine figure. In the end, Arius leaves us with a salvation that is accomplished not by God himself but instead by human achievement. Arianism is thoroughly pagan in outlook and an outright denial of the God and Christ of Scripture.

One last point that is crucial to note in regard to Arius, especially given his importance in later centuries, is his advocacy of a "Logos-flesh (*sarx*)" Christology. This expression refers to a Christology that "assumes that the Logos and flesh are directly conjoined in Christ and that Christ has no human soul."[87] In light of the later Apollinarian heresy, the debate over whether Christ has a human soul is of critical importance. As Chalcedon will later argue, one cannot maintain the biblical teaching of Christ's full humanity without a corresponding affirmation that the Son took to himself a human soul with all of its mental and psychological capacities. But as Grillmeier notes, Arius argued that the first-created Logos took to himself only a human body and *not* a human soul. In Christ, then, there were not two natures "but only one composite nature,"[88] and thus "the Logos has become 'flesh', but not 'man', for he took no soul."[89] In the end, Arius leaves us with a Jesus who is impossible to square with Scripture, for his Jesus, exalted though he may be, is simply a creature, not worthy of our trust and worship, and certainly one who cannot satisfy God's own righteous requirements and save us from our sin.

After Arius there were those who followed in a similar direction.[90] Like Arius, later Arians sought to preserve God's unity and transcendence, given their almost Gnostic view that God could not have direct contact with the material creation. For them, Jesus is simply a creature, an intermediary figure—a god of lesser status than the Father—who is God's agent in creation, but mutable, imperfect in his knowledge, and unworthy of our worship. In every way, early Arians departed from Scripture and ended up in the ditch, yet their departure was so serious that the church had to address it, which is what occurred at the Council of Nicaea.[91]

---

[87] Ibid., 238; cf. Galot, *Who Is Christ?*, 226–228.

[88] Grillmeier, *From the Apostolic Age to Chalcedon (451)*, 244.

[89] Ibid.

[90] Robert Letham provides a helpful summary of six key theological beliefs of early Arianism: (1) God was not always Father, for there was not always a Son; (2) the Son is a creature; (3) the Son is changeable by nature; (4) the Son's knowledge of God and of himself is imperfect; (5) the Son was created by God as an instrument by which he created the world; (6) the Trinity, if we can even speak of such, is of unlike *hypostases* (Letham, *Holy Trinity*, 113). Any unity is only moral, not ontological; the Son is dependent on the Father's will, not his essence.

[91] Some of the biblical texts Arians appealed to include Colossians 1:15, where the fact that the Son is the firstborn of creation was interpreted temporally and not in terms of the Son's rank over creation; and texts that speak of the Son as dependent upon the Father (e.g., John 5:19–29) or of the Father as greater than the Son (e.g., John 14:28; cf. Mark 13:32–33; Luke 2:52). Arians interpreted the divine titles applied to Jesus—*theos*, Lord, Son—as simply expressions of Jesus's uniqueness in sharing in the grace of God. They also appealed to Proverbs 8, which

The Council of Nicaea (325)

The Roman Emperor Constantine called 318 bishops, primarily from the East, to assemble in the city of Nicaea to resolve the growing conflict between Arius and his supporters and Alexander, the bishop of Alexandria, and his supporters. The Arians, who were confident of victory, boldly presented their statement of faith, a document drawn up by Eusebius of Nicomedia. It clearly denied the Son's deity, which stunned a majority of the bishops, and it was roundly rejected. In its place the bishops wrote a creed affirming Christ's full deity, thus rejecting Arius's teaching and those who taught it. The concern of the Council was to confess belief in one God, the true Father, and his true Son, thus affirming that the Son is not a creature. Not much was said about the Holy Spirit; that would come later, at Constantinople (381). Today, what we call the Nicene Creed is really the product of the councils of Nicaea and Constantinople, even though most of the original creed is preserved in the later one. The first creed is as follows:

> We believe in one God Father Almighty maker of all things, seen and unseen:
> And in one Lord Jesus Christ the Son of God, begotten as only-begotten of the Father, that is of the substance (*ousia*) of the Father, God of God, Light of Light, true God of true God, begotten not made, consubstantial with the Father, through whom all things came into existence, both things in heaven and things on earth; who for us men and for our salvation came down and was incarnate and became man, suffered and rose again the third day, ascended into the heavens, is coming to judge the living and the dead.
> And in the Holy Spirit.
> But those who say, "There was a time when he did not exist," and "Before being begotten he did not exist," and that he came into being from non-existence, or who allege that the Son of God is of another *hypostasis* or *ousia*, or is alterable or changeable, these the Catholic and Apostolic Church condemns.[92]

KEY AFFIRMATIONS OF NICAEA

The most significant teaching of Nicaea was the Son's full deity—something the church had always confessed but which was now under dispute, given Arianism. Repeatedly the bishops stressed the deity of the incarnate Son, but unfortunately not without some ambiguity which would require later clarification.

---

presents wisdom as a created reality. One of the reasons why appeals to Proverbs 8 carried such weight was due to people like Justin Martyr arguing that Christ is the "wisdom" of Proverbs 8. This almost universal interpretation embroiled the church in controversy about the precise nature of the relationship between the Father and Son, especially when the Arians argued that Proverbs 8:22 showed that the Son is a created being. Contra the Arians, Nicene theologians employed two exegetical strategies: (1) the Son was "created" when he became incarnate; (2) the creation of wisdom was actually the creation of wisdom's image in creatures as they were brought into existence. However, it is questionable whether this line of exegesis is helpful or necessary. On this point, see Bruce K. Waltke, *The Book of Proverbs: Chapters 1–15*, New International Commentary on the Old Testament (Grand Rapids, MI: Eerdmans, 2004), 126–133.

[92] Hanson, *Search for the Christian Doctrine of God*, 163; cf. Letham, *Holy Trinity*, 115–116.

From Nicaea, though, there are at least four important affirmations that underscore Christ's deity and the purpose of the incarnation.

First, the Son's deity is taught in the phrase that the Son is "of the substance (*ousia*) of the Father." Athanasius explains the importance of this reference.[93] It was not enough to say that the Son was "from God," since the Arians agreed that all creatures come from God; rather, the bishops had to use extrabiblical language to convey the truth that the Son is not created. In saying that the Son was "of the substance of the Father" and then later that he is "consubstantial (*homoousios*) with the Father," the bishops were going on record "that the being of the Son is identical to the being of the Father."[94] Yet, as noted above, at this point in history, a clear distinction between *ousia* (nature) and *hypostasis* (person) had not yet been drawn, as evidenced in the last anathema. It is for this reason that some interpreted Nicaea as affirming modalism, which is not the case; however, it took another half-century to remove this ambiguity.

Second, the Son's deity in relation to the Father is also taught in the phrases stating that the Son was "begotten not made" and "begotten as only-begotten of the Father." Arians had affirmed that the Father was "unbegotten" (*agennētos*) and "uncreated, eternal" (*agenētos*) while the Son was "created" (*genētos*) and "begotten" (*gennētos*). Nicaea affirms the former but not the latter by stressing that the Son was eternal *and* uncreated (*agenētos*) and thus deity, while also begotten of the Father (*gennētos*) in terms of the eternal generation of the Son—"begotten not made" (*gennētos non genētos*). Nicaea is clear: the Son is *not* a creature, and there is an eternal, personal Father-Son relation and ordering—a topic to be developed in later Trinitarian reflection.

Third, in Nicaea's affirmation that the Son was "true God of true God" it distinguished itself from Arianism and taught the deity of the Son. Arians could accept that the Son was "from God," but to say that he was "true God" entails "that he was of the same nature as the Father."[95]

Fourth, Nicaea also places the entire discussion of the incarnation within the overall plan of God to save us from our sins. It speaks of the incarnation and the work of Christ "for us men and for our salvation," thus highlighting the fact that these bishops were not interested in merely an academic theorizing but in confessing a Lord and Savior who can meet our deepest need, namely to take our humanity upon himself and become one with us in order to save us from our sins. In other words, the soteriological purpose of the incarnation is foundational to getting the identity of Christ right; understanding who he is, is crucial to affirming what he does.

---

[93] See Athanasius, *De Decretis* 5.19–21 (NPNF² 4:162–164); cf. Letham, *Holy Trinity*, 116–118.
[94] Letham, *Holy Trinity*, 117; cf. Galot, *Who Is Christ?*, 228–229.
[95] Grillmeier, *From the Apostolic Age to Chalcedon (451)*, 268.

Problems Nicaea Did Not Resolve

The Council clearly argued for the deity of the Son, Jesus Christ our Lord, and for the Son's personal distinction from the Father (contra modalism). In fact, Nicaea insisted that unless the Son was of the same nature as the Father (*homoousios*), he is not fully God. Nicaea, however, was unclear regarding how all of this fit together, and specifically it was unclear on the following points.

First, Nicaea was unclear in its use of language. The Arian bishops continued to stress that the Greek word *ousia* could mean an individual subsistent thing like a person, given the synonymous use of *ousia* and *hypostasis* at this time. Thus to affirm that the Father and the Son are *homoousios* could be interpreted as saying that they are identical in their persons, which would be an affirmation of modalism. Nicaea did not intend this, since their use of the word, as Donald Fairbairn notes, was "to emphasize the full equality and identity between the Son and the Father, but the word turned out to be problematic because some feared that it might imply that Father and Son were a single person."[96] It was not until after Nicaea that this use of the language was clarified so that *homoousios* underscored the fact that all three persons, Father, Son, and Holy Spirit, subsist in or possess the same, identical divine nature as the one true and living God.

Second, there is no question that Nicaea affirmed that the Son was distinct from the Father, yet it did not adequately explain how this can be so while God still remains one. The heart of the problem was the failure clearly to distinguish "nature" from "person." The technical theological meanings that eventually developed were *not* in use for most of the fourth century, and as Letham reminds us, "it is anachronistic to project those meanings back to an earlier time when they simply did not apply."[97] At this moment in history there simply was not a single word for what God is as three, that commanded universal agreement. It was not until *hypostasis* (person) was uncoupled from *ousia* (nature) that the church was able to say with greater clarity how the three persons share or possess the same identical nature yet are distinguished by their personal properties and relations.

Third, Nicaea did not address the question of whether Christ had a human soul, something the Arians denied. Even Athanasius, the defender of Nicene orthodoxy, at least prior to 362 was unclear on this point.[98] While Tertullian

---

[96] Donald Fairbairn, *Life in the Trinity: An Introduction to Theology with the Help of the Church Fathers* (Downers Grove, IL: IVP Academic, 2009), 45–46. Robert Letham also observes that at Nicaea, *ousia* and *hypostasis* were used synonymously, which created the modalist confusion (see Letham, *Holy Trinity*, 115–121).

[97] Letham, *Holy Trinity*, 119.

[98] For a discussion of Christ's human soul in Athanasius's Christology, see ibid., 130–133; Bray, *God Has Spoken*, 325–329. Grillmeier argues that, prior to 362, Athanasius accepted that Jesus had a human soul, but in practice he attached little theological significance to it (Grillmeier, *From the Apostolic Age to Chalcedon (451)*, 308–328). For the most part, Athanasius usually wrote of the incarnate Christ in terms of a union of the Logos with a body or flesh, implying that the assumed humanity is physical only. Yet, after the denial of Christ's human soul by

had already insisted on the existence of Christ's human soul, the defenders of orthodoxy did not challenge Arius's negation. This was probably due to their desire to defend Christ's deity, yet the status of Christ's human soul needed attention. It was not until after Apollinarius's denial that this issue came to the forefront, and by the Council of Chalcedon (451) the church clearly affirmed that the Son took to himself a human body *and soul*.

Yet, regardless of the problems Nicaea left unresolved, in responding to various heresies and wrestling with legitimate questions raised by Scripture, the orthodox confession of the church was beginning to emerge with greater clarity and theological precision. Between Nicaea and Chalcedon even greater clarity would emerge, a topic we turn to in the next chapter, as we continue to investigate the ecclesiological warrant for the church's confession of Christ.

Apollinarius (a man who was closely aligned with Athanasius), Athanasius did stress Christ's full humanity and realized the importance of affirming, what the Chalcedonian Definition would later make clear, that Christ had a full human nature, including a body and soul, and that unless he had a full humanity he could not function as our Redeemer and head.

EIGHT

CHRISTOLOGY FROM
NICAEA TO CHALCEDON:
THE EMERGENCE OF ORTHODOXY

The years between Nicaea (325) and the Council of Constantinople (381) were important ones for Trinitarian and Christological development. Even though the Nicene Creed was the official doctrine of the church, the Arian influence continued and a number of linguistic and theological matters needed resolution. As discussed in chapter 7, it took time to create a common theological vocabulary that established the crucial "nature-person" distinction. Also, more work was needed to set forth the personhood of the Son and Spirit as distinct from the Father yet subsisting in the same identical nature. To complicate matters, the state began to play a greater role in theological disputes, as evidenced by the unfortunate seesaw struggle between emperors who affirmed either orthodoxy or some version of Arian theology.[1] During this time, the role of Athanasius and the three Cappadocian theologians was significant as they helped clarify and conceptualize Trinitarian orthodoxy, which paved the way for Constantinople and laid the foundation for the Council of Chalcedon (451) and its Christological formulation.

In order to set the stage for our discussion of the Council of Chalcedon, and to continue unpacking the ecclesiological warrant for orthodox Christology, let us reflect on this important era in three steps. First, we will describe three theological developments between Nicaea and Chalcedon that were foundational for Trinitarian and Christological orthodoxy. Second, we will outline

---

[1] For a discussion of the history, see Harold O. J. Brown, *Heresies: The Image of Christ in the Mirror of Heresy and Orthodoxy from the Apostles to the Present* (Garden City, NY: Doubleday, 1984), 118–144; Lewis Ayres, *Nicaea and Its Legacy: An Approach to Fourth-Century Trinitarian Theology* (Oxford: Oxford University Press, 2006), 1–130; David F. Wells, *The Person of Christ: A Biblical and Historical Analysis of the Incarnation* (Westchester, IL: Crossway, 1984), 95–97.

three false Christologies—all of which positively helped the church crystallize her thinking about Christ at Chalcedon. Third, we will turn to Chalcedon and unpack its significance for the emergence of orthodoxy as well as address some of the issues it left unresolved for further post-Chalcedonian Christological development.

FROM NICAEA TO CHALCEDON: CRUCIAL THEOLOGICAL DEVELOPMENTS

During this time, three theological developments occurred that catapulted the church forward in Trinitarian and Christological discussion. First, at the Synod of Alexandria (362), the church finally achieved terminological clarity in regard to the "nature-person" distinction. Second, the church clearly stated that the subject or *person* of the incarnation is God the Son living on earth as a man and *not* a man who is simply indwelt by the Son. Third, the church affirmed that the Son took to himself a human body *and* soul, thus insisting on a "Word-man" versus a "Word-flesh" Christology. Let us now develop each of these points in turn.

Developments in the "Nature-Person" Distinction

As heresy drove the church to greater linguistic and conceptual clarity, Athanasius and the Cappadocian theologians are often credited with achieving clarity in the "nature-person" distinction, even though Tertullian and others employed it more than a century earlier.

In regard to Athanasius (c. 295–373), it is an understatement to say that he was a central figure in the defense of pro-Nicene theology, specifically the deity of Christ.[2] Athanasius, the archbishop and patriarch of Alexandria, spent roughly one-third of his forty-five years as bishop in exile due to imperial opposition. His opponents viewed him as inflexible, intolerant, and a single-issue man, but in truth he was a hero of the faith. After he was appointed bishop of Alexandria in 328, he faced opposition on two main theological fronts: modalism and Arianism. Against Marcellus of Ancyra, who appealed to Nicaea to defend modalism due to terminological confusion between *hypostasis* and *ousia*, Athanasius argued for the *distinctness* of the Father from the Son, yet for the Son's full deity.[3] Against Arianism and its varieties, he argued for the full equality and deity of the Son with the Father. Unless the Son is truly God, Athanasius insisted, specific biblical teaching is false. For example, it would be false to affirm that the Son is the full revelation of God, that he does the divine work of redemption, that he is to be worshiped, and

---

[2] See Athanasius, *On the Incarnation of the Word* 1–57 (NPNF² 4:36–67); idem, *Four Discourses Against the Arians* 1–4 (NPNF² 4:306–447).
[3] See Robert Letham, *The Holy Trinity: In Scripture, History, Theology and Worship* (Phillipsburg, NJ: P&R, 2004), 122–145.

that we are united to him by faith. All of these truths are impossible if the Son is only a creature.

What is crucial to see in Athanasius's arguments, as Robert Letham notes, is how Athanasius moves from economic relations between the divine persons to eternal, immanent relations. Knowledge of the triune God and the salvation we receive, Athanasius insisted, comes through the Son, so that whatever is in the Father is in the Son and whatever the Father has, the Son has. Since the Father is not a creature, neither is the Son. Instead one must think of the Son as having no beginning and as being in eternal relation to the Father. Also, Athanasius conceived of the unity of the persons in terms of the Father, Son, and Spirit mutually indwelling each other, what later was called *perichoresis*.[4] In these ways, Athanasius provides the conceptual apparatus to help the church think of the oneness of the divine nature *and* the distinctions between the divine persons.[5] Letham states Athanasius's contribution this way: "His elaborations of the deity of the Son and the Spirit in the one being of God, and of the relations of the three in their mutual coinherence, were quantum advances in understanding and huge milestones on the path to a more accurate view of the Trinity,"[6] and thus of Christology.

Alongside Athanasius's contribution was the work of the three Cappadocian theologians, who helped establish further conceptual clarity in regard to the "nature-person" distinction: Basil of Caesarea (329–379), Gregory of Nazianzus (329–390), and Gregory of Nyssa (335–395). These men strongly affirmed *homoousios* by insisting on the full deity of the Son and the Spirit, including their eternal, personal distinctions from the Father. Along with Athanasius, their efforts helped the church to make the "nature-person" distinction by establishing two crucial points.[7]

First, they taught that God is *one* in "nature," a unity (not uniformity), who reveals himself as possessing a single will, a single activity, and a single glory. All three persons, Father, Son, and Spirit, subsist in the divine nature and possess the same divine attributes equally, not as three separate beings but as the one true and living God. When thinking of the divine nature, it does *not* belong to a general category to which each of the persons belong, parallel to how the human race is a species to which every individual human belongs. In the case of humans, "humanity" is not identical with any particular number

---

[4] Ibid., 139–144.
[5] On this point, see ibid., 144–145; cf. Thomas F. Torrance, *Trinitarian Perspectives: Toward Doctrinal Agreement* (Edinburgh: T&T Clark, 1994), 15; R. P. C. Hanson, *The Search for the Christian Doctrine of God: The Arian Controversy 318–381* (Edinburgh: T&T Clark, 1988), 444–445, 644–645. Athanasius, at the Council of Alexandria (362), argued that *ousia* and *hypostasis* could be used in different senses and thus it was possible to speak of three *hypostases* in the one nature (see Athanasius, *Synodal Letter to the People of Antioch 5–8* (NPNF² 4:484–485).
[6] Letham, *Holy Trinity*, 145.
[7] For a more detailed treatment of this discussion, see Brown, *Heresies*, 150–152; Letham, *Holy Trinity*, 146–166. Letham argues that Basil was the first to use *hypostasis* to denote the way in which God is three, yet strongly arguing that the Father, Son, and Spirit are inseparable in nature (Letham, *Holy Trinity*, 149).

of human beings, nor even with all humans in existence at any given time. In contrast, the divine nature, as Brown notes, "is identical with God, and subsists in and only in the three Persons. . . . The divine Persons are distinct, yet they cannot be separated from the godhead or from one another."[8] Thus, the Father, the Son, and the Spirit are identical in nature—they are one God. Or, as Letham summarizes, "It follows from this that the one identical divine being is shared by the Father, the Son, and the Holy Spirit. All three persons are of one substance (*consubstantial*). All three are of the identical being (*homoousios*). There is only one essence or being of God, which all three persons share completely."[9]

Second, this one God is a plurality, or better, a trinity of *hypostases* or "persons." Because God acts with a single will toward the created world, it is possible to observe their personal distinctions only by God's self-disclosure in Scripture and by their *external* or *economic* works (*opera ad extra*). In thinking about the divine persons' *internal* or *immanent* relations (*opera ad intra*), the Cappadocians employed the biblical vocabulary analogically and distinguished the *persons* (*hypostases*) of the Godhead by speaking of the *relations* between them and the *properties* of each person: ingenerateness (Father), begottenness or generation (Son), and procession (Spirit), all the while insisting that all three persons possess the same, identical nature and attributes.

Donald Fairbairn explains it this way: "The Son is begotten by the Father, and the Spirit proceeds from the Father. . . . That is to say, the relation between the Son and the Father is not identical to the relation between the Spirit and the Father, even though all three persons possess identical characteristics."[10] Thus, all three persons eternally possess the same attributes and subsist in the identical divine nature in communion and union, yet the Father, Son, and Spirit are distinguished from each other by their unique personal properties and relations one to another. Each of the persons are God-equal to each other, thus removing any hint of the subordinationism that had previously plagued the church, yet there is also an order (*taxis*) between the persons that is preserved in the expression "*from the Father through the Son by the Holy Spirit*"[11]—relations which cannot be reversed and which help distinguish the persons from each other.

On the basis of these conceptual distinctions, the church was able to give better theological clarity to the doctrine of the Trinity, as evidenced in the Council of Constantinople (381). This Council was the final conclusion of the Arian controversy, and it crowned the efforts of Athanasius and the three Cappadocian theologians by rejecting all forms of subordinationism (including

---

[8] Brown, *Heresies*, 146.
[9] Letham, *Holy Trinity*, 177.
[10] Donald Fairbairn, *Life in the Trinity: An Introduction to Theology with the Help of the Church Fathers* (Downers Grove, IL: IVP Academic, 2009), 53.
[11] Letham, *Holy Trinity*, 179.

Arianism) and modalism and by rewriting the Nicene Creed so that it included a "third article" about the Holy Spirit and the church. It stressed that God is one being, yet this one God consists eternally of three distinct persons. Each of the persons shares completely in the one identical divine nature and is thus of the same nature (*homoousios*), and each person is God in himself. Furthermore, in order to explain how such a numerical identity between three distinct persons was possible, the church built on the insights of Athanasius and the Cappadocians by reflecting on this wondrous mystery by taking its cue from John 14:10–11—"I am in the Father and the Father is in me"—i.e., the idea of *perichoresis* or "coinherence."[12] Within the one Godhead, the church argued, the three persons coinhere in each other, interpenetrate each other. Donald Macleod explains this idea well:

> Taken temporally, *perichoresis* means that the Father, Son, and Holy Spirit occupy and fill the same time (or the same eternity). Each is unoriginated (*agenētos*), endless and eternal. Taken spatially, it means that each person and all the persons together occupy and fill the same space. Each is omnipresent while remaining unconfused with the others. Each fills immensity. Beyond that, each contains the other; each dwells in the other; each penetrates the other, and each conditions the mode of the existence of the other. None, not even the Father, would be what he is without the others.[13]

The church has always admitted that attempting to explain the Trinity and specifically the unity of the intratrinitarian personal relations is difficult since in human experience no analogy to it exists. Some appeal to the marriage relationship, but even here it fails to deliver, since in God's existence, as Macleod notes, there are neither physical nor mental barriers to complete coinherence, since the divine persons possess the same nature. As God reveals himself and acts in the world, whether in creation, providence, or redemption, he reveals himself and acts as the one God. Yet the one God who reveals himself and acts in this world is triune. Since all three persons coinhere in a single nature, there is no action of one person that does not involve the action of the others, just as there is no relationship with the nature of God apart from a relationship with the persons. Yet, because the persons are distinct, even though the acts of the triune God are common to all three, each person does not act in the same way.[14]

---

[12] Greek, *enperichoresis*; Latin, *circumincessio* or *circuminsessio*. John of Damascus describes *perichoresis*: "The subsistences dwell and are established firmly in one another. For they are inseparable and cannot part from one another, but keep to their separate course within one another, without coalescing or mingling, but cleaving to each other. For the Son is in the Father and the Spirit: and the Spirit in the Father and the Son: and the Father in the Son and the Spirit, but without any coalescence or commingling or confusion. And there is one and the same motion: for there is one impulse and one motion of the three subsistences, which is not to be observed in any created nature" (John of Damascus, *An Exact Exposition of the Orthodox Faith* 1.14 [NPNF² 9:17b], in Donald Macleod, *The Person of Christ*. Contours of Christian Theology [Downers Grove, IL: InterVarsity Press, 1998], 141).

[13] Macleod, *Person of Christ*, 141.

[14] In Patristic thought, or better, pro-Nicene orthodoxy, this is called the doctrine of "inseparable operations." Because each person of the Godhead equally subsists in the divine nature thus constituting one God, Father, Son,

As Macleod states, "The triune God creates; but the Father creates as Father, the Son as Son (or *Logos*) and the Spirit as Spirit. Each works in his own proper way."[15] The same may be said for all of God's actions, especially redemption. The Father redeems as Father by sending his Son; the Son redeems by becoming incarnate, representing his people in his life and death, and substituting himself on the cross for our salvation; the Spirit redeems by applying the work of the Son to us, so that the entire triune Godhead receives all glory and praise.

Why is this discussion important for Christology? For this reason: it was not until the church achieved conceptual clarity on these matters that Christological development could proceed. After Constantinople, Trinitarian formulation was placed on a firmer footing than previously in church history. Once agreement occurred here, and especially in the crucial "nature-person" distinction, more detailed Christological reflection could occur. By this time, Arianism had been defeated, and no longer was Christ's deity in question. Now the church had to wrestle with *how* to relate the deity and humanity of Christ together, and *how* to conceive of the unity of Christ's person. Furthermore, it was during this time that the formal lines of debate were established so that even in later periods of church history, people still remain within these basic parameters. In fact, it seems that later centuries are merely adding periodic footnotes to the previous discussion and defending the earlier views from current denials of orthodoxy.

Thinking Clearly about the Subject (Person) of the Incarnation

Related to the Trinitarian discussion is the question of the subject of the incarnation. Given the "nature-person" distinction, we need to ask the question, *Who*, precisely, became incarnate? *Who* is the subject of the incarnation? Scripture is clear: "the *Word* became flesh" (John 1:14). It was the *person* of the Son *who* became incarnate. Two important points follow from this assertion.

First, in the incarnation it was *not* the divine nature that became flesh or assumed a human nature, as if "natures" are acting, personal subjects. Nor did the Father or the Spirit become flesh; instead it was God the Son, the second *person* of the Godhead, *who* became flesh. Prior to the incarnation, the Son from eternity, along with the Father and Spirit, equally shared, possessed, and

---

and Holy Spirit inseparably act as one (i.e., all three persons are involved in every divine act). Yet because the persons are distinct, each person acts *as* Father, Son, and Spirit, even though in that action the divine persons enact a single agency, which reflects the intratrinitarian *taxis* and relations of the persons within the divine life (*ad intra*). Thus, the work of the Father, Son, and Spirit are inseparably the work of the three *ad extra*, yet the divine persons act as one according to their personal relations *ad intra*. Keith Johnson states this doctrine via Augustine: "The Father acts with the other divine persons according to his mode of being 'from no one' (unbegotten). The Son acts with the other divine persons according to his mode of being 'from the Father' (generation). The Spirit acts with the other divine persons according to his mode of being 'from the Father and the Son' (procession) (Keith E. Johnson, *Rethinking the Trinity and Religious Pluralism: An Augustinian Assessment* [Downers Grove, IL: IVP Academic, 2011], 119).

[15] Macleod, *Person of Christ*, 142.

subsisted in the one divine nature and thus lived in perfect communion and love, mutually indwelling one another. It is for this reason that the Father, Son, and Spirit are fully and equally God, even though as persons they are irreducibly distinct, a fact demonstrated by the incarnation.

Second, to affirm that the subject of the incarnation is the *person* of the Son is *not* simply to say that the Son is one person who possesses two natures, as true as that statement is. Rather, it is to affirm that at the center of Christ's being is the person of the Son living on earth as a man. This affirmation is over against those in the early church who thought of Christ more as a man who was indwelt by God the Son.[16] The incarnation is the personal act of the divine Son who deliberately, voluntarily, and sacrificially chose to take on the form of a servant and make himself poor in obedience to his Father's will and for our salvation (Phil. 2:7; 2 Cor. 8:9).

In addition, we must also affirm that the Son continued to be who he had always been as God the Son. His identity did not change, nor did he change in ceasing to possess *all* the divine attributes *and* performing and exercising all his *divine* functions and prerogatives. Yet now, in taking a human nature into personal union, he is able to live a fully human life and enter into a whole new range of experiences and relationships. The Son, as the personal subject of the incarnation, is now able to experience life in a human body and in a human soul. He experiences human pain, human temptations, and even tastes death. Again, as Macleod notes, "Before and apart from the incarnation, God knew such things by observation. But observation, even when it is that of omniscience, falls short of personal experience. That is what the incarnation made possible for God: real, personal experience of being human."[17]

What this entails, then, is that the baby conceived by the Holy Spirit in Mary; who was born; who grew in wisdom, in stature, and in favor with God and men (Luke 2:52); was the same divine *person* who had eternally been the Son in relation to the Father and Spirit. The incarnate one was not simply a man in whom God dwelt, or even a man uniquely empowered by the Spirit of God. Instead, Jesus of Nazareth is God the Son living personally on earth and experiencing what it means to be human—for us and for our salvation. In fact, the church insisted on this because this is precisely what Scripture teaches and this is precisely the kind of Redeemer we need. We need a Savior who is a man to represent us; but more than this, we need the Lord to come and save. Salvation is of the Lord, and unless it is the Lord who comes, suffers, and dies

---

[16] Fairbairn argues this point in *Life in the Trinity*, 139–145; cf. Donald Fairbairn, "The One Person Who Is Jesus Christ: The Patristic Perspective," in *Jesus in Trinitarian Perspective: An Intermediate Christology*, ed. Fred Sanders and Klaus D. Issler (Nashville: B&H, 2007), 80–113. Some examples of those who taught this include Diodore of Tarsus, Theodore of Mopsuestia, and Nestorius. Nestorius was condemned at the Council of Ephesus (431), and Diodore and Theodore were condemned posthumously at the Council of Constantinople (553).
[17] Macleod, *Person of Christ*, 186.

on the cross, then his death would have no power or efficacy to accomplish our salvation. And the Son, as the second person of the Godhead, did this by taking a human nature with its entire range of capacities into his own divine person alongside the divine nature that he had eternally possessed. Fairbairn captures this emphasis with his statement that "the fundamental assertion of the early church was that the one person who is Jesus Christ is God the Son. It was God the Son as a person (not just the divine nature) who came down from heaven. It was God the Son as a person who united humanity to himself (not two natures united to make a new person)."[18]

What makes this possible is that the *person* of the Son, who possesses the divine nature, is able to act in and through both natures.[19] Prior to the incarnation, the Son acted in and through the divine nature (along with the Father and Spirit), but now, as a result of the personal action of the Son in obedience to his Father and by the agency of the Spirit, *he* is also able to act in and through his human nature. This understanding assumes that a "nature," whether divine or human, consists of attributes, characteristics, or capacities that make it what it is. But it also assumes that "natures" never exist by themselves; they always have a "person" in whom the nature resides. In the case of the incarnation, then, Fairbairn, along with the church, has drawn the following conclusion:

> God the Son—one of the three and only three persons who possessed the divine nature—added to his own person a complete human nature, a full complement of the characteristics and components that make one human. In this way, the same person—the second person of the Trinity—was both divine and human. He was divine because from all eternity he had possessed the divine nature. After the incarnation he was also human because he took upon himself "flesh," that is, all the characteristics that define one as a human being. Because this same person, whom we now call Jesus Christ, was both divine and human, he was able to live on two levels at the same time. He continued to live on the divine level as he had done from all eternity—sharing fellowship with the Father, maintaining the universe (see Col 1:17) and whatever else God does. But now he began to live on a human level at the same time—being conceived and born as a baby, growing up in Nazareth, learning Scripture as any other Jewish boy would, becoming hungry, thirsty and tired, and even dying.[20]

Obviously this affirmation raises a number of legitimate yet difficult questions regarding the incarnate Son, not least the coherency of it—something we will return to in Part IV. Throughout church history, whether it was Arianism or other heretical views, and especially since the Enlightenment, one of the ap-

---

[18] Fairbairn, *Life in the Trinity*, 143–144.
[19] See Gerald Bray, *God Has Spoken: A History of Christian Theology* (Wheaton, IL: Crossway, 2014), 320–322, 350–365; cf. Geerhardus Vos, *Christology*, vol. 3 of *Reformed Dogmatics*, trans. and ed. Richard B. Gaffin Jr. (Bellingham, WA: Lexham, 2014), 48–55.
[20] Fairbairn, *Life in the Trinity*, 140.

peals of non-orthodox Christologies has been their surface ability "to explain" areas of mystery. For example, in nineteenth-century kenoticism, much of its appeal is that it can "explain better" the psychology of the incarnate Son. Its "solution" was to deny that the experience-knowledge of the incarnate Son operated on two levels simultaneously. Instead it argued that the experience-knowledge of Jesus was merely human. The problem, however, is that this explanation surrendered the biblical teaching *and* the church's affirmation that the incarnate Son was able to live simultaneously a divine and human life due to his possessing two natures.

Later in the Reformation period, as we will discuss in chapter 9, the church's affirmation that the Son was able to live on two levels simultaneously became known as the *extra Calvinisticum*. As E. David Willis explains, "The so-called extra Calvinisticum teaches that the Eternal Son of God, even after the Incarnation, was united to the human nature to form One Person *but was not restricted to the flesh*."[21] But it is crucial to note, the *extra* was not new to Calvin; it was what the church had always affirmed, given that the subject of both natures was the *person* of the Son. That is why Willis rightly argues that Calvin's *extra* should be labeled the *extra Catholicum*,[22] since the church has always deemed it necessary to confess that, because the subject of the incarnation is God the Son, our Lord Jesus, even in the state of humiliation, continued to live, act, and experience as both God and man. The *person* who is able to do both of these things is the same before and after the incarnation, yet in obedience to his Father and in reliance upon the Spirit, the Son continued to exercise his divine prerogatives as the Father allowed and consistent with this messianic mission, while also living a fully human life as our new covenant head.

Understanding the Incarnation in a "Word-Man" versus "Word-Flesh" Framework

En route to Chalcedon, the church also had to wrestle with the nature of Christ's humanity. One of the unresolved questions from Nicaea was whether Christ had a human soul, and thus a complete human nature. While Tertullian and others had already insisted on the existence of Christ's soul, Arius denied its reality and argued for some kind of composite nature in Christ. Even staunch defenders of Nicene orthodoxy such as Athanasius were not completely clear on this point, at least prior to the church's rejection of Apollinarius's denial of Christ's human soul, at Constantinople in 381.[23] For example, in his refutation

---

[21] E. David Willis, *Calvin's Catholic Christology: The Function of the So-Called Extra Calvinisticum in Calvin's Theology* (Leiden: E. J. Brill, 1966), 1 (emphasis mine).
[22] Ibid., 153.
[23] See Aloys Grillmeier, *From the Apostolic Age to Chalcedon (451)*, vol. 1 in *Christ in Christian Tradition*, trans. John Bowden, 2nd rev. ed. (Atlanta: John Knox, 1975), 308–328; cf. Jean Galot, *Who Is Christ? A Theology of*

of Arianism, Athanasius makes no mention of Christ's human soul, and seems to think of the incarnation as the Son assuming a human body but not a soul. This is one of the reasons why he attributes the spiritual qualities of Christ to the *Logos*, whereas his passions are attributed to his body. After the Apollinarian controversy, however (see below), the church carefully insisted that the Son, in the incarnation, assumed a human body *and* soul.

In the early church, broadly speaking there were two ways of thinking about Christ's human nature: "Word (*Logos*)-man" versus "Word (*Logos*)-flesh." In the Arian debate and later with Apollinarius, the church insisted that a "Word-man" view was necessary to account for the biblical teaching. The need for a Word-man Christology was especially evident in the post-Chalcedonian discussion regarding the "will" issue, as represented by the church's insistence that the incarnate Son had two wills (*dyothelitism*, a Word-man view) over against the one will view (*monothelitism*, a Word-flesh view). We will return to this debate in chapter 9. At this juncture, we simply want to distinguish these different views and highlight their significance for the emergence of an orthodox Christology. However, before we do so, we need to dispel a common yet inaccurate way of linking these two views to the "schools" of Antioch and Alexandria.

For much of the twentieth century, many have identified the "Word-flesh" view with Alexandria and "Word-man" with Antioch. As the story goes, the Alexandria school focused more on Christ's deity and downplayed his humanity while the Antioch school emphasized Christ's complete humanity. This commonly accepted view also distinguished each school by their overall philosophical orientation, which, proponents argued, affected not only their Christology but also their exegesis of Scripture. Alexandria was more Platonic in orientation and thus favored allegorical exegesis, while Antioch was more Aristotelian in outlook and thus favored a literal reading of Scripture. Also, as the story goes, it was at Chalcedon that there was mediation between these two schools, so that the Chalcedonian Creed is best viewed as a *negative*, kind of compromise statement; it says nothing positively about Christ, only who he is *not*.[24]

The problem with this historical construction is its reductionism. Minimally it assumes the following points, all of which are disputed by current patristic scholarship: (1) these schools were uniform and well represented in the early church; (2) the Antiochenes took Scripture and Christ's humanity seriously

Incarnation (Chicago: Franciscan Herald, 1981), 230. Letham, *Holy Trinity*, 130–133, disputes this point, but see the helpful discussion in Bray, *God Has Spoken*, 325–329.

[24] This view is expressed, for example, in Roger E. Olson, *The Story of Christian Theology: Twenty Centuries of Tradition and Reform* (Downers Grove, IL: InterVarsity Press, 1999), 201–235.

while the Alexandrians did not; (3) the so-called schools' different Christologies were due to their different exegetical methods.

The truth of the matter is that the separation between these two traditions resulted, as Fairbairn contends, "from different ways of refuting the theological challenge of Arianism, which argued that since God the Son suffered and died, he must have been passible and therefore less than the Father."[25] In response, the "Antiochenes" argued that the one who suffered and died was not God the Son, and thus they could still affirm that God the Son was impassible and equal to the Father. But, as Fairbairn notes, "This led them to a Christology that divided the Logos from the man Jesus and understood salvation as a human march, following Jesus, from what Theodore called the first age (one of imperfection and mortality) to the second age (one of perfect *human* life)."[26] It was for this reason that the "Antiochenes" tended to read the Old Testament in a more literal way, but it was their overall theology that produced this kind of interpretation, not any particular desire to take history more seriously.[27]

By contrast, the Alexandrian view refuted Arianism by affirming that it was the *person* of God the Son who suffered, but that he suffered in his human nature, not in his divine nature, thus employing the crucial "nature-person" distinction. This led them to a different Christology, which, it is important to note, is the orthodox view of the church, namely, that God the Son was the active subject at every point in our salvation (in relation with the Father and Spirit)—in his incarnation, life, death, resurrection, ascension, and so on. Thus, Alexandrian exegesis of texts describing Christ, as Fairbairn notes, "ascribed all of his actions and experiences to the Logos himself, but divided between what the Logos did that was in keeping with his divine nature, and what he did that was in keeping with his newly adopted human way of living. Antiochenes (especially Nestorius) dealt with the same passages by ascribing some actions to the Logos and others to the man Jesus."[28] The upshot is this: differences among these "schools" have more to do with different theologies about Christ and salvation in their response to Arianism than with different emphases in exegesis.

If we follow this historical correction, then what results? It is this: we must *not* think of two different, well-developed "schools," but rather we must think of two different approaches to theology, salvation, and Christology. If we think of "Antiochene" thinkers—primarily three main individuals, Diodore of

---

[25] Donald Fairbairn, "Patristic Exegesis and Theology: The Cart and the Horse," *WTJ* 69/1 (2007): 10.

[26] Ibid. Fairbairn argues that, behind the "Antiochene" approach, specifically that of Nestorius and Theodore of Mopsuestia, was a different view of salvation, what he labels a "two ages" view. In contrast, orthodoxy understands human history in terms of creation, fall, and redemption, what he labels a "three ages" view (idem, "One Person Who Is Jesus Christ," 92–96).

[27] See Fairbairn, "Patristic Exegesis and Theology," 10–14.

[28] Ibid., 11.

Tarsus, Theodore of Mopsuestia, and Nestorius (who were all condemned by the church)—we must view their Christology as non-orthodox. As Fairbairn notes, all three of these thinkers "viewed Christ divisively (and thus placed their emphasis on the assumed man, rather than on the divine Logos)."[29] So, in our discussion of Word-man versus Word-flesh, we will not link these views to different schools; instead we will link them to the central issue of the nature of Christ's humanity. With this caveat in place, let us now describe these two approaches.

What, then, is a "Word-flesh" view and its implications for understanding Christ's humanity? The view is this: in the incarnation, the Son (*Logos*) replaces the human soul and enters into a union with the human body so as to form a human being, but, it is crucial to note, what is lost is the full humanity of Christ.[30] Why so? Because normally the church identified with the human soul an entire human psychology that includes within it reason, will, intellect, emotions, etc. But without a human soul in Christ, or even a replacement of it by the Son, a Word-flesh view undercuts Christ's full humanity and has difficulty accounting for how the incarnate Son could experience the whole range of human experiences and relationships and, most significantly, act as our Redeemer. In addition, Word-flesh approaches tended either to endorse one-nature views of Christ (*monophysitism*), or some kind of blended nature, instead of two natures.[31]

By contrast, a "Word-man" view insists that in the incarnation the divine Son assumed a complete human nature—body *and* soul—and thus a complete human psychology, including the entire activity of knowing and willing. Building on the "nature-person" distinction, this view maintained that the *person* is the subject of his nature who acts in and through his nature. In terms of Christology, then, the *person* of the Son, given that he has assumed a full human nature, is now able to live a fully human life, alongside how he has always lived in relation to the Father and Spirit. But to live a human life the Son needed more

---

[29] Ibid., 14.

[30] See Grillmeier, *From the Apostolic Age to Chalcedon (451)*, 247. This view did not operate with a clear "nature-person" distinction. It tended to think of God as a *personal nature*, thereby attributing the linking process between the Word and the humanity of Christ to the *nature* of the Logos as much as to his *person*, which was only the manifestation of that nature. This is why "Word-flesh" views tend toward one-nature views, nature being understood as "self-determining being." In the incarnation, the Son assumed manhood and united it to himself, without in any way changing as a result. The process of union in one nature through incarnation did not destroy Jesus's deity or humanity, which were held together by a *transfer of attributes* from the former to the latter. This device was used to explain the miracles of Jesus, which appeared to attribute superhuman powers to his body. Jesus walked on water because his divine nature expressed itself in his flesh, etc. The problem, however, with such a view is that it could not account for the full humanity of the incarnate Son. How could Jesus have been thirsty on the cross? How could he not know certain things? The "Word-flesh" view had only inadequate answers to these questions since they attributed the weakness/ignorance of Jesus to the Logos accommodating himself to our fleshly limits.

[31] For example, Apollinarius affirmed a "single nature" (*mia physis*) in Christ, as did monophysitism. In both views, the Word assumes a body, and the unity that results is parallel to the body-soul unity in us. As Galot rightly notes in regard to Apollinarius, "The unity is so complete that it is impossible to distinguish the properties of each by relating some of them to the flesh and the others to the Word," hence a single nature (Galot, *Who Is Christ?*, 232).

than a mere body or flesh; he also needed a human soul in order to will, act, and experience *as a man*.

As the church traveled the road to Chalcedon, her understanding of Christ's humanity became more precise by embracing a "Word-man" view. Scripture clearly insists on Christ's full humanity, and the church knew that she could not account for this teaching unless a Word-man view was embraced. Ultimately, the church knew that what was at stake was salvation. If the Son did not personally assume our full human nature and live and die in our place as the *man* Christ Jesus, how could he redeem us? In addition, as the Word-man view stressed, it was not enough for Christ to have one nature or two incomplete natures; *he*, as the divine Son, needed *two natures*, thus explaining how he is fully God and fully man simultaneously.

With these theological developments in place, let us now turn to three heresies that arose in the years between Nicaea and Chalcedon, which resulted in further Christological clarity. In the church's response to these heresies we discover once again the "positive" side of heresy: greater clarity and precision in the church's wrestling with the wonder and glory of the incarnation.

From Nicaea to Chalcedon: False Christological Paths

After the establishment of Trinitarian orthodoxy, further Christological clarity resulted which eventually led to the Chalcedonian Definition. Specifically, greater precision was achieved in the "nature-person" distinction, the nature of Christ's humanity, and the unity of his person as three false views regarding Christ were rejected. Let us think through this development by first seeing what the church rejected before we turn to the positive formulation of Chalcedon.

Apollinarianism

Apollinarianism is the view attributed to Apollinarius, bishop in Laodicea (315–392), who was a staunch defender of the deity of Christ and Nicene orthodoxy. He was a very good friend of Athanasius, but given his aberrant Christological views, specifically in his understanding of Christ's human nature, Athanasius and the three Cappadocian theologians later opposed him. His view was rejected by several church councils, including the Synod of Alexandria (362) and most significantly the Council of Constantinople (381).

Apollinarius's view represented a classic "Word-flesh" understanding of the incarnation. He affirmed that God the Son was consubstantial with God the Father, thus fully God, yet in the incarnation the Son took to himself an *incomplete* human nature, i.e., a human body ("flesh") but *not* a human soul.[32] He

---

[32] Technically, Apollinarius was a trichotomist, who affirmed that human beings were comprised of body, soul, and spirit, over against dichotomists, who affirm only a body and soul. In the incarnation, the divine Logos displaced

sought to avoid the idea that the incarnation was a mere "God dwelling in man." Instead, as Grillmeier notes, for Apollinarius the incarnation "only comes about if divine pneuma and earthly sarx together form a substantial unity in such a way that the man in Christ first becomes man through the union of these two components."[33] In other words, in Christ there is a substantial union of one heavenly element (Logos) and one earthly element (human body). To be sure, the "parts" of the God-man Christ are not equivalent. As Grillmeier explains, "The divine pneuma maintains its preeminence throughout. It becomes the life-giving spirit, the effectual mover of the fleshly nature, and together the two form a unity of life and being"[34] with the divine pneuma, or Logos, that which directs and energizes the flesh, similar to the Form-matter scheme of Aristotle.[35]

The end result is that Christ has one nature (*mia physis*), not two—a composite union, a "living unity"[36] of the divine Logos and human flesh which forms the self-determining individual we know as Jesus of Nazareth. For Apollinarius, given this composite unity and "one-nature" view of the incarnation, in Christ there is a real exchange of attributes (*communicatio idiomatum*), i.e., some kind of blend of deity and humanity so that Christ is "fully God and fully man" *not* in a two-nature sense with the person of the Son subsisting in both natures, but in a composite, one-nature sense, or what Grillmeier labels a "natural unity."[37]

Primarily on soteriological grounds, the church strongly rejected this view: Christ cannot represent and redeem us if he does not assume a complete human nature. Gregory of Nazianzus stated the church's position well in his famous statement, "What is not assumed is not healed."[38] For Christ to serve as our representative covenantal head and substitute, he *must* assume a complete human nature—body *and* soul—otherwise our redemption is incomplete.[39] In

the human spirit (*nous, pneuma*). So while Christ was fully God, he lacked a "complete" human nature such as we have. Apollinarius held to a very literal interpretation of John 1:14—"the Word became flesh"—meaning that the Logos assumed a human body *alone*. A major implication of his view is that Christ's human nature does not have a human will or mind, a view similar to later monothelitism ("one will"), which also was rejected by the church.

[33] Grillmeier, *From the Apostolic Age to Chalcedon (451)*, 331.

[34] Ibid., 333. Brown makes the same observation (see Brown, *Heresies*, 164). The human body of Christ was not preexistent; it came to exist at the moment of conception, but in the incarnation the flesh of Christ was deified in consequence of the energizing effect of the Logos. As Brown comments, "Christ, like all other humans, was a body of flesh animated and formed by a nous, but with the significant difference that the Nous of Christ was not a human spirit but the divine Logos" (ibid.).

[35] Brown makes this point (ibid., 163–164). Apollinarius equated the biblical concept of flesh with the Aristotelian view of matter, and the biblical concept of spirit with the Aristotelian view of form. It is the spiritual form that animates and gives true character to the matter, and this is done in humans by the human intellect or *nous*, but in Christ it is done by the Logos himself. That is why in the incarnation the Logos became flesh, but not a man like ourselves, since he did not take on a human intellect or *nous*.

[36] Grillmeier, *From the Apostolic Age to Chalcedon (451)*, 336.

[37] Ibid., 338.

[38] Gregory of Nazianzus, "To Cledonius the Priest against Apollinarius," in *Christology of the Later Fathers*, ed. Edward R. Hardy (Philadelphia: Westminster, 1954), 218.

[39] For example, the argument of Hebrews 2:5–18 makes this point: in order for Christ to act as our new covenant head and as our great High Priest, he must be fully human and fully God. Later in the medieval era, Anselm (1033–1109) develops this important theological point in his famous *Cur Deus Homo* (Why the God-Man?).

rejecting this view, the church drew a line in the sand: a proper Christology is necessary for soteriology, and to have a Redeemer who actually redeems, he must be fully God *and* fully man.

Furthermore, in the church's rejection of Apollinarianism three important issues resurfaced. First, as the church carefully distinguished "person" and "nature" in Trinitarian theology, she also had to do so in Christology and contend for two natures in Christ, not one. Second, the church rejected "Word-flesh" Christologies as inadequate, thus affirming the reality of Christ's human soul, which includes in it a human will, mind, and psychology.[40] Third, the church insisted that the unified active subject (person) of Christ is the divine Son who added to himself a complete humanity, and thus the person is *not* a composite union constructed by the combination of Logos and human flesh, nor is it, as Nestorius would later contend, a conjunction or union of two personal beings. Instead, the active subject is the eternal Son who assumed a human nature with all of its capacities, thus allowing *him* to live a fully human and divine life.

Nestorianism

Nestorianism is identified with Nestorius (381–451), the Archbishop of Constantinople (428–431), who was condemned at the Council of Ephesus (431). There is a legitimate debate about whether Nestorius himself was Nestorian, and there is no doubt that the debate between Nestorius and Cyril of Alexandria, who brought the charges against him, was very heated. In what follows, we will assume that Nestorius held to what is called Nestorianism.[41]

Nestorianism is often identified with a "Word-man" approach to Christology, yet it flounders on the question of the unity of Christ's person. Nestorius's concern, following his teacher, Theodore of Mopsuestia, was to emphasize the full humanity of Christ, contra Apollinarius, and thus the full deity and humanity of Christ in two natures. Yet in stressing Christ's two natures, he left unexplained Christ's "person" and how the two natures are unified in him. In speaking of the union of "person" (*prosopon*), he conceived of it as a composite union, but not a composite in the way Apollinarius taught, namely the combining of divine and human natures to create the *prosopon* of Christ. Instead, as Fairbairn explains, Nestorius viewed it as a composite union which consisted of "the conjoining or uniting of two personal subjects

---

[40] On this point, Demetrios Bathrellos rightly notes that what Apollinarius excluded from the humanity of Christ "was a rational soul as the centre of thought and willing activity," and thus, similar to some contemporary Christologies, he "came very close to identifying human hypostasis with human mind" (Demetrios Bathrellos, *The Byzantine Christ: Person, Nature, and Will in the Christology of Saint Maximus the Confessor* [Oxford: Oxford University Press, 2004], 11).

[41] For a helpful and nuanced discussion of Nestorius, see Bray, *God Has Spoken*, 329–350.

(the Logos and the man) so that they can be called a single *prosopon*,[42] thus the charge of teaching *two* persons in Christ.

Fred Sanders captures Nestorius's view of Christ's "person" in this way: "The one person who is Jesus Christ seems to be, for Nestorianism, the result of the incarnation or a way of talking about what these two vastly different entities, God the Son and the man Jesus, are doing together."[43] Thus there is a personal union in Christ but it is a personal union of a composite nature with the accent placed on the personal subject of Christ *as the assumed man*. Fairbairn illustrates Nestorius's view by comparing it to a firm composed of two partners, one of whom is never actually seen but whose influence is continually felt in all the firm's decisions. The visible partner is analogous to the man Jesus, yet the Logos is the one who stands behind him. Words such as "Christ," "Son," and "Lord," "refer to the corporate unity created by the cooperation between the two. The unity is a semantic one because the one name 'Christ' signifies the pair of partners, but the actual personal centre of Christ's being, in this understanding, is the man Jesus himself."[44] Nestorius, then, expresses the unity in Christ, but only in an external appearance sense. That is why the "person of the union," as Bathrellos notes, "signified merely an external unity between the divine and human in Christ."[45]

Behind Nestorius's view, along with his teacher, Theodore, is a different conception of salvation and grace.[46] Fairbairn characterizes their view of salvation as a two-act dispensational scheme: humanity's natural condition was one of mortality, mutability, and imperfection (first act or stage) and salvation is the movement toward a radically different state of immortality, incorruption, and perfection (second act or stage). In describing the first act, Theodore, for example, is unclear as to whether it is the result of a historic fall in which, in Adam, we fell from a morally good condition. He seems to assume that this stage is the state of humanity from the beginning. If so, then, salvation is not a restoration of fallen humanity to its original condition, but "rather the elevation of humanity to an entirely new condition."[47] Also, in such a view of salvation, God's grace is viewed as cooperative, enabling humans to reach the second stage with Christ serving as the supreme example of God's grace at work in him. Christ's life is the first life which passes from the first to the second stage, and as a result, his fulfillment of the Mosaic law "acquitted us of the

[42] Donald Fairbairn, *Grace and Christology in the Early Church*, Oxford Early Christian Studies (Oxford: Oxford University Press, 2003), 21.

[43] Fred Sanders, "Chalcedonian Categories for the Gospel Narrative," in *Jesus in Trinitarian Perspective*, ed. Fred Sanders and Klaus D. Issler (Nashville: B&H, 2007), 21.

[44] Fairbairn, *Grace and Christology*, 23.

[45] Bathrellos, *Byzantine Christ*, 19.

[46] In the following, I am indebted to the exposition of Fairbairn, *Grace and Christology*, 28–62; idem, "One Person Who Is Jesus Christ," 80–113.

[47] Fairbairn, "One Person Who Is Jesus Christ," 93; idem, *Grace and Christology*, 32–34.

debt of the lawgiver, his baptism gave us a model of the grace of our baptism, his obedience was a perfect model of the life of the gospel, and his crucifixion and resurrection destroyed the ultimate enemy (death) and showed us the new, immortal life."[48] In this way, in the language of Hebrews 2:10, Christ is the *archēgos* ("pioneer" and "trailblazer"), who crosses to the second stage, and who opens up salvation for us.[49]

It is for this reason, along with the conviction that the Logos could not suffer or die, that Theodore and Nestorius place a huge emphasis on Christ's humanity and thus clearly distinguish his deity and humanity. For Nestorius, the Logos did not participate in the human events of Christ's life.[50] The sharp distinction between deity and humanity in Christ leads Theodore and Nestorius to treat Jesus's humanity as if it were an independent man or subject,[51] and as if the role of the Logos were in terms of his co-operation with the actions of the assumed man.[52]

No doubt, Theodore and Nestorius affirm that Christ is utterly unique: God's indwelling in him was not exactly the same as his indwelling in us.[53] Jesus received grace and indwelling in a complete sense since he was fully united with the Logos and, as Fairbairn notes, "he has received such divine co-operation and power that God can be said to have accomplished all things through him, and after his resurrection from the dead, he has received honour equal to that of God the Logos. He is both the supreme example of grace and a unique case of grace."[54] Yet in the incarnation the stress is on the *assumed man*, and the union is explained more in terms of the indwelling of the Logos, so that the single *prosopon* in Christ is a "way of referring to the co-operative unity between the Logos and the assumed man by using titles that apply to both."[55] As Fairbairn concludes, this way of viewing Christ entails that "One cannot conclude that he [Nestorius] sees the single personal subject in Christ as being the Logos."[56] In fact, it is precisely on this point that Cyril and the later Chalcedonian Definition stand in direct conflict with Nestorius. For orthodoxy, the personal subject in Christ is the eternal Son, but for Nestorius it is some kind of composite.[57]

This partly explains Nestorius's use of the term *Christotokos* ("Christ-bearer") instead of Cyril's (and Chalcedon's) use of *Theotokos* ("God-bearer") in reference to Mary. Given the Logos's transcendence, Christ's two natures,

---

[48] Fairbairn, *Grace and Christology*, 44.
[49] See ibid., 44–45.
[50] See ibid., 53–54.
[51] See ibid., 42; cf. ibid., 54–55.
[52] See ibid., 43.
[53] See ibid., 46–48.
[54] Ibid., 48.
[55] Ibid., 58.
[56] Ibid.
[57] See ibid., 58–59.

and most importantly, that the personal subject in Christ is a composite union of two personal subjects (the Logos and man) and not solely the divine Son, Nestorius rejected the term *Theotokos*. For Nestorius, Mary bears only Christ's humanity with its own *prosopon*, and since the Logos as God is distinct from the man, *Theotokos* must be rejected. Cyril (d. 444), on the other hand, insisted on *Theotokos*, because he was concerned to preserve the *unity* of Christ's person *and*, along with orthodoxy, to view the single personal subject in Christ as the eternal Son, not a composite union of two personal subjects. Because the personal subject of both natures is the Son; because neither nature expresses itself except in union with the Son as each nature's active subject; and because anything said of one of his natures can be said about him as the Son, it is necessary to say that Mary is the "God-bearer" in the sense that Jesus, who was born of Mary, is the incarnate Son and not just a human being indwelt by the Logos. *Theotokos*, then, was not really a statement about Mary; instead it underscored Christ's deity *and* the fact that the personal subject of Christ is the eternal Son who now subsists in two natures.[58]

This debate also entailed further conclusions that separated orthodoxy from Nestorianism. For example, in regard to the question of whether God can suffer, both Cyril and Nestorius agreed that God was impassible. In contrast to Theodore and Nestorius, however, Cyril affirmed that God the Son, as the active subject of the human nature, is able to live a fully human life and thus experience in that human nature suffering and death. In Cyril's famous words, Christ "suffered impassibly," or to be more precise, the Son impassibly made his own the sufferings of his own human nature. Cyril was not saying that there was any change or diminution of Christ's divine nature, since in the incarnation the Son assumed a complete human nature *in addition to* his divine nature, but it did entail that the Son is now able to live a divine and human life.

The church's rejection of Theodore and Nestorius's Christology was often nasty, as evidenced in the Cyril-Nestorius polemics, but it was necessary. Ultimately at stake were two crucial issues. First, the unity of Christ's person. Nestorius simply could not explain it and instead appealed to a composite union of two personal subjects (the Logos and the man), but Scripture does not say that Christ's human nature is an independent person acting in some relation to the divine Logos. Instead, Scripture draws a consistent picture of a *single* person, the divine Son, acting as a unified subject now in two natures, a point that Chalcedon will strongly confess. In fact, it is only when we affirm

---

[58] Though theologically correct, the use of *theotokos* today is problematic. Theologically, it is correct that the person who was born of Mary was the Son of God. But Macleod rightly asks whether it is kerygmatically proper (Donald Macleod, "The Christology of Chalcedon," in *The Only Hope Jesus: Yesterday, Today, Forever*, ed. Mark Elliott and John McPake [Fearn: Christian Focus, 2001], 86–87). This is especially pertinent since many in church history have distorted the term to ask more about Mary as the "mother of God" than about Jesus as the "Son of God."

this critical point that we can avoid any hint of "adoptionism"—something Nestorius had a difficult time avoiding.

Also at stake was the vital relation between Christology and soteriology. Ultimately the Nestorian debate was over competing views of Christ *and* salvation. In sharp contrast to Theodore and Nestorius's two ages understanding, Scripture affirms a creation, fall, redemption structure, as we discussed in Part II, chapter 3. In regard to salvation, this requires more than a uniquely graced man who serves as humanity's example and trailblazer; it requires one who is *God* the Son. The human problem is a serious one: we stand condemned before the holy God of the universe, and the only solution to our peril is if *God himself* acts to save, in order to satisfy *his own* righteous requirements. Scripture is clear: the triune God must save, and he alone can do it. Salvation is God's work, and it is only God the Son incarnate who can redeem us. We do not need merely a man indwelt by and/or joined in some kind of union with God the Son; what we need is the divine Son assuming our human nature into his own person so that *he* can represent us and act on our behalf as our new covenant head and substitute.

Monophysitism

Monophysitism is identified with Eutyches (380–456), a presbyter and leader of a monastery at Constantinople, who was condemned at Chalcedon in 451. Eutyches taught that as a result of the incarnation Christ's human nature was taken up, absorbed, and merged into the divine nature, so that both natures were changed into one new nature—a nature which now was a kind of divine-human composite. This view is also called *monophysitism*—that the incarnate Christ had one (*monos*) nature (*physis*), not two.

Eutyches's view was basically a version of a "Word-flesh" Christology. As Sanders points out, for Eutyches, the mixing of the two natures "does not produce a third substance equally identifiable as divine and human. Because divinity is infinitely larger than humanity, the result of the Eutychian mixing of natures is not an even compound but a mostly divine Christ."[59] Even though this view is different from Apollinarianism, the result is similar: in this "new" nature we have an overpowering divinity and a submerged humanity. Probably more consistently, later monophysites insisted that the union of two natures resulted in a *tertium quid* which was neither divine nor human, but the result of every form of monophysitism is that Christ is neither truly God nor truly man—a view contrary to Scripture and leaving us with a Jesus who cannot redeem.

---

[59] Sanders, "Chalcedonian Categories for the Gospel Narrative," 22; cf. Macleod, *Person of Christ*, 184. For Eutyches, the deity of Christ completely absorbs his humanity as a result of the incarnation.

The Council of Chalcedon (451): Christological Orthodoxy

In October 451, 520 bishops gathered at Chalcedon to wrestle with the ongoing Christological disputes within the church. Most of the church's bishops were from the East, while only four came from the West—two from North Africa and two who were legates of Pope Leo of Rome. Yet, Western influence was great, due to Leo's *Tome*—a letter which was written prior to the Council and which would be incorporated into the Chalcedonian Creed.[60] As with the earlier Nicene Creed, the Chalcedon Definition remained a center of controversy for many decades, but it was never set aside and, as Brown notes, it became "the second great high-water mark of early Christian theology: it set an imperishable standard for orthodoxy"[61] as it confessed the deity and humanity of Christ in the classic formulation of "two natures, one person." As such, it rejected all previous false Christological views and presented a positive understanding of Christ's identity. In a series of statements it clearly distinguished "nature" from "person." In regard to "person" it asserted that the active subject of the incarnation, "the one and the same Christ," is none other than the eternal Son, who is consubstantial with the Father and the Spirit but who has now assumed a complete human nature so that *he* now subsists in two natures—natures that are *not* confused or changed but retain all of their attributes.

The Creed of Chalcedon

The Chalcedonian Definition states,

> In agreement, therefore, with the holy fathers, we all unanimously teach that we should confess that our Lord Jesus Christ is one and the same Son, the same perfect in Godhead and the same perfect in manhood, truly God and truly man, the same of a rational soul and body, consubstantial with the Father in Godhead, and the same consubstantial with us in manhood, like us in all things except sin; begotten from the Father before the ages as regards His Godhead, and in the last days, the same, because of us and because of our salvation begotten from the Virgin Mary, the *Theotokos*, as regards His manhood; one and the same Christ, Son, Lord, only-begotten, made known in two natures without confusion, without change, without division, without separation, the difference of the natures being by no means removed because of the union, but the property of each nature being preserved and coalescing in one *prosopon* and one *hupostasis*—not parted or divided into two *prosopa*, but one and the same Son, only-begotten, divine Word, the Lord Jesus Christ, as the prophets of old and Jesus Christ Himself have taught us about Him and the creed of our fathers has handed down.[62]

---

[60] For a discussion of the events surrounding Chalcedon and its theology, see Grillmeier, *From the Apostolic Age to Chalcedon (451)*, 520–557; Bray, *God Has Spoken*, 350–365.

[61] Brown, *Heresies*, 181.

[62] Cited from J. N. D. Kelly, *Early Christian Doctrines*, 5th rev. ed. (London: A & C Black, 1977), 339–340.

Chalcedon's Significance and Its Key Christological Points

Why is Chalcedon important? For this reason: it sought to summarize and address every problem that had plagued the church in regard to Christ's identity.[63] It sought to curb speculation, to clarify the use of language between East and West, and as such, it acts as a definitive statement and road map for all later Christological reflection. It argued against:

docetism: the Lord Jesus was perfect in manness, truly man, consubstantial (homoousion) with us according to his manness, and born of Mary

adoptionism: it argued for the personal subsistence of the Logos "begotten of the Father before the ages"

modalism: it distinguished the Son from the Father both by the titles of "Father" and "Son" and by its reference to the Father having begotten the Son before the ages

Arianism: it affirmed that the Lord Jesus was perfect in deity, truly God

Apollinarianism: it confessed that the Lord Jesus was "truly man of a reasonable soul and body; . . . consubstantial with us according to his manhood; in all things like unto us"

Nestorianism: it affirmed Mary as theotokos, not in order to exalt Mary but in order to affirm Jesus's true deity and the fact of a real incarnation (it also spoke throughout of one and the same Son and one person and one subsistence, not parted or divided into two persons, and whose natures are in union without division and without separation)

monophysitism: it confessed that in Christ there were two natures without confusion and without change, the property of each nature being preserved and concurring in the one person

Five points capture the heart of the Definition. First, Christ was truly and perfectly God and man. Both the deity of Christ and his humanity are equally preserved and emphasized in order for him to serve as our great High Priest and mediator and to win salvation for us.[64]

Second, "person" and hypostasis are viewed as the same thing. In so doing, Chalcedon provides a clearer distinction between "person" and "nature." Person is seen as a principle in its own right, not deducible from nature, or as a third element from the union of the two natures.[65] A new person does not come into existence when the human nature is assumed, nor does it result in two persons. Instead, Chalcedon affirms that the person of the incarnation is the

---

[63] See Galot, Who Is Christ?, 243–244.

[64] On this point, see Grillmeier, From the Apostolic Age to Chalcedon (451), 547.

[65] This conclusion about the Chalcedonian Definition needs to be nuanced. Chalcedon is still slightly ambiguous on this point. Given Chalcedon's indebtedness to Cyril of Alexandria, the Definition understood the personal unity of Christ to be identified with the person of the Son. However, as Grillmeier notes, Chalcedon applies the word hypostasis "not to the one Logos-subject" but "to the final form of him who had assumed flesh," thus leading to the question of whether hypostasis is used to denote the divine person of the Son or the end-product of the union (Aloys Grillmeier, From the Council of Chalcedon [451] to Gregory the Great [590–604], vol. 2, part 1 in Christ in Christian Tradition, trans. Pauline Allen and John Cawte (Louisville: Westminster John Knox, 1995), 277). This point of contention would be further clarified at Constantinople in 553, where it is the former which is affirmed.

eternal Son, the second person of the Godhead. Furthermore, it is a *person*, not a nature, who becomes flesh, and that is why the incarnation is a personal act of the Son, who took "the form of a servant" (Phil. 2:7) in a deliberate, voluntary, and sacrificial way.[66] It is the *person* of the Son who is the *one* acting agent and suffering subject. Does this imply change in the Son? Not in the sense that the person of the Son changed his identity or ceased to be what he always was. Even as the incarnate Son, he continued to possess all the divine attributes and to perform all his divine functions and prerogatives. Nevertheless, again, as Macleod rightly notes,

> [T]here is real change: change in the sense that in Christ God enters upon a whole new range of experiences and relationships. He experiences life in a human body and in a human soul. He experiences human pain and human temptations. He suffers poverty and loneliness and humiliation. He tastes death. . . . Before and apart from the incarnation, God knew such things by observation. But observation, even when it is that of omniscience, falls short of personal experience. That is what the incarnation made possible for God: real, personal experience of being human.[67]

Third, Christ's human nature did not have a *hypostasis/person* of its own (*anhypostasia*), which entails that Jesus would not have existed had the Son not entered the womb of Mary.[68] There was no "man" apart from this divine action, but as a result of this action, the Son, who possessed the divine nature from all eternity, now adds to himself a human nature with a full set of human attributes which allows him to live a fully human life, yet he is not completely limited or circumscribed by his human nature. This is why, as Fairbairn reminds us, the fathers of the church spoke of God the Son doing some things qua *God* and doing other things qua *man*. "The same person did things that were appropriate for humanity and other things that were appropriate, or even possible, only for God. But the person who did these things was the same, God the Son."[69] Thus, Jesus is far more than a man who is merely indwelt by God the Son; he is God the Son living on earth as a man, accomplishing our redemption as the Lord.

One of the entailments of Chalcedon, which certainly is true to Scripture, is that whenever we look at the life of Christ and ask, *Who* did this? *Who* said this? *Who* suffered death for us? the answer is always the same: God the Son. Why? Because it is not the divine or human nature which acts and thus does things; rather it is the *person* of the Son acting in and through his divine and

---

[66] See Macleod, *Person of Christ*, 185–186.
[67] Ibid., 186.
[68] In chapter 9, we will discuss how *anhypostasis* was better understood as *enhypostasia*.
[69] Fairbairn, *Life in the Trinity*, 140. Bray states it this way: "In the incarnate Christ, the divine *hypostasis* controlled each of its two natures (*physeis*), giving the person of the incarnate Son the freedom to employ them as he chose without being constrained by either of them" (Gerald Bray, *God Is Love: A Biblical and Systematic Theology* [Wheaton, IL: Crossway, 2012], 129).

human natures. It is the *Son* who was born, baptized, tempted, transfigured, betrayed, arrested, condemned, and who died. It was the *Son* who shed his blood for us to secure our salvation. It is in the *Son* that all of God's righteous demands are met so that our salvation is ultimately of God. It is the *Son* who also rose from the dead and who now reigns as King of kings and Lord of lords. Once again, Macleod beautifully captures this truth:

> In him [the Son], God provides and even becomes the atonement which he demands. In him (in his flesh, within the finitude of his life-time, the finitude of his body and the finitude of his human being) God dealt with our sin. He is a man: yet the man of universal significance, not because his humanity is in any sense infinite but because it is the humanity of God. . . . In him, God lives a truly human existence.[70]

Fourth, there is no union of the natures that obscures the integrity of either nature. Within God the Son incarnate the Creator-creature distinction is preserved; there is no blend of natures, or "transfer of attributes" (*communicatio idiomatum*) producing some kind of *tertium quid*. Yet, this does not entail that the two natures are merely juxtaposed, lying side by side without contact or interaction. Instead, there is a "transfer of attributes" in the sense that the attributes of both natures coexist in the one person. This is why Scripture can say that God the Son incarnate can simultaneously uphold the universe (Col. 1:17), forgive sin (Mark 2:10), become hungry and thirsty, grow in wisdom and knowledge (Luke 2:52), and even die. This is why the Son, as the subject of the incarnation, in all of his acts and experiences involves both natures, each in its own distinctive way. As Karl Barth would later express this point, in the incarnate Son, "God Himself speaks when this man speaks in human speech. God Himself acts and suffers when this man acts and suffers as a man. God Himself triumphs when this One triumphs as a man."[71]

Fifth, the Son took to himself a complete human nature, which was comprised of a "rational soul and body." Chalcedon insists that Jesus's humanity, in order to be a complete humanity, had to be more than a body; it had to consist of a full human psychology similar to our own. Chalcedon, then, clearly distinguishes "person" from "soul" *and* it locates the "soul" as part of the human nature. In doing so, it insists on a "Word-man" Christology. It rejects the idea that the Son replaces the human soul, and implicitly asserts that Christ had a human will and mind, even though this latter affirmation is not formalized until the Sixth Ecumenical Council in 681.[72]

In a nutshell, these five points capture the heart of the Chalcedonian

---

[70] Macleod, *Person of Christ*, 190.
[71] Karl Barth, *Church Dogmatics*, 4.2, trans. G. T. Thomson (Edinburgh: T&T Clark, 1956), 51.
[72] See Grillmeier, *From the Apostolic Age to Chalcedon (451)*, 547; cf. Galot, *Who Is Christ?*, 284.

Definition. Even though the Creed is not identical to Scripture in authority, nonetheless it is a statement that sets forth the basic points we must confess, articulate, and defend in regard to Christ's identity. As a confessional statement, it establishes the parameters the church must theologize within in order to capture accurately the Jesus of the Bible.[73] As Chalcedon's preamble asserts, it was written against the backdrop of Scripture and the entire patristic tradition, and as Grillmeier notes, "Few councils have been so rooted in tradition as the Council of Chalcedon."[74] In this way, as Brown acknowledges, the Chalcedonian Definition "became our standard for measuring orthodoxy; where either its affirmation of Christ's deity or of his humanity is rejected, it means that historic orthodoxy has been abandoned. . . . The Creed of Chalcedon is not a theological program, but rather a set of limits; beyond its confines, theology almost invariably will degenerate into skepticism, unbelief, or heresy."[75]

With that said, however, there has been a sustained attack upon the Definition, especially since the Enlightenment era. Most of this attack is due to the rejection of historic Christianity and its replacement with other worldviews, as we outlined in Part I, yet some from within the church have also criticized it. Let us briefly turn to some of those criticisms as we conclude this era in history.

Three Criticisms of Chalcedonian Christology

First, as we noted in chapter 7, some have criticized Chalcedon for its dependence on Greek philosophical thinking in its use of such terminology as *ousia*, *hypostasis*, etc. As the criticism goes, due to this influence, biblical teaching has inadvertently been distorted and Christology is reduced to mere metaphysical speculation. For a variety of reasons this criticism is inaccurate.

On the one hand, the issue is not the use of extrabiblical philosophical language, since all theologizing inevitably does so. Instead, the issue is whether that language, whatever century it is taken from, leads to a distortion of biblical language and teaching. On the other hand, even though fifth-century words were employed, Chalcedon uses them in very un-Greek ways. For example, as we have discussed, nowhere in Greek thought is the "nature-person" distinction made, but the church distinguished between *ousia* and *hypostasis* because Scripture demanded it. In addition, as Macleod perceptively notes, the theology of Chalcedon is radically un-Greek:

> Greek theology was sympathetic to the idea of theophanies (gods in human form) and to the idea of divine adoptions, in which a god might take control

---

[73] See A. T. B. McGowan, "Affirming Chalcedon," in *The Forgotten Christ: Exploring the Majesty and Mystery of God Incarnate*, ed. Stephen Clark (Nottingham: Apollos, 2007), 44–47.
[74] Grillmeier, *From the Apostolic Age to Chalcedon (451)*, 550.
[75] Brown, *Heresies*, 183–184.

of a human personality. But Chalcedon is the language of incarnation. It speaks of the enfleshment of a divine person. Here, God himself enters upon an earthly, historical existence, so that we can say that this man is the Son of God and that in this particular individual God lives a truly human life. That goes far beyond both theophany and adoption. . . . . That, as far as I can see, is a profoundly un-Greek concept.[76]

But this criticism goes further. Related to the above objection is the question of whether it is necessary to continue to employ the same words Chalcedon used or whether we can translate fifth-century terminology into contemporary language. Is it possible, for example, to translate *hypostasis* and *ousia* and the metaphysic that undergirds them into more current vocabulary? In theory, most would agree with Macleod that this is possible; as he reminds us, "it is no more difficult to lift the language of *ousia, phusis* and *hypostasis* into our own time than it is to lift the language of St Paul (*morphe, homoioma* and *eikon,* for example)."[77] Yet, as Part IV will discuss, the translation issue is not easy, especially when people are not simply translating old terminology into new, but actually changing the meaning of the terms.[78]

Second, Chalcedon has also been charged with being dualistic, i.e., it appears to place the two natures side by side within the one person, with each nature retaining its own attributes, thus leading to the practice of attributing some aspects of Jesus's existence to his human nature and others to his divine nature, without any specific relationship between them.[79] So, for example, in the case of impassibility and immutability, Leo affirms, and many others following him, that Jesus "was capable of death in one nature and incapable of it in the other."[80] Chalcedon, then, teaches that the historical Jesus has a kind of *dual* existence, as God and as a man. But how do we make coherent sense of this?

In truth, answering this objection takes us to the heart of theologizing about the incarnation. How one answers this criticism distinguishes various Christological formulations, and Part IV is our attempt to do so. At this point, however, it is enough to say that the reason why Chalcedon was necessary was to avoid various heretical attempts to answer this question unbiblically. In fact, Chalcedon serves as a warning and guard against the attempt to overcome the dualism. Chalcedon, along with Scripture, holds in tension the unity of the one divine person, the Son, who, as a result of the incarnation, now subsists in two

---

[76] Macleod, "Christology of Chalcedon," 79.
[77] Ibid., 78.
[78] As we will discuss in Part IV, today people are using the "person-nature" language but redefining it in such a way that it does not mean what Chalcedon meant by these terms.
[79] A. N. S. Lane, "Christology beyond Chalcedon," in *Christ the Lord: Studies in Christology Presented to Donald Guthrie,* ed. Harold H. Rowdon (Downers Grove, IL: InterVarsity Press, 1982), 268.
[80] Cited in Macleod, "Christology of Chalcedon," 79n4.

natures. Scripture and Chalcedon refuse to blend the dual natures of Christ or surrender the unity of the person acting in and through those natures. Also, as Macleod insists, Chalcedon does positively insist "on the existential unity of the person, Jesus. It emphasizes that although there are two natures, there is but one *hypostasis* or *prosopon*. This means that, without claiming to solve the problem, it stresses the unity without pretending to explain it."[81] In the end, Chalcedon makes clear that we must affirm, as Scripture does, that all the actions of Christ are actions of the person. *He* is the agent of all the actions; speaker of all the words; and subject of all the experiences; and as a result, Chalcedon does not parcel out our Lord's actions, words, and experiences as between the two natures. In truth, it seeks to do justice to the Bible's presentation of Christ without resolving the dualism perfectly, and as such, it serves as a warning to all those who attempt to do so.

Third, similar to the charge of dualism, Chalcedon is often criticized for being *docetic*, despite affirming the full humanity of Christ. Where does this charge arise? From the fact that the Creed states that the Son assumes a human nature "without a human person" (*anhypostasia*). And, as the objection goes, "How meaningful is the ascription to Christ of a full and complete human 'nature' (including a human mind and will) if that 'nature' cannot function as ours does?"[82] (i.e., not normally as ours does, *with* a human person). How do we affirm the self-activating character of the man Jesus without giving rise to two subjects or two persons and thus falling prey to the Nestorian heresy? And is not Chalcedon's denial of Christ having a human person an implicit admission of docetism?

At the heart of this charge is making sense of Jesus's human limitations, specifically his limitations of knowledge and power (see Mark 13:32; Luke 2:52), if the acting subject of the incarnation is the divine Son. We will address this issue in the next chapter in our discussion of the post-Chalcedonian developments of *enhypostasia* and the "will" debates, but presently, it is crucial to remember that Chalcedon's affirmation of *anhypostasia* was not saying that anything was lacking in Christ's humanity; instead it was a denial of two acting subjects in Christ and thus a rejection of Nestorianism and/or adoptionism. To affirm the existence of a human person alongside the person of the Son would mean that Jesus was *not* in fact the incarnate Son but simply a man who was especially friendly with the Son. Furthermore, given that Chalcedon used "person" in an ontological, not psychological, sense, it is not denying the completeness of Christ's human psychology, since that is part of his human nature. Rather, Chalcedon is affirming that the one active

---

[81] Ibid., 80–81.
[82] Bruce L. McCormack, "The Person of Christ," in *Mapping Modern Theology: A Thematic and Historical Introduction*, ed. Kelly M. Kapic and Bruce L. McCormack (Grand Rapids, MI: Baker Academic, 2012), 153.

subject of the human experiences of Christ was the divine Son, and thus a real incarnation had taken place.

Where does this now leave us? E. L. Mascall states it well: "Chalcedon is the truth and nothing but the truth, but is not the whole truth."[83] In other words, Chalcedon sets the parameters and puts in place the guardrails by which Christological discussion now takes place, yet it is not the final statement and, in fact, it spurs us on to further reflection within its boundaries. Ultimately it is only Scripture that can serve as our final authority, but we neglect the Chalcedonian Definition at our peril. What is needed is further reflection on Scripture in light of Chalcedon, and, in fact, this is precisely what occurred in the subsequent years of church history. Chalcedon did not end all Christological discussion; instead it continued to guide and direct further thought in light of more questions and challenges. We now turn to this development.

---

[83] E. L. Mascall, *Whatever Happened to the Human Mind? Essays in Christian Orthodoxy* (London: SPCK, 1980), 29.

NINE

POST-CHALCEDONIAN CHRISTOLOGY: THE ESTABLISHMENT OF ORTHODOXY

Even though the Chalcedonian Definition served as the parameter-setting creed for orthodoxy, it was not the final word, and further reflection was necessary in subsequent years. In fact, the Creed left a number of issues unexplained. One issue, for example, was making sense of the hypostatic union and how to think of Christ existing as "one person in two natures." The Definition accurately paved the road on which our thinking of the incarnation ought to travel, yet the Definition left at least two items unclear, hence the reason why different Christological views remained even until our present day.

First, more work was needed on how to preserve the unity of Christ's "person" while equally stressing the integrity of his two "natures." The wording of Chalcedon, ". . . the difference of the natures being by no means removed because of the union, but the property of each nature being preserved and coalescing in one *prosopon* and one *hypostasis*," could falsely give the impression, as Robert Letham admits, "that Christ was some form of schizoid, for whom some things could be related only to one part of him and other things to another part,"[1] which, for many, could imply some kind of Nestorianism that surrendered the unity of Christ's person. This point is especially significant since, at this time in history, most people assumed that a "nature" required a "person" in a one-for-one fashion. Thus, if Christ has two natures then he must have two persons (i.e., Nestorianism); or conversely, if he has one person then he must have only one nature (i.e., monophysitism); but both of these views are biblically inadequate.[2] How, then, do we explain the Creed's strong

---

[1] Robert Letham, *Union with Christ: In Scripture, History, and Theology* (Phillipsburg, NJ: P&R, 2011), 28.
[2] On this point, see Demetrios Bathrellos, *The Byzantine Christ: Person, Nature, and Will in the Christology of Saint Maximus the Confessor* (Oxford: Oxford University Press, 2004), 33–35. Bathrellos notes that many anti-Chalcedonians were keen on repeating the phrase "there is no nature without a hypostasis" (ibid., 34). He also

emphasis on the unity of Christ's person, given its affirmation of two natures? Conversely, if we affirm that Christ has two natures, which Scripture requires, then how do we affirm that the eternal Son is the one acting subject?

These questions were exacerbated by another factor: Chalcedon left ambiguous precisely *who* the subject of the incarnation is. Even though Chalcedon repeatedly used the eightfold repetition of "the same" to highlight the unity of subject underlying all of Christ's operations, and identified the one subject as the eternal Son (contra Nestorianism), it also stressed the reality of the two natures and recognized the integrity of Christ's humanity (contra monophysitism) within the union itself. In doing so, however, as Dennis Ferrara observes, Chalcedon could give the impression (contrary to its intention) that the "person" of Christ implies some kind of "consequent or composite rather than the pre-existing subject in Christ."[3] It is this seemingly built-in tension which required further explanation; more clarity was required to make sense of the unity of Christ's person as the eternal Son (and not as some kind of composite of the two natures) and how the Son relates to his two natures and lives and acts in them. In fact, what was ultimately required was breaking the assumption that a "person" always relates to a "nature" in a one-for-one fashion, in order to account for how the Son subsists in two "natures."

Second (and related to the first), more work was needed on what constituted a complete humanity and whether Christ's humanity was complete. Even though Chalcedon clearly affirmed that Christ was fully man ("the same consubstantial with us in manhood"), it also affirmed that the "person," or active subject of the incarnation, was God the Son, contra Nestorianism. By doing so, Chalcedon insisted that the single "subject" who acts in and through the human "nature" is the divine Son, not a composite of two "persons"—one divine and one human. In Christ there is only one active subject, who is the eternal Son who has made a human nature his own. As Cyril of Alexandria contended, and as affirmed by Chalcedon, it is the Son who is the personal subject of the incarnation, who alone "activates" the mind and will of his human nature. Yet this affirmation raised a legitimate question which Chalcedon did not address: If the Son is the active subject of the human "nature," "[h]ow meaningful is the ascription to Christ of a full and complete human "nature" (including a human mind and will) if that "nature" cannot function as ours does?"[4] If the human nature of Christ was never allowed to function like ours, with a *human* person as the acting

---

notes that there is justification for this view since, for us, "human nature exists only as, in, and through particular human persons" (ibid.). But in the case of Christ, Chalcedon affirmed that his one person subsisted in two natures.
[3] Dennis M. Ferrara, "Hypostatized in the Logos," *Louvain Studies* 22/4 (1997): 317.
[4] Bruce L. McCormack, "The Person of Christ," in *Mapping Modern Theology: A Thematic and Historical Introduction*, ed. Kelly M. Kapic and Bruce L. McCormack (Grand Rapids, MI: Baker Academic, 2012), 153.

subject, and instead the acting subject is a divine person, then in what sense is Christ completely human like us? Or, as Bruce McCormack rightly asks, "[H]ow do we affirm the self-activating character of the man Jesus without giving rise to two subjects?"[5]

This question was especially pressing since Chalcedon denied that the Son united himself to a "human person" (contra Nestorianism). Instead, the Creed insisted that the Son united himself to a full complex of human attributes, i.e., a human nature, *without* its person (*anhypostasia*). But does not *anhypostasia* imply that Christ was lacking a complete humanity? Was Chalcedon a return to some form of Apollinarianism and/or monophysitism?

Given these unresolved items, it is not surprising that, after Chalcedon, debate continued in various sections of the church. Chalcedon set the basic parameters for orthodoxy, but it required more clarification, which is precisely what occurred in the later Councils held at Constantinople in 553 and 681. Further Christological thought also ensued in the medieval and Reformation eras, which paved the way for greater precision and which better established orthodox Christology.

In this concluding chapter of Part III, we will discuss the high points of Christological development from the sixth century through the Reformation era.[6] Our focus is on four crucial post-Chalcedonian developments which brought greater clarity, especially in the two areas left unresolved from Chalcedon. By so doing, we will finish our discussion of the *ecclesiological warrant* for Christology. This will set the stage for Part IV, in which, in light of Scripture and the tradition, we will seek to commend a warranted, orthodox, evangelical Christology for today.

What are the four crucial issues to be discussed? First, we will reflect on the *anhypostasis/enhypostasis* distinction, further developed at the Fifth Ecumenical Council (553), and which helped clarify the hypostatic union and how the Son subsists in two natures. Second, in light of the Reformation debates on the Lord's Supper, we will discuss how a proper understanding of *communicatio idiomatum* developed, thus paving the way to grasp better the relationship between the two natures of Christ and their union in the one person. Third, we will unpack the significance of the *extra Calvinisticum* for orthodox Christology, especially as a way of maintaining the robust Scriptural presentation of Christ as the *divine* Son incarnate. Fourth, we will conclude with a discussion of the "will" debate at the Sixth Ecumenical Council (681), which clarified further the "person-nature" distinction. Let us now turn to each of these issues.

---

[5] Ibid.
[6] For a helpful discussion of this era, see Gerald Bray, *God Has Spoken: A History of Christian Theology* (Wheaton, IL: Crossway, 2014), 350–402.

The Nature of the Hypostatic Union:
The Anhypostasis-Enhypostasis Distinction

Chalcedon bequeathed to us a number of legitimate questions. Given the Creed's emphasis on the integrity of the two natures and the appropriate attributions made to each one, how do we make sense of the *unity* of the person of Christ without veering into the ditch of Nestorianism? If Christ has two natures, each of which retains its integrity, must he not also have two persons? How is it possible to have a nature without a corresponding acting subject? Chalcedon's answer: In the incarnation, the Son assumed a human nature which was *anhypostatic*, i.e., "without a person." But this raised a further conundrum. If the Son united himself to a human nature *without* a *human person*, then in what sense is Christ's humanity complete? This question was especially pressing given the use of the word *anhypostasia*, since as Donald Macleod reminds us, "*An-hypostasia* is in its very form a negative. It is the denial of *hypostasis*."[7] And if not carefully explained, it could give the impression that there was something lacking in Christ's humanity. In fact, it was due to Chalcedon's lack of clarity on this point that subsequent debates resulted which allowed for monophysitism and Nestorianism to continue.

Before we turn to the church's response to this challenge, it is important to remember what the Chalcedonian Definition intended to deny *and* preserve in its affirmation of *anhypostasia*. Chalcedon was *not* intending to minimize the full humanity of Christ, otherwise we cannot make sense of its insistence on Christ's two natures fully retaining their attributes. Nor was Chalcedon denying, as Macleod notes, "that Jesus Christ was an individual or that his humanness was markedly individual. He was not just some kind of amorphous mass of human-ness."[8] Christ's humanity was distinguishable from that of every other human being. He had personal traits just as we ourselves have, yet his traits were also unique to him, which distinguished him from others. "He dared to be himself at the human level. He was not somebody else. He had a quality and a style of his own."[9] Thus, the assertion that the incarnate Son did not have a "human person" was *not* intended to deny his full humanity; instead, it was intended to deny that our Lord's human nature had an independent existence apart from its subsistence in the person of the Son. When the Son became incarnate, he did not assume a fully existing man, i.e., a human person and nature, but instead added to himself a human nature and gave to that human nature its "person" in and through the person of the Son. We can even

---

[7] Donald Macleod, "The Christology of Chalcedon," in *The Only Hope Jesus: Yesterday, Today, Forever*, ed. Mark Elliott and John McPake (Fearn: Christian Focus, 2001), 88.

[8] Ibid., 88–89. See Ivor Davidson, who makes the same point in his article, "Theologizing the Human Jesus: An Ancient (and Modern) Approach to Christology Reassessed," *IJST* 3/2 (2001): 138.

[9] Macleod, "Christology of Chalcedon," 89.

say, to use contemporary language, that the Son in assuming a human nature had a "personality," i.e., a complex of characteristics which distinguish one individual from another, since Christ's human "personality" is best understood in reference to his human nature with all of its human capacities/attributes, including a human body and soul.[10]

So, then, what was *anhypostasia* affirming? It was affirming that there is only *one* active subject (person) in Christ and that *that* person is the Son, hence its rejection of Nestorianism. Or, to state it as Macleod does, "the human nature of Jesus does not stand in an 'I-Thou' relationship to his divine nature. The two natures are not individual agents able to act on each other as do, for example, two people who love each other. They are not able even to act *with* each other, as two independent individuals might. Far less are they able to act against each other."[11] *Anhypostasia*, then, rules out any idea of dual agency, thus preserving the unity of person: that the one person of the incarnation is the divine Son; that the union between his two natures is because both natures belong to one and the same person; and that it is "persons" who are active subjects and agents, not "natures," thus insisting that it is the Son who is "the Agent behind all of the Lord's actions, the Speaker of all his utterances and the Subject of all his experiences."[12] *Anhypostasia*, then, intends to make sense of the biblical data and the wonderful truth that it was the eternal Son who became flesh, not by "adopting" an existing human person, but by assuming a human nature and in that nature now living and experiencing a human life.

Given the potential confusion of the word, however, is there a better way of stating it? By the Second Council of Constantinople (553), *enhypostasia* was the word enlisted, and since then it has been used by theologians to state better how Jesus is *one* person who subsists in two natures. Let us first explain the concept before discussing its development in the Patristic era.[13]

---

[10] Ibid.; cf. Davidson, "Theologizing the Human Jesus," 138.

[11] Macleod, "Christology of Chalcedon," 89.

[12] Donald Macleod, *The Person of Christ* (Downers Grove, IL: InterVarsity Press, 1998), 189.

[13] There is a dispute over the historical development of *enhypostasia* and who originated it. Due to the influence of Friedrich Loofs's work, Leontius of Byzantium (485–543) was credited with coining and developing the concept. Yet, a number of historians have shown that Loofs's work is inaccurate and that Leontius of Byzantium is not the originator of the term. Instead, it is best traced back to Leontius of Jerusalem, a contemporary of Leontius of Byzantium. Aloys Grillmeier, *The Church of Constantinople in the Sixth Century*, vol. 2, part 2 in *Christ in Christian Tradition*, trans. Pauline Allen and John Cawte (Louisville: Westminster John Knox, 1995), 271, shows that Loofs mistakenly identified the two Leontiuses as one and the same person. The concept of *enhypostasia* was also given further refinement by John of Damascus (675–749), and then later picked up by theologians in the medieval, Reformation, and Protestant orthodoxy eras. For this discussion, see Friedrich Loofs, "Leontius von Byzanz und die Gleichnamigen Schriftsteller der Griechischen Kirche," in *Die Lehre der zwölf Apostel, nebst Untersuchungen zur ältesten Geschichte der Kirchenverfassung und des Kirchenrechts*, ed. Adolf von Harnack, Texte und Untersuchungen zur Geschichte der altchristlichen Literatur 3/1–2 (Leipzig: J. C. Hinrich, 1887). For proponents of Loofs's thesis, see, e.g., Herbert M. Relton, *A Study in Christology: The Problem of the Relation of the Two Natures in the Person of Christ* (London: SPCK, 1917), 69–83; R. V. Sellers, *The Council of Chalcedon: A Historical and Doctrinal Survey* (London: SPCK, 1953), 308–320. For a criticism of Loofs's thesis, see Grillmeier, *Church of Constantinople in the Sixth Century*, 181–270; idem, *From the Council of Chalcedon (451) to Gregory the Great (590–604)*, vol. 2, part 1 in *Christ in Christian Tradition*, trans. Pauline Allen and John Cawte (Atlanta: John Knox, 1987); Bathrellos,

The Concept of Enhypostasia

Enhypostasia is a clarification and development of anhypostasia.[14] Instead of thinking of Christ's human nature *without* a hypostasis or human "person" (suggesting that he was lacking a complete humanity), we should think of Christ's human nature being accorded its personal identity, not in a human *hypostasis* but in the *hypostasis* of the Son by whom it was assumed and to whom it was joined. Christ's human nature, then, is not simply *im-* or *non*-personal (*a-hypostatic*); instead it is more accurately *in*-personal (*en-hypostatic*) as it is individualized as the humanity of God the Son. No doubt, the Son continues to subsist in the same, identical divine nature along with the Father and the Spirit, but at the point of conception, the Son gives to his human nature its *hypostasis* so that now *he*, the Son, is the active subject of both natures simultaneously.

What is the significance of stating it this way? Ultimately it helps clarify more precisely how Christ is one person subsisting in two natures. How? By avoiding any idea that there are two active subjects in Christ *and* that his human nature is lacking anything. In terms of the latter, Macleod captures this crucial point in these words:

> The import of *enhypostatos* is that the human nature of Christ, although not itself an individual, is individualized as the human nature of the Son of God. It does not, for a single instant, exist as *anhypostatos* or non-personal. As embryo, foetus, infant, child and man it is *hypostatos* in the Second Person of the Trinity. The flesh is his. The form of a servant is his. The likeness of men is his. The obedience unto death is his.[15]

How did the concept of *enhypostasia* develop in Christology? In order to answer this question let us briefly turn to some of the key people who were pivotal in its development.

Leontius of Byzantium

It is disputed how much Leontius contributed to the development of *enhypostasis*.[16] Demetrios Bathrellos, however, insists that Leontius did contribute to our understanding of the concept by arguing two important points. First,

---

Byzantine Christ, 34–59; U. M. Lang, "Anhypostatos-Enhypostatos: Church Fathers, Protestant Orthodoxy and Karl Barth," *Journal of Theological Studies* 49/2 (1998): 630–657.

[14] For a definition of the words, see Richard A. Muller, *Dictionary of Latin and Greek Theological Terms* (Grand Rapids, MI: Baker, 1985), 35, 103.

[15] Macleod, *Person of Christ*, 202. Wells captures the import of *enhypostasia* from a different angle. In light of it, he says, in Christ "we come face to face with God. We meet him, not subsumed under human flesh, not merely associated with it, not merely accompanying it, not merely shining through it, but in undiminished moral splendor, giving to that humanity the moral completeness which has been missing from the time of that fall. Though human, Jesus is properly accorded our worship, for he is God; though human, his is the world and his is the church, for he is God. Though human, he is the conqueror of sin, death, and the devil, for he is God" (David F. Wells, *The Person of Christ: A Biblical and Historical Analysis of the Incarnation* [Westchester, IL: Crossway, 1984], 178).

[16] See note 13 above for the discussion surrounding this debate.

Leontius fully embraced the "person-nature" distinction of pro-Nicene theology, and rightly argued that every "nature" must have a *hypostasis* in order to exist. By *nature* he meant the essence or "whatness" of a thing, and by *person/ hypostasis* he meant the "who-ness" of the nature. In distinguishing person from nature, he argued that the person is "neither consubstantial with nor separated from the human nature but co-subsists with it."[17] Also, to further distinguish person from nature, Leontius insisted that a nature is not self-subsistent; only a *hypostasis* is that, and a nature only subsists/exists in a *hypostasis*.[18]

But if every nature must have a *hypostasis*, does this not raise a potential problem, something which the anti-Chalcedonians capitalized on? Bathrellos describes the problem: "What the anti-Chalcedonians wanted to prove by appealing to this principle is that, since there is no nature without a person, if there is in Christ a second (human) nature, as Chalcedon claimed, there is also inevitably in him a second (human) person, which is to be rejected as sheer Nestorianism."[19] Leontius's response leads to his second contribution to the development of *enhypostasia*.

Leontius argues that Christ's human nature would require a human person *if* it existed in separation from the Son, but this never occurs. In Christ, his human nature, from conception, subsists *in* the person of the Son, without losing or compromising his divine nature.[20] Leontius introduces, as Letham explains, the idea of "Christ's humanity as *enhypostatos* (existing in a *hypostasis*—roughly, "person"—of another nature). Christ's human nature subsists in the *hypostasis* of the divine nature. Thus, the human nature in Christ is both *anhypostatos*—having no existence of its own independently—and also *enhypostatos*—subsisting *in* a *hypostasis* of another nature."[21]

By this explanation, Leontius has begun to give an explanation for the *one* person of Christ *and* how the two natures are "in" the person *and* how all the operations of both natures are attributed to the Son. But, as most admit, more explanation is required, and it is Leontius of Jerusalem who provides it.[22]

Leontius of Jerusalem

The concept of *enhypostasia* was developed more completely by Leontius of Jerusalem.[23] He not only insisted that the one subject in Christ is the "person/ hypostasis" of the eternal Son, but also he consistently applied what Chalcedon

---

[17] Bathrellos, *Byzantine Christ*, 42.
[18] See ibid., 43.
[19] Ibid.
[20] Ibid.
[21] Letham, *Union with Christ*, 30.
[22] Bathrellos concedes this, while endorsing Leontius of Byzantium's input (Bathrellos, *Byzantine Christ*, 45).
[23] See Ferrara, "Hypostatized in the Logos," 318. Grillmeier argues that with Leontius of Jerusalem "the history of a great christological concept begins" (Grillmeier, *Church of Constantinople in the Sixth Century*, 282); Cf. Lang, "Anhypostatos-Enhypostatos," 632–657; Davidson, "Theologizing the Human Jesus," 140.

intended but had left slightly ambiguous. In addition, he freed himself from the underlying assumption that had locked the debate, namely, the belief that nature-person necessarily go together in a one-to-one fashion. Leontius agreed that a "nature" without a *hypostasis* is impossible, but then argued that while a "nature" cannot exist without a *hypostasis*, it need not have its own, since it can be "hypostasized" in another. As applied to the incarnation, Leontius proposed that Christ's human nature was *not* without a *hypostasis*; Christ's human nature was accorded its personal identity in the person of the Son.[24] As Grillmeier notes, this is why, for Leontius, "Christ is only one *hypostasis* in the real two natures."[25] Christ's human nature was not simply *im*-personal (*anhypostatic*), but *in*-personal (*enhypostatic*). Thus the "becoming" of the incarnation does *not* imply, as Davidson reminds us, "that God *qua* God indwells or is metamorphosed into a man, but that God the Son subsists personally as a man."[26]

By explaining *enhypostasia* with the idea of in-subsistence, Leontius of Jerusalem helps explain better not only the unity of Christ's person but also how the unity of Christ's two natures is found in the one *hypostasis*. In Christ, then, his humanity has no independent existence by itself, since it was and always is the humanity of the divine Son; yet his humanity remains humanity, and it is not confused with his deity. Also, Leontius nicely explains how Christ's human nature is fully human and lacking nothing, yet due to the action of the Son, it is *he* who lives a fully human life, subject to the contingency and vulnerability of human existence.

In addition, Leontius helps make sense of why it is that Christ's work can meet our every need as our great Redeemer, High Priest, and new covenant head. Why? Because Christ's work is truly a divine-human work, and it is because his humanity subsists in the person of the Son that his life, obedience, and work *as a man* is also a *divine* work. In Christ, then, as Wells reminds us, "we see all that Adam was intended to be, but never was, all that we are not but which we will become through resurrection"[27] and union with him,[28] yet we also see in him the dawning of the new age and the inauguration of the kingdom, something which only God can do. In him, we find our Lord and Redeemer, as well as our sympathetic High Priest and elder brother.

The Second Council of Constantinople (553)

The Second Council of Constantinople accomplished a number of goals and helped solidify the concept of *enhypostasia*. Emperor Justinian I (483–565) called

---

[24] For examples from Leontius of Jerusalem's *Contra* (or *Adversus*) *Nestorianos*, which describes *enhypostasia*, see Grillmeier, *Church of Constantinople in the Sixth Century*, 271–312; Lang, "Anhypostatos-Enhypostatos," 640–648.
[25] Grillmeier, *Church of Constantinople in the Sixth Century*, 285.
[26] Davidson, "Theologizing the Human Jesus," 140.
[27] Wells, *Person of Christ*, 178.
[28] For a development of the link between incarnation and union with Christ, see Letham, *Union with Christ*, 19–141.

the Council to unite the churches and to clarify the Chalcedonian Definition.[29] A series of anathemas underscored the unity of Christ's person, while another set stressed the distinction of the two natures. Canon II ascribed two births to the God-Logos, the one from eternity from the Father, without time and without body, and the other in time at the incarnation. Canons III and V denied Nestorianism by affirming that the God-Logos who worked miracles and the Christ who suffered cannot be separated, since it is the one and the same Son who became flesh. Behind this affirmation is the Chalcedonian teaching that Christ's unity is a true union, not a mingling or a division. In addition, the Council affirmed that our Lord is only one person/*hypostasis*, who is none other than the eternal Son, the second person of the Trinity. The Council also denied monophysitism, in Canon VIII, by stating that the Son subsists in two natures, both of which retain their integrity after the incarnation. Canon IX declares that worshiping Christ in two natures is one act of worship directed to the incarnate Son.

In all these statements, Constantinople II affirms, clarifies, and develops Chalcedon. As Grillmeier notes, instead of weakening Chalcedonian terminology, this Council takes it to its "logical continuation" and it uses and applies the main concepts of Chalcedon in a "clearer and more unambiguous" manner.[30] After Constantinople II, *enhypostasia* became standard in the church. In the East it finds it clearest exposition in John of Damascus, and in the West it was employed by Aquinas, the Reformers, and the post-Reformation Protestant Scholastics.[31] As the concept was consistently applied to Christology, here are some of its more salient implications:

Some Christological Implications of Enhypostasia

1. *Our Lord Jesus Christ was personal, as a man, by virtue of the union of his human nature in the person of the eternal Son.* As a person, the Son gave personal identity to the human nature that he had assumed without losing or compromising his divine nature. Neither, as Bavinck reminds us, did the Son "become a person in and through human nature, for he was that from eternity,"[32] nor for a moment did *the man* Jesus exist apart from the union of natures in the one divine person. "The Son increated it within himself and, by creating, assumed it in himself."[33] This implies, then, that *the man* Jesus from

[29] See Grillmeier, *Church of Constantinople in the Sixth Century*, 438–475; Leo Donald Davis, *First Seven Ecumenical Councils (325–787): Their History and Theology* (Wilmington, DE: M. Glazier, 1983; repr, Collegeville, MN: Liturgical Press, 1990), 244–246; Bathrellos, *Byzantine Christ*, 54–56.

[30] See Grillmeier, *Church of Constantinople in the Sixth Century*, 456–457.

[31] See Ferrara, "Hypostatized in the Logos," 311–327; Davidson, "Theologizing the Human Jesus," 129–153; Lang, "Anhypostatos-Enhypostatos," 630–657; cf. Geerhardus Vos, *Christology*, vol. 3 of *Reformed Dogmatics*, trans. and ed. Richard B. Gaffin Jr. (Bellingham, WA: Lexham, 2014), 39–57.

[32] Herman Bavinck, *Sin and Salvation in Christ*, vol. 3 of *Reformed Dogmatics*, ed. John Bolt; trans. John Vriend; Grand Rapids, MI: Baker Academic, 2006), 307.

[33] Bavinck, *Sin and Salvation in Christ*, 307; see also a fine statement of this in Zacharias Ursinus, *Commentary on the Heidelberg Catechism*, trans. G. W. Williard (Phillipsburg, NJ: P&R, 1992), 210.

the moment of conception was personal by virtue of the union of the human nature *in* the divine Son, who alone is the sole personal subject in Christ.

2. *The incarnation is a dynamic act on the part of the person, i.e., the Son, alongside the Father and the Spirit in triune relationship and action.* Scripture is clear: "*the* Word became flesh" (John 1:14). Scripture denies that the other triune persons became incarnate; it was only the Son. Given that the works of the divine persons are harmonious and indivisible, however, each divine person is involved in the incarnation according to their mode of relation or subsistence, yet it is only the Son who becomes incarnate. And, even in the case of the Son, it is not the divine nature which assumes a human nature; rather, it is the person of the Son.

3. *The human nature of Christ had everything any other human has in its unfallen condition except independent personal existence apart from the person of the Son.* Enhypostasia not only has the effect of particularizing Christ's humanity, it also insists, as Bavinck notes, that it is the Son, "who as subject lived, thought, willed, acted, suffered, died, and so on in and through it [human nature] with all its constituents, capacities, and energies."[34] The fact that Christ's human nature did not receive a distinct completion of existence of its own in an independent self was not the result of any deficiency. On the contrary, it was part of the triune God's eternal plan for the Son to become one with us, to assume a particular human nature, and to give to that nature its person in union to the divine Son, in order to accomplish all of God's saving purposes.

One crucial implication of *enhypostasia* is that Christ's humanity is fully human and thus he is like us in every way except sin, yet this does *not* entail some kind of universal or vicarious humanity that opens the door to universalism. The fact that the Son has become one with us in his humanity does not result in salvation for all people. Macleod states this point well: "His humanity is that of Everyman. But he is not Everyman. He is the man, Christ Jesus; and the only humanity united to him hypostatically is his own."[35]

It is for this reason that we must carefully define what is meant by the "vicarious humanity" of Christ. Thomas F. Torrance, for example, argues that when Jesus was born, baptized, suffered, raised from the dead, and ascended, "we were born again, baptised by the Spirit, suffered, died, rose again and ascended with him."[36] But who precisely are the "we" Torrance is referring to? If the "we" means all people without exception, Scripture does not allow for such a view, nor will appeal to *enhypostasia* allow it either. As Macleod

---

[34] Bavinck, *Sin and Salvation in Christ*, 307.
[35] Macleod, *Person of Christ*, 202.
[36] Thomas F. Torrance, "The Vicarious Humanity of Christ," in *The Incarnation: Ecumenical Studies in the Nicene-Constantinopolitan Creed* (Edinburgh: Handsel, 1981), 139.

perceptively notes, "Christ is true God, but he is not the whole godhead; and he is true man, but he is not the whole of humanity."[37] This requires that we think carefully about the nature of the union between Christ and human beings. *Enhypostasia* does not by itself secure the salvation of every human being; instead, what it secures is the reality of the incarnation and the fact that in Christ, God and man can coexist as one. But how we come to share in his redemptive work is not automatic. It is possible to be human and yet not to be "in Christ" since, as Macleod soberly remarks, "although the incarnation unites Christ to human nature it does not unite him to *me*. I become one with him only in the compound but yet single reality of covenant-election-calling-faith-repentance-sealing."[38]

4. *Since it is the divine Son who gave a personal identity to Christ's human nature and is now able to live, think, will, and act in and through his human nature (and his divine nature), we can say that **the Son** is now able to live a fully human life (and a divine life).* Enhypostasia helps answer the question, Does Jesus possesses a human "I"? The answer is no, if by "I" we mean a human person. Yet, the Son, by assuming a human nature, is now able to live a fully human life since it is the Son who lives and acts as the subject of his actions and operations in and through his natures. Precisely because the Son has assumed a human nature, *he* has a real human consciousness, will, and psychology: *he* is able to think and act in a truly human way. Also, as the Son, he does *not* modify what a human nature is, yet *he* knows himself as the Son in and through his humanity, though he is not completely circumscribed by his human nature, given that *he* subsists in two natures.[39]

5. What is the conceptual underpinning for *enhypostasia*? As noted in Part II, the underpinning is the biblical teaching that humans, though creatures, are *imago dei*. In the Patristic, Medieval, and Reformation eras, *enhypostasia* was sometimes allied to philosophical notions of substance, for good or ill. But as Wells suggests, the concept of "enhypostatic union" does not require such conceptuality, even though it may be helped by it, since scripturally speaking, it is the *imago dei* that underpins the concept. As Wells reminds us, the *hypostasis* of Christ is not a union of two entirely different properties. It is not as if we were

---

[37] Macleod, *Person of Christ*, 203.

[38] Ibid.

[39] Today, some have sought to explain this by distinguishing between Jesus's self-consciousness and consciousness. Self-consciousness is related to the "person," while consciousness is related to the "nature." In Jesus there is only *one* self-consciousness, yet given that the Son subsists in two natures, there are two levels of consciousness, which entails that the Son can simultaneously experience a divine and a human life. John Murray, for example, argued this point. He noticed that in Scripture Jesus speaks and acts in terms of a divine, filial self-consciousness even though he speaks and acts as a man. Murray writes, "the inference would seem to be that our Lord's *self*-identity and *self*-consciousness can never be thought of in terms of human nature alone. Personality cannot be predicated of him except as it draws within its scope his specifically divine identity" (John Murray, "The Person of Christ," in *Systematic Theology*, vol. 2 of *Collected Writings of John Murray* [Carlisle, PA: Banner of Truth Trust, 1977], 138–139). Cf. Philip H. Eveson, "The Inner or Psychological Life of Christ," in *The Forgotten Christ: Exploring the Majesty and Mystery of God Incarnate*, ed. Stephen Clark (Nottingham: Apollos, 2007), 60–61.

uniting a frog and a prince in one *hypostasis*. The physical qualities of a frog and a prince are so different and their mental capacities are so different that it is hard to see how such a union could occur. But this is not the case with the Lord Jesus. Why? Because humanity is created in God's image, and whatever *imago dei* means, at its heart is the idea that what constitutes humanity, what sets it apart from mere animal life, are capacities the originals of which are found in God. As Wells states, "Human nature as created is the echo of which the Creator is sound. He is the original, and we are derivative."[40] Thus, if God is the original, then the derivative finds its meaning only in relation to the original. Ultimately, "[w]hat it means to be truly human is revealed in and by God himself. That being the case, a perfect humanity, one unspoiled by sin, would not only coalesce naturally with the divine but would, in fact, find its perfection in the divine from which it is derived."[41] Hence, to speak of Christ's human nature coming to personal union in the divine Son in no way diminishes Christ's humanity; rather it confesses that Jesus is "God in whom our human nature, without its sin, has come to perfect realization, to moral completion, to perfect union."[42]

The *Communicatio Idiomatum* Debate: The Relationship of the Two Natures to the One Person

Closely related to the discussion of *enhypostasia* is the question of the relationship between the two natures of Christ. On the basis of Scripture, Chalcedon affirmed that, as a result of the incarnation, the Son now subsists in two natures, and that these two natures are united in the person of the Son. Chalcedon denied, contra monophysitism, that the natures were merged into one another or changed, since each nature retained its own attributes. Thus, in Christ, the Creator-creature distinction is not violated, yet both natures are not merely juxtaposed, lying side by side in the one person without contact or interaction. So what exactly is the relationship?

Some in the Patristic era, as Macleod notes, hinted that the relationship between the two natures was one of *perichoresis*, so that Christ's divine nature completely permeated his human nature even though each nature remained distinct. John of Damascus represents this thought when he writes, "He imparts to the flesh His own attributes by way of communication in virtue of the interpenetration (*perichoresis*) of the parts one with another."[43] Some then inferred that Christ in his humanity on earth already possessed complete knowledge, that all the gifts of which the human nature was capable were given him all at

---

[40] Wells, *Person of Christ*, 178.
[41] Ibid.
[42] Ibid.
[43] John of Damascus, *An Exact Exposition of the Orthodox Faith* 3.3 (NPNF² 9:46b–48b), in Macleod, *Person of Christ*, 194.

once at his incarnation, and that any increase in wisdom must be understood only subjectively, not objectively.[44]

The problem with this view, however, is threefold. First, it cannot explain adequately Jesus's growth in wisdom and knowledge (see Luke 2:40, 52). Second, it flirts with monophysitism, or minimally, third, the idea that Christ's divine nature dominates his human nature as if the natures are active agents. If not careful, such a view treats our Lord's humanity in a docetic fashion, which ultimately undermines the basis of our salvation. For these reasons, the church, instead of developing *perichoresis* Christologically, limited it to discussion of how the triune persons share the same, identical divine nature. In its place, the language of *communicatio idiomatum* ("the communion in attributes") was used to think through the relationship between the two natures. Macleod states it this way: Each nature "retained its own distinctive attributes, but between them there was some kind of communion."[45] But what exactly is the nature of this communion? Answering this question clarifies better how to think of the relationship between Christ's two natures and their union in the Son.

Throughout church history people have differed in answering this question, yet, minimally, almost all have agreed that *communicatio idiomatum* entails that the attributes of each nature are to be predicated to the person (see, e.g., Acts 20:28; 1 Cor. 2:8; 1 John 1:1, 7).[46] This is why Scripture can say, in reference to the *person* of the Son, that *he* is almighty, omniscient, eternal, and so on (all attributes of the divine nature), since *he*, as the Son, subsists in the divine nature and all the attributes of that nature are predicated of *him*. Yet, Scripture also says that this same Son is weak, ignorant, embodied, and even mortal (all attributes of the human nature).

How can Scripture say this simultaneously? Is Scripture merely speaking incoherently? No, and for this reason: the attributes of each nature, because they are united in the person of the Son, are predicated of *him* as the Son. Thus what is true of each nature is true of *him*, since *he*, as the Son, is the active subject of both natures.[47] In the incarnation, the Son does not give up

---

[44] See Bavinck, *Sin and Salvation in Christ*, 256–259; Jean Galot, *Who Is Christ? A Theology of the Incarnation* (Chicago: Franciscan Herald, 1981), 337–357. For how various theologians in the Patristic era treated the ignorance of Christ by minimizing Christ's humanity, see Lionel R. Wickham, "The Ignorance of Christ: A Problem for the Ancient Theology," in *Christian Faith and Greek Philosophy in Late Antiquity: Essays in Tribute to George Christopher Stead*, ed. Lionel R. Wickham and Caroline P. Bammel, Supplements to Vigiliae Christianae, vol. 19 (Leiden; New York: E. J. Brill, 1993), 213–226. For example, Athanasius and Cyril treated Christ's self-ascription of ignorance as "condescension to our human nature" (ibid., 223), while the Cappadocians interpreted such limitations as related to the economy of the incarnation (ibid., 224). Either way, there is not a full appreciation for the humanity of Christ.

[45] Macleod, *Person of Christ*, 194.

[46] For a helpful summary of *communicatio idiomatum* and the various senses of *communicatio* used in Christology, see Muller, *Dictionary of Latin and Greek Theological Terms*, 72–75; Stephen R. Holmes, "Reformed Varieties of the *Communicatio Idiomatum*," in *The Person of Christ*, ed. Stephen R. Holmes and Murray A. Rae (New York: T&T Clark, 2005), 70–86; Vos, *Christology*, 60–74.

[47] Classical Christology is not reticent to explain biblical language in terms of Christ's two natures, yet it always predicates what is true of those natures to the person. As Bray notes, "Orthodox Christology thus believed in a

his divine nature but assumes a new nature, a new mode of existence, and so makes human experiences his own—human experiences that can be predicated of *him*. This understanding of *communicatio*, then, not only requires a proper "person-nature" distinction; it also retains the Creator-creature distinction in terms of the natures. It is *not* affirming that the attributes of the natures are comingled; instead, it is teaching that what is true of the natures is also true of the person, so the *communicatio* is real in respect to the person but only verbal in respect to the natures.[48]

Building on this conception of *communicatio*, two other senses of "communion" were affirmed in the development of Christological thinking. First, there is the "communication of mediatorial operations" (*communicatio apotelesmatum* or *operationum*), namely, the idea that due to the union of the natures *in* the Son, all the works of our Lord Jesus Christ, specifically the final result of that work (*apotelesma*), bear a divine-human character. Why? Because, as Bavinck notes, "they all have as their efficient cause the one undivided personal subject in Christ; they were all performed by Christ with the cooperation of his two natures and with a double working (*energeia*), and in the result nevertheless again form an undivided unity inasmuch as they are the work of one person."[49] Thus in all of our Lord's acts and experiences, especially in his saving work for us, both natures are involved, since the natures are united in the Son and the Son is their active subject. It is for this reason that Christ's work is all-sufficient, effective, and triumphant as our new covenant head who defeats sin, death, and the Evil One.[50]

Second, there is the "communication of gifts or graces" (*communicatio charismatum* or *gratiarum*), namely, the idea that, from conception, Christ's human nature was adorned with all kinds of glorious gifts, so that his humanity is elevated above all creatures and in his human nature the Son does works and exhibits powers of God alone. In the Patristic and Medieval eras these "gifts and graces" were explained primarily by arguing that the Son, in uniting himself to a human nature, gave to that nature these graces by virtue of his divine nature. But one must exercise caution and *not* assume some kind of "transfer of attributes" between natures or think that the natures are act-

---

divine person who manifested himself in and disposed of the capacities of two natures. On the cross the divine person suffered and died for us in his human nature, thereby neatly combining the sacrifice of God on our behalf with the doctrine of an impassible and immortal deity" (Gerald Bray, "Christology," in *New Dictionary of Theology*, ed. Sinclair Ferguson and David F. Wright [Downers Grove, IL: InterVarsity Press, 1988], 139). For example, think of Christ's omnipresence. In the ascension (John 16:28; 17:11; Acts 1:9–11), *he* ascended and is no longer present until he returns. Yet in his divine nature, the Son is omnipresent (see Matt. 18:20; 28:20; John 14:23). Or, think of the Son's eternality. Jesus could say he was thirty years old, yet also, "Before Abraham was, I am" (John 8:58; cf. 1:1–2). The former applies to his human nature while the latter applies to him as God the Son.

[48] See Bavinck, *Sin and Salvation in Christ*, 256–259; Gregg R. Allison, *Historical Theology: An Introduction to Christian Doctrine* (Grand Rapids, MI: Zondervan, 2011), 377–379; Macleod, *Person of Christ*, 193–196.

[49] Bavinck, *Sin and Salvation in Christ*, 308.

[50] See Vos, *Christology*, 56–64.

ing agents. Probably a better way of thinking about this "gifts and graces" is Trinitarian, specifically in terms of the Son-Spirit relation.

As discussed in Part II, Scripture links the Spirit's work to the incarnate Son very closely. Jesus was not only conceived by the Holy Spirit, he was also given the Spirit without measure (John 3:34), thus enabling him to live and act in obedience to his Father as our Redeemer. From womb to tomb, the Spirit was the constant companion of the incarnate Son, and it is the Spirit's unique indwelling, empowering, and anointing work that best makes sense of these "graces" and of "Christ's supernatural abilities as well as his moral and spiritual pre-eminence."[51] This is not to deny that all of the Son's actions are his actions, or to suggest that he merely acts as a Spirit-empowered man, but it is another way of speaking of the work of all the divine persons in Christ, especially the work of the Spirit, in order to accomplish and fulfill God's eternal plan of redemption.

In the post-Reformation era, John Owen developed this point well.[52] In wrestling with the relationship between Christ's two natures, Owen, following Chalcedon, refuses to compromise the integrity of each nature, but he also refuses to follow the Patristic tendency to account for the "gifts and graces" in Christ by appealing to Christ's divine nature.[53] Instead, he appeals to the work of the Spirit, the same Spirit who is in *perichoretic* relation with the Father and Son and who shares the same identical divine nature. It is this Spirit who, along with the Father and Son, inseparably acts to bring about our salvation in and through the incarnate Son. Given the Spirit's intratrinitarian personal relation, or mode of subsistence, to the Father and the Son, he is the divine person who creates and sanctifies Christ's human nature and fills it "with grace according to the measure of its receptivity."[54] This explains why it is the Spirit who is the constant companion of the Lord Jesus, filling, strengthening, empowering, and communicating grace to him. Owen clearly states that these "graces" communicated by the Spirit to Christ's human nature do not transgress the limits of that nature, and as such, the Son, in his human nature, is not infused with omniscience or given infinite knowledge. As Owen comments, Christ's human nature remains fully and completely human, yet the Spirit fills him with light and wisdom "to the utmost capacity of a creature; but it was so, not by being changed into a divine nature or essence, but by the communication of the

---

[51] Eveson, "Inner and Psychological Life of Christ," 56.

[52] For a discussion of Owen's view, see Tyler R. Wittman, "The End of the Incarnation: John Owen, Trinitarian Agency and Christology," *IJST* 15/3 (2013): 284–300.

[53] Bray gives the example of Athanasius as one who argued for Christ's "gifts and graces" by virtue of his divine nature (Bray, "Christology," 139). Athanasius argued that the humanity of Christ borrowed divine attributes, or at least that the divine nature gifted the human nature as and when required. So, in reference to Christ's knowledge, Athanasius argued that "Jesus pretended to be ignorant of the date of his return, for example, in order to convince his disciples that he was truly human" (ibid.). This is not an adequate explanation of the biblical data.

[54] John Owen, *The Works of John Owen*, ed. William H. Goold, 16 vols. (London: Banner of Truth, 1965), 3:168.

Spirit unto it without measure."[55] Appealing to Isaiah 11:2–3 and other texts, Owen better explains this sense of *"communicatio"* in Christ, and as Macleod rightly concludes, following Owen, "This indwelling, rather than any grace of union, is the biblical explanation for the moral and spiritual pre-eminence of Christ."[56]

Here, then, are three ways the church has spoken of the *communicatio* relationship between Christ's two natures as united in his persona. In all these ways, we gain greater clarity regarding the integrity of the two natures and how the Son acts in those natures. Yet, despite this basic way of thinking about the relationship between Christ's natures and his person, the Reformation era witnessed a sharp debate between Lutherans and Reformed theologians on this very point, which once again brought the issue to the forefront and brought further clarity in our Christology. Let us briefly address this debate, not only as a continuation of the larger *communicatio* discussion but also as a polemic that helps bring greater precision to our theologizing about Christ.

Reformation Debates on the Lord's Supper and Christology

What do *communicatio* polemics in Christology have to do with the Lord's Supper, specifically the debate over Christ's presence in the elements?[57] On the surface it seems that there is no relationship between these debates, but, as is often the case, appearances are deceptive. The Reformed argued that the nature of Christ's presence in the Lord's Supper was spiritual; the Lutherans contended that Christ's presence was a local, physical presence "in, with, and under" the elements, i.e., consubstantiation. In order to explain how the body of Christ (physical, finite, localized, now risen, ascended, and seated at the right hand of the Father) is *physically* present in the Lord's Supper, the Lutherans advanced an innovative understanding of the *communicatio* and correspondingly of the nature and effects of the hypostatic union (*effecta unionis*).

In agreement with the first sense of *communicatio*, the Lutherans, along with the entire church, granted that the attributes of the two natures were communicated to the *person* of the Son; however, the Lutherans went further. Thinking that one of the consequences of the hypostatic union was an intimate communion of the two natures, each with the other, Lutherans insisted that some of the attributes of Christ's divine nature, specifically omnipotence, omniscience, and omnipresence, were also communicated to his human nature. The *Book of Concord*—representing the official Lutheran position—

---

[55] Ibid., 1:93.
[56] Macleod, *Person of Christ*, 196.
[57] See Allison, *Historical Theology*, 379–381; Muller, *Dictionary of Latin and Greek Theological Terms*, 72–74; Geoffrey W. Bromiley, "The Reformers and the Humanity of Christ," in *Perspectives on Christology: Essays in Honor of Paul K. Jewett*, ed. Marguerite Shuster and Richard Muller (Grand Rapids, MI: Zondervan, 1991), 97–104.

contended that Christ's two natures were not simply placed alongside each other "as if two boards were glued together";[58] instead, due to this "indescribable union," the relationship between Christ's two natures was similar to a rod of iron permeated at every point by the fire that heats it, or similar to the union of soul and body in humans.[59] In the end, Christ's human nature, due to its union with the divine nature, was elevated, and this *genus majesticum* ("genus of majesty") is the basis for asserting that the *physical* presence of Christ (now localized in heaven) is "in, with, and under" the elements in the Lord's Supper (on earth).

The Reformed rejected the Lutheran view. In fact, they charged the Lutherans with "mixing" Christ's two natures, similar to monophysitism—something denied by Chalcedon. The Lutherans denied this charge by insisting that Christ's natures were not transformed essentially by their communion. "Neither is one [nature] transformed into the other. Rather, each retains its own essential characteristics, which never become the characteristics of the other nature,"[60] and thus, divine attributes never become predicates of Christ's human nature even though the human nature is granted a share in them by virtue of the hypostatic union.

The problem for the Lutherans, however, was making sense of their view, and all of their explanations seemed wanting. For example, they distinguished between the "operative attributes of God" (e.g., omnipotence, omnipresence, and omniscience) and "quiescent attributes" (e.g., infinitude, eternity), and then argued that it is only the former attributes that are communicated to Christ's human nature, not the latter ones. Or, they appealed to the distinction between the incarnation (the assumption of flesh) and the self-emptying. They then insisted that in the "incarnation" the Son, as the subject, makes "the human nature, which is inherently finite, fit for the indwelling of the fullness of deity and imparting to it the above-mentioned divine attributes [operative]."[61] However, in the "self-emptying," the God-man, as the subject, allows for some kind of divestiture of attributes first imparted to him. But what exactly is this divestiture?

In the seventeenth century, Lutherans differed in their response. Some argued that Christ refrained only from the *public* use of these divine attributes, so that in the self-emptying the attributes were used, but in a hidden/latent manner. After Christ's resurrection, the attributes were then expressed visibly and publicly, even though they existed "invisibly already from the hour of his conception."[62] Of course, as Bavinck rightly notes, if care is not taken,

---

[58] The Epitome of the Formula of Concord 8/5.
[59] Ibid.
[60] Ibid., 8/2.
[61] Bavinck, *Sin and Salvation in Christ*, 3:258.
[62] Ibid.

an implication of such a view is that Jesus's entire human development, "his growth in knowledge and wisdom, his hungering and thirsting, suffering and dying, became mere appearance."[63] Others preferred to say that in the moment of self-emptying, "Christ totally ceased to use the attributes communicated to him. Though he retained them, he retained them only as a capacity but did not use them. Only after his exaltation did he also exercise them."[64]

Reformed theologians were not convinced. They regarded the Lutheran view as distorting Chalcedon's understanding of the *communicatio*, resulting in at least three problems.

First, in regard to internal consistency, Lutherans must explain why there is no reciprocity in the *communicatio*. The divine nature communicates its attributes to the human, but why not vice versa, especially since they appeal to the hypostatic union for their support? For example, John Mueller contends that "If the incarnation is at all real, then also the communication of divine attributes to the human nature must be real, since by the personal union not only the person, but also the divine nature, which cannot be separated from the person, has entered into communion with the human nature."[65] But why only one way? As Macleod points out, "if we look at the New Testament there is much more evidence of human properties being predicated of the divine than of divine properties being predicated of the human. Certainly if such phrases as 'the blood of God' and such statements as 'They have crucified my Lord' were taken at face-value they would lend support to the idea of the humanization of the divine rather than to that of the divinization of the human."[66] Interestingly, as Kenotic Christology later arises out of Lutheranism, this point is accepted. The problem, however, with either form of argument is that Christ's two natures are confused by some kind of "blending," thus compromising the Creator-creature distinction. It is far better to conceive of the *communicatio* as Chalcedon did, namely, what is true of both natures is "communicated" to the person, but there is no *communicatio* between the natures.

Second, in regard to Christ's human nature, a Lutheran view seems to compromise it.[67] To attribute omnipotence, omniscience, and omnipresence to Christ's human nature, from the moment of conception, is to destroy any sense of what a human nature is; it is to lose the biblical teaching regarding Christ's own human development; and ultimately it robs us of a Redeemer who can truly represent us as our mediator.

Third, Lutheran Christology is in danger of losing the crucial biblical

---

[63] Ibid.
[64] Ibid.
[65] John T. Mueller, *Christian Dogmatics: A Handbook of Doctrinal Theology for Pastors, Teachers, and Laymen* (St. Louis: Concordia, 1955), 275.
[66] Macleod, *Person of Christ*, 197; cf. Vos, *Christology*, 73, who makes the same point.
[67] Vos, *Christology*, 73–74.

distinction between the states of humiliation and exaltation in Christ's work, a distinction which we argued in Part II is central to New Testament Christology.[68] In choosing to become incarnate and humbling himself to the point of death (state of humiliation), the Son lived and acted in his humanity and truly experienced a human life as our representative head. As he lived his life, nothing of his deity was removed, yet he chose, in obedience to his Father and in relation to the Spirit, to obey the Father's will as the last Adam, and by his obedience, effectively achieved and secured our eternal salvation. In order to do this, there was a real "communication of gifts and graces," as noted above, which Scripture affirms and Lutheranism undercuts. In addition, as a result of his obedient work, Scripture affirms that there was a real transition from the state of humiliation to that of exaltation (Phil. 2:9). Yet, Lutheranism has a difficult time accounting for Christ's glorification in his human nature, given their view that "from the moment of conception he possesses the majesty of the divine," since "Such a glorification would have been impossible if the human nature of Christ were already in possession of the divine majesty simply by virtue of the incarnation itself."[69]

Furthermore, Scripture does not allow, even in Christ's glorification, the communication of divine attributes to his human nature. The theological rule of "the finite is not capable of containing the infinite" applies to the human nature of Christ in the states of both humiliation *and* exaltation.[70] As Macleod comments, "Even in the case of the Mediator there are clear limits to the idea of *theiosis*."[71] No doubt, Christ's human nature is glorified to a degree far beyond what he possessed on earth and even far beyond what was true of Adam before the fall. Christ's humanity can share in the glory of God, and it can serve as the revelation of God. It can, as Macleod notes, "subdue all creation to itself and exercise dominion over heaven and earth. It can sit in the very centre of the throne (Rev. 7:17). But it remains human, and not even the most extravagant language used of the glory of Christ should betray us into forgetting that."[72] Ultimately, to say that omnipotence, omniscience, and omnipresence are communicated to Christ's human nature is, in reality, to make it something it is not.

What is the lesson learned from this debate alongside our discussion of *enhypostasia*? Minimally, one recurring lesson is this: in Trinitarian and Christological formulation we must carefully make the "nature-person" distinction. If we think of the incarnation as the divine *nature* becoming incarnate instead of the *person*, we will introduce insurmountable problems. On this point, Bavinck perceptively notes that many Christologies, including Lutheran, inadvertently

---

[68] See Bavinck, *Sin and Salvation in Christ*, 258.
[69] Macleod, *Person of Christ*, 198.
[70] Bavinck, *Sin and Salvation in Christ*, 258.
[71] Macleod, *Person of Christ*, 198.
[72] Ibid.

make this mistake. A Lutheran view of the hypostatic union entails that the divine nature communicates to the human nature some of its attributes, as if the natures were active subjects. However, as Bavinck insists, we must constantly affirm along with Chalcedon, not only that the Creator-creature distinction is true of Christ, but also that it is "the *person* of the Son who became flesh—not the *substance* [the underlying reality] but the *subsistence* [the particular being] of the Son assumed our nature. The unity of the two natures, despite the sharp distinction between them, is unalterably anchored in the person."[73]

Furthermore, it is the *person* of the Son who is the active subject *in* two natures, so that the Son is able to live a fully divine life *and* a human life in his natures. What is true of the natures is predicated of the Son, and the Son, in his entire life, acts in a divine-human way. It is only this development of Chalcedonian orthodoxy that secures space for real human development in Christ, for a real distinction between the states of humiliation and exaltation, and for the fact that the one who accomplishes our eternal salvation is God the Son incarnate.

The *Extra* (*Calvinisticum*)

We now turn to the *extra Calvinisticum*, or what E. David Willis more accurately labels the *extra Catholicum*, given its almost universal status in the church prior to John Calvin.[74] Before we describe what is meant by this expression and its significance for Christology, let us first review three key building blocks from orthodoxy that are required to make sense of it.

First, the *person* of the Son is the active subject of the two natures (*enhypostasia*). The natures are *not* active agents; rather, it is the divine Son who acts in and through the capacities of his natures. Second, the two natures remain what they are—"without confusion" and "without change"—and whatever is true of the natures may be predicated of the *person* (*communicatio idiomatum*). Third, when the Son assumed a human nature, this not only allowed him to live and experience a human life, it also meant that he continued to share with the Father and Spirit the divine nature and a divine life. When the Son became incarnate, this did *not* result in a change in the divine nature; the Son did not cease to be what he had always been, even in the exercise of his divine attributes, hence the Scriptural teaching that the incarnate Son, in relation to the Father and Spirit, *continued* to sustain the universe (Col. 1:15–17; Heb. 1:1–3).

From these building blocks, the church taught the *extra Catholicum* (*Cal-*

---

[73] Bavinck, *Sin and Salvation in Christ*, 259.

[74] See E. David Willis, *Calvin's Catholic Christology: The Function of the So-Called Extra Calvinisticum in Calvin's Theology* (Leiden: E. J. Brill, 1966). See also the fine discussion of the *extra Calvinisticum* in Paul Helm, *John Calvin's Ideas* (Oxford: Oxford University Press, 2004), 58–92; Andrew M. McGinnis, *The Son of God Beyond the Flesh: A Historical and Theological Study of the* Extra Calvinisticum (London: Bloomsbury T&T Clark, 2014).

vinisticum), or simply, the *extra*. What is it?[75] The *extra* is the view that, in the incarnation, the Son not only retained his divine attributes *but also continued to exercise* them in Trinitarian relation. It also insists that, since the Son now subsists in two natures, *he* is not completely circumscribed by the limits of his human nature; the Son is able to live a divine life *outside* (*extra*) his human nature while simultaneously living a fully human life in his human nature.[76] From the moment of conception, the Son humbled himself. In so doing, he did not override the limitations of his human nature. The Son, in his human nature, lived like we do and accepted the limitations of that nature as our representative, covenant head, and mediator. Yet, in order to account for the *incarnate* Son's continual, cosmic exercise of his divine attributes (e.g., Col. 1:17), the church insisted that the Son's exercise of his deity is "outside" his human nature and life. Thus, from conception onward, the Son lived his life *totus in carne et totus extra carne*, that is, totally in the flesh and totally *outside* or apart from the flesh.[77]

The *extra* is a consistent affirmation throughout church history.[78] For example, Augustine affirms it in a number of places. In his *Letters* he writes, "Christian doctrine does not hold that God took on the flesh, in which He was born of the Virgin, in such wise as to abandon or lose His care of the government of the world, or to transfer this care, reduced and concentrated, so to speak, to that small body."[79] Augustine continues in the same vein, stressing that, though incarnate, the Son retained and exercised all of his divine attributes undiminished. He writes,

> And we think that something impossible to believe is told us about the omnipotence of God, when we are told that the Word of God, by whom all things were made, took flesh from a virgin and appeared to mortal senses without

---

[75] For a discussion of the *extra*, especially in Reformation and post-Reformation theology, see Muller, *Dictionary of Latin and Greek Theological Terms*, 111. Muller writes, "The Word is fully united to but never totally contained within the human nature and, therefore, even in the incarnation is to be conceived of as beyond or outside of (*extra*) the human nature" (ibid.).

[76] Willis explains the *extra* in this way: "The so-called extra Calvinisticum teaches that the Eternal Son of God, even after the Incarnation, was united to the human nature to form One Person but was not restricted to the flesh" (Willis, *Calvin's Catholic Christology*, 1). It was first called the *extra Calvinisticum* by Lutheran theologians who used it in a negative way in the context of the debates over the presence of Christ in the Lord's Supper. Yet what Calvin, along with the entire church, was seeking to preserve was the reality of the divine Son continuing to subsist in the divine nature and the full reality of the Son's deity, even as the incarnate one.

[77] In describing the *extra*, Oliver Crisp captures two points that distinguish classical Christology from more non-classical views. First, in the incarnation the divine Son "retains all his essential divine attributes," and second, "these divine attributes [are] exercised throughout the period of the incarnation" (Oliver D. Crisp, *Divinity and Humanity* [Cambridge: Cambridge University Press, 2007], 142). At its heart, the *extra* affirms that the Son while incarnate is also "simultaneously providentially sustaining the cosmos" (ibid.).

[78] Willis observes that the *extra* was widely held in the Patristic era, but by theologians who occupied varying Christological positions. Yet what united the diverse Christologies, which the *extra* helped make sense of, was the attempt of most people to keep together "(1) the impassible and immutable character of God and its correlate, the reality of Jesus Christ's atoning suffering and (2) the constancy of God's ordering of the universe and the identity of this ordering God with the Savior" (Willis, *Calvin's Catholic Christology*, 49–51).

[79] Augustine, "Letter 137," in *St. Augustine: Letters 131–164*, trans. Wilfrid Parsons, The Fathers of the Church, vol. 3 (Washington, DC: Catholic University of America Press, 1953), 20.

destroying His immortality or infringing His eternity, or diminishing His power, or neglecting the government of the world, or leaving the bosom of the Father, where he is intimately with him and in him.[80]

Cyril of Alexandria expresses the same truth when he writes,

> . . . When seen as a babe and wrapped in swaddling clothes, even when still in the bosom of the Virgin who bore him, he [the only-begotten Word of God] filled all creation as God, and was enthroned with him who begot him. For the divine cannot be numbered or measured and does not admit of circumscription. So confessing the Word [to be] hypostatically united, we worship one Son and Lord Jesus Christ, neither putting apart and dividing man and God, as joined with each other by a union of dignity and authority—for this would be an empty phrase and no more—nor speaking of the Word of God separately as Christ, and then separately of him who was of a woman as another Christ, but knowing only one Christ, the Word of God the Father with his own flesh.[81]

In this quote from Cyril, notice his strong emphasis on the unity of the person, the natures united in the person, the unchangeableness of the Son in his unity with the Father, and the Son's existence even beyond his human nature, so that the Son simultaneously is *in* the creation, yet *he* also rules, sustains, and governs that very same creation. J. N. D. Kelly, in reference to Cyril, says, "The Logos, as he [Cyril] liked to say, 'remains what He was'; what happened was that at the incarnation, while continuing to exist eternally in the form of God, He added to that by taking the form of a servant. Both before and after the incarnation He was the same Person, unchanged in His essential deity. The only difference was that He Who had existed 'outside flesh' (*asarkos*) now became 'embodied' (*ensōmatos*).[82]

Athanasius also teaches the *extra*. In his work *On the Incarnation of the Word*, Athanasius gives one of the clearest Patristic expositions of the *extra* in these words:

> For he [Christ] was not, as might be imagined, circumscribed in the body, nor, while present in the body, was he absent elsewhere; nor, while he moved the body, was the universe left void of his working and providence; but, thing most marvelous, Word as he was, so far from being contained by anything, he rather contained all things himself; and just as while present in the whole of creation, he is at once distinct in being from the universe, and present in all things by his own power—giving order to all things, and over all and in all revealing his own providence, and giving life to each thing and all things,

---

[80] Ibid., 22–23. For more statements from Augustine, see Willis, *Calvin's Catholic Christology*, 44–48.

[81] Cited in Willis, *Calvin's Catholic Christology*, 59; see T. H. Bindley, ed., *The Oecumenical Documents of the Faith*, 3rd ed. (London: Methuen, 1925), 214.

[82] J. N. D. Kelly, *Early Christian Doctrines*, 5th rev. ed. (London: A & C Black, 1977), 319.

including the whole without being included, but being in his own Father alone wholly in every respect—thus, even while present in a human body and himself quickening it, he was, without inconsistency, quickening the universe as well, and was in every process of nature, and was outside the whole, and while known from the body by his works, he was none the less manifest from the working of the universe as well.[83]

The *extra* is also taught in the medieval era,[84] yet it is famously identified with Calvin. In fact, the term is pejoratively applied to him by Lutheran theologians in the Reformation polemics regarding the Lord's Supper.[85] In the *Institutes* Calvin refers explicitly to the *extra* in two places: first, in his treatment of the incarnation in Book 2, and second in his discussion of the Lord's Supper in Book 4. Here is the quote from Book 2:

They thrust upon us as something absurd the fact that if the Word of God became flesh, then he was confined within the narrow prison of an earthly body. This is mere impudence! For even if the Word in his immeasurable essence united with the nature of man into one person, we do not imagine that he was confined therein. Here is something marvelous: the Son of God descended from heaven in such a way that, without leaving heaven, he willed to be borne in the virgin's womb, to go about the earth, and to hang upon the cross; yet he continuously filled the world as he had done from the beginning![86]

---

[83] Athanasius, "On the Incarnation of the Word," in *Christology of the Later Fathers*, ed. Edward R. Hardy, trans. Archibald Robertson (Philadelphia: Westminister, 1954), 70–71.

[84] See Willis, *Calvin's Catholic Christology*, 34–44. In the medieval era, there was a Christological distinction made between *totus* and *totum*, which is similar to what becomes known as the *extra Calvinisticum*, even though in the Reformation the *extra* is used more in relationship to the Lord's Supper debates. *Totus* refers to the "whole person" and *totum* refers to the "natures." Thus, to speak of Christ as *totus Christus*, i.e., "the whole Christ," is another way of saying that the *person* of the Son was united to a human nature but *he* also has an existence and reality beyond or outside (*extra*) that human nature and is thus omnipresent because *he* subsists in the divine nature and, by virtue of his deity, he is omnipresent, omnipotent, eternal, etc. On the other hand, to speak of Christ as *totum Christi*, i.e., "all of Christ," refers to the natures of Christ and it means that in his human nature Christ is not eternal, omnipresent, omnipotent, etc. On this distinction, see Muller, *Dictionary of Latin and Greek Theological Terms*, 305. Aquinas also uses this distinction: "Not even in the hypostatic union is the Word of God or the divine nature comprehended by the human nature. Although the divine nature was wholly united to the human nature in the one Person of the Son, nevertheless the human nature did not comprehend the whole power of the divinity was not, as it were, circumscribed" (Thomas Aquinas, *Summa Theologica*, 3.10.1.2).

[85] We can see the influence of Calvin in the Heidelberg Catechism, question 48, which describes the *extra*: "Question: But if his human nature is not present, wherever his Godhead is, are not then these two natures in Christ separated from one another? Answer: Not at all, for since the Godhead is illimitable and omnipresent, it must necessarily follow that the same is beyond the limits of the human nature he assumed, and yet is nevertheless in this human nature, and remains personally united to it."

[86] John Calvin, *Institutes of the Christian Religion*, John T. McNeill, trans. Ford Lewis Battles (Philadelphia: Westminster, 1960), 2.13.4. In Book 4, Calvin writes in reference to the Lord's Supper, "But some are carried away with such contentiousness as to say that because of the natures joined in Christ, wherever Christ's divinity is, there also is his flesh, which cannot be separated from it. . . . But from Scripture we plainly infer that the one person of Christ so consists of two natures that each nevertheless retains unimpaired its own distinctive character. . . . Surely, when the Lord of glory is said to be crucified (1 Cor. 2:8), Paul does not mean that he suffered anything in his divinity, but he says this because the same Christ, who was cast down and despised, and suffered in the flesh, was God and Lord of glory. In this way he was also Son of man in heaven (John 3:13), for the very same Christ, who, according to the flesh, dwelt as Son of man on earth, was God in heaven. In this manner, he is said to have descended to that place according to his divinity, not because divinity left heaven to hide itself in the prison house of the body, but because even though it filled all things, still in Christ's very humanity it dwelt bodily (Col. 2:9), that is, by nature, and in a certain ineffable way. There is a commonplace distinction of the schools to which I am not ashamed to refer: although the whole Christ is everywhere, still the whole of that which is in him is not everywhere. And would

Calvin reflects the sentiments of the church from the Patristic era to his own. In order to preserve all that Scripture says about God the Son incarnate, we must insist on the *extra*. Paul Helm, in discussing the *extra* in Calvin, makes the simple observation that Calvin argued for it because "if the Incarnation is truly the Incarnation of the Son of God, then it must preserve the divinity of the Son of God unaltered or unimpaired. For otherwise it would not be a true incarnation of the Son."[87] Helm further insists that Calvin, along with the church, even allowing for poetic license, would not be pleased with the couplet from Charles Wesley's Hymn, "Let Earth and Heaven Combine": "Our God contracted to a span; Incomprehensibly made man." As Helm notes, "In Calvin's view, God was not contracted to a span in the Incarnation but, rather, was in union with that which is only a 'span'—that is, with human nature."[88]

Helm concludes his discussion of Calvin's Christology and captures the heart of the *extra* with these words: "For Calvin, Jesus of Nazareth, being God the Son incarnate, was God in the closest union with human nature that it is possible to be, but he was not identical with human nature, nor mixed with it."[89] Willis makes the same point. In Calvin, the Incarnation is a reassertion of Christ's rule of creation which has rebelled in Adam in the fall. In the Incarnation, the Son's life and power were never exhausted "by his fleshly accomplishments,"[90] and the Son's "eternal properties were exercised by Christ during the Incarnation not by the humanity of the One Person but by the divinity of the One Person."[91] Thus, as Willis concludes regarding Calvin's Christology, "In the Incarnation, the Son of God left heaven only in such a way that he continued to exercise his dominion over creation; the Incarnation was the extension of his empire, not the momentary abdication of it."[92] Furthermore, Calvin, along with orthodoxy, affirmed a strong asymmetry between the person of the Son and the human nature he assumed—an asymmetry underscored by the *extra*. In the incarnation, the person of the Son has ontological priority, to use Helm's words, over the human nature since *he* exists before the existence of the human nature that he assumed. That is why the person of the Son can act independently of the human nature he assumed, since "his human nature has never acted and cannot act independently of the person of the Word."[93]

Yet, in affirming the *extra*, Calvin is *not* seeking to minimize Christ's humanity. Calvin insists on the full humanity of Christ; without it, we have no

---

that the Schoolmen themselves had honestly weighed the force of this statement. For thus would the absurd fiction of Christ's carnal presence have been obviated" (ibid., 4.17.30).
[87] Helm, *John Calvin's Ideas*, 62.
[88] Ibid.
[89] Ibid., 65.
[90] Willis, *Calvin's Catholic Christology*, 76.
[91] Ibid.
[92] Ibid.
[93] Helm, *John Calvin's Ideas*, 71.

Redeemer. In fact, for Calvin, the *extra* is indispensable to making sense of the voluntary obedience of the Son as our mediator. What is saving in Christ's teaching, miracles, and death is not simply that they occurred but that they occurred *voluntarily*. As the last Adam and obedient Son, as our great prophet, priest, and king, Christ fulfills his office as our mediator by undoing the first Adam's work by the whole course of his obedience. The *extra* guards this truth because, as Willis notes, "that doctrine points to the fact that throughout his humility in the flesh, Christ was not compelled to become incarnate or to adhere to his whole course of obedience. The redemptive activity of the incarnate Lord was a free movement of the Eternal Son."[94]

For Calvin, then, the incarnation and the self-emptying of the Son (*kenosis*) is best interpreted under the heading of *krypsis*, i.e., concealment or veiling.[95] As Willis notes, for Calvin, "The *kenosis* was the concealment, not the abdication, of the Eternal Son's divine majesty."[96] Once again, this is not intended to diminish Christ's humanity; rather it is intended to uphold it along with the Son's full deity. Interestingly, Calvin, unlike some in the Patristic and Medieval eras, does not downplay Luke's statement that Jesus "grew" in wisdom.[97] For Calvin, statements like this should not embarrass us; instead they reveal the truth that the Son chose to become our Redeemer. For our salvation, the divine Son chose to subject himself to ignorance, not of necessity, as with us, but because of his love and obedience to his Father, and out of love for his people. In the end, it is for these reasons that the *extra* undergirded Calvin's entire Christology. As Willis rightly notes, the *extra* functioned for Calvin "as a medium for professing the unity of the person of Jesus Christ without displacing mystery with speculation, and it is a way of accounting for the freedom of Christ's obedience which is his redemptive work."[98]

Given the importance of the *extra* in historical theology, it is surprising how quickly it is rejected or replaced with something else. The *extra* is crucial in helping the church to explain the full scope of the Scriptural presentation of the incarnation and how the Son functioned in and through both natures, yet as we will discuss in Part IV, it has been rejected by various Kenotic Christologies. But it is important to remember that since the Patristic era, through the medieval and Reformation eras, and even to our own day, the church has argued that the *extra*, along with *enhypostasia* and a proper understanding of *communicatio idiomatum*, is essential to a biblically and theologically faithful, orthodox Christology. How exactly we explain all of these pieces of a robust Christology, especially the dual activity of the Son that the *extra* requires, is

---

[94] Willis, *Calvin's Catholic Christology*, 85; cf. Calvin, *Institutes of the Christian Religion*, 2.16.5.
[95] See Willis, *Calvin's Catholic Christology*, 80–82.
[96] Ibid., 80; cf. *Institutes of the Christian Religion*, 2.13.2.
[97] See Calvin's commentary on Luke 2:40.
[98] Willis, *Calvin's Catholic Christology*, 100.

not easy. Yet in order to do justice to all of the Scriptural data, let alone the tradition, it is necessary to uphold these Chalcedonian developments, including the *extra*. That is why the church has thought it necessary to affirm that, in the incarnation, the divine Son has taken to himself a human nature and, as a result, as Bray writes, the Son, our Lord Jesus Christ, is able "to live and work in each of his two natures according to their respective attributes."[99]

THE MONOTHELITE-DYOTHELITE CONTROVERSY

We now turn to one last post-Chalcedonian issue as we round out our discussion of orthodox, classical Christology. The issue centers on the seventh-century "will" debate. In Protestant and Evangelical theology, the conclusions of the post-Chalcedonian Councils are either little known or ignored. This is especially true of the Third Council of Constantinople (681). For example, John Macquarrie, a critic of orthodoxy, described the conclusions of the Council as the "*reductio ad absurdum*" of Chalcedonian Christology,[100] and he is not alone in his assessment. In the Council's rejection of monothelitism (Christ has one will) and its affirmation of dyothelitism (Christ has two wills, one divine and one human), Macquarrie and others see the larger problem of distinguishing "person" from "nature," maintaining a consistent two-nature Christology, and dividing up what is predicated of each nature, to name a few problems.

For at least two reasons these negative assessments ought to be rejected. First, at the heart of this debate is the person-nature distinction, which is crucial for Christian theology. Second, in light of the person-nature distinction, it is hardly arbitrary to think through what belongs to a "person" versus a "nature." Furthermore, the church has given reasoned explanations to defend dyothelitism over against monothelitism. Not only is this a matter of church tradition; it is also well grounded biblically and theologically, which we will discuss. Interestingly today, within and outside of evangelical theology, many are either unaware of this debate or are embracing the monothelite viewpoint again.[101] Contrary to such opinion, we will argue that the "will" debate is not esoteric; rather, it is a necessary development of Chalcedonian orthodoxy that helps clarify and make better sense of the biblical data regarding the identity of Christ and the nature of the incarnation. We will discuss the "will" debate in three steps: first, why the church thought the "will" debate was important;

---

[99] Gerald Bray, *God Is Love: A Biblical and Systematic Theology* (Wheaton, IL: Crossway, 2012), 200.

[100] John Macquarrie, *Jesus Christ in Modern Thought* (London: SCM; Philadelphia: Trinity Press, 1990), 166.

[101] There is a recent trend in evangelical Christology to adopt monothelitism. Some of the reason is due to the fact that currently we tend to identify "person" with the person's will and we do not sufficiently distinguish "person" and "nature" as in the past. In the Patristic era, the Word-flesh Christologies of Arius, Apollinarius, et al., also identified "person" with "soul," "will," "mind," which orthodoxy rejected. This is why Grillmeier sees monothelitism as a continuation of the Word-flesh Christology of Apollinarius (Aloys Grillmeier, *From the Apostolic Age to Chalcedon [451]*, vol. 1 in *Christ in Christian Tradition*, trans. John Bowden, 2nd rev. ed. [Atlanta: John Knox, 1975], 33).

second, the basic concern of monothelitism and their overall arguments; third, a defense of dyothelitism as represented by Maximus the Confessor.

The Importance of the "Will" Debate for Christology

Why did the church think the will debate was important? Three reasons may be given. First, the church insisted that dyothelitism was necessary to uphold the full humanity of Christ over against monophysitism and Apollinarianism. Monothelitism was viewed as a variation of these older heresies. How so? Just as Apollinarianism and monophysitism identified "will" with "person," so monothelitism continued these problematic features of Word-flesh Christologies.[102] Also, placing "will" in "person" and not in "nature," and arguing that Christ's one will is a divine one seems to entail that Christ's human nature does not have a human will. But as Macleod notes, "For one thing, whatever doubts may attach to the definition of will, it is clear that there can be no true human nature without the ability to make human choices."[103] How are we to conceive of a human nature apart from a human will?

Furthermore, Chalcedon affirmed that Christ's human nature consisted of a body *and a soul*, and it did not identify "soul" with "person." Why? Because it sought to make sense of Jesus's ordinary human desires, longings, preferences, aspirations, and aversions. In addition, John 6:38—"For I have come down from heaven, not to do my own will but the will of him who sent me"—seems to require not only a metaphysical distinction between the will of Jesus and the will of the Father, but the logical possibility that Jesus's natural preferences might not always coincide with the wishes of the Father.[104] All of these data seemed to require that, in Christ, a true human will was at work, ultimately seen in the garden of Gethsemane, where Jesus must choose between two ways and two wills—"nevertheless, not as I will, but as you will" (Matt. 26:39).

Second, the church argued that dyothelitism was crucial for soteriology.[105] Picking up the famous maxim of Gregory of Nazianzus, "what is not assumed is not healed," the church insisted that Jesus cannot be our Redeemer without a human will, since it is by the Son's obedience *as a man*, in his life and death, that he accomplishes our salvation and serves as "the model for all

---

[102] There is a legitimate debate over the background of monothelitism. Some have argued that it originated from Cyrillian Christology, given Cyril's emphasis on the unity of the person in Christ. For a convincing argument that monothelitism is unorthodox, see Bathrellos, *Byzantine Christ*, 89–97. For a discussion on monothelitism as a heresy, see Kallistos Ware, "Christian Theology in the East, 600–1453," in *A History of Christian Doctrine*, ed. Hubert Cunliffe-Jones (Edinburgh: T&T Clark, 1978), 181–225. Ware argues that monothelitism was "a revival of the heresy of Apollinarius" (ibid., 188).

[103] Macleod, *Person of Christ*, 179.

[104] See ibid.

[105] See Maximus the Confessor, *Disputatio cum Pyrrho*, in *The Disputation with Pyrrhus of Our Father among the Saints, Maximus the Confessor*, trans. Joseph P. Farrell (South Canaan, PA: St. Tikhon's Seminary Press, 1990); cf. Ware, "Christian Theology in the East," 188.

Christians."[106] But how is all of this possible if the incarnate Son has not assumed a human will? Bathrellos captures this point well: "In the monothelite Christology, Christ's salvific human obedience to the Father is eliminated, and his humanity is relegated to a state of passivity. But such a Christology could not be sustained theologically."[107]

Third, dyothelitism is necessary for Trinitarian theology. "Will" is best located in the *nature* of God, not the person, thus in pro-Nicene Trinitarianism, what is common to all three divine persons is their operation, power, nature, and deity, including a shared will. Yet the Father shares the one will in accordance with his mode of subsistence *as the Father*, and the same is true of the Son and Spirit.[108] But since monothelitism places the "will" in the *person*, it seems to entail two serious implications. If there is only one will in God, which orthodoxy has affirmed, then this would require that there is only one person, hence modalism. The only alternative is to insist that there are three wills in God, but this runs the risk of surrendering the divine unity. Today, the latter implication is endorsed by many social Trinitarians, who argue for three wills in God, locating "will" in the persons, yet disputing the charge that they are ceding God's unity. We will return to this point in Part IV in our discussion of current evangelical Christologies.

Overall, the church insisted that the "will" debate was important. Obviously the monothelites thought otherwise, and it is to their concerns that we now turn.

Monothelitism: Its Basic Concern and Arguments[109]

Monothelitism was the occasion for the Lateran Council (649) and Constantinople III (681). Sergius, Patriarch of Constantinople, argued that due to the union of the two natures in the one person, one must think of a single "energy" or operation in Christ, the theandric (divine-human) operation, which was identified with the divine will. Such an argument placed Christ's "will" in his "person," instead of locating it in his "nature," thus rejecting what Constantinople III would endorse, namely that Christ has two wills, one divine and one human.

In addition, monothelitism also stood contrary to Chalcedon (451), which taught that Christ had a rational soul, endowed with consciousness and choice, *and* that Christ's human soul was not identical with his person. Monothelitism, however, reversed this understanding on both counts. In fact, if they spoke

---

[106] Thomas A. Watts, "Two Wills in Christ? Contemporary Objections Considered in the Light of a Critical Examination of Maximus the Confessor's *Disputation with Pyrrhus*," *WTJ* 71 (2009): 467.

[107] Bathrellos, *Byzantine Christ*, 98.

[108] For a fine summary discussion of these points, see Gilles Emery, *The Trinity: An Introduction to Catholic Doctrine on the Triune God*, trans. Matthew Levering (Washington, DC: Catholic University Press, 2011), 83–158.

[109] In what follows, I am indebted to Bathrellos, *Byzantine Christ*; Watts, "Two Wills in Christ?," 455–487.

of a human will at all in Christ, they only did so, as Bathrellos notes, by say-ing that "Christ appropriated *our* human will and accommodated *our* way of willing."[110]

Why this reversal? What was their concern? Basically, it was to preserve the unity of Christ's person as one acting subject, since they agreed with Chalce-don that the unity in Christ was *not* a blending of two natures but a union of natures in his *person*. Yet, they believed that they could maintain such a unity of person only by affirming a single will in Christ, since a double will would destroy this unity. Thus, monothelites argued that neither Jesus's human soul nor his body ever acted except by the divine will of the Son. The cry of agony in Gethsemane was *not* an expression of a distinction between the human and divine wills in Christ; instead it was an expression of the fact that Christ was truly suffering anxiety and distress in contemplation of his approaching death. Five basic arguments capture their view, arguments which continue today.[111]

First, monothelites argued that the biblical grounding for dyothelitism is lacking. Jesus speaks of his own will in the Gospels, thus distinguishing it from that of the Father (e.g., John 5:30; 6:38). These data imply that the Son has a singular will alongside the will of the Father. Also, Jesus never refers to his "wills" as if he has two of them, which is best explained by tying "will" to "person." Also, monothelites insisted that the standard appeal to Gethsemane (Luke 22:42) is inconclusive. Today, J. P. Moreland and William Craig raise this objection. They write, "Passages in the Gospels usually used as proof texts of this doctrine—such as Jesus' prayer in Gethsemane, 'Yet, not my will but yours be done' (Lk 22:42)—do not contemplate a struggle of Jesus' human will with his divine will (he is not, after all, talking to himself!), but have reference to the interaction between Jesus' will ('my will') and the Father's will ('yours')."[112]

Second, monothelites argued that "will" is *not* located in nature, since it is the *person* who engages in acts of willing. Macquarrie asserts this point: to ascribe two wills to Christ proceeds "on the false assumption that there is a faculty or organ of the mind called the 'will' which has the function of making decisions. . . . But a little reflection on the use of language shows that the 'will' is nothing but the activity of willing, and this is an activity of the whole person. The will is simply the self in action."[113] It is best, then, to think of "will" in terms of a "person" choosing, or the acts of willing by a person. If that is so, then to speak of two wills is unnecessary.[114]

---

[110] Bathrellos, *Byzantine Christ*, 97.

[111] Watts lists seven contemporary arguments against dyothelitism that are very similar to those given in the seventh century (Watts, "Two Wills in Christ?," 456–458).

[112] J. P. Moreland and William Lane Craig, *Philosophical Foundations for a Christian Worldview* (Downers Grove, IL: InterVarsity Press, 2003), 611.

[113] Macquarrie, *Jesus Christ in Modern Thought*, 166–167.

[114] Bathrellos gives the Patristic example of Pyrrhus, who argues this point (Bathrellos, *Byzantine Christ*, 80).

Third, monothelites argued that two wills entailed two persons, which denies Christ's unity and flirts with Nestorianism. If "will" means acts of willing by a person, then to say that Christ has two wills seems to require two distinct persons. Friedrich Schleiermacher argued this point. He asserted, "If Christ had two wills, then the unity of the person is no more than apparent."[115]

Fourth, monothelites argued that two wills in Christ would either oppose one another, which is unbiblical, or conform to one another, which would make one of the wills superfluous.[116] As to the former option, if Christ's wills oppose each other, this seems to undercut the sinlessness of Christ, since his human will would go against his divine will. Yet, as to the latter option, if Jesus's human will always conformed to his divine will, why then speak about two wills, since "[o]ne or the other will is always simply a superfluous accompaniment of the other."[117]

Fifth, some monothelites reasoned that, even if arguments for two wills were cogent, it did not eliminate speaking about Jesus as having one will in another sense, a sense which is essential for preserving the unity of Christ's person. Some allowed for the possibility that we could speak of Jesus having two wills, yet there are also good reasons to say that Christ has only one will, specifically emphasizing Jesus's volitional unity as a person.[118] In this way, some monothelites thought they could uphold the concern of dyothelites while arguing for one will.

Dyothelitism and the Contribution of Maximus the Confessor

What was the response of the church to these arguments? At Constantinople III (681) the church rejected monothelitism and embraced dyothelitism. A number of key figures were involved, but the most significant theologian was Maximus the Confessor (580–662). Even though he died in exile prior to the Council, it was his influence that carried the day.[119]

Maximus viewed monothelitism as a dangerous continuation of Apollinarianism, monophysitism, and the Word-flesh Christologies of the previous era. Conversely, he viewed dyothelitism as a necessary extension and further articulation of the Chalcedonian Definition. Even though the "will" debate did not officially take place until the seventh century, dyothelitism is found in such

---

[115] Friedrich Schleiermacher, *Christian Faith*, ed. H. R. Mackintosh and James S. Stewart (Edinburgh: T&T Clark, 1999), 394. For a similar objection, see Moreland and Craig, *Philosophical Foundations*, 602; Wolfhart Pannenberg, *Jesus: God and Man*, trans. Lewis L. Wilkins and Duane A. Priebe (London: SCM, 1968), 294.

[116] Bathrellos describes Pyrrhus as using this argument (Bathrellos, *Byzantine Christ*, 82).

[117] Schleiermacher, *Christian Faith*, 394; cf. Pannenberg, *Jesus: God and Man*, 293–294.

[118] This argument turns on the distinction between "real" and "verbal" monothelitism. Watts explains the distinction: "Real monothelitism argues that Christ has one will alone. Verbal monothelitism is more subtle: it argues that it is possible to *speak* of one will alone in Christ, in some sense, even if it is also possible to speak in another sense of two wills" (Watts, "Two Wills in Christ?," 459).

[119] For a helpful discussion of Maximus the Confessor, see Edward T. Oakes, *Infinity Dwindled to Infancy: A Catholic and Evangelical Christology* (Grand Rapids, MI: Eerdmans, 2011), 153–160.

figures as Athanasius, the Cappadocian theologians, Leontius of Byzantium, and Leontius of Jerusalem.[120] Yet it was due to Maximus's work that the debate and discussion advanced. Let us describe Maximus's defense of dyothelitism in seven points:[121]

1. Maximus works with a clear "person-nature" distinction.[122] He follows the orthodox tradition by thinking of "nature" in terms of *what* is common to a thing and of "person" in terms of the *who* or subject of the nature. Person is characterized by subsisting by itself, while nature subsists in the person, and it is for this reason that Maximus asserts that there is an ontological priority of person over nature. Also, true to Chalcedon, in Christ the "person" is the divine Son who has eternally shared the divine nature with the Father and Spirit and now subsists in two natures.

2. How does Maximus define "will"? Maximus makes two crucial distinctions. First, he distinguishes between the "faculty of will" (*thelēma/thelēsis*), integral to all rational beings, by which they are capable of willing, *and* the "object of will" (*thelēton/thelēthen*), namely that which is willed by those who possess this faculty.[123] In terms of the latter, God and humans have at times the same "will," but in regard to the former, they do not, given the Creator-creature distinction. As Watts explains, this distinction enables Maximus to clarify exactly what is doubled in Christ: "In arguing that Jesus has two wills, he [Maximus] does not mean that Jesus always willed two different (and possibly contradictory) things at once; rather, he means that he had the *ability* to will as man and the *ability* to will as God."[124] Maximus illustrates this distinction by drawing an analogy with the eye. Just as we distinguish between "the faculty of sight" (i.e., the eye itself) and "what is seen," in a similar way we can distinguish "the faculty of will" (i.e., the *capacity* or *ability* of will) from "what is willed."[125]

Before leaving this distinction, it is important to note that Maximus also wrestles with the nature of "the faculty of will." Watts notes that Maximus's conception of the "will" is similar to Jonathan Edwards's understanding in two ways. First, Maximus would have agreed with Edwards's definition of "the faculty of the will" as "that faculty or power or principle of mind by which it is capable of choosing."[126] So, for example, in relation to human *nature*, there comes the power or the ability to will. It is due to this understanding that Maximus places "will" in nature and not in "person," since he cannot

---

[120] See Bathrellos, *Byzantine Christ*, 51–54.
[121] See Maximus the Confessor, *Disputatio cum Pyrrho*.
[122] See Bathrellos, *Byzantine Christ*, 99–116.
[123] See Watts, "Two Wills in Christ?," 460–461, 473–475; cf. Bathrellos, *Byzantine Christ*, 119.
[124] Watts, "Two Wills in Christ?," 473 (emphasis mine); cf. Bathrellos, *Byzantine Christ*, 119.
[125] See Maximus the Confessor, *Disputatio cum Pyrrho*, 8–9.
[126] Jonathan Edwards, *Freedom of the Will*, ed. Paul Ramsey, Works of Jonathan Edwards, vol. 1 (New Haven, CT: Yale University Press, 1957), 137.

conceive of how to do justice to Jesus willing *as God and as man* apart from doing so. To locate the "will" in person is to lose Christ's full humanity and his ability to act *as a man*.[127] Furthermore, involved in this "natural" will are both instinctual desires and the ability to choose.[128] In Christ, because of his human will, the Son not only instinctively willed to eat, to drink, and to sustain life *as a man*; he also chose and deliberated *as a man*. Second, Maximus, like Edwards, to use current language, would have viewed the will as more compatibilistic than libertarian. He viewed freedom as "not the ability to choose anything at all, but the natural inclination towards what is good without ignorance or hesitation."[129] Thus, similar to Edwards, Maximus agreed that the will's freedom lies in the turning of a rational creature toward the natural object of its desire, which in our case is to serve and obey God.[130] As Watts explains, "He [Maximus] therefore refused the dilemma that the will is either entirely free to choose anything, including its own desires, or entirely bound such that the willer has lost all responsibility. . . . For . . . Maximus, the will cannot be seen as something separate from the nature in which it inheres."[131] It is a "natural" will in that it acts according to the nature in which it inheres. This again is another reason why Maximus strongly opposed placing "will" in the "person" since, as Watts explains, "that would imply that the will stood somehow over nature, rather than existing as a property and function of it."[132]

Alongside this first distinction is a second one, namely the "will" as a "natural" thing that consists of specific capacities/abilities *and* concrete acts of willing which "persons" do. By this distinction, Maximus can speak of a person who wills *and* of his will in the same way we speak of a person who thinks *and* of his intellect.[133] In Christ, there is one willer (Son) who has two wills—divine and human—and these two wills are not identified with the one person.[134]

3. How does Maximus put all of this together? By employing the person-

---

[127] Watts, "Two Wills in Christ?," 485.
[128] See Bathrellos, *Byzantine Christ*, 120–126.
[129] Watts, "Two Wills in Christ?," 469.
[130] See ibid., 469, 475.
[131] Ibid., 475–476.
[132] Ibid., 476.
[133] See Bathrellos, *Byzantine Christ*, 168–172.
[134] As applied to the Trinity, there are three "willers" (persons) who share the same identical will (nature). The one ability to will as God is actualized in and by the three persons. Because the one will does not refer to specific acts or to specific agents of willing, we must distinguish between the willing of the three persons, even though what they will is the same thing at all times because they share the same will by subsisting in the one, identical divine nature. Watts helpfully relates "will" and perspectives: "Thus, when the Father wills to send the Son and the Son obeys, the action is one and the will is one, but the Father and the Son have different perspectives on the same action, since they are distinguished as agents" (Watts, "Two Wills in Christ?," 480). The Father, Son, and Spirit are distinguished as agents by their personal properties, and the church historically has done this by appealing to the relations between the persons: the Father has the incommunicable property of paternity; the Son has sonship and eternal generation; the Spirit has eternal procession. In fact, as Letham argues, it is the eternal, immanent relations between the divine persons that grounds the economic relations (Robert Letham, *The Holy Trinity: In Scripture, History, Theology, and Worship* (Phillipsburg, NJ: P&R, 2004), 397–404. So in the case of Christ, his human obedience is based in his eternal relation to the Father as the Son.

nature distinction,[135] Maximus contends that the "will" is part of nature; that natures subsist in the person; and that it is the person, as the subject of the nature, who wills and acts in and through the nature.[136] So, in the case of Christ, the Son, as a result of the incarnation, wills and acts in and through both natures and thus wills and acts *as God* and *as man*.[137] In thinking of Christ's human nature, it is the Son who is the subject of all of his human attributes and activities. Thus, in Christ the human will is actualized in terms of specific acts of willing by the person in which it subsists. Also, in regard to Christ's human will, as Watts notes, "Maximus is able to refuse the dilemma that Jesus' human will would be either opposed to God (since entirely free) or superfluous (since compelled). It is neither: Jesus actively obeys as man, maintaining the self-determination of the human will, yet according to the natural inclination of the will towards God."[138] The wills perfectly coincide, since the two natures are united in the person who is the active subject of both natures.[139]

By this explanation, Maximus explains the "will" issue better than previous theologians did. In fact, Maximus's explanation is better than the later statement of Constantinople III, which sought to resolve the "will" issue in favor of dyothelitism! The reason for this is that, at Constantinople III, Pope Leo's *Tome*—one of the documents of Chalcedon—continued to exert a huge influence. Specifically, the *Tome* states the following about the "natures": "Each 'form' [nature] *carries on its proper activities in communion with the other.* The Word does what belongs to it, and the flesh carries out what belongs to it. The one shimmers with wondrous deeds, the other succumbs to injury and insult."[140] If not carefully nuanced, one could interpret the *Tome* as teaching that "natures" are acting subjects instead of "persons" and, if not careful, it could almost sound Nestorian.[141] Leo was certainly *not* Nestorian, but his words, given their place in Christological development, could leave open this possible misinterpretation.

In fact, this is how Constantinople III has been interpreted. McCormack, for example, argues that the Council clearly decided that action belonged to the natures, and this is correct to a point. The Council affirmed that in Christ there are "two natural volitions or wills . . . and two natural principles of action" with the human will always and at every point in subjection to the divine will. . . . "Each nature wills and performs the things that are proper to it in a

---

[135] Oakes makes this point in *Infinity Dwindled to Infancy*, 157–160.
[136] See Galot, *Who Is Christ?*, 284.
[137] See Crisp, *Divinity and Humanity*, 47–48, 63, 71.
[138] Watts, "Two Wills in Christ?," 477.
[139] See Letham, *Holy Trinity*, 395–396; cf. Galot, *Who Is Christ?*, 283–286.
[140] Richard A. Norris Jr., trans. and ed., *The Christological Controversy* (Philadelphia: Fortress, 1980), 150 (emphasis mine).
[141] See Richard Norris Jr., "Chalcedon Revisited: A Historical and Theological Reflection," in *New Perspectives on Historical Theology: Essays in Memory of John Meyendorff*, ed. Bradley Nassif (Grand Rapids, MI: Eerdmans, 1996), 148; Watts, "Two Wills in Christ?," 477; Bathrellos, *Byzantine Christ*, 163–164, 176–185.

communion with the other."[142] However, should we conclude that the Council made the "human 'nature' [look] even more like a second 'subject' than ever it had in the early church"?[143] Not if the Council is interpreted in light of Maximus.[144] Chalcedonian orthodoxy, as viewed through later developments, insists that "natures" do not act; only "persons" do. As Bathrellos astutely observes, Maximus does not make "the natures *subjects of willing*"; in fact, nowhere does Maximus say that each nature *wills*, rather, for Maximus, "*the willing and acting subject in Christology is the person of the incarnate Logos.*"[145] In this way, Maximus protects the unity of Christ's person in willing and acting, while simultaneously preserving the distinction of natures and their attributes. As Watts nicely comments, "any talk of nature acting must be understood as referring to the person in whom the nature subsists,"[146] since a human nature subsists not by itself but in particular persons and it is the person who is the subject of willing and acting.

4. How does Maximus apply his insights to the garden of Gethsemane? For Maximus, Gethsemane is a crucial test case which proves dyothelitism. It is in Gethsemane that we see most poignantly the Son acting in and through his human will, in all of its instinctive, rational, and self-determining aspects. Unlike previous theologians (e.g., Gregory of Nazianzus) who argued that Christ's human will was deified so that the opposition spoken of in the prayer between the will of the Father and the will of the Son was only revelatory for us, or Athanasius who attributed Christ's shrinking from death to his human will while he maintained his commitment to the Father with his divine will, as if the two wills were opposed to each other,[147] Maximus gives a better and more consistent interpretation of the text.

Maximus interprets Jesus's prayer as the Son acting in and through his human will in *both* petitions, thus doing justice to the *human obedience* of the Son to the Father. Maximus insists that in this prayer the Son *as man* addresses his Father as *he* chooses to obey even unto death, recoiling at the reality of bearing God's wrath for us. For Maximus, then, "the subject who says 'let this cup pass from me' and the subject who says 'not as I will [but as you will]' are one and the same. . . . both the desire to avoid death and the submission to the divine will of the Father have to do with the humanity of Christ and his human will."[148]

It is only by affirming that Christ has a human will that we can do justice

---

[142] Norman P. Tanner, ed., *Nicaea I to Lateran V*, vol. 1 in *Decrees of the Ecumenical Councils* (Washington, DC: Georgetown University Press, 1990), 128–129.
[143] McCormack, "Person of Christ," 155.
[144] John of Damascus states it in a way similar to Maximus (see Norris, "Chalcedon Revisited," 147–151).
[145] Bathrellos, *Byzantine Christ*, 182 (emphasis his).
[146] Watts, "Two Wills in Christ?," 477.
[147] See Bathrellos, *Byzantine Christ*, 140–142
[148] Bathrellos, *Byzantine Christ*, 147.

to the obedience of the Son *as a man* which is so foundational to Christ's work for us. The Son, in his humanity, as Macleod reminds us, "had ordinary human desires, longings, preferences and aspirations. Just as truly, he had human aversions. Under these influences he made decisions and pursued options in the same way as we do ourselves."[149] In Gethsemane, all of this comes to a head, where in a very real sense—a sense that we will never fathom—Jesus does not want this cup and he recoils from the thought, yet as the obedient Son who loves his Father, and in his humanity, *he* aligns his human will with the will of his Father, as *he* chooses to act as our representative substitute. Instead of viewing Jesus's humanity as a passive instrument of the divine will (which would imply a Nestorian separation between the person of the Son and his own flesh),[150] dyothelitism views the Son as the subject of the incarnation, who wills in and through his human nature, and is "active in obedience at all times as the Son obeyed the Father according to his humanity."[151]

5. Is there biblical evidence suggesting that Christ has a divine will? If will is located in the nature, then every passage that speaks of the deity of Christ would entail that Christ has a divine will. However, since this is what is at dispute, two specific examples will suffice which specifically speak of Christ having a divine will. First, Jesus's lament over Jerusalem (Matt. 23:37; Luke 13:34) makes sense only if the will spoken of here is a divine will. Since Jerusalem had been killing prophets for far longer than Jesus had been humanly alive, Jesus speaks as the patient and long-suffering Lord of the Old Testament who desired or willed (*thelō*) to call his people back to himself.[152] Second, John 5:21 is also instructive. Maximus argued the following: "Indeed, just as the Father raises the dead and gives them life, so also the Son gives life to whomever he wishes (*thelō*)."[153] The word "so," as Watts argues, "indicates that the Son gives life according to the same nature as the Father."[154]

6. What about "verbal" monothelitism? Even if we acknowledge two wills in Christ, should we not also *speak* of one will alone in Christ due to his volitional unity as a person? Some have spoken of a kind of "synthetic" nature arising from the union of the two natures. Can we also speak about a "synthetic" will, i.e., two natural wills are united in the person? Watts describes Maximus's response to this proposal. He points out that when the Patristic theologians spoke of a "synthetic" nature, it in no way meant a "third kind" of nature; rather "it was a way of speaking about the one hypostasis."[155] Also, to

---

[149] Macleod, *Person of Christ*, 179.
[150] See Watts, "Two Wills in Christ?," 485.
[151] Ibid.
[152] Ibid., 472.
[153] Maximus the Confessor, *Disputatio cum Pyrrho*, 47–48, in Watts, "Two Wills in Christ?," 472.
[154] Watts, "Two Wills in Christ?," 472.
[155] Ibid., 462. Watts appeals to Constantinople II and the following anathema to prove this point: "If anyone uses the expression 'of two natures,' confessing that a union was made of the Godhead and of the humanity, or the

speak of a "synthetic will" composed of its components "would suggest that there is a synthesis of all the other properties of Christ's two natures, such as 'the Uncreate and the created . . . the Infinite and the finite . . . the Undefined and the defined . . . the Immortal and the mortal . . . the incorruptible and the corruptible'."[156] In the end, a synthetic or composite will would entail a composite nature, which Scripture and Chalcedon strictly forbid.[157]

In addition, it is illegitimate to appeal to *communicatio* as some monothelites did.[158] As noted above, the proper application of *communicatio* in Christology is to affirm that what is true of the natures is true of the person, yet the natures do not change nor are they mixed. As Watts notes, "We may speak of the man Jesus having a divine will, or the divine Son having a human will." But we cannot speak of a common will by *communicatio*, as if there were an exchange of properties between the natures, for if we do, as Maximus noted, "then thou art really saying that there is not one will but two wills."[159]

7. Is this debate an important one? Maximus and the church certainly thought so. Unless there is good reason to think otherwise, dyothelitism is a legitimate conclusion and a further clarification and development of Chalcedonian Christology. Furthermore, the overall debate is not esoteric. What is ultimately at stake is the full humanity of Christ and whether Jesus is our all-sufficient Redeemer. If Gregory's maxim is correct—"whatever is not assumed cannot be redeemed"—then if Jesus is lacking a human will he is not fully human. And if he cannot choose *as a man* then he cannot stand in our place as the last Adam and obey as our covenant head.

---

expression 'the one nature made flesh of God the Word,' and shall not so understand those expressions as the holy Fathers have taught, to wit: that of the divine and human nature there was made an hypostatic union, whereof is one Christ; but from these expressions shall try to introduce one nature or substance (made by a mixture) of the Godhead and manhood of Christ; let him be anathema" (ibid., 462n37).

[156] Ibid., 462; cf. Maximus the Confessor, *Disputatio cum Pyrrho*, 14–15.

[157] See Bathrellos, *Byzantine Christ*, 99–101.

[158] Maximus cites Pyrrhus as an example of a person who appeals illegitimately to *communicatio* (see Watts, "Two Wills in Christ?," 462–463); cf. Maximus the Confessor, *Disputatio cum Pyrrho*, 16.

[159] Maximus the Confessor, *Disputatio cum Pyrrho*, 16, in Watts, "Two Wills in Christ?," 463.

Part III is now complete. By walking through historical theology, we have not only discovered the need for orthodoxy but have seen its emergence and its establishment by unpacking the basic contours of orthodox, classical Christology. The Chalcedonian Definition and its later developments have provided the church an overall consensus regarding the identity of our Lord Jesus Christ—at least until recent times, when there has been a departure from that consensus. Part I sought to explain the reasons for the departure. Scripture alone is our magisterial and final authority in our theological conclusions (thus Part II of this work). Yet the weight of tradition, which serves as a ministerial authority—what we have called the ecclesiological warrant—must not be neglected, given its wisdom and theological precision, especially in the area of Christological formulation, and thus Part III.

Throughout Part III, we have employed the image of a traveled road. Every road leads to a specific destination, and every road establishes set parameters within which to travel. There is freedom and flexibility for the traveler as long as he remains within the basic boundaries. In Christology, Chalcedon and its later developments have established orthodoxy for the church. People may differ at various points, but as the laboratory of historical theology has demonstrated, various heresies over time have taken many too far on either side of the road, which results in disaster. Yet as we have also discovered, heresy has a positive effect because it drives the church to become theologically precise. Surely one of the lessons to learn from historical theology is that any departure from established orthodoxy must be undertaken with extreme care and clear biblical warrant. This is not to say that nothing new can be said about Christ today. As theologians, we must constantly apply God's word to our lives and address current challenges. However, we must do so carefully, first making sure our theology is biblically warranted, and second, confirming that it stands on the shoulders of past giants.

In Part IV, we turn to the subject of a warranted Christology for today, taking what we have learned from Scripture and historical theology, and setting forth the glory of our Lord and Savior—God the Son incarnate—in light of some contemporary challenges. As we do this, we will expound and defend classical, orthodox Christology and interact with some current views within evangelical Christology which we find inadequate.

IV

A WARRANTED CHRISTOLOGY
FOR TODAY

The concern of this work has been to provide a contemporary articulation of classical Christology for evangelicals today. Given our modern/postmodern culture, our need to take the Bible on its own terms, and our place in church history, the first three parts of this volume have provided epistemological (Part I), biblical (Part II), and ecclesiological (Part III) warrant for the critiques, conclusions, and defenses to be set forth in this final part.

The church has always been pressed into theological action by two causes, one greater and one lesser. The greater cause is the call of God for his church to proclaim his glory in the salvation of his people and his sovereign rule over the world. The lesser cause is the historical harassment of heresies and the contemporary challenges to the traditional formulations of orthodoxy. The earlier work in these last few chapters of warranting the Christological conclusions will now help (1) to clear the confusion in current attempts to identify the person of Jesus Christ; (2) to formulate and articulate a biblical Christology under the magisterial authority of Scripture and the ministerial guidance of historical theology; and (3) to defend this orthodox Christology against charges of incoherency. The hope for this volume as an argument for a fully warranted, orthodox Christology is that it will serve the church in its worship of God in Christ and in the proclamation of his great name in this generation and those that follow.

Chapters 10–12 will take up the contemporary challenges made to orthodox Christology by what has come to be known as kenotic Christology, or kenoticism. The seeds of kenoticism planted in the nineteenth and early twentieth centuries have produced two variants today within evangelicalism, the ontological and the functional kenotic Christologies. While they differ in significant respects, both create problems in doing justice to all that Scripture says about Christ. After critiquing kenotic Christologies for their departure from and/or tension with classical Christology, chapter 13 will present a contemporary formulation and articulation of the orthodox identity of Christ. Specifically, this formulation urges that three affirmations must be made in light of the biblical presentation and historical confirmation that Jesus Christ is God the Son incarnate. Finally, chapter 14 will address the apologetic issue of whether orthodox Christology is logically coherent and will then consider two perennial theological questions regarding Jesus's knowledge and his in/ability to be tempted and/or to sin.

TEN

CONTEMPORARY CHALLENGES
TO ORTHODOX CHRISTOLOGY:
KENOTICISM—A MIDDLE WAY?

In Part III, we unpacked the development of orthodox Christology in light of the Chalcedonian Definition. Until the Enlightenment, this "classical Christology" was *the* way of thinking about the identity of Christ. As discussed in Part I, in the period of the Enlightenment and with the subsequent rise of classic liberalism, a rejection of orthodoxy occurred. This rejection came about mostly because of entire worldview shifts—shifts that radically departed from historic Christian theology. Yet, in the nineteenth and early twentieth century, a group of theologians, first on the Continent and later in the United Kingdom, attempted to reformulate "classical Christology" along a "new" path, that is, a *kenotic* path. They did not embrace the Enlightenment *Zeitgeist* entirely, but they were dissatisfied with the traditional view. As a result, they forged a *via media* or "middle way" which, though rejected by many today, still continues to influence current Christological formulation both outside and within evangelical theology.[1]

In Part IV, as we transition to offering a warranted Christology for today, based on the biblical and ecclesiastical warrants in Parts II and III, we first want to set the stage by discussing the challenge of kenoticism to orthodox Christology. Since kenotic Christology views itself as providing a "new," "better," and "middle" way to theologize about Christ, it is important to think through what its proposal is and to evaluate it in light of Scripture and historical theology.

---

[1] Kevin J. Vanhoozer, *Remythologizing Theology: Divine Action, Passion, and Authorship* (Cambridge: Cambridge University Press, 2010), 139–177, argues that kenotic thought's influence has thoroughly affected theology proper and Christology so that it is now viewed as a "new" orthodoxy, especially outside of evangelicalism.

In this chapter, we will describe nineteenth- and early twentieth-century kenoticism, thus establishing a baseline from which to compare and contrast earlier forms with current varieties. Then in chapter 11, we will discuss the impact of kenoticism on current evangelical Christology. Even though evangelical theology does not completely identify with early kenoticism, there is a clear spectrum of views today that are influenced by features of kenotic thought, all of which result in a departure from classical Christology, some more radical than others.[2] In chapter 12, we will critique and reject evangelical kenoticism. Our overall argument is that these "newer" Christological views are not "better," and that as a *via media* they fail. Ultimately, they do not account for *all* of the biblical data, and the "old" path, as developed in Part III, is still the best way to make sense of the biblical presentation of Jesus as God the Son incarnate.

KENOTIC CHRISTOLOGY (1800–1950)

All kenotic Christologies seek to understand the incarnation by taking their cue from Philippians 2:5–11.[3] Appeal is made to the verb *kenoō*, in verses 6–7—"who, though he was in the form of God, did not count equality with God a thing to be grasped, but emptied himself (*ekenōsen*), by taking the form of a servant, being born in the likeness of men." Kenoticism insists that, in assuming our humanity, the divine Son "emptied himself," that is, "in some way [the Son] limited or temporarily divested himself of some of the properties thought to be divine prerogatives, and this act of self-emptying has become known as a 'kenosis'."[4]

All kenotic Christologies also represent a distinctively non-Chalcedonian approach to Christology, albeit some more so than others. Specifically, they are non-classical in proposing that in the incarnation the Son ceased to possess certain attributes of deity in order for him to become truly human. In seeking to explain the wonder and glory of the incarnation, kenoticism explained it in ways that the church had not previously done.[5] For example, should we think of all of God's attributes as essential to him (which is what the church previ-

---

[2] B. E. Foster, "Kenoticism," in *New Dictionary of Theology*, ed. Sinclair B. Ferguson et al. (Downers Grove, IL: InterVarsity Press, 1988), 364, notes how the current status of kenoticism is difficult to assess, since it is not a popular way of expressing the nature of the incarnation among evangelicals. Yet, as chapter 11 will demonstrate, many of the major themes of kenoticism have been incorporated into current evangelical Christologies.

[3] For a description of kenotic Christology, see David Brown, *Divine Humanity: Kenosis and the Construction of Christian Theology* (Waco, TX: Baylor University Press, 2011); Donald G. Dawe, *The Form of a Servant: A Historical Analysis of the Kenotic Motif* (Philadelphia: Westminster, 1963).

[4] C. Stephen Evans, "Introduction," in *Exploring Kenotic Christology: The Self-Emptying of God*, ed. C. Stephen Evans (Oxford: Oxford University Press, 2006), 4.

[5] Thomas R. Thompson makes this point in quoting Friedrich Loofs: no theologian prior to this time ever taught "a theory of the *kenosis* of the Logos as would involve an actual supersession of His divine form of existence by the human—a real 'becoming-man', i.e. a transformation on the part of the Logos" (Thomas R. Thompson, "Nineteenth-Century Kenotic Christology: The Waxing, Waning, and Weighing of a Quest for a Coherent Orthodoxy," in *Exploring Kenotic Christology*, 75n1).

ously affirmed), or are some of the divine attributes merely accidental? Related to this question is a correlative one: Is it even possible to think of God losing or setting aside any of his attributes and still being God? Historically the church has answered no, but kenotic theologians answered in the affirmative.[6] In addition, if one thinks it is possible to set aside certain divine attributes except what is essential to God, then is this condition temporary or permanent? If temporary, then during his earthly existence, did Christ have any recourse to his divine attributes—since seemingly Christ, in his glorified state, will have access to them in the future? Or, should we affirm that these divine attributes were denied him from his conception and forevermore? If the latter is true, then in what sense can we affirm that the incarnate Son is truly God?

Nineteenth-Century Continental Kenotic Christology

In wrestling with these perennial Christological questions, kenoticists in the nineteenth century walked a fine line between orthodoxy and "modernism." They aligned themselves with the historic confessions of the church, yet they also accepted the results of historical criticism, and it is for this reason that Thomas Thompson views the Christologies of this era as a mixture of the "classical" and the "modern." Over against Hegel's philosophy and classic liberalism, kenoticists affirmed the doctrine of the Trinity and "the eternal, personal pre-existence of the Son,"[7] though in the end, their understanding of the incarnation differed substantially from classical thought. The goal of these theologians was admirable: to make "a little more understandable how it is that the pre-existent Son can enter into a fully human condition while retaining both his divinity and unity of person."[8] Yet their proposals raised more questions than they solved. On the Continent, there was a spectrum of three views (as represented by their proponents), to which we now turn.

---

[6] Interestingly, the historical precursor to kenoticism in Germany was the prior debates generated by post-Reformation Lutheranism and Calvinism. On this point, see David F. Wells, *The Person of Christ: A Biblical and Historical Analysis of the Incarnation* (Westchester, IL: Crossway, 1984), 133–136. As discussed in chapter 9, Lutheranism and Reformed thought differed on the nature of the *communicatio*. Lutheranism allowed for a real "transfer of attributes" from the divine nature to the human, but not vice versa. Within Lutheranism, two streams of thought developed, which the *Formula of Concord* (1576) sought to reconcile. On the one hand, John Brentz argued that the Son's "relative" attributes (omnipotence, omniscience, and omnipresence) were communicated to his humanity. In the case of omnipresence, he argued for different forms of omnipresence in Christ's humanity which entailed that Christ could be both localized (ubiquity *in loco*) and universalized (ubiquity *in Logo*). For Brentz, this meant that the divine glory of God the Son was not in any way diminished in the incarnation. On the other hand, Martin Chemnitz interpreted the *communicatio* from the divine nature to the human more intermittently. Due to the union of natures in the Son, the Son can always choose to use the human nature in ways that are beyond the normal bounds of human limitations, such as extra-physical powers including omnipresence. The *Formula of Concord* sought to reconcile these two schools of thought: one arguing that the omni-attributes were always present, albeit concealed, with the other school arguing that even though these divine attributes were present in capacity, they were rarely exercised. Due to the influence of the Enlightenment, the *communicatio* debate shifted in a different direction in the nineteenth century. Now the debate was not over when, where, and how Jesus had access to his divine attributes; instead, it centered on whether it was even possible that he had any access to these attributes.

[7] Thompson, "Nineteenth-Century Kenotic Christology," 77.

[8] Ibid., 77–78.

GOTTFRIED THOMASIUS (1802–1875)[9]

Thomasius begins by laying out his confessional starting points. He affirms his belief in the Trinity and the personal preexistence of the Son. He agrees with the church that any legitimate Christology must affirm simultaneously the true deity, humanity, and unity of Christ's person, yet he rejects the Lutheran divinizing of Christ's humanity and the affirmation of the *extra*. In regard to the *extra*, he is convinced that it compromises the unity of Christ's person and results in a kind of "twofold mode of being, a double life, a doubled consciousness."[10]

The only alternative, then, is to argue that the person of the Son, in voluntarily assuming a human nature, undergoes some kind of kenosis, hence "the self-limitation of the Son of God."[11] What happens is that there is "a divesting of the divine mode of being in favor of the humanly creaturely form of existence, and *eo ipso* a renunciation of the divine glory he had from the beginning with the Father."[12] Thus, the Son in assuming our humanity becomes completely subject to the limits of space, time, and human development. In this self-limitation, Thomasius insists, the "essence" of deity is not destroyed nor are the two natures confused, yet, as David Wells notes, the divine consciousness of the Son now exhibits itself only "within the bounds of human possibility and under the conditions of human growth."[13] In other words, due to the incarnation, the Son's divine prerogatives, such as knowing all things, exercising divine power, and being fully present, are no longer his.

Given this understanding, the question naturally arises: In what sense is the incarnate Son still God, if he no longer has his divine "mode of being," or if his divine prerogatives are not his? Thomasius's answer: "Nothing is lacking in him which is essential for God to be God."[14] Thomasius explains what he means by making a distinction in the divine attributes between the "immanent" or "moral" attributes and the "relative" or "physical" attributes. As Thompson explains, "Attributes that pertain to the former, such as absolute power (of self-determination), truth, holiness, and love are essential to deity and thus retained by the Son in his incarnate state; those that pertain to the latter, such as omnipotence, omniscience, and omnipresence are deemed not essential to deity by Thomasius and can thus be relinquished by the Incarnate

---

[9] See Gottfried Thomasius, "Christ's Person and Work," in *God and Incarnation in Mid-Nineteenth Century German Theology*, ed. and trans. Claude Welch (New York: Oxford University Press, 1965). Cf. Bruce L. McCormack, "The Person of Christ," in *Mapping Modern Theology: A Thematic and Historical Introduction*, ed. Kelly M. Kapic and Bruce L. McCormack (Grand Rapids, MI: Baker Academic, 2012), 163–166; Brown, *Divine Humanity*, 42–55.
[10] Thomasius, "Christ's Person and Work," 46–47.
[11] Ibid., 40.
[12] Ibid., 48.
[13] Wells, *Person of Christ*, 136.
[14] Thomasius, "Christ's Person and Work," 56.

Son without any loss of divinity."[15] Thus Thomasius's conception of kenosis is that it involves the relinquishing of certain divine attributes in their use *and* possession, but not all of them. In addition, Thomasius believes that the loss of "relative attributes" is only temporary, since the Son regains them in his exaltation, so that now, "[W]e say that the glorified Christ is omnipresent, omnipotent and omniscient."[16]

Thomasius's view has a number of important consequences. First, he argues that some of the divine attributes are *not* essential to God *and* he radically pares down what those attributes are. Second, contrary to orthodoxy, he denies, in Christ's earthly existence, "the full actuality of divine attributes in the Incarnate Christ."[17] Third, he affirms that the triune personal relations have experienced change specifically in the divine consciousness of the Son in relation to the Father and Spirit, and that during the incarnate Son's earthly existence there was a temporary cessation of the Son's cosmic activity of sustaining and upholding the universe.[18]

J. H. AUGUST EBRARD (1818–1888)

In contrast to Thomasius, J. H. August Ebrard interpreted Christ's kenosis as "an exchange of his pre-existent eternal form or mode of being (*Ewigkeitsform*) for a temporal one (*Zeitlichkeitsform*)."[19] In other words, instead of relinquishing certain divine attributes and retaining others, the Son, in assuming our humanity, retains *all* of his attributes but possesses them "only in proportion to the human mode of existence."[20] This entails that the omniattributes (omniscience, omnipotence, and omnipresence) are *not* surrendered but are now available to Christ and capable of being expressed only in a way consistent with his humanity. Omnipotence, then, remained in an applied form in Christ's ability to perform miracles but only within his own limited sphere of influence, not cosmically, which is difficult to reconcile with Scripture and church tradition.[21] Or, omniscience is exercised by Christ as an "ability to see through objects and persons"[22] while the divine attribute of omnipresence is exercised as an "ability to go wherever, over land or sea."[23] Yet one wonders,

---

[15] Thompson, "Nineteenth-Century Kenotic Christology," 83; cf. Thomasius, "Christ's Person and Work," 67–69.
[16] Thomasius, "Christ's Person and Work," 76. Thomasius, working within a Lutheran view of the *communicatio*, employs it with a twist. With the Lutheran tradition, he argues that at the exaltation there is a transfer of divine attributes to Christ's human nature. Thomasius departs from the tradition, however, with his understanding that during the state of humiliation the *communicatio* was from the human nature to the divine.
[17] Thompson, "Nineteenth-Century Kenotic Christology," 84.
[18] See Thomasius, "Christ's Person and Work," 81–82.
[19] Thompson, "Nineteenth-Century Kenotic Christology," 86.
[20] Ibid.
[21] This limitation is difficult to reconcile with Scripture and tradition in two areas. First, it denies that the incarnate Son continues to exercise his divine attributes during his earthly existence, thus questioning whether he is *fully* God. Second, it compromises the Son's real humanity by giving his humanity powers that we do not normally have.
[22] Thompson, "Nineteenth-Century Kenotic Christology," 86.
[23] Ibid.

as Thompson charges, how Ebrard's view has not also undercut Christ's true humanity, unless we think that humans by nature have these same kinds of powers and abilities.[24]

Regardless, this is how Ebrard seeks to uphold the church's confession of Christ as one person in two natures. However, contrary to the *extra*, the Son now only has a life and existence that is limited to the space-time world. Furthermore, Ebrard's view adds two more points that distinguish it from classical thought. First, in assuming our humanity, the Son is no longer impeccable (unable to sin) but peccable (able to sin). Second, contrary to Thomasius, Ebrard contends that the Son's decision to renounce his eternal mode of being is now permanent, which has a number of massive implications for our understanding of the possibility of change within the triune personal relations *and* of God's immutability.

W. F. Gess (1819–1891)

In contrast to Thomasius, and going even further than Ebrard, W. F. Gess applies kenosis to *all* aspects of the incarnation, thus undercutting Christ's full deity. In the incarnation, the divine Son relinquished "all attributes, powers, prerogatives, and glory,"[25] including both the essential and the relative attributes, and he did so permanently. In the Son's *becoming* flesh, he not only assumes a human soul, he is also metamorphosed into one; in Christ *all* of the divine attributes are *permanently* relinquished. The only difference between a human soul and the Son, then, is that the Son became a soul by kenosis, whereas the human soul is the result of creation.

Gess's view is the most extreme form of ontological kenoticism, since it denies that the incarnate Son is "fully God." Gess draws three radical Christological conclusions. First, he argues that the Son's eternal self-consciousness is relinquished at the moment of conception, only to be gradually regained through the normal course of his human development. Second, he insists that the incarnate Son cannot exercise any divine power, and that any divine power exercised by Christ is not done by him but solely by the Father and the Spirit. This conclusion not only denies the incarnate Son's ongoing cosmic functions; it also rejects a staple of pro-Nicene theology, namely, the inseparable operations of the triune persons. Third, in regard to the triune relations, ever since the incarnation, the personal relations have undergone change. As a result of the incarnation, for example, the Son never exercises his divine attributes, as he did before.

These three views (i.e., Thomasius, Ebrard, and Gess) represent kenotic

---

[24] See ibid.
[25] Ibid., 87. For a helpful summary of Gess, see Brown, *Divine Humanity*, 62–69.

Christology as promulgated on the Continent, but kenoticism was not limited to Europe. It was also developing in the United Kingdom, where it was typically less speculative and more orthodox than its European counterpart. Yet, even in the United Kingdom, it challenged classical Christology and sought to offer a *via media*. Let us briefly describe this form of kenoticism as represented by three key proponents.

Early Twentieth-Century British Kenoticism

CHARLES GORE (1853–1932)

For the most part, Charles Gore was a cautious churchman, who desired to uphold traditional church confessions and orthodoxy. For example, he affirmed the conclusions of Nicaea and Chalcedon; however, given his embrace of some higher-critical conclusions, he was concerned to reconcile Anglo-Catholicism and liberalism, especially in the area of biblical criticism. He struggled with the authorship of certain Old Testament books and statements Christ made about them, such as the Mosaic authorship of the Pentateuch and the unity of Isaiah, which seemed to go against what he thought critical scholarship had disproved. For Gore, the kenotic theory appeared to offer a potential way out of the difficulty.[26] By it, he thought he could maintain a robust view of Christ's deity yet also affirm that, in the incarnation, the Son "emptied" himself and thus "accommodated" himself to current "false" ideas, thus teaching a view of Old Testament authorship which we now "know" is incorrect.[27]

How does Gore develop his kenotic Christology? In this way: as a result of taking on our humanity, Christ's knowledge was limited and thus was no different than that of his contemporaries on matters related to history, science, and other matters. In other words, Christ's knowledge was circumscribed by his humanity, and during his earthly existence Christ had no access to his divine knowledge—a modification of classical Christology especially in regard to the *extra*.

Gore explained his view in a way similar to Thomasius: In the incarnation, the Son relinquished or set aside what was not essential to God and whatever was incompatible with humanity, especially his exercise of omniscience, and lived entirely within the limits of his human nature.[28] Yet, Gore also believed that the Son did not set aside his divine consciousness or will *and* that he

---

[26] See this point in James Carpenter, *Gore: A Study in Liberal Catholic Thought* (London: Faith Press, 1960), 156. For a helpful description of Gore's theology, see Brown, *Divine Humanity*, 126–144.

[27] See Charles Gore, "The Holy Spirit and Inspiration," in *Lux Mundi: A Series of Studies in the Religion of the Incarnation*, ed. Charles Gore, 12th ed. (London: John Murray, 1902), 265. For a similar view today, see Peter Enns, *Inspiration and Incarnation: Evangelicals and the Problem of the Old Testament* (Grand Rapids, MI: Baker Academic, 2005).

[28] Gore writes, "He so emptied Himself as to assume the permanent characteristics of the human or servile life: He took the *form* of a servant" (Charles Gore, *The Incarnation of the Son of God*, Bampton Lectures [London: John Murray, 1898], 158).

continued to sustain the universe (Col. 1:17)! Most admit that Gore is trying to marry two incompatible Christologies—classic and kenotic—a view that is highly unstable.[29]

P. T. FORSYTH (1848–1921)

P. T. Forsyth, a Scottish theologian, is also well known for his kenotic Christology.[30] Similar to Gore, Forsyth thought it possible through kenoticism to reconcile the perceived results of biblical criticism with statements of Christ regarding the authorship of various Old Testament books. In addition, he was uncomfortable with orthodoxy in its use of the terms "nature" and "person." For him, these were metaphysical categories which led to unnecessary problems, including the adoption of such kenotic categories of "relative" and "essential" attributes.[31] For Forsyth, Christology should abandon these categories and instead think about how two "modes of being" are related in Christ and think in "moral" categories.[32] By doing so, he insisted, many of the criticisms against classical Christology could be avoided.

How, then, did Forsyth conceive of the incarnation? As Wells explains, what happened in the incarnation was that "the attributes of the eternal, divine Word contracted from a condition of being actual to one of being potential. This contraction was itself the result of a monumental moral act within the Godhead, and the slow, progressive recovery of Godness in its wholeness within the life of the human Jesus was itself also an act of moral conquest."[33] Forsyth rejected Thomasius's explanation of how this took place; instead, he argued that the self-emptying was genuine and that such a reduction is possible only because "God's greatness is, in fact, so great that his self-limitation becomes a possibility, for his greatness is moral, not physical."[34]

Forsyth also rejected the way in which classical Christology spoke of Christ's natures being united in his *person (enhypostasia)*, given its metaphysical overtones. Instead, he spoke of Christ's deity and humanity meeting in a saving action, as the "mutual involution of two personal movements raised by the whole scale of the human soul and the divine."[35] In other words, as Wells explains, what distinguished the human in Christ "was the emergence of personality by moral struggle," and what distinguished the divine "was the self-retraction and coworking in the common cause of saving lost men and women."[36] Forsyth also rejected any notion that Christ had two wills, or two

---

[29] See Donald Macleod, *The Person of Christ* (Downers Grove, IL: InterVarsity Press, 1998), 206–207.
[30] See P. T. Forsyth, *The Person and Place of Jesus Christ* (Boston: Pilgrim, 1909).
[31] See ibid., 229.
[32] See ibid., 307.
[33] Wells, *Person of Christ*, 137.
[34] Ibid.
[35] Forsyth, *Person and Place of Jesus Christ*, 333.
[36] Wells, *Person of Christ*, 138.

levels of consciousness, in the same "person." What his view entailed is a divine Son who lived his life completely circumscribed by his humanity and "who consented not to know with an ignorance divinely wise, and who emptied himself in virtue of his divine fullness."[37]

HUGH ROSS MACKINTOSH (1870–1936)

Hugh Ross Mackintosh is one of the last modern kenoticists, and as such, he attempts to unite previous kenotic views on the Continent and in the United Kingdom. His view is similar to previous kenotic views in three ways. First, he accepts orthodox teaching regarding the Trinity, the full deity and humanity of Christ, and the unity of Christ's two natures in one person.[38] Second, he affirms what all kenotic views do, namely that in the incarnation, "[s]omehow He [the Son] laid aside His Divine mode of existence in order to become man,"[39] and that the Son lived "a life wholly restrained within the bounds of manhood. Outside the conditions imposed by the choice of life as man the son has no activity or knowledge."[40] Third, he is dissatisfied with classical Christology, specifically in its affirmation of *anhypostasia* and the *extra*. As Thompson notes, "Although committed to Chalcedon's intentions . . . Mackintosh is not convinced that its particular 'theoretically-tending' form has best served the church. What he has in view here is the doctrine of the two natures."[41] Specifically, he is concerned that the orthodox construal of the two natures has introduced an untenable dualism into Christology while simultaneously depreciating Christ's true humanity.[42]

What is Mackintosh's solution? First, he rejects Thomasius's distinction between the immanent and relative divine attributes. Given that the world continues to exist and is sustained by God, it is impossible to think that the omni-attributes are not essential to God. Thompson captures Mackintosh's thinking in this regard: "Such attributes *ad extra* become necessary determinations of the Godhead and cannot be easily thought away without also dispensing of the very God-world relation itself."[43] Second, in his earthly existence Jesus did *not* possess the omni-attributes, because in the incarnation these attributes were transposed from a state of actuality to potency.[44] In the case of omniscience, for example, when the eternal passes into time, the Son now knows in a discur-

---

[37] Forsyth, *Person and Place of Jesus Christ*, 294.
[38] See H. R. Mackintosh, *The Doctrine of the Person of Jesus Christ*, ed. Charles A. Briggs and Stewart D. F. Salmond, 2nd ed. (Edinburgh: T&T Clark, 1913), 469–470. Cf. Brown, *Divine Humanity*, 114–120.
[39] Mackintosh, *Doctrine of the Person of Jesus Christ*, 266.
[40] Ibid., 479.
[41] Thompson, "Nineteenth-Century Kenotic Christology," 90.
[42] Mackintosh, *Doctrine of the Person of Jesus Christ*, 294–296.
[43] Thompson, "Nineteenth-Century Kenotic Christology," 92.
[44] Mackintosh, *Doctrine of the Person of Jesus Christ*, 477. Mackintosh states, "It is possible to conceive the Son . . . as now possessing all the qualities of Godhead in the form of concentrated potency rather than of full actuality, *dunamei* rather than *energeia*" (ibid.).

sive and progressive way.[45] Third, Mackintosh knows he must redefine divine immutability, given that the divine Son has changed, so what is immutable in God "is the holy love which makes His essence."[46] In this way, Mackintosh elevates divine love as God's supreme, defining attribute. Fourth, trying to account for Christ's cosmic functions, Mackintosh appeals to the Trinity and contends that "it is a fundamental truth that the world is upheld by God, not by a constituent or part of God."[47] The problem with this explanation, however, is twofold: first, Scripture attributes the cosmic functions to the *incarnate* Son; and second, how do we make sense of the unified and inseparable action of the divine persons?

Mackintosh admits that kenoticism is not without difficulties. Nevertheless, he contends that as a *via media*, it best accounts for Christ's identity in light of Scripture and tradition. In this way, he, and other kenoticists, insisted that their "newer" view was "better," but is this so?

PRELIMINARY EVALUATION OF KENOTICISM

Kenotic Christologies sought to explain the incarnation in ways that were admirable. In contrast to classic liberalism, most kenoticists worked within Trinitarian parameters, thus upholding the reality of the eternal Son and his full deity. In addition, all of them strongly maintained Christ's complete humanity, which is crucial if we are going to have the Redeemer Scripture describes. Wells notes another positive point: kenotic theories rightly emphasized that "[t]he Incarnation and not merely the cross was costly to God. The historical life of Jesus was itself an act of sacrifice by God, and as such it is to be an incitement to devotion."[48] Yet, despite these positives, kenotic theories raised more problems than they solved. In the end, they lacked biblical warrant and historical fit, and at least five major problems resulted.

First, kenoticism failed to maintain a clear distinction between "person" and "nature" and, in fact, redefined how these terms functioned in Trinitarian and Christological theology. In regard to the former, kenoticism confused the person of the Son with his divine nature, thus interpreting the Son's self-emptying as a surrender of his divine attributes, instead of his assumption of a human nature as Philippians 2 teaches. In terms of the latter, kenotic views defined "nature" and "person" differently than historic orthodoxy.

In regard to "nature," many kenotic formulations accepted Thomasius's

---

[45] Mackintosh wrestles with Christ's knowledge: "so Christ, who in virtue of His relation to the Father had Divine knowledge within reach, took only what was essential to His vocation. Though on many subjects He shared the ignorance as well as the knowledge of his contemporaries, yet He had at command all higher truth which can be assimilated by perfect human faculty" (ibid.).

[46] Ibid., 473.

[47] Ibid., 485.

[48] Wells, *Person of Christ*, 138.

distinction between the immanent and relative attributes of the divine nature, thus making the omni-attributes nonessential or accidental. Historically, however, given the traditional classification of divine attributes, *all* of God's attributes were viewed as *essential*, and none as accidental. In addition, such an understanding drastically redefines the nature of God, biblically and historically. As Wells rightly notes, "The only God of whom Scripture speaks is one who is all-powerful, knows everything, and is everywhere. By definition, a god who has diminished power and knowledge is not the biblical God."[49] Some kenoticists, like Forsyth and Mackintosh, tried to evade the issue by switching from metaphysical to moral categories, but most admit they were unsuccessful. Others argued that the deity of Christ was contracted into a mere potentiality, and thus divine passivity. For them, the Son may not have surrendered the divine attributes, but he certainly did not exercise them during his state of humiliation—and even for some, now permanently. But, once again, as Wells rightly insists, "divine passivity can only be distinguished from divine impotence in theory. In practice, a necessary passivity is an operating impotence."[50] Scripture nowhere allows us to think that there is a minimum to deity, and that God can lack power, knowledge, and presence and still be God.

Significantly, this redefinition of "nature" also has soteriological implications. In diluting the Son's deity, at least while on earth, Christ's "ability to save us would also be compromised. The Son of God was able to sacrifice his human nature for our salvation only because the death of that nature was not the end of his existence. In his divinity he remained who he had always been, and it was because of his remaining fully divine that death could not hold him captive."[51]

Alongside kenoticism's redefinition of nature is also how it redefines "person." Scripture teaches that the divine Son, at a point in time, took to himself a human nature. In the kenotic theory, however, when the incarnation takes place, it is as if the divine person has disposed of his divine nature. But as Bray rightly asks, "If a divine person does not have a divine nature, or if his divine nature is somehow quiescent, what content does his personal divinity have? He could be truly divine only as long as he retained the ability to express himself in and through his divine nature."[52] It is for this reason that Scripture teaches, and the church confesses, that Christ's humanity is an *addition* to his deity and not a replacement of it, *and* that the Son is able to live both a fully divine and a fully human life. Kenotic theories so change the life of the divine Son that the self-identity of the Son, along with Trinitarian relations, is greatly compromised and redefined.

---

[49] Ibid.
[50] Ibid.
[51] Gerald Bray, *God Is Love: A Biblical and Systematic Theology* (Wheaton, IL: Crossway, 2012), 202.
[52] Bray, *God Is Love*, 202.

Second, kenotic views cannot maintain the continuity between the preexistent Word/Son (*Logos asarkos*) and the incarnate Son (*Logos ensarkos*), thus implying huge disruptions in the internal relations of the triune persons. No doubt some kenotic views were more radical than others on this point, but all of them, at least minimally, insisted that, during the incarnate Son's earthly existence, his divine self-consciousness was expunged. Along with this assertion was a denial of the *extra*, thus rejecting the Son's ability to live simultaneously a divine and a human life. So, for example, as Macleod reminds us, "[u]p to the moment of his enfleshment, according to this theory, the Son was omniscient. At that fateful moment, however, his knowledge suddenly contracts: from infinity to that of a first-century Jew. That represents a degree of amnesia to which there can be no parallel."[53] That is why kenoticists taught that it is only as the Son grows in his human life that he becomes aware of his divine identity as the Son in relation to the Father and Spirit. But if this is so, then how are we to think of the triune personal relations?

No doubt, the church has confessed mystery at this point, but she has also affirmed one person subsisting in two natures, two wills, a divine and human way of knowing, and the *extra*. This orthodox metaphysic creates a number of legitimate questions, but, as difficult as it is to answer these questions, the classical view explains more of the biblical data and in a more coherent way than does kenoticism. In wanting to offer a "better" explanation, kenotic theories limit the Son to living only in his human nature. But this explanation cannot account for *all* of the biblical data and the church's confession. It undermines the continuity between the preincarnate and incarnate Son, and it renders problematic the internal relations between the triune persons.[54]

Advocates of kenoticism were certainly aware of the difficulty of their position. That is why, in order to restore some continuity between the preincarnate and incarnate Son, most kenotic views filled the gap by assigning to the Holy Spirit the role of the active Son. In this way, "[t]he Spirit became a surrogate for the extinguished, depotentiated Word. In practice this meant that during the incarnate period the divine circuitry was broken, the second person was on a leave of absence from the Godhead, and the Trinity was at best reduced to a 'binity'."[55] Such an understanding also entailed that the relations between the triune persons required some kind of change, either temporarily

---

[53] Macleod, *Person of Christ*, 210.

[54] Baillie insists that the kenotic view results not in a true incarnation but in a "temporary theophany, in which He who formerly was God changed Himself temporarily into man, or exchanged His divinity for humanity" (Donald Baillie, *God Was in Christ: An Essay on Incarnation and Atonement* [New York: Charles Scribner's Sons, 1948], 96). Baillie argues that even if the kenotic theory maintains the *anhypostasia*, the divine Son, in the incarnation, so divests himself of his omni-attributes that there is a loss of deity. If, however, the kenoticist denies *anhypostasia* and regards Jesus now as a human *person*, then we have some kind of metamorphosis taking place. Both of these moves deny the Christian concept of the incarnation. Cf. Louis Berkhof, *Systematic Theology*, 4th rev. and enlarged ed. (Grand Rapids, MI: Eerdmans, 1981), 310.

[55] Wells, *Person of Christ*, 139.

or permanently, thus requiring a redefinition of divine immutability along with a different understanding of the triune persons.

Third, kenotic theories failed to explain how Scripture attributes cosmic functions to the *incarnate* Son (e.g., Col. 1:17; Heb. 1:3). These texts give no indication that the Son temporarily ceased or suspended his divine, cosmic activity during the incarnation or that he was not involved in these actions alongside the Father and Spirit. Furthermore, if, for the sake of argument, one grants the kenotic view, then how do we now conceive of Trinitarian agency? A consistent staple of pro-Nicene theology is that in every divine action, *all* of the divine persons inseparably act (*opera Trinitatis ad extra sunt indivisa*), yet each person acts distinctly according to his mode of relation or subsistence. Thus, in creation, providence, and redemption, the Father, Son, and Holy Spirit act, yet each person acts *as* Father, *as* Son, and *as* Holy Spirit, thus simultaneously preserving the unity and diversity of Trinitarian action. But contrary to the historic understanding of the church, kenotic theories contend that the incarnate Son, at least temporarily (and, for most kenoticists, permanently), no longer acts as the divine Son in relation to the Father and Spirit in the same way as he did prior to the incarnation. This not only fails to do justice to various biblical texts, it also is a serious departure from an orthodox understanding of Trinitarian agency.

This debate is not new. In fact, throughout church history, the question of whether one affirms the "cosmic functions" of the incarnate Son has served as a dividing line between orthodoxy and heresy. On the basis of Scripture, the church affirmed that even in Christ's state of humiliation, as the incarnate Son, he continues to uphold, sustain, and direct the universe *as the divine Son.* Kenoticism cannot make sense of this biblical truth. It is for this reason that William Temple famously asked this question of kenotic proponents in his day:

> What was happening to the rest of the universe during the period of our Lord's earthly life? To say that the Infant Jesus was from His cradle exercising providential care over it all is certainly monstrous;[56] but to deny this, and yet to say that the Creative Word was so self-emptied as to have no being except in the Infant Jesus, is to assert that for a certain period the history of the world was let loose from the control of the Creative word, and 'apart from Him' very nearly everything happened that happened at all during thirty odd years, both on this planet and throughout the immensities of space.[57]

Nineteenth- and early twentieth-century kenotic theories never adequately answered this question. This is why Macleod draws this overall assessment about

---

[56] Temple is not denying the cosmic functions of the incarnate Son. Instead, he is denying that the Son *alone* acts, given the unity of Trinitarian action.

[57] William Temple, *Christus Veritas* (London: Macmillan, 1924), 142–143.

kenotic Christologies: "Any form of kenoticism which involves the idea of a depotentiated *Logos* ('one who had not power which a perfect manhood could not mediate') would be fatal to the Lord's competence to carry out his cosmic functions,"[58] and, as such, must be rejected as unbiblical.

Even for those like Thomasius, who argued that the Son's loss or non-exercise of divine attributes was only temporary, he (and others like him) could not explain the Scriptural texts *and* make sense of how the divine attributes, which were set aside in the state of humiliation, returned in the state of exaltation. The logic of the kenotic view required that, due to the incarnation, some kind of loss, or minimally, non-use of the Son's divine attributes, must occur. But how, then, especially for those who affirmed the temporary nature of this occurrence, do we make sense of the incarnate Son regaining those attributes along with their use? If the incarnation necessitates some kind of loss and the Son remains incarnate now and forevermore, it would seem that the kenotic view must affirm not merely a temporary loss but a permanent one. The only alternative is that, in glorification, what brought about the limitation in the first place—namely, the Son's assuming a human nature—is reversed. But not only is this state of affairs rejected by Scripture; implications of such a view would be disastrous for Christ's ability to be our Redeemer and new covenant head and representative.

Years ago, Donald Baillie challenged kenotic theories at this precise point. Baillie rejects the notion that there is a permanent limitation on the Son, so he presses those who think that the kenosis was merely temporary. If the Son's assumption of a human nature necessarily requires either a surrender or a loss of the omni-attributes, or even a temporary non-use of them, then how do we avoid affirming that this limitation is now permanent? It seems one must affirm either the permanent loss of the omni-attributes and/or their use, or a removal of what brought about the limitation in the first place, viz., the assumption of the human nature. Both of these options Baillie rightly notes are unbiblical and thus unacceptable. He states his challenge this way:

> Was the *kenosis* merely temporary, confined to the period of the Incarnation of the Son of God, the days of His flesh on earth? The holders of the theory would *logically* have to answer: Yes. The presupposition of the theory is that the distinctive divine attributes (of omniscience, etc.) and the distinctive human attributes (of finitude) cannot be united simultaneously in one life: that is why the Incarnation is explained as a *kenosis*. Therefore when the days of His flesh come to an end, Christ resumes His divine attributes, and His *kenosis*, his humanity, comes to an end. His human life is left behind when He ascends to the right hand of the Father. Thus, on the Kenotic theory . . . He is God and Man, not simultaneous in a hypostatic union, but *successively*—

---

[58] Macleod, *Person of Christ*, 209.

first divine, then human, then God again. But if that is really what the theory amounts to—and I do not see how it can be otherwise interpreted—it seems to leave no room at all for the traditional catholic doctrine of the *permanence* of the manhood of Christ.[59]

Even though Baillie is slightly reductionistic in his understanding of kenoticism, since few of them would say that the incarnate Son ceased to be God, nevertheless his point is legitimate. How does kenoticism escape the dilemma of either affirming a permanent loss for God the Son as a result of the incarnation, or some kind of denial of the permanency of his human nature? Both options are unbiblical, and both options reveal the inherent weakness of the kenotic view. In seeking to do justice to the incarnation and to make sense of some of the perennial questions which legitimately occur, the "new" kenotic proposal created more problems than it solved.

Fourth, kenotic views fail to do justice to the entire biblical presentation of Christ (which is the most serious criticism). In this view, the earthly Jesus relinquished his divine attributes, and/or performed no divine functions, enjoyed no divine privileges, and possessed no divine consciousness. But how does this view fit with the biblical data discussed in Part II? The Jesus of the Bible knows he is the eternal Son; he inaugurates God's saving rule, forgives sin, exercises divine power over sin, death, and nature; has divine authority and receives our worship—all actions that identify him as the divine Son and Lord. Kenotic Christology simply cannot affirm this biblical view of Jesus. Macleod captures this point well when he writes,

> It is from such evidence, pointing clearly to the conclusion that Jesus saw himself as divine, acted as one who was divine, portrayed himself as divine and was seen as divine, that the church derived its belief in the deity of Christ. That belief is essential to the life and worship of the church: and fatal to the Kenotic Theory. Whatever the lowliness into which Christ stooped by his incarnation it was not such as to prevent his disciples seeing his glory (Jn. 1:14). If it had been—if the earthly life had disclosed nothing but 'human likeness' (Phil. 2:7)—Christ would never have been worshipped and Christianity would never have been born.[60]

In addition, as noted in our exegesis of Philippians 2 in chapter 4, kenotic theories mishandle the text by misplacing the true nature of God the Son's "self-emptying." They appeal to a text that does not warrant their overall theory. Biblically, the humiliation/humbling of the Son is twofold: first, in taking on our humanity, and second, supremely, in going to the cross. Christ *emptied* himself for the purposes of the incarnation, but he also *humbled*

---

[59] Baillie, *God Was in Christ*, 97.
[60] Macleod, *Person of Christ*, 210–211.

himself unto death. Philippians 2 stresses two great decisions of our Lord: (1) the decision to assume the form of a servant and the likeness of men; (2) the decision to humble himself even further to death on a cross. Yet the text says nothing about his loss of deity, setting aside divine attributes, or even the complete non-use of his divine prerogatives. Instead, the text focuses on the incredible act of "self-emptying" of the Son in adding to himself a human nature. From the moment of conception, and at every moment throughout his life, our Lord chose to live, suffer, and die in order to bear our sin and shame, as our Lord and Savior. By virtue of the incarnation, the Son is now able to live a fully human life and accomplish our redemption. His daily life, culminating in the cross, is a life of *kenosis* by choosing gladly and willingly to submit to his Father's will for our redemption. And as a result of his obedient work, the Father raised him from the dead and gave him a place of exaltation as the Son incarnate. To be sure, he gave up his personal privileges and rights; he humbled himself by choosing to live a fully human life and become our Redeemer, but in all of this, Philippians 2 does not describe the *kenosis* of the Son according to the kenotic theory, since even in the incarnation the Son remains who he has always been, *God* the Son. Kenoticism cannot account for Scripture's entire presentation of Jesus.

Instead of kenoticism's sense of *kenosis*, Philippians 2 and the entire New Testament speak more of *krypsis*, i.e., hiddenness or veiledness. This is not to say that the incarnation was a mere "hiddenness." It was the real addition of a human nature, but it was not the reduction or renunciation of his deity. In becoming incarnate, the Son not only accommodated himself to human weakness; he also veiled his glory, which is seen clearly only by revelation and God's sovereign grace. As Jesus lived a fully human life, as he was tempted in the wilderness to turn rocks into bread, he clearly had the ability to exercise his divine power and authority, as is evidenced on other occasions such as his pronouncing forgiveness of sins, raising Lazarus from the dead, calming the storm, and feeding the five thousand. But, as Macleod notes, there is a difference between Jesus *not* exercising his divine power in his wilderness temptation and his exercise of divine power in the feeding of the multitude. In the former, Jesus was tempted to use his power for himself; in the latter, he used it for the glory of God and for others. Macleod beautifully expresses this truth:

> [Jesus] denied himself the exercise of his divine might and energies, but in other directions these energies were frequently put forth: for example, in per-forming the cosmic functions of the *Logos*, in healing the sick and in destroy-ing the works of the devil. But they were not put forth in his own interest. In particular, they were not put forth to protect him from the implications of his decision to become incarnate and bear the sin of the world. Never once does he in his own interest or in his own defence break beyond the parameters of

humanity. He had no place to lay his head; but he never built himself a house. He was thirsty; but he provided for himself no drink. He was assaulted by all the powers of hell; but he did not call on his legions of angels. Even when he saw the full cost of *kenōsis*, he asked for no rewriting of the script. He bore the sin in his human body, endured the sorrow in his human soul and redeemed the church with his human blood. The power which carried the world, stilled the tempest and raised the dead was never used to make his own conditions of service easier. Neither was the prestige he enjoyed in heaven exploited to relax the rules of engagement. Deploying no resources beyond those of his Spirit-filled humanness, he faced the foe as flesh and triumphed as man.[61]

Fifth, kenoticism is impossible to reconcile with the Chalcedonian Definition. Even though kenotic theorists attempt to remain within Chalcedonian orthodoxy, their formulation revises it at almost every point. For example, in correctly emphasizing the humanity of Christ, they reduce his deity, something Chalcedon explicitly forbids. For the most part, as Macleod notes, "the language of kenoticism is monophysitic, starting from the premise that the idea of two consciousnesses and two minds and two wills in one person is simply absurd. An authentic human life is possible on such terms only at the expense of the divine; if he was a man, he could not have been God."[62] Christ had the human property of ignorance but not the divine property of omniscience. But such a view directly denies what Chalcedon affirms, namely, "one and the same Son, the same perfect in Godhead and the same perfect in manhood, truly God and truly man"—or, that each nature, deity and humanity, retained its own distinctive properties even in the hypostatic union. All of this has to be denied or at least massively redefined by kenotic theories. Even Chalcedon's emphasis on the "one divine person" who subsists in two natures loses its punch in kenotic views since if the Son, in the incarnation, sets aside his divine characteristics and infuses himself into a human subject or takes upon himself a human nature by reducing himself to the dimensions of that humanity, then, as Wells astutely observes, "in joining with humanity there is little reason to speak of the need of unity when the possibility of disunity is no longer there!"[63] Or, as Wells continues to remark, "The self-reduced Logos and the human center of the man Jesus simply become the coordinates of the same self-consciousness. The one person could never be a composite of elements essentially contradictory or different, and therefore to say that Christ was 'one' was as unexceptional as saying that people today are 'one'."[64] In all these ways, kenotic theories are out of step with the affirmation of the church.

---

[61] Ibid., 220.
[62] Ibid., 209–210.
[63] Wells, *Person of Christ*, 139.
[64] Ibid.

Kenotic Christology in the nineteenth and early twentieth century attempted to provide a "newer," "better," and "middle" way between Chalcedonian orthodoxy and classic liberalism, but it failed. Yet it is important to note that the influence of kenoticism is still alive today, both outside and within evangelicalism. Before we provide a warranted Christology for today, we must first investigate whether current evangelical kenoticism fares any better than its older variety.

ELEVEN

EVANGELICAL CHRISTOLOGY

AND KENOTIC INFLUENCES

As outlined in the previous chapter, kenotic Christology was a *via media* attempt by theologians to reformulate Chalcedonian orthodoxy along a "new" and "better" path. These thinkers did not embrace the Enlightenment *Zeitgeist* entirely, yet they were dissatisfied with orthodoxy. What resulted was a "reconstructed" Christology, which, we argued, failed in regard to biblical and ecclesiastical warrant. Most orthodox Christians, including later evangelicals, rejected this attempt to recast Christology, yet today, in evangelical Christology, there is an unmistakable kenotic influence resulting in more diversity of thought than is often recognized.[1] In fact, broadly conceived, there is a spectrum of three viewpoints: the "newer" views known as ontological and functional kenotic Christology versus the "older" classical view.[2]

In this chapter, our intent is to sketch these "newer" Christological views, both of which incorporate some form of kenoticism. Then in chapter 12, we will offer some critical reflections and draw the same conclusion we did for the earlier kenotic views, namely that these "newer" views do not account for *all* of the biblical data, and that the "old" path is better. This will pave the way for chapters 13–14, which will commend the classical view for evangelicals today.

---

[1] Contra Macquarrie, who argued that kenotic Christologies "turned out to be no more than an episode in modern thinking about the person of Jesus Christ" (John Macquarrie, *Jesus Christ in Modern Thought* [London: SCM; Philadelphia: Trinity Press, 1990], 250). In fact, kenoticism is having an immense influence both outside and within evangelicalism. On this point, see Kevin J. Vanhoozer, *Remythologizing Theology: Divine Action, Passion, and Authorship* (Cambridge: Cambridge University Press, 2010), 105–177; cf. Philip Clayton and Arthur Peacocke, eds., *In Whom We Live and Move and Have Our Being: Panentheistic Reflections on God's Presence in a Scientific World* (Grand Rapids, MI: Eerdmans, 2004); John Polkinghorne, ed., *The Work of Love: Creation as Kenosis* (Grand Rapids, MI: Eerdmans, 2001).

[2] For these categories, see Oliver D. Crisp, *Divinity and Humanity* (Cambridge: Cambridge University Press, 2007), 118–153. In Christological discussion, "ontological" refers to some kind of change in the Son's divine nature as a result of the incarnation, while "functional" refers to the Son retaining all of his divine attributes but choosing not to exercise them either temporarily or permanently, due to the incarnation.

ONTOLOGICAL KENOTIC CHRISTOLOGY (OKC)

In recent years, a small number of evangelical philosophers and theologians have rehabilitated some points of earlier nineteenth-century kenoticism.[3] Believing it was dismissed too hastily by orthodox and liberal theologians alike, they are rethinking Jesus's deity and humanity in kenotic terms once again. Their aim, as C. Stephen Evans describes, is to provide "a viable kenotic theory" and to do so "within the boundaries of Christian orthodoxy, broadly and generously conceived."[4] They are convinced that the kenotic approach makes better sense of Jesus's humanity than classical Christology, while preserving Jesus's deity as God the Son. Let us outline the view in five points.

First, what is the relationship of OKC to orthodoxy? Advocates of ontological kenotic Christology insist that they are fully orthodox because they accept the church's confession of the Trinity, the Son's eternal preexistence, and the full deity and humanity of Christ. Additionally, in order to show that OKC is a species of orthodoxy, Stephen Davis asserts the following points: (1) Jesus really performed miracles, even though these miracles were not done by his own divine power but by the Spirit's power at work in him; (2) Jesus is essentially God and *not* a mere man who had his humanity enlarged by a few divine properties; and (3) the incarnate Son remained as the second person of the Trinity; he was *not* temporarily excluded from the Trinity as a result of his "setting aside" certain divine attributes.[5] Given these affirmations, OKC advocates insist that their view is consistent with Chalcedon, yet they argue that the Definition did not fully explain what a "nature" or a "person" is; Chalcedon only established the broad parameters for Christological thought, and therefore we are free to "redefine" these concepts differently than the church did.[6]

Second, what is the overall view of ontological kenotic Christology? OKC proposes that in the incarnation the divine Son "gave up" or "laid aside" certain divine attributes or properties normally belonging to deity, thus choosing to "fully enter into the life of a human being" and limiting himself to these experiences without completely relinquishing his divine nature.[7] Some OKC proponents view this divestment as temporary, only for the state of humilia-

---

[3] See C. Stephen Evans, ed., *Exploring Kenotic Christology: The Self-Emptying of God* (New York: Oxford University Press, 2006); Anna Marmodoro and Jonathan Hill, ed. *The Metaphysics of the Incarnation* (New York: Oxford University Press, 2011); Stephen T. Davis, *Christian Philosophical Theology* (New York: Oxford University Press, 2006); idem, *Logic and the Nature of God* (Grand Rapids, MI: Eerdmans, 1983); Stephen T. Davis, Daniel Kendall, and Gerald O'Collins, eds., *The Incarnation* (New York: Oxford University Press, 2002); Stephen T. Davis, Daniel Kendall, and Gerald O'Collins, eds., *The Trinity: An Interdisciplinary Symposium on the Trinity* (Oxford; New York: Oxford University Press, 1999); Ronald J. Feenstra and Cornelius Plantinga Jr., eds., *Trinity, Incarnation, and Atonement: Philosophical and Theological Essays* (Notre Dame, IN: University of Notre Dame Press, 1989).
[4] Evans, "Introduction," in *Exploring Kenotic Christology*, 5.
[5] These points are taken from Davis, "Is Kenosis Orthodox?" in *Exploring Kenotic Christology*, 113.
[6] See Evans, "Introduction," 1–2, who views Chalcedon this way.
[7] See Evans, "Kenotic Christology and the Nature of God," in *Exploring Kenotic Christology*, 196; Davis, "Is Kenosis Orthodox?" 113.

tion, and after the Son's glorification he resumes possession of all the divine attributes.[8] Others view the divestment as permanent.[9]

Third, what are the perceived strengths of OKC? Over against the classical view, OKC advocates suggest at least three advantages: First, it helps reorient our thinking about God by giving us a God who fully shares our human condition and who, in Jesus, endures "the human situation in the same way that all of us must," i.e., without "hidden divine powers in reserve."[10] Such a view of God is one we can identify with—one who is not distant, immutable, and impassible—but one "who can fully empathize with us."[11] Second, it avoids the classical view's tendency to overemphasize Christ's deity at the expense of his humanity and thus avoids docetism and Nestorianism.[12] Third, it can better answer the charge of logical inconsistency because it does not resort to the perceived problematic features of the classical view—e.g., two wills and minds, reduplicative strategies, and the *extra*.[13]

Fourth, the real "novelty" of ontological kenotic Christology centers on its understanding of Christ's divine nature. Before we discuss this point, let us first discuss the concept of a "nature" in terms of current philosophical and theological discussion in order to situate OKC in light of that discussion.

Currently, in the debate regarding what a nature is, specifically a human nature, a contrast is made between an abstract and a concrete nature.[14] When Christ's human nature is viewed as *abstract*, it is viewed as a property or a set of properties, necessary and sufficient for being human, that the Son adds to himself. As Oliver Crisp notes, one can think of the Son adding an abstract nature to himself in either a two- or three-part way. The two-part option entails that the Son assumes the property of "having a human body" with the Son *becoming* a human soul; the three-part option entails that the Son assumes the properties of "having a human body" and "having a human soul," where the soul is distinct from the Son.[15] In contrast, a *concrete* nature is not viewed merely in terms of properties; instead it is viewed as a concrete particular. In

[8] See Davis, "Is Kenosis Orthodox?" 112–138; Feenstra, "Reconsidering Kenotic Christology," in *Trinity, Incarnation, and Atonement*, 128–151.
[9] See Evans, "The Self-Emptying of Love: Some Thoughts on Kenotic Christology," in *Incarnation*, 263–267; idem, "Kenotic Christology and the Nature of God," 200–202, who defends this possibility.
[10] Evans, "Introduction," 7.
[11] Ibid.
[12] For this charge, see ibid., 3, 7–8.
[13] John Hick charges the classical view with rational incoherence (John Hick, *The Metaphor of God Incarnate: Christology in a Pluralistic Age*, 2nd ed. [Louisville: Westminster John Knox, 1993]; idem, "Jesus and the World Religions," in *The Myth of God Incarnate*, ed. John Hick [Philadelphia: Westminster, 1977], 178). Feenstra defends the rational superiority of OKC (Feenstra, "A Kenotic Christology of Divine Attributes," in *Exploring Kenotic Christology*, 144).
[14] See Oliver Crisp, *Divinity and Humanity*, 34–71; see also Alvin Plantinga, "On Heresy, Mind, and Truth," *Faith and Philosophy* 16/2 (1999): 182–193. For a helpful categorization of current views, see Hill, "Introduction," in *Metaphysics of the Incarnation*, 1–19. For a discussion applied to the divine nature, see William Hasker, *Metaphysics and the Tri-Personal God* (Oxford: Oxford University Press, 2013), 50–54.
[15] See Crisp, *Divinity and Humanity*, 41–49.

the case of Christ's human nature, the Son adds to himself a specific human nature, i.e., a particular instance of human nature that has certain properties. Similar to the abstract view, one can think of the addition of a concrete nature in a two- or three-part way. A two-part view, which would entail Apollinarianism, thinks of the Son as assuming a concrete human body, while he, as the Son, replaces the human soul. A three-part view argues that the Son assumes a concrete human nature consisting of a body-soul composite. Historically, the church has affirmed that God's nature is one and concrete, and that in the incarnation, Christ is composed of three "parts": the person of the Son and the divine nature, and a human nature consisting of a body *and* soul composite, even though, admittedly, it is anachronistic to speak this way of Patristic theology.[16]

In light of these categories, OKC adopts an abstract view over against a concrete view, even though this is not monolithic.[17] The implication is that at the incarnation, the divine Son becomes human by assuming properties necessary and sufficient for being human, while retaining what is *essential* to deity. In stressing the word *essential*, we are now able to discuss how OKC understands the divine nature.

Similar to earlier kenoticism, ontological kenotic Christology rejects the classical view that *all* of God's attributes are *essential* to him; instead, it distinguishes between "essential" and "accidental" attributes.[18] Historically, orthodoxy affirmed that in the incarnation the Son retained *all* of his divine attributes—e.g., omnipresence, omnipotence, omniscience, eternality, etc.—and thus continued to be *homoousios* with the Father and Spirit; it also affirmed that the incarnation was an act of *addition*, not subtraction. This, however, is not the position of OKC. The challenge, then, is to explain how the Son remains *fully* God given his divestiture of *some* of the divine attributes in the incarnation. By employing the essential-accidental distinction, OKC denies that the Son "gives up" his divine nature completely; instead he only "gives up" its *accidental* attributes.

But how does one decide which attributes are which? OKC's answer: by theologizing about the divine nature *in light of the incarnation*. In making this move, OKC rejects the methodological approach of "Anselmian or classical theology," by taking a page from Karl Barth (even though Barth would reject OKC), and arguing that we know only what is *essential* to God

---

[16] Hasker demonstrates that the pro-Nicenes adopted a concrete view of the divine nature, which certainly entails the same for the human nature of Christ (Hasker, *Metaphysics and the Tri-Personal God*, 62–67).

[17] See Hill, "Introduction," in *Metaphysics of the Incarnation*, 8–10.

[18] See Davis, "Is Kenosis Orthodox?" 115–116. Davis gives the following definitions: An *essential property* of x is an attribute that x has and cannot lose without ceasing to exist or ceasing to be x. An *accidental property* of x is an attribute that x has but *can* fail to have and still be x. For example, three-sidedness is an essential property of a triangle, while having hair or an arm is an accidental property of a human.

in Christ. So, for example, Scripture teaches that the incarnate Son is *fully* God yet lacking in knowledge. In order to make sense of this, we must rethink omniscience and omnipotence (indeed, *all* of the divine attributes) in such a way as to affirm that the incarnate Son is divine *and* non-omniscient, non-omnipotent, etc. From this observation, we then conclude that the omniattributes are *not* essential to deity; instead they are accidental and only true of God *simpliciter*.[19]

In their "redefining" of the divine nature, it is not surprising that OKC advocates depart dramatically from classical theology, yet they insist their view is true to Chalcedon and is rationally coherent. How so? As long as we redefine omniscience (or any divine attribute that is inconsistent with being truly human) as x is *essential* to God "unless-freely-and-temporarily-choosing-to-be-otherwise,"[20] then it is logical to affirm that the incarnate Son is *truly* God, because he retains all of the *essential* divine attributes. As it turns out, OKC theorists propose, any divine attribute which is inconsistent with being truly human is simply placed in the "accidental property" category and thus "given up" without any loss of deity. Ronald Feenstra states it this way: We can affirm that "the kenotically Incarnate Jesus Christ, although temporarily non-omniscient, would still be able to possess the attribute of omniscience-unless-kenotically-incarnate."[21]

In the end, OKC explains the incarnation as follows: the *divine* Son temporarily chooses for the purpose of our redemption to "set aside" certain divine attributes, yet he remains *essentially* and *truly* God as long as those attributes he "sets aside" are accidental and *not* essential. After the Son's earthly work is finished, he can return to being with the Father and Spirit, "unchangeably and unalterably omniscient."[22] In this way OKC confesses that "Jesus Christ during his life on earth was both truly divine and, during his freely chosen, temporary, redemptive self-humiliation, not omniscient."[23]

This proposal, regardless of protestations to the contrary, is difficult to reconcile with Chalcedon. No doubt, given their redefinition of the divine nature, OKC is able to affirm in a formulaic sense that Jesus Christ is *fully* God and *fully* man, one person who subsists in two natures. However, in what sense is OKC in continuity with Chalcedon if it jettisons the entire theological substructure undergirding Chalcedonian terminology? Classical Christology never employed the "essential-accidental" distinction vis-à-vis the divine attributes, yet this distinction is foundational to OKC. Davis valiantly attempts

---

[19] On this point, see Feenstra, "Kenotic Christology of the Divine Attributes," 158–164; Evans, "Kenotic Christology and the Nature of God," 190–217.
[20] Davis, "Is Kenosis Orthodox?" 118.
[21] Feenstra, "Kenotic Christology of Divine Attributes," 153.
[22] Ibid., 154.
[23] Ibid.

to demonstrate how OKC is consistent with Chalcedon when he writes, "The kenotically incarnate Logos is indeed 'of one substance with the Father' because the Father's nature or substance just is the set of his essential properties, which the theory insists Christ had."[24] Yet OKC and Chalcedon are not defining the divine nature in the same way and are thus equivocating on their use of *homoousios*.

Fifth, ontological kenotic Christology is "novel" not merely in its redefinition of "nature" but also in its redefinition of "person," which entails some important Christological and Trinitarian implications.[25] For OKC, "person" is best defined as a "distinct center of knowledge, will, love, and action";[26] in Trinitarian theology, this idea requires an acceptance of three wills in God, and in Christology, the endorsement of monothelitism (because the will is located in the person). Historically, classical Christology rejected this understanding of person and instead, in the words of Boethius, defined person as an "individual substance of a rational nature."[27] Even though these two definitions seem similar, they are not. In the latter definition, the person is an "I" or an "active subject" that subsists in a nature, i.e., a subsistent individual who is the agent of his nature. The "rational nature" is best understood as a concrete particular consisting of a body-soul composite, and it is in the nature that the *capacities of will and mind* are placed. This is why classical Christology has always affirmed dyothelitism and has affirmed that, in the incarnation, the divine Son subsists in two natures, and that *he*, as the Son, acts in and through the capacities of each nature.

OKC theorists, however, locate the capacities of the nature, i.e., will and mind, in the person; hence its embrace of monothelitism. This redefinition of person is also seen in OKC's equation of "person" *and* "soul," so that in humans, the soul of the human nature is identified as the "person," and in Christology, the "person" of the Son replaces, or better, *becomes* the soul of the human body. In contrast, Chalcedon clearly distinguished the "person" from the "soul" in its confession that the Son assumed a human nature comprised of a body *and* a "rational soul."

This redefinition of "person" is evident in Thomas Thompson and Cornelius Plantinga. In discussing the kenotic strategy, they suggest that the Logos limited "his divine powers, prerogatives, attributes, and/or glory so as to be compatible with a humanity as animated by a human rational soul—that is,

---

[24] Davis, "Is Kenosis Orthodox?" 121.
[25] See Thomas R. Thompson and Cornelius Plantinga Jr., "Trinity and Kenosis," in *Exploring Kenotic Christology*, 165–189, for a helpful discussion of how OKC advocates redefine person, along with its Trinitarian implications.
[26] See Cornelius Plantinga Jr., "Social Trinity and Tritheism," in *Trinity, Incarnation, and Atonement*, 22. Cf. Hasker, *Metaphysics and the Tri-Personal God*, 19–25.
[27] Cited in Gilles Emery, "The Dignity of Being a Substance: Person, Subsistence, and Nature," *Nova et Vetera* 9/4 (2011): 994 (English edition). For the original source, see Boethius, *Liber de Persona et Duabus Naturis*, chapter 3, "A Treatise against Eutyches and Nestorius," 85, in his *Theological Tractates*.

to be and live as a human person."[28] They make sense of this by positing "a strict identity between the Logos and Christ's human rational soul."[29] Given this strict identity, we can now think of the true nature of the Son's kenosis. In the incarnation the divine Son freely chose to assume the properties of a human nature by assuming a human body and *becoming* a human soul, and in this sense, a human person. In this choice, the divine Son "gives up" certain divine attributes which are incompatible with human existence and truly becomes a human person, even though he remains *fully* God, in the sense described above.[30] In other words, by an act of kenosis, the person of the Son becomes a human—a human soul by self-limitation—one unitive consciousness completely within the bounds of a human body.

At least two implications follow from OKC's understanding of "person." First, it must reject the reality of the *extra*, as taught historically by the church. Why? Because for OKC, the *extra* is metaphysically impossible since *kenosis* entails that the Son is, at least temporarily, circumscribed by the limits of his human body. Second, it also requires an embrace of social Trinitarianism, the affirmation that in God there are three distinct centers of consciousness, will, mind, and agency.[31] The classical view, in contrast, argues that the three persons are distinct yet also share the same capacity of will because they possess the same identical concrete nature. Thus, for OKC, the oneness of the Godhead is not found in the three persons sharing the same identical nature; instead, the divine persons are one because "God is like a community,"[32] a perichoretic unity of Trinitarian persons by which the divine persons have "unity of purpose, fellowship, communion, hospitality, transparency, self-deference, or just simply the love among Father, Son, and Spirit."[33] Furthermore, bound up with this social view, OKC advocates also reject a staple of pro-Nicene theology, viz., the affirmation of the inseparable operations of the divine persons. As Thompson and Plantinga willingly concede, "To the objection that this sunders the *indivisa* of Trinitarian persons and their operations, we confess the transgression."[34]

Here, then, is OKC in a nutshell. Even though it confesses to function within the parameters of orthodoxy, at almost every point it redefines the terms and theological entailments of the Chalcedonian Definition. In chapter 12, we

---

[28] Thompson and Plantinga, "Trinity and Kenosis," 170.

[29] Ibid.

[30] See Richard Swinburne, "The Coherence of the Chalcedonian Definition of the Incarnation," in *Metaphysics of the Incarnation*, 156–160.

[31] On this point, see Richard Swinburne, *Christian God* (Oxford: Oxford University Press, 1994), 182; Thomas H. McCall, *Which Trinity? Whose Monotheism: Philosophical and Systematic Theologians on the Metaphysics of Trinitarian Theology* (Grand Rapids: Eerdmans, 2010), 12–15, 87–105.

[32] Stephen T. Davis, "Perichoretic Monotheism: A Defense of a Social Theory of the Trinity," in *The Trinity: East/West Dialogue*, ed. Melville Y. Stewart (Dordrecht: Kluwer Academic, 2003), 42.

[33] Thompson and Plantinga, "Trinity and Kenosis," 183–184.

[34] Ibid., 189.

will evaluate whether this "new" path is "better" than the old one, but before we do, let us now describe the functional kenotic viewpoint.

FUNCTIONAL KENOTIC CHRISTOLOGY (FKC)

Within evangelical theology, a functional kenotic approach to Christology is more common and less radical. Not all who espouse this view would employ the "kenotic" label, given some of its connotations, but most would not object. Representative examples from biblical studies to systematic theology to philosophical theology, while differing at points, are: Gerald Hawthorne, Klaus Issler, Garrett DeWeese, William Craig, J. P. Moreland, and Millard Erickson.[35] In our description of the view, we will proceed in two steps: first, we will describe the basic viewpoint; and second, we will outline two representative examples of the view.

Overview of FKC

Even though there are various nuances among FKC advocates, the view is best understood by setting it over against classical Christology and OKC in four steps.

First, in regard to the "divine nature," FKC agrees with classical Christology, over against OKC, that the "essential-accidental" distinction is illegitimate. As such, the incarnation is *not* a "giving up" of any of the divine attributes; instead the incarnate Son is fully God and continues to possess *all* of the divine attributes as one who is *homoousios* with the Father and Spirit.[36]

Second, in regard to "person," FKC agrees with OKC by defining "person" as a distinct center of knowledge, will, and action, thus locating will and mind in the person, hence its endorsement of monothelitism.[37] Additionally,

---

[35] See Gerald F. Hawthorne, *The Presence and the Power: The Significance of the Holy Spirit in the Life and Ministry of Jesus* (Eugene, OR: Wipf & Stock, 2003); Klaus Issler, *Living into the Life of Jesus: The Formation of Christian Character* (Downers Grove, IL: InterVarsity Press, 2012); Garrett J. DeWeese, "One Person, Two Natures: Two Metaphysical Models of the Incarnation," in *Jesus in Trinitarian Perspective*, ed. Fred Sanders and Klaus D. Issler (Nashville: B&H Academic, 2007), 114–153; J. P. Moreland and William Lane Craig, *Philosophical Foundations for a Christian Worldview* (Downers Grove, IL: InterVarsity Press, 2003), 597–614. Millard Erickson is slightly different because he endorses dyothelitism and does not emphasize the role of the Spirit as much as the other advocates, yet the functional kenotic emphasis is strong (see Millard Erickson, *The Word Became Flesh: A Contemporary Incarnational Christology* [Grand Rapids, MI: Baker, 1991]). In addition, see Bruce A. Ware, *The Man Christ Jesus: Theological Reflections on the Humanity of Christ* (Wheaton, IL: Crossway, 2013), who embraces a similar view yet is sufficiently nuanced that it is difficult to know where to place him.

[36] See Moreland and Craig, *Philosophical Foundations*, 607. Cf. Ware, *Man Christ Jesus*, 16–24.

[37] DeWeese, "One Person, Two Natures," 144–149; Moreland and Craig, *Philosophical Foundations*, 611–612. On the issue of monothelitism, it is difficult to locate Bruce Ware, yet currently he seems to affirm dyothelitism. As Kyle Claunch suggests in "God Is the Head of Christ: Does 1 Corinthians 11:3 Ground Gender Complementarity in the Immanent Trinity?" in *One God in Three Persons: Unity of Essence, Distinction of Persons, Implications for Life*, ed. Bruce A. Ware and John Starke (Wheaton, IL: Crossway, 2015), 88, Ware seems to affirm three distinct wills in the immanent Trinity tied to each divine person, thus entailing one will in the person of Christ. Yet, in private conversations, Ware wants to affirm some kind of "doubleness" in regard to the will of Christ. In recent days, Ware has clarified his view in regard to the number of wills in the triune Godhead. Ware now affirms one will in God, which all three divine persons share. In this affirmation, Ware, along with pro-Nicene orthodoxy, views the will as a capacity or faculty of the divine nature, and when applied to Christology, this entails two wills in Christ. On this point, see Bruce Ware, "Knowing the Self-Revealed God who is Father, Son, and Holy Spirit – Guest Post

many FKC theorists equate "person" with "soul"[38] so that in the incarnation, the person of the Son (which includes a distinct will and mind) now acts and functions through the limits of a human body, with the divine person/soul of the Son *becoming* the soul of the human body. For FKC, this is the most distinctive departure from classical thought, since Chalcedonian Christology always placed the capacity of will in the nature, not the person, hence its endorsement of dyothelitism. Also, classical Christology *never* equated the person with the soul. As we will argue in chapter 12, it is at this point that both OKC and FKC face the difficult challenge of making sense of Christ's complete humanity, even though both views strongly affirm it. Both kenotic views insist that it is the *classical* view that cannot account for Christ's humanity. But if Christ has only one *divine* will, then making sense of Christ's humanity apart from his possessing a distinct human will is difficult.[39] Furthermore, most FKC theorists think of Christ's human nature as abstract rather than concrete.[40] In so doing, the incarnation is understood as the Son assuming the properties of a human nature, including the property of being a human soul; hence, the understanding that the Son *becomes* a human soul. On the surface this sounds rather Apollinarian, as some willingly admit; however, as Crisp helpfully explains, it is not necessarily so. Crisp clarifies the view: technically, a FKC does not say "that the Word *replaces an existing human soul*. Instead the Word becomes the soul of the body of Christ."[41]

Third, functional kenotic Christology also differs from the classical view in regard to the incarnate Son's *exercise* or *functional* use of his divine attributes during the state of humiliation. Specifically, FKC denies that the incarnate Son *exercises his divine attributes* in upholding the universe and performing miracles, yet, it must be admitted that within this view there is a spectrum of thought regarding the Son's use of his divine attributes. Some FKC advocates contend that the Son *never* uses his divine attributes; all of his "divine" acts are done by the power of the Spirit, similar to but greater than previous Spirit-empowered men. Others modify this stance by acknowledging that the Son *occasionally* uses his divine attributes, but that *predominantly* the Son lives his life as we do—not in his deity but in his humanity—dependent upon the

---

by Bruce Ware," at https://secundumscripturas.com/2016/07/04/knowing-the-self-revealed-god-who-is-father-son-and-holy-spirit/ (accessed July 25, 2016).

[38] DeWeese, "One Person, Two Natures," 147–148; Moreland and Craig, *Philosophical Foundations*, 608–610. From private conversations with Bruce Ware, he does not equate person with soul, thus distinguishing himself from FKC. Yet, in many places, he is sympathetic with the overall perspective.

[39] Crisp, *Divinity and Humanity*, 59, raises this challenge: "Possession of a will is constitutive of being either a human or a divine entity. So, if Christ is fully human he must have a distinct human will. And if he is fully divine he must have a distinct divine will." Yet, given OKC's and FKC's definition of "person," it seems that Christ has only a distinct divine will and *not* a distinct human will.

[40] See, e.g., Moreland and Craig, *Philosophical Foundations*, 597–614.

[41] Crisp, *Divinity and Humanity*, 50.

Spirit, and through whom the Spirit acts.[42] Here is another point where a FKC is *not* merely a species of the classical view.[43] Why? Because even though classical Christology unequivocally affirms that the Son lives a fully human life, it rejects the view that the incarnate Son is limited *only* or even *predominantly* to living a human life by the power of the Spirit. Given that the classical view places the capacities of will and mind in the natures, it is able to affirm the *extra*, which affirms that the incarnate Son can act in and through both natures and thus continue to live a fully human *and* a fully divine life. FKC, on the other hand, given its view of one divine will and mind in the person, has a difficult time accounting for the *extra* and thus making sense of how Scripture says, for example, that the incarnate Son continued to uphold the universe by his own exercise of divine power (e.g., Col. 1:15–17; Heb. 1:3).[44] No doubt, similar to classical Christology, FKC affirms the full deity of Christ, yet it departs at significant points: its minimizing of Christ's *continuing exercise* of his divine attributes on earth, its commitment to monothelitism, and its difficulty in affirming or rejecting the *extra*.

Fourth, FKC is often associated with the term "Spirit-Christology."[45] One reason for this association is its indebtedness to Gerald Hawthorne's conclusions in his important monograph *The Presence and the Power*.[46] In this work, Hawthorne investigates the role of the Spirit in Jesus's life and ministry from conception to exaltation. He, along with many FKC advocates, is convinced that we have not done justice to the Spirit–incarnate Son relationship and, in fact, that this relationship is a missing piece in our understanding of the incarnation. Following Hawthorne, FKC contends that the Son, in becoming a man, "willed to renounce the exercise of his divine powers, attributes, prerogatives, so that he might live fully within those limitations which inhere in being truly human."[47] In the incarnation, then, the divine attributes are not "given up";

---

[42] Hawthorne, *Presence and the Power*, 208–219, represents the former view, while DeWeese, "One Person, Two Natures," 67; Issler, *Living into the Life of Jesus*, 113–129; and Ware, *Man Christ Jesus*, 32–33, represent the latter view. For a similar view, see Myk Habets, *The Anointed Son: A Trinitarian Spirit Christology* (Eugene, OR: Pickwick, 2010), 118–187, 260–267.

[43] Contra Peter Forrest, who identifies the functional kenotic view as "quasi-kenotic" and then views it as a version of classical Christology (Peter Forrest, "The Incarnation: A Philosophical Case for Kenosis," *Religious Studies* 36/2 [2000]: 127–140).

[44] Making sense of the cosmic functions of the incarnate Son separates the classical view from its kenotic variations. For example, Issler (*Living into the Life of Jesus*, 125n31) explains Colossians 1:17 and Hebrews 1:3 in this way: In a preincarnate decision the Son temporarily delegated his cosmic functions to the Father and Spirit, even though the text does *not* say this. In private conversations with Bruce Ware, even though he adopts so much of a FKC view, he also affirms the *extra*, once again making him difficult to place completely within this camp.

[45] "Spirit-Christology" is understood in a number of different ways on a spectrum of liberal to orthodox. For a helpful discussion of this point, see Habets, *Anointed Son*, 1–9.

[46] For a discussion and critique of Hawthorne, see Mark L. Strauss, "Jesus and the Spirit in Biblical and Theological Perspective: Messianic Empowering, Saving Wisdom, and the Limits of Biblical Theology," in *The Spirit and Christ in the New Testament and Christian Theology: Essays in Honor of Max Turner*, ed. I. Howard Marshall, Volker Rabens, and Cornelis Bennema (Grand Rapids, MI: Eerdmans, 2012), 266–284. Within evangelicalism, Hawthorne's influence is large. Outside it, Spirit-Christology is influenced by such people as Karl Barth, Karl Rahner, Jürgen Moltmann, Ralph Del Colle, James Dunn, Colin Gunton, and Roger Haight.

[47] Hawthorne, *Presence and the Power*, 208.

instead, they become "potential or latent within this incarnate One—present in Jesus in all their fullness, but no longer in exercise,"[48] so that the incarnate Son chooses to live his life completely circumscribed by his human nature (or mostly so) and "within the bounds of human limitations."[49] Thus when it comes to how Jesus has supernatural knowledge and exercises supernatural power in his miracles, FKC insists that Jesus does so, *not* by the use of his divine attributes, but by the power of the Spirit.[50] Thus, in all of the incarnate Son's actions, even actions traditionally viewed as *divine* actions (such as his miracles), Jesus performs them by the Spirit, in a way similar to other Spirit-empowered men and parallel to the Spirit's work in us. This is why Jesus can serve as our example, as he shows us how to live our lives in dependence on the Spirit—although he is the paradigm, interpreted more quantitatively than qualitatively.[51]

Here, then, is functional kenotic Christology in a nutshell. The strengths of it are numerous, especially in drawing our attention to the biblical data regarding the Spirit–incarnate Son relationship and highlighting the theological significance of Christ's humanity. Yet it remains to be seen whether it can deliver on its promises. Before we turn to constructive criticism, given FKC's growing influence within evangelical theology, let us explain the view in more detail through two representative examples.

Two Representative Examples of FKC

GARRETT DEWEESE AND KLAUS ISSLER (FKC 1).[52]

In a helpful description of a current FKC, Garrett DeWeese and Klaus Issler outline their view over against classical Christology, especially in their redefinition of "person." We will primarily follow DeWeese's presentation with supplementation by Issler in two steps. First, we will describe their basic understanding of the Chalcedonian Definition and its problems. Second, we will outline the key metaphysical and theological entailments of their view.

THE CHALCEDONIAN DEFINITION AND ITS PROBLEMS

Before DeWeese outlines his proposal, he first locates it within the boundaries of Chalcedon. He nicely summarizes the development of Christology through Constantinople III (681). Even though there were various Christological twists

---

[48] Ibid.

[49] Ibid., 212. As noted, Hawthorne thinks that the incarnate Son *never* exercised his divine attributes, while others like DeWeese, Issler, and Ware think he *occasionally* did so, but rarely.

[50] It seems that Hawthorne and other FKC advocates assume that the exercise of the incarnate Son's intrinsic deity is mutually exclusive with his dependence on the Spirit, something Chalcedonian Christology would deny.

[51] Hawthorne, *Presence and the Power*, 219.

[52] See DeWeese, "One Person, Two Natures," 114–153; Klaus Issler, "Jesus' Example: Prototype of the Dependent, Spirit-Filled Life," in *Jesus in Trinitarian Perspective*, 189–225. These two chapters nicely represent their version of FKC with DeWeese providing the theological-philosophical explanation and Issler giving the biblical argument.

and turns, he correctly identifies the basic Christology of Chalcedonian orthodoxy.

However, despite its being the established Christological orthodoxy until the modern era, DeWeese disputes the suitability of the classical understanding of "person," especially as defined by Boethius.[53] He lists a number of problems with the definition, but two are noteworthy. First, he is convinced that the classical view cannot avoid Nestorianism. In every case other than Christ's human nature, normally an individual human nature *is* a human person, so what exactly is lacking when Christ's human nature is sustained by a divine person? In other words, what keeps Christ's human nature from being also a human person and thus leading us to affirm two persons in Christ?[54] Second, he finds problematic the classical view's location of will and mind in the nature. He asks, How can *one* person have two wills and minds? How can we make sense of the relationship between Christ's divine and human will, and would not Christ's divine will always override his human will, thus minimizing his humanity?[55] DeWeese insists that the classical view results in "Christ's human will/mind/consciousness becom[ing] little more than a theoretical entity with no observable consequences in the life of Christ. Christ's exemplary role as a perfect man simply evaporates."[56]

Given his rejection of the classical view of "person," DeWeese suggests an alternative. Even though he knows his view is a departure from the tradition, he insists that Chalcedon only established the parameters of Christology; it did not stipulate the meaning of "person" and "nature." Thus, as long as our Christological proposal remains within the Chalcedonian formula—"Jesus Christ is one person in two natures"—theology is free to propose alternative explanations.[57]

THE METAPHYSICAL AND THEOLOGICAL COMMITMENTS OF FKC 1

Three points capture the basic proposal. First, DeWeese carefully defines the crucial terms "person" and "nature." Similar to OKC, "person" is defined as "an individual with suitably complex mental capacities,"[58] which, for DeWeese includes both agency *and* the capacities of will and mind.[59] Also, like OKC,

---

[53] DeWeese, "One Person, Two Natures," 125.
[54] See ibid., 127–128.
[55] See ibid., 133.
[56] Ibid. DeWeese's discussion of dyothelitism is confusing. First, he seems to think that the classical view argues that "natures" are acting subjects, which entails that Christ's human nature "consciously recognizes and worships its divine personal *suppositum*, the Logos" (ibid., 134). This is incorrect. The classical view affirms that the *person* is the acting agent in and through the capacities of the nature, and as such the Son is the only acting agent in Christ. Second, DeWeese quotes Donald Macleod (ibid.) to buttress his point that natures are not acting subjects (which classical Christology affirms!), but does not seem to realize that Macleod affirms dyothelitism.
[57] Ibid., 137.
[58] Ibid., 117.
[59] See ibid., 138. "A *person* is an individual with an appropriately complex and structured set of mental properties, faculties (a natural grouping of capacities) and higher order capacities, unified by internal relations."

he identifies this concept of "person" with the biblical concept of the soul: "[sometimes] the biblical word *soul* is used as synonymous with a person."[60] Interestingly, DeWeese insists that the Patristic theologians defined "person" in basically the same way, which is simply false. Even though it took time for *hypostasis* to be uncoupled from *ousia*, Chalcedon never equated "person" with "soul," nor did later councils locate the *capacities* of will and mind in the "person."

DeWeese defines "nature" as an abstract property and not as a concrete particular. He says, "A *nature* is a complex property that includes all properties essential to an individual's being a member of a kind."[61] It is the abstract "whatness" of a kind, "an abstract thing" that must be instantiated in and exemplified by a particular, and it does not have concrete existence on its own.[62] When both person and nature are joined, he insists that an actual person is an "individual *together with a nature*,"[63] with the capacities of will and mind located in the person.

Second, employing these definitions, DeWeese turns to his proposal. The divine Son, the second person of the Trinity, who essentially and necessarily instantiates the divine nature, now assumes the set of properties that define a human nature so that Jesus is now fully God and fully human. Furthermore, "[s]ince a person has a mind and will, and a nature does not, Christ had one mind and one will, which belong to his divine person."[64] During the incarnate Son's earthly ministry, he "voluntarily restricted the exercise of his personhood capacities to the range of thoughts, sensations, volitions, perceptions, etc., that can be exercised by a person operating with the normal limitations of human nature, including being embodied as an organism of the species *Homo sapiens*."[65]

This voluntary restriction, however, is not the same as in OKC. As DeWeese insists, in becoming human, the Son did not "set aside" certain divine attributes, since the Son "possesses the divine nature essentially,"[66] and thus he cannot "give up" divine attributes and still be God. Rather, DeWeese affirms a *functional* kenoticism: the Son voluntarily chooses to exercise his personhood through his human nature, "gaining information about the world through the perceptual faculties of his human body, learning and storing memories through the instrumentality of his human brain, living a perfect human life by his perfect obedience and complete dependence on the Holy Spirit."[67]

---

[60] Ibid., 117, 140.
[61] Ibid., 141.
[62] See ibid., 141–142.
[63] Ibid., 142.
[64] Ibid., 144.
[65] Ibid., 145.
[66] Ibid., 146.
[67] Ibid.

As DeWeese unpacks his monothelite model, he seeks to explain how Christ can will *as a man* even though he has only one *divine* will and mind. Repeatedly, DeWeese talks *as if* Christ has a *human* will and mind, even though metaphysically he does not, and accordingly, his explanation is difficult to follow. For him, Christ's "human mind" refers to the mode of operation of the divine mind "functioning with the constraints of (voluntarily limited by) Jesus' human nature and the organs of a human body."[68] Yet, somehow, DeWeese insists that even though the divine mind functions under the constraints of the human body, the Son is still able to function "gloriously and perfectly according to the divine nature, never sleeps, never ceases to be omniscient."[69] Yet if this is so, then in what sense is Christ thinking and acting humanly—if there is no distinct human will and mind? It seems that DeWeese is trying to affirm some notion of the *extra* but without the traditional metaphysical grounding for it. Ultimately, DeWeese suggests that we should think of Christ's "human mind and will" as a subset of the divine mind and that the divine mind is "largely subliminal"[70] during Jesus's earthly ministry.

In a similar way, DeWeese explains how Christ has a "human soul" when metaphysically there is none, at least in the Chalcedonian sense of the Son adding to himself a concrete human nature comprised of a body *and a soul*. Since DeWeese operates with an abstract nature view, *and* equates soul with person, he cannot distinguish the two as Chalcedon did. Instead he asserts that "Christ's soul was human (in virtue of the soulish aspects of the person of Christ functioning according to his human nature)."[71] In other words, just as there is metaphysically no distinct human mind and will in Christ, there is no human soul; instead the person of the divine Son (which includes the divine mind, will, soul) chooses to *act* and *function* through the limits of his human body, and it is in this way that we can affirm that Jesus is *fully* human.

DeWeese anticipates the charge that, if there is no metaphysically distinct human mind, will, and soul then what about Gregory's maxim—"what is not assumed cannot be redeemed"? He responds by appealing to his abstract view of human nature, placing the soul in the person, and then arguing that "a soul is what a person *is*."[72] By doing this, he is convinced that his monothelite model is a return to the guiding insight of Cyril of Alexandria, who rightly insisted that the person of the Son is the acting subject of the incarnation. Thus, DeWeese not only mistakenly thinks that the classical view treated "natures" as acting subjects; he also appeals to Cyril, who did not embrace monothelitism.[73]

---

[68] Ibid.
[69] Ibid.
[70] Ibid.
[71] Ibid., 147–148.
[72] Ibid., 149 (emphasis his).
[73] For the historical discussion of these points, see Part III.

Third, to round out this proposal, Issler now adds the work of Hawthorne to the mix. Similar to Hawthorne, Issler insists that the incarnate Son lived his life on earth as a man in perfect obedience to the Father and in complete dependence on the Spirit. Jesus, though fully God, lived his life as one indwelt and empowered by the Spirit. However, *pace* Hawthorne, Issler suggests that Jesus's dependence on the Spirit was *not* exclusive; instead it is more in the category of "predominantly dependent."[74] By this he means that "Jesus lived normally within his own human power, relying on the divine resources of the Father and the Holy Spirit, while using his own divine power infrequently, if at all."[75] Issler thinks this accounts for the biblical data better since on rare occasions Jesus seems to use his divine power. But other than these rare examples, Jesus predominantly lived his life as a man in complete dependence upon the Father and Spirit, which serves as a role model for us. Obviously Jesus is unique in that he has the Spirit in full measure, but like Hawthorne, Issler views this more quantitatively than qualitatively.[76]

What about the supernatural elements in Jesus life? Other than a few rare examples, Issler proposes that Jesus's miracles, knowledge, and ability to withstand temptation, while all done by Christ, are done by the Spirit's agency through Christ.[77] After all, Issler argues, "most of the supernaturally oriented activities of Jesus were not unique to him alone but are also performed by 'mere' humans, which supplies additional evidence for the dependency proposal."[78]

Issler and DeWeese are convinced that this FKC proposal better explains some of the perennial issues in Christology. For example, in explaining how the Son who is fully God is limited in his knowledge, Issler suggests that the Son, prior to the incarnation, agreed to allow the Spirit to become a dynamic firewall to Jesus's divine mind so that either Jesus knew things only through

---

[74] Issler lays out three logical options in terms of Jesus's access to divine power: (1) Jesus was occasionally dependent upon the Father and Spirit, but mostly he used his own divine power; (2) Jesus was predominantly dependent upon the Father and Spirit, while he normally lived within his own human power; (3) Jesus was exclusively dependent upon the Father and Spirit and lived completely within his own human power (Issler, "Jesus' Example," 202–205). He then adds two more options: (1) Jesus exclusively used his own divine ability and he was never dependent on the Father and Spirit, and (2) Jesus used his own divine ability about half the time and the other half he depended on the Father and Spirit (Issler, *Living into the Life of Jesus*, 114). As we will argue in chapter 12, from a classical view, this is a very strange form of argumentation. Pro-Nicene Trinitarian thought argues that at no time do the persons of the Godhead ever act "in their own power" apart from the other divine persons, as if the divine persons are doing their own thing in their own resources and power, independent of each other. As applied to Christology, the Son's actions are always *his* actions as the *divine* Son, but always in relation to the other divine persons, hence the classic affirmation of inseparable yet distinct actions of the triune persons. Given the incarnation, the divine Son is now able to act in and through his human nature (and divine nature), but always in relation to the Father and the Spirit.

[75] Issler, "Jesus' Example," 202.

[76] See ibid., 214.

[77] Issler, "Jesus' Example," 204, lists five times when Jesus acted in "his own power" and not in dependence on the Father or Spirit: (1) Jesus forgiving sins (Mark 2:1–12); (2) Jesus being transfigured (Matt. 17:1–13); (3) Jesus displaying his glory at Cana (John 2:11); (4) Jesus responding to the soldiers' question with "I am" as a direct self-disclosure of his deity (John 18:6); (5) Jesus yearning for his preexistent glory with the Father (John 17:5). To this, Bruce Ware, *Man Christ Jesus*, 32–33, adds Jesus raising Lazarus from the dead (John 11:1–44) and the efficacy of the atonement.

[78] Issler, "Jesus' Example," 214.

his human nature, or the Spirit kept his divine knowledge dormant in his sub-conscious mind. "Accordingly, the Spirit would then permit Jesus' increasing awareness within his limited human consciousness in a way that would be appropriate at each stage of Jesus' growing years."[79] In a similar way, Issler explains the "cosmic functions" of the Son. In a preincarnate decision, the Son "temporarily delegated to the other members of the Trinity his usual divine du-ties, such as sustaining the universe (Col 1:17: Heb 1:3)."[80] Jesus's impeccability is explained by the distinction between metaphysical and epistemic possibility. The former affirms that Jesus could not sin, due to his divine nature; the lat-ter, that "although Jesus knew he was God, he was *not certain* that his divine nature would override his human nature to prevent him from sinning. Due to this uncertainty he struggled in his humanity against temptation."[81]

Obviously, this proposal has theological entailments *not* limited to Chris-tology, specifically its affirmation of a "social" understanding of the Trinity, but in the end, its proponents view it as a "better" formulation than the clas-sical view.

William Lane Craig and J. P. Moreland (FKC 2)

Our second example is the proposal of analytic philosophers J. P. Moreland and William Lane Craig in their work *Philosophical Foundations for a Chris-tian Worldview*. Their view is very similar to DeWeese/Issler's proposal, and we will unpack it in the same two steps.

THE CHALCEDONIAN DEFINITION AND ITS PROBLEMS

Craig and Moreland also survey the high points of Christological debate and development in the early church leading to the Chalcedonian Definition. They strongly endorse the basic formula: Jesus Christ is fully God and fully man, one person in two natures, yet like FKC 1, they insist that Chalcedon did not explain precisely how Christ is this, since Chalcedon only established "chan-nel markers for legitimate christological speculation; any theory of Christ's person must be one in which the distinctiveness of both natures is preserved and both meet in one person, one Son, in Christ."[82] Additionally, they admit that Christological development did not end with Chalcedon. Specifically they discuss Constantinople III (681), which rejected monothelitism, and similar to FKC 1, they do not think this Council is binding upon the church. In fact, they insist that dyothelitism is wrongheaded and "in danger of dividing the person

---

[79] Ibid., 215. For a more detailed explanation of the "firewall" idea, see Issler, *Living into the Life of Jesus*, 125.
[80] Issler, *Living into the Life of Jesus*, 125n31.
[81] Ibid., 121. Issler's explanation is strange, since the idea that the divine nature would override his human nature presupposes that "natures" are acting agents, instead of "persons" who act in and through "natures."
[82] Moreland and Craig, *Philosophical Foundations*, 601.

of Christ"[83] and resulting in Nestorianism. In their discussion of Reformed Christology, they struggle with the rational coherence of speaking of two wills and minds in Christ. They ask, "[H]ow is it that one does not wind up with two persons, a human person subordinate to a divine person?"[84] As with FKC 1, Craig and Moreland contend that it is on this point that classical Christology needs rethinking.

In their desire to provide a "better" model, Craig and Moreland unequivocally reject OKC, primarily because it stumbles in maintaining Christ's deity. Agreeing with classical Christology, Craig and Moreland reject any attempt to make God's most prominent attributes merely "contingent properties of God and therefore that he may yield up these nonessential properties and yet continue to be God."[85] If Christology is to be reworked, it has to be done along *functional* kenotic grounds, not ontological.

THE METAPHYSICAL AND THEOLOGICAL COMMITMENTS OF FKC 2

Three steps describe Craig and Moreland's basic proposal. First, they accept the Chalcedonian Definition as representing the biblical teaching that in Christ there is one person who exemplifies two distinct and complete natures, one human and one divine. In addition, they argue that the divine Son takes to himself an abstract human nature and thus the property of being human. As a result of this action, Christ has an "individual essence" in that there is a unique individual who is Jesus Christ, but he also has two "kind-essences," i.e., "Christ exemplified all the properties that constitute humanity and all the properties that make up deity."[86] These natures are distinct in that they do not combine to make one "theanthropic" essence belonging to Christ, for that would make the incarnation essential to the second person of the Godhead, which is false. Only the divine nature belongs essentially to the Logos, but due to the incarnation, he assumed a human nature contingently.

As noted, Craig and Moreland strongly reject OKC on the grounds that it is problematic to think that the Son "gave up" various divine attributes. In agreement with classical thought, the essential-accidental distinction cannot be applied to the divine nature; God *cannot* lose any of his attributes and still remain God. They reject OKC proposals to redefine the divine nature by saying that God has "essential properties like being-omniscient-except-when-kenotically-incarnate, which he never surrenders and which are sufficient for deity."[87] They view this attempt as "explanatorily vacuous" and, ontologically

---

[83] Ibid., 602.
[84] Ibid., 603.
[85] Ibid., 605.
[86] Ibid., 606.
[87] Ibid., 607.

speaking, "it is not clear that there even are such properties as being-omni-scient-except-when-kenotically-incarnate." These definitions evidence an air of arbitrariness and, if accepted, lead to further problems. For example, if the Son temporarily relinquishes his omnipotence but then gets it back again, then "he never in fact ceased to be omnipotent, since omnipotence is a modal property concerning what one *can* do."[88] Or, consider the divine attributes of necessity, aseity, and eternality. These attributes cannot be given up temporarily, for they are by nature permanent attributes. But if this is so, then how can we make sense of Christ's death, unless they are given up? The only answer, insist Craig and Moreland, is to argue along with classical Christology that Christ died only in his human nature, while attributes such as necessity, aseity, and eternality are preserved in the divine nature. But if this is the case (which even OKC proponents must acknowledge in regard to *some* of the divine attributes), then why not say the same for the other divine attributes as well? Christ can be omniscient, omnipotent, and omnipresent in his divine nature but not in his human nature—which, they observe, is precisely what orthodoxy has taught.[89] In the end, the OKC solution fails; it is better to remain within the classical parameters, especially vis-à-vis the divine nature.

Second, contrary to classical Christology and similar to Apollinarius, Craig and Moreland propose that the Logos was the rational soul of Jesus. Here they depart most significantly from Chalcedon and, like FKC 1, redefine what a "person" is. In agreement with all kenotic views today and with social Trinitarianism, they define person as a distinct center of consciousness which includes within it knowledge, mind, will, and action.[90] They propose that the divine Word shares some common constituent which unites the two individual natures, and they explain this union, building on the insights of Apollinarius. They suggest that in the incarnation the Word does *not* replace an existing human soul; instead the Word *becomes* the soul of Christ's human body. Since the Word is the image of God, it also contains "perfect human personhood archetypically in his own nature."[91] The result, then, is this: "[I]n assuming a hominid body the Logos brought to Christ's animal nature just those proper-ties that would serve to make it a complete human nature. Thus the human

---

[88] Ibid. (emphasis theirs).
[89] Ibid., 608.
[90] See ibid., 583. In reference to the Trinity, Craig and Moreland explain that "in God there are three distinct centers of self-consciousness, each with its proper intellect and will." Craig then connects self-consciousness with person-hood: "God is an immaterial substance or soul endowed with three sets of cognitive faculties each of which is suf-ficient for personhood, so that God has three centers of self-consciousness, intentionality, and will" (William Craig, "Trinity Monotheism Once More: A Response to Daniel Howard-Snyder," *Philosophia Christi* 8/1 (2006): 10). For a helpful summary of Craig and Moreland's view of the Trinity, see McCall, *Which Trinity? Whose Monotheism?*, 28–39, and Hasker, *Metaphysics and the Tri-Personal God*, 139–146.
[91] Moreland and Craig, *Philosophical Foundations*, 608.

nature of Christ was complete precisely in virtue of the union of his flesh with the Logos."[92]

On this basis, Craig and Moreland affirm that Christ possessed a complete human nature comprised of body and soul, yet, their proposal is a departure from Chalcedon. Chalcedon does *not* teach that the divine Son became the soul of Christ's human body;[93] rather, it affirms that the Son added to himself a human nature which was comprised of a human body *and* soul.[94] Craig and Moreland, then, similar to OKC advocates and FKC 1, not only redefine "person" to include within it the capacities of mind and will, but also equate "soul" with "person," resulting in a sophisticated monothelitism. They suggest that their view is supported by the biblical teaching that humans are image-bearers. Since we reflect God, *not* by virtue of our animal bodies but as "persons" (souls), God already possesses the properties sufficient for human personhood prior to the incarnation. The only thing the Word lacks is corporeality, which happens in the incarnation.

Additionally, Craig and Moreland insist that their view is consistent with *enhypostasia*. They correctly state that *enhypostasia* means that Christ's human nature did not have its own human *hypostasis*, but instead it became "personal" only in its union with the Word and thus "[t]he *hypostasis* of the human nature is identical with the divine person."[95] Yet, it is important to note that even though their language and formulation is similar to Chalcedon, it is *not* the same. Classical Christology teaches that the divine Son is the *person* of the human nature, but it does *not* teach that the Son *becomes* the human soul of Christ's human nature. Instead what the Son assumes and becomes the *person* of, is a concrete human nature comprised of a body *and* a human soul and its corresponding capacities of will and mind. In Craig and Moreland's view, "the Logos completes the individual human nature of Christ by furnishing it with a rational soul, *which is the Logos himself*,"[96] yet it is this equation of "soul" with "person" that Chalcedon denies, along with their redefinition of "person."

Third, instead of employing the reduplicative strategy, namely, that the Son acts and thinks as a man qua his human nature, and as God qua his divine nature, to explain the human limitations of the incarnate Son, Craig and Moreland postulate a subliminal self as a more adequate explanation. Given

[92] Ibid.

[93] Even though Craig and Moreland say they avoid Apollinarianism, they seem to affirm it. On this point, see Crisp, *Divinity and Humanity*, 45n18. Crisp quotes John A. McGuckin, "Apollinaris of Laodicea," in *The Westminster Handbook to Patristic Theology* (Louisville: Westminster John Knox, 2004), 21–22, and notes the similarity of FKC 2 to Apollinarianism: "The Logos constituted humans as the image of God. The image was particularly located in the *nous*, the spiritual intellect. This was also the seat of personhood (mind and soul). In the case of Jesus the Logos did not need to assume a human mind (logos or rationality), as he himself was the archetype of all intellect. In this one case the image was not anthropologically needed as the original was present, replacing it" (ibid.).

[94] It is best to think of Christ's human nature as *concrete*, even though this terminology is anachronistic.

[95] Moreland and Craig, *Philosophical Foundations*, 609.

[96] Ibid., 610 (emphasis mine).

that the Word becomes the soul of Christ's human body, and given that there is only one divine will and mind in Christ, how do we explain his human limitations, specifically his lack of knowledge (e.g., Mark 13:32)? Classically, the church has argued that in the incarnation the Son assumed a human nature consisting of a body *and* a soul and its corresponding capacities of a human will and mind. As a result of this action, the divine Son is now able to live a fully human life in and through the capacities of his human nature, while never completely limited or circumscribed by his human nature since he continues to possess the divine nature. Thus, when Jesus is presented as tired, weak, and not knowing something, classical thought has employed the reduplicative strategy via the *communicatio*. Christ's human weaknesses are true of *him* qua his human nature; the affirmation of his eternality (John 8:58) is true of *him* qua his divine nature. In this way, classical Christology employs the *communicatio*, *extra*, and *enhypostasia* to make sense of how Jesus, the incarnate Son, is fully God and fully man.

Craig and Moreland, however, cannot employ this strategy, given their redefinition of person and their rejection of two wills and minds in Christ. They must explain how, in the *single* mind of the divine Son, who is necessarily omniscient, he lacks knowledge and experiences temptation. What is their proposal? They postulate that in the "person" of Christ, or, to state it another way, in the one divine, omniscient mind of the Son, there are *two* levels of consciousness. By drawing on explanations from depth psychology, they suggest that "there is vastly more to a person than waking consciousness."[97] So in the case of Christ, the Son's divine mind now has levels of consciousness within it and, they suggest, "at least for the state of humiliation,"[98] the divine aspects of the Son's mind remain "largely subliminal."[99] Thus, "Jesus possessed a normal human conscious experience. But the human consciousness of Jesus was underlain, as it were, by a divine subconsciousness."[100] During Jesus's earthly existence, "the Logos allowed only those facets of his person to be part of Christ's waking consciousness which were compatible with typical human experience, while the bulk of his knowledge and other cognitive perfections, like an iceberg beneath the water's surface, lay submerged in his subconscious."[101] As applied to the will, they argue that the one divine will acts, but now under the limitations of a human body. The will of the Word is now the will of the human nature, exercised through a body, thus bringing about some kind of "human willing" experience, even though there is no distinct human will.

What is the perceived advantage of their view? Craig and Moreland insist

---

[97] Ibid.
[98] Ibid., 611.
[99] Ibid., 610.
[100] Ibid.
[101] Ibid., 611.

that it offers a more satisfying account of Jesus's knowledge and growth as a man. In his conscious experience, Jesus grows in knowledge and wisdom; in his conscious experience, Jesus is tempted, even though he is impeccable, given his one divine will, since in his conscious experience he does not know he is impeccable. "In his waking consciousness, Jesus is actually ignorant of certain facts, though kept from error and often supernaturally illumined by the divine subliminal. Even though the Logos possesses all knowledge about the world from quantum mechanics to auto mechanics, there is no reason to think that Jesus of Nazareth would have been able to answer questions about such subjects, so low had he stooped in condescending to take on the human condition."[102]

More examples could be given to illustrate OKC and FKC, but hopefully these representative proposals demonstrate the diversity and range of thought in current evangelical Christology.[103] No doubt, there are specific nuances between various views, but overall, in evangelical theology, there is a basic spectrum of three views—OKC, FKC, and established orthodoxy. In the next chapter, we turn to critical reflection and argue that these "newer" views are inadequate. The better option regarding a warranted Christology for today is established orthodoxy.

---

[102] Ibid., 612.

[103] In this regard, it is helpful to think briefly through Erickson's position in *The Word Became Flesh*. Erickson's view is more classical in orientation, yet it still falls under the category of a functional kenotic view, except that Erickson affirms dyothelitism and two minds in Christ (see 556–560). After Erickson describes some of the metaphysical grounding to the incarnation (507–530), he turns to discussion of the logic of it (531–576). After rejecting various heresies throughout church history (e.g., docetism, adoptionism, and the strong ontological forms of kenoticism), he suggests a FKC by which the incarnate Son chooses not to exercise his divine attributes. For example, the divine Son chose not, for a period of time, to exercise his omnipresence and omniscience. Erickson states, "It was not that he was pretending that he could not use [the omni-attributes]; he really could not" (549). Or, "what we are saying is that [the Son's] basic powers were not lost, but only the ability to exercise them" (550; cf. 551–576). At this point, Erickson distinguishes between the Son's active and latent attributes. In the incarnation, Erickson proposes, the Son's divine attributes became latent such that his knowledge "may have been limited in actual exercise by his consciousness; being related to a human personality and particularly to a human brain" (556). But given that Christ had two minds and wills, per classical Christology, we can affirm that the divine Son did not give up anything of what he was and had, but added to himself a human nature and "thus restricted somewhat the conditions under which his divine qualities could be exercised" (558). As the Father allowed, the Son had access to and use of his divine attributes, but for the most part, during his time on earth, the Son chose to act in and through his human nature. In regard to Christ's exalted state, Erickson maintains that the incarnate Son is less restricted than in his state of humiliation, yet there is still some kind of "permanent modification in the Second Person of the Trinity, but the limitations are greatly reduced" (576). It is best to categorize Erickson's Christology as a FKC, yet admit that he is more classical in his acceptance of dyothelitism. However, his explanations of Jesus's temptations, (non)-exercise of his divine attributes, etc., are more aligned with a FKC.

TWELVE

EVANGELICALS AND
KENOTIC CHRISTOLOGIES:
A "NEW" AND "BETTER" WAY?

In the last chapter, we described the spectrum of thought within current evangelical kenoticism.[1] What should we think about these "new" Christological views? Much could be said: we offer five critical reflections with the goal of showing that the "classical" view is still to be preferred. Similar to earlier kenoticism,[2] these "newer" views attempt to make "better" sense of Christ's identity, but at key points their formulation flounders in terms of biblical and ecclesiastical warrant,[3] and thus more problems result.

THE CHALCEDONIAN DEFINITION AND THE BURDEN OF PROOF

Even though ontological kenoticism (OKC) and functional kenoticism (FKC) claim formal adherence to Chalcedon, they depart from it at significant points, especially in OKC's redefinition of the divine nature and in both of their redefinitions of "person," their equation of "person" with "soul," and their endorsement of monothelitism.[4] Even though some try to downplay these differences,[5] one must legitimately ask, how far can we redefine our terms in

---

[1] Hereinafter when the phrase "evangelical kenoticism" is used, I intend it to refer to evangelicals who espouse some form of kenotic Christology. I do not intend to affirm that such views are in fact consistent with evangelical theology.

[2] See our discussion in chapter 10.

[3] See our discussion in Parts II and III.

[4] As noted in chapter 11, the Chalcedonian Definition assumes a different concept of person than is used today. Chalcedon distinguished person from soul, and later Councils affirmed dyothelitism, thus locating the capacities of will and mind in the nature. Today, however, person is redefined to include the capacities of will and mind, identified with soul, and monothelitism is embraced.

[5] See Ronald J. Feenstra, "A Kenotic Christology of Divine Attributes," in *Exploring Kenotic Christology: The Self-Emptying of God* (Oxford: Oxford University Press, 2006), 156. C. Stephen Evans, "Kenotic Christology and the Nature of God," in *Exploring Kenotic Christology*, 195n13, admits that OKC's redefinition of the divine nature is novel. He insists his view is still Chalcedonian, however, because it fits within Chalcedon's broad boundaries.

ways that conflict with the Chalcedonian Definition before the Definition takes on a different meaning? Our point is *not* that confessions are equal to Scripture and can never be improved upon. Confessions are secondary standards and thus open to correction and, no doubt, adherents to either form of evangelical kenoticism insist that such rethinking is necessary. Nevertheless, given the consensus of established orthodoxy, one must exercise extreme care in such rethinking. One must demonstrate that classical Christology, properly understood, is first, unbiblical, and second, theologically inadequate, before it is so easily dismissed. Oliver Crisp captures this point well: "It seems to me that someone dissenting from the findings of an ecumenical council of the Church should have a very good reason—indeed, a very good *theological* reason—for doing so."[6] Once again, this is *not* to say that Christological reflection should cease; it is to say, especially for these "new" views, that they must demonstrate that they are more biblically and theologically faithful than the classical view, something not yet done.[7]

PROBLEMS WITH OKC'S THEOLOGICAL METHOD

One of the critical problems for ontological kenotic Christology is its redefinition of the divine nature. Before we turn to the reasons for this assessment, let us first reflect on OKC's theological method for determining the "essential-accidental" distinction in God. What warrant do they give?

Following a recent trend in theological method, Ronald Feenstra suggests that we start with the incarnation as our control for theology proper.[8] He rejects "Anselmian theology," which starts with a maximal view of God's greatness and then moves to Christological reflection. Instead, he suggests that we

---

But even John Hick, *The Metaphor of God Incarnate: Christology for a Pluralistic Age*, 2nd ed. (Louisville: Westminster John Knox, 1993), 73, criticizes OKC for rejecting "much of the traditional Christian understanding of God." Cf. Richard Swinburne, *The Christian God* (Oxford: Clarendon; New York: Oxford University Press, 1994), 232–233.

[6] Oliver D. Crisp, *Divinity and Humanity* (Cambridge: Cambridge University Press, 2007), 35 (emphasis his). In a similar cautionary note, William Hasker, *Metaphysics and the Tri-Personal God* (Oxford: Oxford University Press, 2013), 10, in application to Trinitarian theology warns, "[I]f we are not willing to be trinitarian skeptics, I submit that we will do well to take seriously the consensus of the universal Church, rather than going off in a fundamentally different direction on our own." Cf. Brian Leftow, "Anti Social Trinitarianism," in *Philosophical and Theological Essays on the Trinity*, ed. Thomas McCall and Michael C. Rea (Oxford: Oxford University Press, 2009), 97, who makes the same point.

[7] Jordan Wessling, "Christology and Conciliar Authority: On the Viability of Monothelitism for Protestant Theology," in *Christology: Ancient and Modern Explorations in Constructive Dogmatics*, ed. Oliver D. Crisp and Fred Sanders (Grand Rapids, MI: Zondervan, 2013), 151–170, questions Crisp's appeal to conciliar authority in regard to dyothelitism. Wessling argues that unless we can demonstrate that the Council makes decisions on issues that directly undermine the gospel, mere appeal to the Council's rejection of monothelitism is not sufficient to reject the view as heretical. This may be true, but the burden of proof is on monothelites to warrant their departure from the Councils, since they were viewed as the consistent development of Chalcedon. Critics must show that: (1) dyothelitism is unbiblical or, minimally, not required; (2) it is theologically incoherent and thus inadequate; and (3) monothelitism does not undercut other central theological truths, e.g., Trinitarian theology and Jesus's humanity. Our contention is that monothelitism fails in these areas.

[8] See Feenstra, "Kenotic Christology of Divine Attributes," 158–164. For a discussion of the theological method employed by kenoticism, see Kevin J. Vanhoozer, *Remythologizing Theology: Divine Action, Passion, and Authorship* (Cambridge: Cambridge University Press, 2010), 139–177.

reverse the direction.[9] Feenstra writes, "If Christians use Anselmian methods to articulate their concept of God, they must use these methods only insofar as they reflect what Scripture says about God. And if there is any conflict between the deliverances of Scripture and the deliverances of the Anselmian method, Christian theologians should favour what Scripture says."[10] For example, given that Jesus is described as growing in knowledge, ignorant of certain events, and limited in power, Feenstra proposes that our understanding of omniscience, omnipotence, and all of the divine attributes must be defined in light of Christ. On this basis, OKC argues that omniscience, omnipotence, and omnipresence are *not essential* to deity: these attributes only apply to God *simpliciter*, i.e., plainly and without qualification, apart from the incarnation.

But is this method correct? Feenstra is correct that we must theologize about the divine nature from Scripture, but is it correct to move from the incarnation to theology proper? To what extent does the incarnation dictate our understanding of God's nature? As plausible as it may sound, this approach is problematic and reductionistic. Kevin Vanhoozer registers this concern when he reminds us that, "While a Christological concentration is entirely appropriate in light of the canonical witness (Lk. 24:27), however, a Christological *reduction* is not."[11] Why not? Vanhoozer gives two important reasons.

First, "Jesus Christ reveals God neither *de novo* nor *ex nihilo*. On the contrary, the identity of Jesus is inextricably tied up with the identity of God already established by his covenant with Israel."[12] In other words, God's self-revelation does not start in the New Testament; it begins with creation, shows itself in providence, redemption, and judgment, and ultimately finds its fulfillment in Christ. As one moves from creation to Christ, the triune God discloses more about himself, and even though God's plan reaches its fulfillment in the incarnate Son, God's fundamental nature does not change. What God *is* prior to the incarnation is in direct continuity with what he is after the incarnation. In fact, we know what God's nature *is*, and thus what it means for the Son to be fully God, only in light of God's self-description in the Old Testament. It is too reductionistic to begin with Christ and work backwards. *All* Scripture is our norm, starting in creation, and it is the *entire* canon that defines God's nature.

Second, one cannot consistently apply this Christological reduction, since Jesus is both God *and* man, the Son who subsists in *two* natures. This demands that we must distinguish actions and characteristics that are divine *and* those

---

[9] Sometimes the Anselmian method is identified with natural theology, or what today is labeled onto-theology. In light of the influence of various trends in theology, not least postmodern epistemology, severe criticism has been leveled against this approach, often inaccurately, dismissing it as hopelessly influenced by modernism and contrary to Scripture. For a helpful evaluation of this debate, see Vanhoozer, *Remythologizing Theology*, 81–138.
[10] Feenstra, "Kenotic Christology of Divine Attributes," 162.
[11] Vanhoozer, *Remythologizing Theology*, 418.
[12] Ibid.

that are human. As Vanhoozer observes, "If Jesus' history completely reveals—or, what is more, constitutes—God's very being then it becomes difficult to identify which properties are human and which divine. Does the incarnate life of Jesus reveal that God is a sleeper (because Jesus sleeps)? Yes, Jesus reveals God in bodily form (Col. 1:19), but does it follow that everything Jesus does in the body is equally revelatory of God?"[13] Instead, one has to consider what is human, what is divine, how the person of the Son acts in and through both natures, and how the attributes of both natures are predicated of the person (*communicatio*). But in predicating human attributes to the person, we must preserve the fact that the one person is also deity—the nature of which we discover from *all* of Scripture.

Oliver Crisp adds a third reason for rejecting OKC's theological method. After correcting the story that classical theology did not work from a preformed view of God to the incarnation, Crisp insists that OKC's proposal is *not* a "better" explanation than the church has given. OKC's appeal is that it is more coherent than orthodoxy and that it upholds Christ's humanity better. But to make their case, OKC has to redefine their terms and reinterpret Scripture in novel ways. Is this really necessary? Instead, as the church has done, we start from the entire canon, we take seriously that the Son *added* a human nature, and then we conclude, contrary to OKC, that Christ retained his omniscience in his divine nature but his human nature was not omniscient.[14] Why is this option not better? It makes more sense of Scripture, it requires no redefinition of God's nature, and it is consistent with the consensus of the church. There is simply no reason to reinvent theological method as OKC attempts to do.

Problems with Redefining the Metaphysics of the Incarnation

Problems with the Divine Nature

In regard to the redefinition of the divine "nature," the main problem is with ontological kenotic Christology over against classical Christology and functional kenotic Christology, and its difficulty in sustaining the deity of Christ.[15] There are at least two reasons to reject its proposal.

First, OKC's view is not really an improvement on earlier kenotic views, in that it lacks serious *biblical* warrant. What David Wells says about earlier

---

[13] Ibid., 419.

[14] Crisp, *Divinity and Humanity*, 131, rightly asks, "Why not, with the host of classical theologians who thought about this matter with care and rigour, think that the Word retains his omniscience but that the human nature of Christ is not omniscient? Why not say that, in the hypostatic union, the Word interpenetrates the human nature of Christ, but the converse is not the case, such that the human nature of Christ simply does not have certain properties or predicates that the divine nature of Christ does? This seems to me to be entirely in keeping with the tradition without conceding that the Incarnation involves the Word relinquishing certain divine properties."

[15] Both Stephen T. Davis, "Is Kenosis Orthodox?," in *Exploring Kenotic Christology*, 135–136, and Feenstra, "Kenotic Christology of Divine Attributes," 154, acknowledge this problem. Interestingly, OKC's redefinition of the divine nature is more congenial to panentheism (cf. Evans, "Kenotic Christology and the Nature of God," 202–205; Vanhoozer, *Remythologizing Theology*, 105–177).

forms of kenoticism rightly applies to this one: "The only God of whom Scripture speaks is one who is all-powerful, knows everything, and is everywhere. By definition, a god who has diminished power and knowledge is not the biblical God."[16] Scripture simply does not allow a minimal conception of God's attributes; a God who lacks certain divine attributes is simply not God. OKC offers a logical way of speaking of Christ's deity, but *not* one with biblical and ecclesiastical warrant.[17]

Second, OKC's view is arbitrary and inconsistent. As Craig and Moreland rightly assert, to say that God has "essential properties like being-omniscient-except-when-kenotically-incarnate, which he never surrenders and which are sufficient for deity" is not only "explanatorily vacuous," but, ontologically speaking, "it is not clear that there even are such properties as being-omniscient-except-when-kenotically-incarnate."[18] Furthermore, as Crisp points out, such a view is arbitrary. He writes, "It is very difficult indeed to know where to draw the line demarcating contingent and essential properties. For if omniscience turns out to be a contingent rather than an essential divine property, then what are we to make of omnipotence, omnipresence, eternity or benevolence, to name four other divine attributes traditionally thought to be essential to the divine nature?"[19] Ultimately, the entire procedure looks ad hoc. In addition, why only stop at certain divine attributes? Why not, as Craig and Moreland suggest, consider the divine attributes of necessity, aseity, and eternality?[20] After all, how can we make sense of Christ's death unless he relinquishes these attributes? The very fact that OKC does not do so demonstrates something of its arbitrariness. Even more problematic is how this view can affirm that the incarnate Son is *homoousios* with the Father and the Spirit, if the Father and the Spirit retain *all* of the divine attributes while the Son does not, even temporarily. For the state of humiliation, not only is the Son *not* of the same substance as the Father and Spirit, but also the divine persons do not possess the divine nature equally, which smacks of a quasi-Arianism.[21]

Problems with Person

What about both views' understanding of "person"? Even though FKC disagrees with OKC regarding the divine nature, in agreement with OKC over

---

[16] David F. Wells, *The Person of Christ* (Westchester, IL: Crossway, 1984), 138.

[17] Crisp, *Divinity and Humanity*, 126, makes this same point. For a better discussion of God's nature and attributes, see John S. Feinberg, *No One Like Him: The Doctrine of God* (Wheaton, IL: Crossway, 2001), 233–374.

[18] J. P. Moreland and William Lane Craig, *Philosophical Foundations for a Christian Worldview* (Downers Grove, IL: InterVarsity Press, 2003), 607. Even Thomas Senor, who affirms an OKC, admits that its redefinition of the divine nature has an "air of artificiality about it" and, in the end, "it appears to be ad hoc" (Thomas Senor, "Drawing on Many Traditions: An Ecumenical Kenotic Christology," in *The Metaphysics of the Incarnation*, ed. Anna Marmodoro and Jonathan Hill [Oxford: Oxford University Press, 2011], 105).

[19] Crisp, *Divinity and Humanity*, 132.

[20] See Moreland and Craig, *Philosophical Foundations*, 608.

[21] See Crisp, *Divinity and Humanity*, 127n18.

against classical thought it redefines "person" in more contemporary terms: a distinct center of knowledge, will, and action, thus placing the capacities of will and mind in the person rather than in the nature.[22] The classical view, however, following Boethius's definition—"A person is an individual substance of a rational nature"[23]—does *not* place the capacities of will and mind in the person but in the nature. It views the "person" as an agent, or an "I" who subsists in a "rational nature." This is why the classical view insists that the divine Son, in assuming a concrete human nature, became human by adding to himself a human body *and* soul (including a human will and mind), and as a result, is now able to live a fully human life in and through the capacities of his human nature. In addition, the classical view also affirmed that the incarnate Son is *not* limited to living his life merely through his human nature because, as the Son, *he* continues to possess the divine nature in relation to the Father and Spirit, and is thus able to continue to live a divine life (thus the *extra*).

Why do both kenotic views reject the traditional view of person? A number of reasons are cited, but the most significant is that the classical view leads to Nestorianism. By placing will and mind in the nature, they insist that this seems to entail that Christ has two persons, one divine and one human.[24] Is this charge correct? How do we resolve the differences between a classical view of *person* and the current one? Let us focus on three points.

First, in the literature there is often confusion regarding the classical view. Almost uniformly the charge is that it is Nestorian, but the church consistently rejected Nestorianism by holding to a classical view of person, whether at Chalcedon or at Constantinople III.[25] A better explanation for the charge is either a misunderstanding of the classical view or the assumption that the only viable definition of *person* is the current one, which is then read back on the earlier discussion.

Evidence for this latter explanation is not hard to find. For example, in the discussion of "person-nature" there is a lot of confusion. Evans seems to think that the classical view teaches that the divine nature becomes incarnate *instead of the divine person.* He states curiously, "We must ask the question

---

[22] See Cornelius Plantinga Jr., "Social Trinity and Tritheism," in *Trinity, Incarnation, and Atonement: Philosophical and Theological Essays*, ed. Ronald J. Feenstra and Cornelius Plantinga Jr. (Notre Dame, IN: University of Notre Dame Press, 1989), 22; cf. Hasker, *Metaphysics and the Tri-Personal God*, 19–25.

[23] Cited in Gilles Emery, "The Dignity of Being a Substance: Person, Subsistence, and Nature," *Nova et Vetera* 9/4 (2011): 994; cf. Richard A. Muller, *Dictionary of Latin and Greek Theological Terms* (Grand Rapids, MI: Baker, 1985), 223–227. As Emery and Muller discuss, when Boethius speaks of "an individual substance," he does not mean an individual as a "substance" separate from the *substantia* of the other divine persons (in the case of the Trinity), or, in the case of Christ, that he is only one substance. Instead, "individual substance" is best understood as individual *subsistence*, or the incommunicable subsistence of a rational nature, so that the *person* (Latin: *persona*; Greek: *hypostasis*) is an agent, an "I" who subsists in a nature and acts in and through the nature (ibid.).

[24] This argument is common. For example, Moreland and Craig argue that "it is extraordinarily difficult to preserve the unity of Christ's person once platonism and two distinct wills are ascribed to the Logos and to the individual human nature of Christ" (*Philosophical Foundations*, 611); cf. Evans, "Kenotic Christology and the Nature of God," 199.

[25] See Crisp, *Divinity and Humanity*, 64–65.

what it means for the divine nature to become incarnate, to become enfleshed and live a bodily life."[26] Or, elsewhere Evans speaks of the person of the Son *becoming a human person*, which is not the classical view.[27] Possibly, Evans is confused on this point since he, along with most OKC and FKC advocates, equates "person" with "soul," things that Chalcedon distinguished.[28] In fact, it is due to this equation that the current view of person locates the capacities of will and mind in the person *and* requires some form of social Trinitarianism (although there are different varieties), since all of the divine persons are viewed as "distinct substances or beings,"[29] each person with his own distinct will and mind.

Today, it is on the subject of the *will* and *mind* that the current view of person differs most significantly from the classical. It is not accidental that current views are monothelite while the classical view is dyothelite. Why? William Hasker helps answer this question by speaking of "will" in terms of three distinct applications: "it can refer to the *content* of one's will (the state of affairs that is willed), or to the *act* of willing, or to the *faculty or capacity* of willing."[30] In Trinitarian application, if "will" is used in terms of *content*, then all three persons will the same thing and hence have "one" will. But if we locate "will" in the person in terms of "acts of will and faculties of willing,"[31] then each divine person has a distinct will (thus three wills in the Godhead), and correspondingly, in Christology, Christ has only one will (monothelitism).

Hasker's discussion of the current view of person is helpful, yet, unfortunately, he does not explain well the classical view. Hasker perceptively distinguishes between (1) the *content* of one's will, (2) the *act* of willing, and (3) the *faculty* or *capacity* of willing, but he conflates (2) and (3) and locates both of these in "person." But the classical view distinguished (2) and (3) in relation to the "person." A "person," classically, is an agent or "I" (an individual subsistence) who *acts* in and through his "rational nature" (body and soul), so that (2) is identified with the "person" and (3) with the "nature." Thus, in pro-Nicene Trinitarianism, the Father, Son, and Spirit, because they are distinct persons, *act* as persons according to their mode of subsistence, or according to their eternal, immanent relations. The Father, then, *acts* as

---

[26] Evans, "Kenotic Christology and the Nature of God," 197.
[27] See ibid., 213. Evans writes, "A decision on the part of the Son of God *to become a human person* by assuming human nature and living in a bodily form . . ." (ibid., emphasis mine).
[28] See C. Stephen Evans, "The Self-Emptying of Love: Some Thoughts on Kenotic Christology," in *The Incarnation: An Interdisciplinary Symposium on the Incarnation of the Son of God*, ed. Stephen T. Davis, Daniel Kendall, and Gerald O'Collins (Oxford: Oxford University Press, 2002), 271; see also Garrett J. DeWeese, "One Person, Two Natures: Two Metaphysical Models of the Incarnation," in *Jesus in Trinitarian Perspective*, ed. Fred Sanders and Klaus Issler (Nashville: B&H Academic, 2007), 117, 140; Moreland and Craig, *Philosophical Foundations*, 608.
[29] Stephen T. Davis, "The Metaphysics of Kenosis," in *Metaphysics of the Incarnation*, 122.
[30] Hasker, *Metaphysics and the Tri-Personal God*, 206 (emphasis his).
[31] Ibid., 207.

the Father, the Son *acts* as the Son, and the Spirit *acts* as the Spirit. However, contrary to the current view, the classical view of person places the *faculty* or *capacity* of will in the nature,[32] thus entailing two wills in Christ, one for each nature.

This is also why pro-Nicene theology insisted that the divine persons act inseparably, i.e., the Father, Son, and Spirit *act* according to their eternal relations (mode of subsistence) but "in virtue of their common nature, and consequently the effects of the divine action always have for their source the entire Trinity."[33] Thus, the Father, Son, and Spirit all *act*, yet they *act* in and through the capacities of the one single divine nature that they equally possess and share. Because the nature is where the *capacity of willing* is located, we can say that the three persons *act* as distinct persons according to their eternal-immanent relations, in and through the *capacities* of the divine nature, which includes the same will. As this understanding is applied to Christology, the classical view affirms that the *one* person, the divine Son, given that he has two natures, also has two wills in terms of (3) and *not* (2). In Christ, then, the divine Son is the acting agent who acts in and through his natures, and now, as a result of the incarnation, is able to act *as a man according to his distinct human will*. This is why the divine Son can now live and experience a fully human life, even though he is not entirely circumscribed or limited by his human nature because he continues to subsist in the divine nature. If these distinctions, however, are not acknowledged, it is no surprise that there is confusion regarding the classical view, and why current views (which place (2) and (3) in "person") constantly raise the Nestorian charge.

Second, it is important to stress that the differences between the classical and current views of person are *not* minor. In fact, these differences serve as one of the main reasons for current revisions of classical Christology. If one adopts the current view, it should not surprise us that the classical view is no longer seen as credible *and* that various "adjustments" are required. Why? Because given that in Christ there is only one divine person (which includes in that person *one divine will and mind*), then how can we make sense of a Jesus who is truly human and exhibits limitations of knowledge if that one divine person is omniscient in the full sense of the word? This is why OKC proposes that, in order to make sense of the incarnation, the divine Son must be able to "give up" certain divine attributes such as omniscience, because it is inconsistent with being a human.[34] Or, from the FKC side, the rationale for kenosis is largely due to trying to make sense of how the Son's *one* divine mind

---

[32] See Gilles Emery, *The Trinitarian Theology of St. Thomas Aquinas* (Oxford: Oxford University Press, 2007), 51–127, 338–412; cf. Jean Galot, *Who Is Christ?* (Chicago: Franciscan Herald, 1981), 279–313.
[33] Gilles Emery, *Trinity, Church, and the Human Person* (Naples, FL: Sapientia, 2007), 128–129.
[34] See Davis, "Metaphysics of Kenosis," 129.

can lack knowledge, given that the capacities of will and mind are located in the person.[35]

On these points, it is crucial to note that classical Christology does *not* wrestle with these issues in exactly the same way as evangelical kenoticism does. Why? Simply put, because of their differing conceptions of "person." For example, the classical view allows for the metaphysical possibility of there being two wills and minds in Christ because the *capacities* of will and mind are located in the nature and not in the person. The divine Son, then, who is the agent of his natures, *acts* in and through both natures. This entails that the person of the Son, due to the incarnation, is able to live a fully divine life (as he has always done) and now a fully human life (because he assumes a concrete human nature, i.e., a body and a soul). This also allows for the employment of a proper sense of *communicatio idiomatum* along with the reduplication strategy so that what is true of the natures is predicated of the person. Thus, what is true of the divine nature (e.g., omniscience, omnipotence, omnipresence) may be predicated of the Son and likewise in relation to what is true of the human nature (e.g., growing in wisdom and knowledge, experiencing weakness, being tired). Yet, as the *extra* affirms, because the Son subsists in two natures, he is *not* limited or completely circumscribed by his human nature. The incarnate Son, in relation to the Father and the Spirit, consistent with his mode of subsistence from eternity, continues to act *as the Son* and now as the incarnate Son. But, once again, it is crucial to note that this classical understanding is *not* available to the kenotic viewpoints, given their redefinition of person.

Third, where does this leave us? Obviously the classical and current views of "person" are different. How, then, do we decide which view is correct? For the sake of argument, we will assume that both views are rationally coherent, so ultimately, we must decide in regard to their biblical-theological fit, namely, which view best accounts for *all* the data regarding Christ? In our final two reflections, we will question whether the "new" kenotic paths really meet this standard over against the "old" path of classical Christology.

Problems with Trinitarian Relations and Agency

Both views of evangelical kenoticism affirm some form of social Trinitarianism, given their understanding of person, yet not all social Trinitarians are equal, despite their family resemblances.[36] Given the major difference between

---

[35] Hence Craig and Moreland's proposal of two levels of consciousness within the *one* divine mind and the subliminal nature of the Son's divine knowledge (see Moreland and Craig, *Philosophical Foundations*, 610–612).

[36] On this point, see Hasker, *Metaphysics and the Tri-Personal God*, 81–163; Thomas H. McCall, *Which Trinity? Whose Monotheism? Philosophical and Systematic Theologians on the Metaphysics of Trinitarian Theology* (Grand Rapids, MI: Eerdmans, 2010).

OKC and FKC on the divine nature, we will address some of the Trinitarian implications of each view separately.

Some Trinitarian Implications of OKC

Even though there are numerous implications of OKC for Trinitarian-Christological theology, we will focus on three. First, as noted above, given OKC's redefinition of the divine nature, the divine persons are radically reconfigured in terms of their sharing of the divine attributes, especially in light of the incarnation. Not only does this create insurmountable problems for affirming that Christ is *homoousios* with the other divine persons (which makes it difficult to affirm Christ's deity), it also results in a triune God who for a period of time looks more binitarian than Trinitarian—implications which are not acceptable.[37]

Second, OKC has great difficulty maintaining the continuity between the preexistent Son (*Logos asarkos*) and the incarnate Son (*Logos ensarkos*), thus implying huge disruptions in the internal relations of the triune persons. For example, in the incarnation, as the Son "gives up" his omniscience, even if only temporarily, his divine self-consciousness would be almost completely expunged. As Donald Macleod noted in regard to earlier kenotic views, the result would be "a degree of amnesia to which there can be no parallel."[38] On this issue, as difficult as it is for us to explain the psychology of the incarnate Son, the "older" path is better. Unlike OKC, classical Christology thinks of the divine Son as subsisting in two natures, which allows for the metaphysical possibility of two ranges of consciousness in Christ, given that mind and will are capacities of natures. Even though we are left with plenty of unknowns, this explanation makes better sense of the biblical data, which speaks of Christ's legitimate human growth without expunging the Son's divine self-consciousness, which was his from eternity. OKC simply cannot do justice to this full range of biblical data.

Third, OKC has difficulty accounting for the biblical teaching regarding the cosmic functions of Christ. Scripture attributes various cosmic functions to the *incarnate* Son (Col. 1:17; Heb. 1:3). Additionally, Scripture does not teach that the Son's sustaining of the universe ceased for a period of time. In fact, Scripture speaks of all three persons—Father, Son, and Spirit—acting together in every *ad extra* work, including that of providence (John 1:1–3; cf. Gen. 1:1–3; Col. 1:15–20; Heb. 1:1–3). OKC, contrary to Scripture, proposes that

---

[37] In the incarnation, if the Son "sets aside," i.e., no longer has, certain divine attributes, even temporarily, there is a period of time when Jesus does not equally share the same divine nature and attributes as the Father and the Spirit. If this is so, then it is difficult to see how the Son is *homoousios* with the Father and the Spirit. For a further discussion of these points, see Crisp, *Divinity and Humanity*, 127–131.

[38] Donald Macleod, *The Person of Christ* (Downers Grove, IL: InterVarsity Press, 1998), 210.

the incarnate Son temporarily "set aside" those divine attributes necessary to carry out his cosmic activity, but in that case how do we explain these biblical texts? Evans, in a fairly typical way, suggests that normally all three persons are involved in these cosmic actions, but given the incarnation, the Father and Spirit carry out the work *without* the agency of the Son. He writes, "In some way the activity of each person of the Trinity must involve the activity of each of the others. I see no reason why, if the second person of the Trinity became incarnate and divested himself of omnipotence and omniscience, what we might call the sustaining work of this person in creation could not be carried on by the other persons."[39] Would this then lead to the incarnate Son being dependent on the Father and the Spirit in ways that he was not before? Evans tackles this question by admitting that there are asymmetries in the relations of the persons, so it is not a problem to think of this occurring.[40]

The problem with this explanation, however, is twofold. First, Scripture does not teach it. Cosmic functions are directly attributed to the activity of the incarnate Son. Second, it makes the Trinitarian personal relations divided and lopsided. Not only do the divine persons not act together, which is a denial of pro-Nicene theology and tantamount to undermining Trinitarian monotheism; there is also an asymmetry among the persons that speaks of a fundamental inequality. On this understanding, not only is it difficult to make sense of how all three persons are *homoousios*, but nowhere does Scripture distinguish the divine persons in terms of their possession/non-possession or use/non-use of the divine attributes. Instead, Scripture teaches that the divine persons equally possess the divine nature and act together in every divine action according to the persons' eternal relations. OKC, in the end, undercuts the biblical presentation of Trinitarian agency, and its "new" path is far too costly in regard to biblical-theological fidelity.

Some Trinitarian Implications of FKC

In terms of the Trinity, the approach of a functional kenotic Christology is much better than an ontological kenotic Christology. In the incarnation, the Son does not set aside certain divine attributes; instead, the self-limitation of the Son is *functional*, as he chooses not to exercise his divine attributes. In his humanity, the Son relies on the power of the Spirit to live, act, and obey the

---

[39] Evans, "The Self-Emptying of Love," 259. Evans also suggests that it is not impossible to think that "*one* person of the Trinity could not freely empty himself of such properties, secure in the knowledge that the Father and Spirit will continue providentially to guide creation, and perhaps even secure in the knowledge that he will someday be rewarded by them with the restoration of all the divine prerogatives" (idem, "Kenotic Christology and the Nature of God," 213–214). Stephen Davis agrees and suggests that the Son "planned ahead, made arrangements, settled matters ahead of time" (Stephen T. Davis, "Jesus Christ: Savior or Guru?" in John B. Cobb et al., *Encountering Jesus: A Debate on Christology*, ed. Stephen T. Davis [Atlanta: John Knox, 1988], 54).
[40] See Evans, "Self-Emptying of Love," 259n28.

Father's will for our salvation. Even though this view has a lot of strengths, however, there are at least two problems in Trinitarian terms.

First, FKC has difficulty accounting for how Scripture presents the deity of Christ in his life and ministry. As argued in Part II, Jesus's inauguration of the kingdom, his teaching, and his miracles are not merely Spirit-empowered acts; they are ultimately acts identified with Yahweh. The Jesus of the Bible knows he is the eternal Son; he forgives sin and exercises divine power; he has divine authority and receives worship. How can this identification with Yahweh be made? Because the very works of the incarnate Son testify to who he is (e.g., John 5:16–30). No doubt, all of these actions are done by one who is a man, yet one cannot simply explain Jesus in merely human terms, or even in terms that place him in the category of Spirit-empowered men of the past. His identity is thoroughly divine, and in everything he says and does he demonstrates that he is God the Son incarnate. Scripture teaches this truth most clearly in those texts that attribute cosmic functions to the *incarnate* Son, not merely the Son prior to his incarnation or merely as glorified (Col. 1:17; Heb. 1:3). The only way we can make sense of these texts is to acknowledge that, in his state of humiliation, the Son *continues to exercise* his divine attributes *as the Son* in relation to and united with the Father and the Spirit.

It is at this precise point, however, that the view of FKC stumbles. On one end of the spectrum, some FKC views claim that the Son *never* exercises his divine attributes while on earth, and on the other end, some claim that the Son *sometimes* does, yet *predominantly* the Son's unique actions are done by the power of the Spirit at work in him. But, contra classical Christology, no FKC advocate claims that the Son *continually* exercises his divine attributes—something that is necessary if the ongoing work of providence is to continue. Given FKC's redefinition of person, which entails a denial of two wills and minds in Christ, it is difficult to maintain the classical view of the *extra*. Classically, the *extra* affirmed that the Son, in assuming a human nature, is not limited to it. As a result, the incarnate Son, in relation to the Father and Spirit, continues to carry out cosmic functions; furthermore, these divine actions are not viewed as a violation of Christ's humanity, because his divine attributes remain attributes of the divine nature alone and they are not shared with his human nature. The Son, then, as the acting agent, is able to act in and through both natures even while on earth, including upholding the universe qua his divine nature.

How, then, do proponents of FKC explain these cosmic functions attributed to the Son? Similar to OKC, Issler suggests that the Son in a preincarnate decision "temporarily delegated to the other members of the Trinity his usual divine duties, such as sustaining the universe (Col 1:17; Heb 1:3)."[41] But this

---

[41] Klaus Issler, *Living into the Life of Jesus* (Downers Grove, IL: InterVarsity Press, 2012), 125n31.

explanation runs into the same problems as discussed above, namely, Scripture does not explicitly teach it, it potentially surrenders the unity of Trinitarian agency, and it results in a change in the content of the personal deity of the Son. As Gerald Bray rightly asks, if the Son's "divine nature is somehow quiescent, what content does his personal divinity have? He could be truly divine only as long as he retained the ability to express himself in and through his divine nature?"[42] In other words, FKC so changes the life of the divine Son that the self-identity of the Son, along with Trinitarian relations, is redefined.

The second Trinitarian problem FKC introduces is that it overemphasizes the Son-Spirit relationship and is not sufficiently Trinitarian in thinking through the Father-Son-Spirit relations. Due to the influence of Hawthorne, many FKC advocates believe that the role of the Spirit in the life of Christ is the key to making sense of the incarnation. Their proposal is that the incarnate Son either *never* (e.g., Hawthorne) or *rarely* (e.g., DeWeese, Issler, Ware) exercises his divine attributes. Instead, the divine Son lives his life *solely* or *predominantly* in a human body, with all of its corresponding limitations, *and* as one who is indwelt by, empowered by, and dependent upon the Spirit. In regard to the supernatural activity of Christ, FKC argues that *all* or *most* of Christ's unique actions were done by the Spirit. For example, Ware makes this point by asking, why did Jesus need the Spirit of God to indwell and empower his life? After all, he was fully God, so what could the Spirit add to his deity? Nothing. But if we ask what the Spirit could contribute to his *humanity*, the answer is, "everything of supernatural power and enablement that he, in his human nature, would lack."[43] Or, referring to Matthew 12:28, Ware says, "Jesus does not claim to have performed this miracle by his divine power and authority as God. Rather, he attributes the power used in this miraculous exorcism and healing to the Spirit at work in and through him."[44] There are, however, at least two problems with this view in regard to Trinitarian relations and agency.

The first problem centers on the agency of the Son. In regard to his supernatural actions, it is as if the Son disappears and the acting agent is the Spirit. Think, for example, of Jesus's raising the dead or walking on the water or feeding the five thousand; FKC claims that *all* of these actions were done, *not* by the agency of the Son but by the Spirit. Given that the Son *never* or *rarely* exercises his divine attributes, these actions are not the Son's actions *as a man* (unless we affirm that humans can exercise omnipotence), but actions done by the Spirit. Similar to the Spirit's agency in other Spirit-empowered people,

---

[42] Gerald Bray, *God Is Love: A Biblical and Systematic Theology* (Wheaton, IL: Crossway, 2012), 202.

[43] Bruce A. Ware, *The Man Christ Jesus: Theological Reflections on the Humanity of Christ* (Wheaton, IL: Crossway, 2013), 34. Although Ware does not embrace every point of a FKC, he is referenced here to illustrate how many advocates of a FKC think of the Spirit-Son relationship in regard to the agency of the incarnate Son. Cf. also Myk Habets, *The Anointed Son: A Trinitarian Spirit Christology* (Eugene, OR: Pickwick, 2010), 118–187.

[44] Ware, *Man Christ Jesus*, 36.

though admittedly greater, it is *not* the human who does the work (nor, in the case of Christ, the divine Son), but the Spirit who works through humans as instruments to accomplish his mighty power. If this is the case, however, then what has happened to the agency of the Son in all of his actions? Does the Son merely become *passive* in the doing of his own actions? Not only is the Spirit viewed as strangely "external" to the Son, which from a Trinitarian perspective is not so, but the divine Son as the *person* of the incarnation is also removed from the activity of his human nature, which renders problems for our understanding of the hypostatic union.[45] Oliver Crisp points this out when he argues that such a view seems to assume that *God the Son*, as the person and acting agent of the natures, never acts directly "in" and "through" his human nature. Such action after the assumption of his human nature is only ever mediate, through the work of the Holy Spirit.[46] But surely, as Crisp insists, "[I]f the human nature of Christ is 'owned' by God the Son, it seems very strange that he is not the divine person *immediately* acting upon, or through, his human nature."[47] In fact, given the intimate relation between the Son and his assumed human nature, we must not remove the divine Son from his own human nature and replace it with the "external" action of the Spirit upon him.[48] Is there a better way of explaining this?

There is indeed a better way, and it leads to stating the second problem: the FKC model fails to be sufficiently Trinitarian. It rightly emphasizes the Son-Spirit relationship, which is obviously part of the biblical data; however, it does not satisfactorily think through the Father-Son-Spirit relations as a whole. After all, it is not enough to focus simply on the Son-Spirit relations; we must also account for John's Gospel, for example, which stresses predominantly the Father-Son relations.[49] In other words, it is not enough to appeal to the Spirit's work without wrestling with how all three persons relate to one another. What is needed is a more robust appeal to Trinitarian agency that includes within it a classical understanding of the person-nature distinction and inseparable operations;[50] when this is done, we are convinced we can make better sense of all the biblical data. Think, for example, of John 5:19–30. Here we are told

---

[45] Remember a crucial rule of Christology: *persons* are acting agents, not natures. See Geerhardus Vos, *Christology*, vol. 3 of *Reformed Dogmatics*, trans. and ed. Richard B. Gaffin Jr. (Bellingham, WA: Lexham, 2014), 50, 64.

[46] See Oliver D. Crisp, *Revisioning Christology: Theology in the Reformed Tradition* (Farnham; Burlington, VT: Ashgate, 2011), 100–102.

[47] Ibid., 102.

[48] For a further development of this point, see Crisp, *Revisioning Christology*, 103–107. Crisp argues that the intentional acts of Christ originate in the person. Given that the Son acts through *his* nature "then there appears to be no metaphysical room for the interposition of another divine person between the intentions of God the Son (i.e., his agency) and the intentional actions brought about in his human nature. In short, for the actions of Jesus of Nazareth really to be the actions of God the Son Incarnate, they must be actions that originate with God the Son" (ibid., 105).

[49] See the excellent treatment of Trinitarian agency in Andreas J. Köstenberger and Scott R. Swain, *Father, Son, and Spirit: The Trinity and John's Gospel*, NSBT 24 (Downers Grove, IL: InterVarsity Press, 2008), 165–186.

[50] For a full account of Trinitarian agency, see Emery, *Trinity, Church, and the Human Person*, 115–153.

that Jesus can do *nothing* on his own initiative, but *only* what he sees the Father doing. And then Jesus quickly adds, he can do *everything* his Father does, i.e., create and sustain the universe, judge all people, give eternal life, and, in this context, heal on the Sabbath! The Son's personal, filial relation to his Father—a relation from eternity—now explains why the Son obeys his Father's will, why he does not pursue his own initiative, why he is completely dependent upon his Father, and how he acts *as the Son* in relation to his Father. In truth, one can just as easily explain the Son's actions, dependency, lack of knowledge, and so on in terms of the Father-Son relationship, as FKC advocates attempt to do by appealing to the Son-Spirit relationship, yet to do so would be reductionistic. Instead, we must explain how all three persons relate *ad intra* and then think through how these personal relations show themselves in the divine economy *ad extra*. When we do this, we can better make sense of the incarnation in terms of Trinitarian relations and agency, as classical Christology has always sought to do.

A Classical View of Trinitarian Relations and Agency

Let us briefly describe the classical understanding of Trinitarian relations and agency and its application to Christology, especially as a better explanation than evangelical kenoticism.

Pro-Nicene theology teaches that, even though the divine persons share the same identical nature, they are distinguished by their *personal* relations to each other, i.e., by their mode of subsistence—paternity, sonship, and procession. In addition, the way the divine persons subsist in the divine nature *ad intra* is also how the divine persons act *ad extra*, thus underscoring the fact that there is nothing accidental or arbitrary in the divine relations.[51] Moreover, in God's works *ad extra*, since the divine persons equally possess the same nature, all three persons act inseparably yet distinctly, according to their mode of subsistence. Thus, in creation, providence, and redemption *all* three divine persons act inseparably and together, yet they act *as* Father, *as* Son, and *as* Spirit, and specific actions terminate on the divine persons differently. In regard to the Son's relation to the Father, what characterizes it is the Son's filial dependence upon the Father, yet, the "Father enjoys *personal* priority in the *taxis* (order) of the triune life, not ontological superiority, for the Father and the Son hold all things in common: one divine name (John 17:11), one divine power (John 5:19, 21–22), one divine identity (John 10:30)."[52] As the Son, who is *personally* distinct from the Father, he is the filial recipient of everything from the Father.

---

[51] On these points, see Zacharias Ursinus, *Commentary on the Heidelberg Catechism*, trans. G. W. Williard, 2nd American ed. (Columbus, OH: Scott, 1852; repr, Phillipsburg, NJ: P&R, [1985]), 135–137.
[52] Köstenberger and Swain, *Father, Son, and Spirit*, 123.

In terms of the Spirit's relation to the Father and Son, what characterizes it is the eternal procession of the Spirit from both, as he shares all things in common except that which distinguishes him. As the triune God acts *ad extra*, all three persons act together, yet according to their eternal *personal* relations. Thus, Scripture speaks of the Father initiating and sending, as the one who acts "through" the Son "in" the Spirit. The Son is the one who is sent and "through whom the Father creates and accomplishes all things: In the Trinity, the Son is the only one who acts in this way, as befits his property of Son, Word, and Image of the Father."[53] The Spirit is the one who proceeds from the Father and the Son and "by whom or through whom the Father and Son act, in virtue of his property of Love and Gift."[54]

As applied to the incarnation, all three persons act inseparably, yet distinctly, and with the specific action of adding a human nature terminating on the Son alone. In the incarnate Son's actions, all of his actions are *in filial relation* to his Father, *through* the Spirit, and in such a way that all three divine persons are involved. It is for this reason that one should not attribute an action to one divine person without involving the other two, yet the unified actions of the persons also reflect their distinctions. This is why Crisp, in stating pro-Nicene orthodoxy in regard to the Spirit's action, insists that "any action of the Spirit is *ipso facto* an action involving God the Son, since both are divine persons subsisting in the one Godhead."[55] To be sure, God's actions do terminate on specific divine persons according to their immanent relations within the Godhead. For example, sustaining the human nature of Christ is an action that terminates upon the Spirit rather than the Son, while the assumption of a human nature is an action that terminates upon the Son, not the Spirit. But, as Crisp notes, a proper understanding of Trinitarian relations and agency never views the Son as "merely a spectator, looking on whilst his human nature is manipulated by the Holy Spirit."[56] Even if the Spirit's unique work is tied to the sustenance of Christ's human nature, it is still a work of all three divine persons—*the Son included*. The agency of the Son never disappears, even as incarnate, so that all of his actions are *his* actions, but always in relation to the Father and Spirit.

This classical view of Trinitarian relations and agency is better able to make sense of the relations of the divine persons in the incarnation. It is the Son who becomes incarnate precisely because he is the Son. Even though the Son is *homoousios* with the Father and Spirit, his possession of the divine nature reflects his mode of subsistence, as is true of the Father and Spirit. As Scott Swain and Michael Allen rightly note, "There is a personal order in the one

---

[53] Emery, *Trinity, Church, and the Human Person*, 133.
[54] Ibid. See also Scott R. Swain and Michael Allen, "The Obedience of the Eternal Son: Catholic Trinitarianism and Reformed Christology," in *Christology: Ancient and Modern*, 74–95.
[55] Crisp, *Revisioning Christology*, 102.
[56] Ibid.

true God. Almighty power is possessed by all three divine persons, though it is not possessed in the same way. The Son possesses Almightiness (omnipotence) in a filial way, whereas the Father possesses the same attribute in a paternal manner,"[57] and the same is true of the Spirit.

If this is so, then it is insufficient to explain *all* or *most* of the actions of the Son by the Spirit. Instead, we must explain the actions of the *incarnate Son* as *his* actions *and* the outworking of the triune relations in light of the incarnation and his redemptive work. The Son, then, acts in and through his two natures *in filial relation* (obedience and dependence) to his Father and *through* the Spirit. *As the Son* who continues to possess the divine nature, he is able to exercise his divine attributes and does so, for example, in his ongoing cosmic actions. Yet, the Son, even as the incarnate Son, never acts on his own; the Son always acts in filial relation to his Father *and* through the Spirit, which he has always done. Thus, in the incarnation, even though it is the Son who added to himself a human nature, the Son's relations and actions continue to be done according to his mode of subsistence, *as the Son*. The divine, *ad intra personal* relations never change, but we come to know these relations on the stage of history as the Son becomes incarnate, acts in obedience to his Father's will *through* the Spirit, and lives and dies as our new covenant representative and substitute. It is this classical account of Trinitarian relations and agency that better accounts for *all* of the biblical data including the exercise and non-exercise of the divine prerogatives of the incarnate Son in fulfillment of God's eternal plan.

Problems with the Humanity of Christ

One of the great strengths touted by evangelical kenoticism advocates over against classical Christology is the ability to account for Christ's humanity. However, given their redefinition of "person," it seems that it will be *more difficult* to uphold Christ's full humanity, first in making Christ's humanity unlike ours; and second, in making sense of how Christ either retains his humanity in the state of exaltation or is not permanently limited and thus changed in his ability to act as God the Son. Let us turn to each of these points.

Is Christ's Humanity Like Ours?

Scripture teaches that Christ's humanity is like ours in every way except sin (e.g., Heb. 2:14, 17; Rom. 8:3). This is not an insignificant point: If Christ is not fully man he cannot represent us as our new covenant head. Our salvation requires not only that Jesus be fully God but also that he be fully human,

---

[57] Swain and Allen, "Obedience of the Eternal Son," 90.

and Scripture does *not* diminish his full humanity. Kenotic Christology makes much of this point and constantly charges classical Christology with docetic tendencies. We are told repeatedly that evangelicals stress Christ's deity more than they do his humanity,[58] yet given how OKC and FKC redefine person, it is the kenotic views that seemingly face problems in regard to accounting for Christ's humanity being like our own.

For starters, both views seem to equate the person with the soul, and thus, in the incarnation the Son *becomes* a human soul, or in the words of Craig and Moreland, "the Logos completes the individual human nature of Christ by furnishing it with a rational soul, which is the Logos himself."[59] But if this is so, then one cannot think of a distinct human soul that the Son assumes, contra the Chalcedonian Definition. Or think of how both views place the capacities of will and mind in the person, thus necessitating one will and mind in Christ, namely, the Son's *divine* will and mind. Similar to the problem with the soul, however, in Christ there is no *distinct* human will or mind, once again contrary to the classical affirmation of dyothelitism. The best that can be said is that the divine person of the Son has a will that in the incarnation has two aspects to it, but this is *not* the same as two distinct wills,[60] thus making it difficult to see how Christ's humanity is like ours. If the Son does not act, think, grow in wisdom and knowledge, express human emotions, and so on, in and through *the capacities of a human soul, will, and mind*, it is difficult to think how he is like us, and it is difficult to account for the biblical Jesus.[61]

At this point, what both kenotic views often do is to assume some kind of "doubleness" in Christ, similar to classical Christology yet without the metaphysical underpinning for it. So, for example, when it comes to consciousness, both views talk about a divine and human consciousness, or a divine subliminal knowledge and a human conscious knowledge. So, once again, as Craig and Moreland suggest, in Jesus's conscious experience, he learns. "Even though the Logos possesses all knowledge about the world from quantum mechanics to auto mechanics, there is no reason to think that Jesus of Nazareth would have been able to answer questions about such subjects, so low had he stooped

---

[58] For example, see this charge in Gordon D. Fee, "The New Testament and Kenosis Christology," in *Exploring Kenotic Christology*, 25, and Habets, *Anointed Son*, 53–88.

[59] Moreland and Craig, *Philosophical Foundations*, 610.

[60] See Crisp, *Divinity and Humanity*, 57–61.

[61] To counter this charge, monothelites often reject the idea that the Son added to himself a concrete human nature and instead say his human nature was an abstract one. If so, as Wessling explains, the human nature of Christ is a property, or collection of properties, that are sufficient for the possession of a complete human nature. In that case, "Christ has both a divine and human will in the sense that he has properties that are sufficient for both wills, even if not two distinct wills. . . . So, then, the idea would be that the will of the Logos, in virtue of taking on certain human properties—mental and affective properties perhaps—comes to possess everything sufficient for being a human will, even while retaining that which is sufficient for a divine will" (Wessling, "Christology and Conciliar Authority," in *Christology: Ancient and Modern*, 157). The problem with this explanation is that Christ does not have a *distinct* human will and that, for most kenoticists, the mental and affective properties Christ takes on are not tied to a human soul since, in equating person with soul, the only soul Christ has is his own divine soul.

in condescending to take on the human condition."[62] Or, "the Logos allowed only those facets of his person to be part of Christ's waking consciousness which were compatible with typical human experience."[63] On the surface this explanation sounds plausible until we first remember, there is only *one* divine mind/soul in Christ, and second, how do we conceive of the *one divine mind* having levels of consciousness and knowledge? Even though the classical view has its challenges, at least it can make sense of how the divine Son, who now subsists in two natures, can continue to live a fully divine life *and* a human life, given his assumption of a concrete human nature comprised of a human body *and* a distinct human soul.

The same may be said of how kenotic views speak of a divine and human willing in Christ, yet their view allows for only *one* divine will. For example, Craig and Moreland argue that Jesus possessed "a typical human consciousness,"[64] and as such, Jesus had "to struggle against fear, weakness and temptation in order to align his will with that of his heavenly Father."[65] In fact, "[t]he will of the Logos had in virtue of the Incarnation become the will of the man Jesus of Nazareth."[66] The implication of this view, then, is that "[i]n his conscious experience, we see Jesus genuinely tempted, even though he is, in fact, impeccable. The enticements of sin were really felt and could not be blown away like smoke; resisting temptation required spiritual discipline and moral resoluteness on Jesus' part."[67]

As far as it goes, all of this is fine, and in fact it agrees with classical Christology because it implicitly assumes some kind of "doubleness" in terms of the will. But given that FKC is committed to one will, how is the *divine* Son susceptible to human choices and resisting temptation in his humanity when there is no distinct human will and only a *divine* will? How does the Son act *as a man* if the capacities of will and mind are located in the person? Classical Christology, in its affirmation of two wills, can speak of the real temptation of the incarnate Son because the Son is able to live a fully human life *and will as a man*. It can make sense of the obedience of the Son *as a man*, which is so foundational to Christ serving as our Redeemer. This point is especially seen as Christ's obedience comes to a head in Gethsemane, where the Son, acting as our covenant head, aligns his human will with the will of his Father, as he chooses to forego his rights and to lay down his life for us and thus accomplish our redemption.

Ultimately, every view of Christology must wrestle with Gregory of

---

[62] Moreland and Craig, *Philosophical Foundations*, 612.
[63] Ibid., 611.
[64] Ibid.
[65] Ibid.
[66] Ibid.
[67] Ibid., 612.

Nazianzus's famous maxim, "What is not assumed is not healed."[68] If the Son has not assumed a human nature like ours, that is, a human body *and* soul, then it is difficult to see how the incarnate Son can serve as our new covenant head and mediator and obey *as a man* for our salvation. How can he serve as our covenant representative and substitute? Only if Christ possesses a distinct human will can he render obedience to God in *our* place. Only if Christ possesses a human soul and mind can he take *our* place on the cross. As Bray soberly notes, "Sin is manifested by acts of the mind and will, not by inert skin and bones, so if Jesus did not have a soul he could neither have sinned himself nor become sin for us."[69] Even though kenotic views affirm in the strongest terms the humanity of Christ, their Christological formulation leaves us with a Christ whose humanity is *not* like *ours* in every way.[70]

Are Christ's Human Limitations Permanent?

Scripture and church tradition teach that the incarnation is not a temporary act but a permanent one. In addition, Scripture distinguishes between the states of humiliation and exaltation. Even in the state of humiliation, "whatever the lowliness into which Christ stooped by his incarnation it was not such as to prevent his disciples seeing his glory (Jn. 1:14). If it had been—if the earthly life had disclosed nothing but 'human likeness' (Phil. 2:7)—Christ would never have been worshipped and Christianity would never have been born."[71] Instead of the *kenosis* of the kenotic viewpoints, it is best to think of Christ's humiliation as *krypsis*, i.e., hiddenness or veiledness. In taking on a human nature, the Son not only accommodated himself to human weakness, he also veiled his glory, which is seen only by divine revelation.

As Jesus lived a fully human life, he had the ability to exercise his divine power and authority, but he chose to obey his Father's will for us and for our salvation. As the Son, he continued to live and act in Trinitarian relation to his Father and the Spirit as he had always done from eternity, but now as the *incarnate* Son he is able to live a fully human life in order to redeem us. During his life, acting as the last Adam, in filial obedience to his Father, sometimes Jesus denied himself the exercise of his divine might and energies for the sake of the mission. At other times, as the Father allowed and in relation to the Spirit, he exercised those energies, and in the case of his cosmic functions, he continually

---

[68] Gregory of Nazianzus, *To Cledonius the Priest against Apollinarius* (Ep. 101) (NPNF² 7:440).

[69] Bray, *God Is Love*, 569.

[70] There are other entailments as well. If the mind is placed in *person* and there is no distinct human mind, then how can the Son grow in wisdom and knowledge, if he has only a divine mind? How does he serve as a role model for us? Or, what about Christ's death? If his soul is that of the person of the Son, then at death, when his body is placed in the grave, severed from his divine soul, what has happened to the hypostatic union? Do we still have an incarnation? Contrary to such a view, classical Christology insists that even in Christ's death, the incarnation continues because the person of the Son still continues to subsist in the divine nature *and* the human soul.

[71] Again quoting Macleod, *Person of Christ*, 211.

exercised his divine power in Trinitarian relation. Never once, though, did our Lord act in his own interest, because he always acted in light of who he is as the eternal Son. Even as he faced the cross, he willingly and gladly bore our sin and deployed no resources beyond those which his Father allowed *and* in relation to the Spirit. After his resurrection and ascension, the incarnate Son returned to his previous glory with the veil now removed, and presently the Lord Jesus rules at the right hand of the Father, interceding for his people, and from this posture of rule, he will come again in glory to consummate what he inaugurated in his first advent. In his glorified state, at which we get a glimpse in his transfiguration (Matt. 17:1–13 par.), and more completely post–resurrection and ascension (John 20–21; Acts 1; 9:1–9; Rev. 1:9–20; 5:1–14; 19:11–18), our Lord remains fully God and fully man, but the veil is now pulled back. In his glorified state, Jesus, as God the Son incarnate, continues to act through both natures as he relates to his people as the head and mediator of the new covenant, but it seems that the exercise of his deity is much more prevalent than during the state of humiliation.

Classical Christology, with its person-nature distinction and its affirmation of two natures, two wills, and two minds, is able to make sense of the Son's asymmetrical acting and living through both natures, as well as the transition from earth to heaven, from humiliation to exaltation, and from *krypsis* to glorification. But can the kenotic views do so? Both OKC and FKC insist that *kenosis* is at the heart of the incarnation. To be sure, they affirm this truth differently, yet there is an overall similarity of approach, especially given their redefinition of person and their equation of person with soul. For both viewpoints, in Christ there is only one person and thus one *divine* mind and will, and, it seems, that in the Son's adding to himself a human body and becoming a human soul, there are *necessary* and *permanent* limitations that result, almost as if the state of humiliation continues without a proper transition to the state of exaltation. In other words, in the Word becoming flesh, even if, as FKC advocates affirm, the Son continues to possess the divine nature in the robust understanding of it, the Son's ability to act as *God the Son* seems permanently limited.

We see a glimpse of this, for example, in Hawthorne's unpacking of the incarnation: "In becoming a human being, the Son of God willed to renounce the exercise of his divine powers, attributes, prerogatives, so that he might live fully within those limitations which inhere in being truly human."[72] In fact, Hawthorne contends, unless this took place, we could not account for the unity of Christ's person as both human and divine, thus making it difficult "to think of Jesus as being in reality a genuinely human being."[73] In other words,

---

[72] Hawthorne, *Presence and Power*, 208. See also Issler, *Living into the Life of Jesus*, 109–129.
[73] Ibid., 214.

in becoming a man, the divine Son *necessarily* covered himself with a created, limited, and finite human nature so that, even though Christ is fully God, he cannot express those divine attributes inconsistent with his humanity. While the Son's divine nature is fully present and intact, the manifestation of it is not allowed full expression, given the reality of the incarnation.

But a question must be asked: What about Christ's postresurrection state? Are the limitations of his incarnation now permanent? Given that the Son is now and forevermore the *incarnate* Son, can he now express only those divine attributes consistent with his humanity? Is his inability to express divine attributes inconsistent with his humanity tied only to the state of humiliation (even though, as Scripture teaches, even on earth the divine Son continues to uphold the universe)? Furthermore, in glorification, is the veil pulled back and the full glory of the Son displayed, or is this inability to express his divine attributes bound up with the very nature of the Son's taking on a human nature so that now the Son *cannot* permanently express the full range of his divine attributes?[74]

An affirmation of the permanent limitations of the incarnate Son seems consistent with the kenotic viewpoint, even though some advocates try to avoid this conclusion. It is consistent because of how the kenotic view defines "person." From their equation of person with soul and their placing of will and mind in person, it seems to follow that unless Christ's humanity is shed in his glorification, there are now permanent limitations on the Son in his expression and use of his divine attributes. Unlike the classical view, kenotic views do not affirm two wills and two minds in Christ, thus making it difficult to conceive how, in glorification, the Son can return to a full exercise of his divine attributes. Think for example of the Son's omniscience tied to his divine mind. If the adding of a human nature requires the necessary contraction of knowledge, or the divine consciousness becoming subliminal, then how does the Son return to a full, conscious, omniscient knowledge, given that he has only one mind and that it was the addition of his human body that brought about this contraction? In exaltation, if the glorified Christ returns to his previous state and can exercise all of his divine attributes, then how is he still truly human? On the other hand, if the glorified Christ can exercise all of his divine attributes and retain his humanity, then why cannot he do it in the state of humiliation as well, which, if admitted, seems to undercut the rationale for the kenotic view? It seems that a consistent kenoticism requires that either the Son must remove his humanity in order to return to the full exercise of his divine attributes, or there

---

[74] Bruce Ware is difficult to understand on this question. Although he affirms the *extra*, he seems to imply that the incarnation has brought about permanent limitations, not merely for the state of humiliation but forevermore. See Ware, *Man Christ Jesus*, 21–23, 43–45. He states, "[W]hen Jesus took on our human nature and accepted his dependence on the Spirit, it seems that he accepted this as his way of life forever, from that moment forward without end. . . . when he became also human, he became forever dependent on the Spirit" (44–45).

are permanent limitations entailed by the incarnation.[75] If those alternatives are not acceptable, then the other alternative would be to return to a classical Christology with its corresponding metaphysical commitments.

This is not a new challenge. As noted in chapter 10, Donald Baillie raised this same problem and posed the same dilemma.[76] Denying that there were permanent limitations on the Son, Baillie pressed the kenotic view to account for how *kenosis* was merely temporary, since it seemed to require either some kind of permanent loss or the surrendering of Christ's humanity. If the logic of the position demands that it was necessary for the Son to give up certain divine attributes (or not to exercise them) in order to become incarnate because divinity was inconsistent with a truly human life, then the exalted Son either still lacks these attributes (or does not exercise them) or he is no longer truly human—options that Baillie, classical Christology, and Scripture find untenable. How do kenoticists respond? There are three responses.

First, a few deny the perpetual humanity of Christ, which is impossible to reconcile with Scripture and the historical confessions, and which ultimately robs us of our new covenant mediator now and forevermore.[77]

Second, more kenoticists affirm that Christ's limitations are permanent. Evans, representing OKC, proposes that the glorified Christ remains fully human yet continues not "to possess all of the traditional divine properties."[78] This entails that the Son's preincarnate possessing and exercise of the divine attributes has changed beginning at the incarnation, and that the change is now permanent. What this implies for the triune personal relations, Evans suggests, is that "[t]he resumption of the traditional divine properties can be understood as accomplished by the power of the Father and the Spirit, who bestow glorification on the Son, who merits it by virtue of his sacrificial life and death."[79] Concerned that this results in asymmetrical relations and inequality among the divine persons, Evans admits that everyone affirms some kind of "asymmetries in the relations enjoyed by the persons of the Trinity,"[80] but it is difficult to see how Evans can affirm that the Son is *homoousios* with the Father and Spirit, because the Son does not possess the divine attributes in the same way. Historically, pro-Nicene orthodoxy has spoken of the ordering (*taxis*) among the divine persons according to their eternal, immanent relations, but it has also consistently affirmed that all three persons equally possess

---

[75] Crisp, *Divinity and Humanity*, 135, also raises this dilemma.

[76] See Donald M. Baillie, *God Was in Christ: An Essay on Incarnation and Atonement* (New York: Charles Scribner's Sons, 1948), 97. For questions regarding how the kenotic theory can make sense of the return to omniscience in Christ's exaltation, see John S. Lawton, *Conflict in Christology: A Study of British and American Christology from 1889–1914* (London: SPCK; New York: Macmillan, 1947), 142–143.

[77] See David Brown, *The Divine Trinity* (London: Duckworth, 1985), 234, 257, who defends this option. Feenstra, "Reconsidering Kenotic Christology," in *Trinity, Incarnation, and Atonement*, 147, strongly rejects this option.

[78] Evans, "Kenotic Christology and the Nature of God," 200; cf. idem, "Self-Emptying of Love," 265–266.

[79] Evans, "Kenotic Christology and the Nature of God," 200.

[80] Evans, "Self-Emptying of Love," 267.

the same identical concrete divine nature. On the other hand, Evans and those like him, in affirming permanent limitations of the incarnate Son, ultimately must reconfigure Trinitarian theology in unorthodox ways.[81] Within a FKC view, those who embrace permanent limitations will affirm that the incarnate Son continues to possess the divine nature equally, yet the Son-Spirit relation has now permanently changed from what it was prior to the incarnation, which now results in a different *taxis* from what it was in eternity past.

Third, probably the best response that fits with the Scriptural presentation of the glorified Christ is that the incarnate Son's limitations are temporary for the state of humiliation and *not* in the state of exaltation, even though Christ is permanently the incarnate Son. From the OKC perspective, Feenstra argues for this position by distinguishing between the incarnation, i.e., the Son's becoming human, which is permanent, and *kenosis*, i.e., the Son's emptying himself of certain divine attributes, which is temporary. Feenstra suggests, "The Incarnation need not involve his emptying himself of attributes such as omniscience. . . . The Incarnation does not, in itself, require the Son of God to lack attributes such as omniscience. The Son of God can *be*, and perhaps can even *become*, incarnate while possessing such attributes. The Incarnation simply is the Son's taking on human nature,"[82] while the *kenosis* is something different.

If this is the case, however, then why argue for an OKC, because this is precisely what a classical Christology has always affirmed. Feenstra responds by saying that *kenosis* is necessary in order for the Son to share our lot and to accomplish our redemption; it is not necessary in order to become human. But, once again, is it really necessary for the Son to set aside certain divine attributes in order to accomplish our salvation? If the Son can become truly human without *kenosis*, then it seems that Feenstra has undercut the very rationale for his view. Also, classical Christology, which affirms incarnation and *krypsis*, can certainly account for Christ's full and complete humanity and his accomplishment of our redemption, and it can do so in ways that avoid the problematic features of kenotic Christology.

CONCLUDING REFLECTION

Christological reflection and formulation, whether ancient or contemporary, is not an easy task. Yet, in truth, it is our highest calling as Christians, as we seek to think God's thoughts after him, to bring our entire thought captive

---

[81] In order to avoid permanent limitations on Christ, Evans suggests the possibility that Christ's glorified body may be compatible with "reacquiring and possessing the traditional divine attributes," and as such, in his glorified body he reassumes all the traditional theistic attributes (Evans, "Self-Emptying of Love," 265). The problem with such a view is that Christ's glorified human nature no longer looks human. What evidence is there that human nature, even in a glorified state, is able to be deified in the way that Evans proposes? Scripture gives no indication of this, and the church has carefully kept Christ's divine and human natures distinct, thus preserving the Creator-creature distinction even in the incarnation.

[82] Feenstra, "Reconsidering Kenotic Christology," 148.

to Christ, and rightly to think about the glory and wonder of God the Son incarnate, our Lord and Redeemer. In such a task, there is a lot to think about, to reflect on, and about which in prayer to ask our triune God for wisdom. Biblical, theological, historical, and philosophical data have to be weighed carefully. There are a lot of pitfalls to avoid, and given the importance of the subject matter, it requires our full attention, devotion, and care.

Over the years, the church has wrestled with the identity of the Lord of glory and the wonder of the incarnation, and for the most part, it has spoken in a unified voice until recent days. Even though our theologizing about Christ is never complete, one must propose "newer" formulations with great trepidation, especially given the consistent Christological voice throughout the ages. "Newer" understandings are welcome, but they must always be tested in light of Scripture and the wisdom of the past. Our verdict is that the "old" Christological path, properly understood and explicated, is still the better way to theologize about our glorious Redeemer today. The "newer" kenotic views claim to offer a "better" and "middle" way, but we have found them wanting. In the next two chapters, as we conclude this work, our aim is to "pull together" the pieces of our investigation and set before ourselves the "old" path as the better option for evangelical theology today.

CHRISTOLOGICAL FORMULATION:
THE ORTHODOX IDENTITY
OF JESUS CHRIST

We have finally come to the end of an argument for classic Christology in our contemporary culture. We have explored a lot of information in many different categories to answer the question that Jesus himself asks his disciples: "But who do you say that I am?" (Matt. 16:15). More than a diverse and in-depth investigation, however, the parts of this volume attempt to provide the kind of warrant necessary to answer Jesus's question with confidence and authority in our own day. For the church to know in truth, faithfully confess, and effectively bear witness to the identity of Christ amid the contemporary culture, we must carefully think through the justification required for the conclusions we make. This means that to identify Jesus Christ correctly and declare him within the church and to the world, we must stand on firm epistemological, biblical, ecclesiological, and theological grounds.

Part I worked through epistemological warrant for the identity of Christ by first recognizing the nature of current confusion in Christology and then tracing the cause of this confusion to the worldview shifts of the Enlightenment, modern, and postmodern periods of intellectual history. The strict rationalism and humanistic hubris of the Enlightenment turned the prevailing thought of culture away from the revelational epistemology that reigned into the Reformation era and made it nearly impossible to accept the supernatural as reasonable. This trend continued into modernity and climaxed in a skepticism toward the existence and authority of God and a specific rejection of the Scriptures as his authoritative, inerrant word. And even when postmodernism arose to challenge some of the foundations of modernity, the epistemological skepticism merely shifted to deny the possibility of a universal perspective and interpretation, whether God exists to provide it or not. In this context, the church must return to and explain the rational superiority of a biblical epistemology. The anti-supernatural rationalism of the Enlightenment and the relativistic-pluralistic mind-set of postmodernity cannot seriously challenge the biblical worldview. These rival epistemologies merely reject as a priori unreasonable and impossible the reason, theology, and metaphysics presented in the Scriptures. The Scriptures, however, stand as the only authoritative interpretation of redemptive history in general and of the person and work of Christ in particular precisely because this revelation is given by God himself.

Part II worked through biblical warrant for the identity of Christ by recognizing the authoritative structure of the Scriptures. The Bible is authoritative both in what it says and in how it says it. In fact, the content and form of Scripture cannot be separated without losing or misunderstanding the truth that God has revealed about himself and his plans and promises for humanity and the rest of creation. All things must be interpreted according to God's plans and promises as they have developed across the epochs and through the covenants of redemptive history. And this certainly includes the identity of Christ. In short, the biblical storyline presents Jesus Christ as the eternal and divine Son who assumed a full and sinless humanity to become the true image of God, perfectly obedient Son, great Davidic king, faithful covenant partner, and last Adam that God has always demanded and promised. In fact, in Christ, God himself came in the flesh to inaugurate God's own kingdom on the earth by redeeming a new humanity and restoring it to vice-regent glory over all creation—a work possible only for the God-man.

Part III worked through ecclesiological warrant for the identity of Christ by standing on the shoulders of past theologians to learn the lessons of historical theology. Through every century and generation, the Lord has led the church to synthesize properly all of the biblical data in light of various challenges, denials, and legitimate questions as an exercise in *doing theology*, or better, "faith seeking understanding." Over time, especially from the Council of Nicaea to the Council of Chalcedon, a consistent Christology emerged. To be faithful to the Scriptures and respond to the questions and heresies of the time, the church made careful and sometimes novel use of the linguistic-conceptual resources made available in the culture by God's common grace. Specifically, the church made biblical and theological use of *hypostasis* and *ousia* to confess in the Chalcedonian Definition that Jesus Christ is the Son of God, one *person* with a fully *divine nature* and a fully *human nature*. Even with such specialized terminology and concepts, however, a "classical Christology" took hold in the church from East to West and developed into an established orthodoxy as the church's theologians worked out the implications of Chalcedon. What we now know as classical Christology describes the identity and significance of Jesus Christ with biblical authority and theological coherence and precision: he is God the Son incarnate.

With this epistemological, biblical, and ecclesiological warrant in place, Part IV has worked through theological warrant for the identity of Christ by first critiquing kenotic Christologies that claim to offer a "newer" and "better" understanding of who Jesus is. Within evangelicalism, two different versions of kenoticism attempt a *via media* between classical Christology and those more informed by the Enlightenment and its epistemological heritage. No doubt these kenotic views differ substantially at key points, yet they do have a couple of features in common. Both ontological and functional kenoticism attempt to remain within the church's confessional standards and account for the biblical data, yet both views also attempt to reformulate the established orthodoxy regarding the identity of Christ, with the ontological variety doing so much more radically than the functional version. Theological reformulation itself is not problematic; in fact, it is good and even necessary at times. But theological reformulation must always be warranted. We must have good reason—epistemological, biblical, ecclesiological, and/or theological reason—to say something different or differently than the church has confessed throughout history. In short, the kenotic Christologies make unwarranted changes to classical Christology by redefining the "person-nature" distinction, which leads to a number of serious implications as discussed in chapter 12. Making this theological critique of kenotic Christology, however, has helped to sharpen the theological conclusions we need to make in this penultimate chapter.

JESUS CHRIST IS GOD THE SON INCARNATE

Ultimately, the thesis of this entire work is one theological conclusion with many parts. Based on the warrant and critique of the previous chapters, we must confess that the identity of the Jesus of the Bible is that he is God the Son incarnate. Each part of this volume and every chapter in each part has contributed to this identity statement. A biblical-revelational epistemology provides the intellectual and rational power to receive and understand the biblical presentation of the eternal Son's incarnation, which means, as the church has come to confess, that Christ is the God-man, the divine person of the Son with two natures, one divine and one human. We can now articulate three more specific affirmations that mark the contemporary boundaries of a classical Christology. For clarity, we can place these affirmations in three categories: the subject, the metaphysics, and the economy of the incarnation.[1]

---

[1] These three affirmations both consolidate and amplify Oliver Crisp's four desiderata that he argues comprise the minimal confession for an orthodox Christology (see Oliver D. Crisp, "Desiderata for Models of the Hypostatic

*The Subject of the Incarnation: God the Son Is the Person of Christ
in Eternal Trinitarian Relation with the Father and the Spirit*

"The Word became flesh" (John 1:14). Based on the magisterial authority of
the entire biblical presentation and the ministerial authority of the church's
traditional confession, we now know that John tells us that the *who*, the *subject*, the *person* of the incarnation is the Word or the Son from eternity. This
one and the same person is both eternal and divine: he "was with God" (*pros
ton theon*) and he "was God" (*theos ēn ho logos*) (John 1:1). The person
who has existed eternally as Son in relation to God the Father and in divine
fellowship with the Father and the Spirit is the same person who made the
willing and obedient decision to become incarnate. The second person of the
Trinity, through whom all things were created and who has always sustained
and always will sustain all things, is the same person who assumed a created
"human nature, body and soul, into union with himself so that he now has
a human nature of his own."[2] The Son who shares in the divine nature as the
Covenant Lord of all creation is the person of Christ, the same one, the same
subject who acts as our Redeemer and head of the new covenant, new humanity, and new creation.

In stating it this way, Scripture and Christian theology clearly, carefully,
and consistently distinguish between the *who*, the *subject*, the *person* of the incarnation, and the *what*, the *object*, the *nature* of the incarnation. This distinction between person and nature began as a theological necessity to make sense
of and articulate the self-revelation of the one God—Father, Son, and Holy
Spirit. To be consistently biblical, we must make a real distinction among the
Father, the Son, and the Spirit without separating them into three Gods. Thus
the church confesses that there are three divine persons who share in one divine
nature, such that there is only one God. In this theological sense, *divine nature*
refers to *what* an object is: God, a divine being with a corresponding perfection
of attributes and capacities. *Human nature* refers to *what* constitutes humanity: a body-soul composite with corresponding capacities, such as will, mind,
and emotions. In contradistinction to nature, *divine person* refers to the *who*, *I*,
active subject that subsists in the divine nature and acts through its capacities:
the Father, the Son, and the Spirit are each a divine person. Similarly, *human
person* refers to the *who*, *I*, *active subject* that subsists in a human nature and
acts through its capacities. A nature does not act. A person acts through a

---

Union," in *Christology Ancient and Modern: Explorations in Constructive Dogmatics*, ed. Oliver D. Crisp and Fred
Sanders [Grand Rapids, MI: Zondervan, 2013], 19–41). Crisp proposes these four points: "1. Christ is one person.
2. Christ has two natures, one divine and one human. 3. The two natures of Christ retain their integrity and are
distinct; they are not mixed together or confused, nor are they amalgamated into a hybrid of divine and human
attributes (like a demigod). 4. The natures of Christ are really united in the person of Christ; that is, they are two
natures possessed by one person" (ibid., 29, 40).

[2] Robert Letham, *The Message of the Person of Christ* (Downers Grove, IL: InterVarsity Press, 2013), 120.

nature, never vice versa. In the incarnation, then, the person of the Son, who subsists eternally in the one divine nature, acted to assume a human nature.

While we must distinguish between *person* and *nature*, the precise definition and metaphysical content of each remains a matter of debate in the church. In fact, as noted in our discussion of kenoticism, different views of *person* result in crucial variances in Christological formulation. Today, in contrast to classical theology, *person* is defined as a "distinct center of knowledge, will, love, and action."[3] Moreover, this definition insists that the capacities of will and mind are located in the *person* and not in the *nature*. For this reason, many today argue for a social Trinitarianism that entails three distinct wills and minds in God. The equally problematic Christological corollary is monothelitism: if will and mind are located in the person and Christ is one person, then Christ has only one will and mind. In addition, current views often identify *person* with *soul* and locate various psychological personality traits in the *person* as well. As discussed in our survey of historical theology in Part III and our critique of evangelical kenoticism in chapter 12, this redefinition of *person* and *nature* departs from classical theology and Christology and creates more problems than it solves.

In light of the ongoing debate, it will be helpful to develop this first Christological affirmation by constructing the classical view of *person* and then considering its coherence and Trinitarian context.

THE CLASSICAL UNDERSTANDING OF PERSON

According to the classical view, *person* (1) is ontologically distinct from *nature*; (2) is the active subject or the "I" of a *nature* and that *nature* is the metaphysical location of the attributes and capacities, including will, mind, and psychological components; and (3) is *not* the same as a soul.

The best-known definition of *person* that captures the basic parts in a unified description is the one we have learned from Boethius: "an individual substance of a rational nature."[4] By "individual substance," Boethius referred not to a concrete object but to the *I* or *active subject subsisting* in a nature: the "subsisting singular that exists through itself and in itself, according to an irreducible mode, as a complete whole, a 'hypostasis' that exercises the

---

[3] Cornelius Plantinga Jr., "Social Trinity and Tritheism," in *Trinity, Incarnation, and Atonement: Philosophical and Theological Essays*, ed. R. J. Feenstra and C. Plantinga Jr. (Notre Dame, IN: University of Notre Dame Press, 1989), 22; see William Hasker, *Metaphysics and the Tri-Personal God* (Oxford: Oxford University Press, 2013), 19–25.

[4] Cited in Gilles Emery, "The Dignity of Being a Substance: Person, Subsistence, and Nature," *Nova et Vetera* 9/4 (2011): 994 (English edition). For the original source, see Boethius, *Liber de Persona et Duabus Naturis*, chapter 3, "A Treatise against Eutyches and Nestorius," 85, in his *Theological Tractates*. For a helpful discussion of Boethius on this point, see Eleonore Stump, "Aquinas' Metaphysics of the Incarnation," in *The Incarnation: An Interdisciplinary Symposium on the Incarnation of the Son of God*, ed. Stephen T. Davis, Daniel Kendall, and Gerald O'Collins (Oxford: Oxford University Press, 2002), 206–218.

act of existing on its own account."[5] By "rational nature," Boethius referred to the essence of a thing endowed with intelligence, which includes within it the capacities (will, mind, etc.) through which the subsisting subject can act. In Chalcedonian terms, then, a rational human nature is the body-soul composite. Regarding this basic distinction and relationship between *person* and *nature*, Herman Bavinck provides a good summary: a person is "the owner, possessor, and master of a nature, a completion of existence, sustaining and determining the existence of a nature, the subject that lives, thinks, wills, and acts through nature with all of its abundant content, by which nature becomes self-existent and is not an accident of another entity."[6]

In addition to the distinction between person and nature, we must also distinguish between *divine* and *human* persons. Historically, theology has maintained that the categorical difference between the Creator and his creatures prevents a univocal relationship between divine and human persons but allows an analogical comparison. The divine person is the archetype; the human person is the ectype. Divine and human persons, then, are necessarily similar and necessarily dissimilar—there is continuity and discontinuity between these metaphysical realities.

To use the words of Aquinas and Calvin, each divine person is a "subsisting relation."[7] The three divine persons are relations that subsist in God's single essence. Moreover, each divine person, "while related to the others, is distinguishable by an incommunicable quality."[8] And the incommunicable personal property that distinguishes the divine persons is the *ad intra* relationship between the persons that manifest in God's *ad extra* actions. So the Father is distinguished by the personal property of paternity; the Son by sonship (or eternal generation); and the Spirit by eternal procession. Divine persons, unlike human persons, subsist in the same identical divine nature. And because they possess the single, same nature *equally*, the Father, Son, and Spirit must be distinguished as persons by their *different modes* of subsistence: the Father subsists in the divine nature *as the Father*; the Son subsists *as the Son*; and the Spirit subsists *as the Spirit*.[9]

Human persons, on the other hand, are not subsisting relations. Rather, each human person subsists in its own concrete nature; no human person subsists in more than one concrete nature; and no human person shares the same

---

[5] Cited in Emery, "Dignity of Being a Substance," 995.
[6] Herman Bavinck, *Sin and Salvation in Christ*, vol. 3 of *Reformed Dogmatics*, ed. John Bolt, trans. John Vriend (Grand Rapids, MI: Baker Academic, 2006), 306; cf. Brian E. Daley, "Nature and the 'Mode of Union': Late Patristic Models for the Personal Unity of Christ," in *Incarnation*, 193–196.
[7] Thomas Aquinas, *Summa Theologica*, q. 40, a. 2 ad 1.
[8] John Calvin, *Institutes of the Christian Religion*, 2 vols., ed. John T. McNeill, trans. Ford Lewis Battles (Philadelphia: Westminster, 1960), I.xiii.6.
[9] For a discussion of this point, see Emery, "Dignity of Being a Substance," 997–1001; cf. Gilles Emery, *The Trinitarian Theology of St. Thomas Aquinas* (Oxford: Oxford University Press, 2007), 51–150.

concrete nature with another human person. Individual human beings, then, are identified by both the *principle of subsisting* (i.e., the person or the active subject of the nature) and the *principle of distinction* (i.e., a concrete human nature with *this* flesh, *these* bones, and *this* soul). All concrete human natures are the same *kind* of nature, but not the same *instance* of a human nature. Yet a human person is similar to the divine persons in that a human person does subsist in and act through a corresponding nature. Keeping the person-nature distinction, we can say that, as the analogue of the divine persons, a human person is a particular active subject that subsists in an individuated human body-soul composite (i.e., distinguished from others of the same kind).[10]

Given the biblical presentation, the required theological coherence, the guidance of theological tradition, and the metaphysical options, the classical view of person remains the most compelling. First, we should opt for the view that does justice to *all* of the biblical data and their theological entailments. As discussed in Part III, the classical view of person accounts for the real distinction between the divine persons and their unity and full participation in the one divine nature that is demanded by the biblical presentation. Other views, including the kenotic redefinition of person, fail at either real distinction or full participation, thereby collapsing the divine persons into one or separating the divine nature into three Gods. Second, the classical view of person deserves theological deference because it was adopted and taught by the church for centuries as a crucial part of properly understanding the doctrine of the Trinity and orthodox Christology. Any other view bears the burden of proof, and we should not depart from the classical view without clear proof that it is in error, or that a better option has come forth in terms of biblical grounding and/or theological reasoning. Third, given the biblical and theological superiority of the classical view, we should not abandon or redefine it unless it is shown to be incoherent. Relying on the Christological work of Jean Galot, we can see that the classical view of person is also superior in its rational coherence to all other offerings.[11]

Galot argues that the classical distinction between person and nature not only accounts for all of biblical data, it also makes the best sense of the data and presents them in the most rationally coherent manner. Galot admits that, in our experience, "person and nature are so intimately linked that we perceive them together and we do not dichotomize their respective roles."[12] Yet even in

---

[10] On this point, see Emery, "Dignity of Being a Substance," 997–1001.

[11] In particular, see Jean Galot, *Who Is Christ? A Theology of the Incarnation* (Chicago: Franciscan Herald, 1981); cf. Klaas Runia, *The Present-Day Christological Debate* (Downers Grove, IL: InterVarsity Press, 1984), 105–109.

[12] Galot, *Who Is Christ?*, 287. Galot notes that in common usage, we do not distinguish between person and nature, but usually mean three things by "person": (1) a reference to the entire individual, i.e., the person together with the nature he possesses; (2) a synonym for soul; and (3) a reference to various personality traits (ibid., 283–313). This current usage, however, does not reflect the theological use of "person" in the tradition of Trinitarian and Christological formulation.

our psychological experience, it is possible to distinguish person from nature according to the classical-theological understanding. For example, self-discovery of our own person happens "essentially in our relations with others."[13] Consciousness of *I* comes only in relation to a *you*. As different *I*'s interact, each discovers the incommunicable character that makes it an *I* in relation to *you*'s.

Moreover, Galot suggests that in order to make sense of ourselves, "[e]very person also possesses a reality not of the relational order, what might be called a substantial perfection."[14] Galot identifies this substantial perfection as the soul and body and our possession of a concrete human nature. In distinguishing between the two, "[n]ature embraces the rich reality of body and soul, including the faculties of thought and action. The person is the relational entity that energizes the nature by directing its activity toward others in knowledge and love."[15] In this sense, we can think of a person as "a relation that possesses a reality of its own."[16] But we must quickly add that "[t]his relation does not derive its reality from nature."[17] Galot insists that even in our own experience, we have some sense that our person is the subject of all the activities of our nature, and that our nature is governed by our persons: "while the human person is not, rigorously speaking, his human nature, person personalizes nature to the point of totally possessing it. In this sense, the nature is identified with the person."[18]

Galot's discussion minimally demonstrates the coherence of the classical distinction between person and nature and its explanatory power for Christology. Bringing the person-nature distinction over into Christology helps make sense of the biblical presentation of the incarnation and the continuity between Christ's humanity and ours. We can agree with Scripture that God the Son became a man with no change in his divine nature by explaining that the divine person of the Son personalized a human nature created for him. The person of Christ exists as the God-man because he subsists in the divine nature and in a human nature. The Son continued to be God, subsisting in and acting through the divine nature that he has shared with the Father and Spirit from eternity. And the Son came to be all that it means to be a man: a person subsisting in and acting through a human body-soul. As Klaas Runia explains, "[The Son after incarnation] had a truly human mind, will, consciousness and personality. His birth, his life, his suffering, his death, they were all truly human in the full sense of the word."[19]

---

[13] Ibid., 295.
[14] Ibid., 298.
[15] Ibid.
[16] Ibid., 299.
[17] Ibid.
[18] Ibid., 300.
[19] Runia, *Present-Day Christological Debate*, 107. By "personality," Runia is not referring to a human *person* (*hypostasis*) but to the unique human personality traits and psychological makeup of Christ's human nature.

And the person-nature distinction also helps us make sense of how Jesus could stand face-to-face with the Jewish leaders and declare that he is the covenant God of Israel: "Truly, truly, I say to you, before Abraham was, I am" (John 8:58). The person who made this Yahwistic statement, the person of Christ, is the person of God the Son. The second person of the Trinity, who subsists in the one divine nature with the Father and Spirit as Yahweh, is the active subject who assumed a human nature and acted through it to say, as a man, that he is God, the Creator–Covenant Lord. While his human nature was created for his assumption of it, the divine person of the Son is divine, eternal, and uncreated. The person of the Son (and all the divine persons) "does not belong to the becoming of creatures, but is situated in the 'to be' of God."[20]

The classical person-nature distinction, then, allows us to make the most fundamental Christological formulation with rational coherence in faithfulness to the biblical presentation: the *divine person* of the Son, subsisting in the *divine nature*, did not become a human person but assumed a *human nature*, such that the same *I* is the *person of Christ* that now subsists in the *divine nature as God* and in a *human nature as a man*. Through the divine nature, the person of Christ acts as God. And through his human nature, the person of Christ "asserts itself within a human consciousness and in human language. It is the divine 'I' of a man who is living a genuinely human life."[21] The subject of the incarnation is the person of the Son, the person of Christ, God the Son incarnate.

THE DIVINE PERSONS AND THEIR RELATIONS

In their work on John's Gospel, Andreas Köstenberger and Scott Swain conclude that "when it comes to understanding Jesus' identity and mission ('Christology'), John urges us to perceive Jesus' identity and mission in a Trinitarian light. John's Christology is a *Trinitarian* Christology."[22] Similarly, Klaas Runia argues that the rationality of the incarnation is grounded in God as triune; apart from understanding the eternal relations of the divine persons, we cannot make sense of Jesus as God the Son incarnate.[23] And Bavinck observes how this connection between God's triune existence and the incarnation of Christ makes biblical Christology unique: "the incarnation has its presupposition and foundation in the trinitarian being of God. In Deism and pantheism there is no room for an incarnation of God."[24]

The incarnation and identification of Christ, then, depends upon how

---

[20] Galot, *Who Is Christ?*, 321.

[21] Ibid., 322.

[22] Andreas J. Köstenberger and Scott R. Swain, *Father, Son, and Spirit: The Trinity and John's Gospel*, NSBT 24 (Downers Grove, IL: InterVarsity, 2008), 111 (emphasis theirs).

[23] Runia, *Present-Day Christological Debate*, 106.

[24] Bavinck, *Sin and Salvation in Christ*, 274.

the Father, Son, and Spirit have related from eternity. We can explore this connection to make more specific Christological conclusions by answering three questions: Why did the Son alone become incarnate? How does the incarnate Son relate to the Father? How does the incarnate Son relate to the Spirit?

Before we begin with these questions, however, we need to recognize that much of our discussion will rely on a particular biblical-theological axiom: the ontological is revealed in the economic—what something is will be made known in how it functions. In terms of the Trinity, the *ad intra* relationships are revealed in the *ad extra* work of the divine persons—the eternal relations among the divine persons are revealed in how they function in the history of redemption. As noted above, the Father, Son, and Spirit subsist in the single, same divine nature such that they must be distinguished by their immanent personal relations or mode of subsistence in the divine nature: paternity, sonship, and eternal procession. Moreover, based on the ontological-economic axiom, the divine persons are also distinguished in their external actions in the execution of God's decree on the stage of human history. The divine persons subsist in the divine nature *ad intra* according to a specific *taxis*: their personal relations are not arbitrary or interchangeable. Therefore, the immanent, eternal relations can be fittingly seen in the external, economic activity of the divine persons, including the incarnation.[25] More specifically, all *ad extra* work of the divine persons is unified because they subsist in and act through the single, same divine nature. Yet because the divine persons work *ad extra* according to their *ad intra* relational *taxis*, specific actions within the inseparable operations of God terminate on specific divine persons according to a corresponding economic *taxis*.[26]

In summary, then, we can say regarding the divine *ad intra* relations that the Father has priority not in nature but in mode of subsistence in the divine nature; the Son depends upon the Father not in nature but in personal filiation; the Spirit proceeds from the Father and the Son not in nature but in personal spiration. Regarding the *ad extra* economy, the entire Godhead acts in unity, but the Father initiates and acts through the Son and in the Spirit; the Son obeys the Father and works in the Spirit; the Spirit executes the acts of the Father and Son in power.

With the proper *ad intra* and *ad extra taxis* in mind, we can now address the connection between God's triune existence and the incarnation of Christ.

---

[25] See Gilles Emery, *Trinity, Church, and the Human Person* (Naples, FL: Sapientia, 2007), 115–153.

[26] On this point, see Robert Letham, *The Holy Trinity: In Scripture, History, Theology, and Worship* (Phillipsburg, NJ: P&R, 2004), 383. Letham summarizes the *taxis* among the divine persons: The works of God are *"from the Father through the Son by the Holy Spirit*: the reverse movement in our response to God's grace is *by the Holy Spirit through the Son to the Father"* (emphasis his). Additionally, even though the divine persons are equally fully God, the *taxis* always follows a specific order, namely, "the Father sends the Son, and the Son never sends the Father. The Holy Spirit proceeds from the Father, but the Father never proceeds from the Holy Spirit or the Son."

The Son alone became incarnate because it was fitting for his unique, filial mode of subsisting in the divine nature in relation to the Father and Spirit. As the divine agent of creation and eternal image of God, it was fitting and proper for the Son to become the radiance of the glory of God as a man by assuming and acting through a created human nature. Gilles Emery explains that "[it] belongs properly to the Son to be the one through whom the Father creates and accomplishes all things: In the Trinity, the Son is the only one who acts in this way, as befits his property of Son, Word, and Image of the Father."[27] It was fitting, then, that the eternal Son *of* the Father *in* the Spirit should become the obedient Son in the flesh and accomplish the will of the Father as a man in the Spirit. Scott Swain links the incarnation of Christ to the connection between the eternal and economic relationship and work of the Father, Son, and Spirit: "The story of Jesus, as it unfolds in his filial relationship to his Father in the power of the Spirit, is simply *the being of the triune God in the temporal, self-manifesting, self-communicating execution of his eternal resolve to become our God.* This shows the relationships in the incarnation or economic Trinity are already rooted in the immanent. . . . Jesus is the Son living out in human form his eternal relationship with the Father in the Spirit for our saving benefit."[28]

The incarnate Son relates to the Father in divine-filial dependence as he has from eternity. The person of Christ continues to possess and act through the divine nature as God the Son incarnate. Yet the divine Son now also possesses and acts through a truly and fully human nature that is subject to the same creaturely finitude and weakness as all other instances of human nature. In terms of doctrinal formulation, a classic Christology affirms the two natures of Christ, which means that the Son can and does act through divine attributes and through the analogous but limited capacities of a human body and soul. As both God and man, however, the controlling metaphysical reality is the biblical identification of Christ as the eternal Son of the Father. As the Son of God, *he* is the one through whom the Father by the Spirit created all things; and *he*, in relation to the Father and the Spirit, is the one who continues to sustain and govern all things even in his incarnation. And the same Son of God also lives in absolute dependence upon God as a man: "Jesus depends upon the Father for his life ([John] 5:16), power (5:19), knowledge (8:16), message (7:16), mission (7:28), instruction (14:31); authority (17:2), glory (17:24) and love (10:17)."[29] During his earthly incarnate works, the Son could do only what he saw his Father doing; Christ was a man directly and strictly under the authority of God

---

[27] Emery, *Trinity, Church, and the Human Person*, 133.
[28] Scott R. Swain, *The God of the Gospel: Robert Jenson's Trinitarian Theology* (Downers Grove, IL: InterVarsity, 2013), 190, 192 (emphasis his).
[29] Köstenberger and Swain, *Father, Son, and Spirit*, 118.

the Father. Yet this position-relation was not new; the Son has always depended upon the personal priority of the Father.[30]

The Son's incarnate obedience is not a violation of his deity but the truest expression of his divine-filial relation to the Father: "The Son's obedience to the Father's charge does not compromise the Son's authority to act but rather establishes it. He is the free Lord of all—including his own death—*as* the Son who obeys the Father."[31]

The incarnate Son acts in divine-filial relation to the Father through the Spirit, as he has from eternity. The Spirit's role in relation to the Father and Son expresses "the perfect union of the Father and the Son in love."[32] Moreover, it is through the Spirit that both the Father and the Son act. And this is true for the Son-Spirit relationship even before the incarnation. So even after the incarnation, the Son does not relate to the Spirit in precisely the same way that we do. In contrast to other humans, the Son's action in and through the Spirit is not the result of the Spirit's external action upon the person of Christ. The incarnate Son is not just a greater example of a Spirit-empowered man. Rather, the Spirit is *internal* to the Son in that they both subsist equally and fully in the divine nature. This mutual indwelling of the Son and Spirit (along with the Father) means that when the Spirit acts, the Son acts.[33] The agency of the Spirit, then, in the life of the incarnate Son is no different from the way the divine persons have related from eternity. Even though it is correct to affirm that the incarnate Son acts by the Spirit, this does not deny that the Son is also acting. Owen explains this implication of the divine inseparable operations in full Trinitarian terms:

> [T]he *immediate actings* of the Holy Ghost are not spoken of him *absolutely*, nor ascribed unto him *exclusively.* . . . It is a saying generally admitted, the *Opera Trinitatis ad extra sunt indivisa.* There is no such division in the external operations of God that any one of them should be the act of one person, without the concurrence of the others; and the reason of it is, because the

---

[30] Given this divine-filial relation, we can better make sense of such texts as John 14:28 (cf. 1 Cor. 15:27–28), which speak of the *priority* of the Father in relation to the Son. Scripture teaches that the Father enjoys *personal* priority in the *taxis* (order) of the triune life, but not ontological superiority. The church has captured this truth by describing the Father as the *fons divinitatis*. The Father is the source of the Godhead not in generating the deity/nature of the Son (and the Spirit) but in the priority of his personal relation to the Son and Spirit. All that the person of the Son (and Spirit) has is received from the person of the Father. The full equality and deity of the Son (and Spirit) is not diminished by the Father's personal priority, because all share fully and eternally in the divine nature. For a helpful discussion of these points, see ibid., 184.

[31] Köstenberger and Swain, *Father, Son, and Spirit*, 122 (emphasis theirs).

[32] Swain, *God of the Gospel*, 201.

[33] See Tyler R. Wittman, "The End of the Incarnation: John Owen, Trinitarian Agency and Christology," *IJST* 15/3 (2013): 298–300; cf. Swain, *God of the Gospel*, 204, fn. 45; John Owen, *The Works of John Owen*, vol. 3, ed. William H. Goold (Carlisle, PA: Banner of Truth, 1965), 161–162. Owen argues that the Spirit is the "*immediate, peculiar, efficient cause* of all external divine operations: for God worketh by his Spirit, or in him immediately applies the power and efficacy of the divine excellencies unto their operation; whence the same work is equally the work of each person" (ibid., emphasis his).

nature of God, which is the principle of all divine operations, is one and the same, undivided in them all.[34]

We must say, then, that the Son now has two natures, such that he lives a fully divine and a fully human life in filial relation to the Father through the Spirit. According to the divine nature, the Son continues to perform his cosmic functions in the Spirit as he has from the beginning. And according to his human nature, the Son has in the Spirit "all the graces necessary for growth in wisdom (Lk 2:52) and obedience (Heb 5:8) [and] the leadership required for executing his divinely given mission (Mk 1:12; Lk 4:1–21). . . . The Spirit progressively enables Jesus to become a truly perfected human being (Heb 5:9), the paradigm for a renewed filial humanity (Gal 3:26–28)."[35]

In light of the eternal and economic relations of the divine person, then, we can have Swain summarize our first affirmation regarding the identity of Christ: "Jesus is the Son living out in human form his eternal relationship with the Father in the Spirit for our saving benefit."[36]

The Metaphysics of the Incarnation: The Divine Person of the Son Subsists Forever in the Divine Nature and in a Full and Sinless Human Nature

The incarnation is an act of addition, not subtraction. The eternal Son has subsisted in the single, same divine nature with the Father and Spirit from eternity. And as we just discussed, the Son alone assumed a human nature in history. Neither the person of the Father nor the person of the Spirit assumed a human nature; they continue to subsist only in the divine nature. The person of the Son also continues to subsist in the divine nature, but now this particular divine person also subsists in a human nature. In addition to possessing the perfection of all the divine attributes, the incarnate Son also possesses a human body and soul. The Son did not change or lose or set aside any divine attribute or aspect of the divine life when his divine person came to subsist in a human nature. In short, the divine person of the Son who shares in the divine life by his subsistence in the divine nature now also lives a human life by his subsistence in a human nature.[37] The Son added a human dimension to his personal, divine life.

Moreover, the nature assumed by the divine Son is fully human and completely sinless. The incarnate Son's human body and soul have all of the attributes and capacities of original humanity in full measure, giving the divine

---

[34] John Owen, *The Works of John Owen*, vol. 3, ed. William H. Goold (Carlisle, PA: Banner of Truth, 1965), 161–162 (emphasis his).

[35] Swain, *God of the Gospel*, 205.

[36] Ibid., 192.

[37] As discussed in Part III, change in the perfections of the divine nature is a theological-metaphysical impossibility, as is change in the ontology of a divine person. As we will see, however, the identity and experience of a divine person can change without diminishing his metaphysical perfection.

person the experience of a fully human life. And his human nature is unfallen ontologically and morally and untainted by effects or transgressions of sin, even though the Son fully experienced in many ways the effects of living in a fallen world. The Son does not share in the guilt or disposition of the original sin of humanity, and he in fact never committed a sin, which means that the real human temptations he did experience were that much more intense. As a man, through a fully and sinless human nature, then, the divine person of the Son has obeyed the Father in the Spirit to experience the perfection of human pleasure and to stand against the tempest of human temptations on our behalf.[38]

By taking on *our humanity*, Christ became the first man of the new creation, our great mediator and new covenant head. As *this man*, Christ reverses the work of the first Adam and forges ahead as the last Adam, our great trailblazer and champion (*archēgon*; Heb. 2:10). God the Son incarnate is perfectly qualified to meet our every need, especially our need for the forgiveness of sin. According to the storyline of Scripture, only the God-man—the Son incarnate—could mediate the reconciliation of God and man by offering himself as a sinless, sufficient, substitutionary sacrifice such that God himself redeems his people as a man (1 Tim. 2:5–6; Hebrews 5–10). As the *divine* Son, Christ alone satisfies God's own judgment upon sinful humanity and demand for perfect righteousness. As the *incarnate* Son, Christ alone identifies with sinful humanity in his suffering and represents a new humanity as our great and glorious Covenant Lord. As J. I. Packer explains, "Without incarnation there would have been no God-man, and without the God-man there would have been no mediation, no revelation of redemption. . . . The enfleshing of the Son was thus integral to God's plan of salvation, and the glory of Christ's unique person must be seen as an aspect of the glory of the Gospel itself."[39]

To understand better the Son's identity as this unique God-man who is glorious in salvation, we can leverage the doctrines of *anhypostasis* and *enhypostasis* discussed in Part III. The human nature of Christ never had a separate human person; it only had its subsistence in the person of the divine Son. When "the Word became flesh" (John 1:14), he assumed a human nature that did not have a corresponding human person. The divine Son is the only self-conscious,

---

[38] J. I. Packer gives us an accurate and engaging portrait of how the incarnation of the divine Son allowed him to live a fully human life for us: "The Son of God lived a fully human life before birth, through birth, infancy, childhood, and adolescence, into adulthood. He experienced a wide cross section of human relationships in the family and beyond. He knew what it was to be taught and learn from Scripture, and daily to pray, and to battle with the various forms of temptation that challenge wisdom and virtue. He entered into all the realities of love and hospitality, of joy and disappointment, of popularity and unpopularity, of pain, grief, and torture, agony of mind and body, and death. Moreover (here is mystery again), His relation to our race was such that every element of human experience became His in principle, in an archetypal, generic, and inclusive way. In other words, the experience of human life that He had enables Him to enter empathetically into every bit of human experience as such, . . . and to help us in all our attempts to grapple with them. 'Because he himself has suffered when tempted, he is able to help those who are being tempted' (Heb. 2:18; see 4:15), whatever form their temptation may take" (J. I. Packer, "The Glory of the Person of Christ," in *The Glory of Christ*, ed. John H. Armstrong [Wheaton, IL: Crossway, 2002], 52–53).
[39] Packer, "Glory of the Person of Christ," 54.

self-asserting, active subject of Christ. From the moment of the virgin conception, the eternal Son "took into his own divine person a complete set of human characteristics and components—including everything that pertains to humanity—so that from then on he is said to possess a human nature as well."[40] The direction of metaphysical movement here is crucial. The Son did not come to an existing human being or even human nature to form an artificial or *ad hoc* union. Rather, through the virgin conception, God created a new human nature for the Son, who assumed that nature as part of his subsistent existence. In contrast, believers are indwelt by the Spirit without any change in their metaphysical identity. The Son, however, did not indwell a human body-soul composite. The person of the Son chose to subsist in a human nature in the same way that he subsists in the divine nature. As the divine nature has been from eternity, the human nature of Christ is now part of his permanent metaphysical identity.

To clarify and communicate this new metaphysical identity of Christ, the church developed and deployed the concepts of *anhypostasia* and *enhypostasia*. Building on the person-nature distinction and affirming that Christ's human nature was a concrete particular comprised of a human body and soul, *anhypostasia* teaches that the divine Son assumed a human nature "without a human person" or a human "I." The human nature of Christ never had an independent existence apart from its personal identity in the *hypostasis* of the divine Son by whom it was assumed and to whom it was joined. In the post-Chalcedonian era, this concept was developed by the language of *enhypostasia*, which stressed the same truth but with more precision: Christ's human nature subsists *in* the person of the Son, i.e., it is "in-personal," and as such, the Son is now the acting subject of both his divine and his human natures.

The great Christological point of *an-enhypostasia* is that the human nature of Christ never composes a human person distinct from God the Son.[41] And the glorious implication for Christological identification is that Christ alone is the unique and complete God-man of our salvation. *Enhypostasia* makes sense of the incarnation while stressing the unity of Christ's person. The same eternal Son of the intratrinitarian Godhead who eternally possesses and shares the divine nature with the Father and Spirit now subsists forever in a human nature such that he lives and acts in both natures forever. In Jesus, we truly meet God face-to-face; we meet him, not indwelling or overshadowing

---

[40] Donald Fairbairn, "The One Person Who Is Jesus Christ: The Patristic Perspective," in *Jesus in Trinitarian Perspective*, ed. Fred Sanders and Klaus Issler (Nashville: B&H Academic, 2007), 108.

[41] Insisting that classical Christology is not Nestorian, Oliver Crisp concludes that "the human nature is never in a position to form a supposit distinct from God the Son, which, on the medieval way of thinking, is a necessary condition for the instantiation of personhood—presuming the Boethian definition of person" (Oliver D. Crisp, "Compositional Christology without Nestorianism," in *The Metaphysics of the Incarnation*, ed. Anna Marmodora and Jonathan Hill [Oxford: Oxford University, 2011], 59).

human flesh, nor merely associated with it, but in full and wonderful glory. Although we behold him as a man, he is much more; he is the Lord, the divine Son who humbles himself and veils his glory by becoming one with us. It is *God the Son himself* who dwells among us to speak, act, live, love, rule, and redeem for our good and his glory.

To summarize our second affirmation regarding the identity of Christ, then, we can say that the Son willingly changed his metaphysical identity from a divine person subsisting in the divine nature to a divine person subsisting in both the divine nature and a full and sinless human nature created for him, becoming God the Son incarnate for the sake of a new humanity.

The Economy of the Incarnation: God the Son's Divine and Human Natures Persist Fully and Distinctly as He Acts through Each according to Its Attributes

In addition to the metaphysics of the incarnation, *enhypostasis* also helps us pay careful attention to the economy of the incarnation in making our third Christological affirmation. In the incarnation, the divine Son personalized the human nature created for him. The divine person did not become or replace a human person but assumed a human body-soul composite into his metaphysical identity. Jesus Christ, thus, does not possess a human person (*anhypostasis*). The one and only person of Christ is the divine Son. When Jesus speaks, thinks, wills, and acts, he does so as the eternal divine Son. Moreover, because natures do not act, we cannot ascribe the words and works of Christ to his divine or human nature. All that Scripture ascribes to Jesus relates always and only to the divine person of the Son, whether he acts through his divine nature or through his human nature.

INCARNATE ECONOMY AND ENHYPOSTASIA

As applied to the deity of Christ, *enhypostasia* entails that the divine Son still exercises his divine prerogatives as the incarnate Son (e.g., Col. 1:15–17; Heb. 1:1–3). Contrary to various forms of kenoticism, the Son did not set aside certain divine attributes or their exercise when he assumed a human nature and became a man. The perfections of the divine nature cannot change and the person of the incarnate Son continues to subsist in and act through the divine nature. For example, the incarnate Son continues to "[uphold] the universe by the word of his power" (Heb. 1:3b) because "in him all things hold together" (Col. 1:17). Some scholars (most in kenotic Christology) attribute this power of sustaining the existence and integrity of the universe to the agency of the Spirit. While the Spirit—and the Father—is involved according to the inseparability of all Trinitarian action, however, the biblical texts at issue directly ascribe these cosmic functions to the incarnate Son without mentioning the Spirit.[42] Jesus does sometimes intentionally choose not to exercise a particular divine prerogative. But the point here is that the Scriptures present Jesus Christ performing the works that only God himself can perform.

As applied to the humanity of Christ, *enhypostasia* entails that the divine Son lives as a true man with the normal physical, mental, volitional, emotional, and psychological attributes and capacities of original humanity. Jesus experiences the wonder and weaknesses of a completely human life. But we must remain clear-minded that the one who experienced this human life was the divine person of the Son. We must say, then, that God the Son grew in wisdom, grew tired, ate fish, drank wine, wept tears, suffered torture, died on a cross, gave up his spirit, and was forsaken by the Father.[43] "My God, my God, why have you forsaken me?" (Matt. 27:46) is not the cry of a human nature; it is a cry of a person. It is the eternal Son who bore our sin and the Father's wrath and experienced suffering, death, and forsakenness we cannot fathom, so that we would not have to fear it.

So far we have affirmed that Jesus accomplishes all of his works through either his divine or his human nature. To consider more closely how Jesus acts through each nature, we can apply two doctrines: the *communicatio idiomatum* and the *extra Calvinisticum*.

INCARNATE ECONOMY AND THE COMMUNICATIO

Along with the *unity* of Christ's person as he subsists in and acts through his divine and human natures, we must also maintain that these two natures remain distinct and unaffected by each other. In the incarnation the two natures of Christ are not blended, nor are they changed. Each nature retains its own attributes and integrity, maintaining the Creator-creature distinction even in the hypostatic union of deity and humanity.

Traditionally, the church has used the *communicatio idiomatum* ("communion of attributes") to explain the relationship between Christ's two natures and their union in the Son. Although various conceptions of the *communicatio* have been developed, the church has agreed on at least two points: each nature retained its own attributes; the attributes of each nature are predicated of the Son because he is the subject/person of both natures. We can benefit from the explanatory power of this doctrine for the economy of the incarnation by

---

[42] For another example of Jesus's ability to act through the divine nature, consider his handling of Satan's temptation. Satan tempted Jesus in the wilderness to turn rocks into bread (Matt. 4:1–11). The temptation makes sense only if Jesus has the ability to change one substance into another (cf. water into wine, another example, in John 2:6–11). Experiencing hunger, then, was the result of Jesus's specific choice not to exercise the power of his divine nature, not an imposed limitation of that nature.

[43] In a famous statement, Cyril said that the incarnate Son experienced "impassible suffering" (cited in Fairbairn, "One Person Who Is Jesus Christ," 107). Human experiences such as suffering and death happen to a *person*. In Christ, the divine did suffer in his human nature.

considering some ostensibly contradictory biblical data and reflecting on the theological coherence of the incarnation.

Some biblical presentations of Christ seem to conflict with others. For example, Scripture tells us that the Son ascended into heaven and will return someday in the future (see John 16:28; 17:11; Acts 1:9–11); yet it also tells us that the Son is now present with us to the end of the age (see Matt. 18:20; 28:20; John 14:23). The *communicatio* helps us explain why there is no real contradiction here: the Son qua his human nature is no longer with us, but the Son qua his divine nature is omnipresent, with his people on earth and at the same time with the Father and Spirit in heaven. And the same *communicatio* principle applies to make sense of two more examples: Jesus's eternal existence and his birth, and Jesus's omnipotence and weariness. By utilizing the *communicatio*, we can affirm that the former apply to the Son qua his deity, while we can also affirm that the latter apply to the Son qua his humanity. And again, the *communicatio* keeps the divine-human distinction in place to help us in our faith seeking understanding regarding the death of Christ (Luke 23:46; 1 Cor. 15:3). The person of Christ experienced death through his human nature, including physical pain and the separation of his human body and soul. The divine person of the Son did not cease to exist in the death of Christ but continued subsisting in his divine nature and in his human soul. But through his human attributes and capacities, the divine Son did experience the reality of death such that he purchased the church "with his own blood" (Acts 20:28). God does not have blood to shed. But what is true of his human nature is also true of God the Son incarnate. Thus we must confess that God the Son died.

As a final example, the *communicatio* principle helps us resolve one of the most contentious issues arising from the biblical text: the perfection of God and the suffering of Christ. The clear truth that Christ suffered, even to the point of death on a cross, is used by some scholars as reason to reject a particular perfection of God—his divine impassibility. These scholars argue that since Christ suffered and Christ is God, then God suffers and is therefore subject to change in his divine nature.[44] But consistently applying the *communicatio* highlights the metaphysical misdirection of this argument for reconceiving the divine nature.

First, the *person* of Christ suffered, not the divine nature. In the suffering

---

[44] For a discussion of this trend in current theology, see Kevin J. Vanhoozer, *Remythologizing Theology: Divine Action, Passion, and Authorship* (Cambridge: Cambridge University, 2010), 124–138. Vanhoozer notes that the "relational" turn in theology has substituted classical thought for a "kenotic-perichoretic panentheism." He also makes the astute observation that relational theists have lifted the concept of perichoresis out of its original Trinitarian context, which sought to explain how the divine persons mutually indwell one another. These relational theists elevate perichoresis to a general principle to explain the God-world relation, just as they have lifted *kenosis* out of its Christological context and made it a general principle to redefine the divine nature (cf. Thomas G. Weinandy, *Does God Suffer* [Notre Dame, IN: University of Notre Dame, 2000]).

of Christ, it is the Son as the acting subject of his human nature who experiences the physical, emotional, and relational pain and loss. Second, the Son suffered, not the Father or Spirit. All three divine persons are unified in every divine action. But each act terminates on each person according to their *ad intra* relations and mode of subsistence in the divine nature. In this case, only the Son became incarnate, suffered, and died, not the Father or Spirit.[45]

The *communicatio* does not deny that the Son's suffering affected the other divine persons. The perfect intimacy of the eternal Trinitarian relations did not diminish upon the incarnation of the Son. The Father and Spirit are present with the Son in his suffering. Because they are with him in every work, the Father and Spirit cannot be absent from the Son's suffering during his works of humiliation. The Father and Spirit do not suffer in the same way as the Son. Neither the Father nor the Spirit was crucified. But both the Father and the Spirit were in *perichoretic* relationship with the Son when he suffered. In the Son's crucifixion, then, the Father and Spirit related to the beloved Son *as one enduring crucifixion*. And the divine nature certainly has the capacity for the complete range of thoughts, desires, and emotions, and therefore the Father and Spirit could respond properly and fully to the suffering of the Beloved. The cost of redemption was paid by all three divine persons, but each according to his unique personal relation.

The *communicatio*, then, helps us explain that the *Son suffered as a man*, while the Father and Spirit suffered as God: "he suffers in a divine manner, that is, his suffering is an expression of his freedom; suffering does not befall God, rather he freely allows it to touch him. He does not suffer, as creatures do, from a lack of being; he suffers out of love and by reason of his love, which is the overflow of his being."[46] Yet even here, we must quickly add that the Son suffered obediently to the Father and victoriously in the Spirit. The Father's plan in the incarnation was crucifixion for the redemption of man and the glory of the Son, who would be raised and enthroned over heaven and earth in the power of the Spirit.[47]

Moreover, the *communicatio* is an important part of explaining the coherence of the incarnation because it allows us to employ the reduplicative strategy. Critics charge that classical Christology must predicate contradictory

---

[45] Contra Bruce McCormack, "Karl Barth's Christology as a Resource for a Reformed Version of Kenoticism," *IJST* 8 (2006): 247–248; cf. Vanhoozer, *Remythologizing Theology*, 422–426.

[46] Vanhoozer, *Remythologizing Theology*, 422–426.

[47] Vanhoozer develops this point in four parts: (1) the Son assumed our humanity "not simply to identify with our sufferings (i.e., empathize) but to rid us of them (i.e., by becoming our substitute)"; (2) Christ's death was not as a victim; the cross was part of God's eternal plan and it was not "a belated 'response' to something the human hero said or did"; (3) Christ died as the obedient Son in relation to his Father so that "[e]ven Jesus' so-called 'passive' obedience (i.e., submitting to divine judgment) has an 'active' dimension"; (4) in his suffering, Jesus communicates to us the God who loves us by "freely pour[ing] out his own life for others" (Vanhoozer, *Remythologizing Theology*, 429–430).

properties/attributes to one and the same person.[48] How can the same Son be simultaneously unlimited and limited in power, omnipresent and spatially located, eternal and temporal, etc.?

The *communicatio* reminds us that we are not predicating contradictory attributes of the same person *in exactly the same way*. For example, the Son is omnipotent, omniscient, omnipresent, and eternal because what is true of the divine nature is true of the person who subsists in the divine nature. The Son, however, also subsists in a human nature. So we must reduplicate the predication of attributes to the Son, this time according to his human nature. The Son, then, is weak, unknowing, and spatially and temporally located because what is true of a human nature is true of the person who subsists in the human nature. The *communicatio* and reduplication do leave us with plenty of mystery and paradox regarding the incarnation of God the Son, but not logical incoherency or contradiction.[49]

Having applied the *communicatio* to the economy of the incarnation, we can now add to our affirmation that while Jesus accomplishes all of his works through either his divine or his human nature, those natures remain distinct and retain their full integrity even as each contributes to the predication of divine and human attributes to the Son. To complete this affirmation, we can apply the doctrine of the *extra* to consider the relationship between the divine and human natures of Christ.

INCARNATE ECONOMY AND THE EXTRA

The Son is the subject of the incarnation, who acts through his divine and human natures without violating the integrity of their respective attributes and capacities. But this does not mean that the Son can never act in a way that would be impossible for a mere human. It is true that, as a man, the person of the Son is limited to the abilities of a normal, sinless, but not supernatural human nature. Yet it is also true that the Son lives and acts according to the perfections of the divine nature. Traditionally, the church has employed the *extra* to do justice to the entire biblical presentation of Christ by affirming that the divine Son is not completely circumscribed by his human nature.[50] The Son has ontological priority over his human nature because the divine person

---

[48] For a defense of the logical coherence of the reduplicative strategy itself, see Eleonore Stump, "Aquinas' Metaphysics of the Incarnation," in *Incarnation*, 211–218.

[49] For a more detailed and technical discussion, see Stump, "Aquinas' Metaphysics of the Incarnation," in *Incarnation*, 217. On the point discussed here, Stump concludes, "Consequently, there is no reason for denying that Christ can have properties borrowed from either his human nature or his divine nature. . . . Because each of the incompatible properties is had in its own right by a different constituent of the whole and because they attach to the whole only derivatively, in consequence of the fact that the whole has these constituents, there is no incoherence in attributing both otherwise incompatible properties to the whole" (ibid.).

[50] It is important to remember that the *extra* was not only a Reformation teaching; it has been part and parcel of classical Christology, at least up until the Enlightenment era.

is eternal and thus has a divine life independent of the body and soul he assumed at his incarnation. Moreover, the Son continues to subsist in the divine nature as the second person of the Godhead. The *extra*, then, affirms that the Son can and does act through the divine nature in ways that he could not act through his human nature.

Contrary to a common caricature, the *extra* was not intended to diminish Christ's humanity. The *extra*, rather, seeks to confess and preserve the integrity of Christ's full humanity. From conception on, the Son humbled himself by taking on a human nature, and he did not override its limitations. Yet the Son also continued to exercise his divine attributes "outside" (*extra*) the reality of his human life. In his humanity, then, we should not think of Christ as going through his days thinking about the entire universe, since all of his cosmic functions are done "outside" his human life. Furthermore, when the *extra* is combined with *krypsis*, we gain a clearer understanding of the nature of his *kenosis*: the incarnation brought a real concealment but not an abdication of the eternal Son's divine majesty. The Son became *one with us* to live primarily *as one of us* and then to die *for us*, all in obedience to his Father's will.

Given how the church has distinguished *person* from *nature*, there is nothing contradictory in asserting that the Son can simultaneously act through both natures to accomplish different works, even where the divine works are impossible for the human nature. Some kind of asymmetrical relationship between the Son's living, speaking, and acting in and through his natures must be postulated, which is probably one of the most difficult areas for us to conceive. A human being is only one person subsisting in one human nature; we are neither divine persons nor do we subsist in two different natures. Conceiving of the asymmetrical relationship between the Son living and acting in his divine nature and his living and acting in his human nature surpasses our comprehension. But that does not mean that this part of the incarnate economy is not true—only that it is largely unknown to us. And even still, the *extra* helps us to make this theological-metaphysical confession of Christ.

The best way to account for the asymmetrical relationship in Christ is in terms of the Trinitarian relations worked out in redemptive history for the sake of the Son's incarnational mission. The Son lives out his divine and human lives in relation to the Father and the Spirit *and as our Redeemer*. Against all forms of kenoticism, the Son does not renounce his divine attributes or even the use of them. Instead, the Son's entire life is best viewed through the lens of his *filial* dependence on the Father in the Spirit. The Son does nothing except what he knows the Father wills him to do. When the Father does not will that the incarnate Son actualize some divine power or access some information out of his omniscience, the Son obeys and refrains. The Son did not abandon the use of his divine attributes; he could have turned rocks into bread or come down from the cross, but it was not his Father's will. Moreover, the Son's eternal and divine *filial* relation to the Father can be seen in redemptive history precisely because the Son always lives and acts to fulfill the divine plan of the Father. In the incarnation, neither the Son's deity nor his humanity is diminished. As the Father allows, and by the Spirit, the divine Son, the Lord of Glory, lives, speaks, acts, obeys, wills, rules, and saves as both the Creator–Covenant Lord and our great Redeemer.

Having now also applied the *extra* to the economy of the incarnation, we can finalize our affirmation that while Jesus accomplishes all of his works through either his divine or his human nature, those natures remain distinct and retain their full integrity even as each contributes to the predication of divine and human attributes to the Son. And yet, the ontological priority of the divine person of Christ to his human nature means that he will continue to exercise his divine prerogatives as God the Son even while he lives and works primarily as a man to accomplish his incarnational mission of redemption.

THE GLORY OF GOD THE SON INCARNATE IN REDEMPTION

This summary form of the theology of the incarnation reinforces the overall thesis of this work, namely that the identity of our Lord Jesus Christ is God the Son incarnate. In this chapter, we have pressed further to provide three affirmations of classical Christology. We must maintain these affirmations regarding the theological-metaphysical identity of God the Son incarnate to be faithful to the Bible's own terms, to be consistent with the established and well-tested orthodoxy of the church, and to commend a theologically coherent evangelical Christology to our generation and those who follow us.

However, as important as it is to state theologically who Jesus is, and to do so in a way that is faithful to Scripture and the teaching of the church, we cannot leave it here. Given who Jesus is, we must also be led to worship, adoration, faith in him alone, and a glad and willing submission to his Lordship in every area of our lives. In Jesus Christ, God the Son incarnate, we see the Lord of Glory, who has taken on flesh in order to become our all-sufficient Redeemer. By sharing our common human nature, the Son of God is now able to do a work that we could never do. In his incarnation and cross work, we see the resolution of God to take upon himself our guilt and sin in order to reverse the horrible effects of the fall and to satisfy his own righteous requirements, to make this world right, and to inaugurate a new covenant in his blood. In Jesus Christ, we see the perfectly obedient Son taking the initiative to keep his covenant promises by taking upon himself our human nature, veiling his glory, and winning for us our eternal salvation.

Our Savior and Redeemer is utterly unique. This is why there is no salvation outside of him. He is in a category all by himself in who he is and in what he does. In fact, because our plight is so desperate, due to sin, the only person who can save us is God's own dear Son. It is only as the Son incarnate that our Lord can represent us; it is only as the Son incarnate that he can put away our sin, stand in our place, and turn away God's wrath by bearing our sin. Only Jesus can satisfy *God's* own righteous requirements, because he is one with the Lord as God the Son; only Jesus can do this *for us* because he is truly a man and can represent us. Identification requires representation, and in all these ways our Lord is perfectly suited to meet our every need. Without the incarnation and Christ's entire obedient work, there is no salvation for humanity. To turn Lessing's language on its head, Jesus is a historical particular who has absolute universal significance for humanity, and apart from saving faith in him and him alone, we stand under God's judgment and condemnation.

But in this regard another critical point needs to be stressed. Scripture is clear that in order to understand, know, and adore Jesus correctly, we must also, by God's grace, come to realize our own lostness and sin before God. Our greatest need as humans is to be reconciled and justified before the holy God and judge of the universe. This is something our secular, postmodern culture does not understand, given its rejection and substitution of Christian theology for false worldviews. But to understand the biblical Jesus correctly, to come to know him rightly, and to place all of our confidence in him personally, we must also come to know something of our own guilt before God and why it is that we need the kind of Redeemer he is. For it is not until we know ourselves as lost, under the sentence of death, and condemned before God, that we can even appreciate and rejoice in a divine-human Redeemer. It is only when we realize that we cannot save ourselves that we clearly see that *he* is the Redeemer we need. Yet, for people who by God's grace come to see their need of him, then the Jesus of the Bible is not only understood for who he is but he is also embraced, loved, and adored as Lord and Savior.

Before we are done with our journey in this work, however, there is one more task to complete. Theology does not end with mere description of Jesus's identity or theological *construction*. Theology must also engage in the *apologetic* work of defending the Bible's teaching against various challenges and legitimate questions, as we have already been doing in chapters 10–13. Throughout the ages but especially in our day, orthodox Christology is often charged with being logically incoherent. In the final chapter, we will respond to this charge from the Christological formulation developed in this chapter, and we will also address two perennial and legitimate theological questions which the biblical data raise regarding Christ's knowledge and his in/ability to sin. These last issues are related to the issues of coherence, but they also reflect legitimate questions that are important to address as an exercise in "faith seeking understanding." It is to these topics we now turn.

FOURTEEN

DEFENDING THE THEOLOGY OF
GOD THE SON INCARNATE

Systematic theology not only describes but it also defends biblical and theological formulation. It is not enough to engage in theological *construction* alone; we are also called to make sense of it and to always be prepared "to make a defense to anyone who asks you for a reason for the hope that is in you" (1 Pet. 3:15). Theology, then, engages in an important *apologetic* work in commending and defending the Bible's teaching against various challenges and legitimate questions, and this is extraordinarily important when it comes to proclaiming what is the center and heart of all Christian theology—the person and work of Christ.

In this final chapter we turn to one of the most significant challenges against orthodox Christology, namely the charge of rational incoherence. In addition and related to the coherency issue, are two perennial and legitimate theological questions that need to be addressed: What does God the Son incarnate know, given that he is fully God and fully human? And how do we make sense of Christ's temptations as a man, if he is fully God?

IS ORTHODOX CHRISTOLOGY LOGICALLY COHERENT?

Despite the church's attempt, throughout history, to describe carefully and explain the identity of Jesus Christ, many critics and skeptics are not convinced in at least two ways. First, they are not convinced of the *truthfulness* of the incarnation, which apologetics seeks to address in an entire worldview defense. Our work would be part of such an overall defense, but such a defense would also include much discussion that is outside the purview of this work. Second, critics contend that the very concept of the incarnation is logically *incoherent*—a charge that theology cannot ignore. Given our conviction that God does not teach contradictory truths, especially in regard to Christ's identity, it is incumbent upon the church to show that the incarnation, although beyond our ability to comprehend fully, is logically coherent. In what follows we will address this issue in three steps: (1) outline the basic charge of various critics; (2) describe how we will answer the charge; and (3) respond to the charge in four points.

The Charge That Orthodox Christology Is Logically Incoherent

The incoherency charge is made by Christians and non-Christians alike, although for different reasons. When some Christians level the charge, it is directed to a specific understanding of the incarnation which they want to modify and improve upon. One of the reasons for the rise of kenoticism, for example, is to answer non-Christian critics who insist that classical Christology is incoherent, thus offering a "better" answer.[1] On the other hand, when non-Christians level the charge, their interest is not to provide a better alternative but to reject the Christian position as entirely untenable. In previous chapters, we have sought to address the in-house debate over which Christological formulation is "better." Our primary concern now is to address the charge raised against the orthodox view from non-Christians.

John Hick and Michael Martin are two recent examples of thinkers who level the incoherency charge against classical Christology. In a variety of places, Hick "accepts" the incarnation if viewed as a religious *myth* that tells us something of Jesus's importance as a religious leader, but if taken *literally*, i.e., as actually occurring, it is logically incoherent.[2] Similar to Hick, Martin charges classical Christology with the same incoherence.[3]

What exactly is the charge? It is this: It is irrational to attribute to one single individual contradictory attributes. If deity is understood as possessing specific attributes such as eternality, immutability, omniscience, etc., and God has these attributes necessarily, while humans are temporal, limited in power and knowledge, etc., then how can these attributes be predicated of the same individual simultaneously? Jonathan Hill captures the core of the argument: "But these two lists of properties are inconsistent, in the sense that a single individual could not possibly instantiate all of them. A single individual cannot, for example, be both temporal and atemporal, or omniscient and yet also limited in knowledge. It seems, then, that a single individual cannot be both

---

[1] For example, see C. Stephen Evans, "The Self-Emptying of Love," in *The Incarnation: An Interdisciplinary Symposium on the Incarnation of the Son of God*, ed. Stephen T. Davis, Daniel Kendall, and Gerald O'Collins (Oxford: Oxford University, 2002), 251–252, who charges classical Christology with being logically problematic, hence his kenotic proposal.

[2] For example, see John Hick, "Jesus and World Religions," in *The Myth of God Incarnate*, ed. John Hick (Philadelphia: Westminster, 1977), 178; idem, *The Metaphor of God Incarnate: Christology in a Pluralistic Age*, 2nd ed. (Louisville: Westminster John Knox, 2006).

[3] See Michael Martin, "The Incarnation Doctrine Is Incoherent and Unlikely," in *Debating Christian Theism*, ed. J. P. Moreland, Chad Meister, and Khaldoun A. Sweis (Oxford: Oxford University Press, 2013), 404–413.

fully human and fully divine. But the doctrine of the incarnation tells us that Christ *was* fully human and fully divine. That doctrine, then, seems to be incoherent."[4]

Responding to the Incoherency Charge: The Overall Strategy

How do we respond to this serious charge? Let us outline the overall response in three points.

First, in responding to the charge, we are *doing* theology. *Doing* theology, specifically Christology, is an exercise in "faith seeking understanding," which seeks to apply all that Scripture says about Christ in a biblically faithful and theologically coherent way. Since Scripture is our final authority and epistemological warrant for our Christological conclusions, we are warranted to believe what Scripture says about Christ because Scripture teaches it. This entails that we must let Scripture speak on its own terms regarding Christ's identity, and if tensions arise among the data, our reason must never reinterpret or eliminate the data simply because we do not grasp fully *how* it all fits together.

Second, drawing *logical* conclusions from Scripture for Christology must be done carefully. In fact, what does it mean to be *logical*, and how do we demonstrate logical consistency in our Christological conclusions? First, at the most basic level, we must have sufficient data to draw logical conclusions correctly. Our premises, derived from Scripture, must be true, but we must have enough data to appeal to, otherwise determining what is logical or not is difficult. It is precisely at this point, however, that problems arise. Even though Scripture is true, infallible, and inerrant, it is *not exhaustive* in its teaching, especially in everything pertaining to the incarnation.

Christian theology distinguishes between *archetype* and *ectype* knowledge, both related to the Creator-creature distinction.[5] *Archetypical* knowledge refers to the perfect knowledge of God, whereby he knows himself and all things comprehensively, including all propositional truths and possibilities, as well as their logical relations. His understanding is infinite and without error. This is why for God there are no mysteries or unknowns. For example, it is *not* a mystery to him *how* he exists as three persons subsisting in one identical divine nature, or *how* the deity and humanity of the Son are united in the one person. Yet our knowledge, as creatures, is only *ectypical*, i.e., a finite subset

---

[4] Jonathan Hill, "Introduction," in *The Metaphysics of the Incarnation*, ed. Anna Marmodora and Jonathan Hill (Oxford: Oxford University Press, 2011), 3. At the heart of the charge is the "principle of the indiscernibility of identicals." This principle specifies the necessary conditions for "identity." For example, an object *x* is identical with an object *y* only if every property had by *x* is had by *y*, and vice versa. In Christology, we affirm that Jesus is one and the same individual as God the Son but then predicate contradictory attributes of that same individual, which is contradictory, especially given the Creator-creature distinction.

[5] For a discussion of the *archetype-ectype* distinction in theology, especially in reference to our knowledge of God, see Richard A. Muller, *Post-Reformation Reformed Dogmatics: The Rise and Development of Reformed Orthodoxy, ca. 1520 to ca. 1725* (4 vols.; Grand Rapids MI: Baker, 2003), 3:164–170.

of his knowledge, which also includes Scripture. No doubt, our knowledge is true and objective, because it is a subset of God's perfect knowledge, rooted and grounded in God's self-disclosure. But even the true and objective knowledge we receive from Scripture is still finite. God has not revealed everything about himself and the world; what he has revealed is sufficient for us and our salvation, but it is not exhaustive. That is why for us *mysteries* are inevitable; mysteries *not* as contradictions, but in terms of *unknowns*. We, as finite creatures, simply do not know everything. The Creator-creature distinction, and its corollary the *archetype-ectype* distinction, is never erased, even in the consummated new creation.

Third, as we apply this understanding to the incoherency charge, given our *ectypical* knowledge, three points require emphasis.[6] First, in drawing *logical* conclusions, we must make sure that all of our premises are warranted by Scripture *and* precisely in the manner in which Scripture presents them. Second, it is not surprising that *tensions* will arise in the biblical data, i.e., "unknowns" or "mystery," because God has not exhaustively disclosed everything to us.[7] Thus, when Scripture predicates of the one and same Son both omnipotence and weakness, omniscience and growth in knowledge, if our exegesis is correct, we are not only within our epistemic rights to maintain this tension—we *must* do so. But someone objects, is it not irrational or contradictory to predicate conflicting attributes to the same person? *How* is that possible? Our answer is, in terms of the *how*, we are not completely sure, yet we are warranted to believe it is true because Scripture teaches it. Scripture is our epistemological warrant for knowing what is *logically* possible and impossible, yet given our *ectypical* knowledge, this does not entail that we can fully explain every *how* question. On some of these matters, we simply do not know enough. Third, even though *unknowns* are inevitable in Christology, *we must reject contradictions in our theologizing*. The warrant for this assertion is our doctrine of God and his *archetypical* knowledge. For the triune God of Scripture there are no contradictions, and although Scripture is not exhaustive, it is *his* Word and thus it is true and noncontradictory. In Christology, then, we must unpack the truths of Scripture knowing that these truths are coherent *and* we must show that there are no necessary contradictions in our theologizing about Christ, even though we may not be able to explain fully all the *hows*. Theology does not demonstrate *how* everything fits together; instead, it demonstrates that there is a *possible* way that the biblical data are noncontradictory.[8]

---

[6] On these points, see James Anderson, *Paradox in Christian Theology* (Eugene, OR: Wipf & Stock, 2007).

[7] Not everything in theology is a mystery, and as such, we must not appeal to mystery too quickly. It is only after we have done our exegesis of the relevant biblical data and have stayed true to how Scripture presents the tensions within the biblical data, that we can appeal to mystery on matters that Scripture does not fully address.

[8] See John S. Feinberg, "The Incarnation of Jesus Christ," in *In Defense of Miracles: A Comprehensive Case for God's Action in History*, ed. R. Douglas Geivett and Gary R. Habermas (Downers Grove, IL: InterVarsity Press,

Responding to the Incoherency Charge: Four Summary Points

How do we demonstrate that there is no necessary contradiction in Christology? First, we must place our entire discussion within an overall Christian worldview, rooted in the Bible's own presentation of Christ, and specifically in relation to a proper view of the triune God of Scripture. As Katherin Rogers rightly notes, "The question of the reasonableness of believing in the Incarnation can properly arise if you take it that there exists a God who acts as an agent in the world. On the assumption that there is no such God, the epistemic probability of the Incarnation is nil."[9] I would further add, we must affirm not only a God who acts in the world but also the specific triune God of Scripture. As argued in Parts I–II, apart from the entire framework of Scripture, talk of an incarnation, let alone trying to make sense of it, is difficult indeed. This is why this work began by placing Jesus within the Bible's own storyline and worldview. Unless we do this, we will not be able to respond to the incoherency charge.

Second, we must define our terms carefully and make some important distinctions, as we have done throughout this work. Specifically, the following terms and distinctions are crucial.

THE PERSON-NATURE DISTINCTION

Without making the distinction of person versus nature, it is impossible to defend the logical consistency of either Trinitarian theology or Christology.[10] As discussed throughout this work, *person* refers to the *who*, or the active subject or "I" of the incarnation, and *nature* refers to the *what*, or that which makes a thing what it is. In the case of God, *what* his being is, is described in terms of his attributes. In regard to a human *nature*, it is *what* constitutes humanity in terms of a body-soul composite with its corresponding capacities of will, mind, emotions, etc. The relation between a *person* and *nature* is that a person *has* a nature, or better, subsists in a nature, and it is the person who acts in and through the capacities of the nature. Natures are *not* active agents; only persons are, so that in the case of Christ, it is the Son who assumes a human nature and now subsists in two natures as the active agent of both natures.

Why is this distinction important? For this reason: unless the distinction is made, we end up in all kinds of inconsistencies. Unless we affirm *two* natures in Christ, for example, we will deny the Creator-creature distinction and create a

---

1997), 228–230, who makes a similar point. Disproving the charge of contradiction involves either showing how everything fits together or demonstrating a *possible* way that a concept can be true and not contradict itself. For further details, see Feinberg's essay.

[9] Katherin A. Rogers, "An Anselmian Defense of the Incarnation," in *Debating Christian Theism*, 394.

[10] See Paul Copan, *Loving Wisdom: Christian Philosophy of Religion* (St. Louis: Chalice, 2007), 156, who makes this very point in his defense of the logical consistency of Christology.

tertium quid which is no longer either deity or humanity.[11] In addition, unless we locate capacities such as will and mind in the natures, it is difficult to make sense of how Christ is simultaneously omniscient and growing in knowledge unless he has two minds, one divine and the other human. If we locate mind in person, it is more difficult to make sense of how in his one mind he is both omniscient and not omniscient simultaneously. In locating will and mind in the nature, however, it is now metaphysically possible, and noncontradictory, to speak of a divine and human way of thinking and knowing. Furthermore, in viewing *person* as the active subject, and placing will and mind in the *nature*, we avoid Martin's confusion of treating minds as different agents and then charging that the classical view is Nestorian.[12] We also avoid Martin's charge that "[i]t is at least dubious whether one person could have two minds,"[13] if person and nature have been distinguished and defined as orthodoxy has done. One last point: distinguishing "person" and "nature" is also crucial in making sense of the reduplication strategy, which is important in responding to the charge that we predicate to the same individual contradictory properties. But before we discuss that point, let us add some more crucial distinctions that are necessary to make logical sense of the incarnation.

THE COMMON VERSUS ESSENTIAL ATTRIBUTES DISTINCTION[14]

Common attributes are characteristics that most individuals of a specific nature will have, while essential attributes are qualities an individual must have in order to be part of that specific nature. In the case of humans, it is *common* for humans to be born on earth, to have a mother and father, to have the ability to reason, to have five fingers, and so on, but these things are not *essential* to being human. In other words, "[s]omeone could be human without having *all* properties *common* to human beings, but one could not be human and lack a quality that is part and parcel of the very essence of human beings."[15] In the case of Christ, he has everything *essential* to humanity, although he does not have everything in *common* with us. Just because his human nature was not

---

[11] In regard to two natures, it is crucial to distinguish between an *individual*- and a *kind-essence*. As Thomas Morris, *The Logic of God Incarnate* (Ithaca, NY: Cornell University Press, 1986), 38, explains: an individual essence is "the whole set of properties individually necessary and jointly sufficient for being numerically identical with *that individual*," and in this case, no one can have more than one individual essence. Applied to Christ, all of his divine and human attributes taken together would constitute his individual essence, which would lead to contradictory assertions. We need to speak of two natures, however, in more of a kind-nature sense: "A natural kind can be understood as constituted by a shareable set of properties individually necessary and jointly sufficient for membership in that kind" (39). Applied to Christ, as an individual, he is a person who subsists in *two* natures, with each nature retaining its full integrity, despite their union in the one person.
[12] See Martin, "Incarnation Doctrine Is Incoherent and Unlikely," 406.
[13] Ibid.
[14] The distinctions utilized are developed by Morris, *Logic of God Incarnate*, and are employed by many people. For example, see Copan, *Loving Wisdom*, 156–157; Feinberg, "Incarnation of Jesus Christ," 231–234; Douglas Groothuis, *Christian Apologetics* (Downers Grove, IL: InterVarsity Press, 2011), 523–526.
[15] Feinberg, "Incarnation of Jesus Christ," 233.

the result of natural reproduction, or because he did not have a human person but instead was "personalized" by the divine Son (*enhypostasia*), this does not entail that his human nature lacked anything *essential* to being human. Christ's human nature has all the essential attributes that comprise a human nature, including a body and soul and its corresponding capacities. As John Feinberg notes, what critics must do, and have not done, "is show that Jesus' humanity lacks any properties that are essential to being a human."[16]

THE FULLY VERSUS MERELY HUMAN DISTINCTION

Some may grant that Christ has whatever attributes are essential to being human, but may still object that because he has divine attributes (which are not essential or common to being human) in virtue of being the Son, it is hard to think that he is truly a man like us. In response, we must distinguish between being "fully" human and being "merely" human. To be *merely* human is to have all attributes necessary and sufficient to humanity and to possess nothing but those attributes. If Jesus is *merely* human, it is difficult to think that he is a man like us, but this is not what we affirm. Instead, we argue that Jesus is *fully* human, which entails that he has all the attributes essential to humanity *and*, different from us, he also has all the attributes essential to deity. Feinberg draws out the implications of this point for our discussion: "the Christian doctrine of the incarnation holds that in order to be fully human, one need not be merely human! Jesus has every essential property possessed by everyone who is merely human (thus he is fully human); but as fully divine as well, he is not *merely* human. Once we understand that Christ's nonhuman properties are not properties of his human nature but of his divine nature, we can see how a *person* who is fully human could have properties that no one who is *merely* human could have."[17]

All of the above distinctions are necessary to conceptualize the incarnation and to avoid the charge of incoherence. It is not logically contradictory to affirm that one person—the divine Son—can subsist in two natures, and can act in and through those natures, although admittedly, we are unlike this. Furthermore, as orthodoxy claims, the Son, in taking on our humanity, assumes a concrete human nature which includes all attributes *essential* to humanity so that he is *fully* human and not *merely* human, which once again is unlike us, but results in no necessary contradiction. In addition, when the critics ask, *How* can the Son become incarnate, given that humans have attributes so different from God, one can say two things. First, human attributes which seem incompatible with an incarnation are essential only to being merely human and

---

[16] Ibid.
[17] Ibid., 234. Cf. Morris, *Logic of God Incarnate*, 65–66.

not to being fully human. Second, as we will discuss below, given that humans are the *imago dei*, there is nothing incoherent in thinking that the *person* of the Son can subsist in a human nature with capacities patterned after God.[18]

Third, the reduplication strategy helps rebut the charge that it is logically incoherent to attribute to one single individual contradictory attributes.[19] At the heart of this strategy are two interrelated points. First, a clear "person-nature" distinction must be made, along with the affirmation that the Son subsists in two natures. Often the critic uses the word "individual" in the "individual-nature" sense, but that is not how it is used in Christology. Instead, Christ as an entire individual is the person of the Son who subsists in two distinct natures, not one. Second, given the "person-nature" distinction, we are *not* predicating contradictory attributes of the same person *in exactly the same way*. For example, in the case of the predication of divine attributes to the Son, we are doing so qua his divine nature, which *he* eternally and necessarily possesses. When we predicate human attributes and capacities to him, however, we are doing so qua his human nature and *not* his divine nature. The Son, by assuming a human nature, now subsists in *two natures*, and when predication of those natures is made to his *person*, it is made in different respects. Of course stating it this way does not entail that we can fully get our minds around it; all it demonstrates is that there is no necessary contradiction in affirming that Christ is one person subsisting in two natures.

At this point, Thomas Morris's two minds view is helpful, although for different reasons than he employs it.[20] In classical Christology, the will and the mind are viewed as capacities of natures that persons subsist in, so that in Christ there are two wills and minds. All of the actions of Christ, then, including willing and knowing, are by the person. In the case of Christ, *he*, as the divine Son, wills and acts through two natures and thus wills and knows *as God* and *as man*. It is for this reason that the reduplicative strategy makes sense, given the metaphysics of classical Christology. The Son is truly able to live a human life and thus to will, act, and think as a man qua his human nature, and the same is also true of his divine life qua his divine nature.

What is the relationship between the two minds? Morris proposes an asymmetrical relationship, which is correct, but his explanation of it is inadequate.[21] Morris proposes that the divine mind knows and has access to everything the

---

[18] See David F. Wells, *The Person of Christ* (Westchester, IL: Crossway, 1984), 177–178, who makes this point.

[19] For a defense of the reduplication strategy, see Stump, "Aquinas' Metaphysics of the Incarnation," in *The Incarnation*, 211–218; idem, "Book Review of Thomas V. Morris, *The Logic of God Incarnate*," *Faith and Philosophy* 6/2 (1989): 218–223; Rogers, "An Anselmian Defense of the Incarnation," 395–401; Groothuis, *Christian Apologetics*, 524–525.

[20] Morris rejects the reduplicative strategy, yet Stump, "Book Review of Thomas V. Morris, *The Logic of God Incarnate*," 219–223, argues that Morris is too hasty in rejecting reduplication, and in his two minds solution he adopts a form of it.

[21] See Morris, *Logic of God Incarnate*, 103.

human mind knows, but the human mind has access to the divine only when the divine mind allows it access. Moreover, Morris argues that as Jesus knew through his human mind alone, he knew only what other humans knew at that time, but since he was not merely human, Jesus had access to information that no mere human could know through his divine mind. Morris illustrates his proposal by various analogies such as dreams, depth psychology, and multiple personalities.[22]

Although Morris is on the right track, his overall explanation is inadequate for two reasons. First, Morris gives the impression that minds are active subjects and thus it is the divine mind who knows and has access to the human mind, and so on. But according to classical Christology, persons are active subjects, not natures, and minds are capacities of the nature. It is better, then, to speak of the Son as the one active subject who subsists in two natures and thus is able, as the Son, to will, act, and know as God and as man. Second, all of the illustrations Morris uses assume two levels of consciousness *in one and the same mind*; however, in Christ there are not just two separate levels of consciousness within the same mind: there are two distinct immaterial minds.[23] In order to support his view better, Morris needs to employ more consistently the classical "person-nature" distinction along with the reduplication strategy. By doing so, he could better affirm how the *person* of the Son can truly know qua his human nature and qua his divine nature, with a similar explanation for other human and divine attributes. If followed, then we can make sense of why contradictory attributes are *not* predicated of the Son *in exactly the same way*, which relieves any necessary contradiction while acknowledging plenty of unknowns that we simply cannot fully fathom.

Some may still object and question *how* two minds function in one person. The short answer is: we do not exactly know. The slightly longer answer is that, given the "person-nature" distinction, and appealing to an asymmetrical relationship between the natures, although we cannot exactly explain the relationship, there is nothing contradictory about it. Moreover, as argued above, when thinking of this asymmetrical relation in Christ, Scripture encourages us to do so in terms of the Trinitarian personal relations *ad intra* which are displayed in Trinitarian agency *ad extra*, and by linking these triune relations to the mission of the Son as our Redeemer and new covenant head. By doing so, we *can* conceptualize how and when the Son "accesses" and lives out his divine *and* human life, even though we cannot explain it fully. But, once again, we must stress that, although Scripture's explanation leaves us with a lot of questions, it is *not* necessarily contradictory.

---

[22] See ibid., 104–106.
[23] See Feinberg, "Incarnation of Jesus Christ," 239–241, who makes this same point.

Fourth, and expanding further on the first point, it is crucial to make sense of the incarnation *within* the Christian worldview, specifically theology proper and a theological anthropology. In truth, questions regarding the coherence of the incarnation center on making sense of how Christ's two natures are united in the one person, the Son, and how *he* is the active subject of both natures. Given the Creator-creature distinction, how can two qualitatively different natures be united in the person, unless one or the other nature is incomplete? Moreover, given that the Son is the *person* of the human nature, how do we make sense of a divine person living, speaking, knowing, and acting in and through a human nature?[24]

In response, we must always remember that, as wondrous and beyond our comprehension as the incarnation is, given that humans are the *imago dei*, as David Wells notes, this truth entails that what constitutes humanity "are capacities and perhaps resultant roles in creation the originals of which are to be found in God. Human nature as created is the echo of which the Creator is sound. He is original, and we are derivative. . . . What it means to be truly human is revealed in and by God himself."[25] Given this fact, it is not strange, although it is glorious, to think that the divine Son is able to be the active subject of his human nature and to live in and through the capacities of it. Central to what a person is, in the classical sense, is a relational subject, and to speak of Christ's humanity coming to its personal completion in the person of the Son, as Wells insists, "in no way diminishes or belittles the full reality of his humanity, but simply recognizes that in this instance the original intention of creation has been fully and finally realized."[26]

It is for this reason that, in Christ, we have one who meets our every need. In him, because he is God the Son, we have a divine Savior who satisfies God's own righteous requirements against us. In him, because he is the Son *incarnate*, we have a mediator who can do for us what we cannot do. The incarnate Son leaves us with much to ponder, but biblically and theologically, it is coherent. By the action of the triune God, terminating on the Son, the incarnation is not

---

[24] See John Hick, "Review of Thomas V. Morris, *The Logic of God Incarnate*," *Religious Studies* 25 (1989): 411–414, who criticizes orthodoxy on these points. He complains that the differences between deity and humanity are so great that it is difficult to conceive of how they are united in one person. Hick, however, wrongly seems to think that orthodoxy claims that by the incarnation something that is human subsequently acquires divine attributes, and that Christ's human mind acquires omniscience. But this is *not* orthodoxy. No one claims that Christ's divine nature took on human qualities or vice versa, since the two natures remain distinct, yet there are remaining questions on how the natures are united in the person.

[25] Wells, *Person of Christ*, 178. There is debate over the exact makeup of the *imago dei*, but, at the bare minimum, it includes reason, emotion, and will—all capacities patterned after God, albeit in a finite, creaturely way. Both God and humans have the capacity to reason, will, and feel, yet God has these capacities as the Creator, and we have them as creatures. If these human capacities were totally different than in God, then it would be difficult to conceive how the person of the Son is able to live and act through these human capacities, but given our creation in the *imago dei*, there is no reason to think this.

[26] Wells, *Person of Christ*, 178. See Gerald Bray, *God Is Love: A Biblical and Systematic Theology* (Wheaton, IL: Crossway, 2012), 568–569, who makes a similar point. Despite the differences between a divine and human nature in regard to the *person*, there is a relational aspect common to both.

humanity growing into deity, but God the Son assuming our humanity and bringing all of God's sovereign purposes to pass, including, wonder of wonders, restoring us, as finite image-bearers, to what God created us to be in the first place, now patterned after Christ's glorified humanity.

REFLECTIONS ON TWO PERENNIAL CHRISTOLOGICAL QUESTIONS

Related to the coherency question are two perennial and legitimate *how* questions: *How* do we make sense of what Jesus knows and does not know, and *how* do we grasp the nature of his temptation as our Lord and covenant mediator?

What Does Christ Know?

A crucial theological question in Christology is making sense of Jesus's knowledge. This question is a legitimate one because the same Scripture that teaches that Jesus is the divine Son also reminds us that Jesus himself admitted that there were things he did not know (Matt. 24:36; Mark 13:32). Moreover, contra the ontological kenotic view, omniscience is essential to Christ as fully God, but if so, then how can Jesus know and not know certain things? Working from within a classical Christology, four points are offered to answer this question.[27]

First, Jesus is the divine Son, who now subsists in two natures, one divine and the other human. As the Son, it is *he* who lives, speaks, acts, and knows in and through both natures. Mind and will are capacities of natures and not of persons, which entails that Christ, as the Son, is able to know and will both *as God* and *as man*, since he has two minds and wills in asymmetrical relation.[28] Taking seriously Christ's deity requires that we affirm that, as the Son, *he* knew all things, including the hour of his return. In his human nature, however, *he* knows as a man, which entails that he knows subject to the same laws of perception, memory, logic, and development as we do (Luke 2:52; cf. Mark 13:32). As Gerald Bray insists, "There is no evidence to suggest that he [Jesus] was specially gifted intellectually or had any remarkable talents, still less that he knew the deep secrets of the universe. . . . although he was a divine person, he was functioning within the parameters of his human nature and could not exceed them without compromising the integrity of his humanity."[29] In fact, Scripture tells us that Jesus, as a man, grew in knowledge *and* that he did not know certain things. How, then, do we make sense of this? Two further interlocking truths need to be put in place, to which we now turn.

Second, we must place this entire discussion within the larger issue of the Trinitarian relations and agency now worked out in redemptive-history in

---

[27] In what follows I am indebted to Macleod, *Person of Christ*, 164–170; Bray, *God Is Love*, 566–574.
[28] For a defense of Thomas Morris's two minds view, see Feinberg, "Incarnation of Jesus Christ," 231–241.
[29] Bray, *God Is Love*, 570.

light of the incarnation. As developed in chapter 13, thinking through how the divine persons relate to one another *ad intra* and *ad extra* is crucial in making sense of when and how the incarnate Son acts and knows. From eternity, the Son, in relation to the Father and Spirit, never acts and knows apart from his divine-filial relation to his Father (and in relation to the Spirit). In assuming a human nature, the Son continues to relate to his Father as he has always done, in absolute dependence, but now as the incarnate Son.

Third and building on the second point, Jesus's knowledge must be viewed in terms of Trinitarian relations *and* his role as our covenant head and representative. When and how the Son "accesses" or knows, speaks, and acts in and through his natures is Trinitarian *and* mediatorial. In other words, Christ, as the Son, in order to accomplish our redemption *as our mediator*, spoke, acted, and knew in dependence upon his Father and in relation to the Spirit, primarily in and through his humanity, unless the Father by the Spirit allowed otherwise. Some have tried to capture this point by stressing that in the incarnation and for the sake of the mission, the Son abandoned the *independent use of* his divine prerogatives, which he, as a man would not have enjoyed, in order to act as the last Adam on our behalf. Certainly this is true, and it helps make sense of why the Son, in the state of humiliation, primarily lives, acts, and knows in his humanity. Yet, we must not stress the notion of "the independent use of" too much, as if to suggest that the Son was ever "independent" of his Father and the Spirit. That is why thinking in terms of Trinitarian relations and the Son's mediatorial work is necessary to explain how the incarnate Son knows in terms of both the divine personal relations *and* his work on our behalf as our mediator.

The best explanation, then, of how and when the incarnate Son acts and knows must "put together" all of these truths. Once again, as noted previously, D. A. Carson is on the right track when he insists that the incarnate Son never acts and knows for himself, but only in relation to his Father and for our sake:

> The Son of God abandoned any use of his divine prerogatives and capabilities which, as a man, he would not have enjoyed, *unless his heavenly Father gave him direction to use such prerogatives.* He therefore would not use his powers to turn stones into bread for himself: that would have been to vitiate his identification with human beings and therefore to abandon his mission, for human beings do not have instant access to such solutions. His mission prohibited him from arrogating to himself the prerogatives rightly his. But if that mission required him to multiply loaves for the sake of the five thousand, he did so. Even his knowledge was self-confessedly limited (Matt. 24:36).[30]

J. I. Packer echoes the same thought. After discussing the Trinitarian relations of the Father and Son and underscoring their full equality yet personal

---

[30] D. A. Carson, *The Farewell Discourse and Final Prayer of Jesus* (Grand Rapids, MI: Baker, 1980), 35–36.

role distinctions, Packer observes that the obedience of Christ to the Father "while he was on earth was not a new relationship occasioned by the Incarnation, but the continuation in time of the eternal relationship between the Son and the Father in heaven. As in heaven, so on earth, the Son was utterly dependent upon the Father's will."[31] Packer then connects the truth of the Trinitarian relations to the mediatorial work of Christ and applies it to the issue of Jesus's knowledge. He suggests that, just as the incarnate Son did not act independently of the Father, he did not know independently either. As we quoted previously, Packer helpfully writes,

> Just as [Jesus] did not do all that he could have done, because certain things were not his Father's will (see Matt. 26:53–54), so he did not consciously know all that he might have known, but only what the Father willed him to know. His knowing, like the rest of his activity, was bounded by his Father's will. And therefore the reason why he was ignorant of (for instance) the date of his return was not that he had given up the power to know all things at the Incarnation, but that the Father had not willed that he should have this particular piece of knowledge while on earth, prior to his passion.[32]

So, Packer concludes, Jesus's limitation of knowledge is *not* to be explained "in terms of the mode of the Incarnation, but with reference to the will of the Father for the Son while on earth,"[33] and we would add, in relation to the Spirit, so that the Son's knowledge is best explained by Trinitarian relations *and* his role as our covenant mediator.

Fourth, as the *incarnate* Son and in his role as our mediator, Scripture teaches that Jesus's knowledge was gained as we gain it: by revelation, both general and special. In the Gospels, as Donald Macleod observes, Jesus is certainly viewed as possessing supernatural knowledge (Matt. 17:27; Mark 14:13; Luke 2:47; 5:4–6; John 1:47; 4:18; 11:14), even though, as Macleod rightly notes, we must distinguish supernatural knowledge from omniscience.[34] In his humanity, the Son knew as we know and received supernatural knowledge in relation to the Father and by the Spirit, as other prophets in Scripture received revelation. But even here, Macleod is right to admit, Jesus's capacity for such knowledge would differ significantly from that of ordinary men given his unique relation to

---

[31] J. I. Packer, *Knowing God* (Downers Grove, IL: InterVarsity Press, 1973), 62. Packer's use of "will" in this context could be misleading, but I am placing it in the context of our previous discussion of the classical understanding of person and will. The point to emphasize is that the Son's knowing in relation to the Father and Spirit *ad extra* is the outworking of the *ad intra* person relations. From eternity, the Son knows *as Son in relation to the Father and Spirit*, and never independently, which continues in a similar way in the execution of God's glorious plan of redemption.

[32] Ibid. Calvin states the same truth in his discussion of Mark 13:32: "Until [Jesus] had fully discharged his (mediatorial) office, that information was not given to him which he received after his resurrection" (cited in Packer, *Knowing God*, 62). For a development of this understanding, see J. I. Packer, "The Glory of the Person of Christ," in *The Glory of Christ*, ed. John H. Armstrong (Wheaton, IL: Crossway, 2002), 48–52.

[33] Packer, *Knowing God*, 63. For a similar explanation see D. Broughton Knox, *Selected Works—Volume 1: The Doctrine of God*, ed. Tony Payne (Kingsford, Australia: Matthias Media, 2000), 233–246.

[34] Macleod, *Person of Christ*, 166–170.

the Father *as Son* and his sinlessness. As Macleod suggests, "[Jesus's] intellect was perfectly attuned to the divine,"[35] and as Son, he "conversed with God as his Son; and he thought as his Son. We may even say that he lived in a thought-world of pure revelation so that, to an extent that we cannot fathom, God disclosed himself not only to his thinking but *in* his thinking."[36] Yet the Son, acting and knowing *as a man*, functioned within the parameters of his human capacities, including his human mind, and thus truly grew in knowledge *as a man*.

Does this entail that Jesus was ever ignorant of something he ought to have known? Can we appeal to this fact to argue that Jesus's knowledge, for example, of science and psychology was only a first-century understanding and thus he made mistakes?[37] Once again, Macleod is helpful in suggesting two truths that must be maintained simultaneously, neither of which entails fallibility—especially given the fact that there are other factors than Christ's humanity which we must account for, namely his unique divine relation to the Father and Spirit. First, as mediator, Jesus was "never ignorant of anything that he ought to have known."[38] As a man, Jesus grew in knowledge, but as mediator he knew all that he needed to know, and he lived and acted in obedience to his Father's will. Second, as mediator, Jesus "had to fulfill his office of Mediator within the limitations of a human body, so he had to fulfill it within the limitations of a human mind."[39] As we observe in the temptation accounts, in obedience to his Father's will and acting on our behalf as our covenant representative, just as our Lord did not draw on his omnipotence to turn rocks into bread, so he chose to know *as a man*, dependently and partially. Following Scripture, Macleod suggests, "[Jesus] had to learn to obey without knowing all the facts and to believe without being in possession of full information. He had to forego the comfort which omniscience would sometimes have brought."[40] As applied to the cross, Macleod insists that Jesus's dependence on his Father for his knowledge was an important factor in his suffering. As Jesus bore our sin, the assurance of his Father's love, the sense of his own sonship, were darkened as Jesus suffered "as the one who does not have all the answers and who in his extremity has to ask, Why? The ignorance is not a mere appearance. It is a reality. But it is a reality freely chosen, just as on the cross he chose not to summon twelve legions of angels. Omniscience was a luxury always within reach, but incompatible with his rules of engagement. He had to serve within the limitations of finitude."[41]

---

[35] Ibid., 167.
[36] Ibid.
[37] For example, see Peter Enns, *Inspiration and Incarnation: Evangelicals and the Problem of the Old Testament* (Grand Rapids, MI: Baker, 2005).
[38] Macleod, *Person of Christ*, 168.
[39] Ibid., 169.
[40] Ibid.
[41] Ibid.

None of this, however, implies fallibility. All that it entails is that the Son, in relation to the divine persons *and* for the sake of the mission, knew what he needed to know, and spoke with divine authority as the Son because all that he said was from the Father in relation to the Spirit, so that his actions and words are also the actions and words of God.

Could Christ Have Been Tempted? And If So, Could He Have Sinned?[42]

Another crucial theological question in Christology is, could Jesus have sinned? This question is not easy to answer, and as such, it requires careful reflection, given the variety of issues involved. Historically, classical Christology has argued that our Lord Jesus Christ experienced temptation like us, yet he faced it as one who was unable to sin, hence the affirmation of the *impeccability* of Christ (*non posse peccare*). The minority report, on the other hand, is that Jesus experienced temptation and that, although he never sinned, he was able to do so, hence the assertion of Christ's *peccability* (*posse non peccare*).

Both viewpoints admit that, in wrestling with the question, one must do justice to the following biblical truths: (1) Jesus never actually sinned. Scripture is clear on this point, so the issue is whether Jesus *could have* sinned, not whether he actually did. (2) Jesus was tempted, and his temptations were genuine (Luke 4:2; Heb. 4:15; 5:5–7). In fact, Kevin Vanhoozer astutely notes how the Gospels begin and end with the temptation of Christ. "The temptation narrative at the beginning of Jesus' ministry (Lk. 4:1–13) is a showcase for the same active suffering that marks another temptation narrative (Lk. 22:39–46), together with the passion narrative, at its end."[43] One must affirm, then, the genuineness of Jesus's temptations: as the obedient Son, from the beginning of his ministry to the cross, he faced trials, temptations, and sufferings for us. Any view that minimizes the reality of his temptations is inconsistent with Scripture. Yet, we must add a caveat: We must strongly affirm the reality of Christ's temptations, but we must not make his temptations the same as ours *in every respect*. Why? Because, as much as Jesus is like us, he is also utterly unique, and his temptations reflect this fact. For example, Jesus was tempted to turn rocks into bread, a temptation that normal humans do not face. He was tempted to use his divine prerogatives instead of walking the path of obedience, and he chose to live in dependence upon the Father in order to become our merciful and faithful High Priest (Heb. 2:17–18). In addition, he faced temptation in

---

[42] We assume dyothelitism in our discussion, which seems necessary even to ask the question of whether the Son could legitimately have been tempted. If we affirm monothelitism, as evangelical kenoticists do, then Christ's one will is a divine will, which seems to undercut his ability to be tempted *as a man*. For a complete discussion of this issue, see John E. McKinley, *Tempted for Us: Theological Models and the Practical Relevance of Christ's Impeccability and Temptation* (Eugene, OR: Wipf & Stock, 2009).

[43] Kevin J. Vanhoozer, *Remythologizing Theology: Divine Action, Passion, and Authorship* (Cambridge: Cambridge University Press, 2010), 430.

Gethsemane, but not by anything within himself, since he was perfectly holy and righteous. Unlike us in our fallen condition, in Christ there was no predisposition to sin and no love of it. The temptation he faced was unique to him *as the Son*, and it was unique to him as our sin-bearer. He rightly and legitimately recoiled at the prospect of losing his communion with his Father for a time; as a man, he rightly wanted to avoid death in this way for many reasons. We must never deny that Christ's temptations were real, indeed more real than we could ever imagine or experience, but we must also affirm that they were utterly unique to him. (3) God cannot be tempted with evil, and God cannot sin (see, e.g., James 1:13).

From within these three biblical truths, the question regarding Christ's impeccability or peccability must be answered. If (2) is upheld, it would seem that the Son, by becoming a man, would be able to sin. After all, as the peccability argument goes, if Jesus could not have sinned, then how is he truly like us? Yet, given that the *person* of the incarnation is the divine Son, would not (3) apply to him and thus render him unable to sin? Ultimately, the challenge is to uphold all three truths simultaneously without minimizing any of them. How shall we do so?

Our answer is that the impeccability position is best. Why? Let us first state the theological rationale for it, working within the parameters of classical Christology, and then offer a brief defense of it. Theologically speaking, if we view our Lord as merely the man Christ Jesus, even though his human nature was unfallen and sinless, he would nevertheless, like the first Adam, be *able to sin*. In this sense, we can say that Jesus's unfallen human nature was *peccable*. But there is more to the identity of Jesus than this, especially when we think of the *who* of the incarnation. Jesus is not merely another Adam or even a greater, Spirit-empowered one. He is the last Adam, the head of the new creation, the divine Son incarnate, and *as the Son*, it is impossible for *him* to sin and to yield to temptation, because God cannot sin. Behind this assertion is the fact that sin is an act of the *person*, not of the nature, and that in the case of Christ, *he* is the eternal Son. As Macleod rightly reminds us, "If he sinned, God sinned. At this level, the impeccability of Christ is absolute. It rests not upon his unique endowment with the Spirit nor upon the indefectibility of God's redemptive purpose, but upon the fact that he is who he is."[44]

Ultimately, the explanation for why Jesus could not have sinned, similar to the explanation for when and how he acts and knows, is Trinitarian. What made it impossible for him to sin was not his divine nature as an acting agent,

---

[44] Macleod, *Person of Christ*, 229–230. Macleod goes on to say, "We may link the subject 'God' with many predicates. The Son of God may suffer, may be tempted, may be ignorant and may even die. But we cannot link God with the predicate 'sin.' God cannot in any situation or for any purpose commit a transgression of his own will. He absolutely cannot be guilty of lawlessness" (230).

but the fact that *he* is the Son, in relation to the Father and Spirit, and *as the Son*, he speaks, acts, and chooses, gladly and willingly, to obey his Father in all things.[45] Herman Bavinck captures this rationale well: "He is the Son of God, the Logos, who was in the beginning with God and himself God. He is one with the Father and always carries out his Father's will and work. For those who confess this of Christ, the possibility of him sinning and falling is unthinkable."[46] In fact, it is this truth that provides the grounding and assurance of the indefectibility of God's sovereign plan, and ultimately explains why, in Christ, all of God's gracious purposes cannot fail. It is also the reason why the last Adam is far greater than the first, and thankfully, why the redemption he secures is gloriously better in every way imaginable.

Given the impeccability position, the question that legitimately occurs is in regard to proposition (2): If Jesus could not have sinned, how are his temptations real and genuine? As noted above, we cannot do justice to Scripture if we deny the reality of Christ's temptations. How, then, do we account for them? Do we need simply to appeal to mystery at this point? Before we appeal to mystery too quickly, we need to think through three issues—all of which provide warrant for making sense of how Christ is impeccable even though his temptations are genuine.

First, we must carefully define what is meant by freedom of choice and must not implicitly assume a specific view without argument. When it comes to human freedom, Scripture presents us as free; i.e., we make choices, we do what we want to do, and we are held responsible by God for our actions. However, nowhere does Scripture define human freedom in a precise way. On this point, we can say that the biblical data regarding the nature of freedom are underdetermined. As we begin to theologize about the nature of "freedom," it is necessary to employ extrabiblical definitions to help clarify what is meant by the concept; yet, as with any extrabiblical concept (e.g., *homoousios*, *communicatio*, etc.), we must accept or reject such concepts and definitions based on their overall fit with Scripture. In the case of "freedom," not all definitions are equal. In the end, each view of freedom must be evaluated by Scripture in terms of its consistency with biblical teaching. Today, in current theological-philosophical discussion, there are two basic views of human freedom: libertarian and compatibilistic.

The most basic sense of libertarian freedom is that a person's act is free only if it is not causally determined. For libertarians, this does not mean that our actions are random or arbitrary. Reasons or causes may play upon the will as one chooses, but none of them is *sufficient* to incline the will decisively in

---

[45] See Bray, *God Is Love*, 578, who makes this point. It reminds us again of the crucial "person-nature" distinction.
[46] Bavinck, *Sin and Salvation in Christ*, 314.

one direction or another. Thus, a person is free only if he could have chosen otherwise than he did; if he could not have chosen otherwise, then his choice is not free in the libertarian sense.[47] On the other hand, the most basic sense of compatibilism is that human actions are causally determined, yet free. In other words, a compatibilist view of freedom perceives the human will as decisively and *sufficiently* inclined toward one option as opposed to another, yet it is still free as long as the following requirements are met: "(1) The immediate cause of the action is a desire, wish, or intention internal to the agent, (2) no external event or circumstances compels the action to be performed, and (3) the agent could have acted differently if he had chosen to."[48] If these three conditions are met, then even though human actions are determined, they are still considered free. In thinking through these two conceptions of human freedom, two points need to be considered: first, most admit that both views are possible in the sense that there is no logical contradiction in affirming either one; second, both views cannot be true. How, then, does one decide between them? Ultimately, one must adopt the view that best fits the biblical data, not our preconceived notion of what human freedom is or ought to be.

What does this discussion have to do with Christ's impeccability? A lot. Many who reject the impeccability of Christ often make the following argument: If Christ is impeccable, it makes no sense to think that he was truly tempted, since he would not be resisting sin *freely*.[49] In other words, Christ's temptations are only genuine or *freely* chosen, if he could always do otherwise, but since impeccability insists that Christ could not have sinned, he "could not have done otherwise" in regard to those temptations. What is crucial to note, however, is that this argument works only if one assumes a libertarian view of freedom, but such an assumption requires a defense. For a number of reasons, libertarian freedom is not the best option, given that it is inconsistent with Scripture and theologically problematic.[50] Compatibilism,

---

[47] David Basinger, "Middle Knowledge and Classical Christian Thought," *Religious Studies* 22 (1986): 416, states it this way: for a person to be free with respect to performing an action, he must have it within his power "to choose to perform action A or choose not to perform action A. Both A and not A could actually occur; which will actually occur has not yet been determined." See also William Hasker, *Metaphysics* (Downers Grove, IL: InterVarsity Press, 1983), 32–44; Michael Peterson et al. *Reason and Religious Belief* (Oxford: Oxford University Press, 1991), 59–61.

[48] Peterson, *Reason and Religious Belief*, 59. The third requirement that Peterson et al. lists is very important: the agent could have acted differently if he had chosen to. Libertarians argue that no one is free who could not have (actually) done otherwise. Compatibilists argue that the meaning of the phrase "could have done otherwise" must be carefully defined. The key issue here is the meaning of *can* or *could*. There are at least seven ways that this expression can be understood. And it is only in one of these ways that the compatibilist cannot affirm "could have done otherwise." However, in the other six ways, it is perfectly appropriate for the compatibilist to affirm that the "agent could have done otherwise," and if being able to do otherwise is the criterion for being free, then a compatibilist can legitimately speak of freedom. On this point see John S. Feinberg, "God Ordains All Things," in *Predestination and Free Will: Four Views of Divine Sovereignty and Human Freedom*, ed. David Basinger and Randall Basinger (Downers Grove, IL: InterVarsity Press, 1986), 26–28; cf. John S. Feinberg, *No One Like Him: The Doctrine of God*, Foundations of Evangelical Theology (Wheaton, IL: Crossway, 2001), 625–676.

[49] For example, see Morris, *Logic of God Incarnate*, 138–146.

[50] For some defenses of compatibilism, see Feinberg, *No One Like Him*, 625–775; John M. Frame, *The Doctrine of God* (Phillipsburg, NJ: P&R, 2002), 119–59; Vanhoozer, *Remythologizing Theology*, 297–386.

on the other hand, is a more biblical and theologically consistent view. Assuming it to be the case, then our choices are viewed as true and genuine, even if causally determined, as long as we choose what we want and our choices are not constrained. As applied to Christ, it is now possible to make sense of how he can resist temptation *freely*, not in the libertarian sense or even because he is constrained to do so, but because he freely chose to according to his wants and desires.[51]

In his defense of this view, John Feinberg draws the analogy between Jesus resisting temptations freely yet according to his desires as the holy incarnate Son, and us, as Christians, who increasingly resist temptation as we progress in our Christian lives. In our Christian lives, due to God's gracious work in us by his Spirit, we increasingly resist sin and love righteousness as our desires are more conformed to Christ. Our growth in grace leads to greater victory over temptation, and all of it is done freely according to our wants and desires. In a similar and greater way, Jesus resists temptation as the Son, according to his holy and perfectly good desires, yet none of this requires that he does so unfreely. As Feinberg writes, "His [Jesus's] acts of righteousness and resisting temptation were causally determined, but not contrary to his wishes, and not solely in terms of his knowledge that he could not sin."[52]

Feinberg continues the analogy even further, to the question of whether a genuine Christian can apostatize. If one is convinced (as I am) that the doctrine of the "preservation and perseverance of the saints" is true, then one maintains simultaneously our security in Christ and the reality of the temptation to turn from Christ. The fact that one is kept in Christ does not make it impossible to be genuinely tempted to deny Christ. But do we resist temptation freely? Does God's protection of us "force" us to resist the temptation to apostatize against our wishes? No. In fact, the opposite is the case: Christians learn to resist temptation out of their love for Christ, and thus in accord with their desires and wants. Feinberg rightly asks, "If this is true of eternally secure believers, why couldn't Christ, despite his necessary goodness, freely resist sin though genuinely tempted?"[53] The only reason to think otherwise is either to assume a libertarian freedom and/or to assume that unless people actually sin, they were never really tempted. But both of these assumptions are incorrect, and as Feinberg concludes, "our own experience shows that there can be real temptation, even if it is impossible for us to sin (as in the case of apostasy)."[54] Thus, in both the example of apostasy and in Christ, there is something that makes it impossible to commit a particular sin, but "in neither

---

[51] For an excellent defense of this view, see Feinberg, "Incarnation of Jesus Christ," 241–245.
[52] Ibid., 243.
[53] Ibid., 245.
[54] Ibid.

case does that impossibility make it impossible to be tempted to sin, nor does it make resistance unfree. An impeccable Savior is no more untemptable than an invincible army is unattackable."[55]

Second, we must remember that even though Jesus was unfallen and could not sin, his temptations were still genuine because, in acting as our covenant representative, and in obedience to his Father's will, unless the Father allowed, Jesus did not always utilize his divine rights. For example, when the Father does not allow him to actualize his power or have some information before him, he does not do so, and it is not there. For the sake of the mission, and in order to accomplish our redemption *as our mediator*, Jesus spoke, acted, and knew in dependence upon his Father and in relation to the Spirit, primarily in and through his humanity, unless the Father by the Spirit allowed otherwise. All of this entails that Jesus's temptations were genuine and real. As the sinless one who could not sin, he still had to choose to forego his rights and privileges for us. He had to choose to go to the cross even though he knew the cost, especially in relation to his communion with the other divine persons. None of these choices was easy, and all of them were made as the sinless, spotless Son, who knew precisely the cost involved. As Macleod once again nicely reminds us,

> We must be careful not to misconstrue the effect of Jesus' sinless integrity at this point. Far from meaning a shorter, painless struggle with temptation it involved him in protracted resistance. Precisely because he did not yield easily and was not, like us, an easy prey, the devil had to deploy all his wiles and use all his resources. The very fact that he was invincible meant that he endured the full force of temptation's ferocity, until hell slunk away, defeated and exhausted. Against us, a little temptation suffices. Against him, Satan found himself forced to push himself to his limits.[56]

Third, we must distinguish between knowing and experience. Some, like Morris, insist that Jesus could not know he was impeccable, otherwise this epistemic certainty would render his temptations non-genuine; however, knowing something to be the case does not necessarily make it easier or unreal.[57] For Jesus, knowing that he is the Son entails that he knows he is impeccable; but he also knows, for example, that choosing to put aside his rights and go to the cross will not only result in excruciating physical pain but will also bring about the spiritual reality of bearing our sin and the loss of Trinitarian communion. The knowledge of this does not make it any easier, and in fact, knowing it leads Jesus, in one sense, not to want it, as Gethsemane vividly demonstrates: "My Father, if it be possible, let this cup pass from me; nevertheless, not as I will,

---

[55] Ibid.
[56] Macleod, *Person of Christ*, 227–228.
[57] See Morris, *Logic of God Incarnate*, 146–153.

but as you will" (Matt. 26:39). Yet our Lord, in glad and willing obedience to his Father's will, and acting on our behalf as our covenant mediator, chose to suffer, to experience the horror of the cross in all of its awful dimensions, and ultimately to experience our judgment for us. Even though he was the sinless and spotless Son and thus unable to sin, his impeccability and the knowledge of it did not exempt him "from the sorrows and sufferings associated with normal human life."[58] Jesus could be tempted to resist even good things, but instead, he set his mind to do his Father's will in order to redeem us. Hallelujah! What a Savior!

---

[58] Bray, God Is Love, 577. Cf. Bavinck, Sin and Salvation in Christ, 315.

Our journey is now complete, but in truth we have barely scratched the surface. As we began this work, we now finish it with the conclusion that there is no greater subject matter than our Lord Jesus Christ. To reflect on the glory, wonder, and greatness of our glorious triune God in the face of Christ Jesus is a privilege beyond our wildest imagination. In fact, our highest calling is not only in thinking about him but in knowing him as our Lord and Redeemer. Truly, to know him, who is life eternal, fulfills the very purpose of our existence, as Scripture reminds us (Col. 1:17).

In fact, such a study as we have been doing takes us to the very heart of the gospel and of all of Scripture. Jesus Christ our Lord is the main subject of Scripture, as God's entire redemptive purposes center in him. The Bible is not a random collection of documents thrown together. Scripture is God's self-revelation, progressively revealed through the writings of human authors. And since Scripture is *God's* word, despite its diversity there is an overall unity to it that unfolds God's unfailing plan—a plan that Scripture asserts is ultimately centered on and fulfilled in the incarnate Son of God and his glorious redemptive work on our behalf.

Furthermore, as we have sought to convey throughout this work, Christology is not merely the starting point of all theological reflection; it is its central point. All theological doctrines either prepare for Christology or are inferred from it. In fact, the entire theology and life of the church makes sense only when it is centered in him. It is for this reason that the incarnation has preoccupied the church now for two millennia; indeed, it is something we will joyously do for all eternity, as we attempt to fathom, but never exhaust, the depth, breadth, and wonder of the Lord of Glory, his incarnation, and his glorious work on our behalf as our Lord, Messiah, covenant head, and substitute. We, as a fallen people, have a great need, and he, the Son incarnate, is the only one who can meet that need.

Given what Scripture says about our Lord, we also need the reminder that our theologizing about him is not merely an academic question, something for theologians to ponder; it is also a matter of life-and-death importance. We began this work by noting that there are many beliefs that distinguish Christianity from other religious and philosophical worldviews, but none so obvious and vital as who Jesus is. The conclusion of this work is that Jesus of Nazareth is not merely another religious figure from history but our only Lord and Redeemer. In a day of rampant philosophical and religious pluralism, it is our joy and privilege to proclaim him who alone can save. We do not do so out of bigotry or intolerance; we do so because of who he is. Jesus *is* God the Son incarnate, and it is precisely for this reason that he is so important. Ultimately our Christological reflections must not lead to idle speculation and curiosity; they must lead to our lives being given to *him* in complete faith, trust, obedience, and worship. As the grand old hymn of the church, "Crown Him with Many Crowns," beautifully exhorts us:

Crown Him with many crowns, the Lamb upon His throne;
Hark! How the heav'nly anthem drowns all music but its own!
Awake, my soul and sing of Him who died for thee,
And hail Him as thy matchless King through all eternity.

Crown Him the Son of God before the worlds began,
And ye, who tread where He hath trod, crown Him the Son of Man;
Who ev'ry grief hath known that wrings the human breast,
And takes and bears them for his own, that all in him may rest.

Crown Him the Lord of life, who triumphed o'er the grave,
And rose victorious in the strife for those He came to save;
His glories now we sing, who died and rose on high,
Who died eternal life to bring, and lives that death may die.

Crown Him the Lord of love! Behold His hands and side—
Rich wounds, yet visible above, in beauty glorified.
All hail, Redeemer, hail! For Thou has died for me:
Thy praise and glory shall not fail throughout eternity. Amen.[1]

---

[1] Matthew Bridges and Godfrey Thring, "Crown Him with Many Crowns," in *Hymns for the Living Church*, ed. Donald P. Hustad (Carol Stream, IL: Hope, 1974).

the

FOUNDATIONS
OF EVANGELICAL
THEOLOGY

series

The Foundations of Evangelical Theology series incorporates the best
of exegetical, biblical, historical, and philosophical theology in order to
produce an up-to-date multi-volume systematic theology with contemporary
application—ideal for both students and teachers of theology.

Visit crossway.org for more information.